D1090345

Dictionary of Literary Biography

Dictionary of Literary Biography Documentary Series

Dictionary of Literary Biography Yearbooks

Concise Series

Dictionary of Literary Biography® • Volume Two Hundred Seventy-Eight

American Novelists Since World War II
Seventh Series

American Novelists Since World War II
Seventh Series

Edited by
James R. Giles
Northern Illinois University
and
Wanda H. Giles
Northern Illinois University

A Bruccoli Clark Layman Book

GALE®

THOMSON
™
GALE

Detroit • New York • San Diego • San Francisco • Cleveland • New Haven, Conn. • Waterville, Maine • London • Munich

Dictionary of Literary Biography
Volume 278: American Novelists
Since World War II,
Seventh Series
James R. Giles and Wanda H. Giles

Advisory Board
John Baker
William Cagle
Patrick O'Connor
George Garrett
Trudier Harris
Alvin Kernan
Kenny J. Williams

Editorial Directors
Matthew J. Bruccoli and Richard Layman

LIBRARY OF CONGRESS CATALOGING-IN-PUBLICATION DATA

American novelists since World War II. Seventh series / edited by James R. Giles and Wanda
H. Giles.
          p. cm. — (Dictionary of literary biography ; v. 278)
"A Bruccoli Clark Layman book."
Includes index.
      ISBN 0-7876-6022-1
      1. American fiction—20th century—Bio-bibliography—Dictionaries.
      2. Novelists, American—20th century—Biography—Dictionaries.
      3. American fiction—20th century—Dictionaries.
      I. Giles, James Richard, 1937– II. Giles, Wanda H. III. Series.

PS379.A554 2003
813'.5409—dc21   2003004439

Printed in the United States of America
10 9 8 7 6 5 4 3 2 1

We dedicate this volume to the members of the 2002 Fulbright American Studies Institute in Contemporary American Literature at Northern Illinois University, with respect and appreciation.

Oscar Iván Albán

Radu Andriescu

Patrycja Baran-Antoszek

Mirian Alicia Carballo de Flores

Okaka Opio Dokotum

Dinali Indira Fernando

Laura Flores Calvo

K. M. Ashraf Hossain

Limpár Ildikó

Sophia Kananyan

Gyu-Han Kang

Natalia Koliadko

Paola Loreto

Salwa Hamed Mohamed Mabrouk

Marwan M. Obeidat

V. E. Ramakrishnan

Chukwunyere Udumukwu

Zhang Xiaoling

And to Studs Terkel, in peace and sanity.

Contents

Plan of the Series

. . . Almost the most prodigious asset of a country, and perhaps its most precious possession, is its native literary product—when that product is fine and noble and enduring.

Mark Twain*

The advisory board, the editors, and the publisher of the *Dictionary of Literary Biography* are joined in endorsing Mark Twain's declaration. The literature of a nation provides an inexhaustible resource of permanent worth. Our purpose is to make literature and its creators better understood and more accessible to students and the reading public, while satisfying the needs of teachers and researchers.

To meet these requirements, *literary biography* has been construed in terms of the author's achievement. The most important thing about a writer is his writing. Accordingly, the entries in *DLB* are career biographies, tracing the development of the author's canon and the evolution of his reputation.

The purpose of *DLB* is not only to provide reliable information in a usable format but also to place the figures in the larger perspective of literary history and to offer appraisals of their accomplishments by qualified scholars.

The publication plan for *DLB* resulted from two years of preparation. The project was proposed to Bruccoli Clark by Frederick G. Ruffner, president of the Gale Research Company, in November 1975. After specimen entries were prepared and typeset, an advisory board was formed to refine the entry format and develop the series rationale. In meetings held during 1976, the publisher, series editors, and advisory board approved the scheme for a comprehensive biographical dictionary of persons who contributed to literature. Editorial work on the first volume began in January 1977, and it was published in 1978. In order to make *DLB* more than a dictionary and to compile volumes that individually have claim to status as literary history, it was decided to organize volumes by topic, period, or

From an unpublished section of Mark Twain's autobiography, copyright by the Mark Twain Company

genre. Each of these freestanding volumes provides a biographical-bibliographical guide and overview for a particular area of literature. We are convinced that this organization—as opposed to a single alphabet method—constitutes a valuable innovation in the presentation of reference material. The volume plan necessarily requires many decisions for the placement and treatment of authors. Certain figures will be included in separate volumes, but with different entries emphasizing the aspect of his career appropriate to each volume. Ernest Hemingway, for example, is represented in *American Writers in Paris, 1920–1939* by an entry focusing on his expatriate apprenticeship; he is also in *American Novelists, 1910–1945* with an entry surveying his entire career, as well as in *American Short-Story Writers, 1910–1945, Second Series* with an entry concentrating on his short fiction. Each volume includes a cumulative index of the subject authors and articles.

Since 1981 the series has been further augmented by the *DLB Yearbooks,* which update published entries, add new entries to keep the *DLB* current with contemporary activity, and provide articles on literary history. There have also been nineteen *DLB Documentary Series* volumes, which provide illustrations, facsimiles, and biographical and critical source materials for figures, works, or groups judged to have particular interest for students. In 1999 the *Documentary Series* was incorporated into the *DLB* volume numbering system beginning with *DLB 210: Ernest Hemingway.*

We define literature as the *intellectual commerce of a nation:* not merely as belles lettres but as that ample and complex process by which ideas are generated, shaped, and transmitted. *DLB* entries are not limited to "creative writers" but extend to other figures who in their time and in their way influenced the mind of a people. Thus the series encompasses historians, journalists, publishers, book collectors, and screenwriters. By this means readers of *DLB* may be aided to perceive literature not as cult scripture in the keeping of intellectual high priests but firmly positioned at the center of a nation's life.

DLB includes the major writers appropriate to each volume and those standing in the ranks behind them. Scholarly and critical counsel has been sought in deciding which minor figures to include and how full their entries should be. Wherever possible, useful references are made to figures who do not warrant separate entries.

Each *DLB* volume has an expert volume editor responsible for planning the volume, selecting the figures for inclusion, and assigning the entries. Volume editors are also responsible for preparing, where appropriate, appendices surveying the major periodicals and literary and intellectual movements for their volumes, as well as lists of further readings. Work on the series as a whole is coordinated at the Bruccoli Clark Layman editorial center in Columbia, South Carolina, where the editorial staff is responsible for accuracy and utility of the published volumes.

One feature that distinguishes *DLB* is the illustration policy–its concern with the iconography of literature. Just as an author is influenced by his surroundings, so is the reader's understanding of the author enhanced by a knowledge of his environment. Therefore *DLB* volumes include not only drawings, paintings, and photographs of authors, often depicting them at various stages in their careers, but also illustrations of their families and places where they lived. Title pages are regularly reproduced in facsimile along with dust jackets for modern authors. The dust jackets are a special feature of *DLB* because they often document better than anything else the way in which an author's work was perceived in its own time. Specimens of the writers' manuscripts and letters are included when feasible.

Samuel Johnson rightly decreed that "The chief glory of every people arises from its authors." The purpose of the *Dictionary of Literary Biography* is to compile literary history in the surest way available to us–by accurate and comprehensive treatment of the lives and work of those who contributed to it.

The *DLB* Advisory Board

Introduction

The isolationist foreign policy to which the United States had been largely committed since the end of World War I was destroyed on 7 December 1941 by the Japanese attack on Pearl Harbor. By the end of World War II, the nation stood unchallenged as a world superpower; its involvement in international affairs had become a given. Under the leadership of President Harry S Truman, the United States undertook the rebuilding of Europe. But even as the most powerful and intact of countries, the United States could not escape being touched by the profound insecurity and moral uncertainty that were part of the legacy of the war.

The full disclosure of the horrors of the Holocaust forced the West to question, as never before, the inherent decency of human beings, and Hiroshima forced it to confront the real possibility of the extinction of all life. Americans could hardly ignore the fact that this potential for human annihilation was the clear result of technology, in which they had for so long posited an almost religious faith.

Moreover, at the end of World War II, the United States found itself, as the leader of the West, engaged in a new kind of international conflict, a cold war that continued for more than four decades. The nation assumed a responsibility to stop the spread of communism and thus became involved in a kind of undeclared conflict with the Soviet Union. International tension escalated in 1950 when communist North Korea invaded South Korea, and President Truman sent American troops to Asia as part of a United Nations police action to force out the invading North Koreans. This conflict lasted until 1953, with more than 150,000 American casualties (killed and wounded).

The Korean War forced Americans into a realization that there were, in fact, limitations to the power of even the strongest of nations and contributed significantly to a pervasive sense of instability and uncertainty in the United States. In 1952, Americans elected as their president Dwight Eisenhower, the former commander in chief of the Allied forces in Europe. Despite Eisenhower's paternal image, the 1950s were haunted by McCarthyism, with writers and other creative artists among the targets of the senator from Wisconsin.

The American writers who began publishing in the late 1940s and early 1950s were inevitably touched by this national mood of insecurity and loss of faith in moral certainty. Not surprisingly, several writers—including Norman Mailer, James Jones, and Gore Vidal—first published war novels; and a recurrent theme in this early World War II fiction is a warning against the imminent danger of an American fascism. Mailer and Jones, in *The Naked and the Dead* (1948) and *From Here to Eternity* (1951), create American generals who openly and unapologetically preach the necessity of strong leaders controlling the weak and directionless masses. This thematic concern was hardly limited to the war novelists; Saul Bellow, William Styron, and Chester Himes also produced fiction that expressed anxiety about the existence of grave internal threats to the preservation of American democracy. In *The Catcher in the Rye* (1951), certainly not a political novel, J. D. Salinger created an emblematic figure for the entire decade of the 1950s in Holden Caulfield, a youth in rebellion against a corrupt society and the "phonies" who personified it. In the novel *The Troubled Air* (1951) and in short stories, Irwin Shaw specifically protested against McCarthyism.

It is impossible to estimate the cost of self-censorship during the 1950s to American literature and to American culture in general. What is clear, though, is that the national mood of the decade inspired a withdrawal by several American writers from any sense of involvement in, or commitment to, the dominant culture of the nation. The clearest example of a literary repudiation of mainstream American society came from the group of writers known as the Beat Generation. Jack Kerouac, William Seward Burroughs, Allen Ginsberg, and Lawrence Ferlinghetti were among the best known of the Beats, writers who sought—in Zen Buddhism, jazz, and drugs—antidotes to what they perceived as the sterile conformity of American life. California, especially San Francisco and its City Lights bookstore, served as the West Coast center of the Beat movement. Columbia University occupied a similar position on the East Coast. Zen was not the only foreign philosophy to influence American literature and American culture in the years after World War II. French existentialism, with its emphasis upon the absence of any ethical system in the external universe and the resulting need for each individual to discover or create his or her own moral truths, had a strong appeal for postwar writers. A kind of fiction that can somewhat loosely be labeled as existential realism began to appear on the American literary scene during the 1950s. Existential overtones are present in the work of many of the important writers to emerge in America since 1945. For instance, perhaps the main consistency in Mailer's constantly evolving literary career has been his self-definition as an American existentialist.

Still, despite the considerable importance of the 1950s to American literature, it seems possible to argue that 1961 and 1962 more clearly represented the end of one era of the American novel and the beginning of a new one. During these two years at the beginning of one of the most turbulent decades in American history, Ernest Hemingway committed suicide, and William Faulkner died. The work of these men, who had dominated the national literary scene for more than three decades, constituted the triumph of modernism in American fiction. The literary modernists, also including F. Scott Fitzgerald and John Dos Passos, were committed to formalist experimentation, narrative irony, and explorations of the subjectivity of time. Hemingway and Faulkner, leading literary figures in their generation, produced a body of writing distinguished by its revolutionary sophistication in narrative technique and approach to characterization. Their work pointed the way for American fiction to go beyond William Dean Howells's "reality of the commonplace."

By the 1960s, the Hemingway-Faulkner legacy had begun to have an inhibiting effect on the American novel. It seemed increasingly difficult to surpass the innovations in modernist technique found in such masterpieces as *The Sound and the Fury* (1929), *Absalom, Absalom!* (1936), and *The Sun Also Rises* (1926). John Gardner advocated a retreat from what he regarded as the excesses of post-1960s American fiction in *On Moral Fiction* (1978). Modernism hardly disappeared from American literature after the war, however; it was practiced by such writers as John Cheever, William Maxwell, James Baldwin, Ralph Ellison, and Stanley Elkin. Cheever, who had been turning out remarkable short stories since the 1930s, published his first novel, *The Wapshot Chronicle,* in 1957 and followed it with *The Wapshot Scandal* in 1964 and *Falconer* in 1977. With his masterpiece, *Invisible Man* (1952), Ellison redirected the African American novel away from the naturalism of Richard Wright. Throughout the decade, American novelists searched for innovative structures that liberated them from the formalism and conscious narrative control of modernism.

The social and political turbulence of the 1960s contributed to the intensely felt need of many writers to escape virtually any limitations on their art. Few decades in American history have begun as hopefully or ended as pessimistically as the 1960s. Shortly after his election to the presidency in 1960, John F. Kennedy was challenged by the civil rights movement led by Martin Luther King Jr. and others. The issue came to a head on 17 June 1963, when King delivered his "I Have a Dream" speech to a crowd of more than 200,000 in Washington, D.C. Kennedy passed a federal civil rights bill to end the old barriers of racial segregation in America. The civil rights struggle inspired many American writers, artists, and entertainers, especially those of African American descent, to become political activists.

Domestically, then, the nation was already in a state of turmoil when Kennedy was killed in Dallas, Texas, on 22 November 1963. The television coverage of the assassination and its aftermath, especially the shooting of Lee Harvey Oswald by Jack Ruby, caused writers and critics to wonder if such a passive medium as the novel could remain viable to an audience trained to respond in such a shockingly instantaneous manner. The murders of Kennedy and Oswald resulted in an obsession with conspiracy theories that is still central to the American consciousness. Don DeLillo, probably the American writer most obsessed with the Kennedy assassination and its aftermath, responded to the paranoia resulting from the events of November 1963 with his *Libra* (1988), which fictionalizes the life of Oswald, depicting him as the pathetic agent of a conspiracy organized by disaffected CIA agents and organized crime.

As a result of America's accelerating involvement in Vietnam, the national mood darkened even more. After Lyndon Baines Johnson's election in 1964, the United States became heavily involved in a confusing war in the Southeast Asian nation that few Americans had previously known existed. Throughout the Johnson presidency, American resources and troops were poured into a struggle that was doomed from the first.

One consequence of the Vietnam legacy was the emergence in the United States of a counterculture. Young Americans of draft age simply began refusing to accept induction into the armed services; and antiwar demonstrations became almost a ritual of daily life on college campuses across the nation. Devoted to opposition to the war, experimentation with sex and drugs, and rebellion against everything associated with the middle-class establishment, the counterculture became highly visible throughout urban America; the residential section of San Francisco bounded by Haight and Ashbury Streets soon became its center. Middle-class and middle-aged Americans had little understanding or sympathy, creating a sharp generational division. In addition, African Americans, especially those in urban centers in the north and on the West Coast, were outraged by the war in Vietnam; they saw a disproportionate number of young black men being drafted to serve in Vietnam and came to believe that resources of potential use in America's inner cities were being wasted in Southeast Asia. The Watts section of Los Angeles in 1966 and the black section of Detroit in 1967 suffered massive outbreaks of rioting and looting.

On 4 April 1968, King was assassinated in Memphis; and on 5 June of that same year, Robert F. Kennedy, in a campaign for the presidency, was shot and killed in Los Angeles just after winning the California primary. Also in 1968 and 1970, national television audiences saw antiwar demonstrators violently clash with police and National Guard troops. It was almost difficult to feel the long-anticipated elation when the United States, in 1969, landed a man on the Moon; still, Neil Armstrong's moon walk represented one of the few seemingly unequivocal triumphs for American technology in the decade. Yet, for the novelist and especially for the writer of science fiction, even this revolutionary scientific breakthrough had ominous overtones, as what had previously belonged to the world of imaginative fantasy became one more aspect of reality.

Inevitably, a decade marked by such turmoil affected the American novel, even calling into question the traditional mimetic role of the novel, as American writers and critics began to wonder if fiction could hope to capture such an elusive reality. Even at the beginning of the decade, in "Writing American Fiction" (1961) novelist Philip Roth expressed doubt concerning this question:

> the American writer in the middle of the 20th century has his hands full in trying to understand, and then describe, and then make credible much of the American reality. It stupefies, it sickens, it infuriates, and finally it is even a kind of embarrassment to one's own meager imagination. The actuality is continually outdoing our talents, and the culture tosses up figures almost daily that are the envy of any novelist.

Throughout the rest of the decade, echoes of Roth's pessimistic analysis became commonplace in literary magazines.

Mailer, among others, wondered if the daily barrage of "information and news" from mass media effectively buried any objective and potentially verifiable reality that might exist. In the 1960s it became fashionable to issue pronouncements of the death of the novel. Seeking alternatives to modernism and traditional realism, American writers began to search for ways to revitalize the novel. The most inventive of them found

ways to use the chaos and contradictions of the time. First in short stories and then in a novel, *Snow White* (1967), Donald Barthelme perfected his technique of narrative "collage," a device that deliberately echoed the fragmentation and randomness of American culture and society. In his first novel, *V.* (1963), Thomas Pynchon transformed the national obsession with plots and conspiracies into an elaborate historical tour de force; in *Gravity's Rainbow* (1973) he explored an even darker and more complex landscape. Two World War II novels, one published at the beginning and the other at the end of the 1960s and based on different modes of narrative experimentation, depicted what almost seemed a different war from the one described in the late 1940s and early 1950s by writers such as Mailer and Jones. With his first novel, *Catch-22* (1961), Joseph Heller coined a phrase, which has since become part of the English and American vocabulary, to describe bureaucratic military irrationality and insanity. Kurt Vonnegut had been a prisoner of war in Dresden, Germany, a city of irreplaceable cultural importance and little military significance, when the Allies destroyed it in a technique known as firebombing. In *Slaughterhouse-Five* (1969) Vonnegut combined literary realism with science fiction to convey the technological horror that he had witnessed.

John Barth, in a 1967 essay provocatively called "The Literature of Exhaustion," concisely expressed the rationale for the continuous search for innovation in fictional technique during the 1960s. Careless readers saw the essay as simply another pronouncement of the death of the novel; and Barth, in places, seems to encourage this kind of misinterpretation. At one point, for instance, he says that he is "inclined to agree" with those who believe that "the novel, if not narrative literature generally, if not the printed word altogether, has by this hour of the world just about shot its bolt." However, the essay turns out to be a plea for the revitalization of the novel. Barth asserts that contemporary writers of fiction who ignore the work of such literary innovators as the Argentine writer Jorge Luis Borges, the Irish playwright Samuel Beckett, and the Russian-born novelist Vladimir Nabokov are doomed to create outdated and irrelevant fiction. Self-consciousness in narration is the key to creating the kind of art that Barth believed has validity; we need, he says, "novels which imitate the form of the Novel, by an author who imitates the role of Author."

The self-conscious, experimental fiction that Barth advocated and that he and others practiced was given different labels, the most common one probably being "metafiction." Assuredly, their work marked a movement of the American novel away from the controlled formalism of modernism and toward narrative openness and play. Whereas Hemingway and Faulkner had perfected techniques ranging from narrative minimalism to complex variations on the stream of consciousness to prevent any overt intrusion of an authorial presence that would destroy the reader's suspension of disbelief, the 1960s practitioners of metafiction devised elaborate methods to expedite precisely such intrusions. In his critical study *City of Words* (1977) Tony Tanner provided an excellent analysis of the fascination that such elaborate and often self-reflective alternate realities as labyrinths, mirrors, and libraries held for these writers. Barth's *Giles Goat-Boy* (1966) epitomizes 1960s metafiction.

Barth's fellow metafictionists include William H. Gass, John Hawkes, Robert Coover, William Gaddis, and Ishmael Reed. Gass published *Omensetter's Luck* in 1966 and debated the morality of metafiction with Gardner. Hawkes produced a horrifying metafictional allegory of World War II in *The Cannibal* (1949) and followed it with *Second Skin* (1964) and *Blood Oranges* (1971), while Gaddis brought a postmodernist perspective to his fictional exploration of the world of art in *The Recognitions* (1955). Reed revolutionized African American fiction even more completely than had Ellison with his experiments in elaborately constructed and resolutely nonmimetic fables, *Yellow Back Radio Broke Down* (1969) and *Mumbo Jumbo* (1972).

There were other ways to respond to the sense that contemporary reality had become too complex and chaotic to be captured by traditional realistic fiction. For instance, one could attempt to erase commonly accepted boundaries between fact and fiction. Describing contemporary events, Truman Capote in *In Cold Blood* (1965) and Mailer in such works as *The Armies of the Night* (1968) combined objective reporting with fictional subjectivity to produce a genre variously called "nonfiction fiction," "faction," or "the New Journalism." Styron in *The Confessions of Nat Turner* (1967) and, almost thirty years later, Madison Smartt Bell in *All Souls Rising* (1995) chose instead to fictionalize the past. Neither novel is a standard historical novel; both instead are meditations on the connections between racial hatred and guilt. Yet, for all the speculation during the 1960s that traditional literary realism had become inadequate to capture external reality, novels such as Hubert Selby Jr.'s *Last Exit to Brooklyn* (1964) and Joyce Carol Oates's *them* (1969) revitalized the tradition of American literary naturalism. Dennis Johnson recreated the world of the American urban proletariat in *Angels* (1968). Subsequently, Russell Banks emerged as one of a group of writers who can be called, in the language of critic June Howard, "latter-day naturalists." His *Affliction* (1989) is a grimly detailed account of the legacy of abuse and addiction in an isolated New

Hampshire family. Dorothy Allison published her own naturalistic account of the abuse of women and children in *Bastard Out of Carolina* (1992).

Too many generalizations have been made about the influence of the 1960s on subsequent American fiction, but the decade was a climactic and defining one for the novel and for American literature. It at least resulted in the necessity of closely reexamining long-standing assumptions about the viability of literary realism and modernism, even if such reexamination resulted in the reaffirmation of either or both of these modes of writing.

For the United States, the 1970s were calmer than the 1960s but still involved some turmoil. By the time the 1973 peace settlement was finally negotiated in Vietnam, 56,000 American troops had died, and the war left a legacy of division and recrimination. The men and women who served in the Vietnam conflict did not receive the kind of homecoming that had traditionally been given to returning American veterans of overseas combat. Some were openly denounced by antiwar demonstrators, while many were ignored.

Only in the late 1970s did the American mass media begin a realistic evaluation of the war and its legacy. Such award-winning American movies as *The Deer Hunter* (1978), *Coming Home* (1978), *Platoon* (1986), and *Born on the Fourth of July* (1989) depicted the nature of military combat in Vietnam and/or the postwar suffering of those who survived it. In addition, a group of American writers, most of them veterans of the conflict, have produced a small but distinguished body of fiction about the war. They have utilized a variety of literary approaches that echo the early realistic–naturalistic World War II novels of Mailer, Jones, and Shaw as well as the later postmodernist works of Heller and Vonnegut. For instance, Larry Heinemann's two novels, *Close Quarters* (1977) and *Paco's Story* (1987), are written in a predominantly realistic mode, while Tim O'Brien's *Going After Cacciato* (1978) experiments with postmodernist narration.

The Watergate scandal in 1972 and the forced resignation from office of President Richard M. Nixon two years later created a sense of national insecurity that lingered into the 1980s. The Nixon presidency was followed by the administrations of Gerald Ford and Jimmy Carter, which remained largely scandal-free but were nevertheless perceived as unfocused and ineffectual. But as the 1980s began, Ronald Reagan, a former motion-picture actor, called "the Great Communicator" because of his intuitive mastery of the mass media, became the first American president since Eisenhower to complete two terms in office. The Reagan presidency represented a return to political conservativism and a repudiation of much of the liberal Democratic agenda that had dominated national politics since Franklin D. Roosevelt's New Deal.

During this period the serious American writer became more alienated from the national mainstream than at any time since the 1920s at least. This alienation was partly, but not entirely, the result of national politics. The influence of the French thinkers Michel Foucault and Jacques Derrida led to new theories, first structuralism and then deconstruction, that questioned traditional assumptions about the nature and purpose of literature and of writing itself. Most structuralists argued that literary texts were interrelated and were not primarily the creation of individual writers but instead were the product of the structure of society's dominant ideas and values. Deconstructionists held that, because of the uncertainty of language itself, all writing must inevitably negate its own apparent meanings. Since these two theories assert that the traditional perception of an individual author of a novel is merely a convention and that the elusiveness of language constantly negates the possibility of any consistent theme or intent in any piece of writing, they challenged and repudiated the traditional view of the novel as a controlled individual work designed to speak to a mass audience.

Following in the tracks of Barth, Gass, Hawkes, and Reed, other exponents of postmodernist experimentation emerged. Walter Abish published two especially radical narrative experiments, *Alphabetical Africa* (1974) and *How German Is It?* (1980). In *The Public Burning* (1977) Coover crafted a postmodern absurdist version of the trial and execution of atomic spies Julius and Ethel Rosenberg in the 1950s. Paul Auster published three novellas under the umbrella title *The New York Trilogy* (1985–1987) in which he combines elements of the detective novel, literary history, and metaphysical speculation into a distinctive narrative form. Michael Chabon's 2000 Pulitzer Prize–winning novel, *The Amazing Adventures of Kavalier and Clay,* is an innovative tale concerning the history of comic-book superheroes. In *The Road to Wellville* (1993) T. Coraghessan Boyle mixed the genres of the historical novel and the fitness manual with the phenomenon of mass advertising (the paperback edition was even marketed inside a mock cereal box).

This new emphasis on the fundamentally arbitrary nature of literature and thus of critical judgments about it led to an extensive reexamination of the accepted canon of American literature. Beginning in the 1970s, feminist critics, merging some aspects of structuralist theory with the ideas of the French psychiatrist Jacques Lacan, argued that the canon had traditionally been established by white males and thus reflected an arbitrary and limited approach to American writing. The feminist critical agenda led to new appreciation for such previously undervalued American women writers as Kate Chopin, Zora Neale Hurston, and Anzia Yezierska. It further brought a new awareness of the stereotypes that male writers have often imposed on their women characters, prompting contemporary women writers to counter such stereotypes. Marge Piercy published *Gone to Soldiers* (1987), a story of World War II as experienced by female protagonists. Jane Smiley viewed Midwestern farm life from a Shakespearean perspective in *A Thousand Acres* (1991) and wrote a parody of the Midwestern land grant university in *Moo* (1995). Writing from her own postmodernist narrative perspective, Kathy Acker created a deliberately assaultive kind of feminist fiction.

The same impulses that produced feminist literary thinking have inspired, especially in academia, a view of literature and the novel as modes of social reform and cultural change. This approach to literature resulted in a new interest in writers from traditionally marginalized social and ethnic groups. Beginning in the 1970s, African American women writers such as Toni Morrison, Paule Marshall, Gloria Naylor, Gayl Jones, and Toni Cade Bambara exercised an influence on the American novel comparable to that of Bellow, Roth, Bernard Malamud, and other Jewish American writers. Jamaica Kincaid, a native of Antigua, and Bebe Moore Campbell have published their own black feminist fiction. Inspired by Isaac Bashevis Singer, the great Yiddish writer who immigrated to America, Bellow and Roth have continued their prolific work. Roth, in his Zuckerman trilogy and his other elaborate narrative experiments in merging fiction with biographical fact, has produced an especially complex body of work. Maxine Hong Kingston, Amy Tan, Gus Lee, and other Asian American writers have emerged, as have Tomás Rivera, Sandra Cisneros, Rolando Hinojosa-Smith, Rudolfo A. Anaya, Ana Castillo, and other Mexican American authors. The fiction and poetry of Scott Momaday, Louise Erdrich, James Welch, Leslie Marmon Silko, and Gerald Vizenor have inspired a Native American literary movement, with Vizenor also functioning as a major theorist of Native American literature. Sherman Alexie has followed Vizenor's lead in his postmodernist fiction. Finally, gay fiction has come out of the underground into which it had been forced. John Rechy, David Leavitt, Larry Kramer, Armistead Maupin, and Edmund White are among the most important postwar gay writers.

This increased cultural diversity has resulted in a questioning of old assumptions about the role of the American novelist in contributing to a voice of national consensus. Postmodernist novelists such as Pynchon and even writers speaking for socially marginalized groups must assume that they are addressing much more restricted and limited audiences than the traditional middle-class readership of fiction. There are, in addition, more prosaic reasons for the contemporary alienation of the serious American novelist from the middle class.

Television has been the communications medium of choice for middle- and lower-class America for more than fifty years; and for almost that long, writers and other intellectuals have bemoaned its shallowness and superficiality. Inevitably, the ubiquitous presence of television in America has trained its audience to respond more readily to instantaneous visual images than to the printed page. The impact of computers has also led to losses in readership. For an ever-increasing number of Americans, serious reading seems to be a lost art requiring too much concentration and too much solitude.

Still, it must be said that, in spite of such barriers, a few serious and important postwar novelists continue to speak to, and sometimes on behalf of, middle-class America. Especially in his Rabbit Angstrom quartet, John Updike depicts the morally ambiguous social rise and fall of an ordinary American and thus echoes the fictional agendas of William Dean Howells. Similarly, John Irving writes long novels that consciously echo the Victorian novels of George Eliot, Charles Dickens, and Anthony Trollope.

Other postwar American novelists have revitalized old fictional genres, many customarily associated with popular culture. For instance, regionalism has reemerged as a dominant force in American writing. William Maxwell, whose *They Came Like Swallows* appeared in 1937, published another lyrical re-creation of the small-town Midwest in *So Long, See You Tomorrow* (1980). Cormac McCarthy, Lee Smith, Clyde Edgerton, Lewis Nordan, Ernest J. Gaines, and Reynolds Price helped revive Southern regionalism, while Jim Harrison, Tom McGuane, and Rick Bass depict the landscape of the American West. After moving from Tennessee to Texas, McCarthy wrote primarily about the American West and Southwest. The prolific John Jakes produced several series of American historical romances.

It is safe to say that in spite of all the late 1950s and 1960s pronouncements of the demise of the novel, American fiction since World War II has been, and continues to be, vital and flourishing. It is distinguished by a diversity in form and subject that makes it a truly national literature.

—James R. Giles and Wanda H. Giles

Acknowledgments

This book was produced by Bruccoli Clark Layman, Inc. Tracy Simmons Bitonti was the in-house editor.

Production manager is Philip B. Dematteis.

Administrative support was provided by Ann M. Cheschi and Carol A. Cheschi.

Accountant is Ann-Marie Holland.

Copyediting supervisor is Sally R. Evans. The copyediting staff includes Phyllis A. Avant, Caryl Brown, Melissa D. Hinton, Philip I. Jones, Rebecca Mayo, Nancy E. Smith, and Elizabeth Jo Ann Sumner.

Editorial associates are Amelia B. Lacey, Michael S. Martin, Catherine M. Polit, and William Mathes Straney.

In-house prevetting is by Nicole A. La Rocque.

Permissions editor and database manager is Amber L. Coker.

Layout and graphics supervisor is Janet E. Hill. The graphics staff includes Zoe R. Cook and Sydney E. Hammock.

Office manager is Kathy Lawler Merlette.

Photography supervisor is Paul Talbot. Photography editor is Scott Nemzek.

Digital photographic copy work was performed by Joseph M. Bruccoli.

Systems manager is Donald Kevin Starling.

Typesetting supervisor is Kathleen M. Flanagan. The typesetting staff includes Patricia Marie Flanagan, Mark J. McEwan, and Pamela D. Norton. Freelance typesetters are Wanda Adams and Rebecca Mayo.

Walter W. Ross did library research. He was assisted by Jo Cottingham and the following other librarians at the Thomas Cooper Library of the University of South Carolina: circulation department head Tucker Taylor; reference department head Virginia W. Weathers; reference department staff Brette Barron, Marilee Birchfield, Paul Cammarata, Gary Geer, Michael Macan, Tom Marcil, Rose Marshall, and Sharon Verba; interlibrary loan department head John Brunswick; and interlibrary loan staff Robert Arndt, Hayden Battle, Alex Byrne, Bill Fetty, Marna Hostetler, and Nelson Rivera.

Dictionary of Literary Biography® • Volume Two Hundred Seventy-Eight

American Novelists Since World War II
Seventh Series

Dictionary of Literary Biography

Sherman Alexie

(7 October 1966 –)

Sarah A. Quirk
Waubonsee Community College

See also the Alexie entries in *DLB 175: Native American Writers of the United States* and *DLB 206: Twentieth-Century American Western Writers, First Series.*

BOOKS: *The Business of Fancydancing: Stories and Poems* (Brooklyn, N.Y.: Hanging Loose, 1992);

I Would Steal Horses (Niagara Falls, N.Y.: Slipstream, 1992);

Old Shirts & New Skins (Los Angeles: American Indian Studies Center, University of California, Los Angeles, 1993);

The Lone Ranger and Tonto Fistfight in Heaven (New York: Atlantic Monthly, 1993);

First Indian on the Moon (Brooklyn, N.Y.: Hanging Loose, 1993);

Seven Mourning Songs for the Cedar Flute I Have Yet to Learn to Play (Walla Walla, Wash.: Whitman College Book Arts Lab, 1994);

Water Flowing Home: Poems (Boise, Idaho: Limberlost, 1995);

Reservation Blues (New York: Atlantic Monthly, 1995);

The Summer of Black Widows (Brooklyn, N.Y.: Hanging Loose, 1996);

Indian Killer (New York: Atlantic Monthly, 1996);

Smoke Signals (New York: Hyperion, 1998);

The Man Who Loves Salmon (Boise, Idaho: Limberlost, 1998);

The Toughest Indian in the World (New York: Atlantic Monthly, 2000);

One Stick Song (Brooklyn, N.Y.: Hanging Loose, 2000).

PRODUCED SCRIPTS: "The Indian Fighter," radio, *The Sound of Writing: National Public Radio's Literary Magazine of the Air,* NPR, 1995;

Sherman Alexie (photograph © 1993 by Rex Rystedt; from the dust jacket for The Lone Ranger and Tonto Fistfight in Heaven, *1993)*

"Because My Father Was the Only Indian Who Saw Jimi Hendrix Play the Star Spangled Banner at Woodstock," radio, *This American Life,* NPR, 1996;

Smoke Signals, adapted by Alexie from his *The Lone Ranger and Tonto Fistfight in Heaven,* motion picture, Miramax, 1998.

RECORDING: *Reservation Blues: The Soundtrack,* by Alexie and Jim Boyd, Thunderwolf Productions, TWPRB95, 1995.

SELECTED PERIODICAL PUBLICATIONS—
UNCOLLECTED: "White Men Can't Drum," *New York Times Magazine,* 4 October 1992, pp. 30–31;
"Flight," *Ploughshares,* 20 (Spring 1994): 38–43;
"A Few Reservation Notes on Love and Hunger," *Left Bank,* 6 (Summer 1994): 94–103;
"The Writer's Notebook," *Zyzzyva,* 10 (Fall 1994);
"Beyond Talking Indian Chiefs," *New York Times,* 23 October 1994, pp. B1, B44;
"Generation Red," *Seattle Weekly,* 20 (15 February 1995): 16–23.

Sherman Alexie's writing has attracted a broad spectrum of readers in a relatively brief span. During his first eight years in publishing, Alexie was awarded the Washington State Arts Commission Poetry Fellowship (1991), the National Endowment for the Arts Poetry Fellowship (1992), the PEN/Hemingway Award for Best First Book of Fiction for the story collection *The Lone Ranger and Tonto Fistfight in Heaven* (1993), and the Lila Wallace–*Reader's Digest* Writers' Award (1994), all before age thirty. Widely anthologized as a poet, essayist, and short-story writer, Alexie has also won distinction for his novels: he received the Before Columbus Foundation American Book Award for *Reservation Blues* (1995). Readers admire his keen eye for contemporary details, his often panoramic narrative style, and the complex tragicomic characters in his novels. He has also become a voice of and for the American Indian community, as evidenced by his work with the American Indian College Fund and his participation in a discussion with President Bill Clinton on race in America on the PBS series *The Jim Lehrer NewsHour* (9 July 1998). Alexie is cautious, however, about serving as a spokesman for his community, observing that Indian (the term he prefers over Native American) writers are often outcasts within their own communities. "We don't really fit in within the Indian community, so we write to try to fit in and sound Indian," he states in a 1999 interview for *Poets & Writers,* "So it's ironic that we become the spokespeople for Indian country, that we are supposed to be representatives of our tribes."

Sherman Joseph Alexie Jr. was born on 7 October 1966 to Sherman Joseph Alexie and Lillian Agnes Cox Alexie in Spokane, Washington. His father was of Coeur d'Alene descent and his mother of Colville, Flathead, Spokane, and white descent. Born hydrocephalic, Alexie underwent a brain operation when he was six months old and was not expected to live; or, if he did survive, he was expected to suffer permanent disabili-

ties. Although his recovery was successful, for the first seven years of his life Alexie did suffer seizures and was regularly medicated. Alexie is a registered Spokane/Coeur d'Alene Indian, and he was raised and educated on the Spokane reservation in Wellpinit, Washington, until he attended Rearden High, a white high school some fifteen miles off the reservation. After graduating with honors, Alexie received a scholarship to study at Gonzaga University in Spokane from 1985 to 1987 and then at Washington State University in Pullman from 1988 to 1991, where, though three credits short, he was awarded a B.A. in American Studies in 1995.

Alexie's sojourn at Washington State University marks the turning point in his writing career. He considered medicine and law before attending Gonzaga, but he loved to read and had a voracious appetite for American writers such as John Steinbeck. At Washington State, Alexie enrolled in a creative-writing course taught by Alex Kuo, also of Indian descent, who became a mentor to Alexie. He gave Alexie a copy of an anthology edited by Joseph Bruchac, *Songs from This Earth on Turtle's Back* (1983), which inspired Alexie to start writing. Kuo's guidance and this exposure to the poetry of other Indian writers spurred Alexie to work on his first collection, *The Business of Fancydancing: Stories and Poems* (1992). Its appearance also marked the end of a five-year period of active alcoholism, an omnipresent disease in Indian communities and a recurring and devastating theme in his novels. In 1995 Alexie married a Native American woman, Diane, with whom he has two sons.

The potential desperation of American Indian life is widely documented, and it not only reveals Alexie's somewhat troubled personal history but also factors into almost every discussion of his novels. As one of the few remaining colonized cultures in the world, American Indians are under pressure to assimilate (thereby relinquishing many of their traditions and culturally inherited mores) or to wage an exhausting battle for pan-Indian unity. The casualties in such a battle range from wounded egos to abandoned reservation HUD homes. Under these circumstances it would seem difficult to find a humorous side of life; yet, Alexie presents humor as a means of cultural survival for American Indians—survival in the face of the larger American culture's stereotypes of American Indians and their concomitant distillation of individual tribal characteristics into one pan-Indian consciousness. Alexie's use of humor illustrates his refusal to create characters that play into destructive stereotypes. He uses the disparity between subject and approach in order to suggest the implicit fragmentation and inherent dislocation of all people, illustrating what many critics would term a postmodern sensibility. The process of embracing such disparate modes of content and form only serves to accentuate the survival aspect of Alexie's humor.

Across all of his works Alexie asks three questions: What does it mean to live as an Indian in this time? What does it mean to be an Indian man? Finally, what does it mean to live on an Indian reservation? These questions haunt the characters of Alexie's novels as they attempt to forge their identities from a broken ethnic history and the damaging stereotypes of popular culture. His portrayal of Indian life does not rely heavily on the set "traditional" Indian forms as defined by literary and cultural critics; instead, Alexie carefully and consciously blends elements of popular culture, Indian spirituality, and the drudgery of poverty-ridden reservation life to create his characters and the world they inhabit. The versions of Indian identity presented in Alexie's imaginary reservation are neither completely Indian nor exclusively contemporary American; his consciousness is informed by both popular culture and ethnic/tribal inheritance. His characters are as likely to listen to Jimi Hendrix as they are to listen to Buffy Sainte-Marie, as apt to watch basketball as they are to watch a powwow. Alexie, and by extension his characters, may not ultimately overcome or in any tangible way resolve the fragmentation of identity that is so much a part of contemporary Indian life, but they do learn how to survive and truly "see" themselves in a contemporary context. One way Alexie answers the questions of identity is to suggest, in his article "White Men Can't Drum" (4 October 1992), that people should "hit the button on the remote control so that everyone can hear the answer." He wants to turn off the media images of American Indians and look at the reality of daily reservation life.

Alexie's career began with his collections of poetry and short prose, *I Would Steal Horses, The Business of Fancydancing, Old Shirts & New Skins,* and *First Indian on the Moon,* all published in rapid succession between 1992 and 1993. The poems tend to use humor to express his struggles with contemporary American Indian reservation life. Though his poetic mode may often be humorous, the subject matter—poverty, starvation, alcoholism, and racism—is somber. In addition, the overall sentiment of his early poetry echoes Alexie's own view, stated in a later interview for *Publishers Weekly* (16 September 1996), that for the dominant American culture, "The most terrifying phrase in the world is when an Indian man grabs the microphone and says: I have a few words to say."

Well-reviewed as a poet, Alexie published his first sustained prose work, *The Lone Ranger and Tonto Fistfight in Heaven,* in 1993. This work is not a linear narrative built around a central or dominant character but is instead a series of stories involving several prominent

characters, many of whom reappear, in slightly altered or otherwise accentuated form, in the novel *Reservation Blues.* There is little plot in these pieces, yet in each a series of seemingly minor actions builds to an emotional or philosophical climax. *The Lone Ranger and Tonto Fistfight in Heaven* can be read as a bildungsroman with dual protagonists, Victor Joseph and Thomas Builds-the-Fire, moving from relative innocence to a mature level of experience. It can also be read as a collection of sometimes interconnected short stories told from a consistent narrative voice—an idea one reviewer, Lindsay Throm, suggested in her 1 September 1993 *Booklist* review. Taken from either perspective, the work clearly represents Alexie's first foray into novelistic territory and perspective.

In order to understand the development of Victor and Thomas in *Reservation Blues,* it is useful to investigate the two characters' senses of identity in *The Lone Ranger and Tonto Fistfight in Heaven.* Victor is a character in crisis. He initiates the first section, "Every Little Hurricane," and he first appears as a child being jarred from bed by violent weather: "a hurricane dropped from the sky in 1976 and fell so hard on the Spokane Indian Reservation that it knocked Victor from his bed and his latest nightmare." Victor's identity is found more in the utopian world of dreams and visions at this early point in the collection than it is in the dystopian physical world. There is the unstated realization that Victor cannot resurrect a pure Indian heritage. He also cannot fully connect with the technologically dominated world of the contemporary reservation, where the "television was always too loud, too loud, until every emotion was measured by the half hour." Victor's identity resists being transformed by either extreme—the idealized past or the technologically driven present—so he adopts fragments of each. At times he is the Indian Victor wanting to connect with his lost heritage, the thirteen-year-old who wanted to "figure out what it meant to be Indian." Victor recognizes his ethnic/cultural inheritance while concurrently reflecting on how distant this inheritance really feels in the context of his contemporary life. By identifying with dominant cultural icons—Creamsicles, *The Brady Bunch,* and rock and roll, to name a few—Victor does carve out a place for himself in the culturally amalgamative present.

Though Victor has great difficulty coping with his heritage, Thomas has little problem recognizing his Indian legacy. For him, the identity struggle is really only to find a contemporary sense of self. Thomas is the "storyteller that nobody wanted to listen to." His life is the sum total of stories: he is revealed through the act of telling them. "We are all given one thing by which our lives are measured, one determination," Thomas states, and his are "the stories which can change the world." Thomas

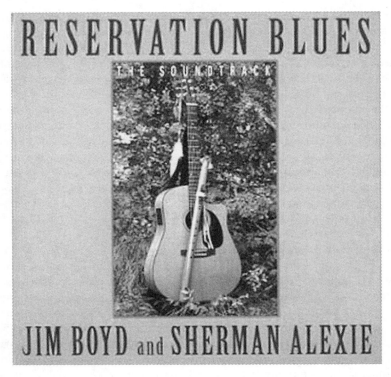

Cover for the album of songs drawn from Alexie's 1995 novel, about an all-Indian rock and blues band

goes beyond the role of the storyteller and at times even appears to be physically and emotionally composed of stories: "I have only my stories which came to me before I ever had the words to speak. I learned a thousand stories before I took my first thousand steps. They are all I have. It's all I can do."

Several characters in *The Lone Ranger and Tonto Fistfight in Heaven*, Victor and Thomas included, can be read as fictional representations of Alexie's own struggle with identity at this point in his career. Given that there is not a singular, guiding narrative voice in this collection, it is unclear at points just who is speaking. In one section, "Imagining the Reservation," the absence of an identifiable "I" makes the story read as Alexie's own words: "Imagination is the only weapon on the reservation." He asks in this same segment, "Does every Indian depend on Hollywood for a twentieth-century vision?", perhaps unaware that he has effectively answered himself through the act of writing the collection.

Critical response to *The Lone Ranger and Tonto Fistfight in Heaven* was positive. Carl L. Bankston III noted in *The Bloomsbury Review* (September–October 1993) that "Alexie blends an almost despairing social realism with jolting flashes of visionary fantasy and a quirky sense of gallows humor." Reynolds Price wrote in *The New York Times Book Review* (17 October 1993) that Alexie "lures us with a live and unremitting lyric energy

in the fast-moving, occasionally surreal and surprisingly comic language of his progress."

In 1995 Alexie published his first full-fledged novel, *Reservation Blues*. Victor and Thomas reappear, as does the reservation setting, though the plot is by no means a continuation of *The Lone Ranger and Tonto Fistfight in Heaven*. The novel focuses on the fleeting musical career of an all-Indian rock band called Coyote Springs. *Reservation Blues* begins, however, with an interloper, the legendary bluesman Robert Johnson, stumbling onto the fictional Spokane reservation. This plot device is another example of Alexie's inclusion of movie stars and musicians in his works. Johnson appears on the reservation because he is "lookin' for a woman" to fix what ails him. The woman in question is Big Mom, the spiritual center of the Spokane reservation community. Johnson's quest for spiritual fulfillment clearly mimics the questing plot so often seen in Alexie's works. This quest, however, is much more direct, and much more Indian, than those pursued by the members of Coyote Springs: Johnson seeks fullness on the reservation, while the band initially seeks fulfillment off the reservation in the white world of record production.

Coyote Springs coalesces after Thomas picks up Johnson's abandoned (or lost) guitar, stating "This isn't my guitar . . . But I'm going to change the world with it." Victor and Junior then join Thomas, and after adding a few more members the band is asked by two wily record executives, Phil Sheridan and George Wright, to audition for a record contract in New York. Sheridan and Wright, though seemingly well intentioned, help bring about the disintegration of the band, a reference to the way in which their historical namesakes, both nineteenth-century U.S. Army generals, attempted to destroy the Spokane tribe.

Reservation Blues alludes to another prominent theme in Alexie's novels, the suggestion that Indians cannot and should not expect fair, unbiased treatment from a country and a culture that have consistently and pervasively sought their destruction. Whether ordering food at a local diner or signing a major record deal in New York, the Indians in this novel cannot expect to be treated fairly. They repeatedly encounter the legacy of greed, genocide, and cultural Manifest Destiny handed down from one generation of white Americans to the next.

Each chapter of the novel commences with lyrics from Coyote Springs blues songs. Each song guides and frames the ensuing chapter, suggesting both thematic content and plot progression. One example is the opening lyrics of the chapter titled "Father and Farther," which state, in part:

> And sometimes, father, you and I
> Are like a warrior
> Who can only paint half his face
> While the other half cries and cries and cries

The chapter that follows this song articulates the frequent Alexie theme of missing and/or absent fathers. Chess and Checkers Warm Water, two Flathead Indian women, recount their father's alcoholism, and Thomas copes with the return of his own alcoholic father. The title song, "Reservation Blues," presents the themes of hunger (both physical and spiritual), desolation, poverty, and despair; the concluding song, "Wake," completes the circular construction of the plot and hints at a certain hopefulness that is rarely present in the novel as a whole. "I can't bury my grief," Alexie writes, "Unless I bury my fear"; and "I think it's time for us to find a way." Alexie later collaborated with Jim Boyd to put these lyrics to music on *Reservation Blues: The Soundtrack* in 1995.

Besides music, basketball is a major device in many of Alexie's works, but it holds a particularly valuable position in *Reservation Blues*. Alexie played basketball in high school and considers the basketball court an appropriate battleground for a twentieth-century reenactment of nineteenth-century Indian-American conflicts. As Peter Donahue writes in "New Warriors, New Legends: Basketball in Three Native American Works

of Fiction" (1997): "In *Reservation Blues,* basketball becomes the means of resistance in the grudge-match that Samuel Builds-the-Fire and Lester FallsApart have with the Tribal Cops." The use of basketball as a controlling metaphor once again suggests Alexie's reconfiguration of contemporary events in light of the historical context of Indian reservations and the essentially conflicted state of contemporary Indian identity. And Alexie himself mingles his writing career with basketball: he applies the discipline of shooting hoops to routine daily writing and is known to take the court between writing sessions.

As in *The Lone Ranger and Tonto Fistfight in Heaven,* the central characters of *Reservation Blues* seek to answer questions of identity and identification: Victor is haunted by an abusive past; Thomas must cope with his father's absenteeism and alcoholism; Junior needs to reconcile his failed relationships with white women and his unsuccessful college experience; and Chess and Checkers need to address their parents' deaths and the death of a younger sibling. All of the characters need to reconcile issues in order to move forward and become individuals in their own rights. They must also come to terms with Alexie's central question of what it means to be an Indian in a country that has forgotten that Indians exist, seeing them instead as artifacts of a distant past rather than members of a living tribe. This concurrent embracing and loathing of one's ancestry is succinctly stated in one conversation between Thomas, Chess, and Checkers:

> "Sometimes," Checkers said, "I hate being Indian."
> "Ain't that the true test?" Chess said, "You ain't really Indian unless there was some point in your life that you didn't want to be."
> "Enit," Thomas said.

Thomas's affirmative "enit" can be read two ways. Since Thomas is the storyteller, it is in one sense a narrative affirmation. Further, since Alexie, like his characters, struggled with many of the same experiences—death of a sibling, alcoholism, a dismal first collegiate experience, and relationships with white women—it is, in another sense, Alexie's own affirmation. Though wryly amusing, this statement gets to the heart of many of Alexie's works—to be Indian is to confront pain, poverty, and alienation, and to laugh in spite of it all.

The female characters in *Reservation Blues* represent Alexie's first real attempt to look at reservation life through women's eyes. Chess and Checkers are, in many ways, the female equivalents of Victor and Thomas. Yet, though they help the band and at times become the focus of the narrative, they are not as fully developed or well-rounded as their male equivalents. In fact, one can also read Chess and Checkers as the authentic Indian equivalents of two non-Indian female characters, Veronica and Betty, who steal the recording contract out from under Coyote Springs. In their commodification of the Indian experience and life, they perhaps reflect Alexie's frustration with both a publishing industry and reading public that seemed to prefer white portrayals of Indian life instead of an authentic Indian voice and concerns.

The critical reception of *Reservation Blues* was not unanimously positive, as it had been with his earlier books. Several critics found the work ill organized, the characters underdeveloped, or the plot and themes unsettling. In "The Exaggeration of Despair in Sherman Alexie's *Reservation Blues*," from the *Wicazo Sa Review* (1995), critic Gloria Bird claims that the novel is "specifically a product, and reflection, of the techno-generation, clever at times, but not the serious literature it's cracked up to be." Another Indian author, Leslie Marmon Silko, in her review for *The Nation* (12 June 1995), relates the plot of *Reservation Blues* to Alexie's life, stating: "It is difficult not to imagine *Reservation Blues* as a reflection of the ambivalence that a young, gifted author might have about 'success' in the ruthless, greed-driven world of big publishing." Other critics found the novel compelling; Howard Meredith noted in *World Literature Today* (1996) that "The art of Sherman Alexie surprises and delights the reader as the dreamlike images and hard-edged realities in *Reservation Blues* find a center on the Spokane Indian Reservation." Meredith finds the tragic nature of the novel, a component Bird considers an exaggerated sense of reality, not at all troubling, stating that "Form and content act in unity to provide a captivating story of the tragic sense of life within a Spokane frame of reference."

Alexie's second novel, *Indian Killer* (1996), is a mystery, a crime that remains unsolved, and a plot line that remains unresolved. Most murder-mystery novels include several characters with both the motive and means to have committed the crime—whatever form that crime may take. *Indian Killer* is no exception. Also in the traditional murder-mystery format, as the plot progresses, the number of suspected killers decreases as more information is revealed, until, in the penultimate moment, the killer is revealed. Alexie, however, eschews such a standard pattern, and in fact reverses it. As *Indian Killer* progresses, the number of potential culprits increases, and the novel does not end with a clear revelation.

In order to understand the progression and sense of order in *Indian Killer,* it is necessary to look at the Ghost Dance and its relevance to the text. The Ghost Dance represents the American Indian belief in a pan-Indian gathering that will cleanse the earth of white

usurpers and bring back the fertility and wholeness of the past. Using the Ghost Dance as metaphor provides a coherent framework within which the characters, their motivations, and Alexie's motivations in *Indian Killer* become focused. The metaphor can be viewed as liberating, both from a sociocultural perspective and in terms of form. With *Indian Killer* Alexie has moved from merely reacting to American racism and oppression to a more active, albeit seemingly destructive, role.

The plot of *Indian Killer* involves a series of murders (the victims are white men) that explodes racial tensions in and around Seattle, Washington. The media, and in particular a right-wing talk-radio host named Truck Shultz, dub the perpetrator the "Indian Killer" because of the killer's penchant for leaving feathers at the scenes of the crimes. This one action of an allegedly demented madman infuriates whites and Indians alike, and it allows Alexie the ability to explore racial tensions and stereotypes. Violent stereotypes are matched with violent repercussions on both sides, and neither Indians nor whites escape having to examine their own identities and the fundamental lies on which they may be based.

John Smith, the central consciousness of the novel, is an emotionally disturbed Indian of indeterminate tribal origin who was adopted almost from birth into a white suburban family. His quest to find a real sense of identity forms one of the many subplots in the novel. While watching a basketball game, John observes:

> So many Indians, so many tribes, many sharing similar features, but also differing in slight and important ways. The Makahs different than the Quinaults, the Lummi different from the Puyallup. There were Indians with dark skin and jet-black hair. Green-eyed Indians. Indians with black blood. Indians with Mexican blood. Indians with white blood. Indians with Asian blood. All of the laughing and carrying on. Many Indians barely paying attention to the game. They were talking, telling jokes, and laughing loudly. So much laughter. John wanted to own that laughter, never realizing that their laughter was a ceremony used to drive away personal and collective demons.

In this remarkable passage Alexie blends his poetic, lyric sensibilities with a strong sense of voice, characterization, and finally, authorial comment.

In his search for identity John encounters Marie Polatkin, a University of Washington student enrolled in an "Introduction to Native American Literature" course taught by a white professor, Dr. Mather. Marie's radical Indian politics clash with Dr. Mather's anthropological view on Indian literatures when she reads that his syllabus includes "three anthologies of traditional Indian stories edited by white men, a book of tradi-

*Dust jacket for Alexie's 1996 novel, a murder mystery that examines racial stereotypes
(Richland County Public Library)*

tional Indian poetry translations edited by a Polish-American Jewish man, and an Indian murder mystery written by some local white writer named Jack Wilson, who claimed he was a Shilshomish Indian." Wilson, a former policeman turned mystery writer, appears later in the novel working out his own search for identity, as does Marie's cousin Reggie Polatkin, an angry, aimless young man, who had a run-in with Dr. Mather over a collection of recorded Indian oral stories.

There is humor in *Indian Killer,* but the humor is more subdued and much darker than in Alexie's earlier work, particularly *Reservation Blues.* Alexie permeates his portrayal of Truck Shultz with an unrelenting series of radio sound-bite racial slurs and ridiculously parodied right-wing clichés that at times take on a satiric, amusing tone. Many of the Indian characters' interactions reveal Alexie's signature humor. But humor is not central to *Indian Killer,* though it is still used to illustrate survival in the face of overwhelming adversity.

Indian Killer met with mixed reviews. Many found the violence too much to bear, but others found the mystery plot enthralling. *Indian Killer* was named one of the

Best of Pages in *People* magazine (30 December 1996). In some ways the positive reviews of his earlier work may have tainted critical reception of Alexie's murder-mystery novel, since *Indian Killer* did mark a radical departure–in style and form–from much of his earlier work. Yet, Richard E. Nicholls, in his 24 November 1996 *New York Times Book Review* endorsement, found this shift of focus logical, observing that "Having explored the way reservation Indians are crippled or overcome by the neglect and assaults of the larger society, he now turns his attention to the experiences of Indians who go out (or are taken out) into the world." Nicholls located many of the persistent themes of Alexie's earlier work in *Indian Killer* and provided a keen assessment: "His vigorous prose, his haunted, surprising characters and his meditative exploration of the sources of human identity transform into resonant tragedy what might have been a melodrama in less assured hands."

The themes of identity formation and survival humor reassert themselves in *Smoke Signals,* Alexie's 1998 motion-picture adaptation of *The Lone Ranger and Tonto Fistfight in Heaven* and a major shift in his career. *Smoke*

Signals takes its plot from one section, namely "This Is What It Means to Say Phoenix, Arizona," but some additional characters and several incidents are adapted from the rest of the collection. Alexie collaborated on the project with director Chris Eyre, a Cheyenne/Arapaho Indian. *Smoke Signals* won two awards at the 1998 Sundance Film Festival and is considered to be the first movie written, directed, acted, and produced by American Indians to ever receive such widespread release.

Since the publication of *Indian Killer* Alexie has focused on his burgeoning movie career. "As I have been working with film," Alexie notes in a *Poets & Writers* interview with Susan Berry Brill de Ramirez (1999), "I've come to realize sitting in a movie theater is the contemporary equivalent of sitting around the fire listening to a storyteller." Alexie divides his time among many pursuits, working on movie scripts, future novels, and poetry simultaneously. Another story collection, *The Toughest Indian in the World,* and a volume of poetry and prose, *One Stick Song,* appeared in 2000. Given his successes at national poetry slams, Alexie seems to have a future in performance as well. According to his official website, <http://www.fallsapart.com>, Alexie made his stand-up comedy debut in 1999 at the Foolproof Northwest Comedy Festival in Seattle. Regardless of the media he chooses, the frequency with which he is anthologized is evidence of his currency. He is a novelist who has altered the ways in which a generation of Indians sees themselves in the media and the ways a host of white readers see Indians in their communities. In doing so, he demonstrates how a novel can be a lyrical, genre-bending tool for self discovery. Alexie will continue to challenge the form, to make it include every facet of his understanding of contemporary Indian life.

Interviews:

Kelly Myers, "Reservation Stories with Author Sherman Alexie," *Tonic* (11 May 1995): 8–9;

Doug Marx, "Sherman Alexie: A Reservation of the Mind," *Publishers Weekly* (16 September 1996): 39–40;

John Purdy, "Crossroads: A Conversation with Sherman Alexie," *Studies in American Indian Literatures,* 9, no. 4 (1997): 1–18;

Dennis West and Joan West, "Sending Cinematic Smoke Signals: An Interview with Sherman Alexie," *Cineaste,* 23, no. 4 (1998): 28–31, 59;

Renfreu Neff, "An Interview With: Sherman Alexie," *Creative Screenwriting,* 5, no. 4 (1998): 18–19, 59;

Susan Berry Brill de Ramirez, "Fancy Dancer: A Profile of Sherman Alexie," *Poets & Writers,* 27, no. 1 (1999): 54–59.

References:

James Cox, "Muting White Noise: The Subversion of Popular Culture in Narratives of Conquest in Sherman Alexie's Fiction," *Studies in American Indian Literatures,* 9, no. 4 (1997): 52–70;

Peter Donahue, "New Warriors, New Legends: Basketball in Three Native American Works of Fiction," *American Indian Culture and Research Journal,* 21, no. 2 (1997): 43–60;

Jennifer Gillian, "Reservation Home Movies: Sherman Alexie's Poetry," *American Literature,* 68, no. 1 (1996): 91–110;

Jane Hafen, "Rock and Roll, Redskins, and Blues in Sherman Alexie's Work," *Studies in American Indian Literatures,* 9, no. 4 (1997): 71–78;

Karen Jorgensen, "White Shadows: The Use of Doppelgangers in Sherman Alexie's *Reservation Blues,*" *Studies in American Indian Literatures,* 9, no. 4 (1997): 19–25;

Ron McFarland, "Sherman Alexie's Polemical Stories," *Studies in American Indian Literatures,* 9, no. 4 (1997): 27–38;

Janine Richardson, "Magic and Memory in Sherman Alexie's *Reservation Blues,*" *Studies in American Indian Literatures,* 9, no. 4 (1997): 39–51.

Rudolfo A. Anaya

(30 October 1937 –)

Roberto Cantú
California State University, Los Angeles

See also the Anaya entries in *DLB 82: Chicano Writers, First Series* and *DLB 206: Twentieth-Century American Western Writers, First Series.*

BOOKS: *Bless Me, Ultima* (Berkeley, Cal.: Quinto Sol, 1972);

Heart of Aztlán (Berkeley, Cal.: Editorial Justa, 1976);

Tortuga (Berkeley, Cal.: Editorial Justa, 1979);

The Silence of the Llano (Berkeley, Cal.: Tonatiuh-Quinto Sol International, 1982);

The Legend of La Llorona: A Short Novel (Berkeley, Cal.: Tonatiuh-Quinto Sol International, 1984);

The Adventures of Juan Chicaspatas (Houston: Arte Público, 1985);

A Chicano in China (Albuquerque: University of New Mexico Press, 1986);

The Farolitos of Christmas (Santa Fe: New Mexico Magazine, 1987);

Lord of the Dawn: The Legend of Quetzalcóatl (Albuquerque: University of New Mexico Press, 1987);

Alburquerque (Albuquerque: University of New Mexico Press, 1992);

Descansos: An Interrupted Journey, by Anaya, Juan Estevan Arellano, and Denise Chávez (Albuquerque: El Norte, 1995);

Zia Summer (New York: Warner, 1995);

Jalamanta: A Message from the Desert (New York: Warner, 1996);

Rio Grande Fall (New York: Warner, 1996);

Maya's Children: The Story of La Llorona (New York: Hyperion Books for Children, 1997);

Farolitos for Abuelo (New York: Hyperion Books for Children, 1998);

Isis in the Heart: A Love Poem (Albuquerque: Valley of the Kings Press, 1998);

My Land Sings: Stories from the Río Grande (New York: Morrow Junior Books, 1999);

Shaman Winter (New York: Warner, 1999);

Elegy on the Death of César Chávez (El Paso, Tex.: Cinco Puntos, 2000);

Rudolfo A. Anaya (photograph by Mimi Anaya; courtesy of the author)

Roadrunner's Dance (New York: Hyperion Books for Children, 2000).

Collection: *The Anaya Reader,* foreword by César A. González-T. (New York: Warner, 1995).

PLAY PRODUCTIONS: *Who Killed Don José?* Albuquerque, N.M., La Compañía, Menaul High School Auditorium, 24 July 1987;

The Season of La Llorona, Albuquerque, N.M., El Teatro de la Compañía de Alburquerque, 14 October 1987;

The Farolitos of Christmas, Albuquerque, N.M., La Compañía, Menaul High School Auditorium, December 1987;

Matachines, Tucson, Ariz., 19 October 1989;

Billy the Kid, Albuquerque, N.M., La Casa Teatro, 11 July 1997;

Angie, Albuquerque, N.M., La Casa Teatro, 10 July 1998.

PRODUCED SCRIPT: *Bilingualism: Promise for Tomorrow,* screenplay by Anaya, Carlos Penichet, and Jeff Penichet, motion picture, Bilingual Educational Services, 1976.

OTHER: "The Writer's Landscape: Epiphany in Landscape," in *Latin American Literary Review,* 5, no. 10 (1977): 98–102;

A Ceremony of Brotherhood, 1680–1980, edited by Anaya and Simón Ortíz (Albuquerque: Academía, 1980);

Cuentos Chicanos, edited by Anaya and Antonio Márquez (Albuquerque: University of New Mexico Press, 1980);

"In Commemoration: One Million Volumes," in *The Magic of Words: Rudolfo A. Anaya and His Writings,* edited by Paul Vassallo (Albuquerque: University of New Mexico Press, 1982): 305–307;

Voces: An Anthology of Nuevo Mexicano Writers, edited by Anaya (Albuquerque: El Norte, 1987);

Flow of the River/Corre el río, introduction by Anaya (Albuquerque: Hispanic Culture Foundation, 1988);

Aztlán: Essays on the Chicano Homeland, edited by Anaya and Francisco Lomelí (Albuquerque: Academía/ El Norte, 1989);

Tierra: Contemporary Short Fiction of New Mexico, edited by Anaya (El Paso, Tex.: Cinco Puntos, 1989);

Who Killed Don José? in *New Mexico Plays,* edited by David R. Jones (Albuquerque: University of New Mexico Press, 1989), pp. 197–231;

"Rudolfo Anaya, An Autobiography," in *Rudolfo A. Anaya: Focus on Criticism,* edited by César A. González-T. (La Jolla, Cal.: Lalo Press, 1990), pp. 359–388.

TRANSLATION: José Griego y Maestas, *Cuentos: Tales from the Hispanic Southwest* (Santa Fe: Museum of New Mexico Press, 1980).

SELECTED PERIODICAL PUBLICATIONS– UNCOLLECTED: "A Writer Discusses His Craft," *CEA Critic: An Official Journal of the College English Association,* 40, no. 1 (1977): 39–43;

"The Courage of Expression," *Century: A Southwest Journal of Observation and Opinion,* 2 (2 December 1981): 16–18;

"Southwest Christmas: A Mosaic of Rituals Celebrates Spiritual, Community Renewal," *Los Angeles Times,* 27 December 1981, IV: 3;

"Still Invisible, Lord, Still Invisible," *AMAE, Journal of the Association of Mexican-American Educators* (1982– 1983): 35–41;

"*The Silence of the Llano:* Notes from the Author," *MELUS,* 11 (Winter 1984): 47–57;

"At a Crossroads: Hispanos Struggle to Retain Values in the Face of Changing Lifestyles," *New Mexico Magazine* (June 1987): 60–64;

"The Myth of Quetzalcóatl in a Contemporary Setting: Mythical Dimensions/Political Realities," *Western American Literature,* 23, no. 3 (1988): 195–200.

Rudolfo A. Anaya is known as a novelist, but his work includes essays, short stories, poetry, and drama. Flourishing as a writer during the 1970s, Anaya has written novels that represent the American Southwest and its historical conflicts, often with traces of autobiography subtly fictionalized and patterned after a literary tradition that includes Mexican/Chicano cultural history and the work of American authors such as James Fenimore Cooper and Henry David Thoreau. The American frontier experience and ideas of the wilderness are thus fused in Anaya's novels, resulting in a style and narrative vision that have appealed to both nonspecialist and scholarly readers. Deeply embedded in the cultural history of New Mexico, Anaya's novels have also been the critical arena for national and international scholarly debates on the analysis and interpretation of Chicano literature.

Rudolfo Alfonso Anaya was born in New Mexico on 30 October 1937 in the village of Pastura. His mother's family had come from Mexico and settled in the Puerto de Luna Valley, adjacent to the Pecos River and south of Santa Rosa. On his father's side, Anaya has roots in the pre–United States history of New Mexico: Anaya's grandfather was one of the original incorporators of La Merced de Atrisco land grant in Albuquerque. According to Anaya, "The land grant which my father's family had helped incorporate consisted of a huge area of land stretching for miles along the Rio Grande in Albuquerque's south valley, and then for miles west into desert as far as the Rio Puerco." A family of farmers and cowboys, Anaya's ancestors lived a rugged life in a desolate land. In a 1990 autobiographical essay Anaya recalls the independent spirit of his mother, Rafaelita Mares, and her resolve to leave her father's valley in 1919 to marry Solomon Bonney, a

Paperback covers for a later printing of Anaya's first novel, about the influence of a curandera
(faith healer) on the life of the narrator (Bruccoli Clark Layman Archives)

man from El Llano Estacado (the Staked Plain, the region buffering Texas and New Mexico). Bonney died in 1925, and Anaya wrote of his mother's situation, "A widow with two small children has no time for a long romance. She married Martín Anaya, a man without pretensions, a man who knew how to work the cattle and the sheep of the big ranchers." Martín Anaya had a daughter from a previous marriage, and he and Mares had seven children: three boys (Larry, Martín, and Rudolfo) and four girls (Edwina, Angelina, Dolores, and Loretta).

Anaya's calling as a writer stems from a regional crossroads of myths (Pueblo, Spanish, Mexican) and of legends (such as the cowboy). In his autobiographical essay Anaya describes being born with the umbilical cord tied around his neck; he was saved by the strong hands of a local midwife known as La Grande, a *curandera* (healer) and a woman of wisdom. In most of his novels and essays he thus associates healing and folk wisdom with personal power. His first lessons in story-

telling were taught by his grandfather, Liborio Mares, from whom Anaya learned the magic of words. The midwife La Grande and Liborio Mares represent in Anaya's memory the origins of his quest as a writer and the foundations of his interest in ancestry, the landscape, and healing. According to Anaya, "All my life I will meet such people, people who understand the power of the human soul, its potential. If I am to be a writer, it is the ancestral voices of these people who will form a part of my quest, my search."

Anaya's parents moved from the village of Pastura to Santa Rosa when Anaya was a baby. These were years spent close to his mother's side, absorbing the Catholicism and folklore of his ancestors, the prayers at the local Santa Rosa de Lima church, and the sense of wonder when exploring beyond the barren hill where the family lived next to several other families. In autobiographical essays published in 1982 and in 1990, Anaya filters memories of his cultural environment and sense of landscape through a literary tradition that he has made his own. In other words, the recollections of his youth in a village of New Mexico, far from being vivid memories of a pastoral youth and way of life, or glimpses of an ethnic culture in its pristine and unpolluted state, have on the contrary been shaped—and, to a great extent, determined—by a literary education and a university training. Anaya redefines New Mexico's wilderness not as a site of Anglo-American conquest or spiritual awakenings but as a place of encounters where peoples of different civilizations meet, meld, and produce a higher form of humanity. Hence, Anaya's heroes represent the transformation of an ordinary person into a human being with special gifts not defined or determined by racial categories. These early experiences, this cultural background, and these literary appropriations constitute the thematic and ideological core of Anaya's first novel, *Bless Me, Ultima* (1972), and of most of his writing.

The family moved to Albuquerque shortly after Anaya completed the eighth grade. In Barelas, a Mexican barrio of Albuquerque, life was shaped by prejudice, revealing to Anaya the meaning of poverty in the context of urban racism and exposing him to the city's version of the *pachuco* (young tough) and to the migration of rural people to urban centers, uprooted by the economic promises of postwar America. His life in Barelas consisted of years of hard work, a cultural transition, and personal growth in spite of the barrio gangs and drugs. Anaya attended Washington Junior High and Albuquerque High School. One afternoon, while swimming in a nearby irrigation ditch, he dove in head first and fractured two neck vertebrae, nearly drowning. He was paralyzed from the neck down and was told by doctors that he might never walk again. After spending a summer in the Carrie Tingley Hospital, resolved to regain the use of his legs and arms, he returned home, walking with the use of a cane. Anaya's mother nursed him through the most difficult period of the paralysis; meanwhile, Anaya wondered if he had been saved for a special role in life. This early awareness of his own mortality was later re-created in his works through figurations of the end of the world, metaphors of death and resurrection in characters with physical disabilities, and narratives recounting the hero's homecoming.

Anaya graduated from high school in 1956 and, inspired by a desire to learn and succeed, he attended business school but soon realized he would make an unhappy accountant. He enrolled in the University of New Mexico, kept the books for a neighborhood bar, and read into the late hours of the night. These were years in which his Chicano friends began to fall behind in the race toward achievement and mobility. "We were Mexican students," he recalls, "unprepared by

high school to compete as scholars. We were tolerated rather than accepted. The thought was still prevalent in the world of academia that we were better suited as janitors than scholars." Anaya adds: "We were different, and we were made to feel different. It was a lonely time; many of us did not survive." The exposure to conflicting ideas and to a secularized version of knowledge also shook Anaya's Catholic faith at its foundations. Literature became a substitute for religion, and writing an act of faith. Anaya attended the University of New Mexico, where he obtained a bachelor's degree in 1963 and a master's degree in 1968, both in English. He began to teach, first at the elementary level, then in secondary schools. During these years he met Patricia Ann Lawless, whom he married in 1966.

The 1960s, a decade of social and political unrest, were inflamed by the idea of Third World peoples' liberation across the globe. To Anaya, this era represented not only the escalating of the war in Vietnam but also the beginning of Chicano student political activism in a nationwide civil rights movement. He distributed petitions to end the war, helped organize the first teachers' union in the Albuquerque school system, and, during the evenings, tried to master the craft of writing. Believing in Anaya's resolve to be a writer, his wife encouraged him.

Anaya wrote his first novel, *Bless Me, Ultima,* during a seven-year period, constantly looking for his own voice and what he calls "the soul" of his narrative. He remembers how the figure of Ultima appeared to him late one night and asked him what he was doing. "I told her," Anaya claims in his 1990 autobiographical essay, "I wasn't satisfied with the story, that it lacked soul. I could imitate the writers I had read, but I couldn't write like me . . . a *Nuevo Mexicano, hispano, indio, católico,* son of my mother and father, son of the earth which nurtured me, son of my community, son of my people." Ultima, he says, taught him how to see and thus articulate his life and world according to his own literary voice. Anaya mailed the manuscript of *Bless Me, Ultima* to various eastern publishers, but all of them rejected it. Shortly after he submitted it to a literary contest sponsored by a small Chicano press at Berkeley, the editors told him that he would be recognized with the 1971 Quinto Sol Publications Award for the best novel written by a Chicano. Having earned a second master's degree in guidance and counseling, in 1971 Anaya was working as director of counseling at the University of Albuquerque. The literary award opened new possibilities for a productive life devoted to writing, teaching, and helping young writers to get published.

In *Bless Me, Ultima* one encounters an interplay of story, plot elements, dream narratives, myth subtexts, and a rhetorical language that can result in multiple interpretations, depending on one's reading emphasis or depth. In addition, the story is based on an extended flashback, thus producing a reading that must distinguish two levels in the narrative: first, the account of an adult narrator (Antonio Márez Luna) as he remembers and reconstructs two extraordinary years in his youth; second, the story proper, which depicts the young Antonio and his life experiences under the guiding hand of Ultima, a *curandera* from Las Pasturas, New Mexico. The time of the story is the 1940s, with references to World War II, to the mourning of lost sons by village women in the region, and to the beginning of the nuclear age at Trinity, New Mexico. The adult Antonio's time corresponds to roughly twenty years later, thus suggesting the violence of another war: Vietnam. With such historical settings for both story and narration, readers of *Bless Me, Ultima* can thus associate the constant allusions to the end of the world in the novel with its broad range of apocalyptic imagery, and the raw background of two major wars of the twentieth century, tacitly posed as nuclear threats to humanity, with the regional conflicts represented by Ultima and the villainous barber Tenorio Trementina.

Interpreted only at the level of the story and its major plot elements, *Bless Me, Ultima* takes the reader into village life in the New Mexico *llano,* to the conflicts between family clans such as the Márez and the Lunas (Antonio's paternal and maternal lineages), and to the resolution that Ultima, as a healer, brings to the regional conflict of good and evil. In the initial encounter between Antonio and Ultima—described in the first paragraph of the novel in a manner that has beguiled generations of readers—Antonio experiences a personal transformation that suggests a rite of initiation into a higher form of life, hence the tendency to interpret *Bless Me, Ultima* as a novel of character development. Ultima intervenes in several regional conflicts, at times against the Trementina sisters (local witches), or against their father (Tenorio Trementina) and, at others, in the company of the young Antonio, as when Ultima cures Lucas Luna of the effects of witchcraft. Although anticipated as early as the first chapter, Ultima's death at the end of the novel forces the reader to reinterpret the entire novel in an act of memory (that is, in a reader's mental flashback to the reading process itself), thus suggesting Antonio's purpose in telling the story of Ultima and of his extraordinary youth. Antonio appears to be driven by a sense of guilt in having played an unwitting part in Ultima's death—thus the insinuation of a confession in the adult Antonio's story and in the manner in which events are organized and described.

Although *Bless Me, Ultima* is a novel that can be read at various levels, it soon divided Chicano literary critics into partisans and detractors. The partisans include critics such as David Carrasco and Robert F. Gish, who in their studies interpret Anaya's novel in the context of Native American culture and religion, or as a novel that portrays the hero's journey as a self-shaping quest akin to art. Among the detractors are critics such as Joseph Sommers, who views Chicano literature as the conscious representation of the urban problems of Chicanos, therefore as the ethnic expression of their political resistance in the United States; he thus sees *Bless Me, Ultima* as an "ahistorical" novel that contributes little to the political goals of the Chicano Movement. In a similar vein, Héctor Calderón reads *Bless Me, Ultima* as a novel that can be "pressed for meaning" as a "flight from history" but which nonetheless legitimizes "The agents of imperialism, the conquistador, and the priest." The critic Enrique R. Lamadrid comments on these and other similar reader biases: "As the first bestseller novel of Chicano literature, it was impossible to dismiss *Ultima*'s introduction of compelling mythic themes into the disjunctive context of the combative and polemical ethnic literatures of the late sixties. *Ultima* was serene in the face of this turmoil, full of conflict, yet non-combative."

Besides illustrating competing approaches to the reading of *Bless Me, Ultima,* at the heart of these differences between partisans and detractors was an attempt to establish a priority between the literary or the political dimensions of the Chicano novel. Interpreted from this perspective, the polemical engagement of these critics over *Bless Me, Ultima* contributed in a significant way to liberating Chicano literature from the ideological constraints of the 1960s as well as to the development of more-sophisticated reading approaches to Chicano novels.

In 1974 Anaya was offered a position at the University of New Mexico, where he was active both in teaching and in organizing a statewide writers' association and summer writing workshops. In these prolific years Anaya also wrote novels, essays, and short stories. A significant achievement is Anaya's publication of two novels that were identified as sequels to *Bless Me, Ultima: Heart of Aztlán* (1976) and *Tortuga* (1979), which completed the narrative cycle known as his New Mexico trilogy. Anaya has declared this trilogy as his fictional autobiography. The recurring themes in these novels are the maturation of youth, the social effects of wars (from World War II to Vietnam), the syncretic fusion of Native American and Mediterranean myths, the New Mexican landscape, and the impact of urbanization on traditional cultures, often allegorized by Anaya in stories of cultural crisis and renewal or in fables of death and resurrection.

Heart of Aztlán is Anaya's experiment with the Chicano political novel. It was published in the year of the

Dust jacket for Anaya's 1992 novel, about a
man's search for the identities of his parents
(Richland County Public Library)

obscure and indirect connection (through a Pueblo Indian) to the legend of the golden carp. Moreover, another of Clemente's sons—Benjamin Chávez—will be a connecting character, a structural element in the overlaps between this novel and those that form part of Anaya's later Albuquerque Quartet (1992–1999). As a character, Antonio vanishes from the narrative, not to appear in any of Anaya's other novels to date.

Heart of Aztlán re-creates Anaya's memories of growing up in Albuquerque during the 1950s, with its urban culture and the emerging Chicano youth expressions, such as teenage gangs of *pachucos*. The novel, consequently, unfolds along three levels as if to suggest the configuration of an emerging Chicano trinity: the urban family, the community, and Aztlán as the Chicano nation. The most obvious candidates for protagonist are Clemente Chávez, who turns into a labor organizer and leader, and his son Jasón, someone with a sensibility and perception reminiscent of Antonio. Both appear to be destined to inherit a blue guitar belonging to Crispín, an old musician endowed with the power of healing, and yet they do not. Crispín symbolizes the ballad tradition of the Mexico–United States border; because he is a singer of ballads or *corridos,* Crispín's music is a repository of deep-seated memories of land loss and disfranchisement. His guitar is more than just an instrument: it represents a cultural legacy and the possibility of a cultural renewal. In his study of *Heart of Aztlán,* César A. González-T. points out this recurrent theme in Anaya's novels: "The novel [*Heart of Aztlán*] has served to distinguish between the uses of traditional myths and the need for the creation of myth in order to establish a basis for universalism in Chicano literature." At the end of *Heart of Aztlán* one senses that Anaya has transformed the Chicano barrio of Barelas (to which this novel is dedicated)—and by extension Albuquerque—into the collective protagonist of this novel. If *Heart of Aztlán* achieved its own degree of success, it also pointed to the limitations of an overtly ideological novel or criticism.

Tortuga reveals that Benjamin has been groomed all along to be the protagonist and true leader of the community. Although he is the prototype of the troubled youth in *Heart of Aztlán,* Benjamin not only inherits Crispín's blue guitar but also embraces his mission in life, namely, to return to Albuquerque with songs of change and renewal. *Tortuga* is the account of Anaya's stay at the Carrie Tingley Hospital; however, as a novel it is patterned after mythical cycles that interconnect the lives of individual characters such as Benjamin (known as Tortuga in the novel because the cast on his body is like a tortoise shell) and mankind generally. Anaya considers *Tortuga* to be one of his best novels, adding that he took his characters "to the depths of despair and

bicentennial of the United States and was hence programmatic in its political as well as mythic intentions. Anaya seems to have anticipated the literary critics who demanded that the Chicano novel politically engage its age, informing readers of the global and urban problems as well as the resolutions. The organizing principle of the novel is the thematic cluster of land dispossession, migration from village to city, and the problems of urbanization, such as racism and two of its manifestations: social and labor segregation. The villagers' migration to Albuquerque, however, is not viewed as a journey to a strange place: Albuquerque is identified as the original site of the mythical Aztlán, the ancient birthplace of the Aztecs. The migration to Albuquerque is thus in an oblique way a homecoming and the foundation of a Chicano community. The leader that emerges from these dispossessed New Mexicans is Clemente Chávez, Jasón's father. Jasón is a character whose role in *Bless Me, Ultima* is not developed but is nonetheless established as important because of his

human suffering, and they find in their hellish existence the faith they need to survive in the world. Perhaps I was finally bringing together my own foundations of faith, finally regrouping from an existential wasteland and giving form to my own credo." No other novel by Anaya achieves a categorical expression in favor of cultural transformation, of the reintegration of society, and of the future as a privileged temporal horizon.

Anaya's early novels have generated a lengthy bibliography of scholarly publications. One source for the study of this phase in Anaya's novels is *Rudolfo A. Anaya: Focus on Criticism* (1990), a collection of essays that includes close readings of Anaya's New Mexico trilogy and of short stories published in *The Silence of the Llano* (1982). In this volume the leading interpreters of *Heart of Aztlán* and *Tortuga* are critics such as Heiner Bus (Germany), Jean Cazemajou (France), María Herrera-Sobek (United States), and González-T. (United States). The international perspectives in these studies illustrate the crossing of borders that remains a major theme in Anaya's writing.

After the New Mexico trilogy, Anaya moved on to other literary projects and activities, trying new genres and reading from his work in various parts of the world. In 1980 he was invited by President Jimmy Carter to read passages from *Bless Me, Ultima* at the White House. A recipient of the prestigious Kellogg Foundation Fellowship, Anaya traveled in China in 1984 and kept a journal, published in 1986 by the University of New Mexico Press under the title *A Chicano in China*. In the 1980s Anaya devoted his energies to the writing of short stories, essays, plays, and children's stories. In addition, he edited several volumes of essays and short prose fiction, and in 1989 he founded the literary journal *Blue Mesa Review*. Anaya's work brought positive recognition: in 1990 he received the Regents Meritorious Service Medal, awarded by the University of New Mexico; between 1990 and his retirement in 1993, Anaya served as Regents Professor at the university.

Anaya's retirement coincided with one of the most productive phases in his literary career, one that remains almost unexplored by Anaya scholars. A significant event was the republication of his novels, including *Bless Me, Ultima,* by Time Warner (1994), marketing his work at both national and international levels. Anaya's most ambitious literary project to date is the Albuquerque Quartet, patterned after the rhythms of seasons. The cycle begins with *Alburquerque* (1992), a title that hinges on historical origins and cultural misinterpretation; as Anaya observes on the first page of the book:

> In April of 1880 the railroad reached *la Villa de Alburquerque* in New Mexico. Legend says that the Anglo stationmaster couldn't pronounce the first "r" in "Albur,"

so he dropped it as he painted the station sign for the city. This novel restores the original spelling: Alburquerque.

The novel opens on a Friday in early April 1992, thereby representing spring; it is followed by *Zia Summer* (1995), which begins in June, also on a Friday, and *Rio Grande Fall* (1996), which starts in early October, hence forming a cycle that will end with a "darkening" season in *Shaman Winter* (1999). This last book takes place on 18 December, three days before the winter solstice, suggesting a promise of resurrection and the rites of spring that Anaya depicts as the refashioning of the self, of society, and of a culture kept in flux by historical conflicts and border tensions. The symbolic design of this narrative cycle is disclosed in a key passage in *Rio Grande Fall*: "Cycles—the seasons of the valley moved in cycles. Each season created its distinct flavors, colors, sounds. The seasons were also reflected in the temperament of the people of the valley."

Always conscious of historical events and important dates, Anaya published *Alburquerque* in 1992 to coincide with the quincentennial of the discovery of America. The frequent allusions in *Rio Grande Fall* and in *Shaman Winter* to the early history of New Mexico include references to Spanish explorers and conquistadores such as Alvar Núñez Cabeza de Vaca, Francisco Vásquez de Coronado, and Don Juan de Oñate, the conqueror of New Mexico in 1598. Framed in this historical context, the intertextual memory of the novel resurrects, as it were, the epic poem by Gaspar Pérez de Villagrá, *Historia de la Nueva México* (History of New Mexico, 1610), which was republished in 1992 in a bilingual critical edition by the University of New Mexico Press. The dedication of *Shaman Winter* reads: "To the ancestors who brought their dreams to New Mexico"; this dedication is significant because it reveals Anaya's revision and expansion of Chicano history and culture by means of literary associations and a myth of historical origins: first, with Villagrás's poem; second, with Juan de Oñate's 1598 Spanish conquest of New Mexico. The novel won the 1992 PEN Center West Award for fiction.

Anaya's narrative language and myth associations continue to reconstruct the sources of a Mexican American cultural tradition, often including the modern idioms of cinema and other forms of popular culture. Anaya interconnects metaphysical elements with current global issues—such as drugs, corporate greed, and social urban decay—thus continuing with the activist ideals of his generation. He combines in his narrative tetralogy structural elements of the conspiratorial plot with notions related to the "double" and to brotherhoods, ancestral revenants, and zoomorphic transfor-

A MYSTERY NOVEL BY THE BESTSELLING AUTHOR OF *BLESS ME, ULTIMA*

RUDOLFO ANAYA

SHAMAN WINTER

Dust jacket for Anaya's 1999 novel, which concludes his Albuquerque Quartet (Richland County Public Library)

mations, joining gothic tales of Dracula and the werewolf with New Mexican variants of the coyote trickster and the pre-Columbian *nagual* (the animal "double" of a shaman), thus proposing the symbolic links between human and animal representations in contexts of worldly machinations and intrigue.

Readers of Anaya will recognize characters from previous novels, such as Benjie and Cindy from *Heart of Aztlán,* who now appear in *Alburquerque* in their adult years as Benjamin Chávez and the artist Cynthia Johnson, the real biological parents of the protagonist, young boxer Abrán González. In this novel, the union of Anglo-Jewish-Mexican bloodlines will produce, according to Anaya, the new racial hybrid: "Chicanos who had one parent who was Anglo or Black or Asian. The new mestizos. They would have to find their identity, as he [Abrán] was trying to find his." Next to a story line of an unknown parentage, self-invention, and confluences of different genealogies, Anaya also develops as a subplot the scramble for land, investments in real estate, the greed of politicians, and the various

plans designed to modernize Albuquerque. The time in the novel coincides with the date of its publication; the season is spring, thus illustrating the promise that America represents in spite of the violence of its history since the era of exploration and conquest. A minor character in *Alburquerque,* Sonny Baca, emerges as the leading character in the next three novels of the cycle.

Beginning with *Zia Summer,* Anaya devotes much of his attention to the theme of conspiracy and the detective work by Sonny, the great-grandson of the legendary lawman Elfego Baca. Sonny must fight the evil influences of Raven, the leader of the Zia cult (an antinuclear protest group made up of women who, obeying Raven's mandates, practice sacrifices and believe in blood rituals) and a Dracula-like gothic figure who for the remainder of the narrative cycle will represent Sonny's "evil twin," or malevolent double. The emphasis of the novel rests on an antinuclear movement and a proposal by the Waste Isolation Pilot Plant (WIPP) to transport "waste material laced with plutonium from Los Alamos Labs down to the WIPP site near Carlsbad." The subplots of *Zia Summer* involve ritual murders and the increasing globalization of Albuquerque's economy. Anaya's thematic treatment of issues related to radioactive waste tied to global greed will logically connect to the theme of the international drug cartels as developed in *Rio Grande Fall.* The action of that novel takes place during Albuquerque's October balloon festival, used by Raven and CIA agents to plot and control the major global cocaine and heroin traffic lines of the South American drug cartels.

Composed of thirty chapters that correspond to the age of its detective hero, *Rio Grande Fall* generates a multilayered plot, beginning with Sonny's cleansing and initiation under the guidance of the *curandera* Lorenza Villa. Other currents include the resolution of three murders, the conspiratorial world of the CIA and of the South American and Mexican drug cartels, and the netherworld of Raven and what he represents, namely the gothic representation of a reversed creation and of an inverted world. Sonny finds himself entangled in the web formed by these mysteries. The novel, therefore, could be initially read as symbolic of his initiation as a sorcerer (thus the coyote *nagual,* or zoomorphic double in the natural world), of his journey to the underworld, and of the figurative death and resurrection enacted at both the beginning and conclusion of the novel. Like Anaya's earlier novels, *Rio Grande Fall* is presented as a puzzle that the reader must assemble as a comprehensive narrative world; as a result, the textual analysis and interpretation turn into activities analogous to detective work. More than just a resolution of the mystery of the narrative, Anaya's novels often carry a double ideological message of human spirituality and the inevitability of historical change.

Both *Zia Summer* and *Rio Grande Fall* associate the confusion and perversion of a world through its scandalous alliances, as is the case with the CIA, the FBI, radioactive waste, the drug cartels, and Raven himself. Moreover, as Sonny's "double," Raven represents the dark Other of the pre-Columbian cosmic twins (the hunter twins in the Popol Vuh, the sacred book of the Quiché Mayans of Guatemala), the biblical Cain in relation to Abel, or the gnostic twin relationship between Christ and Lucifer. Lastly, Raven and Sonny are zoomorphic counterparts, with Raven as master of the air (as a bird), and Sonny as a master of the earth (as a coyote). As a detective and sorcerer in the making, Sonny confronts a world of crime represented by the triumvirate of the CIA/FBI, the drug cartels, and Raven, all of whom seek control of the South American–United States cocaine and heroin traffic. What motivates these parties is money and power, not necessarily the use of drugs: for the CIA, the motive is the financing of right-wing movements in Latin America; for the drug cartels, the buying of entire governments; for Raven, the financing of his antinuclear movement. Among these characters, one also encounters the stock character of the mad scientist in the figure of Dr. Jerry Stammer, who, having invested all of his wealth in laboratory experiments with baboon heart transplants for human beings, and then having lost his money, joins in the drug network in order to continue with his scientific experiments. Anaya's novels thus turn on the themes of corruption in political and scientific circles and of the darkening of the world.

The story that holds the reader's attention in *Shaman Winter* is admittedly new in a Chicano novel. Sonny "dreams" his way back to the 1598 Juan de Oñate expedition, therefore to the early history of New Mexico, followed by the 1846 invasion of New Mexico by Stephen Kearny, then moving on to the present. But Sonny is in a wheelchair, therefore symbolically captive under the power of Raven, the constant foil who now intends to erase Sonny from history by taking hostage four of Sonny's female ancestors. This journey back in time will take Sonny to the realization of his "mixed" ancestry—from a Spaniard by the name of Andrés Vaca and the Indian Owl Woman—and to his discovery that people in New Mexico are all related by ancient blood ties. Chicano cultural identity thus achieves a "cross-national" level in *Shaman Winter,* labeled by Sonny as the new *raza cósmica* or cosmic race (both a concept and the title of a book by Mexican philosopher José Vasconcelos). On a metaphysical level, *Shaman Winter* moves into the realm of reincarnation and the personification of nature's forces of creation and destruction in the characters of Sonny and Raven, respectively. This element suggests a thematic connection to Anaya's previous novels, either in the form of dream narratives, healing figures, convalescent heroes (such as Tortuga and Sonny), or in the positive depiction of miscegenation and the emphasis on the cross-cultural heritage of humanity.

Anaya's novels of the 1990s face global issues and problems—such as environmentalism, biodiversity, and Latin American drug traffic—that other Chicano authors have yet to represent or fictionalize in their work. In terms of critical reception, most Anaya criticism continues to debate and reinterpret the early phase in Anaya's literary life, as exhibited in Francisco A. Lomelí's compilation of transnational perspectives on Chicano literature (2000), in which one discovers how *Bless Me, Ultima* is being read and reinterpreted by audiences in Germany, Italy, Mexico, Spain, and Trans-Baikal Siberia, Russia. Readers of Anaya's work in Russian find in *Bless Me, Ultima* themes and situations that are familiar. Tatyana Voronchenko explains in her contribution to Lomelí's volume: "Like Chicanos, Siberian ethnic minority writers are bicultural and bilingual. Their creativity is marked both by the influence of the Russian environment and an ancestral consciousness. Border culture like Mexican-American culture is a hybrid one. Chicano literature thus in some senses speaks to the Siberian population of a situation that they know."

Rudolfo A. Anaya continues to be active in his art and in his community. He is writing a libretto for an opera based on La Llorona (the Weeping Woman), a prominent figure in Mexican/Chicana folklore that inspired one of Anaya's novellas in 1984 and a 1987 play. In April 2002, Anaya was the recipient of the 2001 National Medal of Arts, presented by President George W. Bush at the White House. A retrospective evaluation of Anaya's novels reveals a constant interplay between story and a language noted for its allegorical intent and the incorporation of myths stemming from diverse backgrounds, such as American Indian, Greco-Roman, Judeo-Christian, and Egyptian. The mythic subtexts in Anaya's novels generally serve as premises to historical conflicts and contradictions, frequently represented by national and world wars. A pacifist, Anaya writes novels with plots that achieve symbolic resolutions, generally with healing forces triumphing over those representing destruction and evil.

Interviews:

"Myth and the Writer: A Conversation with R.A.,"
    New America, 3 (Spring 1979): 76–85;

Bruce Dick and Silvio Sirias, *Conversations with Rudolfo Anaya* (Jackson: University Press of Mississippi, 1998).

Bibliographies:

María Teresa Huerta Márquez, "A Selected Bibliography of Works by and about Rudolfo A. Anaya," in *Rudolfo A. Anaya: Focus on Criticism,* edited by César A. González-T. (La Jolla, Cal.: Lalo Press, 1990), pp. 390–413;

González-T. and Phillis S. Morgan, eds., *A Sense of Place: Rudolfo A. Anaya, An Annotated Bio-Bibliography* (Berkeley, Cal.: Ethnic Studies Library Publications Unit, 1999).

References:

Cordelia Candelaria, "On Rudolfo A. Anaya," in *Chicano Literature: A Reference Guide,* edited by Julio A. Martínez and Francisco A. Lomelí (Westport, Conn.: Greenwood Press, 1985): 34–51;

Roberto Cantú, "Apocalypse as an Ideological Construct: The Storyteller's Art in *Bless Me, Ultima,*" in *Rudolfo A. Anaya: Focus on Criticism,* edited by César A. González-T. (La Jolla, Cal.: Lalo Press, 1990): 13–63;

Cantú, "The Surname, the Corpus and the Body in Rudolfo A. Anaya's Narrative Trilogy," in *Rudolfo A. Anaya: Focus on Criticism,* edited by González-T. (La Jolla, Cal.: Lalo Press, 1990): 274–317;

David Carrasco, "A Perspective for a Study of Religious Dimensions in Chicano Experience: *Bless Me, Ultima* as a Religious Text," *Aztlán,* 13, nos. 1–2 (1982): 195–221;

Michael Anthony Cervantes, "An Analysis of Rudolfo Anaya's Novels as Epics," M.A. thesis, California State University, Los Angeles, 1985;

Reed Way Dasenbock, "Forms of Biculturalism in Southwestern Literature: The Work of Rudolfo Anaya and Leslie Marmon Silko," *Genre,* 21, no. 3 (1988): 307–320;

Lynn M. Fauth, "Tradition and the Indigenous Talent: Rudolfo A. Anaya and the Anglo-American Literary Canon," M.A. thesis, California State University, Los Angeles, 1995;

Robert F. Gish, "Curanderismo and Witchery in the Fiction of Rudolfo A. Anaya: The Novel as Magic," *New Mexico Humanities Review,* 2 (1979): 5–13;

Enrique R. Lamadrid, "Myth as the Cognitive Process of Popular Culture in Rudolfo Anaya's *Bless Me, Ultima:* The Dialectics of Knowledge," *Hispania,* 68 (September 1985): 496–501;

Luis Leal, "Voices in the Wind: Anaya's Short Fiction," in *Rudolfo A. Anaya: Focus on Criticism,* edited by González-T. (La Jolla, Cal.: Lalo Press, 1990): 335–348;

Francisco A. Lomelí and Karin Ikas, eds., *U.S. Latino Literatures and Cultures: Transnational Perspectives* (Heidelberg: C. Winter, 2000);

Antonio Márquez, "The Achievement of Rudolfo A. Anaya," in *The Magic of Words: Rudolfo A. Anaya and His Writings,* edited by Paul Vassallo (Albuquerque: University of New Mexico Press, 1982), pp. 33–52;

Eliud Martínez, *Voice-Haunted Journey* (Tempe, Ariz.: Bilingual Press, 1990);

José Monleón, "Ilusión y realidad en la obra de Rudolfo Anaya," in *Contemporary Chicano Fiction: A Critical Survey,* edited by Vernon E. Lattin (Binghamton, N.Y.: Bilingual Press, 1986), pp. 171–199;

Joseph Sommers, "Critical Approaches to Chicano Literature," in *The Identification and Analysis of Chicano Literature,* edited by Francisco Jiménez (New York: Bilingual/Editorial Bilingüe, 1979): 143–152.

Papers:

An archive of Rudolfo A. Anaya's papers through the publication of *Bless Me, Ultima* can be found at the Zimmerman Library, Special Collections, University of New Mexico.

James Baldwin

(2 August 1924 – 1 December 1987)

Jacqueline C. Jones
Washington College

See also the Baldwin entries in *DLB 2: American Novelists Since World War II; DLB 7: Twentieth-Century American Dramatists; DLB 33: Afro-American Fiction Writers After 1955; DLB 249: Twentieth-Century American Dramatists, Third Series;* and *DLB Yearbook: 1987.*

BOOKS: *Go Tell It on the Mountain* (New York: Knopf, 1953; London: Joseph, 1954);

Notes of a Native Son (Boston: Beacon, 1955; London: Mayflower, 1958);

Giovanni's Room (New York: Dial, 1956; London: Joseph, 1957);

Nobody Knows My Name: More Notes of a Native Son (New York: Dial, 1961; London: Joseph, 1964);

Another Country (New York: Dial, 1962; London: Joseph, 1963);

The Fire Next Time (New York: Dial, 1963; London: Joseph, 1963);

Nothing Personal, photographs by Richard Avedon (New York: Atheneum, 1964; Baltimore & Harmondsworth, U.K.: Penguin, 1964);

Blues For Mister Charlie: A Play (New York: Dial, 1964; London: Joseph, 1965);

Going to Meet the Man (New York: Dial, 1965; London: Joseph, 1965);

The Amen Corner: A Play (New York: Dial, 1968; London: Joseph, 1969);

Tell Me How Long the Train's Been Gone (New York: Dial, 1968; London: Joseph, 1968);

A Rap on Race, by Baldwin and Margaret Mead (Philadelphia: Lippincott, 1971; London: Joseph, 1971);

One Day When I Was Lost: A Scenario Based on Alex Haley's "The Autobiography of Malcolm X" (London: Joseph, 1972; New York: Dial, 1973);

No Name in The Street (New York: Dial, 1972; London: Joseph, 1972);

César: Compressions, l'homme et la machine, by Baldwin and Françoise Giroud, translated by Yvonne Roux (Paris: Hachette, 1973);

If Beale Street Could Talk (New York: Dial, 1974; London: Joseph, 1974);

The Devil Finds Work: An Essay (New York: Dial, 1976; London: Joseph, 1976);

Little Man, Little Man: A Story of Childhood (New York: Dial, 1976; London: Joseph, 1976);

Just Above My Head (New York: Dial, 1979; London: Joseph, 1979);

Jimmy's Blues: Selected Poems (London: Joseph, 1983; New York: St. Martin's Press, 1985);

The Evidence of Things Not Seen (New York: Holt, Rinehart & Winston, 1985); republished as *Evidence of Things Not Seen* (London: Joseph, 1986);

The Price of the Ticket: Collected Nonfiction, 1948–1985 (New York: St. Martin's Press/Marek, 1985; London: Joseph, 1985);

Gypsy & Other Poems (Searsmont, Me.: Gehenna Press, 1989);

Sonny's Blues and Other Stories (London: Penguin, 1995).

Editions and Collections: *Go Tell It on the Mountain* (Franklin Center, Pa.: Franklin Library, 1979);

James Baldwin: Early Novels and Stories, edited by Toni Morrison, Library of America, no. 97 (New York: Library of America, 1998)—comprises *Go Tell It on the Mountain, Giovanni's Room, Another Country,* and *Going to Meet the Man;*

James Baldwin: Collected Essays, edited by Morrison, Library of America, no. 98 (New York: Library of America, 1998)—includes *Notes of a Native Son, Nobody Knows My Name, The Fire Next Time, No Name in the Street,* and *The Devil Finds Work.*

When he died on 1 December 1987, James Baldwin was remembered as a prophet who addressed the causes and results of racial conflict. He spent his entire literary career writing essays, speeches, stories, two plays, and six novels about the inherent untruth of life in this democratic United States and how its citizens ultimately mirror that dishonesty in their lives. Baldwin often said that few were willing to pay the price of the ticket; few were willing to suffer the consequences of being honest.

James Baldwin in Paris, 1960s (photograph by Irmeli Jung; from David Leeming,
James Baldwin: A Biography, *1994)*

Despite his fame as an essayist, Baldwin viewed himself as a novelist. His first novel, *Go Tell It on the Mountain,* was published in 1953 to generally positive reviews. Coming on the heels of Ralph Ellison's acclaimed *Invisible Man* (1952), Baldwin's novel seemed to herald a new era in American fiction. In 1986 it was adapted for television by the Public Broadcasting System (PBS). *Giovanni's Room* (1956) and *Another Country* (1962), which both explore the theme of sexuality, still attract analysis from literary critics. Baldwin's last four novels—*Another Country, Tell Me How Long the Train's Been Gone* (1968), *If Beale Street Could Talk* (1974), and *Just Above My Head* (1979)—all explore the journey of the artist. These novels, among Baldwin's most autobiographical works, have been almost ignored by literary critics, with the exception of *Another Country.* Yet, these novels may be read as Baldwin's best expression of his vision of the terrifying and lonely life of the artist.

Baldwin was born James Arthur Jones on 2 August 1924 in Harlem Hospital to unmarried Emma Berdis Jones. In 1927 she married David Baldwin, who later adopted the boy, making him James Arthur Baldwin. Emma Jones and David Baldwin had eight children together: George, Barbara, Wilmer, David,

Gloria, Ruth, Elizabeth, and Paula. As the eldest, Baldwin helped his mother care for the children. In an early essay titled "Autobiographical Notes" Baldwin described having spent his youth with a child in one hand and a book in the other. An avid reader, Baldwin cited his literary influences as including Henry James, Harriet Beecher Stowe, and Charles Dickens.

While a student at Frederick Douglass Junior High School, Baldwin met Countee Cullen, perhaps the most famous and talented poet of the Harlem Renaissance. Cullen's command of French and his years spent in France inspired Baldwin. The poet encouraged the younger man to apply to Cullen's alma mater, the prestigious DeWitt Clinton High School in the Bronx section of New York City. While at DeWitt Clinton, Baldwin wrote short stories, plays, and poetry. He joined the staff of *The Magpie,* the school literary magazine, and interviewed Cullen in 1942. Baldwin received his high school diploma in January 1942.

With college out of his financial reach, Baldwin was unsure that he could be a writer. Yet, writing seemed like breathing for him. His good friend Emile Capouya had introduced Baldwin to painter Beauford Delaney in 1940. The fact that Delaney, an African

American man, had established himself as an artist affected Baldwin greatly. In one of his last essays, included in *The Price of the Ticket: Collected Nonfiction, 1948–1985* (1985), Baldwin described how Delaney transformed his world: "I walked through that door into Beauford's colors. . . . I walked into music. . . . I began to hear what I had never dared or been able to hear." After meeting Delaney, Baldwin began to envision life as a writer as a legitimate possibility: "Beauford was the first walking, living proof, for me, that a black man could be an artist."

His stepfather's declining mental and physical health had increased the family's reliance upon Baldwin. David Baldwin died on 29 July 1943, the same day that his last child was born. Baldwin wrote of his conflicting emotions in the essay "Notes of a Native Son." David Baldwin's relationship with his stepson was tense and combative; he opposed Baldwin's friends who were not African American and urged the young man to reject the secular world. David was slowly going insane, a condition that became clearer as time passed. Baldwin's conflicting feelings of rage and love for his stepfather, along with the pressure of trying to financially support his family, led him to leave home.

Baldwin's move to Greenwich Village in 1943 coincided with the end of a three-year stint as a youth preacher. He worked a series of jobs and was employed as a waiter at The Calypso restaurant in the Village. This restaurant provided a haven for Baldwin, and it figures prominently in his fiction. Baldwin had begun writing book reviews for magazines and was working on a novel. During this period a mutual friend introduced Baldwin to noted African American writer Richard Wright, who, since the publication and incredible success of his novel *Native Son* in 1940, had become someone against whom success was measured. Wright read a draft of what became *Go Tell It on the Mountain,* and he helped Baldwin to obtain a Eugene F. Saxon Memorial Trust Award to help fund his writing.

In 1948 Baldwin's short story "Previous Condition" was published in *Commentary* magazine. The story focuses on the experiences of Peter, an African American actor, whose race accounts for many of his frustrations. There is a sense of placelessness about Peter; he is not accepted in his Greenwich Village neighborhood, nor does he fit in Harlem. He is searching for something but remains unfulfilled. The story opens with Peter being evicted from an apartment in Greenwich Village because of his race and ends with him sitting in a Harlem bar. Baldwin's symbolic use of geography became a central characteristic of his work.

Baldwin left for Paris in 1948 and returned in 1952 with his first novel, *Go Tell It on the Mountain,* about to be published. Autobiographical in nature, *Go*

Tell It on the Mountain traces the events of John Grimes's fourteenth birthday. John struggles with his religious faith, his feelings for his father, and, more subtly, his sexual attraction to a young man. His mother, Elizabeth, was an unmarried woman with a son when she met Gabriel Grimes, a widowed preacher. Gabriel marries Elizabeth and has three children with her but never really accepts John, who feels unwanted and unloved, even hated, by his stepfather. Throughout the course of the novel John tries to figure out why his father dislikes him, what his relationship is to the church, and just who he is.

The structure of *Go Tell It on the Mountain* is one of its most effective elements. Baldwin, using flashbacks, tells the personal histories of all of the main characters while they are on the threshing floor of the church one Saturday night with John. *Go Tell It on the Mountain* is divided into three sections. Part 1, "The Seventh Day," opens on a Saturday in March as John wonders if anyone remembers it is his birthday. He is performing his usual Saturday morning chores when his mother gives him some change for his birthday. John uses the money to escape to the movies; but he cannot elude the rigid ideas of good and evil that dominate his life at home. When John returns home, the household is in turmoil. His stubborn little brother, Roy, has been injured while fighting with white boys, and Gabriel manages to blame John for the fight. Later, John goes to clean the church for the Saturday night service. Brother Elisha comes to help him, and John's attraction to Elisha is revealed to the reader.

Part 2, "The Prayers of the Saints," presents the life histories of Gabriel, his sister Florence, and Elizabeth. These three adults influence John greatly, and their pasts reveal much about their behavior toward John. The flashbacks of part 2 give depth to the characters and help to make them more sympathetic.

Florence's prayer occurs when she stands at the altar asking for the Lord's help. Her brother is pleased to see her in need and, in his mind, humbled. Actually, Florence is ill, and she seeks to right wrongs before her death. Her prayer recounts the sad events of her childhood and her adult life as a lonely and bitter woman. She grew up to abhor suffering and men, particularly her brother; yet, Florence always shows John affection. All she wants is not to be like her mother: poor, sick, and alone. She is destined, however, to be in a similar situation.

Gabriel's prayer details his life as a rather reckless young man. Drinking, partying, and women filled his days. Even after he experienced a religious conversion, Gabriel continued to sin. He committed adultery and then refused to acknowledge the child who resulted from these encounters. The hypocrisy of Gabriel's negative focus on Elizabeth's illegitimate child is empha-

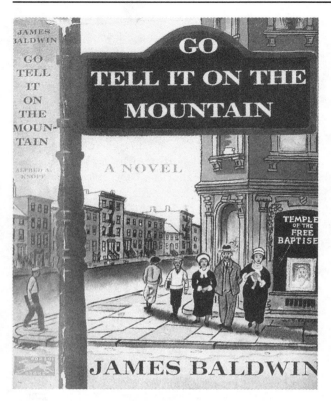

*Dust jacket for Baldwin's first novel, about a fourteen-year-old
struggling with his stepfather and his religious faith
(from James Campbell,* Talking at the Gates:
A Life of James Baldwin, *1991)*

sized to the reader through his relentless haranguing of John. Gabriel emerges as a deeply troubled, hypocritical, sad, and bitter man.

Elizabeth's prayer is perhaps the most poignant. John's mother has an air of resignation about her life with her husband, Gabriel. John had been born illegitimate, so Elizabeth was grateful that Gabriel wanted to marry her and become a father to her son. The only time she resembled anything other than a long-suffering mother was when she was young and with John's father.

Part 3, "The Threshing Floor," centers around John's being saved. He spends the hours from Saturday night to Sunday morning on the threshing floor, giving his life to the Lord. Baldwin describes the experience as a journey from darkness to light. John wants Elisha, in particular, to remember his religious conversion: "'Elisha,' he said, 'no matter what happens to me, where I go, what folks say about me, no matter what *any*body says, you remember–please remember–I was saved. I was *there*.'" The sense of foreshadowing in John's statement implies that someone, someday will accuse him of not loving the Lord; the suggestion is that John's homosexuality will cause him to leave the church. In *Ride Out the Wilderness: Geography and Identity in*

Afro-American Literature (1987) Melvin Dixon argues that John's conversion acts as a liberating force and bodes well for his future: "John Grimes is converted *out* of religion; he is delivered out of the moral authority of the church and of his preacher stepfather, Gabriel."

John's feelings for Elisha are sexual in nature. Elisha guides John through the darkness of the threshing floor and gives him a holy kiss at the conclusion of the novel. The end of the novel appears to be a new beginning for John. He defies his father in the last scene and announces his intention to continue doing so. This aspect of the novel has attracted much critical attention. Dixon sees John's attempt to reconcile his religious faith and his sexual feelings as the central question in the novel. Kenneth Barksdale's review of *Go Tell It on the Mountain* in *Phylon* in 1953 is representative of the critical reception: Barksdale describes *Go Tell It on the Mountain* as "a very fine first novel" and praises its universal appeal.

Although most of the action of the novel takes place in a church, Baldwin's representation of Christianity, particularly as practiced in some African American churches, is tainted with fear and exclusivity. In 1984, however, Baldwin gave his readers a glimpse into what he saw as the themes of the novel: "*Go Tell It on the Mountain,* for example, is not about a church. . . . It's about what happens to you if you're afraid to love anybody." Indeed, love is a central theme in all of Baldwin's works. Love begins with self, and most of Baldwin's protagonists must learn to love themselves before they can have successful romantic relationships.

Baldwin had published a story titled "The Death of the Prophet" in *Commentary* in March 1950 that is actually a sequel to *Go Tell It on the Mountain*. The story, like the novel, is told from the perspective of a third-person narrator. John Grimes is now a young adult living on his own in Greenwich Village. He leaves his family, but, in reality, he flees his father's wrath: "He fought to be free of his father and his father's God." The story traces John's visit to the dying Gabriel's bedside. Gabriel has been in the hospital for two years suffering from paranoia and tuberculosis, and he is in a coma by the time of John's visit. The sight of his father's sunken form leads John to scream and faint. The doctor with whom John speaks implies that an argument between John and his father contributed to his father's current state: after John left home, Gabriel became suspicious of everyone.

John's life is now filled with all those things his father despises: drinking, smoking, partying, and white people. John describes his father's reaction to his young Jewish friend who has come to take John to the movies. John makes his friend go into the hall while he confronts his father: "he looked into his father's eyes. His father looked on him with that distant hatred with which one considers Judas." This scene is reminiscent of the last scene in *Go Tell It on the Mountain* when John looks at his father, in a moment of implied power and rebellion, as he replies to his mother, "I'm ready . . . I'm coming. I'm on my way." John is indeed on his way, out of his father's house and into his own life. "The Death of the Prophet" is as much a story about John's development as it is about the death of Gabriel Grimes.

Notes of a Native Son, a collection of eleven essays, was published in 1955. The title essay makes reference to Wright's seminal novel *Native Son* and to Baldwin's claim as a son of the United States of America. The first section of *Notes of a Native Son* focuses on the representation of African Americans in literature and motion pictures. The second examines the experiences of African Americans in the United States and the effects of racism. Finally, the third recounts Baldwin's experiences in France.

"Notes of a Native Son," perhaps Baldwin's most anthologized essay, is his eloquent attempt to come to some understanding of his father, their relationship, and the idea of legacy. Three important events happened close together: Baldwin's nineteenth birthday, the death of his father, and the birth of his sister Paula. There was also a race riot occurring in Harlem, and all these events caused Baldwin to reflect upon their meanings. Baldwin saw his father's bitter response to racism as a factor in his demise. The most poignant part of the essay involves Baldwin's attempts to reconcile his feelings about his father and to comprehend his father's legacy. David Baldwin strongly disliked white people and, although he acknowledged Baldwin's decision to become a writer, he did not support it.

Baldwin's next book, *Giovanni's Room,* follows the experiences of David, a white American who is living in Paris. David, the narrator, is in flight not only from his country but also from himself and his deepest desires. While his fiancée, Hella, is in Spain, David begins a relationship with Giovanni, a young Italian man; however, he cannot acknowledge this relationship because he refuses to address his homosexuality. Giovanni awakens David's desire for men, and that fills him with emotions: "The beast which Giovanni had awakened in me would never go to sleep again; but one day I would not be with Giovanni anymore. . . . With this fearful intimation there opened in me a hatred for Giovanni which was as powerful as my love and which was nourished by the same roots."

Masculinity and terror are two key themes in *Giovanni's Room*. David is fearful of being considered lacking in manhood and even considers having children to affirm it. David keeps Hella as a tangible sign of his masculinity. Flight is also a major theme as David drinks and travels in an attempt to forget his troubles rather than face them. Giovanni's room represents a

homosexual lifestyle that both entices David and disgusts him. The futility of such a life, at least in David's mind, leads him to renounce Giovanni: "What kind of life can we have in this room?–this filthy little room. What kind of life can two men have together anyway?" Indeed, David, who yearns for societal acceptance, cannot conceive of a world in which two men would live together happily.

Giovanni had come to Paris after leaving Italy when a baby he had fathered was stillborn. He seems desperate for love, and that desperation may be what frightens David as Giovanni clings to him. David runs back to Hella, who has returned to Paris from Spain, and Giovanni is convicted of murdering Guillaume, an old, vindictive gay man who had fired Giovanni from his job as a bartender. David, full of remorse and guilt about Giovanni's pending execution, flees into the arms of a sailor, and Hella tracks him down at a gay bar in Nice.

Even then, David cannot admit his homosexuality. Early in the novel, David announces his intention to ignore his sexuality: "I had decided to allow no room in the universe for something which shamed and frightened me." As his life collapses around him, David tries to explain his feelings to Hella: "'I wish, anyway,' I said at last, 'that you'd believe me when I say that, if I was lying, I wasn't lying to *you*. . . . I mean,' I said, 'I was lying to myself.'" David's indecisiveness and his nonresponse lead Hella to imply that he is not a man. After Hella leaves him for good, David heads back to Paris.

Baldwin had a difficult time getting *Giovanni's Room* published in the United States, largely because of the explicit depiction of homosexual relationships. The critical response to the novel was Baldwin's introduction to the racialized literary world. Many reviewers, such as Leslie Fiedler, seemed disturbed that a novel by an African American writer did not feature any African American characters. In February 1957 James Ivy reviewed *Giovanni's Room* for *The Crisis,* the publication of the National Association for the Advancement of Colored People, under the title "Faerie Queens." He lamented the fact that Baldwin, already known as an advocate for African Americans, wasted his talent writing about a homosexual affair involving white men. Despite David's rather tortured feelings toward his homosexuality, *Giovanni's Room* has been hailed as groundbreaking by literary critics who are interested in gay and lesbian issues.

Baldwin undertook his first trip to the Southern states in 1957 to research articles for *Partisan Review* and *Harper's Magazine*. One of his better-known stories, "Sonny's Blues," was published in *Partisan Review* in 1957. Baldwin returned to Paris during the summer of 1958. In 1959 he won a Ford Foundation grant to complete his next novel, *Another Country*. He continued to give speeches and travel while managing to keep writing.

Published in June 1962, *Another Country* is essentially the story of African American Rufus Scott's adulthood and death and how his demise affects his family and friends. *Another Country* is also the story of Eric Jones, a white Southern gay actor who was Rufus's friend and lover. Their relationship, though not depicted, is the center of the novel.

The first section of the novel, "Easy Rider," centers on Rufus's life, the reasons behind his suicide, and his relationship with Leona, a white Southern woman. His best friend Vivaldo Moore and his sister Ida figure prominently in the novel as well. Richard and Cass Silenski, old friends of Vivaldo, are a middle-aged married couple who are experiencing trouble in their relationship. Section 2, "Any Day Now," begins with Eric in France with his lover Yves. Eric is preparing for a trip to the United States and thus must face everything that he left behind. He is on his way to becoming a successful actor, and returning home will insure his success. Eric's arrival affects the lives of the characters in the novel. Section 3, "Toward Bethlehem," resolves the myriad relationships in the novel.

The novel opens with a memorable image of Rufus, homeless and hungry, walking the streets of New York City. As he walks, Rufus remembers what put him on the street. Readers thus learn the details of Rufus's life in flashback and understand his dilemma: "He was so tired, he had fallen so low, that he scarcely had the energy to be angry; nothing of his belonged to him any-more—*you took the best, so why not take the rest?*" A jazz drummer by profession, Rufus seems lost and emotionally distant. As Rufus performs at his last gig, a young saxophone player inspires the audience and the musicians to reflect on their lives. "*Do you love me?* This, anyway, was the question Rufus heard, the same phrase, unbearably, endlessly, and variously repeated with all of the force the boy had." This question of love, and of self-love, is the one Rufus must answer.

The relationship between Rufus and Leona begins on the night of his last performance. Their eyes meet while Rufus is on the stage, and they continue their flirtation at a party. They consummate their attraction by having sex on a balcony high above Manhattan. Rufus and Leona's relationship allows Baldwin to create a portrait of race relations in the early 1960s. The reaction to the lovers is intense on all sides. Rufus surrounds himself with white people, but his easy acquisition of Leona leads him to madness. He becomes convinced that Leona dates him because of the stereotype of African American men as being sexually superior to white men: "'You know all that chick knows about me? The *only* thing she knows?' He put his hand on his sex, brutally as though he would tear it out."

Baldwin in 1962 (from Quincy Troupe, ed.,
James Baldwin: The Legacy, *1989)*

Thematically, the novel addresses many issues surrounding race and romantic relationships. At the center of any discussion of *Another Country* must be the issue of love, specifically self-love. Rufus cannot bring himself to accept or love all of himself, while Eric does. Thus, Rufus's inaction insures his literal and figurative death, just as Eric's actions insure his survival. The thing that separates them is courage.

Rufus throws himself off of the George Washington Bridge at the end of the first section of the novel. The reader, like his family and friends, spends the rest of the novel attempting to understand what led Rufus to kill himself. His last thoughts are full of clues: "Something in Rufus which could not break shook him like a rag doll and splashed salt water all over his face and filled his throat and nostrils with anguish. He knew the pain would never stop." Rufus's status as an African American man certainly contributed to his death, as he deals with racism throughout his brief appearance in the novel. While some of his actions are certainly horrific, Rufus is ultimately a sympathetic character. Another of his last thoughts is of Eric.

Eric and Rufus's relationship was doomed by Rufus's inability to accept his feelings for another man. He does not accept his homosexuality and punishes Eric for their sexual acts. But as he dies, "He remembered only that Eric had loved him; as he now remembered that Leona had loved him. He had despised Eric's manhood by treating him as a woman, by telling him how inferior he was to a woman, by treating him as nothing more than a hideous sexual deformity." When Eric learns of Rufus's violent relationship with Leona, he recalls their past: "He remembered Rufus' face, his hands, his body, and his voice, and the constant humiliation." Eric fled to France, where he found love with Yves, a white Frenchman.

Just as Rufus is dying, Eric experiences a rebirth. He has been able to define his life for himself and resist the negativity associated with his homosexuality. While he has found happiness in France, he must come to terms with the life that he left in the United States. Eric prospers because he is able to share his hard-won self-love and acceptance with others. All who are intimate with him find themselves transformed. Eric has brief love affairs with Cass, a middle-class wife and mother, and Vivaldo, a young writer. Vivaldo finally acknowledges the futility of his relationship with Rufus's sister Ida, and his writing begins to flourish.

Another Country is the basis for Eldridge Cleaver's attack on Baldwin in his 1968 collection of essays, *Soul on Ice*. Cleaver's views on Baldwin and *Another Country* document the reactions of some black nationalists to Baldwin's fiction. Cleaver describes Rufus as "a pathetic wretch who indulged in the white man's pastime of committing suicide." Cleaver goes on to denigrate Baldwin personally: "There is in James Baldwin's work the most grueling, agonizing, total hatred of the blacks, particularly of himself, and the most shameful, fanatical, fawning, sycophantic love of the whites that one can find in the writings of any black American writer of note in our time." Cleaver's review of the novel is echoed by major African American literary theorists of the period. In *The Way of the New World: The Black Novel in America* (1975) Addison Gayle Jr. offers a fairly typical black nationalist view of the novel: "Rufus has been murdered by an uncaring, unfeeling white society. *Another Country* [is] a novel of vengeance and redemption." Black nationalists such as Gayle and Cleaver condemn Baldwin for making white characters of equal importance in terms of plot to his African American characters. Gayle also accuses Baldwin of accepting the white stereotypes about African Americans. Yet, Baldwin suffered these attacks in silence, preferring not to spar in public with those whom he considered his literary descendants.

Because Baldwin's initial focus is on Rufus, readers are forced to examine the ways in which social norms lead to a denial of identity and to death for the African American bisexual. In his study of gay self-representation in fiction, David Bergman argues that Baldwin is careful to make all his characters bisexual. They are never depicted as "'faggots', by which Baldwin means exclu-

sively and effeminately homosexual." Baldwin expressed his thoughts on homosexuality and race in a 1986 interview with Richard Goldstein of the *Village Voice* (published in *James Baldwin: The Legacy*, edited by Quincy Troupe, 1989):

> A black gay person who is a sexual conundrum to society is already, long before the question of sexuality comes into it, menaced and marked because he's black or she's black. The sexual question comes after the question of color; it's simply one more aspect of the danger in which all black people live.

The "question of color" is what leads Rufus to commit suicide, though his denial of his sexual feelings and his acknowledgment of the sexual acts he performs with Eric play an important role. In "Alas, Poor Richard," his essay on Wright, Baldwin contemplates the cost upon the African American psyche: "But I am suggesting that one of the prices an American Negro pays—or can pay—for what is called his 'acceptance' is a profound, almost ineradicable self-hatred. This corrupts every aspect of his living, he is never at peace again, he is out of touch with himself forever." Rufus has sex with Eric and Leona because he wants their love, but he sees himself as being unworthy of anyone's love. Walking the streets of New York City and contemplating prostituting himself makes Rufus think of Eric: "He glimpsed, for the first time, the extent, the nature, of Eric's loneliness and the danger in which this placed him; and wished that he had been nicer to him."

Harlem, which is characterized in Baldwin stories such as "Previous Condition" and in *Go Tell It on the Mountain* as overly religious and life-threatening, is only a shadowy presence in this novel. The distance between Greenwich Village and Harlem is not just geographic but emotional. Because his friends and lovers are white, Rufus constantly questions these relationships. By situating Rufus in Greenwich Village and surrounding him with white characters, Baldwin draws attention to the absence of African Americans in the life of his principal character. The lack of community for Rufus leads to his fate.

Perhaps *Another Country* is Baldwin's test of the integrationist policies of the 1950s. Both Rufus and Ida Scott attempt to realize their artistic goals in the white world of Greenwich Village and midtown Manhattan. Yet, both characters become pawns in someone else's sexual fantasy. They cannot escape the sexual stereotypes of African Americans and are seen as the black buck and the Jezebel, a promiscuous black woman. Ida personifies the rage of African Americans during the 1960s. Blaming white America for her brother's death, Ida turns her relationships with the white characters in the novel to her advantage. However, her tenuous standing as a jazz vocalist emerges from the opinion of her peers, jazz musicians. She has not endured the requisite suffering, and her willingness to profit from Rufus's suffering dooms her artistic effort.

Another Country is also a critique of conventional notions of masculinity. All of the male characters, with the exception of Eric, struggle with the way in which masculinity is constructed in the United States, and each of them ultimately rejects narrow definitions of a gendered self. Even the minor characters Vivaldo and Richard change their views of themselves as men. Richard had been Vivaldo's high-school English teacher, and the two are engaged in a subtle competition. Each man has been writing a novel for years, but Richard secretly finishes his book and presents Vivaldo with a published copy. Richard's community of family and friends loses respect for him as a writer, however, because they recognize the lack of truth and artistic effort in his commercially successful novel. Richard defines himself by his roles as a father, husband, and provider. He is forced to reexamine his life when his wife commits adultery with a bisexual man. Vivaldo may not be a popular writer like Richard, but readers respect him as an artist because they see the internal struggle and self-examination he undergoes in order to write fiction.

Although his career had been flourishing in France, Baldwin had returned to the United States in 1957 because he felt strongly that he could assist in the fight for civil rights. A significant period in Baldwin's civil-rights activism began in 1963. In addition to giving speeches, Baldwin met with Attorney General Robert Kennedy in an attempt to get federal protection for Freedom Riders and to protest the lack of government action in the area of civil rights for African Americans. Baldwin's second play, *Blues for Mr. Charlie,* ran in New York City from April to August 1964. His first play, *The Amen Corner,* which had premiered in 1955, opened at the Barrymore Theater in New York City in April 1965. Baldwin was also in the process of collecting his short stories for publication as *Going to Meet the Man* (1965) and working on a screenplay, *One Day When I Was Lost: A Scenario Based on Alex Haley's "The Autobiography of Malcolm X"* (1972).

The Fire Next Time (1963), a nonfiction collection including two essays concerning the fate of a racist United States, quickly became one of Baldwin's best-selling books. Baldwin's observations introduced him to a new audience, one that was unfamiliar with his fiction. The positive response to *The Fire Next Time* was a result of its focus on the crucial matter of race. Baldwin's statement that the future of the country was linked to its treatment of African Americans enthralled the country: "The price of the liberation of white people is the liberation of the blacks." He appeared on talk shows and was interviewed many times. With success came fame, and Baldwin

probes the nature of fame in his fourth novel, *Tell Me How Long the Train's Been Gone.*

Baldwin composed *Tell Me How Long the Train's Been Gone* between 1965 and 1967, over several continents and amid much confusion. His inclusion of the dates and locations of the writing at the end of the novel is a testament to the difficulties he encountered. During these years Baldwin was attempting to juggle his writing career with his assumed duties as a spokesperson for African Americans. The demands upon him to speak out against racism continued to increase, while time set aside for writing dwindled. Inevitably, personal doubts and professional criticism began to emerge.

The most compelling portrayal of Baldwin during this period is that offered by Fern Marja Eckman in *The Furious Passage of James Baldwin* (1966). Although she refrains from delving into his sexual liaisons, Eckman succeeds in conveying a sense of the whirlwind within which Baldwin lived. Constantly surrounded by an entourage, Baldwin moved from one speaking engagement to another. Alternatively angry and mellow, the writer was only occasionally sober. Though he was seldom alone, the image of Baldwin that emerged was that of a lonely man. As Eckman says, "he . . . feels himself a stranger everywhere, not least of all within himself." Perhaps more important, Eckman identifies the demands of fame as the source of Baldwin's melancholy. *Tell Me How Long the Train's Been Gone,* with its examination of social and political change, offers Baldwin's most sustained meditations on fame and the impact of celebrity on the artist.

Tell Me How Long the Train's Been Gone is Baldwin's least known novel, and it caused a stir when it was published by Dial Press in 1968. Leo Proudhammer, the protagonist and narrator, is an internationally famous actor who most readers thought resembled Sidney Poitier. The novel tells the story of Leo's failure to analyze and accept himself and the resulting pain and loneliness of living a lie.

Although he frequently wrote about musicians, Baldwin turned to acting for his examination of the African American male artist and the ways in which he is co-opted by fame and his celebrity status. Leo does not inspire sympathy as Sonny did in "Sonny's Blues." His detachment from himself and his life, aided by his profession, becomes infectious. The enticing, almost sensual mystique of the artist and his chosen art form, an integral element in Baldwin's most memorable artistic characters, is clearly missing in *Tell Me How Long the Train's Been Gone.*

Baldwin depicts Leo as being as artificial as the world of the movies he so adored as a child. In Baldwin's fiction, movies are seen by African Americans as windows on the unattainable white world. The young Leo escapes to the dark microcosm of the movies to enter traditional white society in the only role it allows him: that of a voyeur, a visitor. He recalls, "The faces of the movie stars . . . looked like faces far from me, faces which I would never be able to decipher, faces which could be seen but never changed or touched, faces which existed only behind these doors." As an adult Leo seeks to duplicate the distance that he has associated with actors and acting since his childhood.

The accoutrements of celebrity, the special treatment, the adoring fans, are all things that Leo uses to hide from himself: "I am ready: dark blue suit . . . Brazilian cufflinks, black pumps. I am a star again. I look it and I feel it." His only identity, the only one that he can face, is that of a famous actor. Acting becomes Leo's mask. Instead of attempting to gain a secure identity, Leo prefers to adopt one each night at the theater. The title of Leo's next motion picture, *Big Deal,* is Baldwin's commentary on the emptiness of his life and career.

Leo's memories form the three sections of the novel and serve as an introduction to those who had the greatest impact on his life: Barbara King, the white actress who is his former lover and now friend, and his older brother, Caleb Proudhammer. "The House Nigger," the first section of the novel, begins as Leo suffers a heart attack onstage while performing the role of Othello opposite Barbara as Desdemona. Lying in his hospital bed, Leo finally reflects upon his past. Leo's feelings about his sexuality are also revealed in "The House Nigger" as he recalls his two forbidden loves, a white woman and a homosexual man.

The second section, "Is There Anybody There, Said the Traveler," focuses on Leo's youthful experiences with the Actors' Means Workshop and the closeness he once shared with Caleb. Biographer David Leeming notes that several characters in this section are based on acquaintances Baldwin made during the brief Broadway run of his play *Blues for Mister Charlie* in 1964. As the only African American in the theater company, Leo is constantly aware of being out of place. His activities, monitored by distrustful townspeople, lead to his being harassed by the police. The second section of the novel also further explores relationships between the members of the Proudhammer family.

As a young boy Leo learns of the disparity between the races and questions the meaning of democracy. The reality of racism ruins his childhood fantasies. The Proudhammer family consists of a father, an immigrant from Trinidad; a somewhat idealized mulatto mother; the older, rebellious Caleb; and little Leo. One explanation for Leo's estrangement lies in his relationship with Caleb. Disabled by his inability to accept the changes wrought by imprisonment and racism faced by his older brother, Leo does not allow anyone to get close to him. He is intent on not experiencing the transforma-

Back cover of a British paperback edition of Baldwin's 1956 novel, about a white American in Paris coming to terms with his homosexuality (from Campbell, Talking at the Gates: A Life of James Baldwin, *1991*)

tive power of deeply emotional, religious, and sexual life that releases Caleb from his dungeon.

The lack of one consistent emotional and sexual relationship in Leo's life is further evidence of his failure as an artist-hero. Linked by their desire to escape their respective backgrounds, Leo and Barbara sacrifice their personal happiness for public recognition. They meet as young, would-be actors who join a summer theater troupe. One of the most crucial moments in the novel occurs when Lola and Saul San Marquand, the directors of the Actors' Means Workshop, assess Leo's and Barbara's talent. After comparing Leo unfavorably to the legendary black actor Paul Robeson, the San Marquands deliver their verdict. "There is nothing to indicate—ah—in our opinion—that you have any very striking theatrical ability." The San Marquands' unequivocal statement that Leo must be a spectacular actor to compensate for his race leads to his almost exaggerated emphasis on attaining professional success.

Barbara, ever the realist, acknowledges the futility of a romantic relationship with Leo:

> That's the only way we won't lose each other . . . you don't belong to me . . . It means . . . that we must be great. That's all we'll have. That's the only way we won't lose each other . . . you don't belong to me . . . but let's be to each other what we can. But if we do it right . . . we can stretch out our while a very long while and we can make each other better.

This pact neatly removes any guilt from Leo for his selfish treatment of Barbara. Her love for Leo allows him to keep her at a distance lest she crack his armor. Barbara's willingness to accept a platonic friendship, the only relationship Leo offers her, permits him to dictate the nature of their coupling.

The third section of the novel, "Black Christopher," returns to the present as Leo leaves the hospital and resumes his life with Christopher Hall, a young African American activist. While it is often assumed that the inclusion of Christopher was Baldwin's answer to critics who asserted that he was out of touch with the social and political movements in the black community in the late 1960s, Leo's relationship with Christopher is also Baldwin's first depiction of a loving, long-term sexual relationship between two African American men. Christopher forces Leo to reevaluate his life in terms of race and his obligations to the African American community, and, in doing so, Leo finally begins to experience life instead of pretending to live one on stage. Or, as Leo puts it, Christopher defrosts him: "In beginning to thaw, I had to see how I had frozen myself; and, in freezing myself, had frozen Barbara." Christopher redeems Leo by helping him to acknowledge the many identities that define him: being famous, being bisexual, being African American, and being an actor.

Leo's relationship with Christopher can be read as an attempt to reconnect with his cultural past. Christopher, a young activist, remains part of the African American community. Having described Baldwin's writing after *Another Country* as overly political, Houston Baker finds the relationship between Christopher and Leo troubling: "Leo remains unsure of what he must do for or with Christopher. And while he provides material comfort to a degree of understanding, it is impossible to assume he truly understands his young lover." As written, the relationship appears doomed. Leo's uncertainty pervades every facet of his life. At the end of the novel Leo heads off, alone, for a European vacation.

The title of the novel refers to the train as a motif for freedom in African American literature. Thus, "tell me how long the train's been gone" alludes to the length

of Leo's imprisonment, for he has missed the freedom train. The price of Leo's liberation is the courage to face himself. He can only be saved by his recognition and acceptance of his identity as an African American, homosexual man. Leo articulates his inability to be an artist, as Baldwin defines it, through his lifestyle and profession. His upcoming vacation fills him with fear because he will be left alone, without the mask of a role, to confront the real Leo, the one who wants to be an artistic success. Leo typifies a retreat from artistic integrity, an exchange of morality and truth for renown and money.

Autobiographical elements are sprinkled throughout the novel. Like Leo, Baldwin lived in an artists' colony and worked part-time as an artist's model, and he clearly drew upon some of the experiences for the writing of *Tell Me How Long the Train's Been Gone*. James Campbell, one of Baldwin's biographers, views the similarities between character and author as a sign of ineffective writing: "Leo's voice is James Baldwin's voice, but the character can merely mimic his creator, and the result is parody." Leeming, Baldwin's authorized biographer and his secretary during the writing of *Tell Me How Long the Train's Been Gone,* leaves no doubt as to its autobiographical import: the novel "would reflect Baldwin's situation by focusing on a public man's mid-life struggle with himself, his career, and the evil that beleaguers him." Eve Auchincloss and Nancy Lynch quote some of Baldwin's comments on fame, which are strikingly similar to Leo's: "I have a public life—and I know that, O.K. I have a private life, something which I know a good deal less. And the temptation is to avoid the private life because you can hide in the public one." In *Tell Me How Long the Train's Been Gone* Baldwin presents an artist who succumbs to the temptation.

The intense public clamor that greeted all of his nonfiction publications during the 1960s caused Baldwin to question his own effectiveness as a novelist. Many critics and readers either ignore *Tell Me How Long the Train's Been Gone* or point to it as evidence of Baldwin's limited talents as a novelist. In his book-length evaluation of Baldwin's work, Horace Porter mentions this novel only twice. Campbell charges that the novel is overly long and does not have a plot. Negative reviews, its length, and the fact that the novel is not as interesting as its premise have led to its dormant status within the Baldwin canon.

Baldwin's next novel, *If Beale Street Could Talk,* published by Dial Press in 1974, is the story of Tish and Fonny, two young people in love. As Trudier Harris observes in *Black Women in the Fiction of James Baldwin* (1985), it is Baldwin's only novel narrated by a female character. It is also his only sustained examination of heterosexual love. Divided into two sections, *If Beale Street Could Talk* is Baldwin's most profound meditation about the strength of love and the faith that it requires. The first section, "Troubled About My Soul," focuses on Fonny's life just before and just after his arrest. The second section, "Zion," relates the events that occur because of Fonny's arrest.

Tish and Fonny, who have been friends since they were children, fall in love with each other as young adults. Their feelings are not merely affection; each is necessary for the other's existence. The members of Tish's and Fonny's families are prominent and developed characters, and Tish and Fonny go to their families immediately after deciding to get married. Fonny's father, mother, and two sisters provide an interesting contrast to Tish's family. Fonny and his father have a warm, mutually supportive, and loving relationship; but his mother and sisters, described as having light skin and superior attitudes, seem to detest Fonny. In contrast, the closeness of Tish's family is not marred by unrealistic relationships. They fight and love fiercely. Tish's relatives appear to care for Fonny more than his own mother does.

Racism is also at the heart of *If Beale Street Could Talk*. Fonny is arrested for allegedly raping a Puerto Rican woman who later flees the country. The woman chooses Fonny out of a lineup in which he is the only dark-skinned African American man. No one believes in Fonny's innocence except his lawyer, his father, Tish, and her family. Fonny's mother and sisters actively work against him. Baldwin suggests that the African American man is a particular target for racism and holds a tenuous place in the United States:

The same passion which saved Fonny got him into trouble, and put him in jail. For, you see, he had found his center, his own center, inside him; and it showed. He wasn't anybody's nigger. And that is a crime in this fucking free country. You're supposed to be *somebody's* nigger. And if you're nobody's nigger, you're a bad nigger: and that's what the cops decided when Fonny moved downtown.

Thus, Fonny is representative of African American men in the United States and their experiences with attempting to retain their manhood in the face of constant attacks upon it.

Fonny's arrest, its impact on a pregnant Tish and their families, and the attempts to liberate him occupy much of the action of the novel. Tish, her family, and Fonny's father work to keep him optimistic. Knowing that he will be a father helps Fonny to survive being incarcerated. Fonny is also one of Baldwin's artist-heroes, and his sculpting, working with wood and stone, sustains him. His choice of material is revealing, as it suggests that his art is basic, simple, and natural. Fonny describes his two loves as sculpting and Tish. When he is imprisoned, Fonny feels as though he will die without his art. Fonny's father does die at the end of the novel: his suicide takes

Baldwin in 1978 at St. Anne's Hospital in Paris with Beauford Delaney, an artist whose success influenced Baldwin (photograph by Max Petrus; from Leeming, James Baldwin: A Biography, *1994)*

place just as Fonny is about to be released on bail and Tish's baby is due.

Published in the fall of 1979, *Just Above My Head* is Baldwin's last novel, the story of Arthur Montana's life as told by his older brother, Hall. The novel asks whether an African American singer can survive the combination of religion, art, and homosexuality. With the death of Arthur Montana at the age of thirty-nine, one can conclude that the answer is a negative one. The novel is Hall's attempt to understand his brother's death and life. It has taken two years before Hall, seven years older than Arthur, could address these subjects. Hence the relationship between the two brothers is another central element of the novel.

Just Above My Head traces the lives of the Montana family—Paul, Florence, and their sons, Hall and Arthur—and their relationship with the Miller family, comprised of Joel, Amy, and their children, Julia and Jimmy. These two families are bound together by religion, music, and the friendships between the children. Young Julia Miller's calling to preach the gospel irrevocably alters the lives of all the characters in the novel. Her time spent in the pulpit has a negative effect on her family and ultimately destroys Arthur's first serious relationship. Arthur later becomes an internationally famous gospel singer while Hall marries and starts a family. As he approaches middle age, Arthur falls in love with Jimmy, Julia's younger brother, and this union draws the Montanas and the Millers even closer. *Just Above My Head,* told in flashback, is divided into five books: book 1, "Have Mercy," looks at the impact of Arthur's death on his family; book 2, "Twelve Gates to the City," focuses on the influence of religion on the black family; book 3, "The Gospel Singer," concentrates on Arthur's development as a man and a singer; book 4, "Stepchild," examines the love lives of Hall and Arthur; and book 5, "The Gates of Hell," explores the last years of Arthur's life.

Hall, like the unnamed narrator in "Sonny's Blues," is an unreliable narrator on many levels, and yet he claims to view his brother's life with a clarity missing from his own: "He was on stage. He caught the light, and so I saw him: more clearly than I will ever see myself." Technically, it is impossible for Hall to truly know Arthur's intimate thoughts and feelings; he can only claim to know himself. Yet, Hall professes to have a certain insight into his brother's life, despite the fact that the two brothers are separated not only by a seven-year age difference but also by their sexual orientation. Hall is aware of Arthur's homosexuality but feels that he cannot tell this part of his brother's life. Melvin Dixon implies that Hall's status as a heterosexual makes it impossible for him to truly understand Arthur: "Hall's narration of the life of gospel singer Arthur Montana . . . is merely one brother's manipulation of another to come to terms with his conventional responsibilities to family and self." Although he admits to having no knowledge about certain parts of Arthur's life, Hall's relinquishing of the narrative to Jimmy, Arthur's lover, at the end of the novel is unsettling. Is it possible for someone, however close, to know the details of another's life? This question is central in the narrative. Arthur remains for Hall, and consequently for the reader, just above his head, ever present and yet forever out of reach.

Early in *Just Above My Head* the issue of legacy is evoked by Hall's son, Tony, who wonders, two years after his uncle's death, just what kind of man Arthur was. As an adolescent, Tony is in the process of coming to terms with his own sexuality and seems confused about how to deal with taunts that his uncle was a "faggot." Hall's response reveals as much about himself as it does about Arthur:

> I know—before Jimmy—Arthur slept with a lot of people—mostly men, but not always. He was young, Tony. Before your mother, *I* slept with a lot of women . . .

mostly women . . . not always. I'm proud of my brother, your uncle . . . You should be, too. Whatever the fuck your uncle was, and he was a whole lot of things, he was nobody's faggot.

Hall never expressed his pride to his brother, however.

After making love to Crunch, his first male lover, Arthur gleans insight into the meaning of his song: "He was frightened, but triumphant. He wanted to sing." He expresses his deepest feelings though his art. Love means acceptance to Arthur, and this emotion liberates, at least temporarily, his artistic voice. The problem lies in Arthur's search for acceptance from others instead of looking inward. Despite his commitment to expressing honesty in his singing, Arthur is ashamed of his status as a homosexual. His status as an artist-hero is tenuous until he learns to accept himself as a homosexual, Christian, gospel singer; he finally achieves a sense of stability in his personal and professional lives through his union with Jimmy Miller.

Although the church represents the cultural and historical legacy of the African American community in many of Baldwin's works, in his last novel the mood has changed. Early in *Just Above My Head* Hall hints that the church failed Arthur. Certainly his mother, Florence, blames the members of their congregation: "she feels that the people in the church, when they turned against him, became directly responsible for his death." Baldwin also uses Julia Miller, the child evangelist, as a symbol of the hypocrisy of the church. As a child Julia does not truly understand the sermons that she preaches or the lessons that she seeks to impart from her pulpit. The show-business aura that surrounds Julia during her time in the pulpit is presented with a cynical air. In Baldwin's hands religion becomes a cancer that attracts liars and cheats and tears families apart.

Just Above My Head is unusual because Baldwin presents a marriage between two African American men that is recognized and accepted by their families. Commitment is the focus of all of the couplings in the novel, not the quick, hot passion of *Another Country* or the manipulative sexual conquests so prevalent in *Tell Me How Long the Train's Been Gone. Just Above My Head* links sexuality with love, stability, and healing. Crunch heals Julia's wounds from her incestuous relationship with her father by making love to her. He also helps Arthur by showing him that men, black men, can love each other. Crunch senses Arthur's need to be accepted and embraced for who and what he is. Their affair empowers Arthur:

> Still, the step from this perception to articulation is not an easy one. He has faltered and turned back many times. And yet, he knows that, when he was happy with Crunch, he was neither guilty nor ashamed. He had felt a purity, a shining, joy, as though he had been,

astoundingly, miraculously, blessed, and had feared neither Satan, man, nor God. He had not doubted for a moment that all love was holy.

But Arthur must be able to express this same blessed feeling in his musical career. Hall observes that Jimmy had this positive effect on Arthur's art: "Jimmy's presence in Arthur's life, Jimmy's love, altered Arthur's estimate of himself, gave him a joy and a freedom he had never known before, invested him with a kind of incandescent wonder, and he carried this light on stage with him, he moved his body differently since he knew that he was loved, loved, and therefore knew himself to be both bound and free."

African American male homosexuals have been shadowy figures in African American literature. They have been present but not always seen or acknowledged. By making the central character in *Just Above My Head* an openly gay man, Baldwin drops the veil of bisexuality that shrouded many of his previous protagonists. Although Hall implies that Arthur has had sexual relations with women, Arthur never makes such a claim. With Arthur, Baldwin argues for the acknowledgment of African American homosexuals as members of the African American community.

Although Dixon and Kendall Thomas argue that the James Baldwin who is remembered and canonized by some is one who is stripped of his homosexuality, Baldwin has been embraced by younger African American gay writers who were encouraged by his honest exploration of human sexuality in his work. *Go The Way Your Blood Beats* is a 1996 anthology of black gay fiction that takes its title from advice that Baldwin gave to young gay people in a *Village Voice* interview with Richard Goldstein (collected in *James Baldwin: The Legacy*, 1989). Joseph Beam, the late editor of *In The Life: A Black Gay Anthology* (1986), reflected in an essay for *Brother to Brother: New Writings by Black Gay Men* (1991) on what *Just Above My Head* meant to him as a black, gay man: "In *Just Above My Head*, in plain view of the black family, it was possible for two black men to be lovers, and be political, and be cherished for who they were . . . Because he could envision us as lovers, our possibilities were endless."

James Baldwin died on 1 December 1987 of cancer of the esophagus in his home in St. Paul-de-Vence, France. His funeral service was held in the Harlem Cathedral of St. John the Divine, where he was eulogized by Maya Angelou, Amiri Baraka, and Toni Morrison. The appearance of the 1998 two-volume Library of America edition of Baldwin's fiction and nonfiction, edited by Morrison, is recognition of Baldwin's stature in American literature. Yet, this edition excludes *Tell Me How Long the Train's Been Gone, If Beale Street Could Talk,* and *Just Above My Head;* and these works cement Bald-

Baldwin on the set of the 1986 production of his first play, The Amen Corner, *which premiered in 1955 (from Leeming,* James Baldwin: A Biography, *1994)*

win's vision of himself as a novelist. While the Library of America volumes represent a canonization of Baldwin's early fiction, all of his novels offer a potent appraisal of love and life in the second half of the twentieth century.

Interviews:

Richard Goldstein, "Go The Way Your Blood Beats: An Interview with James Baldwin," in *James Baldwin: The Legacy,* edited by Quincy Troupe (New York: Simon & Schuster, 1989), pp. 173–185;

Fred L. Standley and Louis H. Pratt, eds., *Conversations with James Baldwin* (Jackson: University Press of Mississippi, 1989).

Biographies:

Fern Marja Eckman, *The Furious Passage of James Baldwin* (New York: M. Evans, 1966);

W. J. Weathersby, *James Baldwin: Artist on Fire* (New York: D. I. Fine, 1989);

James Campbell, *Talking at the Gates: A Life of James Baldwin* (London: Faber & Faber, 1991; New York: Viking, 1991);

David Leeming, *James Baldwin: A Biography* (New York: Knopf, 1994).

References:

Eve Auchincloss and Nancy Lynch, "Disturber of the Peace: James Baldwin," in *The Black American Writer,* edited by C. W. E. Bigsby, volume 1 (Baltimore: Penguin, 1969), pp. 199–215;

Houston Baker, "The Embattled Craftsman: An Essay on James Baldwin," in *Critical Essays on James Baldwin,* edited by Fred L. Standley and Nancy V. Burt (Boston: G. K. Hall, 1988), pp. 62–77;

Joseph Beam, "James Baldwin: Not a Bad Legacy, Brother," in *Brother to Brother: New Writings by Black Gay Men,* edited by Essex Hemphill (Boston: Alyson, 1991);

David Bergman, *Gaiety Transfigured* (Madison: University of Wisconsin Press, 1991);

Eldridge Cleaver, *Soul on Ice* (New York: McGraw-Hill, 1968);

Melvin Dixon, *Ride Out the Wilderness: Geography and Identity in Afro-American Literature* (Urbana: University of Illinois Press, 1987);

William Farrison, "If Baldwin's Train Has Not Gone," in *James Baldwin: A Critical Evaluation,* edited by Therman O'Daniel (Washington, D.C.: Howard University Press, 1977), pp. 69–81;

Susan Feldman, "Another Look at *Another Country:* Reconciling Baldwin's Racial and Sexual Politics," in *Re-Viewing James Baldwin: Things Not Seen,* edited by D. Quentin Miller (Philadelphia: Temple University Press, 2000), pp. 88–104;

Addison Gayle Jr., *The Way of the New World: The Black Novel in America* (Garden City, N.Y.: Anchor Press, 1975);

Jean-Louis Goundard, *The Racial Problem in the Works of Richard Wright and James Baldwin* (Westport, Conn.: Greenwood Press, 1992);

Trudier Harris, *Black Women in the Fiction of James Baldwin* (Knoxville: University of Tennessee Press, 1985);

Cora Kaplan, "'A Cavern Opened In My Mind': The Poetics of Homosexuality and The Politics of Masculinity in James Baldwin," in *Representing Black Men,* edited by Marcellus Blount and George P. Cunningham (New York: Routledge, 1996), pp. 27–54;

Randall Kenan, *James Baldwin* (New York: Chelsea House, 1994);

Edward Margolies, *Native Sons: A Critical Study of Twentieth-Century Black American Authors* (New York: Lippincott, 1968);

Dwight McBride, ed. *James Baldwin Now* (New York: New York University Press, 1999);

Bruce Morrow and Charles H. Rowell, eds. *Shade: An Anthology of Fiction By Gay Men of African Descent* (New York: Avon, 1996);

Kevin Ohi, "'I'm Not The Boy You Want': Sexuality, 'Race,' and Thwarted Revelation in Baldwin's *Another Country,*" *African American Review,* 33 (Summer 1999): 261–281;

Barbara K. Olsen, "'Come-to-Jesus Stuff' in James Baldwin's *Go Tell It on the Mountain* and *The Amen Corner,*" *African American Review,* 31 (Summer 1997): 295–301;

Gayle Pemberton, "A Sentimental Journey: James Baldwin and the Thomas-Hill Hearings," in *Race-ing Justice, En-Gendering Power: Essays on Anita Hill, Clarence Thomas and the Construction of Social Reality,* edited by Toni Morrison (New York: Pantheon, 1992);

Horace Porter, *Stealing the Fire: The Art and Protest of James Baldwin* (Middletown, Conn.: Wesleyan University Press, 1989);

Shawn Stewart Ruff, ed. *Go The Way Your Blood Beats: An Anthology of Lesbian and Gay Fiction By African American Writers* (New York: Holt, 1996);

Reginald Shepherd, "On Not Being White," in *In The Life: A Black Gay Anthology,* edited by Beam (Boston: Alyson, 1986), pp. 46–57;

Andrew Shin and Barbara Judson, "Beneath the Black Aesthetic: James Baldwin's Primer of Black American Masculinity," *African American Review,* 32 (Summer 1998): 247–261;

Kendall Thomas, "'Ain't Nothin' Like The Real Thing': Black Masculinity, Gay Sexuality, and the Jargon of Authenticity," in *Representing Black Men,* edited by Blount and Cunningham (New York: Routledge, 1996), pp. 55–69;

Robert Tomlinson, "'Payin' one's dues': Expatriation as Personal Experience and Paradigm in the Works of James Baldwin," *African American Review,* 33 (Spring 1999): 135–148;

Eleanor Traylor, "I Hear Music in the Air: James Baldwin's *Just Above My Head,*" in *Critical Essays on James Baldwin,* edited by Fred L. Standley and Nancy V. Burt (Boston: G. K. Hall, 1988), pp. 217–223.

Papers:

An archive of James Baldwin's papers is at the Schomberg Center for Research in Black Culture, New York Public Library.

Russell Banks

(28 March 1940 –)

Denis M. Hennessy
State University of New York, College at Oneonta

See also the Banks entry in *DLB 130: American Short-Story Writers Since World War II.*

BOOKS: *15 Poems,* by Banks, William Matthews, and Newton Smith (Chapel Hill, N.C.: Lillabulero, 1967);

Waiting to Freeze (Northwood Narrows, N.H.: Lillabulero, 1967);

30/6 (New York: Quest, 1969);

Snow: Meditations of a Man in Winter (Hanover, N.H.: Granite, 1974);

Searching for Survivors (New York: Fiction Collective, 1975);

Family Life (New York: Avon, 1975; revised, Los Angeles: Sun & Moon, 1988);

The New World (Urbana: University of Illinois Press, 1978);

Hamilton Stark (Boston: Houghton Mifflin, 1978);

The Book of Jamaica (Boston: Houghton Mifflin, 1980);

Trailerpark (Boston: Houghton Mifflin, 1981);

The Relation of My Imprisonment (Washington, D.C.: Sun & Moon, 1983);

Continental Drift (New York: Harper & Row, 1985; London: Hamilton, 1985);

Success Stories (New York: Harper & Row, 1986; London: Hamilton, 1986);

Affliction (New York: Harper & Row, 1989; London: Picador, 1990);

The Sweet Hereafter (New York: HarperCollins, 1991; London: Picador, 1992);

Rule of the Bone (New York: HarperCollins, 1995; London: Secker & Warburg, 1995);

Cloudsplitter (New York: HarperCollins, 1998; London: Secker & Warburg, 1998);

The Invisible Stranger, text by Banks, photographs by Arturo Patten (New York: HarperCollins, 1999);

The Angel on the Roof: The Stories of Russell Banks (New York: HarperCollins, 2000; London: Secker & Warburg, 2000).

Russell Banks (photograph by Marion Ettlinger; from the dust jacket of The Angel on the Roof, *2000)*

OTHER: *Brushes with Greatness: An Anthology of Chance Encounters with Greatness,* edited by Banks, Michael Ondaatje, and David Young (Toronto: Coach House, 1989);

Mark Twain, *A Tramp Abroad,* introduction by Banks (New York: Oxford University Press, 1996).

Russell Banks has been publishing innovative fiction for more than twenty-five years, gaining praise from critics for his short stories and novels. Although he is primarily a realist, he has experimented with some postmodern techniques and has confronted the reader with unconventional points of view. Banks has stated that voice is a particularly vital part of his storytelling and can help or destroy the effectiveness of the tone and mood of the piece. His short stories work out in brief form the ideas that dominate his novels: the insidious effects of alcoholism, the tenuous relationship of father and son, the changing patterns of community life, and the original sin of racism that affects Americans in their ways of perceiving themselves in a rapidly changing world. His settings range from New England to Florida, Haiti, and Jamaica; however, he is most evocative when he uses the places in which he has lived and worked throughout his life—the semirural, impoverished, cold climates of New Hampshire and upstate New York. Because of his attention to working-class people and the disenfranchised in America, several critics have classified him with "grit-lit" writers such as Raymond Carver, Joyce Carol Oates, and even Denis Johnson, but such comparisons are inadequate to describe accurately his place in American literature in the late twentieth and early twenty-first centuries.

Russell Earl Banks was born on 28 March 1940 in Newton, Massachusetts, to Earl and Florence Taylor Banks; his father was a plumber, as was his grandfather. In 1952 Earl Banks, a violent man and an alcoholic, deserted his family, leaving his wife, three sons, and a daughter. Florence Banks moved the family to Barnstead, New Hampshire, and later to Wakefield, Massachusetts. She sued for divorce, got custody of the children, and undertook a series of clerical jobs to support the family. In reflections on this time in his life, Banks has described his mother as hardworking but self-absorbed and himself as a twelve-year-old called upon to be the male head of a family moving from apartment to apartment, living close to poverty.

At sixteen, Banks left home with a friend in a stolen car, getting as far as Pasadena, California, a trip that cost him a scholarship that had been offered by Phillips Andover Academy. Two years later, in 1956, he again refused entry into upper-middle-class education, this time leaving Colgate University, where he had a scholarship, after only three months on campus. That Christmas he hitchhiked to Miami on a frustrated mission to join Fidel Castro in Cuba. He remained in Miami and married Darlene Bennett, a seventeen-year-old salesgirl, and had a child, Leona Lea, on 13 May 1960. The young family moved to Boston, but Banks left, and the couple eventually divorced in February 1962. Between this time and when he married

Mary Gunst in October of that year, Banks worked in a bookstore in Boston and began socializing with a literary crowd. He quickly became disillusioned with this group; but he began to write.

Banks's experiences suggest the origins of his major themes. In his early writings, as well as his mature work, family strife is intensified by alcohol, violence, and desertion; the reliving of a father's mistakes is a kind of ineluctable doom; and the near-impossible quest to escape the strictures of class and poverty in America are the thematic chords.

Two men who influenced Banks in his early attempts to write were Leo Giroux Jr. and Nelson Algren. Giroux was an unpublished writer, seven years older than Banks, whom he met in Boston. Giroux urged Banks to read and provided him with a list of writers, most of whom he had never known existed. Banks met Algren at the Breadloaf School in Middlebury, Vermont, late in 1962. At the school and in private meetings during long drives, Algren pointed out to Banks the strengths and weaknesses of his writing. Banks credits him with "validating me as a writer."

After Gunst's parents offered to pay for Banks's college education, he enrolled in the University of North Carolina at Chapel Hill in 1964, turning his efforts toward a literary career. While an undergraduate, he founded Lillabulero Press with William Matthews, publishing his *15 Poems* (1967) with Matthews and Newton Smith. He graduated Phi Beta Kappa in 1967. He returned to New England and began teaching writing at Emerson College, Boston, and at the University of New Hampshire at Durham. He and Gunst also had three daughters: Caerthan, born in 1964; Maia, born in 1968; and Danis, born in 1970. The death of his brother Christopher in a train wreck in 1968 greatly affected Banks and is recounted in his short story "Searching for Survivors II." In 1976 Banks was a writer-in-residence at Princeton University and Sarah Lawrence University, and he taught at Princeton until his retirement in 1998. In 1977, after returning from Jamaica, where he spent a Guggenheim Fellowship, he and Gunst divorced. In 1982 he married Kathy Walton, his editor at Harper and Row. He divorced again and in 1988 married poet Chase Twichell. They live in Keene, New York, and Princeton, New Jersey.

Searching for Survivors, Banks's first book of short stories, came out in 1975, as did *Family Life,* his first novel. Robert Niemi, the author of the only book-length study of Banks, considers these stories apprentice fiction, showing Banks's experimentation with styles and techniques, especially metafiction. Banks is obviously looking not just to be fashionable with style but to find a way of putting the painful lessons of his life into words that trick and taunt the reader. Primarily, these short stories became workshops for themes and plots Banks later used in his novels.

Family Life, a short, experimental novel, was published first in 1975, then revised and republished in 1988. Critics in 1975 failed to see anything worthwhile in the book. In 1988, however, perhaps taking Banks more seriously as the author of prizewinning short stories and three novels, they welcomed the novel as a kind of fable criticizing family life in contemporary America. Although Banks made only minor changes, Sun and Moon Press published it with production values much superior to those of the 1975 edition. The significance of this early experimental novel is as a precursor of themes developed in the later work—themes of desertion, infidelity, and brutishness as they work to ruin lives. Lacking the complexity of a novel, it nevertheless reaches into the inner depravity of its main characters, Egress the king and Ruth the queen. Its ferocity is mitigated only by the semijocular tone, characterized by crass obscenity and exaggerated violence. Only the dialogue, which is obviously mid-twentieth-century American, hints at the setting; the time is the mid 1970s, since a novel within the novel, written by Ruth, discusses the Vietnam War. The kingdom, then, is the family of Egress and Ruth and their three boys.

At the outset, Egress is visited by a stranger in a green suit who asks the king for one of the princes to take as a lover: "Any one of them will do. I just have a thing for princes." The language draws attention to itself by its casual obscenity, its oddness when put into the context of a royal court setting. The effect of this ploy is not really funny; it seems more to be an awkward reminder that the problems of the family are universal, timeless in their evil. The king has a homosexual lover, Loon, and the queen has an ongoing sexual relationship with the wine steward. The three sons are cowed by the father's violence toward them and drawn to masculine forms of violence themselves. Readers also learn that Egress's father, Donald the Flailer, beat Egress unmercifully, a hint of the cyclical nature of abuse. Chapter 10 is the novel written by Ruth, which parallels the action of the novel itself: high-school sweethearts marry and have children; sons are tainted by their father's violence and driven apart by the father's call to the Vietnam War; and the mother is unfaithful, begins drinking, and has only halfhearted concern for her husband's return from a POW camp. *Family Life* ends with Egress's banishment from the kingdom by Ruth and the deaths of all the sons through odd forms of violence.

Family Life was obviously written by a young Banks. Contrasted with the meticulous development of character and plot in his later novels, this early work seems to show a budding postmodern experimenter.

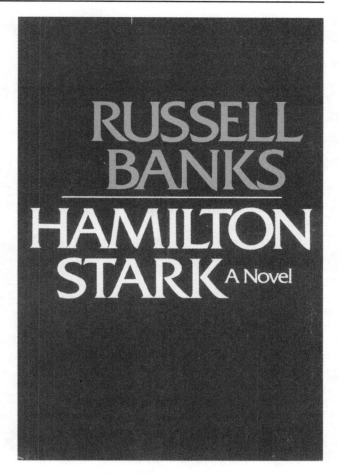

Dust jacket for Banks's 1978 novel, in which characters seek the title character (Richland County Public Library)

He does little of this kind of storytelling in subsequent works. The roots of his themes are evident, however, as are the barely disguised autobiographical details of his plots and the compelling narrative drive. Banks himself has said that it is a book more helpful to him than to the reader.

Hamilton Stark (1978) uses techniques of metafiction similar to those in *Family Life,* but with more satisfying results: more plot, more complexity and depth, and a far more serious purpose. Banks, in the fashion of metafiction writers of the time, lets the main narrator (the author) introduce himself to the reader and discuss the problems of fiction writing, of getting at the truth, of inventing the fiction and having the reader receive it. These poststructural concerns, however, are never allowed to overshadow the narrative. The reader is forced to jump back and forth between various narrators and sources, to hear the author's questions about the reliability of his material, and to read other characters' attempts at fictionalizing the same material. The narrative drive remains strong, giving the reader a complex but lucid view of the title character.

The results of these techniques are helpful to reader and critic alike. In *Hamilton Stark* the biographical connections are not so obvious. The protagonist of this novel is drawn partly in a realistic way, bearing many of the characteristics of the father figure in almost all of Banks's fiction; but there is more to him than realism. Hamilton Stark is depicted as seen through the eyes of his daughter, several of his wives, and the overly sensitive but hardly all-knowing "author" who narrates the story. The character study of the man goes deeper than the legends that surround him in the small town in New Hampshire. The resultant picture is of an Everyman, not perfectly seen so that readers can judge him but seen as completely as possible.

The main narrative voice in the novel, who refers to himself as the author of a book about A., is mild mannered and ordinary. The reader can infer this personality from descriptions of his activities, his reactions to events real and imagined, and his willing suspension of disbelief. One of the motivations for writing his book, this narrator admits, comes from an article he quotes from *The New York Times* that tells of a hermit named Ham who has been living in a "holding tomb" near the Arctic Circle for twenty years. Some of the chapters are simply sections of the novel he is writing, and the summaries at the beginnings serve to set the scene and clarify their literary purpose: "Chapter Five. Back and Fill: In Which the Hero's Ditch, Having Got Dug and the Pipe's Having Been Laid Therein, Gets Filled; Including a Brief Digression Concerning the Demon Asmodeus, along with Certain Other Digressions of Great and Small Interest." The reader, then, is not only taken into the plot but also made aware of the author's necessity and purpose for creating it.

The novel takes place in Barnstead, New Hampshire, a territory Banks knows well. The dialogue, the weather, the thoughts tacit and expressed by the characters are authentically reproduced. According to Niemi, Banks was reading Charles Olson and other Black Mountain poets, along with the New England Transcendentalists, at the time he was writing this novel. He stated to Niemi, in letters and e-mails, that he was prompted by this reading into "a deep investigation into the 'local,' a vertical look into the surround rather than a horizontal one. By keeping things local, I could also keep them personal, without actually being 'autobiographical,' which was anathema to me." As the plot begins, Hamilton Stark has invited his friend to his house for drinks but is not at home. There are bullet holes in his car windows, and he is nowhere to be found. The novel progresses to its end with finding him as its objective, a plot-driven objective and a thematic

one as well. The novel parodies a mystery novel while its true motive is to solve the problem of finding the real in Hamilton Stark.

This novel, then, is a compendium of narrative ploys that authors have used in the past to offer a simulacrum of reality: varying taped first-person accounts by Stark's enemies, wives, and friends about incidents from Stark's life; chapters from another novel written by his daughter; and droll summaries preceding the chapters. There is even the use of the murder mystery to drive the plot—or rather to simulate a plot. The fact that the murder is never really solved makes the point that reality can never really be captured nor truth ever fully realized in fiction. The epigraph from Søren Kierkegaard that Banks uses—"The individual has a host of shadows, all of which resemble him and for the moment have an equal claim to authenticity"—reminds the reader that a full evaluation of any human being can never be communicated, no matter how diligent the attempt.

In a 2 July 1978 *New York Times* review, Ann Birstein described this technique as a kaleidoscope effect with Hamilton as "the brightest piece in a constantly shifting pattern." Her overall evaluation is that the use of metaphor is heavy-handed, that everything has a hidden meaning that might lead the reader to lose interest in the main character's actual worthiness. She avers at the end of the review, though, that Banks's writing makes reading the book worthwhile, and she points to the strength of his writing that critics in the next two decades recognized and praised. Banks combines his postmodern attempts at playfulness of technique with a realism that captures the rigors of blue-collar life: the mind-numbing tedium of digging through damp and cold cellars to fix the plumbing of decaying houses, or the mindless terror of a fistfight started out of lust and anger and ending in broken bodies and spirits. Mainly he describes the dumbfounding realization that men like Hamilton Stark are so insensitive to love and caring that the people around them cannot know or like or get close to them in any way. The insight may be a reflection of Banks's relationship with his father or, as he hints, his relationship with his daughters. Banks began to show in this novel and the short stories of this period a talent for making readers aware of the torments of working-class life.

In *The Book of Jamaica* (1980) Banks further develops his theme of the inability to reach certainty about a man or about anything in life. The four parts of the book are loosely interrelated stories of a young professor's travels in Jamaica in 1976 as he is studying, on a grant, the lives of the Maroons, Jamaican descendants of a slave group that settled on the island after escaping the Spanish in the seventeenth and eighteenth centuries.

Banks is obviously attempting to deal with injustices of race and class in this book, using the island of Jamaica as representative of the New World corrupted by the Old, from the seventeenth century to the 1970s. In a symposium on travel writing, published in *The New York Times* in 1991, Banks cites the Melvillean journeys of *Typee* (1846), *Omoo* (1847), and even *Moby-Dick* (1851) as examples of the novelist using travel to fresh places as a background for the protagonists' awakenings to new elements in life. He says, "I think that since Homer, all travel writing that's of lasting interest—writing that we continue to read, writing that is written by writers as travelers, not travelers as writers—is really written to make a point about home." In *The Book of Jamaica* the journey the professor is taking reminds him of the racial problems in his own country. The deeper he travels into the inner settlements of Jamaica and the closer he comes to the people, the more he learns.

In the first part, "Captain Blood," the first-person narrator tells of a string of incidents involving his attempts to find out more about the actor Errol Flynn, who had spent much of his time luxuriating on the island after his success with movies, especially *Captain Blood* in 1935. The narrator gradually gathers bits of a story about Flynn's putative part in the murder, dismemberment, and disposal of a local butcher's wife. DeVries, the butcher, was tried, convicted, and executed for the murder, but local legend says that Flynn, along with a native doctor and the doctor's son, must have shared the guilt. The narrator's quest, never really explained as to purpose, seems less daunting than the search for Hamilton Stark in the previous novel, but the reader can guess that gossip, an intimidated witness, and points of view biased by race, nationality, and class will foil the investigation. Once again Banks is questioning the efficacy of language in coming to any truth.

In *The Book of Jamaica* are the seeds of themes that become vital to Banks's novels. Race and the barriers that color creates in the New World become an abiding interest beginning with the first section of this novel. Wealth, and the freedom it allows Flynn and other white islanders he befriends, is contrasted to the poverty and desperation of the murder victim and her husband, who is coerced into compliance, forced to dismember and destroy his wife's body. Though readers never discover the concrete facts of the murder—nor do the authorities—it is evident that race and privilege protected the real perpetrators. The murder remains a legend, enhancing the swashbuckling reputation of Flynn while shaming and damning the black servant people.

The narrator, who relates these points in a tone of controlled fury, ends up befriending a black woman, having drinks with her, and sleeping with her in his room. The next morning he gets a note from her,

Dust jacket for Banks's 1985 novel, which interweaves the narratives of two people trying to escape their desperate lives (Richland County Public Library)

regretfully asking for some money to help feed her children, and he pays her $20. If he has any compunction for his own compliance in disgracing black Jamaicans, he does not mention it. The Jamaican patois is something the narrator wants to learn; he believes that it is a tool used by the Jamaicans to shroud their feelings and frustrations. However, this interest is the only effort he makes in "Captain Blood" to get a deeper understanding of their plight.

In the second part, "Nyamkopang," Banks opens in first person using the same narrator, except that the professor has returned to Jamaica from a short stay back in the United States a changed man, wiser presumably from his first brush with Jamaican chaos. This time he has brought his wife and children. Neither he nor his family are ever given names, except he is sometimes called Johnnie by the Jamaicans he gets to know, a name he thinks is given to any white man who seems friendly to the natives. In this section Banks makes clear that his protagonist is on a quest. He feels uncomfortable about the Churches, a couple who rented a house to him for a small amount and instructed him to send the money to a bank in Canada. Although he does not realize it at first, their ploy is to get the money out of the country to relatives, thus avoiding heavy taxes imposed by a new reform regime in Jamaica. The narrator's naiveté at this point alerts the reader to a certain quixotic quality that colors all his descriptions of the injustices he perceives. The reader knows that Johnnie is not so aware of the realities of Jamaica's problems as he thinks, and the inability to understand problems based on race becomes the overriding theme of the novel.

About a third of the way through this section, Banks briefly changes the point of view from first to third person. After attending a dinner party at the Churches', at which Mrs. Church reprimanded one of the black servants by slapping his hand with a kitchen knife, the narrator mulls the incident while walking: "The dreamy American had found himself, for the first time in his life, truly alone. Prior to this, solitude had been abstract and something to admire, had even been a source of pride and something of a lived metaphor for certain of his philosophic beliefs." Now, in solitude, he must think of the moral decisions that come with a reality in which one must take a stand for or against the kind of hateful actions of the Mrs. Churches, and he grows angry at the feeling of isolation. In the next paragraph, he passes over the crest of a ridge, and the point of view returns to first person. Banks uses such changes in narrative voice throughout, even switching to second person in the last part of this section, ironically giving the prose the sound of a travel brochure: "You are having a loud, wonderful time, a hell of a guy." His purpose in this quick shift of point of view, Niemi suggests, is to show his protagonist becoming less subjective, more realistic in his understanding of the plight of the islanders. Banks develops this technique more effectively in his later novels.

The third section of the novel, "Obi," is used to develop the plot while concentrating more on obi, or obeah, a kind of sorcery or magic that is practiced in the Caribbean, Africa, and parts of the southern United States. Third-person narration takes over, and Johnnie is alternately referred to as "the American." Terron, Johnnie's Rastafarian friend, is now "the Rasta." This narrative ploy makes the events seem as though they are told by a more distant, perhaps more cold and objective, narrator. Both of these characters are starting on a journey to visit Colonel Bowra, the leader of Gordon Hall, the Maroon colony on the other side of the island, and bring him back to Nyampokong. The journey is tortuous and filled with much drinking, carousing, and conversation. Bowra performs seemingly

magical feats using his power of obeah, but as Banks describes them the reader is not sure that they are not illusions brought on by the omnipresent rum and marijuana. The meeting of the two regional Maroon leaders is disastrous, and Bowra, shocked by his counterpart's indifference to the murder of one of his own people by the police, orders him killed.

In "Dread," the last section of the novel, Johnnie's family life has deteriorated because of Johnnie's neglect, his rambling travels away from home, and his preoccupation with the study of the Jamaicans. His wife takes the children, leaving him and the island, and he stays alone in the house they had rented from the Churches. Disillusioned, he can no longer side with the wealthy and powerful society that continues to gull Jamaicans. Despite some concessions to principle, he leaves for Florida feeling like an ignorant tourist, confounded by the differences in culture and philosophy that divide the races.

The metaphor of the traveler-protagonist representing man in his search for truth and meaning in life continues in Banks's next novel, *Continental Drift* (1985), although this time Banks uses more of his knowledge of working-class life in New England. The setting is the New Hampshire of *Hamilton Stark* but shifts, as its protagonist Dubois yearns for escape, to Florida; a parallel plot involves a young Haitian woman, Vanise, and her family's attempted flight from Haiti. This novel, which gained much critical attention and praise, was a runner-up for the Pulitzer Prize in 1986. The changes that Banks has made in his style and approach to storytelling in *Continental Drift* are apparent. Characterization is better developed; the narrative voices are as experimental as in his earlier works, but more functional; and the themes of racial and class strife are more powerfully presented, more effectively plotted. Niemi says that Banks becomes more of a realist in his short stories written in the early 1980s, and this book shows the results of that development. *Continental Drift* is about the despair of working-class lives in the United States, using the plight of a poor Haitian family to add perspective.

In a 10 September 1989 *New York Times Magazine* piece on Banks, Wesley Brown says that many readers were put off by the narrative voice and its shift from Dubois to Vanise, which was criticized for being intrusive and condescending. In the article Banks answers that he "deliberately avoided the use of an impersonal narrator because of his belief that the narrator of a novel must be held accountable in the same way as the characters are." Banks is then quoted directly as averring, "The choice of one narrative voice over another is not a technical problem, but a moral one. And to a great extent *Continental Drift* is about the responsibility that goes with telling a story." The narrative voices serve several purposes for Banks. The voice in the

"Invocation" is omniscient, as a storyteller's would be. As the first chapter opens, the voice is still omniscient, but it uses present tense and a taut style and idiom that most resemble those of a sharp-tongued modern-day New Englander. When the story switches to Vanise and the Haitian refugees' experience, the voice reverts to the storyteller's philosophical tone and idiom. Readers are once again reminded of a Joycean influence in Banks, namely the use of narrative voice to imitate the speech and background of the character being treated. This technique heightens the effect of the parallel descriptions of the New Hampshire protagonist and his counterpart, the self-exiled Haitian black woman.

This technique of narration provides a deeper characterization of the principals in the novel. Robert Raymond Dubois is an oil-burner repairman with a wife and two children, a man who works hard for "chump change." Even before encountering the contrasting life of Vanise, the reader can sense the irony of the situation: a man with a healthy family, who owns his own house and has a job that pays him regularly, is suffering paralyzing mental anguish. He feels unfortunate compared to his brother and others who are more successful, earning more money and recognition. Vanise, who is bereft of any physical comforts, any security, or even any home, certainly is in a much more pitiable condition. Dubois is a prototypical blue-collar American working man who loves his wife but carries on a sexual affair with another woman; loves his children but is too self-absorbed to show them love; works a hard day willingly but yearns for the shadowy opportunity that will bring him more of what he wants.

Banks begins the first chapter on Vanise with a narrator who is an observer, close to the action in Haiti but not closely involved. He tells her story sympathetically, with close detail of her miseries and strengths and vulnerabilities. His narration allows him to describe Vanise fully while giving a credible picture of the miserable lives led by all of the people in her predicament.

As Dubois decides, with his wife's agreement and even urging, to relocate to Florida to work at his brother's liquor store, the similarities between Vanise's life and that of the Dubois family become clear. Each is leaving home, shifting to another place, searching for a better life. In one of his narrative interludes, Banks describes the drifting of the earth's plates during the history of the planet, sometimes tearing land masses apart. He is suggesting that people move ineluctably and for different reasons, changing and uprooting their lives. For Dubois, the move is disastrous; his illusions of a better life are quickly squelched by the strange surroundings, the predictably insensitive treatment from his brother, and the choices he is forced to make that endanger his life and his soul.

Dust jacket for Banks's 1989 novel, about a small-town policeman emotionally scarred by his violent, alcoholic father (Richland County Public Library)

The plot in this novel moves more chronologically, clearly, and dramatically than in any of Banks's previous novels. He switches from the Haiti narrative to the New Hampshire and Florida sections without confusion or lessening of intensity. Banks is an innovative and experimental stylist, and *Continental Drift* shows a successful refinement of his literary techniques. He presents Vanise's escape from Haiti as a flight from the cruelty of Aubin, the local police chief and the father of her illegitimate child, as he pursues her for the stealing of a ham that her nephew has taken for their destitute family. This information comes between two chapters that depict Dubois's escape from the unrelenting frustration of his dead-end job and aimless life. The contrast and comparison give the reader a clear picture of the desperation that haunts two separate lives. At the same time, Banks seems to be asking readers to interpret for themselves how comparable the problems are: the one a matter of material need, an urgent need to escape overt tyranny; the other a sensitive man's squirming under the oppression of ennui, loss of self-respect, and a possibly overweening ambition. This question, as it alternates between the two settings, provides much of the dramatic intensity throughout the novel.

Vanise and Dubois seem to be victims in Banks's cosmology of humanity's striving for something better. Dubois is thwarted more obviously by his own greed and pride, made more vulnerable by his naiveté, easily preyed upon by his self-serving brother and a longtime friend. Vanise, clinging to her superstitions and instincts, is a victim of the cruelty and indifference of nature and of corrupt men and their institutions. Aubin, the police chief, had impregnated her, then betrayed her and hounded her out of her home; conniving thieves took her money and raped and cheated her during her escape. On the last leg of her journey, her path finally crosses that of Dubois, who is making extra money to pay his way out of trouble by transporting Haitian refugees to Florida. On an order from his friend and now boss, Ave, Dubois forces the passengers overboard to avoid arrest by the Coast Guard. Although Vanise miraculously survives, Dubois is conscience-stricken. He tries to give his share of the money to Vanise, but she ceremoniously refuses it; the men who have taken him to her then murder him for the money.

The last part of the novel, "Envoi," eulogizes Dubois in a reflective, philosophical, and, to some extent, forgiving voice; it is the voice from the "Invocation." This Prospero-like recapitulation also looks to the future, all-knowingly, and tells of the failures and tragedies that befall Dubois's family as they stumble through their lives without a father. "Sabotage and subversion, then, are this book's objectives. Go my book, and help destroy the world as it is," the voice admonishes and concludes.

Banks hides the hortatory tone of this narrator in the voice of a *loa,* or storyteller, but a comparable tone pervades his next three novels, all telling of the steady slide of family, morality, and restraint in American middle-class life. In *Affliction* (1989) he sets aside his racial themes and concentrates on two weeks of life in the small town of Lawford, New Hampshire, following the trials of Wade Whitehouse, a forty-one-year-old well digger, snowplow driver, and part-time policeman. The plot brings several story lines together, all somewhat familiar to Banks's readers. One involves Wade Whitehouse's marriage to Lillian; they divorce, remarry each other, and divorce again, creating subsequent troubles with custody of their daughter, Jill. Another involves a hunting accident that might have been a murder. The central story, though, is the ongoing conflict between Wade and his father, a battle that highlights Wade's hidden fears and hatred, the results of a childhood and adolescence marred by a domineering, cruel, and violent alcoholic father.

Critics complained again about Banks's narrative voice, which they considered more omniscient than believable; but they were pleased that Banks used fewer experimental techniques in this novel. The first-person narrator is Rolfe, Wade's younger brother, the only brother who has a college education and a comfortable high-school teaching job in Boston, far enough away from Lawford. Wade's two older brothers have been killed in Vietnam, and his sister is married and still living in the area. The use of Rolfe's narrative allows Banks to describe Wade objectively and subjectively through his brother's voice. Rolfe believes that he is free from the terrible scars that Wade suffers from the drunken and bitter treatment at their father's hands, but it is apparent that Rolfe is no more free than Wade himself. This dramatic irony raises questions about the veracity of the narration as well as about some of Rolfe's actions.

Banks uses his characters, principal and minor, to explicate the theme of the novel. His epigraph is from Simone Weill: "The great enigma of life is not suffering but affliction." All of the characters are afflicted and conflicted by weakness of some sort, particularly the passivity and lack of awareness that stem from alcoholism, living in a hermetic backwater, or paranoia; and Banks tracks these traits back to their original affliction, or cause of pain. Wade genetically inherits alcoholism from his father, who also passes on his violent temper and closed personality through his treatment of the boy. These sufferings, as horrible as they are, would not be so poignant without Wade's love for people and his community: "he said it with a wince, a slight twist on his face: he loved the town, and he could not imagine loving any other." Wade is torn, afflicted by a sensibility that sets him apart from the hardly notable drunks and flailers in the town, and it proves to be a fatal flaw.

Each of the other characters exhibits afflictions, seemingly unaware of them. Margie Fogg is attracted to the divorced Wade, though well aware of his most dangerous traits. Lillian, now married to a successful insurance salesman, is justifiably repelled by Wade's incurable failings but unable to shed the hatred and bitterness that hurt their daughter and conflict her own life. Gordon LaRiviere, Wade's boss, is tormented by greed and a cynical insensitivity to the real interests of Wade and the community. Jack Hewitt, a frustrated former minor-league pitcher, has never fully recovered from his disappointments in life, and he passively takes or steals every advantage he can out of the little town. Rolfe, subject to the same heredity and nurtureless upbringing that Wade had, flees from his family and hometown and thinks he has shed the horrible fate of his brother's afflictions. He cannot see that his constrained, careful life has perhaps freed him from pain but doomed him to an insipid existence that is just as much a prison as Lawford could be.

Dust jacket for Banks's 1991 novel, about the aftermath of a school bus wreck in a small town
(Richland County Public Library)

In interviews Banks has said that he had made peace with his father before Earl Banks died in 1979, but he has also admitted the autobiographical foundations of *Affliction*. The denouement of *Affliction* brings no resolution to any of Wade's conflicts. After killing his father, he disappears, much like Hamilton Stark, and Rolfe reports that he will only turn up again by a chance arrest for some petty crime. Readers are left with the idea that there are many such men, afflicted and wandering, punished only by their inner ghosts.

In *The Sweet Hereafter* (1991) narrative voice again takes over as Banks uses four narrators to tell a story of a small town, Sam Dent, in upstate New York near Lake Placid. He used a newspaper account of a real event in Texas as inspiration for the story. Banks characterizes each storyteller more roundly, more convincingly, and more affectingly than in any of his previous attempts. One of the narrators, Dolores Driscoll, is a bus driver whose bus full of children swerved off the icy road on her rural route, killing all but Dolores and Nichole Burnell, a high-school student who is another narrator. Billy Ansel, the father of two of the victims,

and Mitchell Stephens, a lawyer, also narrate their perspectives of the events. Niemi mentions the obvious parallels to director Akira Kurosawa's motion picture *Rashomon* (1950) in its expository approach, but he is accurate in pointing out that unlike Kurosawa, Banks extends the plot with each person's account rather than just giving the same story over and over. Dolores's voice frames the story with the first and final accounts; Billy's is second; Mitchell's is third; and Nichole's serves as the climax of the novel.

Each narrator tells of his or her part in the accident, giving insight into the probability or lack of fault or human error in the terrible calamity. Each also brings in subplot material that is a complication in his or her life, a guilt or human failing that haunts each of them. Dolores seems to be representative of the community, a servant of the people of Sam Dent, the wife and uncomplaining caretaker of a disabled husband, a bus driver who loves her young passengers and her job. Reminiscent of Wade Whitehouse and his service and dedication to the community, she has none of his tragic flaws. As she describes in detail her journey before the accident, she gives a thumbnail sketch of Billy, who always followed behind her so that his children could wave to him from the bus. Her description of Billy as a Vietnam veteran trying to make sense out of life after that war, and after losing his wife to illness and early death, is sympathetic. She also gives insight into the lives of the Walkers, who run a local motel; Risa Walker is the woman with whom Billy is having an affair, and her child is slow, shy, and not as mature as the others his age.

Painfully honest in telling her story, Dolores reveals seeing a dog disappear that fateful morning and then possibly reappear right before the accident, causing her to steer the bus away from it and the road, killing all those children. She says that she erred "on the side of the angels" when she thought she saw the dog or deer or child on the road in front of her, swerving to make sure she would not kill what may or may not have been an apparition. The real fault, then, is putative at best, and Dolores seems willing to take blame if it will help heal her community. Readers then are convinced that the accident was fateful, one of the contingencies life presents that victims and survivors have to live with and suffer.

Billy's narrative, too, is straightforward, unselfconscious and frank. Along with Dolores, he seems to represent the interests of the real community of Sam Dent, the community that would not lower itself to sue for money after such a tragedy. He recalls the details of the morning and is honest and self-effacing in revealing that at the moment of the accident he was thinking about having intercourse with Risa Walker. Billy asks himself about the culpability for the accident, and he reviews the possibilities. He knows that although many people in the town blame Dolores, she is no more culpable than the state of New York, which failed to put up guardrails where the bus went off the road, or the highway department that filled the sandpit with water, or the seatbelts that trapped the children as they tried to escape the sinking bus. He tells of his affair with Risa, which began after his wife died; the change in his life that Vietnam caused; his love and sense of loss for his children; and his coldness, which is a way of protecting his grief. He is a character that readers will forgive, favor, and admire.

Billy also tells of his meeting with the lawyer, Mitchell Stephens, who is trying to get Billy to join the parents who are suing for millions of dollars. He rebuffs Stephens and stands alone against the outside interests that will destroy the community and its integrity. As Stephens narrates the next segment, the sophisticated, somewhat cynical lawyer emerges not as a stereotypical opportunist but as a man of average moral character, a father who has lost a child—a child who is not dead but caught up in drug addiction and who calls him periodically for money. He is polite with prospective clients in Sam Dent, but his narrative is peppered with condescension and cynicism about these people. Banks appears to be making him not a sympathetic character but, more subtly, a pitiable one. Stephens underestimates Dolores's honesty and Nichole's canniness, and this irony gives the novel a sly, almost comical tone.

The depth and skill of Banks's characterization are apparent in Nichole's account of the events. She is intelligent and innocent, but there is a hint of her disingenuous understanding of the treachery in adult life that makes her an almost fearsome character and shows how inaccurate Stephens was in appraising her as a witness. The accident has made her perceive more clearly than ever her parents' greed, contrasted with Billy's principled stubbornness; she sees her own father's selfish lust when she realizes he no longer will abuse her sexually because she is now confined to a wheelchair by the accident. She knows also how wrong public opinion can be when she sees the town exile the blameless Dolores. Sensing all these things, she testifies at the trial that Dolores was going much faster than the speed limit and lost control because of it. Her lie loses Stephens's case and frees the town from further damaging litigation.

In the final section Dolores tells of her enjoyment as she watches from the stands at the county fair as her old car is used in the demolition derby as a target for punishment, as a victim that wins the derby. As she and her husband, Abbott, are leaving the stands, neighbors help her with Abbott's wheelchair. Perhaps the community has started healing, but it will never be the same, never feel its former self-righteousness and sense of innocence when it compares itself to the cruel and greedy world outside its borders. Stephens tempted these people with a plan to cash in on their worst tragedy; if not for a teenager's crafty lie, the town would have given in to this temptation.

Motion-picture versions of *Affliction,* with a screenplay by Paul Schrader (1997), and *The Sweet Hereafter,* with a screenplay by director Atom Egoyan (1997), were well received critically and popularly. Both novels, bleak and wintry, capture a mood that works well on the screen; setting often characterizes the lives of Banks's people.

Banks's outrage at the racial and class problems of late-twentieth-century America is clear in *Rule of the Bone* (1995), his most direct attack on what he feels are its most serious problems. He chose to portray the decay of contemporary moral values by making the protagonist-narrator of this novel a fourteen-year-old boy, Chapman "Chappie" Dorset. The language he uses and the facts of his life and adventures closely parallel Mark Twain's *Adventures of Huckleberry Finn* (1884). Chappie, who later changes his name to Bone, has a missing father, is forced into homelessness, steals to live, and takes up with a black man who acts as a surrogate father and role model for him. Also like Huck, he meets his father later in the novel, only to be disappointed. Transplanting the story to upstate New York and into the shopping-mall culture of the late twentieth century allows Banks a framework for his novel that can show how the problems of race and class have changed or remained the same. He also can comment on the plight of disenfranchised children in an adult world that has lost its way.

Chappie introduces himself in language that echoes Twain's: "You'll probably think I'm making a lot of this up just to make me sound better than I really am or smarter or even luckier but I'm not." In a 7 May 1995 *New York Times* review of the book, Jonathan Franzen mentions the likeness not only to Twain's Huck but also to J. D. Salinger's Holden Caulfield—except, he notes, Bone is more generic and less funny than Holden, and different also in being immune to pop culture. The reason for these differences, Franzen explains, is that Bone never had the home that Holden had to go back to.

One by one Bone catalogues his miseries, which are the torments of children in this age: divorced parents, abusive stepfather, indifferent mother preoccupied with other problems, unsupervised time alone, and temptations of marijuana and alcohol to relieve the torpor of everyday life. Banks creates empathy through the boy's honesty, his twisted sense of integrity, and a fierce sense of loyalty and friendship that seems to fill the void left by lack of family ties. When he steals rare coins that had been secreted in a closet, he finds out they were really his grandmother's and were meant as his inheritance; he most likely would never have gotten these coins from his stepfather, Ken, who hid them. He eventually is banished from the house.

He takes refuge with his sixteen-year-old friend, Russ, who is sharing a place with a group of bikers, and spends most of his time in malls. Bone has fantasies about going back with Christmas presents and being taken in by Ken and forgiven. He is also assumed to be dead at one point. Bone in fact has been forced to get away from his "family" of bikers, Adirondack Iron, and keep traveling. He and Russ stay for a time in the town of AuSable in a burned-out school bus that turns out to be the very bus in which the children of Sam Dent perished. Asked why he used this coincidental image, Banks told a *Paris Review* interviewer in 1998 that he felt that the object of death and turmoil in *The Sweet Hereafter* should represent new life and a new chance for a young person in trouble.

One of Chappie's decisions when he realizes he "must be a criminal now" is to get a tattoo. From the drawings offered by the tattooist he picks a skull and

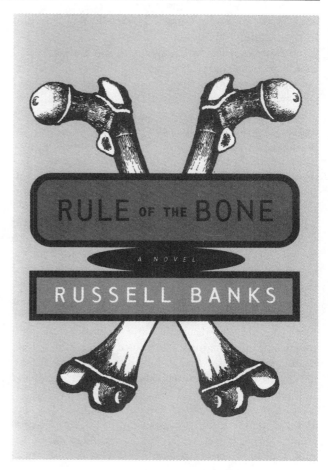

Dust jacket for the 1995 novel in which Banks created a contemporary version of Huckleberry Finn (Richland County Public Library)

crossbones, minus the skull, because it reminds him of the Peter Pan pirates. He feels the new nickname Bone will be appropriate, and Russ says, "Bone is hard, man. Fucking hard. It's universal, man." Indeed, Bone is becoming tougher. In a subsequent foray, he and Russ break into a summer home, eating any available food and burning the furniture for warmth. Picked up by Buster Brown, a dangerous child molester who is holding a girl captive, Bone rescues the girl, Rose, nicknamed Froggy. He takes her back to the bus in AuSable and finally helps her to get home. At the bus, he meets its new inhabitant, I-Man, and feels he has met his best friend. At this point the story has begun to take shape as a bildungsroman. Bone has not merely hardened; he has made choices for himself. At least one of his decisions, the one with Froggy, is motivated by a selfless sense of right. Seeing the child used and victimized by Buster Brown, he can see his own sorrow and acts to save her. In doing so, he not only lifts a wad of money from Froggy's perverted captor but also meets the counterpart to Twain's Jim, I-Man, who will help him learn even more about life.

Several of Banks's major and minor themes and motifs are apparent. Chappie is an alien in an indifferent world, a world seeming even more cruel because of the boy's sensitivity and awareness of what should be. Violence exacerbated by abuse of alcohol and drugs appears constantly. Dramatic contrasts in class and privilege, such as the summer house used only for vacations by its owners, Bib and Maddy Ridgeway, but used as a lifesaving last refuge for the boys, confront the reader. People with money and power, then, wittingly or unwittingly victimize the disenfranchised; whether the criminal Buster Brown or the complacent Ridgeways do the victimizing makes little difference to the victims. The theme of race also runs throughout the novel. As in other novels, Banks does not force the reader into making abstract connections with themes. The characterization of the young protagonist is detailed and personal enough to evoke empathy. The plot is complex, dramatic, and realistic, but with touches of the romantic. The choice of narrator was no doubt prompted by Twain, but the voice is realistic for the late twentieth century, and the idioms real and unforced.

The second half of the novel takes I-Man and Bone to Jamaica, and by this time I-Man has become Bone's surrogate father. His advice is informed by his philosophy, which emphasizes self-reliance and confidence when faced with problems or evil. From this point on the boy's courage is tested, as are his wits and resourcefulness, and he learn how to show the love he has begun to feel for the people around him. He remembers Bruce, a friend who died in a fire back in the bikers' house—probably trying to save Bone, whom he thought was inside—and he realizes he loves him. He loves Froggy, not for anything she did for him but for what she was. Of course he loves I-Man for the strength and acceptance he modeled.

Banks's use of imagery is at times romantic, sometimes obvious, but within the context of this novel apt, if a bit outlandish. The resurrection of the bus from *The Sweet Hereafter* is a bold ploy. Even the reappearance of Ave and his boat, *Belinda Blue*, fits neatly into Banks's purposes. Captain Ave hires Bone to help cook for and serve paid guests he is carrying to a nearby island, and Bone uses the $200 pay to make his next move. He is given a small cubby in which to sleep, and Banks describes it as shaped like a coffin; readers are reminded how Ave's ship—and Dubois—helped to send other desperate people to their deaths in *Continental Drift*. In the chapter Banks calls "Bone Phones Home," an allusion to the 1982 movie *E.T. the Extra-Terrestrial*, Banks reminds the reader of Bone's alien status in

Jamaica. Bone, like the unnamed narrator of *Book of Jamaica*, knows that he will never get used to a multiracial world in which he is not in the majority.

The call he makes is answered by Russ, who tells him of his own boring life and his grandmother's death and presents to Bone a reminder of the pointless life they have lived. Bone tells him he wants to come home, though, and change his life, maybe even go to college. Russ is surprised, but the reader has been prepared for this change in Bone and understands his growth. Another call he makes "home" is to Froggy's mother, who tells him in her dope-addled voice that the girl is dead. This call constitutes a perfect image for Bone's desperate loneliness. The novel ends with Bone pondering the stars and the people he loves at last.

Cloudsplitter (1998) is a departure for Banks, an historical and biographical novel about an enigmatic figure in American history. Banks spent seven years researching and writing this novel about John Brown, the nineteenth-century abolitionist, who was eccentric and widely believed to be just short of insane. While Banks's previous works had focused primarily on contemporary events, themes in many of his novels involve race, and much of the latter part of Brown's life was spent opposing slavery. Moreover, Banks's main interest in fiction has been the plight of the alienated, black or white, in the Western Hemisphere. Brown was something of an outcast, as were the slaves he helped to freedom in Canada. He looked forbidding, with his beard and shock of hair sticking out defiantly, and his core beliefs were just as resolute and different. Brown, a relatively unlettered man, was an unsuccessful farmer who worked hard with little money to show for it. He begins to emerge, then, as a typical Banks protagonist: race conscious, alienated, and working class.

The novel itself does not follow the historical life only; nor does it purport to stay simply with the facts. Banks makes this approach clear in the author's note that precedes the novel: "the book should be read solely as a work of fiction, not as a version or interpretation of history." James M. McPherson reviewed the book for *Atlantic;* in his article, republished in 2001 in *Novel History: Historians and Novelists Confront America's Past (and Each Other),* he praised the novel but pointed out some historical inaccuracies. In response, Banks refers to his introductory note and says further that he was concerned more with the voices of Brown's son Owen and those of the other characters than with facts. Altering facts, he feels, is sometimes necessary to the artist, and Banks shows a commitment to getting voices right in fiction. One of the main interests in *Cloudsplitter* is the relationship of Owen to Brown, including all of the problems of finding oneself the son of a strong-willed and stubborn father and of dealing with submerged Oedipal feelings, conflicting ideas, and loyalty (although in this novel, problems of alcohol are conspicuously absent).

Cloudsplitter is Banks's longest novel. It is also the only one told in epistolary style and the only one so closely tied with fact, although *Continental Drift* and *The Sweet Hereafter* were suggested by real events. The protagonist-narrator, Owen, is the third son of a strong father who is motivated mainly by his religious beliefs. His diction and tone are stiff and formal, as befits a crudely educated autodidact of the mid-nineteenth century. He shows the honesty and diffidence and conflicted emotions toward the events around him that mark him as a typical Banks narrator. The story is told as Owen writes to Katherine Mayo, who was in reality Oswald Garrison Villard's research assistant. Villard, in 1910, published the most authoritative biography of Brown. In *Cloudsplitter* Owen is supplying Mayo with biographical notes for Villard's book, and the year is 1899. Owen had escaped the Harper's Ferry massacre forty years earlier by running through the field as his two brothers and his father were trapped and executed. As his recollections begin, he tells of attending the ceremony in 1889 at which the remains of his two brothers were interred, finally, at his father's grave site in North Elba, New York. The graves are within sight of Mount Tahawus, which translates from the Algonquin as Cloudsplitter. As the bodies are lowered into the ground, Owen speaks with anger, regret, and guilt. This guilt is a keynote in Owen's commentary throughout the novel, although its exact source is unclear.

The Cloudsplitter mountain of the title, a looming presence for most of the Brown family as they went about their daily lives in Timbuctoo, near North Elba, has been interpreted by some, McPherson among them, as a symbol of John Brown breaking through the cloud of slavery like a lightning bolt. Banks said in the *Paris Review* interview, however, that this tall mountain signifies the awakening of Owen himself, breaking through the clouds of his father's domination and finding the truth and horror of his own beliefs. As the novel progresses, both interpretations seem apt.

Owen is writing primarily for himself, not just to aid a scholar with historic details. From the beginning, he uses words to search out his innermost thoughts. He thinks of discovering his mother, John's first wife, at the moment of her death:

> I unclasped my hands from hers and watched her slip away from me. Her body fell back onto the day-bed and then slid over the lip of the abyss into the darkness. She was gone. Gone. And in that instant, although I was still a child, I understood to the bottom of my soul that I was now alone. I knew, too, that I would remain so for the rest of my life.

CLOUDSPLITTER

A Novel

RUSSELL

Author of THE SWEET HEREAFTER

BANKS

Dust jacket for Banks's 1998 historical novel about the relationship between abolitionist John Brown and his son Owen (Richland County Public Library)

Just prior to this moment he had been talking to his imaginary brother, Fred, the only person besides his mother in whom he would confide. In these memories of a man past middle age Banks shows an introspective personality that has not changed much throughout life. This characterization makes Owen more closely resemble Dubois, Wade, Rolfe, and even Bone in their solitary, brooding sadness.

Set against this introverted boy, almost like a foil, is John Brown: strong, stoical, fiercely religious, and not at all content to brood alone about his beliefs, nor harbor resentments about what he thinks to be right without taking action. The two strands of the novel compete. One is the story well known, if variously misunderstood, of the abolitionist who worked in the Underground Railroad, did battle in the Bloody Kansas wars, and even at his defeat and death at Harper's Ferry, brought America to the realization that it had to make up its mind about slavery. The other is Owen's story, analyzing the gradual growth of the sensitive boy, overawed by his father, into a man knowing his own mind and heart, even if this conversion brings him little happiness.

The plot of the novel is as imaginatively drawn as other Banks novels, despite its attachment to history. Each incident, whether factual or fictive, enhances the development of the novel. Brown's idealistic fervor about slavery was counterbalanced, Owen describes, by his desire to be as wealthy as other Americans. His business dealings in sheep and land speculation, ultimately failures, are described with patience and understanding. Owen also accompanies his father to Boston to hear a lecture by Ralph Waldo Emerson, and as Emerson develops his ideas on the stage in awe-inspiring language, Owen realizes that the famous writer has the same ideas about slavery as does his father, but his refinement of them in language and concept is much more rational than his father's attempts to express them. After the lecture, Brown rises and walks from the hall without joining in the applause, saying, "The man's truly a *boob!* For the like of me, I can't understand his fame." Owen tries to reconcile the apparent differences between the two, but the implication seems to be a judgment of his father as not a great man, not a man of faultless humility. He contrasts his father's reliance for truth on God and Emerson's on Nature, as he understood the lecture, and Owen's beliefs in later life show him to have favored the latter. Brown's attendance at the lecture probably never happened, but Banks is augmenting history to make a point artistically, in this case involving the differences in Brown's abolitionist theories and those of the country's intellectuals. It also shows a young man enjoying the humbling of his overbearing father by a man of greater intellect.

Another element of Owen's maturation involves a friendship with an African American man and a love for his wife. Lyman Epps is a neighbor of the Browns and a coworker in moving slaves along on the Underground Railroad. He and his wife, Susan, live with the Brown family at one point. Owen spends much time with Lyman, thinking about him obsessively. In one of the most effective scenes in the book, Susan explains to Owen that his obvious feelings for her are not mutual and that she feels that he is a good man who should find a white woman to marry. He claims that he cannot. While Lyman and Owen are out cutting new paths one night, Owen realizes that his "thwarted love for Susan was my love for Lyman gone all wrong." In a somewhat contrived scene on the same journey, a mountain lion approaches the two. As Owen hands a pistol to Lyman, he forgets to let the hammer down, and Lyman mishandles the gun and kills himself. The psychology of this incident is dense, but inferences of

homosexual love, racial feelings, and Owen's pointed betrayal of his father's principles of morality and love and justice for African Americans are evident.

Banks reminds the reader periodically of the origins of the narrative by having Owen address Katherine Mayo and add commentary on his feelings about what he is doing. As he begins the Harper's Ferry account, he describes how he has been carrying his father's papers with him for a long while; he cannot explain why, yet he takes care to pack all the documents safely in a salvaged crate, suggesting a sacred duty of keeping a record of his father's plans and ideas for the sake of history. His description of the events on the final day at Harper's Ferry shows this dutiful son in an ambiguous light. He perches himself in a tree overlooking the site of the action and narrates from this distant vantage point the crumbling of the entire venture. He confesses that he climbed to this aerie not only to see but also to escape. The two strands of the novel close together, then: the story of the father, public and private, and the inner story of a man's impossible battle to shed the smothering protection of his father's firm grip.

In these novels the strongest theme has been the father-son relationship in all its complexity, the failures of fathers and sons to "just make contact" as E. M. Forster would insist. The autobiographical elements aside, Banks addresses in these novels a universal theme; but in combining this theme with the problem of race in the Americas and throughout the world, he has taken on as a novelist the most important issues of his time.

Along with McPherson's favorable comments on *Cloudsplitter,* most of which praised the artistry of the book and the sensitivity Banks used in fictionalizing the conflict that might have raged between father and son, critics received the novel appreciatively. Walter Kirn, in his 22 February 1998 *New York Times* review, wrote of it not as historical saga alone: "The dynamic between Owen and his father is beyond dysfunctional or abusive; it's more like a geological condition, as if the father was a massive earthquake and the son a minor aftershock. The only analysis Banks indulges in is moral analysis. His subject is motives, not minds."

Cloudsplitter shows Banks's development as a novelist. In his earlier novels, his use of various narrative voices seemed experimental; in this novel, his use of Owen's point of view is successful and enhances the credibility of the events. In a 1998 interview in *The Writer,* he explained his deliberation in choosing the person, a woman, to whom the sensitive Owen is telling his thoughts in letter form. Owen, with his troubled relationship with his father and his close and tender love for his mother, would have felt more comfortable discussing his most intimate thoughts with a woman. Owen's trust of Mayo is evident. Banks's characterizations have always been a major strength in his fiction, and in *Cloudsplitter,* working with historically real people, he maintains the believability of his characters while going even more deeply into their minds. In a 1998 interview with *Salon* he hints that he is working on a novel that will tell the entire story through a woman's point of view, something he has tried in parts of *Continental Drift* and *The Sweet Hereafter.*

A summary of Banks's contributions to the American novel must include the broadening perspective he has offered readers, an examination of what it is like to live in a society tainted by racism and complicated by rapid changes that leave communities confused about their values. He has developed the eternal themes of filial strife, family conflict, addiction, and the physical and mental trials of the working classes and rural poor. His style has illustrated the imaginative uses of narrative voice and the uses of metafiction and magic realism within the realistic tradition. In a June 2000 *Harper's,* Banks writes that he wants to be part of a national literature that is consciously in touch with all of its people.

The plots, themes, and artistry of his novels support these lofty goals.

Interviews:

Curtis Wilkie, "Grit Lit," *Boston Globe,* 25 August 1991;

Cynthia Joyce, "Russell Banks," *Salon Interviews* (5 January 1998);

Lewis Burke Frumkes, "A Conversation with Russell Banks," *Writer,* 111 (August 1998): 18–21;

Robert Faggen, "The Art of Fiction CLII," *Paris Review,* 147 (Summer 1998): 50–88.

References:

Wesley Brown, "Who to Blame, Who to Forgive," *New York Times Magazine,* 10 September 1989, pp. 52–70;

James McPherson, "Russell Banks's Fictional Portrait of John Brown," in *Novel History: Historians and Novelists Confront America's Past (and Each Other),* edited by Mark C. Carnes (New York: Simon & Schuster, 2001);

Robert Niemi, *Russell Banks* (New York: Twayne, 1997).

Ann Beattie

(8 September 1947 –   )

Miriam Marty Clark
Auburn University

See also the Beattie entries in *DLB 218: American Short-Story Writers Since World War II, Second Series* and *DLB Yearbook: 1982.*

BOOKS: *Chilly Scenes of Winter* (Garden City, N.Y.: Doubleday, 1976);

Distortions (Garden City, N.Y.: Doubleday, 1976);

Secrets and Surprises (New York: Random House, 1978; London: Hamilton, 1979);

Falling in Place (New York: Random House, 1980; London: Secker & Warburg, 1981);

Jacklighting (Worcester, Mass.: Metacom Press, 1981);

The Burning House (New York: Random House, 1982; London: Secker & Warburg, 1983);

Love Always (New York: Random House, 1985; London: Joseph, 1990);

Spectacles (New York: Ariel/Workman, 1985);

Where You'll Find Me, and Other Stories (New York: Linden Press/Simon & Schuster, 1986; London: Macmillan, 1987);

Alex Katz (New York: Abrams, 1987);

Picturing Will (New York: Random House, 1989; London: Cape, 1990);

What Was Mine (New York: Random House, 1991);

Another You (New York: Knopf, 1995);

My Life, Starring Dara Falcon (New York: Knopf, 1997);

Park City: New and Selected Stories (New York: Knopf, 1998);

Perfect Recall: New Stories (New York: Scribner, 2001);

The Doctor's House (New York: Scribner, 2002).

Ann Beattie (photograph by Rollie McKenna; from the dust jacket for My Life, Starring Dara Falcon, *1997)*

Ann Beattie is a novelist and short-story writer whose evocations of American life at the end of the twentieth century have earned her a wide readership and sustained critical engagement for more than two decades. Beattie's fiction explores the emotional and social landscapes of white, middle-class America, focusing most often on members of the baby-boom generation, their coming of age in the turbulent years of the late 1960s and early 1970s, and their efforts to build lives in the ruins of the nuclear family and the suburban idyll their parents' generation had embraced.

Charlotte Ann Beattie was born on 8 September 1947 in Washington, D.C., the only child of Charlotte Crosby and James A. Beattie, a grants-management specialist for the federal government. Beattie grew up in the suburbs of Washington and has described her childhood as "normal and middle-class," noteworthy only

Dust jacket for Beattie's first novel (1976), about a man's listless pursuit of a former girlfriend
(Richland County Public Library)

for her early interest in the arts and her poor academic performance through high school. As an undergraduate English major at American University in the late 1960s she began, in her own words, to "take writing seriously" and to study the writers who eventually influenced her work: F. Scott Fitzgerald, Ernest Hemingway, and John Updike. In 1971 Beattie earned a master's degree from the University of Connecticut and began work on a doctorate in English. By 1972, however, the stories that she had been secretly working on had come to occupy her full attention, and she dropped out of graduate school to pursue a life in writing. Except for brief stints at the University of Virginia (1975–1977) and Harvard (1977–1978), Beattie has since shunned universities and writers' workshops. A lingering distaste for academic life is evident throughout her fiction.

In the early 1970s, under the tutelage of writer J. D. O'Hara, whom she credited in a 1982 interview with having "taken scissors to the ends of" her early stories, Beattie began publishing in magazines and literary journals, including *Atlantic, Virginia Quarterly Review,*

and *Western Humanities Review.* In 1974, after more than twenty rejections, *The New Yorker* accepted "A Platonic Relationship." From then until the mid 1990s, when the editorship of the magazine changed, Beattie published seven or eight stories a year in *The New Yorker,* and her fiction quickly gained a following among literate, upper-middle-class readers. In 1976 Doubleday published both her first novel, *Chilly Scenes of Winter,* and her first collection of short stories, *Distortions.* Since 1976 she has published six novels, six collections of short stories, and a commissioned volume on the painter Alex Katz.

From 1973 to 1982 Beattie was married to musician David Gates, whose encouragement and insights she credits as important in the development of her fiction. In 1988 she married painter Lincoln Perry. By February 1990 Beattie's writing had made her enough of a celebrity that *People* magazine covered her marriage to Perry together with the publication of her novel *Picturing Will* (1989), which had already sold more than fifty thousand copies. The *People* article, accompanied by photographs of the newlyweds, described the couple's "common passion for art," their "domestic harmony," their decision to remain childless, and their influence on each other's work.

Although she has occasionally granted interviews, Beattie has been a reluctant subject of academic criticism, resisting critics' "pretentious guesses" in favor of the essential "mysteriousness" of the stories. At every stage her work has polarized reviewers and literary critics. Many have praised Beattie's technical skill, her acutely detailed surfaces, and what Larry McCaffery called her "coolly dispassionate prose rhythms," which can be unexpectedly infused with emotions ranging from poignancy to droll humor. Others, however, have found Beattie's fiction banal, preoccupied with trivia, insufficiently dramatic, or too much given to what John W. Aldridge called the "bizarre, mysteriously inexplicable, or absurd." Critics have also objected to the passivity of her characters and the sense of futility that attends their search for purpose or meaning. Beattie is frequently classified with writers such as Raymond Carver, Frederick Barthelme, Mary Robison, Tobias Wolff, and Amy Hempel under the term "minimalist." For Aldridge, one of Beattie's harshest and most vocal critics, "minimalism" implies "a method in which what is barely stated about a person or an experience is given a kind of subaqueous luminescence as well as a certain air of menacing fatality by the materials that are left out but the presence of which is nevertheless hauntingly there, lurking just behind the venetian blinds of its shuttered prose."

Set mostly in eastern seaboard cities and towns from Charlottesville, Virginia, to Dell, New Hampshire, Beattie's stories are populated by people who came of age during the Vietnam War and the sexual revolution. In her interview with McCaffery and Sinda Gregory, Beattie dismissed the idea that she speaks for her generation, insisting instead that the people in her fiction "reflect some of my own personal problems and concerns, perhaps to an exaggerated degree but I don't mean them to be taken as representative of the culture." At the same time, these problems and concerns have had resonance for many readers who recognize in them both the pathos and the comedy of the age they live in. Among her most significant themes, recurring throughout her career, are the impermanence of human relationships and the fragility of selfhood in the face of social disintegration and cultural change. Relationships, especially marriages, are made in weakness and false hope; they stifle, disappoint, or go unaccountably sour; they end in relief more often than in regret; and when they endure, they rarely nourish and sustain. Despite Beattie's surprising proclivity for happy, modestly hopeful romantic endings, there is little in her treatment of heterosexual love to warrant much optimism.

An only child, Beattie has a special fascination with sibling relationships. In five of her six novels and in many of her stories, these fraught but inescapable kinship ties figure importantly. More durable than romantic relationships—though no less troubled in some cases—the relationship to a brother or sister can be the most stable and supportive a character has, as it is for Charles and Susan in *Chilly Scenes of Winter*. It can provide a way for jagged fragments of memory to be put together into some kind of coherence, as it does for Marshall Lockard and his brother Gordon in *Another You* (1995). It can simultaneously define and dwarf a person, as it does Bob Warner and his three siblings in *My Life, Starring Dara Falcon* (1997). Sibling relationships can erupt into violence, as one does in *Falling in Place* (1980); for the orphans and virtual orphans who populate so many of the novels and stories, they can also provide shelter and support.

Although she herself is childless, Beattie also has a keen and sympathetic interest in children and frequently features them as important characters. Several critics have observed that Beattie renders children as precocious, adult, even prophetic or redemptive in their understanding of the world, while she commonly portrays adults as child-like in their impulsiveness, their selfishness, their charming or alarming naiveté, and their attachment to toys. Where children are most central to Beattie's novel plots, however, they function as avatars of the age they live in.

Like the writers and philosophers of the postwar period, Beattie is persistently interested in the subject of work—the need for and the difficulty of finding meaningful employment, the absence of a sense of vocation in people's lives, the dullness and anonymity of white-collar work, and the alienation of academic labor. Beyond the immediate matter of meaningful work, however, Beattie's characters are widely afflicted by a more general lack of purpose. A few have a sense of artistic yearning, usually not sufficient to call a vocation; some have a sense of family loyalty or friendship, however disabling or misplaced. Almost none are driven by a strong sense of artistic, religious, or ideological purpose.

Reflecting the aimlessness and passivity of its protagonists, Beattie's early fiction is loosely structured, advancing its plots by indirection, coincidence, and metonymy. In her more recent novels, however, she shows a greater inclination to control and experiment with narrative form. "I'm much more interested in formal issues now," she told interviewer Don Lee in 1995, "in how things are put together, and what I might do on that level to get a trajectory that is more clearly the author's. I know ten ways to move through time, and my interest is in finding the eleventh."

Although Beattie's first novel, *Chilly Scenes of Winter,* has been treated as a love story—Charles's quest to reunite with his former lover Laura, who is married—it is typical of her early work in offering an obsession without a strong narrative telos. Working at a vaguely

Dust jacket for Beattie's 1980 novel, about one summer in the life of a family that is falling apart
(Richland County Public Library)

defined government job in Washington, D.C., and living in a house he inherited from his grandmother, Charles is consumed by thoughts of how to see, talk to, and ultimately win back Laura; but rather than pursuing her through a well-defined course of action, Charles moves listlessly through the days. He grows morose listening to Janis Joplin and remembering a friend's dog that died. He thinks compulsively about food—going repeatedly to the grocery store, checking his wallet for grocery money, pondering what to cook or eat for dinner, and fantasizing about foods Laura used to prepare. Charles's sister, Susan, a college student, comes home to visit and brings a disturbed friend, Elise. Together Charles and Susan try to cope with their mother's alcoholic breakdown, their stepfather's growing dependency, and their own unhappy memories of the past. Charles's friend Sam spends more and more time at the house, eating Charles's food and sleeping with women in Charles's spare bedroom; eventually he moves in to stay. Charles takes Laura's plain, overweight friend Betty on several dates, pitying her but also hoping to hear about Laura. Eventually, Betty reveals that Laura has separated from her husband, a former college foot-

ball player, and is living in an apartment. Charles buys some yellow tulips and takes them to Laura, who fixes him dinner and makes a special dessert, the orange souffle he has been craving. Although theirs is, as Charles puts it, "a story with a happy ending," much remains unsettled at the end of the novel, and the characters' depression and aimlessness threaten to reassert themselves at any moment.

Chilly Scenes of Winter was a Book of the Month Club Alternate Selection and was made into a motion picture called *Head Over Heels* that was released by United Artists in 1979, but the critical reception was mixed and often unfavorable. "It really does seem marvelous," a critic for *Virginia Quarterly Review* observed, "when someone is able to catch the 'accelerated grimace' of a generation"; the same reviewer praised Beattie for her "grace bestowing humor" and her "strong, kindly sanity." But Greg Morris, reviewing the novel for *Prairie Schooner,* counted the novel a disappointment compared to *Distortions,* the volume of stories published at the same time: "the wit and the sharpness of the short stories have been surrendered to the necessities of the longer form. Beattie, rather contrarily, tries to make a short story long, and patience quickly wears thin. . . . The emotions are empty, the jokes tiresome, the problems insufferably dull." Critics looking at the novel retrospectively also had mixed reactions. In his survey of 1970s fiction Frederick Karl included the novel in a list of "mixed and unsatisfactory" early work. T. Coraghessan Boyle, on the other hand, counted *Chilly Scenes of Winter* the best of Beattie's first three novels, unmatched until *Picturing Will*.

Beattie's second novel, *Falling in Place,* reverses the order of the first, treating family disintegration against a background of romantic pursuit. In place of the singular point of view (Charles's) she uses in *Chilly Scenes of Winter,* Beattie adopts a multiple-focus strategy, recounting the events of one turbulent summer through the eyes of several different characters. Set in New York City and suburban Connecticut, *Falling in Place* describes the failing marriage of John and Louise Knapp. John is a Princeton graduate and Madison Avenue advertising man who lives during the week with his mother and his younger son, five-year-old Brandt, in Rye, New York, in order to care for his mother and to be closer to his work in the city. He also carries on a passionate love affair with Nina, a twenty-five-year-old salesclerk at Lord and Taylor. On the weekends John and Brandt rejoin Louise and the older children—Mary, age fifteen, and John Joel, age ten—at home.

Though they try to maintain a semblance of togetherness with family dinners, picnics, and vacations, the atmosphere is tense and loveless. John tells his friend Nick that he is frustrated because he has "married the wrong woman and had the wrong children." Mary has failed high-school English and is a bored, alienated summer-school student who describes the class to her father as "suck-o." At home she fights bitterly with John Joel and dreams of Peter Frampton, listening to his albums and fervently kissing his picture on a poster. John Joel spends his summer eating compulsively, tormenting his sister and being tormented by her, and keeping company with his even more deeply troubled friend Parker. Their mother, Louise, whose point of view is only minimally represented in the novel, leads a self-involved, emotionally unfulfilling life in the suburbs. Despite a grim determination to keep her family together, she is contemptuous of John and only sporadically attentive to her disturbed, hostile children. "She was paranoid about things that were not happening," John says of her late in the book, "and she didn't care about things that were."

But before too many summer weeks have passed, the Knapps' facade of normal family life is destroyed when John Joel shoots his sister with Parker's gun. As Mary recovers, Louise languishes, and John Joel gets intensive psychiatric care. Forced to abandon the illu-

sions he has cultivated about himself and his family, John decides to stop being paralyzed by guilt and duty and to act in his own best interests. On a final, bleak family vacation in Nantucket, he asks Louise for a divorce, determined to leave his false, unfulfilling family existence for a new life with Nina. Although John is highly optimistic about their future together, Christina Murphy points out in her 1986 study of Beattie that the ending of the novel is more ironic than romantic. Beattie, she notes, portrays this new relationship as nearly as shallow and self-deceptive as his marriage was, with Nina drawn to John's affluence and stability and John taken by Nina's youth, her innocence, and her willingness to provide maternal comfort and warmth.

If encroaching middle age and the sorrows of seemingly settled domestic life are relatively new territory for Beattie, *Falling in Place* also includes the unsettled young people familiar from her earlier work. Mary Knapp's summer-school teacher is Cynthia Forrest, a Yale doctoral student profoundly disillusioned by the realities of her summer job and the sullen laziness of the high-school students in her class. "This kind of part-time job was the best thing you could get," she thinks, "and the pay was no good, and your brain—after so much time realizing that she had a brain—was now being challenged by trivia." Cynthia's lover Peter Spangle goes off to Spain at his mother's behest to retrieve his brother; when he returns, he goes to his old friend Nina's apartment for games, pizza, and dope before reuniting with Cynthia in the second romantic, and ironic, ending of the novel; he is what Georgia A. Brown calls a "quintessential Beattie hero: predictably unpredictable, in and out of jobs, cities, countries, apartments, bed." While Spangle is away, a depressed magician named George meets Cynthia in a laundromat and pursues her ardently, even obsessively, with magic tricks, pink sponge rabbits, and plastic roses. These characters are tangential to Beattie's main plot and contribute to what some of Beattie's critics have labeled the "non-cohesiveness" of *Falling in Place;* at the same time they extend and deepen the exploration of romantic wishfulness and unfulfillment in the novel.

Like its predecessor, *Falling in Place* garnered mixed and sometimes hostile reviews. Marni Jackson, writing in *Maclean's,* complained that "Anomie has settled over everything like volcanic ash. . . . the center has gone beyond not holding; it has completely disappeared. . . . The heart of the book is missing, too." Pearl K. Bell, writing in *Commentary,* objected that Beattie has claimed "the chaotic world of post-everything dropouts" as her "private literary fiefdom"; Bell contended that "it is drearily clear that Ann Beattie has nothing fresh to reveal about these disaffected drifters" and that while she writes about the same social world as John

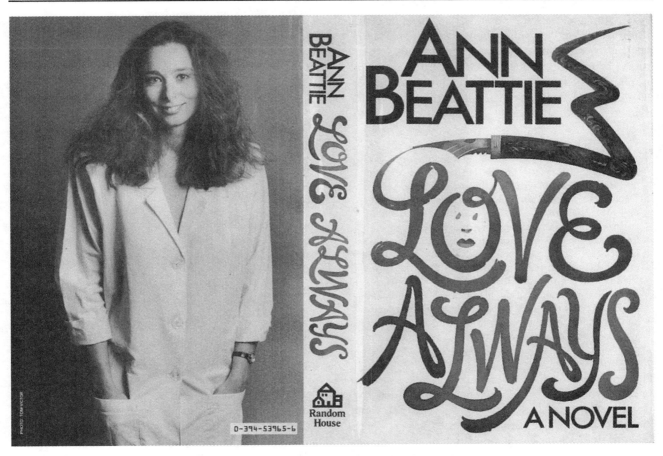

Dust jacket for Beattie's 1985 novel, about the staff of a trendy magazine
(Richland County Public Library)

Cheever, she lacks "his mournful humanity." In contrast, *Virginia Quarterly Review* pegged the book as "not simply its author's best but one of the finest of recent years." Also in her defense, Neil Schmitz found that what sustains *Falling in Place* "is not the acuity of Beattie's characterization or the intensity of the several passions, but the skill with which she weaves pop-ephemerae into her prose. . . . Beattie does not get beyond this surface, because, horribly, there *is* nothing beyond this surface."

In the short stories published during the late 1970s and early 1980s—collected in *Distortions, Secrets and Surprises* (1978), and *The Burning House* (1982)—as in the novels of the same period, Beattie's characters embark on tentative, often unfocused quests. Impelled by restlessness and loneliness, held back by their own passivity, they seek romantic fulfillment, real friendship, meaningful work, and a sense of self in an unhappy, unstable world; if these goals prove false or unattainable, they seek the numbness of drugs, the safety of outworn or dysfunctional relationships, or the security of

continued illusions. Characters change partners, move from city to country or country to city, form resolves, and buy things or give them away, but few are able to alter in any fundamental way the psychic and social circumstances that produce their yearning and despair. Despite the steadiness of her themes, Beattie's tonal range in these stories is considerable—from bleak to darkly comic—and her narrative strategies are complex and interesting, especially her negotiation of the epiphanies that have been a hallmark of the modern short story but that emerge only with irony or awkwardness in the lives of these particular characters and in these particular times.

In her third novel, *Love Always* (1985), Beattie temporarily abandons her neorealist vision of contemporary American life in favor of what Josh Rubin, writing in *The New York Times Book Review,* aptly called a "comedy of manners" set in the Green Mountains of Vermont. This novel is about a group of bright, hip, and wealthy people associated with a magazine called *Country Daze.* In two years the magazine, devoted to social satire and "eclectic" pursuits, "had become the hit of *tout* New York"—proof positive, its founder, Hildon, tells his friends, "that the entire country was coked out." The magazine has just been sold "at a handsome profit." Except for his extraordinary luck and shrewdness, Hildon shares credentials with many other Beattie characters. He is, she writes,

> an only child from a middle class background who went to prep school and to Yale, dodged the draft, was admitted to law school at the University of Virginia and dropped out. A year as a reporter himself, for the Detroit Free Press. Married, no children. Got tired of city life, moved to the country, turned a profit selling real estate and decided to start a magazine. According to Hildon, he had just been in the right place at the right time; instead of the Let's-Open-a-Restaurant dream, he had started a magazine and put a lot of his friends to work. He saw the magazine as an extended family, a continuation of the life he and his friends had led in college. Obviously they were beating the system, and while he didn't think he or this bunch was representative, he was sure that they all felt very lucky and grateful.

The most important of Hildon's friends is Lucy Spenser, who writes an advice column—a "Latter Day Miss Lonelyhearts" as she puts it—under the pen name Cindi Coeur. "Lately," Beattie writes, "Lucy had been thinking that maybe it was time to stop. Just because Jagger was still popping up like a jack-in-the-box, did she really want to be Cindi Coeur at forty? Still, Lucy herself admitted to a morbid fascination with being facile." Hildon is in love with Lucy—indeed, the two have a long-running affair. Lucy herself is in love with Les Whitehall, a pretentious college teacher who left her more than a year ago. In the meantime Hildon's wife, Maureen, who throws lavish, foolish theme parties every summer, is having an affair with Matt Smith, the new publisher of the magazine. Maureen's blend of fury, boredom, and shallowness leads her into a variety of activities, including bizarre sessions of something her mentor describes as "part psychotherapy, part body reconditioning, and part assertiveness training" and noisy feminist raids on a vintage lingerie shop in town.

Also on hand for much of the summer of 1984 is Nicole Nelson, Lucy's fourteen-year-old niece, on hiatus from her role in a popular soap opera called *Passionate Intensity*. Fatherless, Nicole has been in show business since she was a toddler and for several years has been playing the role of Stephanie Sykes, "an abused child from a broken family, a teenage alcoholic who was being rehabilitated by a woman internist and her husband Gerald, a wimpy would-be novelist who felt misunderstood not only by his wife but by the world." A toy company is developing a Nicole Nelson doll, reflecting her popularity and the success of *Passionate Intensity* but also making the real Nicole feel trapped in her own body. A writer has been hired to write a "novelization" of the show and is conducting interviews with all of the principal characters. Nicole's mother, Jane, thinks Nicole needs a vacation from the stresses of her life in California—and she also wants to be free of Nicole so she can spend time with her twenty-five-year-old boyfriend—so she packs her daughter and their massive, troublesome dog, St. Francis, off to Lucy's in Vermont.

Many of the other characters in the novel are also associated with the media. Myra DeVane is a reporter on assignment to do a story about *Country Daze* for the local paper; before the story is over, she also sleeps with Hildon. Edward Bartlett is a photographer whose friendship with Nicole leads to his arrest when he persuades her to help him take nude photographs of himself to send a former girlfriend. Piggy Proctor is a California talent agent and Nicole's surrogate father. Andrew Steinborn, an aspiring novelist who has been hired to write the novelization of *Passionate Intensity*, comes to Vermont with his fiancée, Lillian Worth, to interview Nicole about the character of Stephanie Sykes.

At first Nicole seems likely to fit right in with her aunt's shallow, self-absorbed friends. But she emerges as a precocious and rather sad figure, imprisoned by her famous image, coming into adulthood without a real childhood, real friends, or real protectors. Before the novel is over she expresses with adolescent eloquence the hollowness of celebrity and the absence of pleasure in a world of privilege. Her mother's death in a motorcycle accident late in the novel makes Nicole homeless, rendering literal a circumstance that has been symbolically true for many years.

Jane's violent, accidental death forces a brute reality on characters whose lives have been spent cultivating and pursuing images. Beattie's sardonic depiction of her characters is comically revealing of their delusions and limitations. The excesses, the ambitions, the crude amorality of the privileged are never far from the surface of their story.

Love Always received generally favorable comments from reviewers and critics who liked the combination of serious and comic elements in the book, although in the 15–22 July 1985 *New Republic*, Frank Rich criticized the "flaccidly assembled jumble of melodramatic plot bombshells, buzzwords, and helter-skelter wisecracks." Christopher Lehmann-Haupt, writing for *The New York Times Book Review*, characterized the novel as "almost cruelly satirical" of its shallow characters and praised especially Beattie's "amazing eye for detail" and her ability to "turn our emotions on a dime and send them speeding off in a direction altogether differ-

*Dust jacket for Beattie's 1989 novel, about a man's attempts to protect and care for his stepson
(Richland County Public Library)*

ent from satirical comedy." He also noted how effectively Beattie matches a narrative technique that is "essentially Keystone comedy" with a somber theme, "the failure of love." Alice Hoffman, also writing in *The New York Times Book Review,* likewise praised Beattie's "elegant aloofness," her droll humor, and her keen eye. But Hoffman objected that while Beattie "skillfully raises serious questions about the nature of love and the inability to connect," it is "disappointing that she provides no answers. Her intent is not to analyze but to reveal, and this she does with assurance."

In *Picturing Will,* published four years later, Beattie turns her attention back to the nuclear family and to those interior landscapes of thought and feeling that seemed hardly to exist in *Love Always.* Like the earlier novels, this one covers only a short span of time, a brief season when Will is five-and-a-half years old. The principal characters are Will's single mother, Jody, a passionate photographer; Will's biological father, Wayne, a coarse, exploitative, and finally criminal man with little interest in his son; Wayne's wife, Corky, who is kind to Will when he visits them in Florida but

whose real desire is to have a child of her own; and Will himself. Woven into the third-person narrative are italicized passages in the voice of Mel, the gentle nurturer who courts and eventually marries Jody and becomes Will's truest parent. Secretly a writer, Mel uses a journal to record and reflect on the experience of being a father to Will.

As the novel opens, Jody is working as a wedding photographer in Charlottesville, Virginia. Will plays with G.I. Joe dolls and listens to bedtime stories, making a little kingdom of his home and buffering his mother against the world. Mel visits from New York, where he lives, encouraging Jody in her work and trying to persuade her to marry him. He also cares for Will, tending to him at the playground and displaying his artwork as a real father would. Only the increasing urgency of Mel's desire to marry Jody slightly unsettles the equilibrium of their lives. When Will's friend Wagoner's mother hits and kills a deer—an event that ultimately leads to the breakup of Wagoner's family—the balance is more obscurely disturbed. But two events have even more dramatic effect. First, Jody becomes the protégée of a gallery owner—a decadent, opportunistic, sexual predator whose name, Haverford, Jody changes to Haveabud. Through Haveabud, who does not prey on her, Jody gains an entrée into the New York art world. Second, Will goes to visit his father and stepmother in Florida. Mel drives him, but Haveabud invites himself and a fatherless young boy named Spencer to go along on the trip. At a motel along the way, while Mel tries to sleep off a headache in another room, Will witnesses a bizarre sexual encounter between Haveabud and Spencer, who is older than Will but still a child; when Haveabud falls asleep, Spencer molests Will.

In Florida, further trauma awaits Will. During his visit, Wayne embarks on an extended and violent sexual odyssey, leaving Will in Corky's well-meaning but self-absorbed care. Eventually, Wayne is arrested on drug charges and taken away in handcuffs while his son watches. The next morning Mel comes to rescue him and take him home. In time Mel and Jody do marry and settle in Manhattan, where Jody becomes well known for her art photographs.

In a final, retrospective chapter, set in the twenty-first century (around 2010) and told from the point of view of an adult Will, Mel gives his stepson access to the manuscript he has written over the years. This document, which readers of the novel have already seen portions of, gives voice to Mel's tenderness and uncertainty, his love for Will over many years and his doubts about how to be a good parent. Will weighs Mel's reflections with his own memories of the past and especially of that traumatic time in Florida. "He had been so helpless," Will thinks, "Helpless in the motel room with Haveabud and Spencer. Helpless when the police led his father away—the beginning of the end of Wayne's marriage to Corky." Will goes on to consider the parenting he has received from Jody and Mel. "Jody," he thinks, "was absent too many times and wanted to hear too few things. If not for Mel, he might have been sent to Florida more often. Years later he found out that when Mel got the call to come get him, Mel was furious, because he had wanted all along to stay in Florida in a motel and wait while Will had his visit. If only that could have happened. If only Mel could have been there in fifteen minutes instead of the next morning."

Will's final assessment of Mel, as of his mother, is complicated. He sees in Mel's caretaking "a sort of narcissism difficult to separate, at times, from true involvement"; he sees a willingness to be taken advantage of by Jody and "an almost militant desire that things go well, or at least have a rationale, after the fact." Will recalls Mel's shakiness when he arrived in Florida and remembers that he did not tell Mel what had happened with Haveabud and Spencer because he "realized that he should not bring up anything that might cause further trouble." At the end of the chapter, after he has stayed up late reading Mel's manuscript and thinking about the past, Will recalls a scene from earlier that evening when Mel was playing on the lawn with Will's baby son. This conclusion—Will's measured, insightful sense of the past and his own contentment in the present moment—is almost completely free of the irony with which Beattie has previously approached happy endings.

Picturing Will is among Beattie's most popular and warmly praised novels. Critics welcomed the seriousness, cohesiveness, depth, and even—some critics argued—the uncharacteristic optimism of Beattie's family portrait. Judith Timson, in a *Maclean's* review, called the book "a brilliant meditation on the paradoxical aspects of the parent-child relationship: the need to have children, the desire not to, the compulsion to protect them—and the ultimate failure of most adults to do so." Boyle, writing in *The New York Times Book Review,* praised the novel for its interweaving of the italicized sections "that speak directly to the reader in the intimate way of a diary or monologue. The language is inspired, rhapsodic, and true, and the voice speaks to us of the connection between parent and child." Lehmann-Haupt's response to the novel was more ambivalent; he wrote in *The New York Times* that Beattie "takes us on a strange and disquieting journey. It is like a voyage around the border of a photorealistic tapestry in which every brilliant detail interlocks with its neighbor but never permits the viewer to step back and gain a perspective on the whole."

In *Another You* Beattie again juxtaposes present and past, interspersing her narrative chapters with italicized letters to "Martine" from a lover who signs himself only as "M." For much of the novel the identities of "Martine" and "M," who seem to have lived in a previous generation, are not disclosed; the complicated circumstances referred to in their letters are mysterious, only gradually pieced together into a story. The protagonist is Marshall Lockard, a college English professor disheartened by his unrewarding job and his lack of professional prospects. Marshall's wife, Sonja, a real estate agent, is having a less-than-passionate affair with her boss, Tony Hembley, meeting him for trysts in vacant houses. Unable to have children, Sonja cares tenderly for Marshall's stepmother, Evie, whom Marshall loves but can hardly bring himself to visit in the nursing home.

The novel begins when Marshall gives a ride to one of his students, Cheryl Lanier, who is hitchhiking on a winter night. They go for coffee and end up having drinks, then dinner. Marshall knows he is on dangerous ground but does not discourage the girl's attentions.

Cheryl confides to him her worries about her room-mate, Livan Baker, for whom she has just picked up a prescription for Valium. The girl's distress, Cheryl says, is a result of being sexually abused by one of Marshall's colleagues, Jack McCallum, whom Marshall holds in contempt. At first Cheryl's account is vague, but eventually she fills in some details. Livan was a research assistant to McCallum; on a research trip to Boston, in a "borrowed triplex in Revere," McCallum had tied Livan to the bed and had sex with her.

Disturbed by Cheryl's story, Marshall considers ways to help Livan and bring McCallum to justice. What follows is a tangled melodrama, a story clear to no one and dangerous to everyone it touches. Marshall confronts McCallum, calling him at home. McCallum responds in a bizarre manner, saying he would like to be dead "because when I think about it, the weather is dreary, and our jobs don't mean much in the long run"; he rambles on describing his family problems—his wife's rage, his son's behavior disorder, and his own mood swings. Soon afterward McCallum appears at Marshall's house, arguing that Livan is "psychotic" and the victim of a long-term eating disorder. He produces hysterical, accusatory notes from her as evidence of his innocence. He elaborates—beyond Marshall's toler-ance—his psychiatric and marital problems and his wife's fury at him over the girl's allegations. Finally he is persuaded to spend the night at the Lockards'. The next morning, after Sonja and Marshall have left the house, McCallum's wife arrives and stabs her husband nearly to death.

In the aftermath of these events Marshall continues to try to piece together the story of what actually happened and to weigh his own complicity in the matter, beginning with his flirtation with Cheryl. For no clear reason he begins to have flashbacks to his early childhood and particularly to a conversation with his mother not long before her death. His stepmother, Evie, who cared for him through much of his child-hood, has another stroke and dies. Sonja ends her affair with Tony and confesses her infidelity to Marshall, who is astonished. She also reveals that Evie had slept with Marshall's father while Marshall's mother was still alive, that their affair had gone on for years from the time before Evie left her parents' house in Canada and came to live with the Lockard family as an au pair.

When McCallum is released from the hospital in early spring, he and Marshall head to Florida—McCal-lum to get some sun and Marshall to visit his brother Gordon and Gordon's new wife, Beth. On the way they stop in Buena Vista, Virginia—Cheryl's home-town—ostensibly so that McCallum can locate Cheryl and seek her forgiveness. In fact, what he hopes to do is to reunite with his former sweetheart, Cheryl's mother,

Janet—now an aging, impoverished mother of ten chil-dren. Cheryl reveals that her mother and guidance counselor had urged her to apply at Benson College, thinking that "Professor McCallum here would be my ticket to getting financial aid." Marshall is justifiably astonished by this turn of events, which Cheryl asserts "isn't some cosmic coincidence." The next morning Marshall finds a note from McCallum, who is bailing out of the trip to Florida to stay in Buena Vista and see Janet Lanier again. McCallum also gives what he claims is a full account of his sexual involvement with Livan. Marshall goes on to Florida where, together with his heavy-drinking brother Gordon, he tries to reconstruct the remembered and deeply troubling scene in which his mother told Marshall and Gordon—then only small children—she was going to die. Having recovered some of the knowledge he was seeking, and enervated by the luridness of Florida, Marshall makes up his mind to head homeward.

The final chapter of the novel is a first-person account in Evie's voice of the mènage á trois—Mar-shall's father, Miles; Marshall's mother, Alice; and Evie herself, Eveline Martine Delia Lockard. She recounts her long love affair with Miles, her illegitimate preg-nancy, and the birth of her son, Martin, who was raised as one of Miles and Alice's children until his sudden death at age three. She also describes the scene Mar-shall has been struggling to recall, and she tells about Alice's death from cancer. Her account, written dur-ing her nursing home days, resolves the mystery of the letters and reflects on the more troubling mystery of her stepsons' characters—Marshall's solitude and self-absorption and Gordon's need to live life on the run. It also reflects broadly on the mysteries of human motivation as she wonders, "What would have hap-pened if I had never started with him, let alone been won back through the years by fragments of romantic melodies? Or by an avalanche of letters to which I added a P.S. that was not there: that he loved me."

Sven Birkerts observed in his *New York Times* review of *Another You* that "Ms. Beattie has always dem-onstrated a sure touch when dealing with the vagaries of modern love" and that "she has always been alert to what is ponderously called the Zeitgeist. She has not lost her knack for the former. The ebb and flow of con-flicted emotion between Marshall and Sonja—and between them and the other characters is handled with precision and ease." But Birkerts found the main plot dated and uninteresting; more compelling, he argued, is the subplot divulged in the letters. Other reviewers were harsher in their assessment of the novel. Kim Hubbard, writing for *People,* found Marshall's ennui "contagious" and complained that Beattie's charac-ters seem "hardly more real than the paper dolls

ANN BEATTIE

MY LIFE, STARRING DARA FALCON

A NOVEL

Dust jacket for Beattie's 1997 novel, in which a flamboyant,
out-of-work actress influences a meek housewife
(Richland County Public Library)

Marshall once played with." Martha Duffy in *Time* winced at Beattie's "penchant for artsy or newsy allusions" and deemed the novel dated and inauthentic, "a real disappointment." Michiko Kakutani, on the other hand, took *Another You* as proof of Beattie's development as a novelist; Kakutani wrote in *The New York Times* that Beattie "has learned to use her prodigious descriptive skills to conjure up not only the palpable world of things her characters inhabit, but also their inner world of feelings. In doing so, she has enriched and broadened her fictional universe and produced a novel that, however flawed, radiates an authentic emotional power."

In her 1997 novel, *My Life, Starring Dara Falcon*, Beattie revisits some of the themes of her earlier fiction: the loss of parents, the failure of romantic love, and the emptiness of celebrity. The story is told from the point of view of its protagonist, Jean Warner, who was orphaned as a child when her parents died

in a plane crash; throughout the novel Jean remains haunted by the memory of the day she heard the news of the crash. Jean was raised by her aunt, a troubled woman who gambled away Jean's settlement from the airline and then disappeared from her niece's life. During her sophomore year of college, Jean dropped out to marry Bob Warner and move to Dell, New Hampshire, where she has become part of his large, seemingly close-knit family. While Bob commutes to Boston to get a CPA degree that he thinks will be useful in the management of his family's nursery business, Jean devotes herself to Bob's family, enjoying security and companionship she lacked as a child. She runs errands for Bob's increasingly demanding mother, Barbara, and provides help and company to her frequently pregnant sister-in-law Janey. She makes a little money by typing other people's manuscripts, most notably a dull, sprawling, ever-expanding memoir that ends only when its elderly writer dies.

This happy, if somewhat stifling, life is disturbed by the arrival of Dara Falcon, an out-of-work actress. Although Jean initially dislikes Dara, finding her "self-involved," "excessive," and controlling, she soon becomes fascinated by the newcomer. More than Dara's style, her energy (which Jean characterizes as "willed" rather than "genuine"), or her overt sexuality, what intrigues Jean is Dara's changing life story. "Dara Falcon," Beattie writes, "was once Darcy Fisher. She either had or hadn't been a promising actress. She either did or did not have a baby when she was sixteen." By her own account she spent time in McLean Hospital after a breakdown, may or may not have gotten a scholarship to Radcliffe, and may or may not have had a role in an Andy Warhol movie or a soap opera called *Time of Desire*.

In a short time Dara insinuates herself deeply into the lives of Dell residents. She borrows money, clothes, cars, even lodgings. She breaks up the engagement of Dell native Tom Van Sant and moves in with him. She is instrumental in getting Tom to open a new, upscale garden center that nearly drives the Warner family nurseries out of business. She tries to kindle an affair with Bob's married brother Frank, writing him intimate letters. More than anywhere else Dara insinuates herself into Jean's life and psyche. Where Dara is powerful, Jean is malleable; where Dara is colorful, Jean feels herself to be dull and colorless. As Dara's life story expands and changes, Jean's past contracts into a few bleak facts. When Dara gets the part of Nora in a local production of Henrik Ibsen's *A Doll's House* (1879), Jean staggers under the weight of the revelations in the play. Using information she has elicited from her friend, Dara contrives to get the memoir Jean has been typing turned into a play, produced and paid for by the dead author's fiancé, the wealthy, bisexual Edward Quill. Dara herself is to star in this improbable venture.

Eventually, feeling aimless and suffocated in Dell, Jean separates from Bob and goes to the University of Connecticut to get a degree. Even there Dara continues to play a powerful role in Jean's life, insistent on continuing their friendship across distances, lapses, and outright betrayals. "You only left your husband. You're not trying to leave me too, are you?" she asks Jean. For a time, long after the end of her marriage to Bob, Jean is bound to Dara by a ring Dara has given her for safekeeping. Handed down to Tom Van Sant by his mother, the ring may or may not have signified an engagement between Dara and Tom; when they break up, Dara gives it to Jean to prevent herself, she says, from throwing it away. Only when Jean finally returns the ring to its rightful owner–Tom–does she begin to be free of Dara's destructive influence.

Dara makes one last encroachment on Jean's life by attempting to seduce Liam, the psychology professor with whom Jean has fallen in love. By that point Jean has gained some insight into the nature of their friendship. "She always had the upper hand," Jean reflects, "she was the self-dramatizing, eccentric femme fatale, I was the dutiful little housewife; I was the audience, she the star; for too long, while I had gone on under the delusion that I had been the principal actor in the play that was my life, that play could more properly have been called *My Life, Starring Dara Falcon*." Realizing that Liam's reputation as a womanizer is accurate, Jean leaves him and sets out to discover her own path in the world.

The novel ends where it began, with Jean sitting by a pool in Key West, Florida, reading Dara's obituary in *The New York Times* under the headline: *Dara Falcon, Actress and Playwright*. Jean has married a hotel manager she met while attending a conference on near-death experiences. Though her husband's occupation puts her in a state of ongoing homelessness–they move from city to city and travel often–she welcomes this combination of freedom and romantic companionship. "I still think of him as my big chance," Jean says; "He's my chance to live a moderately eventful, often pleasurable life. My chance for a new start–because, to this day, every moment lived on the lam from Dell and its inhabitants seems a potential new start."

Like many of Beattie's previous novels, *My Life, Starring Dara Falcon*, polarized reviewers. *The New York Times* reviewer Kakutani deplored it, calling it "an ill-conceived experiment" and saying it "embod-

ies the worst flaws of her early and later fiction: the meaningless chatter and anomic cataloguing of the mundane that could turn her weaker stories into formulaic exercises in alienation, and the schematic narrative pyrotechnics that have made her less successful novels awkward and contrived." But Jim Shepard, in *The New York Times Book Review*, found the weaknesses of the novel offset by its considerable strengths: Beattie's characteristically acute observation, her eloquence on "both the quiet aggression within marriages and the pathos of families," her unerring sense of comedy, and her "tenderness and precision" in rendering Jean's life. Lorin Stein's review in the *Yale Review* offers one of the most serious scholarly assessments to date of Beattie's novels. Stein points to several new developments in Beattie's late fiction. He calls *My Life, Starring Dara Falcon* a "troubling" novel, a departure from everything Beattie has written, her "most difficult" and "most intriguing: a tissue of autobiography spun by a woman whose life eludes her." He points out that "Dara's opacity gives Beattie something she has never had before: conversations as battles. There have always been brilliant stalemates in her books . . . but now there are winners and losers, the chance to understand, even the risk of misunderstanding." The effect, he suggests, is a "new, very Jamesian note for Beattie."

In *Park City: New and Selected Stories* (1998) Beattie brings together a generous sampling from the early volumes of short stories as well as her later collections *Where You'll Find Me, and Other Stories* (1986) and *What Was Mine* (1991). She also includes eight new stories, all of them substantial. In the short fiction of the late 1980s and the 1990s Beattie's focus shifts somewhat from the loners and wanderers, temporary connections, and vague longings that occupied her in the early stories. Increasingly, she concerns herself with the domestic lives of adult men and women–their marriages or longstanding partnerships, their growing children, their homes, and their feelings: of sexual jealousy or passion, of satisfaction or regret, of grief at the loss of parents or friends and fear in the face of their own mortality.

In addressing these themes–and they are not so much new as deepened and matured–she continues to trace the profound, still-unfolding social changes that confront Americans born after World War II. With a sustaining interest in formal innovation, a clear eye, and a steady nerve for American life at the end of the century, Beattie is likely to continue to be a major American writer.

Interviews:

Larry McCaffery and Sinda Gregory, "A Conversation with Ann Beattie," *Literary Review,* 27 (1984): 165–177;

Steven R. Centola, "An Interview with Ann Beattie," *Contemporary Literature,* 31 (Winter 1990): 405–422;

Neila C. Seshchari, "Picturing Ann Beattie: A Dialogue," *Weber Studies,* 7 (Spring 1990): 12–36;

James Plath, "Counternarrative: An Interview with Ann Beattie," *Michigan Quarterly Review,* 32 (Summer 1993): 359–379;

Jaye Berman Montresor, "This Was in 1991, in Iowa City: Talking with Ann Beattie," in *The Critical Response to Ann Beattie,* edited by Montresor (Westport, Conn.: Greenwood Press, 1993), pp. 141–154.

Bibliography:

Harry Opperman and Christina Murphy, "Ann Beattie (1947–): A Checklist," *Bulletin of Bibliography,* 44 (June 1987): 111–118.

References:

John W. Aldridge, *Talents and Technicians: Literary Chic and the New Assembly-Line Fiction* (New York: Scribners / Toronto: Maxwell Macmillan Canada / New York: Maxwell Macmillan International, 1992);

Georgia A. Brown, "Chilly Views of Beattie," *Canto,* 3 (August 1980): 165–173;

Joseph Epstein, "Ann Beattie and the Hippoisie," *Commentary,* 75, no. 3: 54–58;

Don Lee, "About Ann Beattie," *Ploughshares,* 21 (Fall 1995): 231–235;

Jaye Berman Montresor, ed., *The Critical Response to Ann Beattie* (Westport, Conn.: Greenwood Press, 1993);

Christina Murphy, *Ann Beattie* (Boston: Twayne, 1986);

Carolyn Porter, "Ann Beattie: The Art of the Missing," in *Contemporary American Women Writers: Narrative Strategies,* edited by Catherine Rainwater and William J. Scheick (Lexington: University Press of Kentucky, 1985), pp. 9–28;

David Wyatt, "Ann Beattie," *Southern Review,* 28 (1991): 145–159.

Madison Smartt Bell

(1 August 1957 -)

David Galef
University of Mississippi

See also the Bell entry in *DLB 218: American Short-Story Writers Since World War II, Second Series.*

BOOKS: *The Washington Square Ensemble* (New York: Viking, 1983; London: Deutsch, 1983);
Waiting for the End of the World (New York: Ticknor & Fields, 1985; London: Chatto & Windus, 1985);
Straight Cut (New York: Ticknor & Fields, 1986; London: Chatto & Windus, 1987);
Zero db and Other Stories (New York: Ticknor & Fields, 1987; London: Chatto & Windus, 1987);
The Year of Silence (New York: Ticknor & Fields, 1987; London: Chatto & Windus, 1987);
The History of the Owen Graduate School of Management (New York: Vanderbilt University, 1988);
Soldier's Joy (New York: Ticknor & Fields, 1989);
Barking Man and Other Stories (New York: Ticknor & Fields, 1990; London: Bloomsbury, 1992);
Doctor Sleep (New York: Harcourt Brace Jovanovich, 1991; London: Bloomsbury, 1992);
Save Me, Joe Louis (New York: Harcourt Brace, 1993);
All Souls' Rising (New York: Pantheon, 1995; London: Granta, 1996);
Ten Indians (New York: Pantheon, 1996);
Narrative Design: A Writer's Guide to Structure (New York: Norton, 1997);
Master of the Crossroads (New York: Pantheon, 2000);
Anything Goes (New York: Pantheon, 2002).

OTHER: "One Art," in *My Poor Elephant: 27 Male Artists at Work,* edited by Eve Shelnutt (Atlanta: Longstreet Press, 1992), pp. 1–15;
Andrew Nelson Lytle, *A Wake for the Living,* preface by Bell (Nashville: J. S. Sanders, 1992);
"Hammerhead," in *That's What I Like (about the South),* edited by George P. Garrett and Paul Ruffin (Columbia: University of South Carolina Press, 1993), pp. 17–23;
"The Mastery of Peter Taylor," in *Critical Essays on Peter Taylor,* edited by Hubert Horton McAlexander (New York: G. K. Hall, 1993), pp. 254–261.

Madison Smartt Bell (photograph by Jerry Bauer; from the dust jacket for All Souls' Rising, *1995)*

SELECTED PERIODICAL PUBLICATIONS– UNCOLLECTED:

DRAMA
"Happy Families Are All Alike," by Bell and Andrew Moore, *Boulevard,* 11, no. 1–2 (1996): 54–75.
FICTION
"Pawnshop," *Vox,* 1 (Spring 1991): 54–55;
"Summertime," *Gentleman's Quarterly* (August 1992): 79–80, 84;
"The Life of Georgie," *Witness,* 6, no. 1 (1992): 68–75;

"I Ain't Blue," *Gulf Coast,* 8, no. 2 (1996): 27–38;

"Leadbelly in Paris," *Oxford American,* 27–28 (1999).

NONFICTION

"Less is Less: The Diminishing American Short Story," *Harper's* (April 1986): 64–69;

"Literature and Pleasure: Bridging the Gap," *Antaeus,* 59 (Autumn 1987): 127–134;

"An Essay Introducing His Work in Rather a Lunatic Fashion," *Chattahoochee Review,* 12 (Fall 1991): 1–13;

"Blood and Guts in the Bookstore," *The World and I* (April 1992): 562–573;

"The Short Story Revival (Or Whatever It Was): An Impressionistic History and Diatribe," *Mississippi Review,* 21 (Spring 1993): 55–66;

"A Propeller on a Skullcap That Spins with Quirky Energy," *New York Times,* 13 June 1993, II: 28;

"Rediscovering the Ageless Pleasures of Rereading," *Boston Globe,* 20 June 1993, p. B42;

"Unconscious Mind: The Art and Soul of Fiction," *AWP Chronicle* (May–Summer 1996): 1, 9–14;

"Soul in a Bottle," *Creative Nonfiction,* 14 (2000): 110–134.

Madison Smartt Bell and his fiction tend to evade easy categories. As a writer who started publishing in the early 1980s, he was never affiliated with either the Minimalists or the "Brat Pack" novelists such as Jay McInerney and Tama Janowitz. Grounded in a rural Southern tradition rather than in urban grunge, he nonetheless seems equally at home in both areas. His style, while descriptive and lyrical, stands against a foreground of taut action with the punch of a thriller. Still considered a young author, he has already garnered Guggenheim and National Endowment for the Arts fellowships, was a finalist for the National Book Award and the PEN/Faulkner Award, achieved publication in the *Best American Short Stories* anthologies, and was named by *Granta* magazine in 1996 as one of the top American novelists under forty. His output includes novels, short-story collections, and a writing manual, not to mention many essays, reviews, and other writings.

Born in Nashville, Tennessee, on 1 August 1957, Bell grew up as an only child in rather unusual circumstances. At the time his parents married, they purchased ninety-six acres in the rural stretches of Williamson County with the intention of living on a farm. His father, Henry Denmark Bell, was a Nashville lawyer who eventually turned circuit judge in Franklin, Tennessee. His mother, née Georgia Allen Wigginton, a talented horsewoman, taught riding lessons and presided over a summer camp while also managing the farmstead. The plan was in part to create the anti-industrial existence described by the Southern Agrarians in the now-famous collection *I'll Take My Stand* (1930). With the help of a hired hand named Benjamin Taylor, who resided on the property as a tenant, the Bells lived a genuine farm life with horses, cows, hogs, sheep, and a garden. As Bell recounts in his autobiographical essay "One Art" (1992), "Mine was an atavistic childhood."

Some of his earliest memories are connected to foaling and farm chores, images that occasionally surface in his fiction. Yet, the Bell household also provided a cultured atmosphere, with family friends such as Andrew Lytle, Allen Tate, and other writers of the Southern Renascence dropping by as guests. Since Franklin is not far from the city of Nashville, Bell seems to have had the best of two worlds, the regularity and placidity of farm life with the proximity of urban sophistication. From ages six to fourteen he was a student at Ensworth school in Nashville. He attended high school at Montgomery Bell Academy, a boy's prep school.

From the time he was a toddler, Bell suffered from chronic asthma and allergies, often taking refuge in books. Perhaps for this reason, his mother taught him to read early, an experience that "put me a little out of sync with the group," as he remarks in "One Art," as well as encouraged a lifelong devotion to the printed word. It also spurred in Bell a habit of narrating his days to himself, often adding "he said" and "she said" to others' voices. His formative reading included a lot of Gerald Durrell and Mark Twain, but he also enjoyed science fiction and the fantasies of C. S. Lewis and J. R. R. Tolkien. He developed a consuming interest in the Southern Renascence, including the works of Tate, Robert Penn Warren (Bell estimates that he read Warren's 1946 novel, *All the King's Men,* more than a hundred times), Flannery O'Connor, William Faulkner, and Peter Taylor. He also reached for less established authors such as Harry Crews and Madison Jones.

Bell always had ambitions to be a writer, though he did not begin seriously until he suffered a collapsed lung in his senior year of high school. Convalescing alone in a room for several weeks spurred him to write what he called in "One Art" his "first real short story," a trifold view of death called "Triptych." Deeming it imitation Ernest Hemingway, however, he put it away in a drawer after completing it. In 1975, enrolling at Princeton, he intended to write but was somewhat intimidated by the wealth of students who had already written. An early short story, "The Structure and Meaning of Dormitory and Food Services" (published in *Lowlands Review,* 1978), gives some sense of the alienation he felt. He therefore left school for a semester to work at the receiving docks of the Ingram Book Company back in Nashville. There he also worked on his writing, including a revision of his first story, "Triptych," changing the style to imitate O'Connor.

Dust jacket for Bell's first novel (1983), about a small-time drug dealer and his associates in a New York City park (Richland County Public Library)

Returning to Princeton after six months, he came under the aegis of Southern writer George Garrett, who gave Bell his first publication by accepting the revised "Triptych" for the *Intro* anthology series. Bell went on to major in English and did extremely well in his studies. Though grateful for mentors such as Garrett and Stephen Koch, Bell admits, "I was a stubborn student who usually wouldn't listen to anything or follow any advice." Still, with the encouragement of Koch, Bell eventually wrote a short unpublished novel called "The Structure of the Telephone Company," splicing Southern agrarianism with telephonic metaphors.

Bell graduated from Princeton summa cum laude in 1979 with several prizes for fiction and a Phi Beta Kappa membership. Though he had written an undergraduate thesis on Madison Jones, and graduate school loomed as an option, Bell says it drifted out of possibility when he forgot to bring the applications home during Christmas break and missed the deadlines. Instead, he ended up after college graduation in the slum-ridden Williamsburg section of Brooklyn, loosely affiliated with a group of other recent graduates and dropouts

interested in moviemaking. He recalls this period as a time spent writing in the mornings and drinking bourbon with beer chasers in downtown Manhattan bars.

Though he had introductions to some agents and hopes of selling "The Structure of the Telephone Company," this sale never came to pass. "What I was doing," he stated in a 1987 *Publishers Weekly* interview, "was writing stuff that was self-consciously Southern." Meanwhile, he held down a variety of jobs, from security guard to photograph research assistant. At the same time, Bell wrote a series of readers' guides for the Franklin Library on figures ranging from Plotinus and Miguel de Cervantes to Leo Tolstoy and Anthony Trollope; he also served as a manuscript reader and copywriter for Berkley Publishing. Of longest duration, however, was his work in the motion-picture cooperative "185," its name derived from 185 Nassau Street, the address of the creative arts building at Princeton. Bell cofounded the group the year he graduated from college. Later, during a stint working on a Radio Televisione Italiana documentary about the rehabilitation of heroin addicts, Bell learned to be a competent sound man and assistant cameraman. Though the group eventually broke up in 1984, he absorbed the kind of technical movie details visible in the short story "Zero db" (1985) and his third novel, *Straight Cut* (1986). He also wrote freelance articles for the magazine *Home Video*. Despite his various activities, Bell felt it was time to focus more on his own writing.

Advised by Garrett to apply to Hollins College in Roanoke, Virginia, a school known for its graduate program in creative writing, Bell made the late deadline and was accepted. Having deferred admission for a year, he went to Roanoke in the fall of 1980. There he tried to rework "The Structure of the Telephone Company" but soon realized that he had reached a dead end. Inspiration finally struck in the form of voices speaking in his head—which is still the way that stories come to him—and he sat down to write for what turned out to be all night. Bell counts this experience as the most uncanny he has ever had. When he emerged, he had the beginning of his first published novel, *The Washington Square Ensemble* (1983), a panoply of street voices that begins and ends in Washington Square Park.

The cohering force in the story is a small-time Italian drug dealer with the street moniker Johnny B. Goode, who loosely employs (and has renamed) four men to sell his wares: Holy Mother, a former Mafia hit man turned junkie who was in Attica during the 1971 prison riot; Yusuf Ali, a giant black Muslim given to reciting long stretches from the Koran; Santa Barbara, a Hoboken-based Puerto Rican interested in voodoo and Yoruba magic; and Carlo, a dumb but handsome Dominican soon asked to leave the group. Additional color is provided by Porco Miserio, an alcoholic part-time hustler and itinerant horn player who has acquired what he calls a storytelling stone that loosens up people's tongues. He has also knocked out Yusuf Ali by wielding the stone in his fist, spurring much of the action in the next chapters.

As each character speaks his piece, a casually brutal background emerges: Holy Mother's induction into the Mafia, for example, or his later savaging at the hands of prison guards, ending in chronic pain and a narcotics dependency; or Yusuf Ali's lonely childhood living in a basement with rats in Hunts Point after his mother was shot in an accidental hit at the wrong apartment. Meanwhile, Santa Barbara seeks out the corpse of a wino and drags him away for a voodoo send-off. The climax of the novel occurs in Washington Square Park, with a Rastafarian mob, a lot of quick action, and the saving grace of Porco's horn. "Music has gone into my writing in a number of ways," Bell wrote in "One Art," "directly as a subject a number of times. It has influenced more subtly the way I make a sentence or a paragraph or even a whole book." As the title word

"Ensemble" suggests, the monologues in the novel come across as jazz riffs, and the dovetailing of all these plot strands resembles musical segues.

Bell wrote most of the novel during his year at Hollins, which ended with an M.A. degree in 1981, a return to Brooklyn, and a recommendation from Garrett to see the literary agent Jane Gelfman. *The Washington Square Ensemble* was published by Viking in 1983 to mostly positive notices. Thomas Ruffen in *The Los Angeles Times Book Review* (27 February 1983) called it "a flawed yet brilliant first book." Ivan Gold, writing for *The New York Times Book Review* (20 February 1983), pointed out that it had "all the faults of a first novel . . . and some of the virtues of a fourth," that it had the bravura of the best debuts and showed the complexity of a seasoned novelist, but that the ending seemed contrived. Only a few reviewers noticed that the novel was as much a duel of philosophies as opposing actions and that the finale has more to do with internal resolution than physical closure. This pattern holds true for most of Bell's fiction.

His second novel, *Waiting for the End of the World* (1985), was roughed out during a stay at the MacDowell Artists' Colony in New Hampshire. Meanwhile, his editor at Viking, Cork Smith, had moved to Ticknor and Fields. Because of the change in publishers and the corresponding uncertainty of a contract, Bell acquired a commission to write about the school of management at Vanderbilt University, resulting in one of his lesser-known books, *The History of the Owen Graduate School of Management* (1988). Bell's livelihood at this point had grown somewhat uncertain.

Waiting for the End of the World draws on the New York scene that Bell experienced during almost seven years in Brooklyn. It has all the tension of a thriller and concerns everyone's Cold War fear: a group hijacking plutonium to make a nuclear bomb. This time Bell's social misfits show a darker cast: Larkin, a bright, selfless former mental patient with a background in music, photography, and alcohol; Mercer, a University of Chicago graduate, former cocaine addict, and drug runner who has killed a member of the mob; Carrera, a foster child in and out of drug rehab, ending up at New York University, where he nurtures dreams of the perfect explosion; Hutton, a divorced Vietnam veteran with the desire to enact his worst nightmares; and Simon, the warped psychologist who organizes them all into a lethally destructive team. Bell also layers in more urban eccentrics, including "the Sparrow," who lives in a welter of record albums and gin bottles, and Porco from *The Washington Square Ensemble,* who reappears with his horn.

The casual atrocities in Bell's fiction are notched up in this novel: one scene involves two policemen who are decapitated and their heads frozen; another concerns an act of sabotage that derails a subway and kills more than a hundred people. The crux is an act of nuclear destruction planned for Times Square. As always in Bell's work, however, there is a philosophical bent: what Simon thinks of as political terrorism, Larkin refers to as "increasing the chaos." The novel is interspersed with wild newspaper stories all leading toward a shadowy apocalypse. Bell also displays his usual interest in the otherworldly, from a manhunt for a diabolist and serial garroter to a fascination with spontaneous human combustion. Meg Wolitzer in *The New York Times Book Review* (18 August 1985) wrote, "The reader is left with a very bleak but sometimes memorable vision of a world out of control." David Remnick, writing in *The Washington Post Book World* (1 September 1985), applauded the "terrific power" of the novel while at the same time noting that Bell was perhaps too impressed with the casual and atrocious anomie at the center of the city. This element, perhaps, is one pitfall in Bell's early work: the shock and enthusiasm of the outsider for what hometown residents live with all the time.

In his next novel, Bell scaled back his structure. *Straight Cut* is based more on a sinister love triangle than a host of aggressive street types. The novel nonetheless depends on the kind of protagonist visible in most of Bell's fiction: an unsteady man, vulnerable and lonely, but with a variety of talents, often including martial arts training and philosophical or mystical lore. Bell's own background is relevant, not the least of which is his movie experience as a sound man. A fascination with martial arts is also a given in Bell's fiction: Bell took up tae kwon do in college and continued this interest, with occasional breaks, up to the level of second-degree black belt. The accompanying stoic philosophy is present, as well—Bell half-subscribes to the adage "Whatever doesn't kill you makes you stronger," along with a feeling of overcoming large odds. In *Straight Cut* protagonist Tracy Bateman, a talented film editor, lying low after the failure of his marriage, gets a call from his reckless former partner, Kevin. The job ostensibly involves some film editing in Rome, but it also turns out to be a front for drug smuggling and money laundering.

Tracy is the sort of thoughtful character who carries around Søren Kierkegaard's *Either/Or* (1843) and also can karate-kick his way out of a mugging. When the movie job turns into an unfinished drug deal, with Tracy's estranged wife, Lauren, as bait, Tracy decides to get even with Kevin. The plot includes international intrigue, two deadly but comical Bulgarian henchmen, and some help from a slightly fanciful former terrorist called Racine. Significantly, the woman in the book, Lauren, has a sustained voice and presence, which signaled a breakout of sorts for Bell.

He soon settled into the rhythm of a book a year. *The Year of Silence* (1987) is the end of what Bell has called his New York trilogy (along with *The Washington Square Ensemble* and *Waiting for the End of the World*). The novel chronicles the drug-overdose death of Marian, a young woman living in New York, as recalled a year later by the various people whose lives intersected with hers in some way, from her semiboyfriend to a panhandling, street-hustling dwarf she befriended with handouts of fruit. If Bell's earlier novels bore a violent impact, *The Year of Silence* carries a mood of bereavement that a *Publishers Weekly* reviewer saw as combining "delicacy and great tensile strength." By this point, some critical consensus had emerged as to Bell's literary strengths: strong, lyrical writing; attention to detail; and a disparate, desperate cast of characters. Bell's images of the city, as Roberta Silman noted in *The New York Times Book Review* (15 November 1987), were "not unlike Céline's Paris."

Zero db, his first collection of short fiction, also came out in 1987. By then, Bell had produced an impressive array of short stories, with publications in such magazines as *Harper's* and *The Hudson Review*. The stories in this volume express the concerns of a writer exploring his territory, though the locale varies from nonacademic life at Princeton to the seamy side of New York and back to the rural reaches of the South. The much anthologized story "The Naked Lady," for example, which first appeared in *The Crescent Review,* is in redneck dialect and concerns both the mystical center of art and how to punch your way out of a biker bar. Like many of Bell's novels, it is built on a singular voice. But the middle grouping, starting with "The Structure and Meaning of Dormitory and Food Services," "Irene," and "The Lie Detector," are semi-autobiographical and trace the life of a loner trying to give some shape to his existence. The last story in the collection, "Today Is a Good Day to Die," signals another departure, chronicling the life of a cavalry lieutenant at the Battle of Little Bighorn.

Bell's second collection, *Barking Man and Other Stories,* came out three years later, in 1990. Though the subjects again show a wide range, there is more focus, and the writing is slightly more restrained, though more politically engaged. The troubling story "Witness," for instance, is about the violent consequences of a stalking and the inability of the courts to do enough for the victim. "Finding Natasha" is a search for romance among the junkies in New York. The title story is a new take on Franz Kafka's *Metamorphosis* (1915), featuring a mild-mannered Briton named Alf who likes to spend time at the zoo and who slowly, inexorably turns canine. Reviews of both story collections were quite positive, ranging from Dean Flower's assessment in the Summer 1990 *Hudson Review* of their "wonderful astrin-

*Dust jacket for Bell's 1989 novel, in which he examines race relations
in the new South (Richland County Public Library)*

gent brevity and clarity" to praise in *The New York Times Book Review* from Anne Bernays, who called them "astonishing" (15 February 1987), and Rick DeMarinis, who judged them "the work of an important and talented writer" (8 April 1990).

Throughout this period, Bell spoke out against minimalism, faux realism, philistine publishers, and whining authors, in articles such as "Less Is Less: The Diminishing American Short Story," which appeared in *Harper's* in 1986 during the so-called short-story renaissance. Criticizing contemporary writers such as Amy Hempel, Ann Beattie, Bobbie Ann Mason, Raymond Carver, and Frederick Barthelme, Bell identified the group traits he considered most disturbing: "a trim 'minimal' style, an obsessive concern for surface detail, a tendency to ignore or eliminate distinctions among the people it renders, and a studiedly deterministic, at times nihilistic, vision of the world." As Bell has repeatedly observed, true minimalism is concentrated from larger material and not simply an exercise in spareness. Bell tends to like "maximalists" such as Cormac McCarthy and risk-takers such as Mary Gaitskill and William Vollmann. In a more embittered vein, in "The Short Story Revival (Or Whatever It Was): An Impressionistic History and Diatribe" (*Mississippi Review,* Spring 1993), he pointed out that there seemed to be more writers of short fiction than there were readers. If there is hope for the survival of both the short story and literature in general, Bell wrote in another essay, "Literature and Pleasure: Bridging the Gap" (*Antaeus,* Autumn 1987), it exists in authors willing to experiment with form, even if that means dabbling in genre fiction. Too often, he argues, so-called literary fiction represents a refuge from reality rather than a confrontation with what is out there. As he states: "the most fundamental delight which literature can offer must have something to do with the perception or discovery of truth." Whether one agrees with Bell, there is no doubt of his increasing stature as a critic, in both essays and reviews.

He also has been teaching (with some gaps) at Goucher College in Baltimore since 1984, where he now occupies the Goucher Chair of Distinguished Achievement. He teaches alongside his wife, the poet Elizabeth Spires, whom he met at a writers' conference in Maine and married three years later, on 15 June 1985. The two have a daughter, Celia, born in 1991. Bell has taught writing at Columbia University, the University of Iowa, Johns Hopkins, the University of

South Maine, and the 92nd Street YMHA in Manhattan. In addition, he has taught literature courses, notably in the modern short story and in political fiction.

Inevitably, as Bell's reputation grew, critics attempted to pin him down with a label. Given Bell's Tennessee background (with both his parents' families in mid-Tennessee as far back as the Civil War), "Southern writer" seemed apt enough—except that Bell had chosen not to write much about the South. *Soldier's Joy* (1989), coming two years after his previous novel, marked a return to his Southern roots and won the Lillian Smith Award that year. The novel takes its title from an old tune about victorious soldiers during the Revolutionary War. The main character, Thomas Laidlaw, recently back from Vietnam, is struggling to reestablish himself on the farm and incidentally to better himself on the banjo. In his leisurely descriptions of posthole digging or saving a motherless lamb, Bell displays the hard-earned farmer's lore he learned as a child. Achieving a Joycean distance, however, he wrote half the novel in England, where he and his wife lived for a year on her Amy Lowell Traveling Poetry Scholarship, and the other half in Iowa City, where he taught fiction.

What starts out as a pastoral existence slowly accelerates to a seminightmare. The kicker is the politics of racism, a subject that eventually erupted in *All Souls' Rising* (1995). Bell notes in "One Art" that *Soldier's Joy* "was written with an explicitly political motive. I never thought I would do such a thing and was a bit horrified to find myself attempting it. But now it seems to me that it is not quite such an anomaly in the body of my work." In *Soldier's Joy* the political cause is represented by Rodney Redmon, a childhood friend of Laidlaw's who happens to be black. Other unwitting provocateurs are Raschid, an Indian who opens "Mosque 37 and Health Food Restaurant" in downtown Nashville; Adrienne Wells, fiddler and possible romantic interest; and Brother Jacob, a charismatic preacher who advocates racial harmony. The novel shows that underneath the bucolic surface of the new South is a rigid intolerance—not exactly news to most, but something that Laidlaw feels he must combat. Teaming up with Ratman, a buddy from Vietnam, Laidlaw builds up (a little improbably) to a face-off with the Ku Klux Klan. At the center of all the conflict, he remains oddly self-sacrificing, fighting for some ideal that he cannot quite articulate.

The critical response to the novel sounded as if everyone had simply been waiting for Bell to return home. Reviews were mostly laudatory, though part of the response was a reaction to the antiracist message of the novel more than the storyline. As more than one critic pointed out, the novel seemed slightly distended, its lyrical sections going on for too long and its violent ending a bit too hyped up. Still, it signaled that Bell had joined the pantheon of noted Southern writers, not just in heritage but also in subject matter.

Bell's next novel, however, is set in London. *Doctor Sleep* (1991) is inhabited by the expatriate American Adrian Strother, a therapeutic hypnotist who cannot cure his own insomnia. The novel features common Bell elements: a mystical core, in this instance the hermeticism of Giordano Bruno, a sixteenth-century renegade Dominican monk; several martial arts scenes; drugs and a series of foul murders in the background; two once-intimate, now semidistant women; and a shady buddy from the past. Adrian is desperate for sleep, and in fact much of the action of the novel takes place in a semifugue state. Adrian's wife has departed, leaving a hole in his life. As with Bell's other unlikely heroes, Adrian strives for salvation through both the body (martial arts) and the mind (gnostic hermeticism). The journey of such a character must of necessity be half brutally physical, half oddly static, with the world as a template for divine presence.

This novel was not the first time Bell had used religious beliefs as a fulcrum in his work. "I was raised as a not very observant Episcopalian," he noted in an unpublished interview (1997), adding that he has flirted with Catholicism under the spell of Graham Greene, as well as with the Russian Orthodox Church and Sufi mysticism from a friend's influence. As Bell emphasizes, the spiritual underpinning of his characters has ranged from Islam to apocalyptic Christianity to Kierkegaardian leaps and existentialism. As for *Doctor Sleep,* Bell commented in a 1995 interview with Justin Cronin, "The book is basically structured as a prayer." Bell seems to have perfected his form, and he has called *Doctor Sleep* his favorite work. The critics gave mixed notices, with the British in particular not quite able to appreciate what David Montrose of *TLS: The Times Literary Supplement* called the "woolly tangle at the centre" (24 January 1992). Bell was disappointed that the hermetic subtext, based partly on Frances Yates's *Giordano Bruno and the Hermetic Tradition* (1964) as well as her *Art of Memory* (1966), seemed to have eluded many readers. Given the hybrid forms in which he works, such oversimplification is always a potential problem.

Save Me, Joe Louis (1993) encompasses both the North and the South, city and country, crime and redemption. The plot follows an unlikely duo, Charlie and Macrae, an educated drifter (from *Waiting for the End of the World*) and an AWOL misfit, respectively. They embark on a series of muggings in which they force their victims to withdraw money from automated teller machines. When the risk becomes too great in the city, they drift southward, picking up a confederate named Porter after a botched liquor-store holdup. They end up on Macrae's family farm, taking care of the livestock and land while tending to Macrae's ailing, near-blind father. As in *Soldier's Joy,* daily agricultural labor is good for the soul, though Bell is again too smart to strictly equate rural existence with the virtuous life. Racism and petty jealousies abide. The romantic interest emerges in the form of Macrae's elusive cousin Lacy. In Bell's fiction the women are active agents but nonetheless represent a shadowy salvation or damnation, a consummation devoutly to be wished and feared. The novel picked up several critical plaudits—including the comment "a remarkable read" from Crews, one of Bell's literary idols, in *The New York Times Book Review* (20 June 1993).

By then, Bell had settled into the niche of a critically acclaimed author with a select following. In order to advance, he needed to expand both his claim to attention and his audience. His concern over race relations led him to historical research, back to the slave revolution in Haiti, and to his magnum opus in 1995, *All Souls' Rising,* which was both a PEN/Faulkner and National Book Award finalist. Part of a projected trilogy, with a massive amount of research blended into the narrative through many voices, *All Souls' Rising* is that most difficult of forms, the large historical novel, in this case an attempt to make sense of the incidents surrounding the Haitian fight for independence. Such a multilayered narrative is too broad and various for any single outlook, and Bell shows the growing conflict through a variety of perspectives, from plantation owners to slaves. But the main viewpoint is that of Dr. Antoine Hébert, a newcomer to the island, who is as appalled and fascinated by the darkness as Joseph Conrad's Marlow. As the embodiment of eighteenth-century science and rationality, Hébert is an apt foil for the characters he meets as he penetrates deeper into Haiti. His antithesis is Riau, a rebel native who is guided by intuition.

On his way to the interior, Hébert encounters Arnaud, an aristocratic planter who beats and also sleeps with his slaves, as well as his wife, Claudine, who is capable of both awesome cruelty and altruism. The panoply of characters includes the brutal insurgent leader Choufleur, who orders people flayed alive; the jovial priest Père Bonne-chance, who has seriously compromised his vow of chastity; and Toussaint-Louverture, a black man who represents the main hope for balance in the midst of the horror. The events commence around 1791 during the first major uprisings. By the time they are over in 1804, the cane fields have been razed, and the earth is littered with mutilated corpses. Bell's scenes of destruction and creation, violence and voodoo, bring out a lyricism that seems almost worshipful. As Bell admitted in an unpublished interview: "Violence is a way to make dramatic points large and clear, and I am attracted (for nar-ratives) to situations where a moral issue can be portrayed, literally, as a matter of life and death." The critical reception was glowing, from John Vernon in *The New York Times Book Review* (29 October 1995) calling the novel both panoramic and iconic, to Ken Ringle at *The Washington Post* (28 November 1995) comparing it to William Styron's *Confessions of Nat Turner* (1967).

All Souls' Rising was a gamble, however, and in order to hedge his bets, Bell also wrote one of his more conventional novels, *Ten Indians* (1996), which came out soon afterward. *Ten Indians* does have some new material, namely a focus on domestic drama. The protagonist, Michael Devlin, is a child psychologist with a steady practice, a stable family life with his wife and daughter, a tae kwon do hobby, and a nagging discontent that he is ineffectual in the world. By now the Bell protagonist is more or less recognizable from book to book: self-aware up to a point, talented, and driven, with one or two weaknesses that involve drugs or alcohol. On the prodding of his tae kwon do teacher, Devlin opens a branch school in a crime-ridden section of Baltimore—learning only gradually that two rival gangs have signed up to be his students. Though the pace is fairly rapid, the concerns raised by *Ten Indians* are similar to those presented on a grander scale in *All Souls' Rising:* the problems of racism and other perceived inequities, and what it would take to heal such seemingly unclosable breaches. Given his Southern background, Bell is certainly sensitive to these problems, though as he pointed out in the Cronin interview, "Now we're coming into a time where national experience is able to serve up experiences of disenfranchisement of one kind or another to almost everyone, irrespective of region." Bell believes the force to change must come from within, from the will of individuals.

At times critics have accused Bell of overproduction (the kind of charge leveled at Joyce Carol Oates and John Updike); his response, however, is refreshingly down to earth: he produces so much, he claims, because he has had to depend on book royalties for a living. Bell is a working writer, one who takes only a weeklong break between books. In addition, he has turned out essays and reviews for such publications as *The Village Voice, The Philadelphia Inquirer, The London Standard,* and *The New York Times Book Review.* He has been commissioned to write screenplays from several of his novels, including a German version of *Straight Cut* called *Choc En Retour* (1993), the title deriving from Haitian dialect for a "shock in return" or boomerang effect (though Bell wrote the script in English). Many of his books have been translated into Dutch, Spanish, Japanese, German, and Danish.

From Bell's years of teaching fiction came a textbook for workshops, titled *Narrative Design: A Writer's Guide to Structure* (1997), in which he presents a series of

Page from the manuscript for Master of the Crossroads *(2000), Bell's second historical novel about Haiti and Toussaint-Louverture (Collection of Madison Smartt Bell)*

stories that demonstrate a blueprint for writing, from linear design and symmetry to tapping into unconscious processes. He likes teaching and believes, unlike some of his contemporaries, that much good writing can emanate from the workshop process. Though worried about pressures of conformity in the classroom, he compares writing skills to those learned in martial arts, noting: "Skills that have been *learned* consciously, through practice and rote repetition, are *deployed* unconsciously, intuitively, instinctively, without the stuttering delay required by a conscious decision." This prescription neatly links craft and imagination.

In 2000 came the second novel in the Haiti trilogy, *Master of the Crossroads*. Taking up where *All Souls' Rising* left off, the plot focuses more centrally on the former slave turned generalissimo, Toussaint-Louverture. Amid the shifting allegiances and brutal clashes of Haitian uprisings, Louverture is observed by characters as various as Claudine Arnaud; the former slave Riau, now a captain under Louverture, and Dr. Hébert, searching for his lover, Nanon, just four of many figures from the previous novel. The start of the novel shows Louverture some years hence, in 1802, imprisoned deep in a fortress. But the bulk of the novel takes place from 1793 on, when the colony of Saint Domingue was ripe for uprising, presenting Louverture with an array of dangerous choices. His very name, *l'ouverture,* or "the opening," represents just such a juncture, as does Legba, the voodoo god of the crossroads repeatedly mentioned.

Bell displays the same love of detail and penchant for violence as in the first Haiti novel, but never gratuitously, given a backdrop where death and mutilation are everyday events. On the other hand, discerning good from evil in such a complicated history is no easy task, and Bell's Louverture remains, as many critics have noted, an ambiguous figure.

Bell has also worked on nonfiction about Haiti from his travels in that country, starting in 1995. The manuscript, still in progress, is called "Soul in a Bottle." His last Haiti novel is tentatively titled "The Stone That the Builder Refused."

Just as *Ten Indians* came soon after the first of the Haiti novels, the comparatively lightweight novel *Anything Goes* (2002) was published not long after the second Haiti installment. An ensemble novel, *Anything Goes* is about the members of a band called Anything Goes (which is also the attitude of its players and the title from one of their songs). The band consists of the hard-living band leader, Perry; the guitarist and hopeful songwriter, Chris; Allston, the drummer, and the narrator, Jesse Melungeon, a bass player holding off repetitive-stress injury with a lot of painkillers. The novel ambles along from musical bars to drinking bars and back, filling in

background along the way, such as the broken home that Jesse came from. Plot complications come with the entrance of singer and siren Stella, attracting both Jesse and his estranged father.

With its backdrop of rock, pop, and blues, *Anything Goes* signals a return to music in Bell's fiction. In fact, the band's original songs were co-written by Bell and Wyn Cooper and put to music on a website at Goucher College: <http://faculty.goucher.edu/mbell/AnythingGoes/anththinggoesportal.htm.>. In the novel itself, the musical references can at times go on too long, as if Bell has to prove his credibility as a musician. The novel is best in its re-creation of a bar band's life, from seedy dives to road trips.

Along with his technique and vision, Bell has developed a tangible ideology. His causes also include an increasing concern for the environment and an antipathy to industrial society, which he feels makes us "irrevocably committed to global suicide by slow poisoning." And though not enthusiastic about New Age cults, he admits in "An Essay Introducing His Work in Rather a Lunatic Fashion" (1991), "We too have a crying need for some viable new mythology." In a 1994 interview with Mary Louise Weaks he spoke of "A universal eschatology that says we are living in the last days." Such beliefs invariably bleed into his fiction. Wherever they appear, in whatever plot that thickens around them, Bell's characters are instantly recognizable: the sensitive and compulsive, the talented but groping, the figures in the maelstrom—looking for some form of salvation.

Interviews:

Sybil Steinberg, "*PW* Interviews: Madison Smartt Bell," *Publishers Weekly,* 232 (11 December 1987): 45–46;

Robert Bradley, "An Interview with Madison Smartt Bell," *AWP Newsletter* (February 1989): 1–3, 5–6;

Mary Louise Weaks, "An Interview with Madison Smartt Bell," *Southern Review,* 30 (Winter 1994): 1–12;

Justin Cronin, "A Conversation with Madison Smartt Bell," *Four Quarters,* 9 (Spring 1995): 13–24;

Jack Stephens, "Madison Smartt Bell," *Bomb,* 73 (Fall 2000): 36–42.

References:

Randi Henderson, "A Flood of Fiction," *Baltimore Sun,* 24 March 1991, pp. H1, H6;

Bill Kent, "Going Straight," *Baltimore Magazine* (May 1989): 52–55, 110–113.

Papers:

An archive of Madison Smartt Bell's manuscripts and correspondence through 1993 is housed at the Firestone Library, Princeton University.

T. Coraghessan Boyle

(2 December 1948 –)

Bonnie Lyons
University of Texas at San Antonio

See also the Boyle entries in *DLB 218: American Short-Story Writers Since World War II, Second Series* and *DLB Yearbook 1986*.

BOOKS: *Descent of Man* (Boston: Little, Brown/Atlantic Monthly, 1979; London: Gollancz, 1979);

Water Music (Boston: Little, Brown, 1981; London: Gollancz, 1982);

Budding Prospects: A Pastoral (New York: Viking, 1984; London: Gollancz, 1984);

Greasy Lake & Other Stories (New York: Viking, 1985);

World's End (New York: Viking, 1987; London: Macmillan, 1988);

If the River Was Whiskey (New York: Viking, 1989);

East Is East (New York: Viking, 1990; London: Cape, 1991);

The Collected Stories of T. Coraghessan Boyle (London & New York: Granta, 1993);

The Road to Wellville (New York: Viking, 1993; London: Granta, 1993);

Without a Hero: Stories (New York: Viking, 1994; London: Granta, 1995);

The Tortilla Curtain (New York: Viking, 1995; London: Bloomsbury, 1995);

T. C. Boyle Stories: The Collected Stories of T. Coraghessan Boyle (New York: Viking, 1998);

Riven Rock (New York: Viking, 1998; London: Bloomsbury, 1998);

A Friend of the Earth (New York: Viking, 2000; London: Bloomsbury, 2000);

After the Plague: And Other Stories (New York: Viking, 2001; London: Bloomsbury, 2001);

Drop City (New York: Viking, 2003).

Much of the appeal of T. Coraghessan Boyle's novels and stories is in his creation of outrageous characters, bizarre situations, and deliberately inflated comparisons. Hip, erudite, and audacious, his fiction is widely praised for its black comedy, incongruous mixture of the mundane and the surreal, wildly inventive and intricate plots, manic energy, and dazzling wordplay. Although he

T. Coraghessan Boyle (photograph © 1995 by Pablo Campos; from the dust jacket for The Tortilla Curtain, *1995)*

has written a few pieces of realistic, psychologically probing fiction, almost all of his novels and stories have used comedy of one sort or another to serve moral purposes such as exposing greed, racism, and cultural insensitivity, satirizing contemporary foibles and obsessions, or deflating pomposity. Boyle has said that people devalue comic writing, which he defines as deadly serious; in an interview published in 1998 he pointed to Flannery O'Connor's "A Good Man is Hard to Find" (1955), which he called "a comic story in a desperate, frightening way."

Born Thomas John Boyle on 2 December 1948 in Peekskill, New York, the grandson of Irish immigrants, Boyle has suggested that the mad, language-obsessed part of him derives from his Irish ancestry. At seventeen he changed his middle name to Coraghessan (pronounced "kuh-RAGG-issun"), a name from his mother's side of the family. His father, a schoolbus driver, and his mother, a secretary, both died of complications from alcoholism before Boyle was thirty. Although his family did not have much money, Boyle was pampered and encouraged to obtain a good education. By his own report his youth was spent "hanging out" and taking a lot of drugs. He began writing in college with an absurdist one-act play about a young boy eaten by an alligator—except for his foot, to which his family builds a shrine in the living room. When the professor and class laughed and applauded, Boyle concluded writing was "a pretty good gig." After graduating from the State University of New York at Potsdam in 1968, Boyle taught high-school English for several years to keep from being drafted. During this period he published "The OD & Hepatitis RR or Bust" in *The North American Review* (Fall 1972) and, primarily on the basis of that story, was admitted into the University of Iowa Workshop. Once at the University of Iowa he began taking literature courses as well as creative-writing courses, earning his M.F.A. in 1974. He became a model student; in his words, "I grew up. Instead of cutting classes, I sat in the front row and took notes." This transformation was because he felt he had found what he was meant to do: for all his irreverence and outrageousness, Boyle is absolutely serious about his writing. He completed his Ph.D. in nineteenth- and early-twentieth-century British literature in 1977 but opted for a creative dissertation. This collection of short stories was later revised and published as *Descent of Man* (1979). Since 1977 Boyle has been a professor at the University of Southern California. In 1993 he moved from Los Angeles to a Frank Lloyd Wright house near Santa Barbara, from which he commutes to USC. He is married to Karen Kvashay, and the couple has three children.

Boyle's orange and black zebra-striped jacket (obtained at a Liberace garage sale), earcuff, new-wave clothes, bad-boy persona, and frequently shocking comments have provided him recognition that is unusual for a hard-working literary craftsman. A tremendous ham who loves attention and giving readings of his work, Boyle is well aware that flash attracts audiences, and he is intent upon being both the best writer he can be and as popular as possible. In this dual commitment he is not unlike Charles Dickens, whose work Boyle studied while earning his doctorate.

The two epigraphs to Boyle's first book, *Descent of Man*—the first from Franz Kafka (words spoken by a "free ape"), the second the one word "Ungowa!" from the 1939 Johnny Weissmuller movie *Tarzan Finds a Son* (1939)—suggest the range and resources of Boyle's stories, which include everything from spoofs of popular culture to learned parodies of various genres. Two of the best stories of the collection, the title story and "Heart of a Champion," involve animals, and like many satirical works remind readers of the nature of the body and the inescapable animal side of human beings. In "Heart of a Champion" the overly humanized, desexualized Lassie disappoints Timmy, her boy master, by her unexpected response to a predatory coyote: "instead of leaping at her adversary's throat, the collie prances up and stretches her nose out to him, her eyes soft as a leading lady's, round as a doe's." The female animal behaves like a female animal, while in "Descent of Man," the human female animal, a researcher, betrays her human lover for her subject, a genius chimpanzee who quotes William Butler Yeats and listens to Wolfgang Amadeus Mozart's *Don Giovanni* (1787). The genre parodies include "We Are Norsemen," an imitation of Old Norse bards, and "Green Hell," which lampoons factual accounts of plane crashes, works such as Piers Paul Read's *Alive: The Story of the Andes Survivors* (1974).

Boyle's first novel, *Water Music* (1981), intertwines the stories of two men's lives. The first is a fictional rogue, Ned Rise, an irrepressible picaresque hero from the London slums. The second is the historical figure Mungo Park, the Scottish explorer who led expeditions to Africa in 1795 and 1805. The upper-class Park and the lower-class Rise are opposite in social background but kindred rebels. The novel follows Park on his African explorations, which include complicated adventures with a variety of native Africans, in counterpoint with Rise's often disreputable or illegal adventures, such as running a sex show and robbing graves. The two men's lives come together during a grueling journey down the Niger River in 1805, from which Park, in historical fact, never returned.

While *Water Music* is historically informed, there is no attempt to make the reader forget he is reading a novel rather than experiencing reality or reading history. The plot flaunts melodramatic devices, including stupendous cliffhangers, complicated coincidences, and even miraculous resurrections—all reminiscent of similar delights in the works of eighteenth- and nineteenth-century novelists from Henry Fielding to Dickens. In an unapologetic "Apologia" Boyle announces that he has been deliberately anachronistic, inventing language and terminology and reshaping historical facts "with full and clear conscience." There are chapter titles such as "Oh Mama, Can This Really Be The End?" and even a recipe for baked stuffed camel, which advises one to dig a trench, bake two days, and serve with rice. *Water Music* offers what became hallmarks of Boyle's works, from deliciously gory descriptions to verbal acrobatics, delivered in a mixture of polysyllabic diction and current colloquialisms.

Reviews of Boyle's first novel mixed praise with criticism. Grove Kroger, in the *Library Journal* (15 November 1981), commented that "Boyle's invention flags at the end, and the explorer himself remains oddly insubstantial" but also claimed that Ned Rise was "one of contemporary fiction's most challenging creations" as a character. Alan Friedman in *The New York Times Book Review* (27 December 1981) asserted, "Hardly ever does the novel allow the reader to enter the world it creates. When bones are crushed or buttocks lacerated, when characters suffer (and, poor dears, how they suffer!) their sufferings seem for the most part contrived to elicit crocodile tears."

Budding Prospects: A Pastoral (1984), Boyle's second novel, stands apart from the rest of his novels because it is based on his friends' actual experiences, uses a first-person narrator, is relatively simple, and has a happy ending. Boyle said in the unpublished interview:

> After *Water Music* I was looking for something contemporary. *Budding Prospects* is a story that I knew well and was involved in and I just wanted to have some fun with the idea of the quotes—the American dream of getting up early and having a good scam and making your fortune. And in the case of the true story as in the fiction, it didn't work. That seems to be a wonderful comment on those ideas and forces you to reevaluate and reassess. As the hero does and as he did in real life.

Beginning with its dual epigraphs, from Benjamin Franklin's preface to his 1757 *Poor Richard Improved* ("Plough deep, while Sluggards sleep; and you shall have Corn to sell and to keep") and Arthur Miller's 1949 play, *Death of a Salesman* ("Why, boys, when I was seventeen I walked into the jungle, and when I was twenty-one I walked out. And by God I was rich"), the novel satirizes American get-rich-quick schemes and unbridled capitalism. The protagonist, Felix Nasmyth, describes himself in the first sentences of the novel: "I've always been a quitter. I quit the Boy Scouts, the glee club, the marching band. . . . I got married, separated, divorced. Quit smoking, quit jagging, quit red meat. . . . About the only thing I didn't give up on was the summer camp." In the last pages of the novel this self-proclaimed quitter, formerly in flight from stability and fatherhood, steadfastly returns to a future of hard physical work, emotional commitment to a woman, and the intention "maybe even—if things went well—to plant a little seed."

Felix is recruited by a devious schemer, Vogelsang, into a million-dollar scheme to grow thirty acres of marijuana on a remote farm in the mountains. Convinced that money is the major goal in life and that their scheme is viable, Nasmyth and two friends spend hilariously grueling months fighting off all kinds of threats to their enterprise: rain, rats, fire, bears, even blackmail. Their original

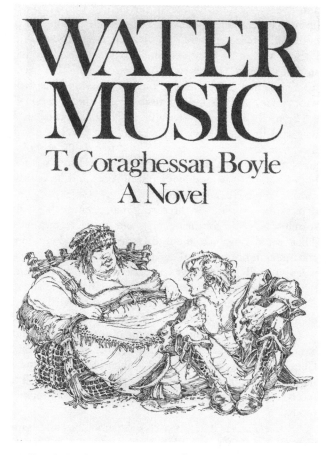

Dust jacket for Boyle's first novel (1981), in which his rogue protagonist encounters the explorer Mungo Park on an ill-fated African expedition (Richland County Public Library)

expected profits shrink as their comic disasters increase. En route the novel exposes the violent redneck subculture of California as well as cynical hippie drifters. Although the ending is economically disastrous for the narrator, it is one of Boyle's rare happy endings, as Felix seems headed for a genuinely good and satisfying life. Boyle has said he gave his pastoral *Budding Prospects* a positive conclusion because he was following the true story, but that in general he resists happy endings both because readers expect them and because they make literature sentimental pablum: "There are never happy endings. They are too simple, too easy. It doesn't work that way."

Boyle again demonstrated his cultural range and versatility in the fifteen stories in *Greasy Lake & Other Stories* (1985), with premises that include everything from Russian high culture to Elvis impersonators. In "The Overcoat II" Boyle updates Nikolai Gogol's classic, setting it in contemporary Moscow consumer hell: "He'd been standing in one line or another since 5:30, when he left the ministry where he worked as a file clerk, and all he had to show for it was eight russet potatoes, half a dozen onions, and twenty-six tubes of Czechoslovakian toothpaste he'd been lucky enough to blunder across while looking for a bottle of rubbing alcohol." In "Rupert Beersley and the Beggar Master of Sivani-Hoota" Boyle spoofs detective stories, while in "The New Moon Party" and "The Hector Quesadilla Story" he combines politics and baseball with fantasy and mythology, respectively. "Ike and Nina" celebrates the imaginary love affair of Nikita Khrushchev's wife and President Dwight D. Eisenhower. While all of these are comic in various ways, the frequently anthologized title story is a departure from most of Boyle's work both because of its autobiographical roots and its darkly serious tone. A coming-of-age story, "Greasy Lake" depicts the evening of three suburban teenage boys in search of an outlet for their energy and frustrated passions. Their wanderings take them to Greasy Lake, where they encounter more and darker adventure than they anticipated, including a ravaged car, battered faces, and a dead biker. A would-be bad boy at the beginning of the story, the narrator is distinctly different at the end; when a girl offers a good time of sex and drugs, saying, "Hey, you want to party, you want to do some of these with me and Sarah?" the chastened narrator is unable even to speak. Generally acclaimed for its wide range of narrative techniques and voices, this second story collection also received praise as serious social commentary in a comic mode.

World's End (1987), Boyle's most ambitious and complicated novel, won the PEN/Faulkner Award for fiction in 1988. The novel traces the intertwined fates of three families living in Peterskill, a Hudson Valley community similar to Boyle's own hometown, Peekskill, New York. With similar patterns of action and emotions occurring in both the seventeenth and twentieth centuries, the novel depicts the conflicts between three families and their descendants: the Van Brunts, a Dutch family of tenant farmers; the Van Warts, overbearing landlords who own the Van Brunt farm; and the Mohonks, displaced Kitchawank Indians. Each of the three families embodies and passes along a repeated trait: for the Van Brunts, it is betrayal; for the Mohonks, it is revenge; for the Van Warts, it is abuse of power.

The twentieth-century protagonist, Walter Van Brunt, investigates his family history, especially that of his father, a left-wing political activist who betrayed his own family and ideals by secretly helping rabidly reactionary mobs attack communists and blacks at a Paul Robeson performance. Walter himself makes a traitorous and eventually disastrous alliance with Depeyster Van Wart, while a descendant of the Mohonks foils Depeyster's desire for a male heir by impregnating Depeyster's wife. Boyle has called *World's End* "a kind of rhapsody on the idea that what we inherit from our parents may preclude the possibility of free will. That there are certain things in the genes

that might be deterministic. . . . Walter Van Brunt certainly winds up being a victim of his biology. If you trace back through history to the characters that preceded him, it's all replicated in a way."

Much of the response to *World's End* was positive; for example, in *The New York Times Book Review* (27 September 1987) Benjamin DeMott praised the novel for providing "space for moral and emotional as well as esthetic reality, producing a narrative in which passion, need and belief breathe with striking force and freedom." Not all of the critical reception to *World's End* was positive, however. In a review in *The New York Times* on 23 September 1987, Michiko Kakutani complained that "there's something mechanical and cumbersome about Mr. Boyle's orchestration of time past and time present" and that the proliferation of characters is such "that we never really get a chance to know them as recognizable individuals."

A stock trader who meets Satan, a talking statue of the Virgin Mary, a public-relations man hired to raise Ayatollah Khomeini's image, and a man forced to wear a full-body condom by his absurdly health-conscious girlfriend all appear in Boyle's third story collection, *If the River Was Whiskey* (1989). Although this volume has some of the zany characters and hyperbolic situations that are Boyle's trademark, it differs from the earlier two collections in its greater topicality, its more insistent connections to the immediate period during which it was written. In a 1998 interview Boyle explained that during the three-year period he spent writing *World's End* he "had been storing up a lot of material. Everything that happened every day in society, everything that happened to me, all the ideas I had to put on hold."

As in earlier collections, several stories have literary sources, including "Me Cago en la Leche (Robert Jordan in Nicaragua)," which spoofingly updates the life of Ernest Hemingway's protagonist from *For Whom the Bell Tolls* (1940), and "The Devil and Irv Cherniske," which satirizes American materialism in an homage rewriting of Washington Irving's "The Devil and Tom Walker" (1824). But the story that received the most attention is "If the River Was Whiskey," a poignant father/son tale that ends the collection. During a summer month at a lakeside cabin a troubled, alcoholic man attempts to become closer to his son, Tiller. Despite these efforts, on the last night the father, who is "beyond drunk," realizes that his wife is leaving him, "which meant that Tiller was leaving him." Although he tries to convince himself that he does not care and that the effort to connect had not been his own idea in the first place, his dream reveals his anguish:

he was out in the boat with Tiller. The wind was blowing, his hands were shaking, he couldn't light a cigarette. Tiller was watching him. He pulled at the oars and nothing happened. Then all of a sudden they were

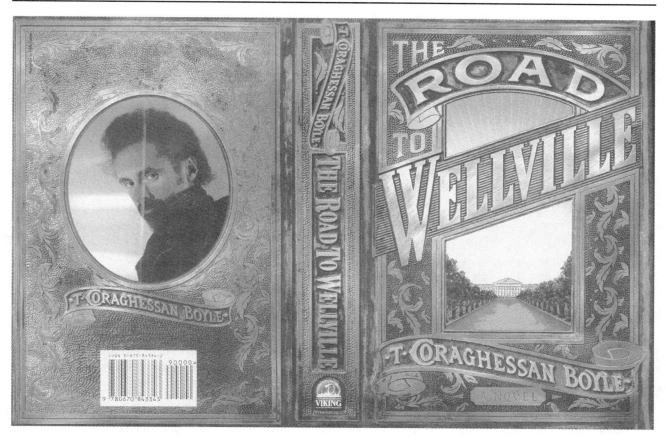

Dust jacket for Boyle's 1993 novel, about the Michigan sanitarium run by Dr. John Harvey Kellogg
in the early twentieth century (Richland County Public Library)

going down, the boat sucked out from under them, the water icy and black, beating in on them as if it were alive. Tiller called out to him. He saw his son's face, saw him going down, and there was nothing he could do.

Elizabeth Benedict commented in *The New York Times Book Review* (14 May 1989), "I know of no other story by Mr. Boyle that is nearly as powerful or poignant" as "If the River Was Whiskey," and many critics have also wished Boyle would write more stories or novels in this vein. But Boyle has said that "There are other writers who write well in that mode," while only he could have written a story like "The Miracle of Ballinspittle" and that if he is "unique in any way it's probably in that sort of story."

Boyle's fourth novel, *East Is East* (1990), was inspired by a newspaper article from a friend who dropped by while Boyle was writing *World's End* and announced he had found Boyle a subject for his next book. In *East Is East* Hiro (hero) Tanaka, a twenty-year-old Japanese seaman, jumps ship off the Georgia coast, swims ashore, and tries to survive as an illegal alien. He is in flight from Japan, where he has been shunned because he is a half-breed: his American father deserted his Japanese mother, a bar hostess who

eventually drowned herself in shame. Hiro arrives full of illusions about America, derived from movies and popular music, and also with a set of samurai ethics as interpreted by twentieth-century Japanese writer Yukio Mishima. Even before Hiro sets foot on shore he collides with Ruth Dershowitz, the other main character, a "Jewish American Princess" (and thus another kind of JAP) who calls herself La Dershowitz. An intensely ambitious and envious would-be writer, Ruth is staying at an artists' colony, Thanatopsis House, on Tupelo Island, largely because she is the lover of the owner's son rather than because of her writing skill. Other writers at the colony, all of whom are satirized, include a man who specializes in "urban Jewish angst," and Ruth's main competitor, Jane Shine, a phony but successful schemer. During Hiro's strenuous physical and psychological trials he hides out in the swamp, in Ruth's cabin, and in the mansion of a dotty old dowager who mistakes him for Japanese American conductor Seiji Ozawa. His final destination on this increasingly dark journey is the swamp of all swamps, the Okefenokee. Ruth's comic parallel tortures are her enemy's glorious public reading at the writers' colony followed by her own dismal reading, which puts some of her audience to sleep. At the end of the novel Hiro honorably commits suicide, while

Ruth, who at first protects him, now uses him as a springboard to a career in journalism, thus selling out personally and professionally.

As is often the case with Boyle's work, critical response to *East Is East* varied greatly. On one hand, in *The New York Times Book Review* (9 September 1990) Gail Godwin praised the novel, calling it "irresistible" and "Boyle's finest yet," adding that "It has the vital language and inventiveness of plot that we have come to expect from him." On the other hand, Oliver Conant suggested in the *New Leader* (12–26 November 1990) that Boyle "should do more with his considerable gifts than squander them on cynical conceits like *East Is East*," while in the November–December 1990 issue of *West Coast Review of Books* Tom Hymes observed that "Only Hiro achieves depth and pathos, and those in only the last few pages."

Set in 1907 and 1908, *The Road to Wellville* (1993) provided Boyle a vehicle for an oblique attack on some dominant modern idiocies–ridiculous self-improvement plans and quack health schemes. The novel (later made into a movie starring Anthony Hopkins) takes place in Battle Creek, Michigan, at the Battle Creek Sanitarium, known as the San to its followers, who historically included in later years Henry Ford, Thomas Edison, and William Howard Taft. Heading the sanitarium is a "man with a mission," Dr. John Harvey Kellogg, a believer in colonic irrigation, vegetarian biologic living, and sexual abstinence. The amazingly popular sanitarium "cures" feature a hideous diet of nut butters, grapes, milk, and mysterious unpleasant substances, plus multiple daily enemas, and special baths during which an electric current moves through a patient's body while his hands and feet are placed in water.

Kellogg's main antagonist is George, one of Kellogg's many adopted children, who despite all of his father's efforts is stubbornly unimproved. Physically unhealthy and repulsive, George resists his father's plans and in the wild climactic scene sets fire to one of the buildings, destroys his father's precious fecal samples, and looses Lillian, the chimp, and Fawn, the pure white vegetarian wolf, on him. Dr. Anus or Dr. Shit, as George unfondly calls him, momentarily falters–"for the first time in his physiologic life, he felt his faith flag"–but he reminds himself that he is "no ordinary man" and in a typical Boyle climax pushes George into a vat of macadamia butter, "baptizing him, purifying him," and also drowning him.

Besides the doctor and his son, the novel follows the actions of two other primary characters. The first is a patient, Will Lightbody, who comes to the San both because his wife, Eleanor, is a health nut and because she has inadvertently ruined Will's health by trying to cure his drinking habit with a potion containing opium. The other important character is a would-be capitalist, Charlie Ossin-ing, who comes to Battle Creek to seek his fortune via a new cereal called Per-Fo (perfect food). Charlie's business adventures and Will's medical and marital adventures include arrest, last-minute escapes, physical torments, and sexual suffering. The novel closes with a coda in which readers learn that the only thing that brought down the sanitarium was the Great Depression and that Charlie becomes a prosperous philanthropist having invented Per-To, the perfect tonic, containing "'Celeriac, Gentian, Black Cohosh, True & False Unicorn Life & Pleurisy Root'–in a forty-percent-alcohol solution ('Added Solely as a Solvent and Preservative')."

Without a Hero: Stories (1994), Boyle's fourth collection, continues his mix of mostly satiric, wild stories and an occasional more realistic, psychological kind. Two of the best stories, "Big Game" and "Filthy With Things," are sharp exposures of yuppie excess, while "Sitting on Top of the World," which closes the collection, is a rather sweet love story of sorts.

Following his pattern of counterpoint and clash between opposites as in *East Is East,* Boyle's sixth novel, *The Tortilla Curtain* (1995), depicts the intersecting lives of two couples living in Topanga Canyon, Los Angeles: Delaney Mossbacher, a liberal nature writer and self-styled pilgrim, and his wife, Kyra, a hotshot real estate saleswoman; and Candido Rincon, an undocumented Mexican pursuing the American dream of a better life while living literally hand to mouth in the canyon with his young, pregnant wife, America. The opposites first meet when Delaney, driving his Acura with its personalized license plate ("Pilgrim"), accidentally hits Candido. From that first collision the novel traces the contrasting lives of the two couples.

The desperate lives of the Mexican couple are depicted with compassion and unnerving realistic detail as they struggle simply to survive. Theirs is a life of hunger, intimidation, and victimization, of brutal, underpaid, dangerous work for which they are pitifully grateful. While the Rincons have barely enough food to survive, the Mossbachers live an indulgent existence and watch their diets. The Mossbachers' primary social concerns are recycling and nature preservation; to the Mossbachers' neighbors, people such as the Rincons are at best invisible, at worst perceived as similar to coyotes, menacing threats to the newly gated subdivision, Arroyo Blanco. While the Arroyo Blanco residents fear people such as the Rincons, one of their own accepted residents, Dominick Flood, is revealed as a more serious, unrecognized economic threat with his white-collar crime. Man-caused and natural catastrophes, fire and flood, provide the climactic plot developments.

While writing *Tortilla Curtain,* Boyle anticipated that politically correct reviewers would fault him for daring to appropriate the reality of people radically unlike him; in his words, "how can I presume to write about Mexicans." However, his depiction of those characters has been admired. For example, in *The New York Times Book Review* (3 September 1995) Scott Spencer praised this aspect of *Tortilla Curtain,* saying it "adds to his fictional range an openhearted compassion for those whom society fears and reviles." Boyle's characterization of the rich white couple has been criticized instead, for asking the reader to take seriously characters who are depicted with contempt. Spencer attacked Boyle for being "the most contemptuous of our well-known novelists," a negative response to Boyle's consciously comic, satiric impulse. Calling *The Tortilla Curtain* "comic by definition only," Boyle explained, "you probably won't laugh out loud but you will know that it is not absolutely naturalistic; it's not played straight. There is something slightly askew there." This satirical impulse, which leads Boyle to introduce Delaney on the opening page as "a liberal humanist with an unblemished driving record and a freshly waxed Japanese car with personalized plates," made some critics once again accuse Boyle of creating flat characters with whom readers cannot identify or sympathize.

Boyle's next novel, *Riven Rock* (1998), like *The Road to Wellville* and *Water Music,* combines historical figures and invented characters, and like *The Road to Wellville* is set in the early years of the twentieth century. In this novel the real people are Stanley McCormick, the insane son of the multimillionaire inventor of the reaper, and his wife, Katherine Dexter, the first female science graduate of the Massachusetts Institute of Technology, who became a committed suffragette and promoter of birth control. Shortly after their seemingly enviable union, Stanley is diagnosed as a schizophrenic and sexual maniac. Despite all the best psychiatric care money can buy, he remains uncured and virtually imprisoned in a family estate called Riven Rock in California, locked away in an all-male world since he loves women "with an incendiary passion that was like hate, that was indistinguishable from hate."

The novel depicts Stanley's decades in his gilded asylum and Katherine's steadfast loyalty to her husband interspersed with flashbacks to their earlier lives. Boyle carefully prevents the reader from reducing Stanley's mental problems to any one cause: madness runs in his family; his mother was domineering and antisexual; his sister was both seductive and mentally ill; and the entire upper-class culture was puritanical. As in other novels, Boyle counterpoints the well-known historical figures with more ordinary fictional characters. By depicting the less extreme love-hate relationships with women of Eddie O'Kane, Stanley's Irish male nurse, the novel effectively makes the theme universal and suggests, as D. M. Thomas observed in *The New York Times Book Review* (8 February 1998), "The male of the species is indeed a riven rock."

Dust jacket for Boyle's 1995 novel, which contrasts the lives of a wealthy white couple and a struggling Mexican couple in Los Angeles (Richland County Public Library)

Responses to *Riven Rock* were mixed. Thomas called Stanley "a memorable character" and the youthful Katherine "a touching creation" whose "personality traits are beautifully interwoven with the spirit of America's Age of Innocence." He concluded that "the book is filled with good writing and richly observed scenes; it has humanity and humor in abundance." But he also faulted the novel for "lack of risk-taking in terms of literary form," for being "traditional and realist." In the 20 January 1998 *New York Times,* Michiko Kakutani argued that the novel once again proved Boyle unable to "create a sympathetic, three-dimensional character and tell a story that engages feelings other than laughter, horror, superiority or contempt."

Set in an ecologically disastrous 2025 on the California estate of a rock star who collects animals to preserve genetic possibility, *A Friend of the Earth* (2000) focuses on groundskeeper Tyrone Tierwater, an aging ecoterrorist, whose former wife, Andrea, suddenly reappears. First-person chapters alternate with third-person chapters set in the 1980s and 1990s to depict Tyrone's progression, inspired by Andrea, from ordinary American consumer to impassioned ecodefender. While full of wildly gory descriptions of extreme weather conditions and biological chaos written in Boyle's signature over-the-top style, the novel also presents with quiet poignancy the accidental death of Tyrone's daughter, Sierra, who falls from a giant redwood in which she was living. Tyrone's solutions to ecological destruction are intemperate and often downright misanthropic, but the environmental passions of the novel are taken quite seriously.

Reviews of the novel were mixed. In *The New York Times* (8 October 2000) Albert Mobilio complained about "slack plotting, motiveless characters and unfruitful time shifting" in the novel; he concluded, "both global catastrophe and one family's painful struggle remain unaffecting." On the other hand, in *The Los Angeles Times Book Review* (10 September 2000), Eric Zency praised the novel: "Part antic comedy, part ecological intelligencer, part heartfelt plaint, *A Friend of the Earth* is a comic novel on grievous themes, a serious exploration of tragic truths." Similarly, Kakutani in *The New York Times* (3 October 2000) asserted that Boyle's novel "manages to be funny and touching, antic and affecting, all at the same time."

After the Plague: And Other Stories (2001), which won the Southern California Booksellers Association Award for best fiction title in 2002, explores a generally dark world of aberrant humans and destruction of all sorts, from personal to ecological. Boyle's opening establishes the theme: "After the plague—it was some sort of Ebola mutation passed from hand to hand and nose to nose like the common cold—life was different." Praising Boyle for the thematic maturity and somber tone of this collection, Jonathan Levi in *The Los Angeles Times Book Review* (30 September 2001) concluded that there is no "finer virtuoso of the American language" than Boyle.

Boyle's next novel, *Drop City* (2003), brings together in 1970 two exemplars of the American spirit—California hippie communards and tough individualist loners trying to live off the land in Alaska. After traveling across the country, the newly self-named Star and Pan join Norm Sender's commune north of San Francisco. When local authorities hassle them, the commune heads north to Alaska to live in a deserted cabin owned by Norm's uncle. In Alaska they encounter Sess Harder, his new wife, Pamela, and other Alaskans homesteading in the wilderness. En route to the violent climax, the excesses and illusions of both groups are exposed. For example, the hippies' dogma of free love is unmasked as denying women the ability to say no, and their supposed lack of sexual possessiveness is exposed as a total sham. Both the hippies and the Alaskan homesteaders are depicted realistically, with positive and negative characters in each group.

Neither completely satirical nor nostalgic, *Drop City* is a convincing evocation of a crucial period of American history and of perennial American types of dreamers. A glowing evaluation in the *Kirkus Review* (March 2003) concluded that the novel is "Probably the fullest picture of the hippie culture of the late '60s since Marge Piercy's early fiction, and one of Boyle's best." While criticizing the most negative character in the novel as being "so one-dimensional he might as well be named Sergeant Evil" and saying that the ending "feels hurried, lopped off," Dwight Garner in *The New York Times Book Review* (23 February 2003) generally praised the novel as "the best, and surely the wooliest, book about that era's communal living and back-to-the-earth movements." He suggested that "in its own sly way, this may be his most affecting and emotionally complex novel since *World's End*." In particular, Garner argued that previous criticism about Boyle's failure to provide "characters we're actually persuaded to feel anything about" is not true in *Drop City*.

In mid January 2003 Boyle said that he was one-third to one-half done with a new novel, "The Inner Circle." It is set in Bloomington, Indiana, from 1939 to 1956, and centers on Dr. Alfred C. Kinsey's sex researches.

Boyle has been hailed as one of the most imaginative contemporary American novelists, and his work enjoys wide popularity. Critical response, however, has been consistently mixed. His novels are frequently faulted for lack of psychological depth and for failure to create intensely realized, complicated characters. Nonetheless, even his harshest critics, such as Kakutani, concede that "When it comes to pitch-black humor, Grand Guignol slapstick and linguistic acrobatics, T. Coraghessan Boyle is a master of his domain."

Interviews:

David Stanton, "T. Coraghessan Boyle," *Poets & Writers Magazine,* 18 (January–February 1990): 29–34;

Elizabeth Adams, "An Interview with T. Coraghessan Boyle," *Chicago Review,* 37 (1991): 51–63;

Bonnie Lyons and Bill Oliver, "Entertainments and Provocations," in *Passion and Craft: Conversations with Notable Writers,* edited by Lyons and Oliver (Urbana: University of Illinois Press, 1998): 42–59.

References:

Theo D'Haen, "The Return of History and the Minorization of New York: T. Coraghessan Boyle and Richard Russo," *Revue Française d'Etudes Americaines,* 17 (1994): 393–403;

Krishna Baldev Vaid, "Franz Kafka Writes to T. Coraghessan Boyle," *Michigan Quarterly Review,* 35 (Summer 1996): 533–547.

Michael Chabon

(24 May 1963 –   )

Patrick Meanor
State University of New York at Oneonta

BOOKS: *The Mysteries of Pittsburgh* (New York: Morrow, 1988; London: Hodder & Stoughton, 1988);
A Model World and Other Stories (New York: Morrow, 1991; London: Hodder & Stoughton, 1991);
Wonder Boys (New York: Villard, 1995; London: Fourth Estate, 1995);
Werewolves in Their Youth (New York: Random House, 1999; London: Fourth Estate, 1999);
The Amazing Adventures of Kavalier & Clay (New York: Random House, 2000; London: Fourth Estate, 2000);
Summerland (New York: Talk Miramax Books/Hyperion Books for Children, 2002; London: Collins, 2002).

Michael Chabon (photograph by Patricia Williams; from the dust jacket for Summerland, *2002)*

Few contemporary American fiction writers begin their literary careers with such public notoriety as Michael Chabon gained with his best-selling first novel, *The Mysteries of Pittsburgh* (1988), which made him wildly successful at the age of twenty-four. Though he has been grouped with other popular young authors in their twenties, such as Bret Easton Ellis, Tama Janowitz, and Jay McInerney, Chabon's work could never be mistaken for their consciously minimalistic style, dark subject matter, and social criticism, or their pessimistic view of the materialistic downside of the American Dream. Chabon himself feels he shares little with the so-called literary Brat Pack: "I never thought I had any connection with 'the usual suspects'; but I suppose that youth was the main handle, an inevitable handle. I just didn't pay much attention to it. I was 23. I thought in terms of what I had in common with Cheever, Nabokov or Flaubert when they were 23. I had high aims" (*Publishers Weekly,* 10 April 1995). Many critics have characterized Chabon's writing as elegant, vividly descriptive, polished, and sophisticatedly fluid, placing his work much closer to that of writers such as John Updike, John Cheever, or even F. Scott Fitzgerald.

Chabon (pronounced shay-bahn) was born in Washington, D.C., on 24 May 1963. His father, Robert, is a physician, lawyer, and hospital administrator; his mother, Sharon, is a retired lawyer. Chabon graduated from the University of Pittsburgh with a B.A. in English in 1984 and earned an M.F.A. at the University of California, Irvine, in 1987, where he worked with novelist and critic Donald Heiney (MacDonald Harris). He also married poet Lollie Groth in 1987. After he won a short-story contest with *Mademoiselle* in that same year, he wrote his master's thesis, *The Mysteries of Pittsburgh;* his adviser, Heiney, was so impressed that he sent the manuscript to Mary Evans, a literary agent at the Virginia Barber Agency in New York City. Evans sold the book to William Morrow Publishers for $155,000 at a private auction—one of the highest figures ever paid for a first novel by a virtually unknown author.

The Mysteries of Pittsburgh made Chabon famous in the highly competitive world of New York publishing. It became a commercial best-seller praised by most members of the critical and academic establishments. Not only were the characters fully and humanly developed, but also the tone of the novel combined humor with the bittersweet poignance of newly discovered romantic love. Most importantly, though, its themes were relevant and contemporary: family conflict, sexual identity, love, the nature of friendship, the role of the "underworld" (both actual and mythical), the fictive roles that the protagonist and his friends consciously and/or unconsciously embody and enact, and, most crucially, the function of memory and nostalgia in their lives. All of these themes culminate in a major epiphanic moment at the conclusion of the novel as Art Bechstein confronts the complex and troubling nature of his personal identity; that is, who he was and what he has become.

One of the most appealing aspects of *The Mysteries of Pittsburgh* is that it is clearly a coming-of-age novel, a bildungsroman in the tradition of Fitzgerald's *This Side of Paradise* (1920), J. D. Salinger's *The Catcher in the Rye* (1951), McInerney's *Bright Lights, Big City* (1984), and Ellis's *Less Than Zero* (1985). The plot centers on Art Bechstein, a recent graduate of the University of Pittsburgh, in the last summer of his youthful innocence. Art simultaneously discovers and defines the most troubling mysteries of his life, all of which become the major themes of the novel. The book is also, according to the critic Douglas Fowler, one of the few good novels "about American college undergraduates, a literary feat of no small magnitude." Chabon structures the novel in the mythic form of the fall of a naive young man from innocence to experience, or from ignorance to knowledge. However, Art Bechstein must enter the painful chaos of the fallen world—that is, the adult world—so that he may begin to define himself as a human being.

Chabon structures *The Mysteries of Pittsburgh* into twenty-three chapters, each with a title that encapsulates its thematic content, summarizes its action, or delineates its characters' individuality. Proper names help the reader understand characters in greater depth and locate them within a literary, historical, and/or mythic context. Chabon frequently uses Cheever's favorite fictional technique, "mythologizing the commonplace," in helping the reader to uncover a particular character's deeper significance. Art Bechstein's first and last names intimate an Arthurian subtext, a prelapsarian world: Pittsburgh as Camelot. Parsing the name Bechstein mythically, and etymologically, reveals more than a casual connection to Arthurian Grail matters.

"Becher" in German means "cup, beaker, goblet, or chalice"; and "stein" is the German word for "stone, rock, precious stone, or gem." Both names allude to Western Europe's most ancient literary and mythic narrative: the quest journey for the Holy Grail, an object that is usually depicted as a chalice or cup. But in its pre-Christian manifestations, the Grail is often a rock, stone, or precious gem.

Art's father, Joe "the Egg" Bechstein, is an important Mafia figure in Pittsburgh and, as such, is literally the king of the underworld, but also mythically, Hades, King of the Underworld. Art's homosexual lover is Arthur Lecomte, whose surname means both "count" and "Count," reinforcing the Arthurian grail connections also embedded in Art's name. Arthur is a delicately beautiful young man who becomes, mythically, the tempter, a male Eve figure.

One of Art Bechstein's major emotional crises in the novel is over his troubling bisexuality, which follows a cyclic pattern: his affair with Arthur alternates with an affair with a beautiful young woman named Phlox. Early in the novel Art identifies another major mystery or secret he must unravel: "I had, after years of searching, finally discovered the nature of my father's work . . . so I came to associate it with shame, and with the advent of adulthood."

Arthur introduces Art to Phlox, whom he had noticed earlier at the entrance to the library. The word "phlox" is the name of a particularly vivid flower—flame-colored, with apposite leaves and flowers. The word comes from the Greek and means both "flame" and "wallflower." Cognates of the etymological root of the word include "shine, flash, burn, and white," all of which suggest the mythical White Goddess, who functions as both a temptress and fatal woman, roles that Phlox embodies throughout the novel. Arthur then prepares Art to meet the mysterious Cleveland Arning, whose reputation he had heard about earlier in the novel: "They had spoken of nearly nothing but his exploits." However, Art becomes aware that while Cleveland's girlfriend, Jane, and Arthur speak of Cleveland as a kind of demigod, his social status had recently been tarnished: "he had fallen, or was falling, or they were all on their way down. They hadn't said it, but I saw it in their fancies, the great epic, the time when Cleveland and Arthur had been two and angelic and fast, was long gone." Art feels that he has entered that lost or fallen world, "at the start of the first summer of my new life, and they tell me that I've come in late and missed everything."

In chapters 8 and 9 Art begins a steamy sexual affair with Phlox, and her role as the temptress is made even clearer. It becomes evident that both Art and his friends are fulfilling roles, consciously or unconsciously; Cleveland revels in his role as the outsider, "Evil Incarnate," resident beatnik, and petty criminal. In chapter 11, "Sex and Violence," Cleveland reveals details of his literary models and his family background. He tells Art about his mother's suicide and his psychiatrist father's hidden life as a homosexual, the ostensible reason for his wife's suicide. But Cleveland's greatest ambition is to assume some role in the Mafia, and he wants Art to help him attain that position. Art resolutely refuses to aid him in any way. However, one of the most anxious moments of the novel is when Cleveland somehow manages to meet Art's father and asks to play a greater role in the underworld—a request that, in effect, seals Cleveland's fate.

In one scene, as Art and Phlox discuss the mystery of Art's mother's death, Patti Page's 1950s hit "Old Cape Cod" is playing on the radio, and Art remarks on how moved he is by it: "This song always kills me." When Phlox asks him why, he reveals one of the most important themes of the novel, one that uncovers the melancholic nature of Art's permanent response to life: "Oh, I don't know. Nostalgia. It makes me feel nostalgia for a time I never even knew. I wasn't even alive." Fowler points to this concept as one of the unifying themes that pervades Chabon's novels and stories: "Perhaps not since the high point of J. D. Salinger's career . . . has a writer of Chabon's fluent gracefulness represented so much nostalgia making melancholy the affluent young. And everywhere in Chabon's fiction there is a valedictory sense of seeing from the outside those emotions that seem to be experienced from the inside only once." Certainly, Art's pervasive sense of nostalgia constitutes the core of his experience of the "fallen world," or the "wasteland" that he now consciously identifies.

Chabon's mythical allusions increase substantially in the last third of the novel, demonstrating that mythologizing the commonplace allows the reader to interpret a narrative on several levels at once. Though *The Mysteries of Pittsburgh* is a story about the painful difficulties of growing up, it is also a story about a Freudian "family romance." When Phlox and Art feud over his friendship with Arthur, Art returns to Arthur, who lives in the Hades-like Shadyside, an actual neighborhood in Pittsburgh. After some irrelevant small talk, the two men fall into bed and engage in passionate sexual activity. One of Art's most agonizing mysteries is revealed as he and his gay alter ego begin a painful but passionate affair, through which Art may begin to understand the desires and needs of his true bisexual nature. For the next several chapters Art's affair with Phlox winds down when she suspects that Art and Arthur are lovers. Phlox's role as "fatal woman" takes on new and alarming dimensions. She sends a vicious letter to Art condemning his homosexuality, which exposes the depth of Phlox's homophobia.

The dramatic conclusion of the novel begins with the self-destructive demise of Cleveland Arning. The chapter titled "The Beast That Ate Cleveland" opens prophetically as Art interprets the signs of Cleveland's chosen destiny: "I imagine it was shortly before dinnertime on the twenty-third of August that Cleveland reentered the world of his earliest childhood, intent on doing it harm." The most extreme form that nostalgia can take is for its victim to attempt either to regenerate or destroy his childhood. Cleveland is so desperate for money that he plans to return to his home neighborhood, Fox Chapel, and rob a wealthy household. After Cleveland steals some valuable jewels, he is shocked that the police are almost immediately on his trail. He suspects Art's father tipped off the police. Cleveland stops at Art's for help, insisting that Art accompany him to his favorite visionary location, the Cloud Factory, so he may hide the jewels there. Art tries to call his father to help Cleveland, but Joe refuses to accept the call. As the police arrive, Art is taken into custody just as Cleveland scales the summit of the Cloud Factory: "In that one long second before he lost his footing and fell head over heels over head, the spotlight hit him strangely, and he threw a brief, enormous shadow against the perfect clouds, and the hair seemed to billow out from the shadow's head like a black banner." Cleveland's fall from the Cloud Factory constitutes the most dramatic moment of the novel. Psychologically, Cleveland's fall destroys all of Art's illusions about his own family.

Even though Cleveland is dead, Art continues to treat him as a spiritual mentor, a father figure, because Art has rejected his own treacherous father. Art resists arrest and is hospitalized after being severely beaten by the police. In this wounded condition he asks the most momentous questions about the most troubling mysteries of his life. He asks his uncle what really happened to his mother, because he now suspects that she was murdered in place of his father in a mob conflict years before. With a nurse's help he makes his escape from the prison-like hospital. When he returns to Arthur, he discovers that his father's thugs have threatened Arthur's life if he does not leave Pittsburgh immediately. The police had found Phlox's antigay letter on Cleveland's body (Art had given it to him earlier) and handed it over to Joe. Art and Arthur decide to flee to Spain to try to begin a new life. Arthur leaves first to escape the thugs, and Art plans to meet him there later.

In the last few pages of the novel, Art explains how the events of his last undergraduate summer have radically transformed him. The "mysteries" of the title were, for the most part, revealed because of his friends and lovers. But Art's most important transformation

Dust jacket for Chabon's first novel, a critical and popular success published in 1988 (Richland County Public Library)

came out of his utter rejection of his father and his destructive underworld. One of the major transforming experiences in most coming-of-age stories is what the great scholar of mythology, Joseph Campbell, calls "father atonement"; that is, the youthful, wounded hero realizes that he has, in a symbolic sense, become "at one" with his father, or has symbolically become his father. Chabon completely reverses that pattern, and Art delivers the clearest thematic statement of the novel: "My father I will never see again. . . . One can learn . . . to father oneself." Though he lost Cleveland, and Arthur is in Majorca, he no longer requires their physical presence "because I can find them so easily in myself." In the concluding paragraph Art summarizes the meaning of his last summer in Pittsburgh by mythologizing the place and his friends and lovers. He cautions the reader, however, to beware of the dangers of memory: "No doubt all of this is not true remembrance but the ruinous work of nostalgia, which obliterates the past, and no doubt, as usual, I have exaggerated everything."

Chabon's first novel thus examines some of the most serious themes of contemporary American literature: how people, consciously or unconsciously, assume fictive roles they then live in; the importance of sexual identity in discovering the heart's true desire; that genuine spiritual transformation always involves pain and suffering; and that an honest life consists of a continuous process of identifying and exposing one's most confounding mysteries. Art Bechstein's struggle to heal himself began by absorbing and utilizing the spiritual energies and examples of his friends and lovers.

Chabon had been writing and publishing short stories between 1987 and 1990, mostly in *The New Yorker* but also in *Gentleman's Quarterly* and *Mademoiselle*. Though he has subsequently become more celebrated as a novelist, there is little question that he is one of the more accomplished and prolific American short-story writers of the 1980s and 1990s. Morrow published Chabon's first collection of short fiction, *A Model World and Other Stories,* in 1991 to solid critical praise. Fowler finds the same themes and characters in the stories that appear in *The Mysteries of Pittsburgh:* "The stories in the collection chart the attempts of each character to make sense out of adulthood by delving into the events of their childhood. . . . At its best, Michael Chabon's fiction depicts the nostalgia his characters feel for their former lives, which they have seen severed from them through an aboriginal emotional crisis." Part 2 of *A Model World and Other Stories* is called "The Lost World" and consists of five interlinked stories tracing the emotional development of the protagonist, Nathan Shapiro. Certainly the title, "The Lost World," defines quite accurately Chabon's most consistent theme: the fall of an innocent from a condition of ignorant bliss into a condition of knowledge or experience. Another thematic pattern found throughout most of Chabon's novels and stories is the transformation of the protagonists' world from a "model" or Edenic one into a "wasteland" or "lost" world.

After the phenomenal success of *The Mysteries of Pittsburgh* and *A Model World and Other Stories,* Morrow gave Chabon a substantial advance so that he could work on his next novel, tentatively titled "Fountain City." By the time *A Model World and Other Stories* was published in 1991, he had been working on "Fountain City" for two years, but the project seemed to be going nowhere. His domestic life was in upheaval; he was divorced in 1991, lived with another woman, and met and married Ayelet Waldman, a lawyer, in 1993. (They have three children, Sophie, Ezekiel, and Ida-Rose.) He also moved six times. After five years and an endlessly elaborating plot that featured Paris and Florida, "utopian dreams and ecological activists, architecture and baseball, an Israeli spy and a man dying from AIDS, a love affair between a young American and a woman 10 years his senior" (*Publishers Weekly,* 10 April 1995), he began to see that his book had no center and no direction. His editor at Morrow, Douglas Stumpf, kept encouraging him, until Chabon had written "1500 pages of what he tried to turn into a 700-page–and still unpublishable–manuscript." From this experience came Chabon's second novel, *Wonder Boys* (1995).

Like Federico Fellini's movie *8½* (1963), a story about the inability to come up with a worthy successor to his early hit *La Dolce Vita* (1960), Chabon's *Wonder Boys* focuses on its protagonist's seeming inability to follow up on his third novel, a critically acclaimed bestseller, *The Land Downstairs.* As critic John Skow put it in the 10 April 1995 *Time:* "Chabon decided to write about a novelist who can't get his next novel written. . . . He pretends optimism to his editor, but the truth is that his half-written book is an unreadable mass of unstrung chapters." *Wonder Boys* is not only an ironic *kunstlerroman* (a novel about the devolution of the artist) but also a roman à clef; its characters, themes, and setting are thinly veiled autobiography. *Wonder Boys* was made into a critically acclaimed movie in February 2000; it was directed by Curtis Hanson, with a screenplay by Steven Kloves, and featured Michael Douglas, Frances McDormand, and Tobey Maguire.

Protagonist Grady Tripp's surname plays on his inability to finish his ever-evolving novel–a work that is "going nowhere," primarily because of his constant use and abuse of alcohol and marijuana. But the name Tripp also becomes a metaphor for his uncanny talent for "tripping" over himself and falling–metaphorically, physically, aesthetically, and spiritually. Because of the comic situations Grady finds himself involved in throughout the novel, he is also a contemporary picaresque hero. The many humorous scenes connect the novel to other comic masterpieces such as Kingsley Amis's *Lucky Jim* (1954), David Lodge's *Small World* (1984), and even Richard Russo's *Straight Man* (1997), all of which are set in academia. *Wonder Boys* follows a serial form and records the disasters of what critic Michael Gorra calls "Grady's lost weekend." Grady is an overweight, middle-aged creative-writing professor at a small liberal-arts college in Pittsburgh. He has been carrying on an extended affair with the college chancellor, Sara Gaskell, who is the wife of Grady's supervisor, Walter Gaskell, chairman of the English department. As the novel opens, the reader learns that Sara is pregnant with Grady's child; she and Walter have not slept together in years. Adding to that pressure, Grady's old college friend and editor Terry Crabtree is arriving to look for new talent at the college's annual WordFest and to take possession of Grady's long-overdue novel, *Wonder Boys.* Even though Grady has been working on it for

seven years, the novel is nowhere near finished. When Terry inquires, Grady lies blatantly: "It's done. . . . It's basically done. I'm just sort of, you know, tinkering with it now, buddy."

Throughout the novel Chabon interweaves the life story of Albert Vetch, who was the first writer Grady had known when Vetch had lived at Grady's grandmother's hotel. He taught English at Coxley College, where both Terry and Grady later graduated. Vetch evolves throughout the narrative into a literary and spiritual doppelganger for both Grady and his most promising student, young James Leer: "He had set a kind of example that, as a writer, I've been living up to ever since." But more importantly, Grady identifies with him because they both struggle with what Grady calls "the midnight disease," habitual insomnia, from which James Leer also suffers. Vetch, a gothic writer of horror stories in the Edgar Allan Poe tradition, had been highly productive for many years up until the time of his wife's suicide. Vetch became for Grady the suffering artist hiding in his Ivory Tower–the turret of the hotel, where Vetch wrote. After his wife's suicide, Vetch took to drink and shot himself in the head. Grady was fourteen when he found the body and was both traumatized and exhilarated by the experience.

One crucially important theme running throughout *Wonder Boys* is the effect of alcohol and drugs on the self-destructive behaviors and creative paralyses of both Grady and Vetch. Grady's recurring falls–his "spells," as he calls them–are the direct result of his drinking and drugging. Chabon juxtaposes the physical falls with the metaphorical, mythic ones to indicate the sorry condition Grady finds himself in at the conclusion of the novel.

James Leer functions as Grady's younger doppelgänger and is his most talented, creative writing student. The other students in Grady's class detest James because they are threatened by his talent; he is a strange and isolated young man, and his gothic stories and obsession with old movies–and movie stars' suicides–infuriate his fellow students. Tripp sympathizes with James's isolation because he himself felt that way all his life, particularly as a youth. James is Grady's artistic disciple, and Grady acts as James's guide and protector, especially from the obvious erotic designs that Terry, a homosexual, unashamedly displays for the vulnerably attractive young man. Early in the evening of the opening events of WordFest, Grady opens Walter Gaskell's safe to show James the black satin jacket that Marilyn Monroe wore, once, the day she married Joe DiMaggio. But as Grady and James are leaving the party, the Gaskells' blind dog, a husky named Doctor Dee, attacks Grady and bites him in his Achilles tendon. James shoots the dog with a "toy" gun he carries with him,

Dust jacket for Chabon's 1995 novel, about a weekend in the life of a creative-writing professor
(Richland County Public Library)

and the picaresque activities of the novel ensue. Grady hides the dead dog in the trunk of his 1966 fly-green Ford Galaxie. From then on, the novel evolves into a series of sometimes melodramatic, but always humorous, madcap adventures, moving from parties to bars to the house of James's grandparents, Howard Johnson motels, and eventually to Grady's father-in-law's home during Passover. Grady wants to protect James from being arrested for shooting Doctor Dee and stealing Monroe's priceless jacket.

As the plot moves along, Grady realizes that most of the information that James has given him about his family is simply fabricated and calls his parents to come and take him home. However, during Grady's troubled ruminations over James's lies, he begins to see similar patterns of dishonesty in his own life. He wonders if the penchant to fabricate is one of the consequences of "the midnight disease": "After awhile you lost the ability to distinguish between your fictional and adult worlds; you confused yourself with your characters, and the random happenings of your life with the machinations of plot." Grady then begins to see that James's fantasies were no more fictional than many writers, including, at times, his own.

After Grady discovers that James's parents are actually his grandparents, he enlists the willing aid of Terry in rescuing James from them; one of the more vivid picaresque adventures in the novel is this deliverance of James from his "prison." While Grady is presented as the savior of innocent and beleaguered youth, Terry happily takes on the demonic role of tempter, ultimately seducing James. Terry also informs James that he wants to publish James's novel, *The Love Parade.* Shortly after James is arrested for his theft, Grady has a deeply disturbing vision of himself as Terry must see him: "He was seeing only the pot-addled author of a bloated, boneless, half-imaginary two-thousand page kraken of a novel, a hoax whose trusting and credulous pursuit had cost him tens of thousands of dollars and, seemingly, his career."

Still, the most painful assessment of his novel comes from another brilliant student, Hannah Green, who had just finished reading the entire manuscript. While she praised the elegant writing as "amazingly beautiful," she makes a devastating comment: "You have whole chapters that go for thirty and forty pages *with no characters at all!*" And Grady must sadly admit that it suddenly occurred to him that, on a certain level, he "had no idea of what the book was really about." However, Hannah's critical comments strike even more deeply into the heart of Grady's creative paralysis when she says: "I wondered how it would be—what this book would be like—if you didn't—if you weren't always so stoned all the time when you write." Grady assured her that "It wouldn't read half as well," but immediately knows that she has identified the cause of his trouble.

Grady and Terry then begin their last picaresque adventure to reclaim Grady's stolen Ford Galaxie, which contains Monroe's satin jacket. On their way, Terry finally gets Grady to admit that he is nowhere near finished with *Wonder Boys*. Terry also admits that he found what he read "a mess" and he really could not recommend it be published. Terry states that, to keep his job, he needs "to hand them something fresh. Something snappy and fresh. Something kind of pretty and perverted at the same time." Grady knows that James's novel qualifies on all counts. As they spot Grady's stolen car and retrieve the precious jacket, the car thief pursues Grady, and Terry drives around the parking lot to pick up Grady. However, the car Terry is driving contains Grady's entire manuscript, and as the door swings open, the wind blows the pages out of the car: "The air was filled with *Wonder Boys*. . . . Pages were . . . brushing up like kittens against my legs." They barely make their escape with just seven pages of Grady's beloved manuscript salvaged.

As the heartbroken Grady arrives back at Word-Fest, Terry comforts him by telling him that the catastrophe may have been a blessing in disguise since the future of the novel was hopeless. Grady weeps openly as he restores Monroe's jacket to Walter Gaskell. However, Grady arrives at the concluding ceremonies of WordFest just in time to hear that Bartizan Press, Terry's employer, has decided to publish James's first novel, *The Love Parade*. James stands up and awkwardly accepts the crowd's applause. As Grady describes it, James "spread out his hands . . . and took his first sweet bow as a wonder boy." Grady also understands why the college and Walter will never press charges against James for either the death of his dog or the theft when he hears Walter announce that Bartizan Press has agreed to publish Walter's book on Marilyn Monroe and Joe DiMaggio, *The Last American Marriage*.

In the concluding pages of *Wonder Boys*, Grady experiences several major revelations: "I had lost everything: novel, publisher, wife, lover; the admiration of my best student; all the fruit of the past decade of my life. I had no family, no friends, no car, and probably, after this weekend, no job." At the very moment of his utter and complete failure, he decides to give the rest of his expensive pot to a young janitor. Grady then begins to lose consciousness and is about to fall over a balcony

when Sara Gaskell saves him. He comes to in the hospital and is told by an internist that his "spells" are actually anxiety attacks caused by his alcohol and drug abuse, and that if Sara had not called the doctor's attention to his wounded tendon, he would have lost his foot. Once Grady's problems with alcohol and pot are identified and acknowledged, his chances of surviving—both physically and spiritually—increase significantly.

The novel concludes with the marriage of Grady and Sara after their leaving the college. She becomes the dean at Coxley College, where Grady and Terry were students and where Vetch had taught long ago. Grady is hired as an adjunct professor to teach creative writing. He ceremoniously buries all the early drafts of *Wonder Boys* in the backyard. He has stopped smoking pot and overindulging in alcohol; he meets each Tuesday night after his workshop with some of his students at the Alibi Tavern. Grady cautions his students to beware of the "incurable disease that leads all good writers to suffer inevitably, the quintessential fate of their characters. The young men listen dutifully, for the most part, and from time to time some of them even take the trouble to go over to the college library and dig up one or another of his novels, and crouch there, among the stacks, flipping impatiently through the pages, looking for the parts that sound true."

The publication of *The Amazing Adventures of Kavalier & Clay* (2000), Chabon's third novel, elevated his literary reputation into the most prestigious ranks of contemporary American novelists primarily because it won him a Pulitzer Prize in 2001. Critics were, for the most part, ecstatic in their praise of its thematic range and depth. At 636 pages it is almost as long as all of Chabon's previous books put together. Ken Kalfus in *The New York Times Book Review* (24 September 2000) listed the most outstanding qualities of the volume: "the depth of Chabon's thought, his sharp language, his inventiveness and his ambition make this a novel of towering accomplishment." Kalfus also called it "a comic epic, generously optimistic about the human struggle for personal liberation." In *Commentary* (June 2001) John Podhoretz favorably compared Chabon with other major contemporary American novelists:

> Sentence by sentence, Chabon has always been an uncommonly good writer, perhaps the best prose stylist of his generation (he is thirty-eight). But there was no hint in his previous novels, the best-selling *Mysteries of Pittsburgh* and *Wonder Boys*, of the proposive force, narrative command, and beguiling wit he displays here.

In defining one of the principal themes of the novel as the abuse of artists by the big publishing houses, R. Z. Sheppard also pointed out in *Time* (24 June 2000) another of the best attributes of the book: "Screwing the talent is an old story, but never before told with as much imagination, verve and affection as can be found in *The Amazing Adventures of Kavalier & Clay*." The novel elaborated on many themes and genres from Chabon's earlier works. It is a bildungsroman for both protagonists, and a *kunstlerroman* because both main characters develop their artistic gifts–Joseph Kavalier as a visual artist, and Samuel Clay as a writer–in spite of their battles with the powerful publishing world of New York City. Podhoretz also pointed out other genres that Chabon employs in the book: "*The Amazing Adventures of Kavalier & Clay* combines fable, magical realism, adventure story telling, Horatio Alger and mordant humor." *Publishers Weekly* (21 August 2000) characterized the work as "an epic novel about the glory years of the American comic book (1939–1954)." But the range and scope of Chabon's scholarly treatment of comic books and their artists raise that genre to a more prestigious level: readers and writers must treat such artists with a gravitas formerly reserved for novelists, short-story writers, poets, and serious visual artists.

The most important theme running through the entire novel is the power of the imagination to produce art and to create ways of escape from both physical and spiritual death. While the novel is about the fall from innocence to experience of both protagonists, it explores ways in which the imagination redeems them from the destructive consequences of their fall. Their art, then, becomes the vehicle by which they transform and redeem themselves in a fallen world.

The Amazing Adventures of Kavalier & Clay is divided into six major sections. In part 1, "The Escape Artist," seventeen-year-old Samuel Louis Klayman–later known as Sammy Clay–is forced to share his Brooklyn bed with a newly arrived cousin from Prague, eighteen-year-old Joseph Kavalier. Both teenagers are obsessed with escape in some form. Joe is from a prominent Jewish family in Prague and has been trained by one of the great stage illusionists, Bernard Kornblum, in Houdini-like magical escapes. In order for Joe to escape the increasing Jewish persecution by the Nazis, Kornblum smuggles him out of Prague in a large box that contains the huge clay figure of the sixteenth-century Golem of Prague. Once Joe arrives in Lithuania, he makes his way east through Siberia and Japan and eventually to the Brooklyn home of his cousin. However, Sammy is obsessed with escaping his own cultural imprisonment and "dreamed the usual Brooklyn dreams of transformation and escape. He dreamed with fierce contrivance, transmuting himself into a major American novelist, or a famous smart person, like Clifton Fadiman, or perhaps into a heroic doctor; or developing, through practice and sheer force of will, the mental powers that would give him a preternatural con-

trol over the hearts and minds of men." Both young men immediately identify themselves as artists on the first night they meet. Though their aspirations are noble and aesthetic, they also are unashamed pragmatists interested in making lots of money by collaborating on projects. Sammy introduces Joe to comic books, and they immediately begin working together on future artistic works.

One of the most impressive aspects of the novel is the sheer amount of interwoven information on the history of the American comic book, and the protagonists share some similarities with the actual creators of *Superman*, which began appearing in 1938. *Superman* was the creation of two Jewish artists, illustrator Joe Shuster and writer Jerome Siegel, both of whom were victimized by the large publishing houses and denied the financial rewards they deserved. The first third of the novel details Joe and Sammy's continuous battles with their publisher to receive even a fraction of the fortune their work begins generating for the corporation. Throughout the book, Chabon alludes to models from which Joe and Sammy learn their trade: *Lil Abner, Krazy Kat, Abbie n' Slats,* and especially Milton Caniff's *Terry and the Pirates.* But Chabon is particularly concerned that the reader become aware that the major connection between Joe and Sammy is language; that is, the generating power of words. All of their collaborative ideas come out of their conversations:

> Every universe, our own included, begins in conversation. Every golem in the history of the world, from Rabbi Hanina's delectable goat to the river-clay Frankenstein of Rabbi Judah Loew ben Bezalel, was summoned into existence through language, through murmuring, recital, and kabbalistic chitchat–was literally talked in life. Kavalier and Clay–whose golem was to be formed of black lines and four-color dots of the lithographer–lay down, lit the first of five dozen cigarettes they were to consume that afternoon, and started to talk.

During their hours of talking they came up with their major creation, a hero who releases people from "the shackles of oppression, he offers the hope of liberation and the promise of freedom." They dub him "The Escapist" and decide he is "an escape artist in a costume. Who fights crime." Toward the end of chapter 7, Joe amplifies their hero's call to adventure and purpose: "He is here to free the world."

One of Chabon's stock motifs appears as an important sign of the characters' heroic attributes: both protagonists are wounded in some way. Sammy was a victim of polio as a child and walks with a limp in his left leg. He also discovers during the course of the novel that he is a homosexual. He is, then, wounded both physically and psychologically. Joe is wounded later in the story: at his listening post in Antarctica during World War II, he is shot by a German and breaks his ankle during their struggle.

Parts 2 and 3, "A Couple of Boy Geniuses" and "The Funny-Book War," show their rise to the top of the comic-book world with the growing popularity of the Escapist, though they run into potential diplomatic problems with the State Department, which accuses their superhero of anti-Nazi behavior; they give their hero's nemeses, who are Nazis and Iron Chain cabal, names like Attila Haxoff or Hynkel or Hassler. The publishers fear a lawsuit because America has not yet entered the European war.

Part 4, "The Golden Age," consists of seventeen chapters and elaborates on the financial and popular success of Kavalier and Clay. The section also shows Sammy falling in love with a handsome young actor, Tracy Bacon; it is his first grudging admission that he may be gay. Tragedy strikes Joe when the Nazis sink the ship carrying his younger brother, Thomas, to America. Joe had spent hefty sums of money arranging for the boy's safe arrival. The disaster psychologically unhinges Joe, who immediately joins the navy and cuts himself off from Sammy and Rosa (Sammy's girlfriend and later wife) and all of his other friends and acquaintances. His suicidal depression finds its only relief in the prospect of actually killing Germans in any possible way. Part 5, "Radioman," depicts his life at a navy listening post in Antarctica, where he ends up the only survivor but determines to kill the one remaining German at his listening post eighty miles away. Joe patches together a seriously damaged airplane and manages to get to his destination. Joe is a modern-day Dedalus who uses his imagination and creates his own methods of escape: he becomes, quite literally, his own escape artist. Though wounded by the German officer, he kills him and is awarded the navy's highest medal, the Distinguished Service Cross. He is commissioned an ensign and is now, officially, a hero in the eyes of the world.

Part 6, "The League of the Golden Key," at twenty chapters, is the longest section of the novel. True to the author's consistent use of mythic characters and themes, Chabon depicts Joe as the "Returning Hero" who, like another trickster and escape artist, Ulysses, is reunited with both his wife and son. His eleven-year-old son, Tommy (named after his dead brother, Thomas), seeks out Joe without knowing Joe is his father. Tommy, also obsessed with magic, befriends many magicians and escape artists in New York; he regularly skips school by forging convincing notes from his mother to present to the school authorities.

Tommy lives in the Long Island suburb of Bloomville, obviously based on Levittown, with his mother,

Dust jacket for Chabon's lengthy children's fantasy, in which a young man and his friends defeat the forces of the trickster figure Coyote (Richland County Public Library)

Rosa, and Sammy, his ostensible father. Sammy has lost much of his money because the bottom had fallen out of the comic-book industry: the superhero lost whatever attraction he may have had to the actual returning heroes of World War II. Through the magicians, Tommy discovers that Joe is actually living on the seventy-second floor of the Empire State Building and is planning a major escapist event by leaping off the eighty-sixth floor. Joe has become exactly what Grady in *Wonder Boys* warned his writing students to avoid: a character in his own work. The escapist event reunites Joe with Sammy and Rosa, and he moves in with them in Bloomville. He reveals to Sammy the enormous project he has been working on for the past twelve years: 4,000–5,000 pages of illustrations of a variety of images, in which the motif of the Golem constantly recurs. He finally realizes, as he shows Sammy a 2,256-page comic book called *The Golem*, that he is telling the story of his own physical and spiritual resurrection: "Joe came to feel that the work—telling his story—was helping to heal him. All the grief and the black wonder that he was never able to express, before or afterward . . . all of it went into the queasy angles and stark compositions, the cross-hatchings and vast swaths of shadow, the distended and fractured and finely minced panels of his monstrous comic book." Joe also comes into the deeper understanding that the function of art–and especially his art–is to escape: "To slip, like the Escapist, free of the entangling chain of reality and the straight jacket of physical laws . . . truly to escape, if only for an instant; to poke his head through the borders of this world, with its harsh physics, into the mysterious spirit world that lay beyond."

Joe moves in with Sammy, Rosa, and Tommy after realizing that he is still in love with Rosa and that Tommy is actually his son. Sammy comes to the realization that he must finally admit to the world that he is gay. Joe also discovers that the money he left for years in the East Side Stage Crafts Credit Union has accumulated into almost $1,000,000. The novel concludes as Sammy decides to leave for Los Angeles, where he may find another Tracy Bacon to love, and Joe finds true happiness with Rosa. Tommy always suspected that Joe was his father and is proud to have found him at last. Joe, in a last gesture of love, offers to buy Empire Comics and give it to Sammy. Whether Joe returns to Empire Comics remains the final mystery of this rich novel.

The thematic range and depth of *The Amazing Adventures of Kavalier & Clay* far exceeds those of Chabon's earlier novels. All three can be viewed as psychological, spiritual, and mythic journeys that seek to create meaning and significance in an existentially empty world. What unites all of them is Chabon's ability to "mythologize the commonplace." However, Chabon's most impressive achievement in the novel is his ability to show the redemptive power of the imagination and how that power can metamorphose the lives of Kavalier and Clay into heroic dimensions. Their gift of narrative–the stories they tell–enables them to transcend time and to transform the temporal into timeless and immutable art.

Chabon's next book was the critically acclaimed *Summerland* (2002), a children's fantasy novel, five hundred pages long. Noting his two older children's intense interest in J. K. Rowling's Harry Potter series, Chabon consciously set out to create his own kind of American magical world, combining elements of Native American and Norse myth and folklore. He had always been a serious admirer of J. R. R. Tolkien and C. S. Lewis, but Chabon wanted to combine his love of fantasy with his equal

enthusiasm for baseball; *Summerland* brings together those two topics in highly imaginative ways.

Summerland features many of the characteristics of what mythologist Joseph Campbell calls the mythological journey of the hero: the call to adventure, the road of trials and dangers, the search for the father, and the hero's attempt to save the world from imminent collapse into a wasteland condition. The unlikely hero of the book is Ethan Feld, a motherless child whose distaste for baseball far outweighs his ability to play the game. His mythological quest begins after his crackpot inventor father is abducted by the prince of darkness, the trickster Coyote, a semi-Satanic figure who intends to use for lethal purposes a substance that Ethan's father has created. Coyote wants to destroy the underlying structure of the universe by poisoning the waters that nourish the Cosmic Tree of the World, Chabon's version of the Edenic Tree and Yggdrasill of Norse mythology, the World Ash Tree or *axis mundi*. The tree supports the four worlds: the Winterlands, the Summerlands, the Middling, and the Gleaming, all of which are woven together into a gigantic cosmic loom. The fate of these worlds ultimately rests on the outcome of a baseball game between Ethan and his friends and the destructive forces of the Coyote. This rich novel presents baseball-playing dwarves, giants, parallel universes, and magic portals, all energized by a doomsday-scenario plot. Chabon structures the novel on a baseball-as-life metaphor, but true to the American tradition, it focuses on the hero's ability to find within himself–with the assistance of friends and wise guides–the inner resources to overcome his flaws and save the world from its fall into a wasteland. Chabon has also written a screenplay for a planned motion-picture version.

Michael Chabon has become, before the age of forty, a highly accomplished novelist, short-story writer, children's fantasy novelist, and screenwriter. Certain recurring themes appear throughout all of his works: coming of age, nostalgia and memory, family conflicts, love, the growth of the artist, friendship, Edenic happiness, and wasteland desolation. However, Chabon consistently exalts the imagination in creating worlds that nourish the spiritual lives of human beings.

Reference:

Douglas Fowler, "The Short Fiction of Michael Chabon: Nostalgia in the Very Young," *Studies in Short Fiction*, 32 (Winter 1995): 75–83.

Annie Dillard

(30 April 1945 –   )

Barbara Lounsberry
University of Northern Iowa

See also the Dillard entries in *DLB 275: Twentieth-Century American Nature Writers: Prose* and *DLB Yearbook 1980.*

BOOKS: *Tickets for a Prayer Wheel: Poems* (Columbia: University of Missouri Press, 1974);

Pilgrim at Tinker Creek (New York: Harper's Magazine Press, 1974; London: Cape, 1975);

Holy the Firm (New York: Harper & Row, 1977);

The Weasel (Claremont, Cal.: Rara Avis, 1981);

Living by Fiction (New York: Harper & Row, 1982);

Teaching a Stone to Talk: Expeditions and Encounters (New York: Harper & Row, 1982; London: Pan, 1984);

Encounters with Chinese Writers (Middletown, Conn.: Wesleyan University Press, 1984);

An American Childhood (New York: Harper & Row, 1987; London: Picador, 1988);

The Writing Life (New York: Harper & Row, 1989; London: Picador, 1990);

The Living (New York: HarperCollins, 1992);

Mornings like This: Found Poems (New York: HarperCollins, 1995);

For the Time Being (New York: Knopf, 1999).

Collections: *The Annie Dillard Library* (New York: Harper & Row, 1989);

Three by Annie Dillard (New York: Harper & Row, 1990)—comprises *Pilgrim at Tinker Creek, An American Childhood,* and *The Writing Life;*

The Annie Dillard Reader (New York: HarperCollins, 1994).

OTHER: Fred Chappell, *Moments of Light,* introduction by Dillard (Newport Beach, Cal.: New South Press, 1980);

Pinions, *Wind on the Sand: The Hidden Life of an Anchoress,* foreword by Dillard (New York: Paulist Press, 1981);

"Singing with the Fundamentalists," in *The Graywolf Annual Three: Essays, Memoirs & Reflections,* edited by Scott Walker (St. Paul: Graywolf Press, 1986), pp. 9–21;

Annie Dillard (photograph by John Montre; from the dust jacket for The Writing Life, *1989)*

The Best American Essays 1988, edited by Dillard and Robert Atwan (New York: Ticknor & Fie[...] 1988).

SELECTED PERIODICAL PUBLICATIO[N] UNCOLLECTED:

POETRY

"The Heart," *Poetry,* 125 (February 1975): 260;

"Quatrain of the Body's Sleep," *Poetry,* 125 ([February] 1975): 262;

"Monarchs in the Field," *Harper's Magazine,* 153 (October 1976): 104;

"Metaphysical Model with Feather," *Atlantic Monthly,* 242 (October 1978): 82;

"Soft Coral," *Antigonish Review,* 48 (Winter 1982): 5;

"The Windy Planet," *Science,* 86 (June 1986): 69.

FICTION

"Life Class," *Carolina Quarterly,* 24 (Spring 1972): 23–27;

"Ethiopian Monastery," *Hollins Critic,* 10 (August 1973): 12;

"Five Sketches," *North American Review,* 260 (Summer 1975): 30–31;

"The Stone," *Chicago Review,* 25 (1975): 152–153;

"Doughnut," *Antioch Review,* 34 (1975–1976): 22–25;

"A Christmas Story," *Harper's Magazine,* 252 (January 1976): 58;

"Utah," *Tri-Quarterly,* 35 (Spring 1976): 96–98;

"Stone Doctor," *Epoch,* 26 (Fall 1976): 63;

"The Living," *Harper's Magazine,* 257 (November 1978): 45–64;

"Ship in a Bottle," *Harper's Magazine,* 279 (September 1989): 68–71;

"A Trip to the Mountains," *Harper's Magazine,* 283 (August 1991): 48–55.

NONFICTION

"The State of the Art: Fiction and Its Audience," *Massachusetts Review,* 23, no. 1 (Spring 1982): 85–96;

"The Joys of Reading," *New York Times Magazine,* 16 May 1982, p. 47;

"Why I Live Where I Live," *Esquire,* 101 (March 1984): 90–92;

"Iotebook," *Antaeus,* 61 (Autumn 1988): 84–87;

"rite Till You Drop," *New York Times Book Review,* 94 (28 May 1989): 1, 23;

"g Back: Correspondence from Fans," *Harper's agazine,* 278 (June 1989): 28–29;

"r Young Writers," *Image: A Journal of the Arts Religion,* 16 (Summer 1997): 65–68;

"c of Time: Cover Story," *Harper's Magazine,* nuary 1998): 51–56;

"*Ttne Reader,* 92 (March/April 1999): 39–

and novelist Annie Dillard entered
ne with a book of poems called
el and a Thoreauvian natural his-
ker Creek. The latter brought the
Pulitzer Prize in nonfiction. It
e of readers that has grown
g volumes. Readers relish
s of nature, her lush and
pirited humor that only
us metaphysical quest.
he success of *Pilgrim at*

Tinker Creek, readers waited for Dillard to assay fiction, and she did so with the 1992 novel *The Living.*

Dillard was born Meta Ann Doak on 30 April 1945. *An American Childhood,* her 1987 memoir, recounts her early life through her high-school years as the elder of two daughters of well-to-do Pittsburgh parents Frank and Pam (Lambert) Doak. Although she never mentions it in the volume, Dillard's ancestors founded a major corporation: American Standard. Dillard was raised in the Presbyterian Church; however, she spent four consecutive summers during her youth at a fundamentalist church camp in the country. "We sang Baptist songs and had a great time," she recalls; "It gave me a taste for abstract thought."

An American Childhood documents Dillard's early interest in nature and art. It also reveals the intensity she has always focused on whatever engages her, be it beetles, baseball, or books. The memoir ends in 1963 as Dillard prepares to leave Pittsburgh to enter college. She chose Hollins College in Virginia for its writing program, and in 1964, following her freshman year, she married her writing teacher, the poet and novelist R. H. W. Dillard. After earning her bachelor's degree from Hollins in 1967 and a master's degree in 1968, Dillard spent 1972 exploring the woods and waterfall of the seventeen-foot-wide Tinker Creek that circled her home in the Roanoke Valley. *Pilgrim at Tinker Creek,* which has been compared persistently to Henry David Thoreau's *Walden* (1854), took Dillard eight months to write, working seven days a week, fifteen and sixteen hours a day, in a tiny library carrel enclosed by cinder block. She has acknowledged that she wrote the book from 1,103 note cards upon which she had collected observations and also passages from her extensive reading.

Pilgrim at Tinker Creek is "really a book of theology," Dillard told *Harper's Magazine* in February 1974; "It's the result of one year's walking around and thinking about what kind of god gave us this kind of world. I decided it must have been a very carefree, exuberant one, saying, 'Here, have a tulip! Have a beetle! Have another beetle!'" Tension, nevertheless, resides in all of Dillard's major works between God's grandeur and human suffering, between the beauty of nature and its destructiveness. In a 1978 interview with Philip Yancey, Dillard acknowledged that as she wrote *Pilgrim at Tinker Creek,* she kept before her the image of suffering people. In return, she found that those who responded "with the most warmth" to the volume were often struggling with cancer or some similar burden.

Dillard was playing second base in a softball game when she learned that the first chapter of *Pilgrim at Tinker Creek* had been accepted by *Harper's Magazine.* Harper's Magazine Press wished to publish the entire volume, and the magazine engaged Dillard as a contrib-

*Dust jacket for Dillard's 1974 account of a one-year cycle of seasons in
the Roanoke Valley (Bruccoli Clark Layman Archives)*

uting editor, sending her to the Galápagos Islands in the summer of 1973. In 1974, *Pilgrim at Tinker Creek* became a best-seller and prizewinner.

In 1976 Dillard left her husband and the state of Virginia to take a position as scholar-in-residence at Western Washington State College in Bellingham. While the Roanoke Valley of *Pilgrim at Tinker Creek* offered an uneasy interface of wilderness and civilization, Bellingham represented another kind of last frontier: the farthest edge of western settlement in the United States proper. Dillard lived in a cedar shake house on an island in Puget Sound, commuting to the mainland to teach courses in poetry and other forms of writing.

"I came here to study hard things—rock mountain and salt sea—and to temper my spirit on their edges," Dillard wrote in her second volume of nonfiction, *Holy the Firm* (1977), sounding again like Thoreau. *Holy the Firm* took fifteen months to write (in contrast to the eight months for *Pilgrim at Tinker Creek*), even though it is only one-fourth the length of the earlier volume. Just as *Pilgrim at Tinker Creek* chronicles the seasons of a year, winter to winter, *Holy the Firm* also employs a chrono-

logical structure: three consecutive November days. The work began as a poem. "I merely wanted to see what was going to happen," Dillard told Yancey; "I simply needed a certain amount of events—whatever might happen—to make a minor point: that days are lived in the mind *and* in the spirit." According to Mike Major, the phrase "holy the firm" has its roots in esoteric Christianity. It represents Dillard's effort "to find a middle ground between pantheism, in which God is indistinguishable from nature, and deism, which posits that God created the world, but then abandoned it." Holy the firm is a created substance; yet, it is beneath the surface of the earth and thus difficult to see.

Dillard described the problems of writing *Holy the Firm* as enormous: "After the second day's plane crash . . . how could I resolve anything on the third day?" Nevertheless she found the shift from the poetry of *Tickets for a Prayer Wheel* to the prose of *Pilgrim at Tinker Creek* and *Holy the Firm* to be "thrilling." "Poetry was a flute, and prose was the whole orchestra," she told Katherine Weber in a 1989 interview. "I'm still spending the energy from that shift." The essence of poetry "is not its pretty language,"

93

she maintains, "but the fact that it has the capacity for deep internal structures of meaning." Dillard says she tried to provide *Pilgrim at Tinker's Creek* and *Holy the Firm* with poetic structures so that nonfiction prose could have the same artistic meaning as poetry.

During her years on Puget Sound, Dillard met Gary Clevidence, an anthropologist. They were married in 1980. In 1979 they moved to Middletown, Connecticut, when Dillard accepted the position of writer-in-residence and adjunct professor at Wesleyan University, a position she maintains, spending her summers in her house in South Wellfleet on Cape Cod. "I came to Connecticut because, in the course of my wanderings, it was time to come back east–back to that hardwood forest where the multiple trees and soft plants have their distinctive seasons and their places in sun and shade," she said in a 1984 *Esquire* article, "Why I Live Where I Live."

Teaching a Stone to Talk: Expeditions and Encounters (1982) offers fourteen narrative essays emerging from Dillard's 1970s sojourns in the Galápagos Islands, South America, Virginia, and Washington. During the early 1980s, after the birth of her daughter, Cody Rose, Dillard began to focus on writing as a subject in itself. *Living by Fiction* (1982), *Encounters with Chinese Writers* (1984), and *The Writing Life* (1989) explore the art and life of writing, while *An American Childhood* captures the awakening of a child–one who happens to be a writer. Also during the 1980s Dillard and Clevidence divorced. In 1986 Dillard read the newly published *Henry Thoreau: A Life of the Mind* by Robert D. Richardson Jr. She admired the book so much that she wrote Richardson a fan letter. She met him and, before the end of the decade, married him.

Dillard's books on writing might be seen as her preparation for writing fiction. She says that *Living by Fiction* was her attempt to understand the meaning of the world by exploring how it is seen by such "contemporary modernist novelists" as Vladimir Nabokov, Jorge Luis Borges, Samuel Beckett, Italo Calvino, William Seward Burroughs, John Barth, Robert Coover, and Thomas Pynchon. She comes to the conclusion that in the hands of these writers fiction has moved "from depth to surface, from rondure to planes, from world to scheme, from observation to imagination, from story to theory, from society to individual, from emotion to mind."

Dillard's novel, *The Living,* reverses this movement. It can be viewed as Dillard's effort to return fiction to the world–in its depth and rondure–and the novelist to observation, story, society, and emotion. Dillard's ambition is even greater: her novel is a rejection of either/or exclusions in favor of both/and inclusiveness. *The Living* offers depth and surface, story and theory, emotion and mind. "I like to be aware of a book

as a piece of writing, and aware of its structure as a product of mind, and yet I want to be able to see the represented world through it," Dillard explains.

The "represented world" in *The Living* is Washington State in the years 1855 to 1897. As Hope Hale Davis wrote in the *New Leader* (10–24 August 1992), the novel offers "all the old-fashioned satisfactions of the 19th-century novel" with "the benefit of 20th-century freedoms and insights." Dillard's research for *The Living* was exhaustive. At least seven historical personages are included among her fictional characters: James J. Hill, the railroad baron; Frederick Weyerhaeuser, the lumber tycoon; the Lummi chief Chowitzit; the Nooksack chief Hump Talem; Tommy Cahoon, a scalped Pullman conductor; George Bacon, a lively mortgage agent; and various Seattle politicians. As with *An American Childhood,* an historical plate of the early settlement adorns the inside covers of the novel. A map of northwest Washington follows the table of contents. As a result, the reader's first experience of *The Living,* like that of the settlers themselves, is through landscape–through geography.

Dillard stretches herself artistically in *The Living.* While *Pilgrim at Tinker Creek* explores a one-year cycle of seasons at Tinker Creek and *Holy the Firm* covers three days on Puget Sound, *The Living* follows the lives of three generations of Western settlers in locales ranging from Baltimore, Maryland, to St. Paul, Minnesota, to Washington State. This novel grew from Dillard's short story "The Living" (1978), which presents the central dramatic crisis: Beal Obenchain's determination to control Clare Fishburn's soul–and the startling result. Don Scheese, in *The Georgia Review* (Spring 1993), described Beal Obenchain as a "shadowy scholar" right out of Nathaniel Hawthorne. A splay-footed giant who lives in a hollowed-out tree stump in the forest, Obenchain represents death and metaphysical evil in the novel. The giant is oppressed by "an airless demon" and kills animals and human beings, it appears, in order to keep from killing himself. When murdering a Chinaman fails to exorcise his demon, Obenchain embarks on a Nietzschean experiment. He intends to dominate another human soul, first by threatening that person with death and then, perversely, by not following through with the threat, leaving his victim in constant anticipation of death.

"Fishburns" is the title of the first of the seven sections of *The Living,* a name uniting suffering–burns–with divine life, the fish as the Christian symbol of Christ. Obenchain randomly chooses Clare Fishburn to be his victim, drawing his name from a bucket, but the two are far from randomly matched. Both are tall men whom Dillard calls "lighthouses," for they represent the opposing beacons of evil and good, wilderness and civi-

Dust jacket for Dillard's 1987 memoir, about the early influences of nature and art
that shaped her as a writer (Richland County Public Library)

lization: Clare lives on "Golden Hill" in the town of Whatcom. As *The Living* unfolds, readers are surprised to find that Obenchain fails in his objective. After suffering a few days of fear, Fishburn finds that Obenchain's death threat merely makes palpable his essential human predicament: he is going to die. This revelation changes Clare beyond measure.

What appears, then, as the evil plot of one man against the life of another (evoking for readers all the suspense of old-fashioned melodrama) is transformed by Dillard into a metaphysical and theological cautionary tale: a summons of mortality. Clare Fishburn, "looking at things as if for the last time," comes to see them "as if for the first time." He sees that society seduces. He discovers that "every chasing after distinction and a backlog of money was chaff and blowing wind" and that "the dazzle of it blinded people, and the clamor of it deafened them." Clare comes to feel he lacks time "to honor all he wanted to honor" and gains an "increasing sensation of participation, of glory, even, in a world of flux."

Obenchain's threat at Christmas thus leads to Clare's awakening in "Spring," the fifth section of the novel, and to his calm during the fall financial "Panic" (section 6). While his neighbors quake and scatter, Clare feels himself "more substantial than before." He participates fully in the life of the community as well as in the natural world. He fathers a daughter and launches a boat.

In the seven sections of the novel Dillard weaves a tapestry of narratives around Clare's awakening: stories of the trials and spirit of Clare's mother, Ada, who was one of the first settlers on Bellingham Bay; the story of Minta Honer and her hops farm and of the young idealist John Ireland Sharp; and stories of the successive decimations of the Lummi and Nooksack Indians and of the exploitation and expulsion of the Chinese. Cycles provide meaningful structure to the novel–cycles of seasons and generations, of boom and bust. *The Living* begins with the Fraser River gold rush of 1858 and ends with the Klondike rush of 1897; in between those years, the coastal settlements vie to become the center of Japanese trade or the terminus for Hill's Northern Pacific Railroad. In the 3 May 1992 *New York Times Book Review* Thomas Keneally noted that within these larger cycles, Dillard keeps returning to human events, "imbuing them with poignancy."

HarperCollins, Dillard's publisher, trumpeted *The Living* as "the literary event of the year" for 1992. It printed one hundred thousand hardcover copies and committed $125,000 to the promotion of the novel; *The Living* went on to become a best-seller. Critical response to the novel has been predominantly positive. The majority of reviewers agreed with Clif Mason, who, in *Western American Literature* (Spring 1993), called the novel the intellectual and stylistic culmination of Dillard's career. Almost unanimously Dillard was praised for her sharp gaze; her rich vocabulary and masterful use of words; her vivid, startling imagery; and the wealth of detail in the novel. While a few critics faulted her control of her historical research, many savored her collector's eye for the arcane knowledge and vocabulary of the Pacific Northwest. In the Winter 1993 *Hudson Review* David Mason, who grew up in Bellingham, vouched for the accuracy of Dillard's depictions, down to the "hazel and alder, and plaguey thickets of blackberry." Other reviewers praised Dillard's re-creation of the racial and cultural insensitivity of the times, especially the insensitivity of the white majority. *Library Journal* (15 March 1992) reviewer Dean James called *The Living* an "unflinching" portrayal of pioneer life at its best and worst—its racism and brutality, its optimism and charity.

Many reviewers noted that *The Living* was true to naturalistic fiction in exploring the impact of natural, social, and economic forces on the people and landscape of Bellingham Bay. Barbara Kingsolver, reviewing the novel for *The Nation* (25 May 1992), saw *The Living* as both Dillard's celebration of the "pure, naïve energy" of capitalism during this time of Manifest Destiny, and her indictment of the shortsightedness of that capitalism. "In the novel's forty year span," Kingsolver wrote, "we watch the town [of Whatcom] rise and fall so many times over, you would think it might learn its lesson. The point may be that a profit-driven economy is incapable of learning lessons, as it has no mind, only an appetite." Kingsolver locates Dillard's indictment of capitalism in the "shrewdly" drawn scene in St. Paul during which railroad tycoon James J. Hill blithely sells off the Washington forests to Frederick Weyerhaeuser for a song, just so his train cars will not have to return from the West Coast empty. Scheese noted, however, that Dillard rejects the romantic view that civilization destroys the wilderness. Instead, she repeatedly portrays the unexpected encroachment of the natural world upon the (barely) civilized one. As with her indictment of capitalism, she shows human society as incapable of understanding and incorporating the harsher lessons of nature.

Also receiving positive notice were the metaphysical and religious dimensions of the novel. Molly Gloss wrote in *The New York Times Book Review* (31 May 1992) that *The Living* is "above all, a novel about the reiterant, precarious, wondrous, solitary, terrifying, utterly common condition of human life." C. D. Albin, writing in *Christian Century* (7 October 1992), found the novel "spiritually and emotionally challenging—and also strengthening," while Scheese ended his lengthy review by declaring that Dillard "has revived the issue of religious faith for her readers . . . no small accomplishment in what some theologians have called a 'post-religious' age."

The major critical disagreements regarding *The Living* have centered on its characters and plot. Many reviewers praised Dillard's character creation: the reviewer for *Booklist* (15 February 1992) found the people in the novel "marvelous" and "complex," and the reviewer for *Christianity Today* (14 September 1992) declared them "vivid and unusual enough to please a Charles Dickens." Many reviewers lauded the range and variety of Dillard's characters. Albert B. Stewart, writing in *The Antioch Review* (Fall 1992), observed that Dillard creates figures "varied enough for a dozen novels," while in *Newsweek* (8 June 1992) Katrine Ames praised the "particularly interesting women" in Dillard's large cast. The reviewer for *Publishers Weekly* (24 February 1992) suggested that Dillard's "indelible characters" are "memorable not so much for specific actions as for the way they live."

Other reviewers, however, found Dillard's characters a significant weakness in the novel, and there were a handful of harsh reviews in prominent publications. Devon Jersild, writing in *USA Today* (13 May 1992), criticized Dillard's "annoying" habit of describing characters' facial structures each time they appear, as if the reader had never met the characters before, and Louise Sweeney, in *The Christian Science Monitor* (22 May 1992), wished Dillard would get inside her characters' hearts. The reviewers for *The New Yorker* (6 July 1992) and *Wall Street Journal* (4 May 1992) found ironic the fact that the characters in *The Living,* for them, failed to seem alive. *The New Yorker* reviewer asserted that both "the setting and the individuals who inhabit it are convincing in a daguerreotype fashion—they seem touchingly antique, that is—but they never completely come to life. As a result, all the loss and death seem wasteful and inefficient rather than truly touching." *The Atlantic* (June 1992) reviewer concurred, stating that "the characters are, unhappily, mostly tissue-paper goody-goodies. The one exception in this virtuous crowd is a psychopath who cannot provide effective

Dust jacket for Dillard's 1992 novel, which chronicles the lives of nineteenth-century settlers in Washington State (Richland County Public Library)

suspense because it is clear from the general tone of the story that he will come to an appropriately bad end." Altogether, the reviewer concluded, "this is a disappointing work."

Those who were disappointed in the novel thus located its weakness in the nexus of character and plot. The suspense of the plot loses its effectiveness when melodrama becomes metaphysics. David Plante most fully articulated this perspective in his assessment for *The Yale Review* (October 1992). "Partway into Annie Dillard's novel *The Living,* I thought she was on to something new," he begins, noting that the

> originality of the book seemed to me to be in how these details of the lives of the characters accrue and themselves become the substance of the book. . . . But after this promising beginning, about one-third of the way into the book, the author seriously damages her work by clamping a plot onto it. . . . The plot . . . never gives the book the structure Annie Dillard evidently thought it needed. It is as though the author thought that without the plot's moral darkness—a Hawthornian moral

darkness—the book would not have the depth she imagined a novel must have to be *true.* But that very intention reduces the plot to a device.

Although *The Living* opened on *The New York Times* best-seller list, the lack of unanimous acclaim may have kept the novel from becoming "the literary event of the year" its publisher hoped—and may have discouraged Dillard from further forays into fiction. In 1994 Harper-Collins published *The Annie Dillard Reader,* which reprints all of *Holy the Firm,* excerpts from *An American Childhood* and *Pilgrim at Tinker Creek,* Dillard's favorite essays and poems, and "a new and changed" version of the short story "The Living"—as if Dillard were still trying to get the story right. In 1995 she offered a new collection of poetry, *Mornings like This: Found Poems,* and in 1999 she published a new work of literary nonfiction, *For the Time Being,* which explores metaphysical questions via chronicles of the lives of newborns, of a family of Mogul horsemen, and of Jesuit paleontologist Teilhard de Chardin. In this work she dwells on a grain of sand and a service of clouds.

The major shift in critical appreciation of Dillard's work during the 1990s has been from noting Dillard's kinship with the nineteenth-century Transcendentalists to appreciating her differences from them. Readers have gone from linking Dillard to Thoreau to finding her affinity with Nathaniel Hawthorne and Herman Melville as well. Dillard has admitted that her favorite book is *Moby-Dick* (1851) and that she likes "the big guys who really go after the big game." *Moby-Dick,* she has said, is the best novel in English, perhaps in any language. "Everything I want to do as a writer is in that book," she has said, "the use of information metaphorically, the insistence on reading every event and every object for meaning." Imaginative acts matter, Dillard believes; in *Living by Fiction* she wrote, "A completed novel in a trunk in the attic is an order added to the sum of the universe's order. It remakes its share of undoing."

Interviews:

Philip Yancey, ed., "A Face Aflame—An Interview with Annie Dillard," *Christianity Today* (5 May 1978): 958–963;

Michael Burnett, ed., "An Interview with Annie Dillard," *Fairhaven Review* (1978);

Katherine Weber, "*PW* Interviews: Annie Dillard," *Publishers Weekly* (1 September 1989): 67–68;

Maureen Abood, "Natural Wonders: Interview," *U.S. Catholic,* 64 (November 1999): 30–33.

Bibliographies:

William J. Scheick, "A Bibliography of Writings by Annie Dillard," in *Contemporary Women Writers: Narrative Strategies,* edited by Catherine Rainwater and Scheick (Lexington: University Press of Kentucky, 1985), pp. 64–67;

Dawn Evans Radford, "Annie Dillard: A Bibliographical Survey," *Bulletin of Bibliography,* 52 (June 1994): 181–194.

References:

"About This Issue," *Harper's Magazine,* 248 (February 1974): 14;

Sandra Humble Johnson, *The Space Between: Literary Epiphany in the Work of Annie Dillard* (Kent, Ohio: Kent State University Press, 1992);

Mike Major, "Annie Dillard, Pilgrim of the Absolute," *America,* 128 (6 May 1978): 363–364;

Scott Slovic, *Seeking Awareness in American Nature Writing: Henry Thoreau, Annie Dillard, Edward Abbey, Wendell Berry, Barry Lopez* (Salt Lake City: University of Utah Press, 1992);

Linda Smith, *Annie Dillard* (New York: Twayne, 1991);

Pamela A. Smith, "The Ecotheology of Annie Dillard: A Study in Ambivalence," *Cross Currents: The Journal of the Association for Religion and Intellectual Life,* 45 (Fall 1995): 341–358;

Richard White, "A Review of Annie Dillard's *The Living,*" in *Novel History: Historians and Novelists Confront America's Past (and Each Other),* edited by Mark C. Carnes (New York: Simon & Schuster, 2001), pp. 109–118;

Steve Wiegenstein, "Nature in Annie Dillard's *The Living,*" in *The Image of Nature in Literature, the Media, and Society,* edited by Will Wright and Steven Kaplan (Pueblo, Colo.: Society for the Interdisciplinary Study of Social Imagery, 1993), pp. 88–93;

Philip Yancey, "This Pulitzer Prize Winner Understands Both Christians and Skeptics," *Christianity Today,* 27 (15 July 1983): 50, 52.

Clyde Edgerton
(20 May 1944 –   )

Sara Elliott
Aurora University

BOOKS: *Raney* (Chapel Hill, N.C.: Algonquin Books of Chapel Hill, 1985; London: Penguin, 1990);

Walking Across Egypt (Chapel Hill, N.C.: Algonquin Books of Chapel Hill, 1987; London: Cape, 1988);

The Floatplane Notebooks (Chapel Hill, N.C.: Algonquin Books of Chapel Hill, 1988; London: Viking, 1989);

Killer Diller (Chapel Hill, N.C.: Algonquin Books of Chapel Hill, 1991);

In Memory of Junior (Chapel Hill, N.C.: Algonquin Books of Chapel Hill, 1992);

Redeye: A Western (Chapel Hill, N.C.: Algonquin Books of Chapel Hill, 1995);

Where Trouble Sleeps (Chapel Hill, N.C.: Algonquin Books of Chapel Hill, 1997).

RECORDINGS: *Walking Across Egypt: Songs and Readings from the Books Walking Across Egypt and Raney,* sung and played by the Tarwater Band: Clyde Edgerton, Susan Edgerton, and Jim Watson, Flying Fish Records, 1987;

The Floatplane Notebooks, abridged, read by Edgerton, Random House Audiobooks, 1989; abridged, read by Edgerton, Winegrass Productions, 1996;

The Devil's Dream: Traditional and Original Music from the Novel by Lee Smith, arranged and performed by the Tarwater Band: Clyde Edgerton, Susan Ketchin, and Bill Butler, Tarwater Productions, 1992;

Raney, abridged, read by Edgerton, Wiregrass Productions, 1996;

Walking Across Egypt, abridged, read by Edgerton, Wiregrass Productions, 1996;

Killer Diller, abridged, read by Edgerton, Wiregrass Productions, 1996;

In Memory of Junior, abridged, read by Edgerton, Wiregrass Productions, 1996;

Redeye, abridged, read by Edgerton, Wiregrass Productions, 1996;

Where Trouble Sleeps, abridged, read by Edgerton, Wiregrass Productions, 1997;

Clyde Edgerton (photograph by Bernard Thomas; from the dust jacket for The Floatplane Notebooks, *1988)*

The Safety Patrol Song (and others), written and performed by Edgerton and the Rank Strangers: Jack King and Matt Kendrick, Durham, N.C., Snow Hill, 2003.

OTHER: "A Four-Blade Case," in *Family Portraits: Remembrances by Twenty Distinguished Writers,* edited by Carolyn Anthony (New York: Doubleday, 1989), pp. 79–92;

"Changing Names," in *New Stories from the South: The Year's Best, 1990,* edited by Shannon Ravenel (Chapel Hill, N.C.: Algonquin Books of Chapel Hill, 1990), pp. 127–133;

"Washing Dishes," in *The Rough Road Home: Stories by North Carolina Writers,* edited by Robert Gingher (Chapel Hill, N.C.: University of North Carolina Press, 1992), pp. 102–117;

"Baby at the Lake," in *Writer's Harvest: An Annual Collection of New Fiction,* edited by William H. Shore (New York: Harcourt Brace, 1994), pp. 137–142;

David Perkins, ed., *Pete and Shirley: The Great Tarheel Novel,* first and last chapters by Edgerton (Asheboro, N.C.: Down Home Press, 1995);

"Send Me to the Electric Chair," in *The Best American Short Stories, 1997,* edited by E. Annie Proulx and Katrina Kenison (New York: Houghton Mifflin, 1997), pp. 215–222.

SELECTED PERIODICAL PUBLICATIONS–
UNCOLLECTED:

FICTION

"Natural Suspension," *Just Pulp,* 3 (Spring/Summer 1980): 70–76;

"Raney and the Psychiatric," *Pembroke Magazine,* 16 (1984): 57–62;

"Songs of Men," *Southern Exposure,* 17 (Spring 1989): 34–39;

"Venom," *Southern Exposure,* 19 (Fall 1991): 37–42;

"Search and Rescue," *Southern Review,* 30 (Summer 1994): 452–461;

"Lucky Strike," *Carolina Quarterly,* 48 (Winter 1996): 82–87;

"Lunch at the Piccadilly," *Carolina Quarterly,* 50 (Summer 1998): 24–31.

NONFICTION

"The Way We Are: Yard Sale," *Southern Style,* 2 (May/June 1988): 5;

"Pan Fried Heaven," *Sophisticated Traveler: The New York Times Magazine,* 16 May 1993, pp. 30–31, 44, 46;

"Notes from the State Fair: What's Spam Got to Do with It?" *Oxford American* (June/July 1996): 48–57;

"Edgerton Playing God," *North Carolina Review of Books* (November/December 1997): 8, 10.

North Carolina novelist Clyde Edgerton is most commonly recognized as a Southern writer, although readers across the United States and around the world identify with his stories of families and relationships. Edgerton is also known for the humor in his writing, and this trait is emphasized in his readings and performances, in which he often theatrically takes on the voices and mannerisms of his characters. In addition to his novels Edgerton has published stories in a variety of publications, and his short fiction has been included in anthologies such as *New Stories from the South: The Year's Best* (1990), and *Writer's Harvest: An Annual Collection of New Fiction* (1994). Edgerton's novels have been named

among the Notable Books of the Year by *The New York Times* and included in the *Publishers Weekly* annual Best Books of the Year list. Teaching and writing have been continually intertwined in Edgerton's career, and he has held both faculty and visiting lecturer positions at colleges and universities in the South. Edgerton's satirical novels are sometimes described as "fast reads," but they also offer serious social commentary. Christianity is a frequent focus of examination in his work, as is the changing cultural landscape of the South. Edgerton's work is character-driven, and he is perhaps best known for his ability to realistically capture the rhythms of Southern speech.

Clyde Carlyle Edgerton was born on 20 May 1944, in Durham, North Carolina, the only child of Truma and Ernest Edgerton. He grew up in the small community of Bethesda, just outside of Durham, surrounded by a wide network of extended family. While Edgerton's father was an insurance salesman and his mother was a homemaker, they both came from farming families: his mother's family raised cotton, and his father's family grew tobacco. Edgerton spent a great deal of time with his relatives, and the old family stories that were told and retold at frequent family gatherings had a significant impact on both his identity and his imagination. Many of these family stories were later worked into Edgerton's novels. The significance of oral tradition and the rhythm of intimate, repeated storytelling are clear influences throughout Edgerton's work.

Three of Edgerton's relatives were also particularly influential in his early life. His mother's two sisters, Oma and Lila, were married but childless; they were almost daily visitors to the Edgerton home. This close contact gave Edgerton particular exposure to women's speech and was an influence in his use of female narrators, particularly in his first novel, *Raney* (1985). His mother's brother, Clem, was also a strong presence in Edgerton's childhood. Clem had lost an arm in World War I and never fully recovered from the trauma, suffering from depression and alcoholism the rest of his life. He moved into the Edgerton home before Clyde was born and lived with the family until 1978, when he committed suicide. The characters of Uncle Nate in *Raney* and Uncle Raleigh in *Where Trouble Sleeps* (1997) are inspired, in part, by Clem.

Throughout his childhood, Edgerton attended church with his parents, and Southern Baptist Christianity was a significant aspect of family life. The religious dimension of Edgerton's background became a major influence on his fiction. In an interview in Susan Ketchin's *The Christ-Haunted Landscape: Faith and Doubt in Southern Fiction* (1994) Edgerton commented, "In the South religion is a serious matter. Questions of good and evil, eternity, and hell fire, are on every street corner, everywhere." Discussing the conflicts created by his specific church experiences and the way they have influenced his writing, he explained:

> In my church, the same older people who loved me like aunts and uncles also refused to consider letting black human beings, created in the image of God, have entry into our place of worship. While I can clearly understand the cultural conditioning which would lead to this paradox–I experienced it myself–my sense of, my beliefs about, what the historical Jesus would do in the church I was raised in . . . creates a kind of excitement, drama, conflict, tension. There is a need to write it out, to understand it, and in the process, to entertain myself and my reader.

Besides having a large family network to socialize with, Edgerton was also popular in his school and community, enjoying hunting and sports with his friends. Like his father, Edgerton was particularly passionate about baseball and played on a team every summer for nine years. He also developed a love of fishing, mostly because of the influence of his Uncle Bob, who lived in Ocala, Florida, and whom the family visited yearly. Another lifelong interest that began in Edgerton's childhood was music. His mother arranged for him to begin taking piano lessons when he was seven. He later learned to play the banjo and guitar, played in rock-and-roll bands in college, and has continued to play in bluegrass and other bands throughout his writing career, often incorporating music into fiction readings and conference appearances.

Edgerton attended Southern High School in Durham County. He was a good student and was selected to attend Boys' State at the University of North Carolina during the summer following his junior year. This participation resulted in the University of North Carolina at Chapel Hill sending him an application for admission during his senior year in high school. After graduating from Southern High School in June 1962, Edgerton entered the university the following September. During high school, Edgerton had enjoyed the essays of Ralph Waldo Emerson and Henry David Thoreau. In his sophomore year of college, he read Ernest Hemingway's *A Farewell to Arms* (1929) and decided that he wanted to be an English teacher.

Throughout college, Edgerton remained committed to the conservative beliefs and views of his upbringing. He worked for the Barry Goldwater presidential campaign in 1964 and published a poem in the school newspaper that was critical of war protestors. Edgerton was also a student in the Air Force ROTC program, and after graduating in 1966 he received a commission and entered the United States Air Force. He served in the Air Force from 1966 to 1971, part of that time as a

fighter pilot in Japan, and part as a forward air controller over Laos. During his service in Southeast Asia he received the Distinguished Flying Cross. While in the Air Force, Edgerton continued to read and was drawn to the naturalism of Stephen Crane. Edgerton also tried some writing of his own, but the work was mostly descriptive paragraphs, which he did not develop into complete stories.

Like many veterans of the Vietnam conflict, Edgerton returned to civilian life with a new suspicion of authority, bred out of resentment of being denied the freedom to question the purposes and justifications of the war. After his discharge from the Air Force, Edgerton decided to pursue a master's degree at the University of North Carolina before beginning his teaching career. The combination of his Vietnam experience and his liberal arts education led to major shifts in Edgerton's political thinking, and in 1972 he worked for George McGovern's presidential campaign. After earning his M.A. in teaching, he took a position teaching English at his alma mater, Southern High School, where he taught for a year before returning to the University of North Carolina at Chapel Hill to pursue a Ph.D. in English education.

While in graduate school, Edgerton met Susan Ketchin, whom he married in 1975. Ketchin, along with campus readers' theater performances of Eudora Welty's "Why I Live at the P.O." (1941) and Flannery O'Connor's "A Good Man Is Hard to Find" (1955), introduced Edgerton to the works of Welty, O'Connor, and William Faulkner. Reading these Southern authors gave Edgerton a new perspective on writing and helped him to understand for the first time that he did not have to imitate the style of Hemingway or Crane to be a writer, and that instead he could write about subject matter from his own life, using the oral rhythms of the storytellers he grew up with. After hearing Welty read her short story "Why I Live at the P.O." on public television one evening in 1978, he began to write short stories with a strong oral quality to them, drawing on his immediate surroundings and on the family tales of his childhood.

After completing his doctorate in 1977, Edgerton accepted a faculty position at Campbell University, a small Baptist school, in Buis Creek, North Carolina, where he taught until 1985. He and his wife bought an older home in the small town of Apex, North Carolina, and Edgerton began to submit his stories to literary journals and magazines. He received 202 rejections before finally having his story "Natural Suspension" accepted for publication in the small periodical *Just Pulp* in 1980. The story is about a boy, Meredith, falling through a weak spot in a kitchen floor into an abandoned well beneath the house. Meredith later became the central character in Edgerton's third novel, *The*

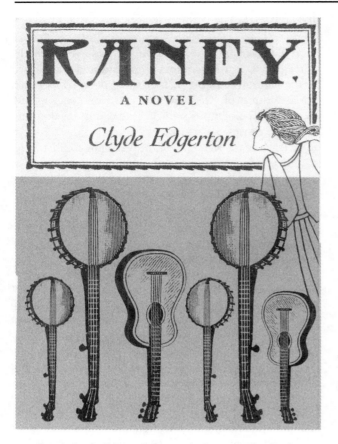

*Dust jacket for Edgerton's first novel, about a couple adjusting
to one another in the early years of their marriage
(Richland County Public Library)*

Floatplane Notebooks (1988), and a revised version of the
story appears as an early scene.

Edgerton continued to teach and write, and while
he and Ketchin were living in Apex, their only child,
Catherine, was born in 1982. Ketchin had taken a seminar on Southern fiction with Louis D. Rubin Jr., a
well-known literary scholar who had recently founded
a small publishing company, Algonquin Books of
Chapel Hill. Sylvia Wilkinson, a Southern writer, upon
reading an early draft of a manuscript Edgerton had
started, suggested that Edgerton take a writing course
with Rubin. After reading several pieces of Rubin's criticism, Edgerton decided to show some of his work to
Rubin, and he submitted parts of a manuscript he was
working on, which had already been rejected by several
New York publishers and agents. After reading the
excerpts, Rubin had Edgerton send the entire book to
his fiction editor, Shannon Ravenel. The manuscript
became Edgerton's first novel, *Raney,* and began Edgerton's long-standing relationship with Algonquin Books
and Ravenel.

Raney, as described on the dust jacket, is "the
story of the first two years, two months, and two days

in the life of a modern Southern marriage." The novel
is narrated in the first person by the title character,
Raney Bell, as she navigates the complicated beginnings
of her marriage with Charles Shepherd. The union portrayed in the novel is, in many ways, a marriage
between the Old South and the New South, conservative and liberal, rural and urban. Raney is from the tiny
fictional town of Listre, North Carolina, where her life
revolves around her immediate and extended family.
She is a dedicated member of the Freewill Baptist
Church, and her personal relationship with Jesus Christ
is central to her life and values. Her education is limited
and her views traditional. Charles is an open-minded
librarian who grew up in Atlanta, attending with limited
enthusiasm an Episcopalian church. He is interested in
the world of ideas and often frustrated with the provin-
cialism of Raney's ever-present family. In spite of their
differences, Charles and Raney are drawn together by
their love of music and their basic good-hearted
natures.

The narrow limits of Raney's world and the distance between her world and Charles's are evident in
the first scene of the novel, as Raney describes an early
encounter between the two families:

> Charles's parents are staying at the Ramada—wouldn't
> stay with any of us—and today, me, Mama, Aunt
> Naomi, and Aunt Flossie ate lunch with Charles's
> mother, Mrs. Shepherd. And found out that she's, of all
> things, a vegetarian. . . . Somehow I thought people
> were *born* as vegetarians. I never thought about some-
> body just *changing over.*

As Charles and Raney settle into married life, Raney
continues to be surprised by Charles's tendency to
question authority, his willingness to drink wine, and
his desire to talk about things other than family and
food, while Charles must cope with Raney's commitment to the views of her family and church leaders, her
unexamined racism, and her prudish attitudes toward
sex. Both partners slowly make concessions and begin
to move toward each other. The novel closes with a
newspaper clipping announcing the birth of their son
and illustrating the ongoing compromises. The baby is
baptized at the Episcopal church, but a reception is held
at the Freewill Baptist Church. Raney's friend Madora
is named godmother, but Charles' best friend, Johnny
Dobbs, the first black person Raney has met, is named
godfather.

Several reviewers compared Raney's honest,
down-to-earth voice with that of Huckleberry Finn and
praised Edgerton's mastery of the rural Southern dialect, particularly his ability to create a believable female
voice. A few critics found the story trivial or saw the
portrayal of Raney as simplistic or patronizing. Most,

though, enjoyed the humor and described the characters as both complex and endearing. In *The New York Times Book Review* (23 June 1985) Carol Verderese concluded: "Like Charles, we are both appalled by Raney's provincial attitudes and awed by her simple wisdom. She is ingenuous but not naïve, and her exploration of life's limitations and possibilities is as poignant as it is funny."

While the general reception of *Raney* was positive, Edgerton soon learned that his most serious critics were his employers at Campbell University. Shortly after the book was published, and just before Edgerton's contract was due to be renewed, he was asked to meet with administrators. Although students and faculty at Campbell were enthusiastic about *Raney,* the president, provost, and dean of liberal arts and sciences had concerns about whether the book furthered the mission of the university. They saw the portrayal of Freewill Baptists in the book as demeaning and felt that the novel took too light a view of sex and alcohol. The controversy was widely reported in both the local and the trade press, and after many tense weeks Edgerton was finally presented a new contract, but without the customary raise and without the tenure offer that Edgerton's department chair had requested. The success of *Raney* and the public controversy at Campbell had led to several job offers from other colleges in the Southeast, so after receiving the unsatisfactory renewal offer, Edgerton resigned and accepted a faculty position at St. Andrews, a Presbyterian college in Laurinburg, North Carolina, where he taught until 1989.

Edgerton's contract at St. Andrews allowed him more time for writing, and he quickly completed his second novel, *Walking Across Egypt,* published in 1987. The first idea for the novel came when Edgerton was visiting with his mother one day, and she told him about accidentally sitting down in a rocking chair from which she had removed the seat to be sent out for repair. She went through the empty space where the seat would have been and was stuck for about fifteen minutes. Edgerton thought the incident was hilarious and went home and wrote a short story about a woman in the same predicament. The story became an early scene in the novel, which develops the unlikely relationship between seventy-eight-year-old Mattie Rigsbee and a juvenile delinquent, Wesley Benfield.

Wesley comes into Mattie's life through his uncle, Lamar, a dogcatcher whom Mattie has summoned to take away a stray dog she has been feeding. Mattie tells her son, Robert, "I got as much business keeping a dog as I do walking across Egypt," a reference to one of her favorite hymns. Like Edgerton's first novel, *Walking Across Egypt* is set in Listre, North Carolina, and Mattie has several qualities in common with Raney. She is a devoted Christian, intimately involved in the lives of her family and community members; she is prone to judging people but also genuinely cares about others; and she is quite concerned with appearances. When Lamar arrives at her home to find her stuck in the chair, she is so worried about one of the neighbors stopping by and seeing her dirty lunch dishes that she asks Lamar to wash them and put them away before he goes to work at freeing her.

Walking Across Egypt also touches on conflicts between Old South, Christian values and a New South, secular viewpoint, with Mattie's two grown children serving as representatives of the latter. Mattie is greatly disappointed that neither her son, Robert, nor her daughter, Elaine, has married or given her grandchildren. Her need to find some way to continue nurturing others is revealed in frequent, detailed descriptions of her cooking for anyone who happens to stop by, even the stray dog. Though Mattie's faith is sometimes simple and naive, she takes her preacher's sermons to heart and tries to act on them. When the preacher quotes Christ's statement in Matthew 25 that "Whatso ye do unto one of the least of these my brethren you do also unto me," she decides that the troubled teenager, Wesley, is the "least of these" and determines to take him in when he is released from the juvenile detention facility. By the end of the novel the stray dog has also rejoined the household, and Mattie is preparing to adjust to her new life.

Reviews of *Walking Across Egypt* were generally positive, with strong appreciation for the realistic dialogue and more comparisons to Mark Twain. Carolyn See's review in *The Los Angeles Times* (30 March 1987) represented one caveat that appeared in the criticism: she commented that the book "teeters on the very edge of terminal cuteness," but concluded, "Mattie is so brave (and resigned) in her loneliness that you have to like her." The novel was adapted by Paul Tomasy as a motion picture starring Ellen Burstyn as Mattie and Jonathan Taylor Thomas as Wesley. Produced by the independent Mitchum Entertainment and filmed in 1998, the movie was screened at several film festivals in 1999 and 2000 and then released on video.

Edgerton's third novel, *The Floatplane Notebooks,* published in 1988, demonstrated an important shift from the lighthearted satire of *Raney* and *Walking Across Egypt.* Although the book does include several comic (even slapstick) scenes, it represents a new depth, complexity, and darkness in Edgerton's work. Ever since writing the 1978 story about the boy falling through the kitchen floor, Edgerton had been working on a longer piece of fiction about a Southern family's experience with the Vietnam War, but he had had a hard time finding an appropriate structure. He was finally able to complete the novel when he decided to tell the story through multiple first-person narrators. This structure, combined with the prominent role of the family burial ground in the story, led to many comparisons with Faulkner's *As I Lay Dying* (1930), although that book was not a significant influence on Edgerton.

The Floatplane Notebooks is again set in Listre and deals with themes of family, community, and faith through the lives of the Copeland family. In an interview in the *Atlanta Journal and Constitution* (23 October 1988) Edgerton described it as "a book about what wars do to people, and about persistence, the lingering of a family through generations." The novel takes its title from the notebooks that the father of the family, Albert Copeland, keeps, ostensibly as a record of the floatplane that he is attempting to build from a kit, but which eventually comprise his version of a family history.

With the stark consequences of Vietnam as a backdrop, the gentle questioning of Christianity that Edgerton began in his first two novels takes a much more serious tone in *The Floatplane Notebooks*. Meredith Copeland, the central character, is never as fully accepting of Christianity as his self-righteous cousin, Mark, is. Mark's hypocritical faith is presented with a far darker view than Raney's or Mattie's more innocent piety. After Meredith has returned from Vietnam with serious injuries, paralyzed and unable to speak, Mark is given the task of going out to find Meredith's wife, Rhonda, who has left him. As he drives to meet her, he contemplates his attraction to her and uses the biblical idea that looking at a woman lustfully is the same as committing adultery to justify betraying his cousin: "It's all a matter of physical geography. I mean if I'm thinking it and she's thinking it, *that's* the *sin,* as they say. Why the hell deprive yourself."

Meredith is not given his own narrative voice in the novel until the third section, after his Vietnam injuries, and his most serious questionings of his family's traditional religious beliefs come at this point, when he cannot voice them to anyone but himself:

> What I'd like to know is what happened to God. Aunt Esther, you got him locked up somewhere, afraid to let him out—afraid he might hear somebody cussing, for Christ's sake? If that's the way it works He ain't ever been in a war. And you figure in a posse of twelve fishermen, you're going to have some nasty language. That's the part that gets left out.

The question of what "gets left out"—of family stories and of history books—is another central theme in the novel. One of the six narrators is a wisteria vine that grows in the family cemetery, telling stories of the family's past and representing the voices of the dead. The vine relates incidents of racism and abuse that do not

appear in any of the traditional family stories repeated by the current generation.

In spite of its tragic vision, *The Floatplane Notebooks,* like Edgerton's earlier novels, is ultimately a hopeful story of family commitment and continuity. The novel closes with the scene of another annual grave cleaning, this time featuring the two newest members of the Copeland family—Meredith's son, Ross, and nephew, Taylor. When the work is done and the picnic is over, the family heads to a nearby lake so that Albert Copeland can try yet again to get his floatplane in the air. This time he finally succeeds, and the paralyzed Meredith, strapped in and wearing a football helmet, experiences the joy and freedom of flight.

Some reviewers were skeptical of the new direction in Edgerton's work. In the *Chicago Tribune* (6 November 1988) Maude McDaniel suggested, "*The Floatplane Notebooks* shows laudable ambitions but fulfills few of them very satisfactorily." Frank Levering, of the *Los Angeles Times Book Review* (6 November 1988), however, described the book as "among the wisest, most heartfelt writing to emerge from the South in our generation," and Barbara Kingsolver's review in *The New York Times Book Review* (9 October 1988) praised the "lighter touch" of the comic elements in the novel: "Occasional farce is controlled and subtly directed toward the story's core. The result is warmly humorous, gossipy, and rich." *The Floatplane Notebooks* was also cited as one of the best novels of 1988 by *Publishers Weekly,* and the book is generally viewed as a turning point in Edgerton's career, establishing him as a major new Southern writer.

As with *Raney,* fundamentalist Christian reaction led to minor controversy surrounding *The Floatplane Notebooks* when a radio preacher in Virginia objected to the inclusion of the novel as optional reading for a local high-school English class. The school board voted to remove the book, but many other high-school and college classes around the country have adopted it into the curriculum.

In 1989 Edgerton was awarded a Guggenheim Fellowship, which allowed him to take a leave of absence from St. Andrew's and complete his fourth novel, *Killer Diller,* published in 1991. In *Killer Diller* Edgerton revisits Mattie Rigsbee and Wesley Benfield from *Walking Across Egypt,* eight years later, with an older, frailer Mattie now living in a nursing home and twenty-four-year-old Wesley living in Back on Track Again (BOTA) House, a halfway house sponsored by the local Baptist college, Ballard University. Edgerton also returns to the omniscient third-person narrator and a more standard chronological structure for this novel. Mattie is more in the background in *Killer Diller* but is still a grandmother figure for Wesley, who is

"Clyde Edgerton is a miner of considerable skill, burrowing into the hillside of humanity to find the ore of characters so pure and so real they might just sit down beside us and tell us a tale."
—Washington Post

"a genius for characterization."
—Atlanta Journal and Constitution

"Those who whine about the lack of quality in contemporary fiction can just quit. Clyde Edgerton epitomizes quality."
—Richmond News Leader

Killer Diller

Clyde Edgerton

Algonquin Books of Chapel Hill

A novel by the author of Walking Across Egypt

Clyde Edgerton

ISBN 0-945575-53-X

Dust jacket for Edgerton's 1991 novel, which continues the adventures of Mattie and Wesley, characters in his 1987 novel, Walking Across Egypt *(Richland County Public Library)*

developing relationships with a wider cast of characters. Most significant, he is serving as a mentor for a mentally retarded teenager, Vernon Jackson, through a Ballard University enterprise called Project Promise, and he is falling in love with Phoebe Trent, a resident of another Ballard-run institution, Nutrition House, a treatment facility for overweight Christians. Wesley has also helped to form a gospel rock band, The Noble Defenders of the Word, and is secretly practicing his preaching technique.

With Christianity once again a focus of examination, *Killer Diller* introduces two extreme examples of Baptist legalism and judgment, Ned and Ted Sears, the president and provost of Ballard University. Though the various Ballard social programs have some genuine merit, the Sears brothers are primarily interested in the good publicity and grant money they can bring to the university. They spend their time convincing aging widows to leave their property to the university, checking to make sure the BOTA residents are not cussing, and making secret plans to obtain funding for a private university airport. With these two serving as foils, Wesley's

bumbling but earnest attempts to become a good Christian and understand the Bible appear innocent, even though he often combs the scriptures for scenes of lust and fornication as a way to justify his physical desires for Phoebe. Ultimately, the conflicts between Wesley's independent understanding of the Bible and the narrow and manipulative Christianity of Ned and Ted Sears lead Wesley to flee BOTA House and hit the road with his band, renamed The Wandering Stars. Just before his departure, Wesley shocks the Sears brothers and the rest of the audience when he gives his testimony at a Ballard-sponsored luncheon and addresses the issue of the two differing creation stories in Genesis, concluding: "If you believe every word in the Bible is absolutely true like some kind of steel trap then you believe both of those versions are absolutely true and if you believe that then you ain't using the brain God gave you."

Critics and readers who were unsettled by Edgerton's startling structure and stark subject matter in *The Floatplane Notebooks* saw *Killer Diller* as a welcome return to the more lighthearted, straightforward writing of *Raney* and *Walking Across Egypt*. Reviewers again responded positively to the humor and to Edgerton's ear for Southern speech, although the overall judgment of the book was mixed. In his review in the *Southern Quarterly* (Fall 1991) Kenn Robbins contended that *Killer Diller* did not live up to the high expectations created by Edgerton's first two novels and claimed that the book was missing "first, new and inventive incidents to hold our interest and, second, a riveting story." In *The New York Times Book Review* (10 February 1991), Lisa Koger also acknowledged that "Occasionally, Mr. Edgerton's sense of humor gets the best of him and he pushes a scene until the characters border on the cartoonish." Overall, her review was enthusiastic, however, and she claimed, "the bottom line is that there's an affecting story, authenticity of voice and moral complexity here." Some of the mixed reactions to the book may be related to its autobiographical roots. When asked by Dale W. Brown in an interview in *Carolina Quarterly* (Winter 1994) if the *Raney* controversy at Campbell University had affected the sharper satire of Christian fundamentalism in this novel, Edgerton replied, "The Campbell experience certainly had a lot to do with *Killer Diller*. That's one reason I feel less comfortable as an artist with that book–because I was scratching my own itch."

In 1991 Edgerton was awarded a Lyndhurst Prize and continued to devote much of his time to writing. His fifth novel, *In Memory of Junior* (1992), shares several characteristics with *The Floatplane Notebooks*. For this complex novel Edgerton again adopted the multiple-narrator structure, expanding the number of voices to twenty-one. The novel is propelled by conflicts over burial sites, inheritances, family secrets, and most important, the nature of "truth." The story, set in Summerlin, North Carolina, in the same fictional county as Listre, revolves around two brothers, Tate and Faison Bales, and their families. The title alludes to one of the central disputes in the book: the question of the text for the tombstone of Faison's stepson. Faison, his wife, June Lee, and her son had agreed to legally change the boy's name from John Moody Jr. to Faison Bales Jr., but before the change could be completed, the boy was killed in a car accident. The other central controversy concerns the fate of the Bales family farm, which is in question because Tate and Faison's father, Glenn, and stepmother, Laura, are both near death, and the inheritance will depend upon which one dies first.

In Memory of Junior confronts, more directly and explicitly than any of Edgerton's other novels, the tensions between an Old South sensibility based on agriculture, traditional values, Christianity, and the acceptance of absolute truths, and a New South, secular view influenced by humanism, postmodernism, and an acceptance of the subjective nature of reality. The two

Bales brothers, who continually aggravate each other, embody these differing worldviews. Tate is a psychology professor, while Faison is a "good-old-boy" hunter and fisherman who sometimes moves houses for a living. While on a fishing trip near the end of the novel, the two brothers have a drunken conversation about their differing ideas about the world and about what constitutes truth. Tate tries to explain the concept of multiple views of reality:

> what somebody *believes* is their whole world. . . . The way something smells is not in this world. It's in our heads, because if it was in the world then you wouldn't have flies landing on shit, because shit would stink to flies, too. . . . In his head it's beauty and in ours it's ugly, ugliness. Who's to say? Who's to say?

Faison can only respond to the argument by saying, "You talk like a damned atheist. . . . You won't ever get over going to college." Faison's friend Jimmy is an even more caustic critic of new ideas. Talking with Tate sets Jimmy off on a diatribe against "these college people" because of a newspaper article he has read recently:

> And what it said was there was this group of feminists and abstractionists or some such at Duke University who are trying to cut out everything that dead white males have ever done. I said to myself, Wait a minute! Wait a *minute!* Think about that. That takes up everything that's ever been done, more or less. . . . These professors are trying to actually destroy all of civilization–or at least the *history* of civilization. . . . If somebody would drop the big one in the middle of every kind of college except the agricultural ones, we'd be one hell of a lot better off as far as I'm concerned.

Ultimately, debates over truth, fact, and perspective are most significant to the lives of the characters when they concern family history rather than world history, and *In Memory of Junior,* like *The Floatplane Notebooks,* acknowledges the silences and untold stories that affect the generations. Stories about the reason that Tate and Faison's mother left when they were young vary, depending on which narrator is speaking, and even after their Uncle Grove reveals that she actually left with another woman, the story is again repressed and replaced with yet another new version of truth.

In spite of the weighty questions dealt with in the novel, *In Memory of Junior* also exemplifies Edgerton's trademark humor, through the realistic voices of the varied narrators and occasional bits of physical comedy. The novel was named a Notable Book of the Year by *The New York Times,* and reviews were overwhelmingly positive, although reviewers differed in their perceptions of the general tone of the book. Shelby Hearon, in *The New York Times Book Review* (11 October

1992), called it a "larky, down-home chronicle" and a "funny, sunny anthology." *Publishers Weekly* (3 August 1992) described it as "a prime example of entertaining, down-home Southern fiction," and *The New Yorker* (30 November 1992) presented it as "benign and bemused small-town comedy from a North Carolina novelist whose sensibility is a sharp as it is gentle." Other reviewers placed a greater emphasis on the cultural criticism in the novel. In her review in the *Southern Quarterly* (Winter 1993) Donnalee Frega argued that "the politics of relevance and the contingency of truth are central issues throughout Edgerton's novel" and asserted, "I believe that this book is Edgerton's finest and most complicated work so far, but it may confuse readers who don't wish to notice the subtly serious social commentary often underlying his hilarious stories."

Although Edgerton continued his social commentary through examination of forgotten history in his next novel, *Redeye: A Western* (1995), the book was a distinct departure for him in other ways. Most significant, *Redeye* is the only one of Edgerton's novels not set in the fictional Listre and Summerlin area of Piedmont North Carolina. As the subtitle indicates, it is in fact "A Western," set in 1890s Colorado and inspired in part by his appreciation for the writing of Cormac McCarthy and by a visit to Mesa Verde National Park. This difference in the setting of the novel also led to differences in Edgerton's writing process. Because he was not dealing with immediate, familiar surroundings, he did extensive research to ensure accurate depictions of the geography, language, and customs of his setting. He read forty books and took more than five hundred pages of notes organized into categories such as horses, clothing, food, geology, and embalming. He also made a return trip to the Mesa Verde area to become more familiar with the landscape and to spend time with some local historians. Clarity of place was so important to Edgerton that one of the first things he did as he began the novel was to draw a map of the setting and tack it to his office wall. When the book was published, the map was re-created on the endpapers. Edgerton managed to retain some of the familiar speech patterns of his own ancestors in the characters by making several of them pioneers who had originated from North Carolina. In Edgerton's fictional universe, the P. J. Copeland family of *Redeye* is related to the Albert Copelands of *The Floatplane Notebooks*.

The structure of *Redeye* again makes use of multiple first-person narrators, with the text of an Old West–style tourist guidebook inserted throughout, serving as a frame narrative. Several intertwined stories revolve around the discovery of ancient Native American cliff dwellings at Mesa Largo. While Abel Merriwether, a rancher and amateur archeologist, understands the historical significance of the site and wants to study and

Dust jacket for Edgerton's 1992 novel, in which two brothers represent the differing values of the Old and New South (Richland County Public Library)

preserve it, a local businessman, Billy Blankenship, wants to exploit the site for profit through tourism. Bishop Thorpe, a Mormon saint, gets involved in the exploration hoping to find proof in the ancient ruins that Jesus visited the area after his resurrection. Blankenship also draws his business partner, P. J. Copeland, into the venture. Copeland and Blankenship have recently learned the new science of embalming and hope to introduce the practice to the area. One example of Edgerton's typical physical comedy with a dark undertone occurs when Copeland and Blankenship attempt to gain publicity for their new business by warning people that unembalmed bodies can explode from heat, and then proving the point by using dynamite to stage the explosion of a "chinaman" killed working on the railroads.

Perhaps the darkest character in the book is the former cowboy Cobb Pittman, who has devoted his life to avenging the Mountain Meadows massacre of 1857, an actual historical event in which Mormon settlers attacked and killed a wagon train of Gentile pioneers. Pittman travels with his dog, Redeye, who is trained to

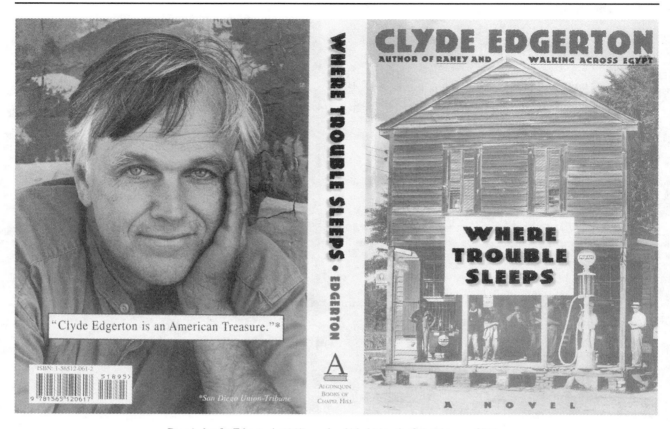

*Dust jacket for Edgerton's 1997 novel, which depicts the fictional town of Listre,
North Carolina, in 1950 (Richland County Public Library)*

attack animal or human by jumping up and latching onto the opponent's nose. Pittman has already killed four of the Mormons involved in the massacre and is on the trail of Bishop Thorpe. With the Mormon massacre an essential background element, *Redeye* again confronts issues of religious hypocrisy and conflicts over the nature of truth and history. The novel also addresses traditional Western themes of violence, freedom from societal constraints, and the exploitation of land and people. P. J. Copeland's niece, Star, newly arrived from North Carolina, highlights the differences between the more civilized East and the wild West: "Somehow I feel that out West I am able to be more honest than I was at home, more open to the new," she says. She uses the freedom of the West to abandon both her corset and her Southern-belle rules of decorum about interactions with men. The complicated nature of the relationships between white settlers and Native Americans is reflected in the two Indian characters, Mudfoot and Lobo, who are manipulated by the Mormons. The novel follows the convention of the Western as it concludes with justice achieved through violence, but it also leaves greater room for uncertainty about the nature of justice, as the ancient ruins of Mesa Largo are fated to become America's first tourist trap.

Redeye met with generally positive reviews, though some critics were skeptical of the complex, wide-ranging plot and of Edgerton's risky attempts to capture the voice of an 1890 Mescadey Indian in the character of Mudfoot. In *Booklist* (15 March 1995) Joanne Wilkinson contended, "Because Edgerton roams so far and wide here, his novel never quite hangs together, but he certainly delivers some hilarious set pieces. The author's many fans, accustomed to the rural North Carolina setting of Edgerton's previous five novels, may be a bit startled by this book's move west, but they'll stick around for the ride anyway." Tim Sandlin, in *The New York Times Book Review* (30 April 1995), noted that Mudfoot "seems contrived," but he was otherwise enthusiastic, describing *Redeye* as "Eudora Welty meets Mark Twain" and claiming, "Edgerton has combined structure, character and style to create a small gem of a novel." The *Library Journal* review (15 April 1995) likewise concluded, "A master storyteller, Edgerton proves that he is in full command of his craft no matter what the setting," and Polly Paddock, in the *Chicago Tribune* (24 May 1995), called *Redeye* Edgerton's "funniest yet . . . filled with winsomely wacky characters and priceless dialogue." Paddock also commented on the darker satire of the novel in her

mention of the Mountain Meadows massacre, noting, "For all the hilarity he can muster, Edgerton wants us to ponder the convoluted thinking that can lead wild-eyed 'true believers' to such atrocities."

In 1995 and 1996 Edgerton and his wife shared the Eudora Welty Chair in Southern Studies at Millsaps College in Jackson, Mississippi, where he continued to work on his seventh novel, *Where Trouble Sleeps* (1997). For this book Edgerton returned to the familiar territory of Listre and to the third-person omniscient narrator, although his use of free indirect discourse allows him to fully develop the voices of several of the main characters. *Where Trouble Sleeps* is set in 1950, when Listre is a smaller, less developed town, with just one blinking stoplight. The small community's life is dominated by the Baptist church and Preacher Crenshaw, yet the beer drinkers at Train's Place are tolerated, to varying degrees. The central conflict in the novel arises when a stranger, Jack Umstead, drives into town in his stolen Buick. Umstead's deceptive attempts to learn enough about the town and its people to plan a robbery while avoiding suspicion serve as a sinister contrast to the earnest efforts of six-year-old Stephen Toomey to understand the world around him and learn the rules necessary to be a good Christian.

Stephen's mother, Alease, is intent on indoctrinating Stephen into a strict moral and cultural code. In the opening scene of the novel, Alease takes Stephen and a neighbor boy, Terry, to a nearby prison to see the electric chair. The reason for the trip, as she explains to the boys, "is so you-all can see what will happen if you ever let the Devil lead you into a bad sin. They'll put you in the electric chair and electrocute you. And little sins can lead up to big sins." Between frequent readings from *Aunt Margaret's Bible Stories* and his own observations of the actions of adults around him, Stephen tries to clarify the all-important moral code:

> Stephen was beginning to get some idea about who was going to hell and who was going to heaven. His mama and daddy and aunts and uncles were pretty clear. Terry's daddy—Mr. Daniels—was pretty clear: He was going to hell for getting drunk and beating up Mrs. Daniels. Mrs. Daniels was going to hell for drinking wine. He, Stephen, would go to hell if he didn't accept Jesus, something he was getting old enough to figure out how to do. . . . A lot of it—getting saved—had to do with visiting old people and going to church every time you were supposed to. . . . And not drinking beer and whiskey.

As the outsider, Umstead, with his thin mustache and ubiquitous yellow shirt, insinuates himself into the lives of the locals, he causes some of them to recognize their own weaknesses, even, ultimately, Alease Toomey. He

indirectly helps Preacher Crenshaw finally give up his lust for the nineteen-year-old Cheryl Daniels. He even confirms the faith of the eccentric church secretary, Mrs. Clark, who has moved into her office. While attempting to rob the church, Umstead is heard by Clark, who calls out, "Is that *You*, Jesus?" Umstead plays along, talking to Mrs. Clark through the office door, quoting scripture, and then convincing her to slide $10 to him under the door. Mrs. Clark cherishes the encounter as a religious experience, but Stephen, in his open-eyed innocence, suspects the truth. When the secretary tells Alease and Stephen about her holy visitor, Stephen asks, "Did he have on a yellow shirt?" Though Umstead serves as a catalyst for redemption, his own goal is deception and theft, and in the end he is brought to justice by the seemingly frail Bea Blaine as he attempts to rob her.

The combination of serious questions about human nature and faith with comic dialogue and physical humor again led to a positive critical reception. In an article in *Renascence* (Summer 2001) W. Todd Martin called *Where Trouble Sleeps* "Clyde Edgerton's criticism of moralistic Christianity" and argued that Edgerton "creates a uniquely textured fiction that exposes the hypocrisy of the misguided morality of some Southern Baptists, couching his criticism within the context of light-hearted humor." Victoria Rebeck, in *The Christian Century* (17 June 1998), noted, "Edgerton's delivery is wickedly funny. His narration is concise and spare," and in *World and I* (April 1998) Robert Gingher commented, "Edgerton's achievement remains the engaging authenticity in his revelation of place, psychology of community, and conflicted human nature." *Publishers Weekly* (23 June 1997) also praised Edgerton's "antic humor and respect for his character's dignity." In *The New York Times Book Review* (28 September 1997) Mark Childress described the novel as "thoroughly appealing" and called attention to the depth of the book by noting that it is "the story of a boy's search for his own salvation. And the seriousness of this underlying quest is what makes the novel ever so much more than just charming."

In the fall of 1998 Edgerton was named Distinguished Visiting Professor of Creative Writing at the University of North Carolina, Wilmington. He continued in that position for four years until he was granted tenure in the fall of 2002 as a full professor. Edgerton and Ketchin separated in 1999, and the couple was divorced in early 2001. In December 2001 Edgerton married Kristina Jones. Edgerton commutes to Wilmington but continues to live in the Durham area, where he writes and occasionally performs music with the Rank Strangers band. Although his writing is consistently identified with his region, Edgerton reaches a wide national and international audience, and his books

Edgerton-7

Aunt Lil reached for his little white ticket slip and put it with hers. ~~On the way out,~~ she'd insist that he pay with her MasterCard.

A cafeteria worker carried Aunt Lil's tray to one of their two favorite tables, they sat, Carl said the blessing, and they began eating. He was never quite sure if he should say the blessing ~~when he ate lunch~~ with her. Unlike his mother and Aunt Sara, Aunt Lil had more or less given up on church. They didn't talk about it. Carl figured that was one of the things they could talk about sometime, now that they were the only two left--and now that he too had drifted away from the shore, as that old gospel song said.

He watched her look around for old friends, ~~didn't say anything about the fact she hadn't seen any in months now.~~ They talked about normal things. He checked his watch a few times.

"Have you met Mr. Flowers?" she asked. "With that fancy white hair." She pictured him rolling in his wheelchair out onto the porch--at Rosehaven--his leg stuck out, straight ahead, a big smile on his red face. He was a dandy.

"The one had the knee operation?" asked Carl.

"Yes. The preacher."

"We talked a little bit the other day."

"Where did you see him?"

"On the porch. You were with me."

"On . . . ?" Why didn't he speak up? He was ~~getting to be~~ mumbling-- like the others. ~~Mumbling.~~

"On the porch. When you were smoking a cigarette. You know, if you'd let me take you up to the hearing aide place I think we could get you fixed up."

"I can hear okay. People's talking has just fell off some."

"I think it's your hearing that's fell off some."

Page from a late draft for a forthcoming novel Edgerton has tentatively titled "Old People"
(Collection of Clyde Edgerton)

are appreciated for their combination of humor with complex critiques of cultural and religious issues.

Interviews:

Bob Summers, "Clyde Edgerton," *Publishers Weekly,* 234 (16 September 1988): 58, 60;

William J. Walsh, "Clyde Edgerton," in his *Speak So I Shall Know Thee: Interviews with Southern Writers* (Jefferson, N.C.: McFarland, 1990), pp. 115–124;

Caroline Harkleroad, "Clyde Edgerton on Fried Okra, Fainting Goats, the Telling of a Good Story, and *Killer Diller,*" *Oxford Review,* 6 (February 1991): 1–2, 19;

Kenn Robbins, "A Conversation with Clyde Edgerton," *Southern Quarterly,* 30 (Fall 1991): 59–65;

Dale W. Brown, "Dusty's Flying Taxi," *Carolina Quarterly,* 46 (Winter 1994): 38–59;

Dannye Romine Powell, "Clyde Edgerton," in his *Parting the Curtains: Interviews with Southern Writers* (Winston-Salem, N.C.: J. F. Blair, 1994), pp. 82–91;

Christopher D. Campbell, "Reading, Writing, and Going to War: An Interview," *War, Literature, and the Arts,* 8 (Fall/Winter 1996): 133–147;

Shelby Stephenson, "Clyde Edgerton: Singing This Song," *Carolina Quarterly,* 48 (Winter 1996): 75–81.

Bibliography:

Hilbert H. Campbell, "Clyde Edgerton's Bibliography, 1980–1998," 25 February 1999 <http://www.clydeedgerton.com/bibliography.htm>.

References:

Angeline Godwin Dvorak, "Cooking as Mission and Ministry in Southern Culture: The Nurturers of Clyde Edgerton's *Walking Across Egypt,* Fannie Flagg's *Fried Green Tomatoes at the Whistle Stop Cafe*

and Anne Tyler's *Dinner at the Homesick Restaurant,*" *Southern Quarterly,* 30 (Winter/Spring 1992): 90–98;

Sara Elliott, "Dead Bodies, Burned Letters, and Burial Grounds: Negotiating Place Through Storytelling in Contemporary Southern Fiction," dissertation, Northern Illinois University, 1998, pp. 102–157;

James A. Grimshaw Jr., "Clyde Edgerton: Death and Dying," in *Southern Writers at Century's End,* edited by Jeffrey J. Folkes and James A. Perkins (Lexington: University of Kentucky Press, 1997), pp. 238–246;

George Hovis, "The *Raney* Controversy: Clyde Edgerton's Fight for Creative Freedom," *Southern Cultures,* 7 (Summer 2001): 60–83;

Cynthia E. Huggins, "Witnessing by Example: Southern Baptists in Clyde Edgerton's *Walking Across Egypt* and *Killer Diller,*" *Southern Quarterly,* 32 (Spring 1997): 91–96;

Susan Ketchin, "Clyde Edgerton: A Garden of Paradoxes," in her *The Christ-Haunted Landscape: Faith and Doubt in Southern Fiction* (Jackson: University of Mississippi Press, 1994), pp. 352–370;

W. Todd Martin, "*Where Trouble Sleeps:* Clyde Edgerton's Criticism of Moralistic Christianity," *Renascence,* 53 (Summer 2001): 257–266;

Michael McFee, "'Reading a Small History in a Universal Light': Doris Betts, Clyde Edgerton, and the Triumph of True Regionalism," *Pembroke Magazine,* 23 (1991): 59–67;

Michael Pearson, "Stories to Ease the Tension," *Hollins Critic,* 27 (1990): 1–9.

Papers:

Clyde Edgerton's papers, manuscripts, and correspondence are collected in the library of the University of North Carolina at Chapel Hill.

Stanley Elkin

(11 May 1930 – 31 May 1995)

David C. Dougherty
Loyola College in Maryland

See also the Elkin entries in *DLB 2: American Novelists Since World War II; DLB 28: Twentieth-Century American-Jewish Fiction Writers; DLB 218: American Short-Story Writers Since World War II, Second Series;* and *DLB Yearbook: 1980.*

BOOKS: *Boswell: A Modern Comedy* (New York: Random House, 1964; London: Hamilton, 1964);

Criers and Kibitzers, Kibitzers and Criers (New York: Random House, 1966; London: Anthony Blond, 1967);

A Bad Man (New York: Random House, 1967; London: Anthony Blond, 1968);

The Dick Gibson Show (New York: Random House, 1971; London: Weidenfeld & Nicolson, 1971);

The Making of Ashenden (London: Covent Garden Press, 1972);

Searches and Seizures (New York: Random House, 1973); republished as *Eligible Men: Three Short Novels* (London: Gollancz, 1974); republished as *Alex and the Gypsy: Three Short Novels* (Harmondsworth, U.K. & New York: Penguin, 1977);

The Franchiser (New York: Farrar, Straus & Giroux, 1976);

The Living End (New York: Dutton, 1979; London: Cape, 1980);

The First George Mills (Dallas: Pressworks, 1980);

Stanley Elkin's Greatest Hits (New York: Dutton, 1980);

George Mills (New York: Dutton, 1982);

Early Elkin (Flint, Mich.: Bamberger Books, 1985);

Stanley Elkin's The Magic Kingdom (New York: Dutton, 1985);

The Rabbi of Lud (New York: Scribners, 1987);

The Six-Year-Old Man (Flint, Mich.: Bamberger Books, 1987);

The MacGuffin (New York: Linden Press, 1991);

Pieces of Soap: Essays (New York: Simon & Schuster, 1992);

Van Gogh's Room at Arles: Three Novellas (New York: Hyperion, 1993);

Mrs. Ted Bliss (New York: Hyperion, 1995).

Stanley Elkin (photograph © by Miriam Berkley; from the dust jacket for Mrs. Ted Bliss, *1995)*

Fond of fracturing readers' expectations, Stanley Elkin made his most profound impact on his fellow writers. Toward the end of his life, his books were falling out of print, and only specialized editions of some novels were widely available. However, literary critics and fellow novelists have continued to champion Elkin's exuberant innovations in fictional form. What sets Elkin's work apart from that of his contemporaries is his restoring to fiction the primacy of rhetoric. While other novelists experimented with minimalist and metafictional aesthetics, Elkin held out for the centrality of style. Readers often come to a novel expecting style and grace but not anticipating the same demands on attention that poetry often requires. In Elkin's novels, however, rhetoric is not merely decoration but is the substance, the raison d'être, of the entire fictional construct. As he said in "The Rest of the Novel" (1990, collected in *Pieces of Soap* [1992]), "For conveying ideas, novels are among the least functional and most decorative of the blunt instruments," and aesthetics and style are "the only subject matter."

Stanley Lawrence Elkin was born in New York City on 11 May 1930 into a family with a love for rhetoric and a gift of gab. His father, Phil Elkin, was a traveling salesman who specialized in costume jewelry and who maintained his success even during the Great Depression, particularly after moving the family to Chicago when Stanley was three. The fledgling writer's love of language was reinforced by his father's rhetoric and enthusiasm as a raconteur, and Elkin went on to create several pitchmen protagonists.

Upon completing his undergraduate education in 1952 and his M.A. a year later at the University of Illinois, Elkin served in the United States Army between 1955 and 1957. He wrote several reminiscences about his idle, generally amusing days in the service, among them "Where I Read What I Read" (1982, reprinted in *Early Elkin* [1985] and *Pieces of Soap*). In 1953 he married Joan Jacobson, with whom he eventually had three children: Philip, Bernard, and Molly. After getting out of the service, Elkin returned to Illinois for his Ph.D., which he completed in 1961. By that time he had also begun publishing short stories and had launched a teaching career. Although he accepted visiting appointments at several universities, most of his academic life was spent at Washington University in St. Louis, where he became Merle Kling Professor of Modern Letters in 1983. After his death the university created the Stanley Elkin Professorship in the Humanities in Arts and Sciences.

Elkin's novels are inevitably variations on the picaresque tradition, in which the plot is organized around the life of a single character whose misadventures lead him to an obsessive preoccupation with the process of becoming himself and discovering what it means to be himself. Elkin's heroes are usually men—few successfully drawn female characters appear in his work. Generally, the women in Elkin's novels are extensions of the egos and consciousness of the men, objects of love, lust, obsession, even occasional cruelty. Only in the late "Confessions of a Princess Manqué" (collected in *Van Gogh's Room at Arles* [1993]) and *Mrs. Ted Bliss* (1995) does Elkin feature a female character as his protagonist. Generally his picaresque form is complemented by the flexibility of omniscient narration, in which the author-narrator has absolute freedom to explore the rhetorical possibilities inherent in any fictional situation. The point of view occasionally shifts, within a paragraph or even a sentence, between the omniscient narrator's voice and that of his central character. Without warning, the speaking voice becomes "I," and readers are within the mind of the hero for a moment, then released to the omniscient narrator's view of the world. This technique is rare, but not unique to Elkin. In two novels, *Boswell: A Modern Comedy* (1964) and *The Rabbi of Lud* (1987), as well as the novella "Confessions of a Princess Manqué," Elkin adopts the first-person central narrative technique, creating characters whose voices are flexible enough to accommodate their creator's rhetorical flourishes.

His first novel, *Boswell: A Modern Comedy,* establishes three important themes and motifs for his entire career as a novelist: the limiting impact of death in human lives; the power of obsession; and the picaresque narrative strategy. Parodying Samuel Johnson's biographer James Boswell, Elkin builds a retrospective account of his hero's life, from adolescence to the failure of his grand enterprise. Elkin's modern Boswell designs a Club to provide a focal point for the celebrities he has cultivated throughout his life; as the "capstone" of his career, it will confirm his importance. Whereas many writers use the first-person retrospective as a means of the character's coming to understand her or his past and the decisions that shaped it, Elkin's Boswell tells his story with ironic innocence: while telling it, he unwittingly condemns himself as a misguided and ultimately parasitic human being, drawing his sense of significance from the notice he can compel the great and the near-great persons of his time to take of him.

Like his historical namesake, Elkin's Boswell is obsessed with celebrities. Many real-life fans and celebrity-hunters seem to derive meaning or self-worth from having met or having acquired a letter or memorabilia from famous people. Boswell, however, is not satisfied with a handshake or an autograph; he wants the whole person. Because his life lacks any existential meaning that he can discern, he pathologically needs to associate with the makers and shakers of his time. One of them refers to him as a "kind of gate crasher, but it's all absolutely high art with him." He builds elaborate campaigns, many of which take several months, to establish contact with a famous person, to bask in the reflected glow of this person's celebrity.

This obsession with great people recalls the sometimes sycophantic interest Johnson's biographer had in the great men of London during the eighteenth century. The historical Boswell early set his sights on the influential literary dictator, then began maneuvering to meet him. Elkin has acknowledged his deliberate use of

Dust jacket for Elkin's first novel, which satirizes Samuel Johnson's celebrity-seeking biographer (Richland County Public Library)

Boswell's name for his modern hero, but the difference is as subtle as it is important: Johnson really was a great man, and much of the preliminary knowledge of his life and opinions comes from his devoted biographer's work. As Thomas LeClair (1974) pointed out, Elkin overtly satirizes his Boswell's quest for association with the "great men" of his time, most of whom Elkin characterizes as silly, foolish, or trivial.

Boswell's obsession with celebrity is grounded in a profound anxiety about his mortality. The novel begins with a grim meditation on death: "Everybody dies, everybody. Sure." Obsessed by thoughts of his own death, Boswell believes that his own persistent awareness of his transience creates in him a unique sense of mortal purpose. An orphan, Boswell needs to define himself in terms other than ancestry. He does so by creating and responding to challenges that can be heroic or downright silly—or both.

On his path to marriage with the beautiful but morally degenerate Countess Marguerite and the culti-

vation of the trend-makers of his day, Boswell undertakes a variety of strange occupations, some never before seen in a serious American novel. His first "great man," anthropologist Leon Herlitz, advises Boswell to "Become a strong man." Taking Herlitz literally, Boswell works out obsessively, becoming a compulsive bodybuilder and beginning his lifelong campaign to attract celebrities. He later wrestles professionally, but, meagerly challenged by that theatrical enterprise, he exaggerates one match with an aging foe who wrestles as "The Grim Reaper" into a mythic confrontation with the Angel of Death. In this funny scene, readers get an important insight into Boswell's character and Elkin's theme: Boswell seeks a challenge worthy of his energy; he moreover associates his need for external self-definition with this desire to take on a great challenge, even if he has to invent the importance he attaches to that challenge. Therefore, after he marries the countess, thereby assuring his lifelong dream of wealth, leisure, and access to great people, Boswell becomes bored; it was just too easy. So he focuses obsessively on his genetic line, a poignant orphan's variation on the mortality theme, and provokes conflict with the notoriously promiscuous countess; he also refuses to acknowledge his bastard son from an earlier affair.

A central motif of *Boswell,* then, is dissatisfaction with any achievement, no matter how deliberately won, so long as mortality remains the undefeatable constant. At the end of the book, waiting outside the meeting of the great and near-great that is to be his lifetime achievement, Boswell leads a mob of protesters in denouncing The Club and all it stands for: "Everybody dies, *et cetera.* Well, not yet, not just yet. . . . Rise and shine, old sleepy slugabed of a self." Reflecting on his life, Boswell has not (as the reader and Elkin have) comprehended the fundamental illusion of his "greatness-by-association" theory; but he has discovered that to become himself, he cannot be content with any achieved goal; he must locate another challenge, whether heroic or zany, and strive for it.

Boswell's obsession is ego-driven. He has little sympathy for those whom he mistreats on the way to his self-definition, including his illegitimate son, his wife, and his business associates. This egocentrism of the quest for self-understanding is a hallmark of Elkin's early novels; it is nowhere more dominant than in his second novel, *A Bad Man* (1967). Leo Feldman is a compulsive vendor who—in his zeal to meet any marketing challenge—arranges abortions (at a time when this procedure was illegal), drug transactions, or even arms sales to a representative of what appears to be a vigilante group specializing in hatred and paranoia. His ethics are negligible, and his hunger for a challenge in selling far surpasses any possible legal or moral consequences of his actions. He wonders at one moment whether a young man for whom he is arranging a gun sale has killed anyone yet, but his concern is quickly distracted by the challenge of a drug sale. Feldman not only conducts evil business practices but also abuses his mentally deficient son, Billy, once symbolically disowning him by telling a parent at a school open house that his son is model student "Oliver B." He moreover abuses his wife, Lily, sexually and psychologically, subsuming her needs in his selfish interests. He mistreats his friend and physician, Dr. Freedman, by lying about illnesses he or Lily allegedly has, in order to get references or prescriptions for surgical procedures or illegal drugs. He deliberately misuses his best friend in youth, Leonard Dedman, by turning their friendship into an ego-serving game of frustrated expectations. He lures an entrepreneurial genius, Victman, away from a major firm, only to disregard every prudent merchandising suggestion Victman makes, thus frustrating him by stifling his creative abilities.

Clearly, then, Leo Feldman is a "bad man" by any ordinary ethical definition—a wicked father, spouse, friend, businessman, employer, and citizen. One chapter, devoted to Leo's childhood, grounds his zeal for commerce in the mad merchandising of his peddler father, whose business ethic Leo surpassed by selling the "unsaleable thing"—his father's body. This character, whom Elkin, in an interview with Doris Bargen for her 1980 study, called "a cruel man with style," is guilty of many sins and several crimes. He is not, however, guilty of the crime for which he is ultimately sentenced to prison. The "present" of the novel is the year Leo spends in the strangest prison in American literature.

A Bad Man grew from an anecdote a friend told Elkin concerning a lawyer who was sentenced to jail for embezzlement. The author wondered what might happen to any middle-class individual incarcerated in the artificial world of prison. As the project matured, his hero became anything but an ordinary man; he became, as his name deliberately puns, an extraordinary egocentric as well as a "felled man." As the novel took shape, it fit into a distinguished tradition of "incarceration novels," in which a prisoner's crime becomes a means of self-discovery, such as Fyodor Dostoevsky's *Crime and Punishment* (1866), Franz Kafka's *The Trial* (1925), Albert Camus's *The Stranger* (1942), and Bernard Malamud's *The Fixer* (1966). But the book with which *A Bad Man* exhibits the closest affinity is Ken Kesey's *One Flew Over the Cuckoo's Nest* (1962), in which the hero is confined in a mental hospital presided over by the cruel, repressive, uptight Big Nurse. The authority figure in Elkin's novel, Warden Fisher, is as uptight and repressive as the nurse in Kesey's book. The prison he runs is much more like a Kafkaesque mental asylum

than a correctional institution. There is little effort at rehabilitation, and none at all if the prisoner, like Feldman, is a "bad man."

This distinction is the crux of the novel: being a "bad man" means being assigned to a segregated population. Bad men are dressed differently than the other convicts and have absolutely no privacy. Feldman is assigned a clown suit; his file has been checked out several times from the prison library, where there are seven copies, but he himself is denied access to it. Therefore, bad men are objects of public discourse, deliberately denied privacy and the opportunity simply to fit into the general prison population. As Feldman learns gradually, bad men are segregated in another way: they will never leave the prison alive.

The problem of being a bad man is compounded by the way in which one acquires this designation. Bad men are not assigned funny suits and death sentences on the basis of their crimes or their pasts. They are designated by the warden's fiat. He instinctively knows who is and who is not a bad man and makes an unappealable decision that has life-and-death consequences. Warden Fisher, Feldman's nemesis, represents himself to the other inmates as the persecutor of bad men. Initially, he tries to persuade Feldman of the banality of evil, of the pettiness of being a bad man. Over and over, he tells or writes Feldman that "Life is ordinary." It appears to Feldman and to many readers that the warden is an apostle of orthodoxy, a man whose passion for the status quo amounts to an obsession with those who challenge or violate it. Even when he meets the warden, Feldman is disappointed because the man looks so ordinary; but Fisher is a zealot presiding over a madhouse-prison. Calling himself a "Fisher of Bad Men," he initiates a public campaign to destroy bad men among the convicts. He calls for the other convicts to share his mission for God: "I am calling for the infusion of the sacerdotal spirit! I need inquisitors' hearts! . . . You [ordinary prisoners] must be warden's familiars. We shall share the power of the keys." Elkin explicitly associates the warden's appeal to the passions and fury of his hearers with those of the Inquisition, the Salem witchcraft trials, or the Joseph McCarthy hearings on Communism during the 1950s—a charismatic hysteria.

However ordinary he looks and however much he insists that life is ordinary, Feldman's nemesis is no ordinary penal official. Fisher arranges for Feldman's opportunity to have sex with the warden's wife and to confront his own mortality by sleeping in an electric chair. Feldman's most important discovery in the entire novel is that "he's one too. The Warden. *He's a bad man too!*" Feldman and the reader know why Fisher is so obsessed with bad men, and readers know, if Feldman does not, that this quality is what constitutes the bad-

Dust jacket for Elkin's 1976 novel, in which the deterioration of a small-business owner's health from multiple sclerosis mirrors a national decline during the energy crisis of the 1970s (Richland County Public Library)

ness in a bad man: an obsession, a compulsion so total that it obliterates all possible moderation. One bad man, Ed Slipper, is obsessed with living to become the oldest convict in America, just as Feldman is obsessed with retailing. Neither is more or less fanatical than Fisher and his obsession with bad men. The difference, however, is that the system provides Fisher with a means to pursue his obsession, whereas it humors a silly one like Slipper's and punishes a dangerous one like Feldman's.

The warden's absolute power is manifested in his making good on his determination that this bad man must die rather than leave the prison. Before Feldman's sentence is up, the warden convenes a kangaroo court with the express purpose of killing Feldman. The goal is to turn the other bad men into killers of one of their own. Even here, the warden's quality as a bad man overwhelms the purpose of the trial. Intrigued by Feldman's defense, that he is not only innocent but "decent" (or ordinary), Fisher proposes the ultimate wager among bad men. He forgives Feldman all his past, to let the entire case rest on Feldman's treatment of Dedman, his friend.

One of Elkin's best novels, *The Dick Gibson Show* (1971), is the picaresque adventure of a nameless man who finds his various identities as "Dick Gibson" or "Ellery Loyola" or "Marshall Maine" or any of the aliases under which he works as a radio personality. It is also a study in extinction, and the lengthy story about the hero's adventures on Mauritius during his army days, with the tales of dodo birds that temporarily escaped extinction, reminds readers that not only species of animals but also elements of popular culture face the necessity of adapting in order to survive.

The Dick Gibson Show considers the degree to which Americans actually depend on their work to define their lives; the relationship between vocation and identity became a major theme in Elkin's work in the 1970s. The hero has absolutely no identity that is not derived directly from the power of his voice as he works at radio stations from Nebraska to Miami. The opening line of the novel informs readers that "When Dick Gibson was a little boy he was not Dick Gibson"; but despite the facts that two episodes concern Dick's visit to his family in Pittsburgh and that he has a few romances, readers never learn his real name. His identity is thus a construction, something he manufactures out of his fascination with radio and his "God-given gift of a voice," which he carefully trains to neutralize regional accents. His life is a series of apprenticeships at rural stations, under a variety of names, until he can create his identity as "Dick Gibson of Nowhere, of Thin Air and the United States of America sky."

In each of the principal episodes Gibson's need to discover his professional self leads him to challenge and ultimately subvert the radio format in which he has achieved success. Although his life can be equated with a quest for the creation and understanding of "Dick Gibson," each stage in this process leads Dick to a delusional paranoia in which he insists on magnifying his own identity through confrontation.

The first major section is Dick's literal apprenticeship. He works at a variety of small stations, under several names, but eventually settles at KROP, an AM station in Nebraska. Calling himself Marshall Maine, he quickly learns that the community depends on the economic power of one large family, the Credenzas, who own most of the farms, the grain elevators, and agribusinesses in the county, as well as its only radio station. Maine adapts his role as a newsman and disc jockey to curry favor with these influential people, seeking or even making up human-interest stories they might like and playing music selected to please them. When they do not take him into their extended family, Maine tries to force a confrontation with the Credenza brothers by deliberately playing music the family will not like or leaving the microphone open while he gossips about family members. He actually welcomes the brothers' visit to the station, thinking that only "through a showdown could he ever negotiate his brotherhood" with them. The reason he loses his job reinforces the theme of his using his work to substitute for an authentic identity. Preposterously fantasizing that the brothers will murder him because he has offended the family, Maine is shocked to discover that he is out of a job simply because everyone stopped listening to the station.

The next stage of Dick's evolution is his journeyman status. At last claiming his chosen identity as Dick Gibson, he broadcasts an all-night, public-affairs, call-in program in Hartford. In this larger market he has achieved some success. But on 9 March 1959 his format goes completely out of control as his normally predictable guests behave erratically. In a "radio drama" (the form is alternately drama and narrative) he searches for a rational explanation for the compulsive, confessional behavior of the pharmacist, the professor, the former model, and the would-be political figure, all of whom seem to compete in telling the most shameful secret. Gibson settles on the new guest, a psychologist rumored to specialize in "mind over matter," as the cause. As his guests' behaviors become progressively irrational, Gibson concludes that Dr. Behr-Bleibtreau is compelling them to tell shameful stories, then lapse into catatonia. Seizing on this explanation, Gibson extrapolates a mythic confrontation by fantasizing that Behr-Bleibtreau will not rest until he has stolen Dick's voice, therefore his professional identity. He even believes the psychologist summons a demon to assist him. What really happens in this episode is ambiguous; but Gibson clearly exaggerates the psychologist's powers to make his own confrontation more meaningful than it is, and in this fantasy he equates his voice with his soul.

As the host of an all-night call-in show from Miami, the hero, having changed his legal name ("he would never *not* be Dick Gibson again"), believes he has found his true calling as a pioneer in an emerging broadcasting format. As in Hartford, when his show succeeds beyond his expectations, he notes a new element of unpredictability in his callers: "Night Letters" turns morbid and solipsistic. Looking again to the logic of confrontational paranoia, Dick suspects that someone is deliberately undermining his program. He concludes that this "enemy" is Behr-Bleibtreau disguising his voice or influencing others to call in and disrupt the show. When he cannot prove this suspicion, he persuades himself that Behr-Bleibtreau will try to kill him, then welcomes this possibility as a vindication of his personal importance. He cultivates situations in which he would be vulnerable to attacks. When no one attacks, Dick must find another plot to energize his life. His need for self-definition takes one last desperate turn

when he decides to hunt down and kill a vendor of arms and hate materials who pollutes the minds of children. Although this mission is an improvement on the ego-centered quests of the past—in this formulation Dick would sacrifice his freedom to rid the world of evil—he comes to realize something about the banality of evil and reluctantly settles back into his created life as a call-in radio host.

Elkin synthesized national phenomena of the early 1970s (the first serious energy crisis, small businesses being absorbed by massive enterprises) with his own health crisis (he was diagnosed as having multiple sclerosis in 1972) to create *The Franchiser* (1976). Ben Flesh, the hero whose name was deliberately selected to remind readers of America's archetypal entrepreneur Benjamin Franklin, undergoes a series of crises in his health as he seeks to take part in the building of a new America.

Ben's goal in business is mixed, partly profit and partly the joy of deal-making. One element results from an overwhelming need to earn money to keep the Finsberg family, whose father was Ben's mentor, economically secure. Unlike any Elkin hero before him, Ben feels intense pressure because of others' needs. He is ruthless, obsessive, and unpredictable in his business dealings, but he is animated by his need to do good instead of by his ego. He is also driven because his body is falling apart on him. A central theme of the episodic structure of *The Franchiser* is Ben's discovering and adapting to his condition, multiple sclerosis. More than any previous Elkin hero, he feels his mortality directly, once lamenting that "plague builds its nest in us." He learns that his life is a series of "remissions" during which he can work and build. But each remission implicitly suggests its opposite: at the most poignant moment of the novel, Ben cries out, "*I want my remission back!*" This complaint against necessity suggests the central theme: that all life, like Ben's, is a series of "remissions," and that humans struggle against deteriorating health and lost opportunity to create their lives.

Ben Flesh creates his life, after his orphanhood, as a man with a zeal for making money by implementing a vision of uniformity. Much as the American commercial, scenic, and conceptual landscapes were transformed by franchises during the second half of the twentieth century, Elkin's hero is a pioneer in that change. He is a franchiser, one who buys the right to operate a business under a national franchise and is subject to its oversight. He thus becomes a local embodiment of a national concern; this point is made humorously when Ben hangs from a Kentucky Fried Chicken sign to give a speech at the opening of his Brooklyn franchise. The point is also made more grimly during a later trip to South Dakota, when Ben has to check into the local hospital because his disease has entered a serious plateau. While he is ill, an unprecedented heat wave, combined with energy shortages, causes his frozen-custard franchise to fail. A fellow patient tells him to "Be hard, Mr. Softee."

Despite the sympathetic portrayal of Ben as a provider for the Finsberg family, a man animated by love as much as by the need for money or power, his goal glorifies consumer culture and the standardization of American life in ways that may trouble many readers. Owning various franchises such as doughnut chains, laundry chains, dance studios, tax preparers, miniplex cinemas, confectioners, and auto parts stores, Ben enthusiastically defines himself as a "true democrat, . . . who would quell distinction, obliterate difference, who would common-denominate until Americans recognized that it was America everywhere." In short, Ben's dream of franchising America would lead to the obliteration of regional distinctions. It would normalize American architecture and culture. Ben's goal, beyond making money and providing for the Finsbergs, is to "costume his country, to give it its visible props . . . Familiar neon signatures and logos, all its *things,* all its *crap,* the true American graffiti." Elkin seemed at the time of this novel to admire Ben's enthusiasm for a process that was well under way in American life. He applauded Ben's vision of himself as the wave of the future, "Speaking some Esperanto of simple need, answering appetite with fast foods." Although Elkin later expressed reservations about his endorsement of Ben's goal, clearly he presented one of the first fictional portraits of the entrepreneur of the late twentieth century.

Elkin also creates challenging links between the hero's disease and America's energy crisis. Bargen was the first to point out that the novel is organized around three trips Ben makes to check on his franchises, and during the 1974 trip Ben loads his beloved Cadillac (his transportation, home, and office) with cans of gasoline for fear that the next station may be out of supply, thus making the auto into a time bomb. Some cities to which he travels experience brownouts, and the Mr. Softee franchise literally melts because of the energy crisis. Elkin directly associates the microsystem, Ben's body, with the macrosystem, America: as his body is falling apart, so is America's energy supply. He calls the brownouts "civilization's demyelination [a symptom of MS]"; he reverses the metaphor by saying, "his own energy crisis unresolved, his body still demyelinating a mile a minute."

The last several chapters of *The Franchiser* treat Ben's final desperate gamble to build a lasting enterprise, a carefully calculated motel that will appeal to families journeying to another new American landscape, Disney World. This dream is more than a commercial one; Ben hopes to create a "place" where there was nothing, in rural Georgia. But things are stacked against Ben: the inn fails, and his dream as well as his fortune with it, because of labor problems and an unexpected reduction in the interstate highway speed limit. Commercially, this franchiser is a failure. He aims high in the end and falls hard; yet, he succeeds in ways few businessmen in American fiction have. Despite his business obsessions, Ben sees the larger picture: that life is itself a franchise and that people live from remission to remission.

After he published the controversial novella collection *The Living End* (1979), which challenged many readers' beliefs about God, the Holy Family, Heaven, and cosmic justice, Elkin returned to a project that had been close to his heart for many years: chronicling the adventures of a family cursed by "blue-collar blood" for several generations. The resulting novel, *George Mills* (1982), was Elkin's personal favorite among his books. Although it was generally well received by critics and won the 1982 National Book Critics Circle Award for fiction, the novel did not appeal to the reading public.

Elkin told interviewer David C. Dougherty in 1991 that his preference for *George Mills,* in spite of the lack of general enthusiasm for the book, comes from its being a "story factory" or a source of inspiration for several self-contained episodes. Individual sections stand out; readers generally agree that the story of "Greatest Grandfather" Mills, published separately as *The First George Mills* (1980), is among the best pieces Elkin ever wrote. While never quite connected with the larger themes of the novel, Elkin's subsequent tale of Florida spiritualists is remarkable in itself. And the narrative of the forty-third George Mills, who finds himself a captive of the Turkish Janissaries at the turn of the nineteenth century, is noteworthy in conception and execution. Some readers, however, question whether the novel lives up to its major premise, a family cursed to a blue-collar tradition; others may ask whether the brilliance of the parts is a sufficient aesthetic quality to justify this long, diverse narrative.

One response to this criticism is that *George Mills* is really about the tyranny of history, especially the received oral tradition. The four Mills descendants on whom Elkin concentrates (all named George by family tradition), by buying into the myth of the "Mills curse," build the notion that dooms the family. As Peter G. Christensen argued in a 1995 article, the subject of *George Mills* is recognizing "the unimportance of history itself."

The narrative is organized into five parts, three of which concern the misadventures of a furniture mover in modern St. Louis and his education at the hands of Florida spiritualists as well as his experiences with his father, who tried in his own way to avoid the

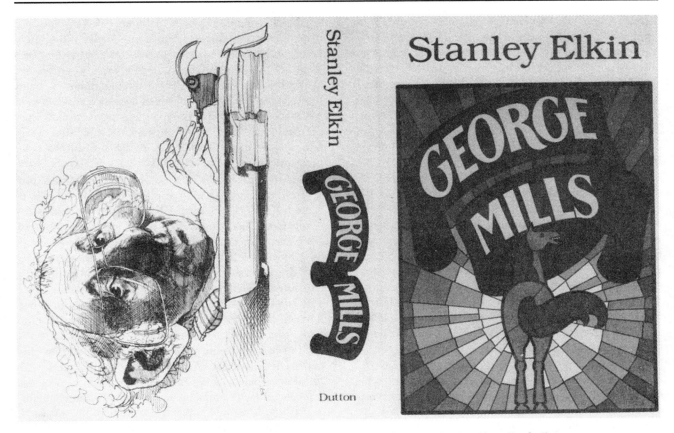

Dust jacket for Elkin's favorite among his novels, the story of four generations in a blue-collar family
(Richland County Public Library)

"Mills curse." The first section, the narrative of "Greatest Grandfather Mills," depicts the origins of that curse. Sent to a Crusade with his lord's worthless son Guillalume, Mills misses a turn, and the two find themselves in a Polish salt mine as captive laborers, then escape and wind their way through Eastern and Mediterranean Europe, "and *that* was the first Crusade." While they are lost in Europe, the mendacious Guillalume, who wants to stay out of the fighting so that he will inherit after his elder brothers are killed in the Crusades, pronounces the family curse on his retainer: "There are distinctions among men, humanity is dealt out like cards." The style of part 1 effectively parodies the motifs of the quest romance, and the anti-quest nature of Guillalume and Mills's adventure is brought to its completion when Guillalume does inherit because his brothers died on their Crusades, whereas he and Mills escaped because of Mills's resourcefulness and good luck. Instead of rewarding Mills for his service with a title or a fief, Guillalume sends him back to the stables, "because it would not do for one so high placed to have as a retainer a man who knew nothing of horses."

The forty-third Mills, whose story comprises part 4, also rubbed elbows with royalty and had adventures that contributed to the family romance. He counsels King George IV of England in keeping secret his affair with Lady Fitzherbert. The style of this section emulates that of Restoration and early-eighteenth-century drama, rich in double entendre, puns, and sexual innuendo. The tone turns to the style of American frontier tales when Mills is sent to Turkey on a mission to the Sultan, then finds himself unwillingly a member of a Turkish military elite known for their ferocity and cruelty. Eventually distinguishing himself as the cruelest among the Janissaries, Mills becomes part of the cadre's folklore, and when he and a friend are sent on a suicide mission, they simulate an attack that results in the Sultan's decision to end the autonomy of the Janissaries forever. Thus the forty-third George Mills is a cause of an historical event but not a beneficiary from it. He and his friend escape into a harem, in which they must pose as eunuchs. The "metaphysical discourse" among the harem women, the servants, and the eunuchs on topics such as whether a eunuch can expose himself are successful parodies of both academic discussions and eighteenth-century salon wit. When George's intact sexuality is revealed, he becomes part of the harem folklore as well, a regenerated eunuch, but he must escape or die. After a contrived escape, this Mills immigrates to America, thus bringing the "blue collar curse" to another shore.

The remaining three chapters tell the somewhat less colorful story of an "average George," a St. Louis eviction specialist in 1980. This section, the largest in the novel, is the key to Elkin's themes about entrapment in history. The forty-third Mills provided a clue to this theme when he exulted in his exploits as the stuff of family legend. His friend elected to stay in the harem, with its charms, knowing he would someday be castrated. Mills chose paternity and therefore escaped. If he remained, "there would be no son. His tale would go untold. And what a tale, he thought." The contemporary Mills, though neither as clever nor as adventurous as his ancestors, elects to escape history. Recognizing that it is his and his descendants' destiny to live as "Oddjob George, Lunchpail Mills, . . . like a priest at a time clock," George resolves to end the curse by never having children.

The contemporary George nevertheless has his own adventure. Having lost his job, he becomes the companion of the bitter, wealthy Judith Glazer, who travels to Mexico in search of quick-fix cures for the cancer that is killing her. Denied the historic theater of his two ancestors, Crusade or Holy War, George has the opportunity for a less spectacular, but more important, heroism. As unappealing as Mrs. Glazer is, George cares for her in Mexico and learns to love her. This journey, combined with his coming to understand his father's efforts at ending the curse, and his refusal to propagate the Mills line, leads to George's escape from history. At the end of the novel he preaches a sermon in which he renounces his sense of being "saved, lifted from life," which he has had throughout the book. George believes he has broken a curse that had power only because the family assented to it.

Elkin's next novel, *The Magic Kingdom* (1985), was inspired when the author, vacationing in London, saw a BBC report concerning a group of terminally ill British children who were recipients of a grant-a-wish foundation, about to embark on an air journey to Disney World. In several interviews Elkin recounted his sobbing painfully at the misery of these children. From this germ, with the playful language becoming increasingly accompanied by a growing philosophical sensitivity, Elkin fashioned his novel.

In constructing this odyssey Elkin cultivates a dual vision of the increasingly widespread social phenomenon of granting a wonderful holiday to dying children. He does not exactly condemn the practice, but he certainly does not endorse it. The grant-a-wish strategy, while well intended, places the children's mortality on display, with the attendant publicity such events often have; and as Elkin points out in *The Magic Kingdom*, what the children may really need is privacy, an opportunity to share their anxiety and resentment of their mortal condition, and a means of accepting their shared mortality. This theme Elkin suggests by emphasizing the symbolic "hidey-hole" in which the children seek refuge from the public display of their physical weakness and the fakery of Disney World.

After several difficult excursions to the rides and several humiliating public displays, one of the children gains forbidden access to a hotel room that caregiver Mary Cottle has rented to secure her own privacy. They transform that room into their own secret place, their hidey-hole, and in this imaginative sanctuary they find the courage to speak of their shared mortality, meaningful exchanges of feelings, and eventually love. The most bitter of the children, Benny, holds the dying Rena in his arms after a cruel intrusion from the outside. A park employee, angry with one of the caregivers, has followed him to Mary's room. He and an ally return disguised as Mickey Mouse and Pluto, and Mickey verbally abuses the children, leading to chaos that sets off Rena's final attack. The important elements of privacy, love, and death are consistently contrasted against the more garish and artificial attractions of Disney World.

The logic of paradox pervades the entire novel. The enterprise itself, undertaken with the best intentions, results in death and humiliation until the children make their own magic kingdom, and even it cannot remain free of the cruelty of the outside world. The children are sympathetic victims, but they are also understandably resentful of their horrid lot in life and at times mean-spirited. The physician who attends the journey, while competent, is more interested in his own fame than in the children's health; the nanny loves only those children in her immediate charge and resents the demands other children make (Elkin calls her a "patriot of the propinquitous"). The principal paradox, however, lies with the motives of the hero and his displacement by one of the caregivers as the real minister to the children's needs.

Unlike all Elkin's novels before it, *The Magic Kingdom* does not revolve around a single, obsessive protagonist. Eddy Bale, the hero, is an ordinary man whose son, Liam, succumbed to a childhood disease, and Eddy cannot escape the guilt he feels because of the boy's death. At one point he engages in a long dream-conversation with his dead son, but ends by seeking Liam's approval, perhaps of the journey as compensation for his inability to help Liam, but certainly for his son's forgiveness: *"How'm I doin?'"* Eddy organizes the expedition out of frustration that Liam's death has destroyed his own sense of purpose (he lost his job, and his marriage fell apart). In Disney World, however, Eddy is powerless to handle the children's needs, and his staff is falling into chaos around him. The real hero to the children is the most unlikely of the characters, Nurse Colin Bible.

The paradoxical discourse of *The Magic Kingdom* is nowhere more pervasive than in Colin's transformation from exploiter of the children to minister to their needs. His lover wants a monopoly on creating wax figures of the children for Madame Tussaud's museum. Colin also believes his boyfriend will benefit from schematic drawings of the Disney World figures and initiates an affair with a park employee to get them. He thus, paradoxically, betrays his beloved to benefit him. This plan backfires and is a direct cause of the employee's initiating the Mickey Mouse prank that leads to Rena's death. Still keeping his lover's interest as his primary goal, Colin gains a consent signature from several children. But while doing so, he leads them to two discoveries that are at the thematic center of the novel.

First, he takes them out to watch the tourists who come to Disney World. Until now, the children have felt that their condition renders them persons observed rather than observers. Watching the fat, lumpy, skinny, "not defective, merely aging or old" tourists, the children come to understand that they are different in degree, not in kind, from the rest of humanity. They are ill-formed, but many who are not in poor health are ugly too. They are dying, but—and it strikes them with the shock of recognition—so is everyone who is alive. Reveling in others' imperfections, they gain a collective, sympathetic perspective on their own. Subsequently, Colin bullies and flirts with a concessionaire so he can take the children to Discovery Island. Out of everyone's judgmental and pitying gaze, the children explore, share, and sunbathe, armed with a new perspective on their broken bodies. For one perfect morning, free of curiosity, pity, and other reminders of their mortality, the children enter a truly magic kingdom: "glad to be alive, they stared at each other and caught their breath." Afterward, they must return and face Rena's death and their own with whatever courage and dignity they can muster.

Although Elkin wrote three more novels and a trilogy of novellas, he never again reached as far artistically or thematically as he did with *The Magic Kingdom*. His next effort, *The Rabbi of Lud,* did not please readers and ultimately did not satisfy Elkin. In his final interview, with Peter J. Bailey in 1995, Elkin said that *The Rabbi of Lud* needed editing. The book has a clever premise, but one that leads toward plot complications rather than character development and theme. Jerry

Goldkorn, the protagonist-narrator, settles in a "funerary, thanatopsical town" in New Jersey, where his primary rabbinical function is burying Jews from New York and New England. His immediate family constitutes the entire Jewish population of Lud. Except for a portion of one chapter, which is represented as a deposition in which Jerry's daughter, Connie, tells about receiving visitations from the Virgin Mary, the entire novel is narrated in the first person. Elkin had avoided this method in his novels since *Boswell,* generally preferring the latitude of complete omniscience. He told Dougherty in 1991 that *The Rabbi of Lud* moved him back to first person because he liked Jerry's voice. The selection of voice is appropriate for one central theme this novel shares with both *The Dick Gibson Show* and *The MacGuffin* (1991): the nature of conspiracy and the consolations of paranoia. Telling his story, Jerry tells readers much more than he intends or realizes about his own repressed motives.

Although he is cocky and irreverent, Jerry suffers from low self-esteem, which led him to his calling in Lud as an alternative to congregational duties, in which he would need to become involved in the lives of members of his synagogue. As a rabbi "lying doggo" he merely consoles families he has never met and buries individuals he has never known. Thus, Jerry is protected from serious involvement in the lives of people, while he can nurture the illusion that his work is meaningful. His low self-esteem stems from two sources. First, he attended an "offshore yeshiva" because his Hebrew was not good enough for him to attend a traditional school. His Hebrew is still poor enough that any sophisticated congregation would be wise to him instantly. Moreover, Jerry once served an apprenticeship as "Chief Rabbi of the Alaska Pipeline." What happened to him in the north country persuaded him that it is best to lie doggo in Lud, with only the dead as neighbors.

An entire chapter tells the story of Jerry's Alaska adventure. A decade before the events of the novel, he offered to trade assignments with Rabbi Petch. During that year he learned two things about himself: that he is subject to uncontrolled enthusiasm, and that if "Alaska's a scam," Jerry is easily conned. After a plane crash he meets a "miracle rabbi," and despite many clues that the man is a con artist, Jerry is eagerly taken in by the appearance of miracle; the man switches the Torahs in Jerry's luggage with worthless parchments, one a crib sheet (which Jerry could probably use) and one blank. Thinking back on the event, Jerry realizes how gullible he was, and how his victimization in this scam undermined his commitment to any religious obligation. He was, however, massively successful in his services north of the Arctic Circle. The problem was that most of the people who came to his Arctic Circle

Dust jacket for Elkin's 1985 novel, about a group of dying children on an ill-fated trip to Disney World
(Richland County Public Library)

services were Gentiles, many of them violently anti-Semitic. The Jews became disaffected and drifted out of contact with organized religion. Jerry's services became notorious for his foul-ups with the phony Torahs the "miracle rabbi" switched, so much so that Rabbi Petch had to travel up and bail Jerry out of the mess he created.

These failures rankle. As a result, Jerry unconsciously decides to play it safe, and despite the protests of his wife, Shelley, and his daughter, he reaffirms his commitment to Lud. Staying there, however, means remaining indifferent to Shelley's and Connie's distress. Connie complains that the family's backyard is a cemetery. Jerry, however, cannot see beyond his cowardice to understand his daughter's need. He ignores Connie's cries for help until she gives her deposition to the town newspaper, embarrassing her father because she claims to have received visitations from the Virgin Mary. Jerry comes to understand how much his pusillanimity has harmed his wife and daughter when, in the eulogy for Joan Cohen, someone he actually knows and loves, Jerry asks forgiveness for the sins "we committed

against Thee by living in the wrong communities"; he quickly amends the recipient of this transgression to "*My daughter*," thus confessing publicly what his own inability to confront the world has cost his family.

Jerry's retreat to Lud has its amusing side as well. Faced with a dull, well-to-do life, Jerry invites paranoia, invented intrigue, and conspiracy to energize his life. Officiating at one funeral, Jerry becomes persuaded that the body is really that of a Nazi war criminal and offends the mourners by his eulogy. He believes many mob families dispose of their inconvenient dead in Lud, and at times he wonders if it is Jimmy Hoffa's final resting place. Late in the novel he sincerely believes a customer in the local barbershop is a hit man. Elkin counters Jerry's paranoia by demonstrating the randomness of life and death: Joan Cohen dies while walking in the autumn, accidentally shot by a hunter. This notion of paranoia as a method of animating one's life through intrigue receives its fullest treatment in *The MacGuffin*.

Although Elkin repeatedly expressed his distaste for political novels as formulaic and agenda driven, the hero of *The MacGuffin* is an aging, savvy ward politician, Robert Druff, who has served for several years as Commissioner of Streets in an unnamed Midwestern city. As Patrick O'Donnell (1995) argues, Druff's conflation of the personal and the political expands to reveal Elkin's despairing analysis of politics as a form of cultural paranoia, of believing that ordered systems can control random events. In this novel Elkin draws upon what Alfred Hitchcock called a "MacGuffin," a device that sets the plot into motion or transforms an ordinary event into an adventure: "spyworthy MacGuffin paraphernalia, . . . whatever got slipped into Cary Grant's pocket without his knowledge or Jimmy Stewart's briefcase when the girl switched briefcases on him." The plot is set into motion by either a chance or a deliberate event. Moreover, plot operates at several levels in *The MacGuffin*. It is by far Elkin's most intricately plotted novel, like a detective story or a Hitchcock movie; it is about the nature and composition of "plots," or schemes to deceive or injure persons; and it is ultimately about the existence of "plots" in human lives—that is, whether people experience or invent the adventures that give their lives narrative coherence and significance.

Like Jerry in *The Rabbi of Lud,* Druff has settled for a second-rate life. He has been a ward heeler and a hack politician, having only once sought a higher office with more responsibility and power. As a political appointee he brokered deals and participated in policy decisions, but only at the perimeters of power. He realizes, as his political career draws toward its end, that the failure to achieve more than he has is because he had "no overview," that is, no political philosophy and no urgent agenda for action. Now nearing sixty, he suffers from several illnesses, and he feels that his time is drawing to a close. His marriage, after a tempestuous courtship he recalls midway though the book, has become routine and dull. He feels estranged from his son, Mikey. In short, he has settled thoroughly into his behind-the-scenes life, and as it ends, he wishes that everything might have been different, maybe better. His MacGuffin is summoned when one of his chauffeurs tells him, "You could have been a contender." This cliché (from the 1954 movie *On the Waterfront*) makes Druff wonder what his life might have been like if it were not for his "bland ambition" (Elkin's pun on the title of Watergate conspirator John Dean's 1976 memoir, *Blind Ambition*).

Druff's depression about the degree to which he created or inherited his "shabby old mortality and downscale being" is countered when too many unexplained coincidences begin to happen, first at the perimeters of his life, then within it. He has long believed one of his drivers was a spy for the mayor, with whom he has a strained relationship. A Palestinian zealot named Su'ad is killed by a hit-and-run driver, and Druff suspects foul play because she was in a crosswalk when it happened. A sensuous buyer named Meg Glorio rekindles Druff's passions, and he develops a campaign to seduce her, only to discover that she may be associated with a complex Oriental-rug smuggling ring Druff has come to suspect may be operating throughout the city, because a man he meets leaving Meg's apartment had recently offered him a bribe to look the other way in the matter of Su'ad's death. Moreover, he believes that a synagogue and the local university are involved in unspecified ways, and eventually he concludes that Su'ad, who was also Mikey's mistress, was an operative in the smuggling ring.

The very complexity of the plotting of *The MacGuffin,* while alluding to other narrative forms such as mystery novels (a genre Elkin personally despised) and film noir (which he loved), suggests the epistemological center of the novel and Elkin's late career. Are things run by chance or by design? All these coincidences persuade Druff that something, or someone, is guiding his career and his personal destiny. Even before these events begin to occur, Druff was animated by "a kind of paranoia, all the compounding interest on disappointment, the wear and tear of ambition." As circumstances begin to hint at a thematically coherent narrative, he becomes persuaded that his life is an adventure, that he has meaning, that he is fated to solve the mystery of Su'ad's death and the smuggling ring, as well as the apparent involvement of the university, the synagogue, and the city government. As O'Donnell observes, his narrative is a mock version of *The Odyssey* as well as a parody of Hitchcock movies and detective novels.

He becomes convinced that he has a literal MacGuffin—a doppelgänger, a manifested and incarnate Fate, with whom he can converse about his adventure. To his MacGuffin, he believes, his life is "raw material" for a themed narrative. This belief gives his life a meaning he never observed before. He can, by theorizing MacGuffin, live a purposeful life, even as he approaches its end. His MacGuffin, therefore, is Druff's desperate attempt to place meaning and pattern in a life that has been random and chaotic. The alternative to having a MacGuffin, he suspects, is that "you had to fall back on your character," which involves accepting one's own mortality and the likelihood that one cannot accomplish anything purposeful in one's lifetime. This theme underlies the comedy and parody of *The MacGuffin*. A life that turns out at its end to be less clear, and less purposeful, than one hoped or expected is also explored in Elkin's posthumously novel, *Mrs. Ted Bliss,* which won the 1995 National Books Critics Circle Award for fiction.

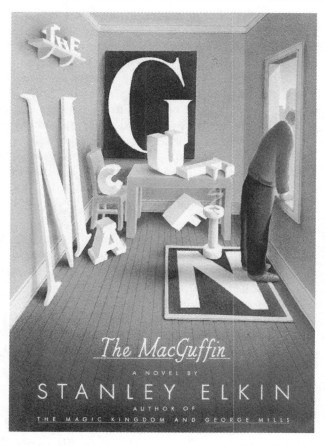

Dust jacket for Elkin's 1991 novel, which parodies Alfred Hitchcock movies as a ward politician uncovers—or invents—a conspiracy
(Richland County Public Library)

Unlike Elkin's novels of the 1970s or 1980s, the final book is not driven by an obsessive hero. Protagonist Dorothy Bliss is a widow who all her life let her husband, Ted, make the important decisions. Surviving Ted in a Miami condominium, Dorothy has to adjust to taking responsibility for her own actions. While Ted bought the autos and paid the bills, Dorothy, who emigrated from Russia as a child and worked only a decade until she married, styled her life that of a "baleboosteh" who remained "content to leave it to others" to make decisions about policy, vocation, even the election of officials. She is bullied by her surviving children to bury Ted in his native Chicago rather than in their adopted Florida, where she would be near him. In her widow's years, as she approaches eighty, Mrs. Ted Bliss must discover that she is also Dorothy—that she has an identity separate from that conferred by marriage and children. She also learns that the world is much more complicated than it appeared to be. Like Jerry in *The Rabbi of Lud* and Druff in *The MacGuffin*, Mrs. Ted has settled for the apparent bliss of a peaceful,

nonconfrontational life until something happens to shock her out of her grief and complacency.

Her "MacGuffin" is the discovery that Ted's Buick LeSabre is worth far more than its book value to certain people. The massive condominium complex into which Ted and Dorothy retired is owned by a cartel of Venezuelan, Colombian, Chilean, and Cuban immigrants who mistrust the American, largely Jewish, retirees for their "failure of imagination." When suave Venezuelan entrepreneur Alcibiades Chitral virtually courts Dorothy, then offers $5,000 more than book value for the automobile and its parking space, Dorothy becomes entangled in a web of adventures that will disclose conspiracy or the appearance thereof. She knows his offer is much too high, having checked the blue book herself, but she cannot drive; the gentleman caller reminds her of movie star Cesar Romero; and the notion of money laundering is "alien to Dorothy's baleboosteh soul." When she is subpoenaed to testify in a federal case against Chitral, whose conviction results in a hundred-year sentence, Dorothy learns much more than she ever wanted to know about the drug trade in south Florida and Ted's less-than-antiseptic past. If her opinion of Ted's life is challenged by what she must learn, her construction of her own character, which she has defined as Mrs. Ted, must undergo a reassessment as well. Her adventures lead her through treatment by a quack recreational therapist whose sudden death may be an accident or may be murder; arranged wins at the dog track, compliments of a South American owner and fixer of south Florida gambling; a strained visit to Chitral in the penitentiary; and the painful disclosure by Ted's business partner that not all the corruption was in south Florida and that not all of it is arranged by South Americans.

Like Druff and Jerry, Dorothy passes through the stages of paranoia, from her belief that things happen by design rather than coincidence, to her accepting a kind of cosmic fatalism as the only response to matters that may be too random and unpredictable. As the novel closes, Hurricane Andrew, one of the most devastating storms of the century, is approaching south Florida, and the streets are jammed with evacuees. Dorothy rides out the storm on the seventh floor of a near-empty condominium. She does not exactly decide to confront one last great adventure; she fails to take action to get away until it is too late, then refuses for reasons she cannot quite understand to have plywood placed over the glass doors.

The novel, and Elkin's fiction, ends with a scene that is at once poignant and preposterous. The old woman, who has refused to act in her self-interest, awaits whatever is coming in the company of a female security guard she has encountered throughout the novel. The women have lost much, and they do not particularly like each other. The guard cannot know whether her mother got away or is trapped or dead; Dorothy cannot discern whether her daughter-in-law's honeymoon cruise placed her in the path of the hurricane. In the midst of this uncertainty and desolation, all the two women have is each other.

Although he became increasingly disappointed over his lack of sales as his career drew toward its close, Stanley Elkin occupies an important place in the America fiction of the second half of the twentieth century. As a teacher at various universities, at the Bread Loaf Writers' conferences, and at dynamic public readings across America, he encouraged and influenced many writers by his example and by his generous criticism of their efforts. His model was that of the artist devoted to his craft, one who persisted in his own commitment to what a novel should be despite frequent disappointments at the lukewarm reception many of his later books received. By both his example as a serious funny writer and his memorable novels, situations, character, and sentences, Elkin made a substantial mark on the fiction of his era.

Interviews:

Scott Sanders, "An Interview with Stanley Elkin," *Contemporary Literature,* 16 (1974): 131–145;

Phyllis Bernt and Joseph Bernt, "Stanley Elkin on Fiction: An Interview," *Prairie Schooner,* 50 (1975): 14–25;

Thomas LeClair, "Stanley Elkin: The Art of Fiction LXI," *Paris Review,* 17 (Summer 1976): 53–86;

Jay Clayton, "An Interview with Stanley Elkin," *Contemporary Literature,* 24 (1983): 1–11;

Richard B. Sale, "An Interview with Stanley Elkin in Saint Louis," *Studies in the Novel,* 16 (1984): 314–325;

Marc Chenetier, "An Interview with Stanley Elkin," *Delta,* 20 (February 1985): 15–25;

David C. Dougherty, "A Conversation with Stanley Elkin," *Literary Review,* 34 (1991): 175–195;

Peter J. Bailey, "'A Hat Where There Never Was a Hat': Stanley Elkin's Fifteenth Interview," *Review of Contemporary Fiction,* 15 (Summer 1995): 15–26.

Bibliographies:

Larry McCaffrey, "Stanley Elkin: A Bibliography 1957–1977," *Bulletin of Bibliography,* 34 (1977): 73–76;

Marc Chenetier, "Stanley Elkin: Bibliographie Selective," *Delta,* 20 (February 1985): 207–214;

William M. Robbins, "A Bibliography of Stanley Elkin," *Critique,* 26 (1985): 169–184.

References:

Peter J. Bailey, *Reading Stanley Elkin* (Urbana: University of Illinois Press, 1985);

Bailey, "Stanley Elkin's Tales of Last Resorts," *Mid-American Review,* 5 (1985): 73–80;

Doris Bargen, *The Fiction of Stanley Elkin* (Frankfurt: Lang, 1980);

Peter G. Christensen, "The Escape from the Curse of History in Stanley Elkin's *George Mills,*" *Review of Contemporary Fiction,* 15 (1995): 79–91;

Robert Edward Colbert, "The American Salesman as Pitchman and Poet in the Fiction of Stanley Elkin," *Critique,* 21 (1978): 52–58;

John Ditsky, "'Death as Grotesque as Life': The Fiction of Stanley Elkin," *Hollins Critic,* 19 (June 1982): 1–11;

David C. Dougherty, "Nemeses and MacGuffins: Paranoia as Focal Metaphor in Stanley Elkin, Joseph Heller, and Thomas Pynchon," *Review of Contemporary Fiction,* 15 (1995): 70–78;

Dougherty, *Stanley Elkin* (Boston: Twayne, 1991);

Thomas LeClair, "The Obsessional Fiction of Stanley Elkin," *Contemporary Literature,* 16 (1974): 146–162;

Larry McCaffrey, "Stanley Elkin's Recovery of the Ordinary," *Critique,* 21 (1978): 39–51;

Patrick O'Donnell, "Of Red Herrings and Loose Ends: Reading 'Politics' in Elkin's *The MacGuffin,*" *Review of Contemporary Fiction,* 15 (1995): 92–100;

Arthur M. Saltzman, "Ego and Appetite in Stanley Elkin's Fiction," *Literary Review,* 32 (1988): 111–118;

"Stanley Elkin and William H. Gass: A Special Feature," *Iowa Review,* 7 (1975);

Alan Wilde, "A Map of Supersensiveness: Irony in the Postmodern Age," in his *Horizons of Assent: Modernism, Postmodernism, and the Ironic Imagination* (Baltimore: Johns Hopkins University Press, 1981), pp. 127–165.

Papers:

Stanley Elkin's personal papers are archived in two separate collections at the Olin Library at Washington University in St. Louis, Missouri.

Irvin Faust

(11 June 1924 -   )

Philip M. Isaacs

See also the Faust entries in *DLB 2: American Novelists Since World War II; DLB 28: Twentieth-Century American-Jewish Fiction Writers; DLB 218: American Short-Story Writers Since World War II, Second Series; DLB Yearbook: 1980;* and *DLB Yearbook: 2000.*

BOOKS: *Entering Angel's World: A Student-Centered Casebook* (New York: Bureau of Publications, Teachers College, Columbia University, 1963);

Roar Lion Roar and Other Stories (New York: Random House, 1965; London: Gollancz, 1965);

The Steagle (New York: Random House, 1966);

The File on Stanley Patton Buchta (New York: Random House, 1970);

Willy Remembers (New York: Arbor House, 1971);

Foreign Devils (New York: Arbor House, 1973);

A Star in the Family (Garden City, N.Y.: Doubleday, 1975);

Newsreel (New York & London: Harcourt Brace Jovanovich/Bruccoli Clark, 1980);

The Year of the Hot Jock and Other Stories (New York: Dutton, 1985);

Jim Dandy (New York: Carroll & Graf, 1994).

SELECTED PERIODICAL PUBLICATIONS—
UNCOLLECTED: "Action at Vicksburg," *New Black Mask Quarterly,* 5 (1986): 101–128;

"The Empire State Is Number Three?" *Confrontation,* 37/38 (Spring/Summer 1988): 25–40;

"Artie and Benny," *Michigan Quarterly Review,* 28 (Spring 1989): 236–257;

"The Blue Seats," *Confrontation,* 42/43 (Spring/Summer 1990): 23–27;

"Bootsie Wants Harvard," *Four Quarters,* 5 (Fall 1991): 50–64;

"Let Me Off Uptown," *Fiction,* 10, no. 1-2 (1991): 73–105;

"Enemy Propaganda," *Confrontation,* 48/49 (Spring/Summer 1992): 30–50;

"The Combat Zone," *Descant,* 33, no. 1 (1993): 2–28;

"Black Auxiliaries," *Literary Review,* 37 (Summer 1994): 545–567;

"Paradise," *Confrontation,* 58/59 (Spring/Summer 1996): 83–107;

"Starring Nohj Anyew," *Literary Review,* 44 (Spring 2001): 548–567;

"B-17," *Literary Review,* 46 (Spring 2003).

Irvin Faust has earned a place in the pantheon of American authors who have attempted to blend fictive narratives into actual historical background. But unlike E. L. Doctorow and Don DeLillo, for instance, Faust customarily writes against the grain, dealing with people who exist outside the mainstream and whose lives are spent in striving to enter it. Since he is also a Jew, Faust is often lumped with writers such as Philip Roth and Saul Bellow, whose work concentrates on the Jewish experience. But Faust has shown himself to be concerned with a much broader segment of Americans, as seen in novels such as *The File on Stanley Patton Buchta* (1970), *Willy Remembers* (1971), and *Jim Dandy* (1994) as well as in many of his short stories. His writing—elliptical in style, varied in structure, freewheeling in its range, deeply evocative of human psychological aberration—exemplifies the fictive social historian at his best.

A native New Yorker, Irvin Faust was born on 11 June 1924 and has lived most of his life in the Morningside Heights neighborhood of Manhattan near Columbia University. His father, Morris Faust, came to the United States to escape anti-Semitism in Poland. Faust's mother, Pauline Henshel, had been born in New York. Faust lived his early life in Brooklyn and Queens in a liberal household. He enlisted in the Signal Corps Reserve at eighteen, a decision inspired by the signal man in the 1942 movie *Wake Island,* starring Brian Donlevy. Called to active duty at nineteen, he was shipped overseas in 1944 and eventually posted to the Sixty-fifth Division of George S. Patton's Third Army in Luxembourg. He later participated in the liberation of the Philippines and then served in the Army of Occupation in Japan.

Irvin Faust (courtesy of the author)

After his discharge Faust entered City College of New York (now part of the City University of New York), received a B.S. in physical education and biology in 1949, and then taught in a junior high school in Harlem from 1949 to 1953. Recognizing a need for a different, more effective way of reaching students, he began to study guidance and counseling at Teachers College of Columbia University and received an M.A. in 1952. He enrolled in the doctoral program there, and his adviser, Raymond Patouillet, suggested that he had a flair for putting words on paper and that an experimental case study he had submitted might be the basis for a doctoral thesis. Faust earned an Ed.D. in 1960, and his dissertation was published in 1963 by Teachers College under the title *Entering Angel's World: A Student-Centered Casebook.*

Meanwhile, he had married Jean Satterthwaite in 1959 and begun to work as a guidance director at Garden City High School in 1960. However, Patouillet encouraged him to take a class at Columbia under R. V. Cassill. His first piece of fiction, a story called "Into the Green Night," was eventually published by *The Carleton Miscellany* in 1961. Other short stories followed until, in 1965, Random House published *Roar Lion Roar and*

Other Stories. This richly varied collection of stories about people whose lives and dreams are shown in often-shattering juxtaposition with the world around them was warmly received.

The events of the Cuban Missile Crisis of 1962 triggered the idea for Faust's first novel, *The Steagle* (1966). This book (the title refers to the wartime merger of two football teams–the Steelers and the Eagles) explores Faust's interest in the blurring of fantasy and reality, which he feels is a key aspect of American life. It also pursues the idea of the Jewish "outsider" who urgently wants to become the "American" of his dreams. Harold Weissburg, the hero of *The Steagle,* is a World War II veteran turned college English teacher who has a strong psychological reaction to the news of the missile crisis. Spurred by the madness of the situation, he seduces a colleague, tells off his department chairman (whose scholarly papers he has meekly ghostwritten), and flies off to Chicago, Las Vegas, and Hollywood– assuming, along the way, several identities, each a product of his adolescent dreams and each tailored to deal with the broad spectrum of people he encounters, ranging from sane and normal to completely mad.

Faust makes strong use of interior streams of consciousness, in this case centered on imagined dialogues with Weissburg's boyhood companion, Mendel. In the course of his journey Weissburg shifts from one fantasy character to another, becoming, variously, Bob Hardy, brother to Andy of the movie family; Rocco Salvato, former high-school bully and present gangster; the fifth horseman of the famed Notre Dame football team; George Guynemer, son of the French flying ace of World War I; Cave Carson, son of doomed spelunker Floyd Collins; and, finally, Humphrey Bogart. Faust shows that he can be not only a serious writer but also a funny one, as his self-described "computer bank" mind serves up an array of historical fact, sports data, and in-depth knowledge of popular music.

As Weissburg plays out his mad leap from suburban family man and academic hustler to high-rolling multiple hero, Faust has portrayed what Richard Kostelanetz has described in *TriQuarterly* (Winter 1967) as "the most perceptive breakdown in all novelistic literature," and readers are made aware of the cultural wasteland that surrounds Weissburg's soul and threatens his mind. *The Steagle* was an impressive first novel that served to catapult Faust into the forefront of American writers of social realism. The motion picture that was made from it in 1971 by Avco-Embassy (produced by Joseph Levine and directed by Paul Sylbert) helped to underscore that reputation.

For his next novel, *The File on Stanley Patton Buchta*, Faust turned again to current events: specifically, the student turmoil of the late 1960s. He imagined a policeman-protagonist who becomes a triple agent almost like the old Czarist provocateurs. Stan Buchta is a Gentile; Faust described him in "Irvin Faust on His Novels" (1991) as "a typically attractive American boy of middle-European background, who drifts and plays his games until personal tragedy catalyzes him, at least for the moment—much the way America drifts and plays games, until an event such as unrestricted submarine warfare in 1916–17, Pearl Harbor in 1941, or Tet in 1968 finally jolts us into action." Buchta is a Vietnam veteran and a college graduate. He is assigned by his superiors to infiltrate a radical left-wing organization, B. U. C. (Believers Under the Constitution), which is in opposition to a proposed new public college to be built on Randall's Island. While undercover, Buchta is asked to join a secret, right-wing, racist, and anti-Semitic group of policemen calling itself Alamo and using the term "Remember" as a rallying cry. Demonstrations and confrontations build toward apocalyptic riots as other groups—the black nationalist Zulus and the Puerto Rican–dominated Ponce (Reform) Democratic Club—take sides and action.

In the midst of all this turmoil Buchta becomes romantically involved with Heidi Korwin, a traditionally liberal Jewish teacher, a relationship that is compromised by his attraction to Darlene Rawson, the aloof black sister of a Zulu leader. The resolution is bitterly ironic when Buchta, forced by circumstance to make his choice, attempts to get the mortally wounded Heidi to a hospital, where she dies.

This book, with its portrayal of an ordinary man caught in confusing and extraordinary circumstances, was not admired by critics, perhaps because its political stance was neither clear-cut nor chic. Yet, it offers many examples of Faust's linguistic virtuosity in isolated sections, such as the Alamo leader's autobiographical treatise and a verbal recapitulation of the British movie *Zulu* (1964).

Faust next began to indulge one of his primary interests, reading history, and to shape the results into historical fiction with a contemporary interplay. His first attempt to do so resulted in a six-hundred-page draft of an historical novel about a Revolutionary War hero. It failed to gel, however, and remains on the shelf. But the impetus was there, and finally, during a Memorial Day parade in which two survivors of the Spanish-American War were marching, an idea was born. In "Irvin Faust on His Novels" he explained, "for years I had been reading about this war and its causes; now I plunged into new research, plucked my main character out of that parade, and began *Willy Remembers*."

In *Willy Remembers*, Faust, again writing against the grain, cast Willy as "a narrow-minded, highly-bigoted German-American who had loved just two things in his 93 years: his two sons and America." The entire book is a monologue, delivered in the first person by Willy Kleinhans as he weaves his personal history with that of his country in a remarkable display of narrative versatility.

Ninety-three years of events are jumbled in the exuberant clutter of Willy's mind. He confuses as much as he reports, including his language, so that when he says, "truth is no stranger to fiction," he is also providing a comic motto for the pervasive, evolving use of history in novels. People and events, data and legends, everything gets confused, conflated, and commingled, emerging whole and coherent in Willy's inimitable, deceptively lucid delivery. Thus, every assassin in American history is called Oswald; Jack Johnson assumes Muhammad Ali's mantle: "I don't think Jack Johnson is helping himself in the fight game with this Black Muslim business"; Admiral Dewey dissolves into Governor Dewey; Teddy Roosevelt becomes Franklin Roosevelt; the pitcher Grover Cleveland Alexander takes on his presidential namesake's portly figure. The artistic use of these "overlapping stereotypes of urban and national memory" was praised by Cassill in *The New York Times* (29 August 1971) for its "Joycean complexity of ambivalence, portmanteau images, and concentric legends."

Willy's story is tragic. He tells of the deaths of friends in Cuba, of his brother and older son in the two world wars, and, in a moving chapter, of the bizarre self-impalement of his younger son while pole-vaulting. His confusions, anachronisms, and tireless one-liners are nevertheless insistently comic. Above all, his voice is unwaveringly authentic, an expression of a century's agglomeration of prejudices in a paradoxically patriotic anthem.

Willy Remembers was warmly received. Cassill wrote:

> I assume I'm in agreement with most of the front-line critics in calling "Roar Lion Roar" one of the best short story collections of the 1960s—and in feeling that neither "The Steagle" nor "The File on Stanley Patton Buchta" quite met the promise of Faust's first book. But—double-happy ending—those two novels now appear as projected lines that close in the fulfillment of "Willy Remembers."

Faust's passion for history continued, and his extensive research into the Boxer Rebellion, an uprising against imperialism in China in 1900, was capped by Richard M. Nixon's trip to China. Faust began to work on a novel that thematically would resemble a Chinese puzzle: a box within a box within a box. The result was *Foreign Devils* (1973), in which Faust demonstrates mastery of his own particular form: the blending of popular history and the disintegrating personality. His new hero is a Jew, a writer, a New Yorker, and a veteran, but his present and past are played off against a brilliant evocation of a vanished America through the use of parody. Sidney Benson (once Birnbaum) is a guilt-ridden writer separated from his Gentile wife and partly supported by his mother's earnings from the family candy store. Sidney's father had run away during the Depression years, and this simultaneous breakdown of family and country is paralleled in the present by Sidney's marital troubles and the war in Vietnam.

So, as President Nixon leaves for Peking, Sidney attacks his four-year writer's block by starting an adventure novel about the Boxer Rebellion. The hero, Norris Blake, will be a reporter—a Gentile, swashbuckling expression of Sidney. Faust presents a nearly perfect parody as he sustains the stilted rhythms and arrogant ideology of the Richard Harding Davis school of foreign correspondence while projecting Sidney's longings for sex and danger.

Dust jacket for Faust's first novel, in which a professor assumes a variety of identities on a mad odyssey spurred by the Cuban Missile Crisis (Richland County Public Library)

As Sidney works on this novel within a novel, he considers his present situation in a series of inner conversations with his "other self"—conscience-editor-censor-superego. They address each other as Captain Bligh and Mr. Christian as they debate Sidney's own story at least as much as the work in progress.

The artful climax of the book comes when Sidney has tracked down his now mute and helpless father, attended by an ancient mistress, in Albuquerque. When he tells the wrecked old man the end of his Boxer novel, the attempted communication between father and son marks a touching, problematic resolution of the need for Sidney, and America, to come to terms with the past.

After finishing *Foreign Devils,* Faust returned to the subject of contemporary America with the idea of approaching it through the eyes of a stand-up comedian. In Faust's view, "by 1974 there seemed to be very

A NOVEL BY THE AUTHOR OF Willy Remembers

FOREIGN DEVILS Irvin Faust

Dust jacket for Faust's 1973 novel, in which a writer struggles to complete a novel about the 1900 Boxer Rebellion in China (Richland County Public Library)

little to laugh at or about in this country." *A Star in the Family* (1975) is the story of Bart Goldwine, whose rise and fall is the subject of a biography-in-progress, with the comic providing wisecracking commentary on his own life. The structure is typically Faustian: time sense and continuity are completely broken up as interviews with some thirty-six people who knew Goldwine intimately or casually are interspersed with biographical segments, offered as "research," which include such disparate material as Bart's bar mitzvah speech, his New York State Regents comprehensive essays, transcripts of taped performances, and reviews of his work or columns about him. Finally, there are segments of autobiographical narration, some of which are interior monologues, that sometimes include other people's voices. Each voice—every nuance of phrasing, tone, attitude, and style—is distinctive and authentic, a demonstration of what may be Faust's greatest strength as a narrative artist.

The thematic material is familiar: the pop-culture allusiveness, commentary on political history and social/sexual mores, the veteran with problems of alcoholism and readjustment, the familial conflicts, and the anomalous mixture of liberalism, patriotism, and prejudice. But this story of a comedian's passage—from class clown and platoon wit to Borscht Belt and Broadway; from television and Hollywood to blacklist and provincial club date and barroom routine-on-demand—made its appearance during the height of Lenny Bruce's popularity. Jerry Tallmer, in an interview with Faust in the *New York Post* on 24 May 1975, observed how most of the critics—and, as a result, the general public—dismissed it as another book about, or using, Bruce, which could not have been further from the actual fact. Faust explained in "Irvin Faust on His Novels" that "Bart Goldwine was cast more in the traditional mode of a Milton Berle or a Jerry Lester." Above all, he was not politically or socially controversial; in fact, he subscribed to the traditional America of his youth.

Faust refers to *A Star in the Family* as one of his "lost babies," a serious work that was shunned for inappropriate reasons. The strength of the novel lies in the character of Bart Goldwine, who, despite his failed marriages, his infidelity, and his brash conceit, has heart and has values. He cares about his family and his country in a way that Faust portrays as redeeming, old-fashioned, and, presumably, disappearing. And when his faltering career is momentarily saved by his successful impression of John F. Kennedy, only to be destroyed by Kennedy's assassination, Faust successfully ties his hero's subsequent decline to that of a nation that has, in his opinion, never fully recovered from the events of 22 November 1963.

In 1978 Faust returned to the subject of World War II—not to write about the war itself, but finally to come to grips with what it meant to his generation. *Newsreel* (1980) deals with a main character who had been raised to heroism by the war and afterward could never stop reaching for that kind of apogee. The title can be taken as an allusion to *U.S.A.* (1930), in which John Dos Passos used a technique of that name as part of a design to integrate political and historical sweep with private fictional individual lives. Faust is writing in a contemporary idiom, and the notorious impinges upon imaginary, ordinary humanity. His particular theme has become the problem of identity, a political/philosophical as well as psychological matter. In "Irvin Faust on His Novels" Faust said that *Newsreel* is his statement on "where middle-aged America is today: clinging to the old, assaulted by the new, even suspecting that the new may have some validity, clutching frantically for a simpler time (the simplest of which was the war), yet still wanting to grow and do the *right* thing."

The narrator is a veteran whose post-traumatic stress disorder revolves around an obsession with Dwight D. Eisenhower. Under Eisenhower's command he had evolved from Manny Finestone, neurotic New York City schoolboy, into Captain Speed Finestone, recipient of a battlefield commission. As Finestone wrestles with his two identities, he enters into two failed marriages (which, with Manny's uncanny eye for the wrong choice, practically segue into each other), and into professions in the theater, journalism, freelance genre writing, and teaching, until finally he is ready to begin a serious work of fiction. Finding his own voice is a metaphor for resolving his identity problem, integrating Manny and Speed, the components of his father and brother, the parts of him drawn into his various relationships with women, and projections into ego-ideal figures such as 1940s disc jockey "Symphony Sid" Torin, baseball player Roger Maris, and Olympic track star (later congressman) Jim Ryun. All these issues somehow turn on his schizophrenic politics, the American dilemma in which patriotism and philosophical ideals are in direct opposition. His liberal attitudes are in constant conflict with his idolization of Eisenhower. Thus, the presidential election of 1952 virtually guarantees an emotional crisis: after working vigorously for Adlai Stevenson's campaign, he cannot bring himself, on the first Tuesday in November, to vote against Eisenhower.

These issues come into sharp focus when Manny enters into a romantic relationship with a young, apolitical, ordinary salesgirl whose single-minded ambition is to work in a shopping mall. For Manny, Maureen O'Brien embodies the American dream. If he can marry her, he can embrace and possess those fugitive values for which he has always spurned the mundane offerings of his time. This proposition is stated in the language of comedy, heavily laced with outright farce, as befits the tale of a pilgrim whose vocabulary has been gleaned from sports pages, movies, political rhetoric, military slang, and sentimental romances.

His ultimate leap for salvation is presented in terms of a polling-booth choice to vote for Hubert Humphrey in 1968. But the resolution of the novel, as well as the final indication of Maureen's substance as a character, comes when, after she has left him, he hears her voice pleading with him to "be a mensch." By responding to that quiet, serious voice, Manny remains undefeated and, "grinning Speed's crooked grin," sits down to write *The Girl in the Mall*.

The reviews of *Newsreel* acknowledged Faust's merits, charm, and novelistic skill; however, most of the reviewers also expressed a curious bafflement about the point he is trying to convey. John Leonard, writing in *The New York Times* (8 April 1980), was able to state more exactly what the engagement of this novel is: "*Newsreel* brilliantly portrays the Jewish romance with American popular culture. It ends in schizophrenia. That the fathers of the Hollywood studios that gave us our images of the American family and the American way were mostly Jewish themselves is not peculiar; it is sad. They took it upon themselves to invent everything to which they wanted to belong." But Leonard went on to link Faust's work with that of other contemporary Jewish writers in America, thus failing to give Faust proper credit for his distinctiveness.

Five years passed before Faust's next book was published, and this one marked a return to his first love, short fiction. *The Year of the Hot Jock and Other Stories* (1985) includes nine offerings from a mature storyteller in complete mastery of his narrative art, combining issues of race and ethnicity, historical figures and events, and elements of sports, gambling, and popular culture. In his usual spare, pointed, elliptical style Faust captures the revealing nuances and manifold variety of New York voices and tone.

In his next novel, *Jim Dandy*, Faust combines the product of extensive historical research and a keen awareness of human nature and popular lore with a high degree of imagination. His hero is Hollis Cleveland (Jim Dandy), a black numbers runner in the turbulent world of New York City in the 1930s. Once again Faust presents a man who can be both ruthless and quixotic but who is, fundamentally, a person of substance. In the course of the novel, people respond to Hollis in several ways as they project their own hopes, fears, ambitions, and aspirations onto him, giving him assumed identities that range from the Scarlet Creeper character in Carl Van Vechten's Harlem novel, *Nigger Heaven* (1926), to Mirambo, black slaver of the Congo. *Jim Dandy* is flight of fancy, myth, dream, and reportage, all woven into a firmly grounded story.

A prologue, set in 1915, depicts Hollis as a child appearing in Tiny Cleveland's minstrel show. The identity of the title character is established: the posturing, ruffled, witty, outlandishly black-faced performer. The bigoted, baiting nature of the audience is also established, as is Hollis's exposure by his father to his tribal African heritage.

The time shifts to 1935. At a posh New York party Hollis is summoned into the presence of his boss, Sol Winograd, who, while exhibiting an almost fatherly regard for Hollis, presents him with an ultimatum: he must pay back some of the money he has been stealing and begin to turn in all receipts in person every month. In response Hollis flees with the money and forged papers under the name of James Dandy. This flight is

*Dust jacket for Faust's 1975 novel, about the rise and
fall of a comedian (Richland County Public Library)*

reminiscent of Harold Weissburg's in *The Steagle,*
except that every identity Hollis assumes is thrust on
him by others rather than self-created. Thus, on a
freighter bound for England, he is assumed by the captain to be one of the actors in the Broadway production
of Marc Connelly's *The Green Pastures* (1930) and by the
cabin boy to be an emissary sent by Eleanor Roosevelt
to investigate oppressive labor conditions aboard ship.

Arriving in London, Hollis is kidnapped by a
dotty nobleman who believes Hollis is Prince Gallifa,
illegitimate son of an archrival of Haile Selassie. Aware
that he is being pursued by Sol's men, Hollis accepts
this identity and arranges to fly to Ethiopia to join the
Italian forces there. His first stop is Paris, where he is
assumed by his pilot host to be a legendary Senegalese
Casanova. When they reach the south of France, he
boards an Italian plane that is subsequently shot down
in Ethiopia by a lone, heroic machine gunner. As the
only survivor, he finds himself in league with a ragtag
group of Ethiopian soldiers who take him to be Christo-

pher da Gama, a descendant of a man who fought for
them in the past. As da Gama he leads a successful
counterattack on a convoy of Italian tanks.

Unwilling to commit himself to further combat,
Hollis proceeds on muleback toward Addis Ababa and,
once again, is mistaken for someone else, in this case
the former emperor Menelik, and is asked to address
the troops. He does so in English, narrating the life of
Joe Louis and concluding with a graphic and inspiring
(even for people who cannot understand him) depiction
of Louis's decisive victory over Primo Carnera of Italy.

Upon arriving in Addis Ababa he acquires still
another identity, that of the Black Devil, hero of African anticolonialism. He meets a Canadian war correspondent whose report of their interview is presented as
another diversionary interlude woven into the story.
Hollis then is summoned to a meeting with Ras Tafari
(Haile Selassie), who offers him a commission in his
army; Hollis refuses, in part because Ethiopia is a slave-
holding state. This issue of slavery weighs heavily on
Hollis. After taking up with a local woman he tries,
unsuccessfully, to stop her from daily visits to the slave
market and falls into a catatonic state.

At this point Faust introduces a counterhero: Max
Josephson, a black World War I ace, whose exploits
and goals in Africa are self-aggrandizing and apolitical.
He is, however, persuaded by the Canadian journalist
to rescue the Black Devil before the Italians find him
and take their revenge. As Max flies away with his som-
nambulant comrade, the sack of Addis Ababa by the
conquering Italian army and residents of the city is
described in chilling yet imaginative—from an aerial perspective—detail.

After an abortive stop in the Belgian Congo, Max
and Hollis arrive in Liberia and begin the climax of
Hollis's African odyssey. By this time Max has promoted himself to the rank of brigadier general and
introduces Hollis as Major James Dandy as they are
made welcome by the president. While Hollis continues
his recuperation, Max attempts to involve his host in an
intricate business scheme centering on control of
Liberian rubber production. The inner workings of
Hollis's mind and memory are revealed as he wrestles
with his consciousness of his African heritage, even
assuming yet another identity—as Mirambo, a black
slaver of the Congo—as he works his way through his
mental crisis. Finally emerging as his usual sardonic,
clear-eyed, independent self, but reflecting all he has
experienced while in Africa, he is now prepared to
become aligned with the native Kru faction in their
fight for recognition in Liberia. Max diffuses a resulting
diplomatic confrontation but then is summoned by the
president, who tactfully suggests that his rubber scheme
would involve too much potential scandal and asks

Maintain maintain willy-voice maintain maintain!

III

NEW YORK, NEW YORK, WAS A WONDERFUL TOWN

    I was ten in the blizzard of '88. Telephone lines in
the snow like dead snakes. Stiff dead Greek. King of the
Hill. Great fun. Well Benjamin Harrison beat Cleveland for
president that year. Cleveland was a hopscotch president,
in, out, in. Wasn't the best in history, but like my father
said, he kept the People's Party out, and that was the main
thing. They named a city after him. Grover, California.
Also a great pitcher. He wound up in a flea circus.
Cleveland beat Harrison in the popular vote. But Nixon got
more states than Kennedy and Hayes jobbed Tilden. Joe
Pulitzer never raked that muck. Roosevelt killed Landon
every way and also the <u>Literary</u> <u>Digest</u>. But the Haymarket
Riot killed the cops and you can't tell me those two wops
were innocent anymore than Tom Mooney, although Izzy and Moe
were honest as the day is long and nailed 5,000 bootleggers,
so not all cops were on the take, but Altgeld which means
Old Gold as in a carton of, though one heck of a governor,
should not have let the bombers go.

    My father and mother got the milk through in '88.
That is how the business really got going. We kept all our
new customers that spring. And worked like hell. Just

Page from the corrected typescript for Faust's 1971 novel, Willy Remembers
(Collection of Irvin Faust)

Max to leave the country. Before leaving, Max tells Hollis that the Krus have asked him to become their leader, but he flies off to cast an appraising eye on "the diamond situation in the Sierra Leone" before deciding.

Hollis, however, wants no more of Africa. He finds his passport for returning home when he encounters Scott Winograd, Sol's son, whom he knows well. Scott is an idealistic Yale graduate who has committed himself to the fight to free Ethiopia from Italian control. When Hollis refuses to join him, Scott hands over a letter from his father. In it Sol tells Hollis he is ready to forget all differences and offers a partnership instead.

Back on home turf, Hollis is once more in complete self-control. He meets with Sol, who attempts to woo him by offering him all of Harlem. When Hollis says no and leaves, Sol sends his goons after him. But Hollis, a step ahead, calls his man at police headquarters, arranges for "Harlem, the Bronx and that piece of Yonkers we talked about," and turns Sol in. In an epilogue, on a "steamy summer night in 1938 a man in a tan gabardine suit" listens to a radio account of Joe Louis's destruction of Max Schmeling while Hollis Cleveland, as Jim Dandy, cakewalks up Fifth Avenue in triumphant celebration.

Jim Dandy is a major novel, arguably Faust's best. It was, however, largely ignored by the critics, though John Leonard and Richard Lingeman both in *The Nation* (26 December 1994) placed it among the best of the year (on lists that had only one other novel, Doctorow's *The Waterworks* [1994]). One exception was Amanda Heller, whose brief review in the *Boston Globe* (14 August 1994) praised Faust as "a writer of power and intelligence" whose "novelist's skills and qualities of mind remain undiminished by the lengthy hiatus." Eddy L. Harris wrote in *The New York Times Book Review* (14 August 1994) that "the imagination and inventiveness of Irvin Faust are powerful enough engines to drive any story," although he added, "What a magnificent tale it could have been if Mr. Faust had been content simply to tell a story."

One major exception to the generally inhospitable reception was a review-essay by Neil D. Isaacs in the *Virginia Quarterly Review* (Autumn 1995), which offered a retrospective of Faust's work. Isaacs remarked that *Jim Dandy* is

> a novel that reworks many of Faust's familiar themes, attitudes, and techniques into something quite new, distinct and distinctive. The challenge of an elliptical style is here compounded by a structure that ranges far behind and beyond the immediate chronological focus of 1935–36. . . . The issue of personal identity merges with dilemmas of ethnic, political, national and racial affiliation. . . . the historical setting is made relevant to contemporary themes. Organized crime is seen as a civilized bulwark against anarchy, just as Mussolini's fascism got the trains to run on time: the price of order is loss of freedom.

Isaacs concluded, "A writer whose entertaining storytelling encompasses such a profound grasp of prejudice, persona, patois, politics, and pathology cannot long remain unappreciated."

Faust remains a self-described compulsive writer. Since he retired in 1997 from his long career as a high-school guidance counselor (a career that he has often said provided him with an effective counterbalance to his fictional work), he has been able to devote full time to his writing. Awaiting a publisher is a new collection of short stories, "Black Auxiliaries," consisting of work completed since *The Year of the Hot Jock and Other Stories,* most of it published separately. Also, a new novel with the working title of "Before the Fiddlers Have Fled," set in the three years before America's entrance into World War II, is nearing completion. It is intended as a re-creation of and tribute to the big-band era. In addition, Faust is writing a mystery novel tentatively titled "The Blue-Eyed Jew."

Few American authors have exhibited the broad reach and originality of Irvin Faust. His work is rich in its examination of the American character as well as entertaining. Faust summed himself up in "Irvin Faust on His Novels": "As a writer I think I have something to say; at the very least, I have a particular vision of the world I'd like to share, a vision that some readers have, in fact, found sympathetic and/or informative."

Interviews:

Jerry Tallmer, "Book and Author," *New York Post,* 24 May 1975, p. 33;

"Irvin Faust on His Novels," in *American Writing Today,* edited by Richard Kostelanetz (Troy, N.Y.: Whitson, 1991), pp. 212–218.

References:

Neil D. Isaacs, "*Jim Dandy* to the Rescue," *Virginia Quarterly Review,* 71 (Autumn 1995): 750–755;

Richard Kostelanetz, "New American Fiction Reconsidered," *TriQuarterly,* 8 (Winter 1967): 279–286.

Papers:

A collection of Irvin Faust's papers is housed at the Mugar Memorial Library, Boston University.

William Gaddis

(29 December 1922 – 16 December 1998)

Christopher J. Knight
University of Montana

See also the Gaddis entries in *DLB 2: American Novelists Since World War II* and *DLB Yearbook: 1999*.

BOOKS: *The Recognitions* (New York: Harcourt, Brace, 1955; London: MacGibbon & Kee, 1962);
J R (New York: Knopf, 1975; London: Cape, 1976);
Carpenter's Gothic (New York: Viking, 1985; London: Deutsch, 1986);
A Frolic of His Own (New York: Poseidon, 1994; London: Viking, 1994);
Agapē Agape (New York: Viking, 2002);
The Rush for Second Place: Essays and Occasional Writings, edited by Joseph Tabbi (New York: Penguin, 2002).

SELECTED PERIODICAL PUBLICATIONS–
UNCOLLECTED: "Stop Player. Joke No. 4," *Atlantic Monthly* (July 1951): 92–93;
"Les Chemin des ânes," *New World Writing,* 1(April 1952): 210–222;
"J.R. or the Boy Inside," *Dutton Review,* 1 (1970): 5–68;
"Untitled Fragment from Another Damned, Thick, Square Book," *Antaeus,* 13/14 (Spring/Summer 1974): 98–105;
"Nobody Grew but the Business," *Harper's* (June 1975): 47–54, 59–66;
"Trickle-Up Economics: J. R. Goes to Washington," *New York Times Book Review* (25 October 1987): 29.

For William Gaddis, writing novels entailed a quasi-religious seriousness, akin, in spirit, to a ceremony of consolation. His novels may appear different from one another on the surfaces; yet, they each return to a set of abiding concerns, including the quest for a sense of purpose, an answer to the central question, "what really is worth doing?" Tony Tanner's evaluation of Gaddis's first novel, *The Recognitions* (1955), as "ultimately . . . a religious book" is relevant to all of his novels, despite the novelist's attempt "to seek authenticity in negation."

Gaddis was born in New York City on 29 December 1922. His father, William Thomas Gaddis, worked "on Wall Street and in politics," and his mother, Edith Gaddis, was an executive for the New York Steam Corporation. His parents separated when he was three, leaving Gaddis to be raised by his mother in Massapequa, Long Island. As a boy he was sent to a Congregationalist boarding school, now defunct, in Berlin, Connecticut. He returned to Long Island to complete both his grammar- and high-school educations. At Farmingdale High School he developed a kidney disorder, the result of the mistreatment of a prior condition, erythema grave. The disorder prevented him from serving in World War II and also led to his withdrawing for a year from Harvard College, which he began attending in September 1941.

Gaddis remained at Harvard until 1945, when the dean asked him to leave following an incident of rowdiness. Before his departure, Gaddis had begun to think of himself as a writer, especially in connection with his contributions to the Harvard *Lampoon*. Regarding these pieces, John Kuehl and Steven Moore wrote, "the majority of Gaddis' *Lampoon* contributions are merely clever, collegiate pieces that give little indication of the immense talent that was to unfold after he left college." Gaddis was not barred from returning to Harvard, but as his possible reinstatement carried with it some restrictions regarding housing, he chose not to return.

After leaving college, Gaddis moved to New York City, where he worked for a year as a fact checker for *The New Yorker*. Gaddis wrote that he spent the next five years "in Central America and the Caribbean, Europe, mainly Spain, and briefly North Africa before returning to complete the partially written novel finally published in 1955." In a 1978 essay, "In the Zone," Gaddis reminisced about his time in the Panama Canal Zone, where he had gone hoping to find work as a journalist. Instead, he worked as a canal machinist and later as a crane operator. He used this material in *The Recognitions* when describing the character of Otto, who travels to Latin

William Gaddis (photograph © Marion Ettlinger)

America with the hope of garnering the kind of experience that might be transformed into literature.

From Latin America, Gaddis returned to New York, where he remained for a brief stay in 1948. At this time he met Sheri Martinelli, the woman who became the inspiration for Esme in *The Recognitions,* a character described by Moore as "One of the strangest yet memorable heroines in contemporary literature." Martinelli was an engaging beauty who, her own artistic ambitions notwithstanding, will probably be remembered more for the inspirational role that she played in the creative life not only of Gaddis, but also of the poet Ezra Pound and the memoirists Anaïs Nin and Anatole Broyard. In *The Recognitions* Esme assumes a muse-like role, especially for the central character, artist Wyatt Gwyon, who uses her as a model for the Virgin in several Flemish masterworks that he forges. Gaddis also reproduces verbatim a long letter that Martinelli had written and presents it as Esme's. The letter, with its strong advocacy of painting as standing in a harmonious relation to truth, appears at a crucial point in the novel. Couched in Platonic terms, it reads, in part: "Rooted within us, basic laws, forgotten gladly, as an undesirable appointment made under embarrassing pressures, are a difficult work to find. The painter, speaking without tongue, is quite absurdly mad in his attempt to do so, yet he is inescapably bound toward this."

By the end of the year Gaddis had returned abroad, this time to Spain, where he spent two years. In Madrid he became an ardent admirer of the Prado's magnificent collection of Flemish paintings, which figure prominently in *The Recognitions.* He also came under the influence of Robert Graves, then living in Majorca, and Graves's book *The White Goddess: A Historical Grammar of Poetic Myth* (1948). In a letter to Moore, Gaddis speaks of hurrying "to talk to Graves and ask for suggestions regarding what religion might a Protestant minister becoming unhinged turn to. He came up with something about Salem witchcraft (I later dug up the Mithras solution elsewhere) but was such a fine and generous man that we had numerous talks and, in fact, he was to become somewhat the physical model for Rev. Gwyon [in *The Recognitions*]." While in Spain, Gaddis also visited the Real Monasterio de Guadalupe in Estremadura, the model for the monastery in *The Recognitions.*

In 1950 Gaddis left Spain for Paris, where he partially supported himself by writing radio plays for UNESCO. He also wrote the short piece "Stop Player. Joke No. 4," published in the *Atlantic Monthly* (July 1951). Gaddis did not stay in Paris for long, and after a parting trip to North Africa, he returned to New York toward the middle of 1951. He spent some time doing magazine work, but his principal aim was to complete his novel, which he had been working on for several years. In December 1952 he signed a book contract with Harcourt, Brace, and with the advance he was able to spend much of the next year and a half finishing the book, finally completing it in the spring of 1954. Robert Giroux, then head of the trade side of Harcourt, was a major advocate for the book and pushed it through a recalcitrant hierarchy. The book, nearly a thousand pages, was copyedited by Catharine Carver, managing editor of the *Partisan Review,* and it was published in March 1955.

Gaddis was thirty-two. Filled with confidence, he married Patsy Black, an actress and later art expert from North Carolina. They had two children, Sarah (born on 10 September 1955) and Matthew (born on 28 January 1958), before divorcing in 1965. He married again, in 1968, to Judith Thompson, although that marriage ended in divorce in 1978.

The Recognitions is difficult to summarize because of its epic size and ambition. The book is divided into three parts: part 1 is largely held together by the character of Wyatt Gwyon, who, even as he slips in and out of parts 2 and 3 and also undergoes a name change, still figures as something like a protagonist, even hero. The question of the hero's role is often raised, beginning with Wyatt's Aunt May, who imprints upon the young Wyatt the notion of the hero as "someone who serves something higher than himself with undying devotion" and who "does not need to question," because the "Lord tells him his duty."

The novel offers a full-fledged examination of mid-century American culture, especially its self-promoting artists. Yet, for all its expanse, Wyatt holds all the disparate elements together and gives them the semblance of reality (though who and what are real is itself a major theme, one that also ties in with that of love). Meanwhile, part 1 of the novel, beginning with the story of Wyatt's parents and their ill-fated trip to Spain (his mother, Camilla, dies en route), is largely about Wyatt's aspirations to be a serious artist, aspirations that are at first frustrated by his Aunt May, whose Calvinism has

no room for image making, and then later by an art establishment whose values seem distorted by economic self-interest and the myopia that comes with a group imperative. Wyatt is certainly talented but not to the point that he can compel others to see the world through his eyes. Yet, even when believing that painting, in its most exalted instances, should afford something akin to a moment of genuine recognition—much in the manner that he experienced when viewing Pablo Picasso's *Night Fishing in Antibes* ("When I saw it all of a sudden everything was freed into one recognition, really freed into reality that we never see, you never see it")—Wyatt allows himself to be seduced into another avenue of artistic production: the forging of Flemish masterworks.

Wyatt's corruption begins innocently enough; he has studied in Germany, has been trained in the European traditions, and now, at midcentury, with his own artistic career ended by a fire that destroyed virtually all of his work, he manages to earn money doing restorations. A chance meeting with art dealer Recktall Brown leads to a Mephistophelean pact, though Wyatt does not at first recognize it as such. Rather, he finds himself enthralled with the prospect of living in the midst of recognitions. Later, when Basil Valentine, the conspiratorial, former Jesuit art historian, taunts Wyatt with his calumny (mindful that the forged Flemish masterworks are technically unparalleled), Wyatt fights back, rejecting the charge, thinking that he has somehow, through his desire and need, circumvented the dishonesty that attaches to almost all forgeries: "No, it's . . . the recognitions go much deeper, much further back." Entrapped by his own isolation and budding delusions, Wyatt begins to imagine himself a member of the Flanders Guild, as one who has taken "the Guild oath, to use pure materials, to work in the sight of God." He is wrong, but the mistake, which he eventually comes to understand and renounce, would appear more pronounced were it not for the fact that the surrounding culture seems mired in a version of this same falsification, where no gesture is more imitated than the announcement of one's own originality.

Wyatt still appears in part 2, but the novel also starts to give greater attention to its large case of artistic aspirants and interlopers. These characters repeatedly seek out one another's company at parties celebrating their own work, or at neighborhood bars such as the Viareggio. Gaddis describes them as

an ill-dressed, underfed, overdrunken group of squatters with minds so highly developed that they were excused from good manners, tastes so refined in one direction that they were excused from having none in any other, emotions so cultivated that the only aberra-

delusional state, and the now resourceless Wyatt goes back to the city, where his overwrought state leaves him also on the precipice of madness.

Part 3 of the novel takes many of the characters to Europe. Wyatt, rebaptized as Stephan (a variation of the name of the first Christian martyr), ends up in Spain after a foray into North Africa, where it is said that he killed a man. In Spain, Wyatt is befriended first by Frank Sinisterra, a good-hearted forger who, nevertheless, was responsible years prior for the death of Wyatt's mother aboard ship because he was impersonating a doctor. When Wyatt meets him in Spain, he is again in disguise, this time as the Rumanian Mr. Yak. Knowing of Wyatt's relation to Camille, Sinisterra treats the younger man like a son. What connects the two men is that they are both penitent souls, a fact that later takes Wyatt to the Real Monasterio de Nuestra Señora de la Otra Vez, where he occupies himself restoring the monastery's canvases. There he is befriended by Ludy, a writer of imperceptible talent, yet important for the reason that as he peppers Wyatt with questions, he manages to elicit answers of some interest, especially as they pertain to Wyatt's failed quest to make art explain existence. The quest, Wyatt now understands, was doomed from the start, not only because existence is not so reducible but also because the work was rooted in a fundamental mistrust. The suggestion is that Wyatt has made a discovery that will positively affect his future.

The novel does not conclude with the story of Wyatt, however, but instead ends with the deaths of several characters, including Sinisterra, Valentine, Esme, and devoted Catholic composer Stanley, most of whom have crossed the ocean to Italy. At the conclusion Stanley is playing, on a cathedral organ, the composition that he has long been working on, which fatally tests the uncertain structural status of the cathedral: "The walls quivered, still he did not hesitate. Everything moved, and even falling, soared in atonement."

The Recognitions took years to complete, with Gaddis thinking that he had written something worthy of attention and praise. As he said in a 1987 interview, "Well, I almost think that if I'd gotten the Nobel Prize when *The Recognitions* was published I wouldn't have been terribly surprised. I mean that's the grand intoxication of youth, or what's a heaven for." The last line of the novel—"He was the only person caught in the collapse, and afterward, most of his work was recovered too, and it is still spoken of, when it is noted, with high regard, though seldom played"—refers to Stanley, although Gaddis later conceded that it was also self-reflexive: "the last line of *The Recognitions* was there with forethought. I knew *The Recognitions* would be highly spoken of but seldom read." The 1955 reviews were

THE RE-COGNI-TIONS

A NOVEL BY

WILLIAM GADDIS

Dust jacket for a later printing of Gaddis's 1955 book, which reviewers called an ambitious, but not wholly successful, first novel (Richland County Public Library)

tion was normality, all afloat here on sodden pools of depravity calculated only to manifest the pricelessness of what they were throwing away.

They are, Gaddis continues, the "people for whom Dante had rejuvenated Hell six centuries before." In part 2 Wyatt, realizing the wrongfulness of his forgeries, attempts to undo what he has wrought. What he does not realize is that no one is going to want to hear his confession; too much has already been invested, by too many people, for them not to do their best to block out whatever revelation Wyatt is prepared to make. Brown tells him: "My boy, you've fooled the experts. But once you've fooled an expert, he stays fooled." Wyatt remains unconvinced, though he goes away for a period, seeking escape from a city and a culture that have, for him, become increasingly "unreal." His escape is also a retreat, for he returns to his minister father's house, thinking that he will resume his own study for the ministry. His father, however, has slipped into a

anything but encouraging. Most reviewers were struck by the author's talent, as was C. J. Rolo, who in the *Atlantic Monthly* (April 1955) spoke of the book as "one of the half-dozen most remarkable first novels published by American writers since the end of the nineteen-thirties" but still called it "a somewhat incoherent semi-failure."

The failure, many thought, stemmed from Gaddis's extraordinary ambition. "This is surely one of the most ambitious novels ever written," conceded the *New Yorker* reviewer, who continued: "it is immensely long and immensely erudite, and for the first few hundred pages continuously disturbing, rather than interesting" (9 April 1955). The Marxist critic Granville Hicks, writing in the *New York Times Book Review* (13 March 1955), offered the most damning of judgments: "The novel is full of episodes that, in a less ambitious work, one would be happy to call promising. Indeed, it is only because Mr. Gaddis, in his first published work, has so ostentatiously aimed at writing a masterpiece—and has made upon his readers demands that only a masterpiece could adequately reward—that one is dissatisfied." Later, in 1962, Jack Green wrote a history of the reception of this novel, titled *Fire the Bastards!*

For Gaddis, the reception of *The Recognitions* was demoralizing. In a 1985 interview, he confessed: "When you're that age, and you spend that much time on that complicated a book, you expect something to happen. And when it doesn't happen, it's very discouraging, to put it mildly. It took a while to recover really. And then I did the same thing all over again . . . Another long, complicated book." Gaddis is referring to his second novel, *J R,* published in 1975. Twenty years, however, intervened between the publication of the first and the second novel, the consequence of both the mixed reception of the first novel and the author's need to provide for his family. At first, he tried to make a living as a freelance writer, but his success fell short of his expectations. He then took a public relations position with Pfizer, a pharmaceutical company. The job allowed him to move his family to Croton-on-Hudson, but it was not work that Gaddis felt comfortable doing, and after four years he quit. His next job involved making movies for the United States Army, until his opposition to the Vietnam War made this endeavor impossible. This army stint was followed by freelance writing for Kodak and IBM corporate executives. With the exception of writing a never-produced play, "Once at Antietam," Gaddis concentrated in the period between *The Recognitions* and *J R* on trying to make ends meet.

Despite its initial reception, *The Recognitions* did begin to acquire admirers. In a 14 July 1974 *New York Times Book Review* article, Tony Tanner wrote:

The Recognitions is written in an awareness of *all* the literary currency of the past which is, as it were, still in circulation. The book's themes and its fierce indictment of the modern world may seem conventional by now, but Gaddis's treatment of them is so dazzlingly original that one never has the sense of mere recapitulation of received ideas. In all this, and in its scope, its witty-serious use of erudition, its endless exploitation of the resources available to a modern text, its brilliant use of language, and, not least, its marvelous humor and range of tone which can combine medieval mysteries with modern science, *The Recognitions* seems to me one of the most important American novels written since the last war.

The increasing recognition helped Gaddis to get not only advances on the second novel but also several grants from such organizations as the Rockefeller Foundation and the National Endowment for the Arts. In time, Gaddis was able to complete the 726-page *J R,* a satire of big business in which an eleven-year-old boy builds a short-lived but huge paper-money empire. Written almost entirely in dialogue, with many voices left unidentified, the novel is unusually difficult. Nor is the dialogue self-contained; one fragmented conversation frequently melts into another. In fact, everything in *J R* is caught up in a continuous flow, and every event, no matter how seemingly discrete, is understood as existing in an inescapable web-like relation to every other. The book is thus a cacophony of voices, or, in the words of George Steiner, "a cancerous mingling of telephone calls, of crossed lines, of dial tones and static that fudges the logorrhea of the American voice" (*The New Yorker,* 26 January 1976). The description is echoed by both Patrick O'Donnell, who perceives the novel "as a kind of talking switchboard" entailing a "radical destabilizing of human agency," and Susan Strehle, who, in *Fiction in the Quantum Universe* (1992), is struck by how the narrative voice "leaps through television lines, or jumps telephone wires," thereby creating "motion and energy inside the text." The novel takes the notion of the unobtrusive author to a new level, which was also part of Gaddis's intent. *J R* won the National Book Award for fiction in 1976.

Of all Gaddis's novels, *J R* probably most challenges traditional notions of human subjectivity. As Gaddis moves toward reducing each character to his or her voice, a certain disembodiment of identity inevitably ensues. Since he is also attentive to the way people's speech patterns often express a circumscribed range of verbal tics and clichés, human individuality begins to seem increasingly suspect. Sometimes the clichés are deliberate, as when a corporate officer, Crawley, uses them to deflect bad economic news: "If you want to quote me you can say the long overdue technical read-

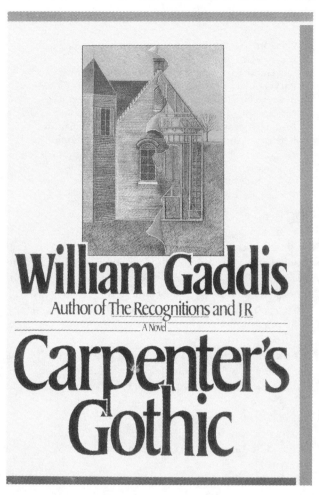

Dust jacket for Gaddis's 1985 novel, his shortest and most pessimistic (Richland County Public Library)

justments taking place in our present dynamic market situation offer no convincing evidence of the sort that has characterized long-term deterioration in past major business downturns." Mostly, however, characters speak in clichés unknowingly.

For Gaddis, the banality of ordinary discourse represents a falling off from a potentially much more vigorous exchange. Edward Bast, an aspiring composer, is sensitive to such failing; in a culture dominated by cash nexus, he obstinately longs to live out a demand that emanates from a divine impulse. Or, as he tells the eponymous character, J R, a sixth-grade child whose education has been waylaid by the community's worship of the bottom line: "That's what I'm trying to, listen all I want you to do take your mind off these nickel deductions these net tangible assets for a minute and listen to a piece of great music, it's a cantata by Bach cantata number twenty-one by Johann Sebastian Bach damn it J R can't you understand what I'm trying

to do, to show you there's such a thing as as, as intangible assets?"

Bast's successes will not be great, either with J R, who will go his own way, or with his own composing, as his desire to write an opera gives way, first, to an aspiration to write a cantata, and then to "writing a piece for the unaccompanied cello." Yet, Bast does not so much fail as, entrapped in the swirl of J R's paper empire, he postpones his potential artistic realization. He is still young, and at the end of the novel, after journeying through despair, he exhibits a renewed commitment to his music.

J R's commitments are of another order. Beginning with a muffled pay-phone transaction, the child manages to build up a financial empire that proves to be no more substantive than the junk bonds that get things rolling. But if it is no more than a paper empire, its creator, J R, proves to be as interesting a blend of mischievous conniving and youthful innocence as Mark Twain's Huckleberry Finn. Whether Gaddis consciously had Huck in mind or not is uncertain, but he expressed in interviews his great appreciation of Twain.

Gaddis's regard for Twain highlights two aspects of his own work that often go underappreciated: his comic and satirical talents. Gaddis told the New York State Writers' Institute that "the review [of *J R*] that made me happiest was a woman in Cleveland, [writing for] the *Cleveland Plain Dealer,* who wrote, 'I was seen laughing in public places until tears ran down my cheeks.' That's the kind of review that you want." As for social satire, Gaddis, like Twain, is motivated by a sense of outrage, stemming from his sense that the United States is "a country of decent people who do terrible things." His fiction repeatedly makes evident the disjunction.

Gaddis was especially drawn to Twain's later, darker work. The shadow is most evident in Gaddis's own dark novel, *Carpenter's Gothic,* published in 1985. The title refers to an architectural style, first made popular in the United States by nineteenth-century architects such as Andrew Jackson Downing and Calvert Vaux, and designed to complement the picturesque landscape of the East Coast, especially places such as Downing's own Hudson River valley, the location of Gaddis's novel. The style was designed in opposition to the geometries of Greek Revivalism. Gaddis, sensitive to the beauty and symbolism of the style, makes the house in his novel something akin to a central character, one not only thematically interwoven with the narrative but also mentioned by its characters.

For Gaddis, writing a certain kind of novel is "something worth doing," especially if it helps its author and readers to front better the mystery of existence. Gaddis, in *Carpenter's Gothic,* imagines himself as working in a spirit akin to humble carpenters, undeterred by the smallness of scale, faithful to the staples of his trade, yet with the desire to do something worthy. As he told Lloyd Grove in a 1985 interview:

> When I started I thought, "I want 240 pages"—that was what I set out for. It preserved the unity: one place, one very small amount of time, very small group of characters, and then, in effect, there's a nicer word than 'cliché,' what is it? Staples. That is, the staples of the marriage, which is on the rocks, the obligatory adultery, the locked room, the mysterious stranger, the older man and the younger woman, to try to take these and make them work.

Carpenter's Gothic is Gaddis's shortest and most tightly structured novel. It is also his darkest, beginning with the first paragraph, describing boys blithely batting a dead dove back and forth. The context is one of ordinary violence, ordinary because it has become so much part and parcel of modern life. The violence is but a shadow of what ensues, for this is a novel of chaos. There remains, however, the paradox that even as Gaddis writes a bleak novel about cultural disintegration, he does so in a poignant and poetic manner, giving rise to the hope that things might not be so mournful as the surface details of the novel suggest.

Many critics found the novel entirely despairing, and not without reason; it is easy to be overwhelmed by the dark influence of protagonist Paul Grimes over the events of the novel. A Vietnam veteran, Paul is a violently disturbed confidence man who has married Elizabeth, the daughter of a now-deceased influential industrialist, with the hope of steering his way into the halls of power. In this pursuit he sets himself up as the public-relations spokesperson for the Reverend Elton Ude, another confidence man. Doing so only heightens Paul's readiness to believe in a conspiratorial "they" determined to bring everyone down. The novel itself is enmeshed in the aura of conspiracies, and it is not always clear when the conspiracies are real and when not. McCandless, an unsuccessful novelist who owns the house of the title, thinks "There's a very fine line between the truth and what really happens," and the reader has multiple opportunities to reflect on the observation. McCandless, for instance, while intelligent and left-leaning, is, in his crusty retirement, almost as prone as Paul to spotting malevolent links. As he tells Lester, with whom he has previously worked in espionage: "–No no no, no it's history Lester, five hundred years of it, your Portuguese sailing into Mombasa plundering the whole east coast, ivory, copper, silver, the gold mines spreading the true faith right up to Zambezi valley slave trading all the way? The whole damned nightmare sanctified by a Papal Bull good God, isn't that what you'd call having business with the Bible?"

McCandless is a cantankerous man whose cynicism and penchant for haranguing people makes him something of a doppelgänger for the more youthful, and politically opposite, Paul. These two characters fight their battles not face-to-face but through others, as Elizabeth astutely recognizes. The recognition fuels her accusation that McCandless has befriended her brother, Billy, only so that he might strike a blow at her husband. In the end, the innocent suffer.

In the 1980s Gaddis's reputation was decidedly on the upswing. While critics tended to find *Carpenter's Gothic* too dark, they acknowledged the quality of writing. This response, combined with the fact that Gaddis had received some of the most distinguished awards in the country—including the National Book Award for *J R*, a Guggenheim Fellowship (1981), a MacArthur Foundation Fellowship (1982), and election to the American Academy of Arts and Letters—solidified his reputation. The first book-length critical studies of his work began to appear, among them Steven Moore's *A Reader's Guide to William Gaddis's The Recognitions* (1982), John Kuehl and Moore's edited collection of essays, *In Recognition of William Gaddis* (1984), and Moore's *William Gaddis* (1989). Both the recognition and the prize money (from not only the MacArthur Foundation but also, later, the Lannan Literary Award for Lifetime Achievement) made full-time writing more feasible. Such benefits also allowed him to settle on Long Island's East End, famous as a home to artists. In addition to the awards, a romantic involvement, lasting several years, with Muriel Oexenberg Murphy, a wealthy New Yorker, may also have helped to ease the author's financial anxieties. In the 1990s he gained more critical attention and additional awards, including being named New York State Author for the years 1993–1995 by Governor Mario Cuomo.

The last novel published in Gaddis's lifetime was *A Frolic of His Own* in 1994. A send-up of the legal profession, ostensibly centered on the legal difficulties experienced by Oscar Crease, a community-college history professor, the novel is also a meditation on justice. Oscar's legal entanglements involve two suits he has lodged: the first has to do with an auto accident in which he was, legally and paradoxically, both the driver and the car-struck victim; the second stems from Oscar's contention that Hollywood, in the form of a blockbuster Civil War movie, *The Blood in the Red White and Blue,* has stolen the general concept of his unpublished play, "Once at Antietam." Neither suit progresses especially well, and while Oscar launches these less with the intention of mining deep pockets than with the wish to see justice done, justice turns out to be a more complicated matter than Oscar, in all his innocence, ever imagined. Oscar may cling to a notion of natural

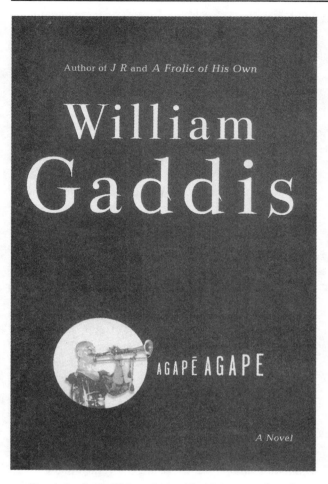

Dust jacket for Gaddis's posthumously published novel (2002),
a "secret history of the player piano"—like the work
Jack Gibbs was unable to complete in J R
(Richland County Public Library)

Wendell Holmes, tries to treat each case strictly in the context of the written law, whether he agrees with it or not. He would, says Christina, "give Jesus thirty days [in jail for contempt] if he could," because special consideration is reserved for no one. The only consideration is the law, those "words, words, words" that, however slippery, serve as a ground for Judge Crease's legal judgments.

Thinking that even the written law is not synonymous with justice, others, including Harry, a corporate lawyer, have shown themselves more inclined to slant the law in the direction of historical, political, and social considerations, so as to make the law more in keeping with present notions of what is right. For Harry, just as important as winning a case is finding its right answer. Harry may like the comforts of corporate practice, but he has not entirely shed the idealism that first took him into law, the belief that law might be "an instrument of justice." Still, his notion of what is right appears an incomplete one. So, while he appears to be a decent man, it is not clear that bending the law in one direction—in accordance with notions of social liberalism—is, in the long run, a better servant to justice than is Judge Crease's strict constructionism.

Unlike Oscar's more Platonic notion, or her stepfather's and husband's more legal and political notions, Christina's notion of justice of the heart works on an intuitive level. She views Oscar's suits as, in truth, having little to do with justice and a great deal to do with the desire to be taken seriously. As she, in response to Harry's more cynical explanation, offers: "because money's just a yardstick isn't it. It's the only common reference people have for making other people take them seriously as they take themselves, I mean that's all they're asking for isn't it?" Christina's notion is intertwined with her sense of people's individual needs (as distinct from their desires). She practices the command to "love thy neighbor as thyself," a command that one character, Madhar Pai, dismisses as "a plain oxymoron," but which the novel suggests may, in fact, be more in sympathy with justice than any other notion.

The last form of justice is the hypothetical justice referred to in the opening line of the novel: "Justice?– You get justice in the next world, in this world you have the law." The line is implicitly dismissive of an ideal, heavenly justice, but it need not be thought of as the voice of the novel, for it is Harry's view, spoken in a skeptical mood. The other possibility, that there is a justice above and apart from that of this world, is left to hang throughout the novel. It is suggested most noticeably in some of the haunting descriptions of nature, a nature that threatens to wrap everything "in a chill mantle of silence." In such passages Gaddis suggests not only the fragility of human life but also the mystery

law, as the most fitting understanding of justice; yet, the novel offers a range of alternatives and wisely suggests that justice resides less in the camp of any one understanding than in the mix of them all. The mix includes common-law justice, most identified with Judge Crease, Oscar's father; justice as fairness, most identified with Oscar's brother-in-law Harry; justice of the heart, most identified with Oscar's half sister Christina; and the hypothetical justice of the next world.

Common-law justice refers to the notion that there is no universal law, no Mount Sinai commandments that can be said to supercede ordinary common law, or that which a community writes down and regards as binding. It gives force to a strict constructionism, the view of Judge Crease, who, in his tenth decade, continues to sit on the bench in the United States District Court for the Southern District of Virginia. Indifferent to local concerns and pressures, Judge Crease, working under the judicial influence of Justice Oliver

adhering to this world that cannot be detached from the question of justice.

Before his death, Gaddis completed one final book: *Agapē Agape* (2002). It is, says his son, Matthew, about "the secret history of the player piano," a history that had long been on Gaddis's mind and that figured prominently in *J R*, in which Jack Gibbs spent the better part of his adult life trying, unsuccessfully, to complete this same work. It is also about an artist who is mindful of his impending death and trying to put his art and his life in some semblance of order.

Gaddis died of prostate cancer on 16 December 1998. He is buried in Oakwood Cemetery, Sag Harbor, New York. He is now thought of as a novelist whose ambition, especially in *The Recognitions* and *J R,* recalled that of Herman Melville, and whose success, in his lifetime, also recalled Melville's success, or lack of, in his own lifetime. Gaddis is best known for dense, philosophically ambitious works that challenge the reader on several levels as he engages complex metaphysical issues.

Interviews:

Tom LeClair, "Missing Writers," *Horizon* (October 1981): 48–52;

John Kuehl and Steven Moore, "An Interview with William Gaddis," *Review of Contemporary Fiction, 2,* no. 2 (Summer 1982): 4–6;

Marie-Rose Logan and Tomasz Mirkowicz, "Interview with William Gaddis," *Literatura na Swiecie, 150,* no. 1 (1984): 178–189;

Lloyd Grove, "Gaddis and the Cosmic Babble," *Washington Post,* 23 August 1985, pp. B1, B10;

Zoltán Abádi-Nagy, "The Art of Fiction: An Interview with William Gaddis," *Paris Review, 105* (Winter 1987): 56–89;

"New York State Writers Institute Reading," moderated by Tom Smith, audiotape, 4 April 1990, Institute Archives;

Smith, "Interview with William Gaddis," *Public Radio Bookshow with Tom Smith,* 21 December 1993;

Dinitia Smith, "Gaddis in the Details," *New York Magazine* (3 January 1994): 34–40;

Gregory Feeley, "An Artist Who Likes to Be Read, Not Heard," *Newsday* (19 January 1994): 55, 87;

"New York State Writers Institute Seminar with William Gaddis," moderated by Smith, audiotape, 14 April 1994, Institute Archives;

Emmanuelle Ertel, "William Gaddis l'obsession de l'erreur," *Entretien* (March 1998): 98–103.

References:

Gregory Comnes, *The Ethics of Indeterminacy in the Novels of William Gaddis* (Gainesville: University Press of Florida, 1994);

Jack Green, *Fire the Bastards!* (Normal, Ill.: Dalkey Archive Press, 1992);

John Johnston, *Carnival of Repetition* (Philadelphia: University of Pennsylvania Press, 1990);

Christopher J. Knight, *Hints and Guesses: William Gaddis's Fiction of Longing* (Madison: University of Wisconsin Press, 1997);

Peter W. Koenig, "'Splinters from the Yew Tree': A Critical Study of William Gaddis' *The Recognitions,*" dissertation, New York University, 1971;

John Kuehl and Steven Moore, eds., *In Recognition of William Gaddis* (Syracuse, N.Y.: Syracuse University Press, 1984);

Moore, *A Reader's Guide to William Gaddis's The Recognitions* (Lincoln: University of Nebraska Press, 1982);

Moore, "Sheri Martinelli: A Modernist Muse," *Gargoyle,* 41 (1998): 29–55;

Moore, *William Gaddis* (Boston: Twayne, 1989);

Patrick O'Donnell, "The Reader's Frolic," *Profils Americains: William Gaddis,* 6 (1994);

Susan Strehle, *Fiction in the Quantum Universe* (Chapel Hill: University of North Carolina Press, 1992);

Tony Tanner, "After Twenty Years, Recognition," *New York Times Book Review,* 14 July 1974, pp. 27–28;

Peter Wolfe, *A Vision of His Own: The Mind and Art of William Gaddis* (Madison, N.J.: Fairleigh Dickinson University Press, 1997).

Papers:

William Gaddis's papers are on deposit at Washington University in St. Louis, Missouri.

John Hersey

(17 June 1914 – 24 March 1993)

David Sanders

See also the Hersey entries in *DLB 6: American Novelists Since World War II, Second Series,* and *DLB 185: American Literary Journalists, 1945–1995, First Series.*

BOOKS: *Men on Bataan* (New York: Knopf, 1942);

Into the Valley (New York, Knopf, 1943; London: Hodder & Stoughton, 1943);

A Bell for Adano (New York: Knopf, 1944; London: Gollancz, 1945);

Hiroshima (New York: Knopf, 1946; Harmondsworth, U.K.: Penguin, 1946); expanded as *Hiroshima: A New Edition with a Final Chapter Written Forty Years after the Explosion* (New York: Knopf, 1985);

The Wall (New York: Knopf, 1950; London: Hamilton, 1950);

The Marmot Drive (New York: Knopf, 1953; London: Hamilton, 1953);

A Single Pebble (New York: Knopf, 1956; London: Hamilton, 1956);

The War Lover (New York: Knopf, 1959; London: Hamilton, 1959);

The Child Buyer (New York: Knopf, 1960; London: Hamilton, 1961);

Here to Stay (London: Hamilton, 1962; New York: Knopf, 1963);

White Lotus (New York: Knopf, 1965; London: Hamilton, 1965);

Too Far to Walk (New York: Knopf, 1966; London: Hamilton, 1966);

Under the Eye of the Storm (New York: Knopf, 1967; London: Hamilton, 1967);

The Algiers Motel Incident (New York: Knopf, 1968; London: Hamilton, 1968);

Letter to the Alumni (New York: Knopf, 1970);

The Conspiracy (New York: Knopf, 1972; London: Hamilton, 1972);

My Petition for More Space (New York: Knopf, 1974; London: Hamilton, 1975);

The President (New York: Knopf, 1975); expanded as *Aspects of the Presidency* (New Haven: Ticknor & Fields, 1980);

John Hersey (photograph by Allison Shaw; from the dust jacket for The Call, *1985)*

The Walnut Door (New York: Knopf, 1977; London: Macmillan, 1978);

The Call (New York: Knopf, 1985; London: Weidenfeld & Nicolson, 1986);

Blues (New York, Knopf, 1987; London: Weidenfeld & Nicolson, 1988);

Life Sketches (New York: Knopf, 1989);

Fling and Other Stories (New York: Knopf, 1990);

Antonietta (New York: Knopf, 1991);

Key West Tales (New York: Knopf, 1994).

OTHER: *Ralph Ellison: A Collection of Critical Essays,* edited by Hersey (Englewood Cliffs, N.J.: Prentice-Hall, 1974);

The Writer's Craft, edited by Hersey (New York: Knopf, 1974).

John Hersey earned early recognition, first as a reporter and then as a novelist. His dispatches from Guadalcanal and Sicily for the Henry Luce magazines *Time* and *Life* made him one of the best-known correspondents in World War II. As the war was ending, his first novel, *A Bell for Adano* (1944), was awarded the Pulitzer Prize in fiction. In 1946 his interviews with six survivors of the atomic bombing of Hiroshima were the peak of his reporting and for the rest of his long career as a writer his most widely known publication. As a journalist after 1946, he wrote occasionally for *The New Yorker* and other publications and was moved to write at greater length about an incident in the Detroit race riot of 1967. But, for more than fifty years following the unexpected Pulitzer, he was primarily a novelist. Given the singular procession of his fiction from his second novel onward, Hersey was, in a special sense, an aspiring novelist. He was always likely to pursue a new subject and a different form. Hersey's fourteen novels reflect not only an unusually wide range of subjects–from the war he covered as a young reporter to the fanciful travels of a Stradivarius violin–but also his persistent examination of the differences between fiction and journalism.

John Richard Hersey was born on 17 June 1914 in Tientsin, China, the youngest of three sons of Roscoe and Grace Baird Hersey, missionaries affiliated with the YMCA. The family lived in the British Concession, which the boys left each day to attend Tientsin Grammar School and later Tientsin American School. While Roscoe Hersey served in France in World War I with a detachment of Chinese coolies, John traveled around the world with his mother and stayed briefly with family in Briarcliff Manor, New York. Returning to Tientsin in time to begin his formal education, he picked up additional fluency in Mandarin. Despite the wartime interruption, Hersey's first eleven years marked him as a "mishkid," a missionary's child, a foreigner who behaved much as the Chinese expected him to, but a foreigner still in the American society to which the family returned when Roscoe Hersey's illness forced him to retire from missionary service.

Hersey's formal education continued in the United States at public schools in Briarcliff Manor, the Hotchkiss School, and Yale University. Of the public schools he has left no memoir. As a scholarship student at Hotchkiss, he gained needed self-confidence. He had several teachers at Hotchkiss whom he recalled fondly, but none as formidable as George Van Santvoord, the polymath headmaster. For a young man who often had the feeling of being a foreigner, Hersey fit into a range of activities at Yale that excited him more than his classes. He wrote for the *News* rather than the literary magazine, was involved with campus politics and not the pacifist movements of the 1930s, and lettered in varsity football as a reserve end behind eventual Heisman Trophy winner Larry Kelley on a team whose coaching staff included law student Gerald Ford.

His combined major in history, arts, and letters influenced his writing career less than his work on the *News* and his senior thesis on the eighteenth-century American painter Jonathan Trumbull. He said in an unpublished 13 August 1987 interview that he believed that a postgraduate year at Clare College, Cambridge, "opened his vision about writing" to something other than the news. Returning to the United States in the summer of 1937, he held his first postgraduate job, which he described in the Winter 1987 *Yale Review,* as "secretary, driver, and factotum" to the novelist Sinclair Lewis. In the fall of the year he joined the staff of *Time,* eager to work for what struck him then as "the liveliest enterprise of its type," although he did not hesitate to submit a scathing essay on the magazine as part of his job application.

Hersey began by working in every department of *Time* except science and medicine, turning news clippings into standard *Time*-style columns. In 1939 he was sent to China and Japan as a correspondent and earned his first byline for *Life* with an article on Ambassador Joseph Grew's "dynamic appeasement" at his difficult post in Tokyo. From Pearl Harbor until 1944, Hersey's work for Luce publications was split between field assignments and "The World War in Review" section of *Time.* He wrote *Men on Bataan* in 1942 based on reports from the magazine correspondents in the Philippines and letters from families of his subjects. The book consists of alternating chapters on General Douglas MacArthur and individuals who served under him, and, of course, was necessarily written in ignorance of what happened to those who survived the Japanese victory. The writer disliked his effort for being, as he said in the 1987 interview, "too adulatory of MacArthur," and he eventually persuaded Knopf to drop it from the list of his books. *Into the Valley* (1943) was his eyewitness account of action in the third battle of the Matanikau River on Guadalcanal, rewritten from a dispatch to *Life* while he recovered from plane-crash injuries incurred on a later rescue mission to the river.

Shortly after Guadalcanal, Hersey was sent to the Mediterranean theater, where he filed a story for *Life* on the work of the American military government (AMGOT) in Licata, Sicily. Both General George Patton and the military governor of Licata became fictional characters in Hersey's first novel, *A Bell for Adano.* The bell of the title was Hersey's invention, a symbol of the work to be done picking up the pieces of society after the war. As Major Joppolo makes his way to Adano's *palazzo di cittá* (municipal offices) on his first day ashore, he notices an empty bell tower, the bell presumably having been removed and melted down for armament. The first Italian he meets in his new headquarters begins to explain the importance of the bell to the town by detailing the townspeople's condition: they have been without bread for three days; the dead are unburied; the water carts have not reached town for several days; and the bell has gone—but he goes on to talk only about the bell. It was seven hundred years old and had rung in every hour of the townspeople's lives. In his first action as governor, Major Joppolo promises to replace it. Meanwhile, the fictional General Marvin roars into Adano and decrees to an astonished Major Joppolo that in order to keep the roads clear for the invasion, no carts will be allowed on the road into town. The story of *A Bell for Adano* follows from Joppolo's realizing that because the carts bring water to the town, he must countermand the general's order if he is to begin his work. The order can be ignored, but only so long as it gets stalled in military communication channels, and Joppolo can build a democratic town government as he addresses the restoration of the town's daily needs and tries to find a new bell before higher authority eventually catches up with him.

A Bell for Adano is vivid and uncomplicated, to some degree the fleshing out of the actual military governor's agenda as Hersey watched it unfold in Licata. Orville Prescott, in *The New York Times* (7 February 1944), judged that Hersey had "gone beyond the horrors and heroics" and to the best of his ability had told the truth. Diana Trilling was harsh in her disagreement: Hersey's "ideas, like his prose, have undergone a conscious, falsifying, and purposeful simplification," she wrote in *The Nation* (12 February 1944). This reaction may be understandable since the novel begins with a foreword begging the reader "*to get to know this man Joppolo well. We have need of him. He is our future in the world.*" The tone scarcely differs from that of the opening paragraphs in most chapters of *Men on Bataan,* but Trilling underestimated the narrative skill of a writer who was determined to tell his story simply because he was dealing with the sum of a man's actions, each of

which offered guidance for rebuilding the postwar world that went beyond the Atlantic Charter or anything else "*so faultless on paper.*"

A Bell for Adano won a Pulitzer Prize, but *Hiroshima* (1946), the account of people surviving the first atomic bomb dropped on Japan, remains Hersey's most widely read book. To understand its effect, especially in the late 1940s, one must remember how unimaginable the destructive power of that single bomb was to those who tried to follow the first news reports—even after the six years between 1939 and 1945 of trying to grasp the enormity of mass bombings of civilians from Warsaw to Tokyo. Of course, this problem faced Hersey as he considered how to report the ruins he saw and the words of survivors he interviewed, and his basic decision was to be objective to the point of silencing the admonitory voice of his early journalism that had broken out even in his first novel.

No discussion of *Hiroshima* can fail to mention either the extraordinary immediate reception of the book or the milestone that it marked in Hersey's career. Its first publication as the full text of the 31 August 1946 issue of *The New Yorker* prompted requests from governmental and scientific bodies for thousands of copies to inform the public beyond the relatively limited circulation of the magazine. Newspapers were permitted to reprint it on the condition that it not be abridged, and the full text was read in a series of special radio broadcasts. Within the canon of Hersey's later books, it is reprinted in *Here to Stay* (1962) and in a 1985 edition with "Aftermath," a later account of the six survivors. In writing *Hiroshima* for *The New Yorker,* Hersey broke with *Life* and Luce, although he had begun his 1945–1946 tour of China and Japan on assignment for both publications. Hersey wrote articles for many magazines and journals during the rest of his long career, but, already immersed in research and planning for *The Wall* (1950), he was primarily a novelist at the time *Hiroshima* was becoming a publishing sensation.

Hersey had written *A Bell for Adano* "at white heat" on a one-month respite from being a war correspondent in 1943, working from firsthand observations of the campaign in Sicily and particularly what he saw in a few days at the office of the American military governor at Licata. *The Wall,* his second novel, came from years of deliberation, planning, and rewriting. It began as an act of conscience when Hersey was posted to the Moscow bureau of *Time* in 1944 and taken by the Russians to a site in Estonia, where he interviewed Benjamin Weintraub, who had just been rescued from a funeral pyre built by Germans to exterminate their Jewish prisoners before they fled the Russian advance. "I did not know. We did not know," Hersey said in a 1989 address at Baltimore Hebrew College about this first intimation of the Holocaust, adding "I could have known. We could have known." Thus, he vowed to tell the story of what Weintraub and other Jews had survived. Many decisions lay between this promise and *The Wall*. He had no special authority for undertaking the task, as he knew in admitting his ignorance. He was not a Jew. He had known no comparable ordeal. "I wish I could convey how shocking, how life-changing, that story was to me in my unknowing state at that time," he said in 1984. He had only a profound, if instant, sympathy born of the Weintraub interview (which took place more than a full year before he began interviewing Hiroshima survivors) to lead him to understand that he must write about what followed from the agony as well as the agony itself.

Shortly after publication of *Hiroshima*, a conversation with an Auschwitz survivor led Hersey to give up any thought of setting a story in the death camps and to write instead about the survivors of the ghettos; he chose the Warsaw ghetto, which he had seen while still posted in Moscow, for "its legendary quality" even before the uprising preceding its destruction. He read *The Black Book of Polish Jewry*, edited by Jacob Apenszlak (1943), and other sources in English before he came upon a cache of documentary material all in Polish or Yiddish. At that point he hired translators, one for each language, to read aloud on a wire recorder in rapid and "intensely moving" English the accounts and memoirs that fed at least half of Hersey's research for the novel. The translators' efforts to convey the voices behind many of the documents helped Hersey decide to give up any thought of third-person narration (even one as detached as that of the reporter of *Hiroshima*) and have the story told by ghetto survivors. This decision led, in turn, to his creation of the "intuitive historian," Noach Levinson, the sole compiler of a four-million-word archive of the life of the Warsaw ghetto. This mass of notations becomes a long novel about the Warsaw ghetto from November 1939, when German restrictions on Jews began to be enforced, to May 1943, when forty-one ghetto residents escaped and the last buildings were razed.

The novel begins with an "Editor's Prologue" that describes how the fictitious Levinson Archive was found after the war by a party of four ghetto survivors. "What a wonder of documentation!" the editor exclaims. This remark and a few others establish a critical relationship between the "editor," Hersey, and his creation, Levinson. The first line of the archive is the archivist's professional notation: "EVENTS NOVEMBER 11, 1939. ENTRY NOVEMBER 17, 1939. N.L." to head his impressions of a major character, Dolek Berson. The archival apparatus has struck many critics as stultifying, even deadening; yet, Alfred Kazin, after

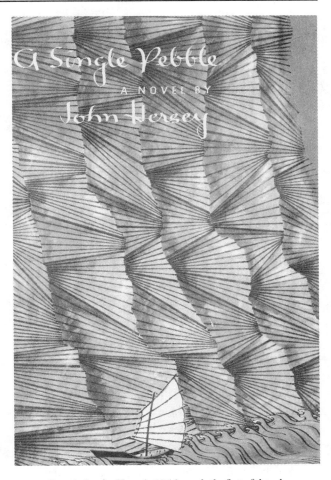

Dust jacket for Hersey's 1956 novel, the first of three he set in China (Richland County Public Library)

admitting initial puzzlement and boredom, proclaims that "the fraternity between Noach and Hersey all through this long book is one of the happiest things I have seen for a long time in our monotonously hard-boiled literature."

The Wall is the story of Jews from many backgrounds who depend on one another as their will to live grows in the face of their prospective annihilation. The archivist's miscellany is beautifully suited for conveying the variety of responses to the Germans' first decrees: those of the militant Zionists, Socialists (with their ties outside the ghetto), and Communists; the people who still call a ghetto street "the best kind of neighborhood"; the wealthy man who assures himself that "money would do everything"; and his daughter (eventually the heroine of *The Wall*), who begins internment by memorizing "the Polish parts" of her life. In the early months of their ordeal the prisoners have almost ignored the extremity of their situation as their acts of resistance forge them into a community. Only when they come up against German cordons at every exit do they seem to realize that they are locked inside the wall. The ghetto community becomes a group of fighters as their numbers dwindle and their living space contracts block by block. Rachel Apt, Berson, and Levinson, three solitaries, become intensely loyal to each other within that community.

The Wall is the culmination of Hersey's early career as a war correspondent becoming a novelist of contemporary history. From the relatively simple process of turning a news story into fiction in *A Bell for Adano,* he found himself "inventing a memory," an archivist's memory, to imagine what had happened in the Warsaw ghetto. That exhausting effort was followed, as he explained in the July 1952 *Yale University Library Gazette,* by a succession of fictions that illustrated both his desire of "going all the way into imaginative fiction" and his recognition that "in trying to tell the truth, the literary artist must dare to lie, to make things up."

The title of *The Marmot Drive* (1953) refers to the efforts of Connecticut villagers to hunt down and exterminate local woodchucks on a weekend in which the son of the village selectman brings his girlfriend, Hester, home from New York to meet his parents. The narrative begins just before the muster in the early morning fog, in which people are heard before they are seen, and young Hester has a limited, fragmented sense of what is going on. Her present confusion is laced with puzzling recollections of arriving in the village, Tunxis, late the day before, meeting the selectman, Matthew Avered, and attending the town meeting that night. Hester observes Avered pitted against the respectable people of Tunxis, who can hardly restrain themselves as he faces them down; "as if they resented his intelligence and wanted to destroy him for it," she muses. Her sympathy for Avered becomes twisted with a possible physical attraction. After all, she hears that Avered had arranged for her to be near him during the hunt while stationing his son at a greater distance. Given much time alone to consider this, she tells herself that she wants to get Avered alone to know the son better, but soon fantasizes embraces with the "experienced, compassionate," older man. As he tries to remove a speck from her eye near the end of the drive, she tries to see "something she can scarcely define" in his eyes. A villager spies Avered bent toward Hester in this compassionate act and turns her surmise of the scene into a case for "a light public whippin'."

What Hester cannot imagine is how suddenly and eagerly the citizens will put the village whipping post to use. She is struck dumb when interrogated on the spot and can proclaim neither Avered's innocence nor her own. Since the story is told entirely from her point of view, and she has fled into the bushes from the punishment that everyone else (presumably, even Avered's son) righteously attends, the whipping cannot be described. The next record of Hester's awareness is of her noting Avered's "far away look" when he leaves the platform. As townspeople laugh at his efforts, he is left to kill single-handedly the few woodchucks who have not escaped the marmot drive.

Although Hersey tried to choose timeless themes and treat them distinctively with his art, readers have been tempted to find some reflection of the early 1950s—loosely, Senator Joseph McCarthy's scapegoating of many public officials—in *The Marmot Drive.* Hersey's career to that point may have led to this habitual approach, but later observers more often see young Hester jolted from her Manhattan workday schedule into a situation beyond any Connecticut suburb, a setting that resembles those of the Puritan villages of Nathaniel Hawthorne's tales. In the same year that *The Marmot Drive* bewildered both readers and reviewers, Hersey, at thirty-nine, became the youngest writer ever elected to the American Academy of Arts and Letters.

In 1946, while Hersey was on assignment for *Life* and *The New Yorker,* he and photographer Dmitri Kessel traveled downriver on a junk through the gorges of the Yangtze River. Their prospective collaboration was unpublished, but by 1956, when Hersey had begun to despair of seeing China again, he wrote *A Single Pebble,* the first of his three novels set in what he called his "natal land" ("natal" rather than "native" perhaps because of his abiding awareness of having been a foreigner growing up in Tientsin). This short tale is surpassingly clear coming after *The Marmot Drive.* It draws upon Hersey's feelings of exile and his questioning of policies and actions in the period when China became "America's lost love" to a wildly mixed group of Americans.

The narrator of *A Single Pebble* is an American hydraulic engineer looking back "half a lifetime ago" to the upriver junk voyage he made through the Yangtze gorges from Ichang to Wanhsien. In his twenties then, he was full of a plan to build a dam that would solve China's problems; he had started out on this trip for the sake of learning anything at first hand that might help him sell his ideas. This engineer not only worships technology but also believes in the power of a single massive technological effort. Although he has learned Mandarin sufficiently to carry on searching conversations with the crew of the junk and is a skillful observer of both terrain and every detail of the labor upstream, he ends his journey with his ambitions intact. And so they remain as he tells his story decades later.

The departure of the junk is delayed a whole day as the cook remains ashore on routine errands. The crew seems not to notice their abrupt idleness or the engineer's unconcealed impatience, and while they are

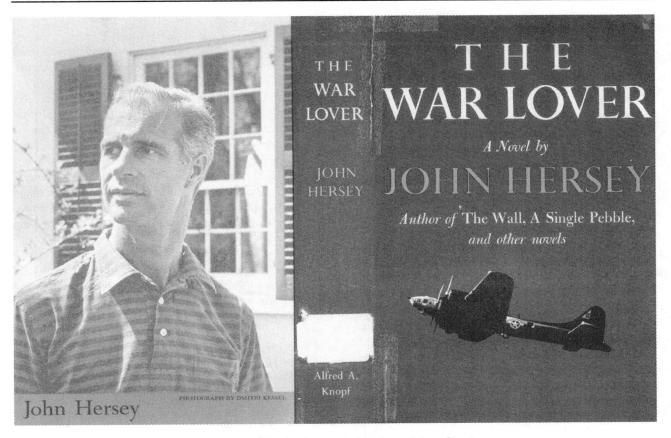

Dust jacket for Hersey's 1959 novel, about the psychology of heroism
(Richland County Public Library)

still tied up to the dock, the American complains that "the Chinese did everything so slowly, carelessly, cheerfully." On the first day of upstream tracking, he begins observing the work of trackers, men on towpaths pulling the vessel against the current toward its destination, steps at a time, for a thousand miles. At first the sight stirs his ambitions, his visions of himself delivering these people from such grinding labor, and he pours out these feelings to the owner's young wife, his only listener. Let the crew propitiate the river god with ritual sacrifices; the engineer would change the river. So strong is his belief that he lets it override the horror he notices in the woman's eyes and eventually even ignores her warning never to say such things to the Old Pebble, the head tracker.

On an intellectual level the engineer understands that changing the river will do away with the labor that marked the tracker's existence. What he has never known and perhaps never will learn is how such a man as the tracker cannot merely accept the conditions of his existence but actually become devoted to the act of overcoming them. One day he imagines his dam as the junk approaches a point in the river between two sheer

cliffs: "a beautiful concrete straight-gravity dam" with "ingenious liftlocks at either side" and "truly hydraulic elevators" beyond which the junks could continue "as on a placid lake." As he lectures his listeners to the limit of his Mandarin vocabulary, Old Pebble stands up as if to strike him and just as abruptly begins speaking to his countrymen in dialect, effectively dismissing lecture and speaker from any shipboard existence.

The next day the junk faces its haul at Wind-Box Gorge, the most dangerous point in the passage from Ichang to Wanhsien. The path arrests the engineer's attention in its starkness: "a ceiling, an inner wall, and a floor of solid rock, with only peril for an outer wall." At that point he sees Old Pebble gaze at a zigzag pattern of square holes on the opposite cliff rising to a height of seven hundred feet where, centuries before, an army had inserted beam ends to make a ladder for tracking at flood stage. Then Old Pebble breaks into a song either of "great happiness or great pain," which spurs him to strain in his harness so that he slips and falls. The engineer perceives something beyond a vision of his dam when he confesses that the minute in which this accident transpired was long enough for him to "come close to sensing the meaning of the most awesome concepts: paralysis, burial, infinity," but not, of course, what moved the tracker. Four months after the tracker's death, the engineer files a fervently optimistic report on the possibilities of a dam in Yellow Cat Gorge, which is dismissed "by sound men as impractical."

A Single Pebble is a remarkable piece of work, both in its departure from Hersey's previous fiction and in its own right as a philosophical tale. It was unreservedly praised by reviewers as "flawlessly conceived" and "written with great sensitivity." Santha Rama Rau wrote in *The New York Times* (10 June 1956), "In a deceptively simple story Hersey has captured all the magic, the terror, and the drama of that extraordinary stretch of water." With this novel Hersey seems to have been freed from the obligation to write a novel of contemporary history or to demonstrate that he could write wholly imaginative fiction.

Hersey's first attempt at war fiction was a fragment, "Sail, Baker, Dog," written aboard the aircraft carrier *Hornet* on his first wartime assignment for *Life*. He put it aside partly in the swarm of activity as he moved on to action in Guadalcanal and partly because it offended *Hornet* aviators on whom it was based: Hersey had written of men who enjoyed war to the point of lusting after it. He did not return to the subject until the late 1950s with *The War Lover* (1959), set in England and the skies over western Europe, as an American B-17 crew undertakes its last bombing mission. The story is told by Charles Boman, the copilot, and is presented in alternating chapters detailing "The Raid" (the day of the present action) and "The Tour" (the set of twenty-four missions). Boman tries to understand his pilot, Buzz Marrow, as the war lover of the title and at the same time to account for changes in himself over the course of the tour. This structure is difficult to maintain unless one realizes that Boman is the life lover whose own story happens to envelop what he relates of Marrow.

Boman has begun his service overseas with the received conviction that "the war will end sooner" if he "can concentrate on hitting the enemy carefully and well." By the time he takes off on the raid, he is committed not only to his duty of getting his crew home alive but also to do "nothing that contributed to the death of anyone." Marrow's love of war is most often expressed in sexual terms, as when he proclaims that flying is "almost as good as getting it." Such a figure, title character or not, is hollow beneath the displays of his monstrous obsession. And war is simple in its barbarous progress compared to the intricacy of building a life, as Boman learns from Daphne, the "dead man's drag," whom he had met just after the mission in which her American lover had been lost.

The story of the tour, enveloping the raid, begins with an early conversation in which Boman does not listen to Daphne "too carefully, for I was thinking of what I could tell her next to impress her with my sensitivity, my kindness, my warmth . . . my high regard for everything." Self-love, deeper than self-esteem, enables Boman's love of Daphne and his attachment to a life beyond his Flying Fortress (which Marrow had named *The Body*). When the crippled craft falls into the Channel on what would have been the last return to base, Boman is in command while Marrow has slipped into a stupor, clinging to the sinking wreck of the fuselage. This last episode of "The Raid" brings the structure together to show how Boman's survival, now that he is within sight of England, has followed from "The Tour" as well as his able command of the doomed Fortress.

The War Lover is Hersey's last effort as a novelist to deal with the meaning of the war he had tried to understand since his assignments for *Life* in 1942. *The Body* is his microcosm of that war, in which some men were given a chance to survive if they loved life enough. Reviewers had mixed reactions to the novel; Arthur Mizener commented in *The New York Times* (4 October 1959) that *The War Lover* became overly detailed "to the point of distracting the reader's attention from the wonderful story," while Whitney Balliett in *The New Yorker* (19 December 1959) called it a "solemn, passionate sermon against war" that became, in describing the flight home, "a remarkably sustained piece of writing."

Between the end of the war and his becoming Master of Pierson College at Yale in 1965, Hersey served with local school boards and national committees studying the teaching of reading and the treatment of gifted students. He was the critic of all bureaucracy, all unfeeling error, that he spotted in the educational establishment. This work led to several articles with national impact as well as his satire, *The Child Buyer*, in 1960.

Hersey's service on these school boards and committees made him thoroughly familiar with the objects he satirizes in *The Child Buyer*. The novel is described with long-winded precision by its subtitle: *A Novel in the Form of Hearings before the Standing Committee on Education, Welfare, & Public Morality of a certain State Senate, Investigating the conspiracy of Mr. Wissey Jones, with others, to Purchase a Male Child*. It is Hersey's modest proposal for dealing with outbreaks of extraordinary intelligence in a typical school system. Two of Hersey's earlier writings led directly to *The Child Buyer*: "The Brilliant Jughead," a 28 July 1945 *New Yorker* article that describes the United States Army's work in combating illiteracy among its troops—particularly its attention toward the individual soldier—and "Intelligence, Choice, and Consent," a 1959 paper for the Woodrow Wilson Foundation, built on a case study of a sixth-grader "who may be very bright," but because of the oversights of a school system focused on the mythical average student, "is a leading talent for the American scrap heap." This child's circumstances foreshadow those of Barry Rudd, the "male child" at the center of *The Child Buyer*.

Barry is not simply a slum child with a high IQ; he is certifiably one mind in a million. He enchants his principal with his brilliance but suffers at the hands of such enemies of the exceptional child as the guidance counselor. Into this setting arrives Wissey Jones, a talent scout seeking the rarest of bright children for United Lymphomilloid (U Lympho), a firm whose "Great Mystery—the Miracle of the Fifty-Year Project" begins with doses of forgetfulness and isolation for its young recruits toward an undisclosed end that promises to serve national defense.

The form of the novel is quite literally the three-day transcript of public sessions of a committee of three state senators (one reasonably open-minded, the second a caricature witch-hunter, and the third who says just enough to demonstrate that he is a moron) and their narrowly efficient counsel. The plot of *The Child Buyer* unfolds in the testimony of witnesses closest to Barry or problems that have arisen in his attempted sale to U Lympho. First reactions to U Lympho's offer range from the anguish of Barry's mother and the outrage of his principal to the enthusiastic endorsement by those who believe that "national defense" must be served by prodigies whose emotions will be controlled by major surgery tying off all five senses. In the final stage of the subject's development he will be connected to computers and will work on problems relating to the Mystery, which is unknown even to the Child Buyer himself, although he guesses that it has something to do with "man's greatest need—to leave the earth."

Each person connected to Barry ultimately agrees to his sale. The last to be won over is the principal, who believes in the "infinite potentiality of young people." In her view, the boy is finished in his present environment and has a chance to do something remarkable at U Lympho. "And if he fails," she says, "if he does forget, and if they do turn him into a machine, he'll be the best." So the brightest adult in Barry's world is made to show how humanism can betray itself in its struggle with mechanism. Finally, Barry himself becomes a party to the agreement. After learning as much as anyone else knows about the U Lympho project, he agrees to go with Wissey Jones because life in service of the Mystery "might be interesting"—more interesting, obviously, than the "enrichment" of his schooling.

B. F. Skinner, inventor of teaching machines who experimented with the "baby box," said in the 10 October 1960 *New Republic* that he thought the situation of *The Child Buyer* "implausible," the book coming from someone who "has wanted to do something about education." Carl Hansen, then school superintendent of the District of Columbia, complained in the same source that the book was satire "as it always is, at the expense of balance," by a writer who may not know that "at the working level, the school demands more good sense than most people think."

Hersey worked on his next novel, *White Lotus* (1965), for five years. It is a young white woman's account of living in slavery and enduring racist oppression in an intricately imagined "Yellow Empire." The novel, published at the early height of the civil rights movement in the United States, develops the narrator's situation in what Hersey calls a "fluid time," within which many events have parallels in an outline of black history in America during the centuries since the arrival of the first African slaves. In his author's note, Hersey suggests that *White Lotus* might be "thought of as an extended dream about the past," where "happenings are vaguely familiar yet different." Readers will thus note parallels between fictional happenings and historical events of which White Lotus herself seems quite unaware. The girl has some memories of a village childhood in Arizona and recalls slight traces of a popular culture outside that village, but she has no memory of how the Yellows conquered her white society (always remembered as white, never American). Many years after the publication of *White Lotus,* Hersey said that its situation was his Tientsin childhood "turned inside out," perhaps what that childhood might have been without the privileges that shielded him from the conditions of his Chinese neighbors' existence.

The story opens with its heroine in the "sleeping bird" stance of her protest movement as she faces the racist Yellow governor of an outlying province. She is poised on one leg, "like a bird perched for the night," staring impassively ahead and showing nothing on her face. She embodies her hard-won existence.

Not only has she struggled to gain her place, but the assimilation into the meager white station of Yellow society has entailed so complete an adoption of the Yellow language that she does not begin to feel literate until she first traces the chevron character for "man." At this point and in this tongue she begins to tell of the six stages of her existence among Yellows: three as a slave followed by three of emancipation. Hersey's achievement in this novel may lie more in the telling than in the tale, in the language that effects her subjugation and assimilation. Even so, Michele Murray in *Commonweal* (5 March 1965) found that Hersey's "regular language, professional quality, smoothness, [and] care for explanation all seem to falsify the slave experience."

THE CHILD BUYER

A Novel *in the Form of* Hearings *before the Standing* Committee *on Education, Welfare, & Public Morality of a certain* State Senate, *Investigating the conspiracy of* Mr. Wissey Jones, *with others, to* Purchase *a* Male Child

JOHN HERSEY

Author of *The Wall*, *The War Lover*, & other novels

Dust jacket for Hersey's 1960 novel, about the failure to educate young geniuses properly (Richland County Public Library)

The narrator is among whites rounded up in Arizona and herded in chains to Santa Barbara, where they are stripped, shaved, and stuffed in the hold of a slave ship. Arriving in the Yellow Empire with nothing of their own, they look upon each new thing as a token of a superior people. They begin thinking of themselves as "pigs" and "sows," as the Yellows call them. The still-nameless girl is sold to a scholar and his dainty wife, whose fine silks only make the chattel feel coarser. As "Shen's White Lotus" she is as much a Yellow master's possession as any scullery maid. When slaves become scapegoats for outbreaks of crime, the scholar concludes that whites deserve only to work as field hands, and White Lotus is sold off to a plantation in Honan. Many hardships there lead to an abortive rebellion, at the end of which her thoughts betray the extreme of her solitary existence: "It now seemed to me that God had abandoned us not by sending a storm, or by failing to fend off a storm sent by the Yellows' deities, but rather had decamped from within each of us, from our natures, from our worthless white souls. Ai, yes, I felt godlessly worthless."

As White Lotus is sold even farther away, to a cotton plantation, Hersey imagines many ranges of slave psychology. His heroine secretly learns Chinese "as though it were the only written language, its texts the only learning." She kowtows to the Yellow gods who had vanquished the white ones, and at a swine-killing she loathes "the very words 'pig,' 'hog,' 'sow'. . . meaning slave, meaning creature with white white skin, meaning myself." An abolitionist movement (the Uncage-the-Finches-Society) and a civil war lead to emancipation. Riots drive White Lotus and her lover to the remote Humility Belt, where they are feared as "smart pigs" in their efforts to "teach some of the world's better ways to the people of our race." Their school is closed by hooded members of the Hall (an organization of Yellow supremacists), provoking no show of emotion by her students: "Ayah! My children were white children, indeed! No emotion whatsoever." White Lotus moves to Up-from-the-Sea ("City of Wonder! City of Modern Times!" Shanghai), settling in slums that make up a white enclave where needle-women lose their sight working at filatures while their jobless men frequent opium dens where they can pretend to be nonwhites. She identifies "mixes" and even some whites who actually pass as "chinkties." More attractive to the Yellows than most white women, she accompanies a Yellow lover to readings by white poets. At this farthest point of her ascent into Yellow society, old friends from the provinces turn up as evangelists of the "Sleeping Bird" protest movement, from whom White Lotus begins to learn a freedom that is "not to be bestowed but grasped."

Most of the mixed reviews in 1965 addressed perceived analogies between black history and White Lotus's account of white captivity in the Yellow empire. Hope Hale, in the *Saturday Review,* admired the novel as a "magnificent . . . absorbing tale" that "sometimes borrows too simply from Negro stereotypes." The length and detail provoked another reviewer for *Time* (29 January 1965) to say that "the point of the piece can be made in an epigram" (which the reviewer did not attempt), "but the author covers almost 700 pages with illustrative incident." *The Times Literary Supplement* (8 July 1965) noted that "the reader's energy is dissipated by the sheer persistence of the author's." Some later commentary echoes these reviews, mostly in summary paragraphs of literary history, but a few studies have focused on *White Lotus* as an instance of Hersey's abiding concern with the conditions of human existence that call for action.

For almost twenty years after *White Lotus* Hersey pursued two callings: writing, at least as prolifically as he had in the years since *The Wall,* and academic assignments at Yale. His term as Master of Pierson College was followed by his appointment as adjunct professor of English, teaching alternating seminars in the writing of fiction and of journalism. The five novels that he published in this period begin with *Too Far to Walk* (1966), a tale of contemporary undergraduate life that draws on the Faust legend, and end with *The Walnut Door* (1977), which portrays a man and a woman creating lives off-campus well after the tumultuous 1960s. His journalistic output also increased.

Too Far to Walk was written before the author's employment at Yale. His Faust character, John Fist, is a college sophomore seemingly in the midst of the familiar slump during which utter boredom has overtaken the drive to achieve whatever he had needed to gain admission to Sheldon College. He has reached the point where he finds it too far to walk to his eight o'clock class. He has barely taken the first steps toward the level of learning Faust had attained before his frustrations had brought him to Mephistopheles. "What do you want?" the Mephisto of this story asks John in his darkened room. The answer is, "Awareness of the entire works . . . and to encompass and understand it all!" Fist thinks he has said that to himself, but his tempter, The Spirit of Playing It Cool, offers him all that he can imagine in exchange for his "immortal, primeval soul."

Hersey's humor in this novel disconcerted reviewers, who claimed that he had dismissed student anxieties and even serious criticism of higher education while ignoring the implications of having a radical professor walk backward in a demonstration so that he can admire the ranks of students marching toward him. The town brothel is furnished like a college dormitory, and Fist's prostitute pays him for answers to her survey questions about student unrest. This satire gives way to the boy's LSD-induced hallucination, which begins with lush Caribbean settings where John is a beachcomber and darkens with the settings of jungle warfare. His parents had been foils in earlier comic episodes, but in the induced terror of his primeval id, he sees his father killed by a sniper and his mother raped by satyrs. He awakens to break off his pact with the forces of evil by saying that he cannot stay on a knife-edge between psychedelic fantasy and objective truth. He walks to his eight o'clock class. The conclusion is abrupt enough to make a reader question whether John has really given up shortcuts to experience and whether his diabolical adventure has given him the wisdom to risk the threat of dullness by giving up fantasy. Hersey's moral, according to Edward Grossman in the *New Republic* (26 March 1966), was that "fooling around with the devil is not a truly deadly business."

Under the Eye of the Storm (1967) traces the experience of two couples aboard *Harmony,* a yawl of "dis-

tinctly unyachty lines." Dr. Tom Medlar, a young liver specialist, is its doting, painstaking skipper, who keeps a detailed log and knows every plank and fitting of his vessel. He has even identified a minute section of dry rot along the keelson, how it got there, and what he can do about it besides brood. He packs all of this particular knowledge aboard *Harmony* for a weekend of sailing with his wife and another couple. They get under way in a fog that delays their awareness of a storm proceeding north from Cape Hatteras; for Tom it is a situation where "you got away from yourself and faced the universe." The men argue over the use of a sailboat while the gale moves toward them. Flicker Hamden, a "computer nut" used to commanding instant solutions, would rely on "even minimal communications" and haul into harbor ahead of any squall, but Medlar insists that "the whole point is being out in it. Coming through it."

Hersey develops one of his best stories by describing the storm blow by blow and detailing what Medlar does to keep his boat afloat. "Exacticism" is Medlar's approach and method; at every moment, he tries to apply what he knows at the wheel of *Harmony.* But the storm hits with its own mysterious force that cannot predictably be met by Medlar's efforts. He knows then that he is "alone with chaos" and the tormenting knowledge that he had neglected to cleanse the keelson of its dry rot. Narrative and thesis are inseparable in Hersey's most compactly philosophical novel, which, however, struck R. V. Cassill of *The New York Times Book Review* (19 March 1967) as "confused and intermittent."

Hersey's next book, *The Algiers Motel Incident* (1968), was a return to nonfiction. Among the many casualties in the Detroit race riots in the summer of 1967 were three young black men shot by the police in the Algiers Motel. Hersey suspected from conflicting early accounts that the incident was a police execution within a system of unequal justice that he had observed earlier at first hand. "Perhaps the whole point of this book," he wrote, "is that every white person in the country is in some degree guilty of the crimes committed in the Algiers."

At the end of each of his years at Pierson College, Hersey had written a report to the alumni summing up activities, with special notice of such events as the arrival of co-education in 1969. At the end of his five-year term in 1970 his unusually long summary of a semester of student unrest was published by Knopf as *Letter to the Alumni.* Hersey reported that a dreaded May Day weekend was notable for being nonviolent because "White Yale began to recognize, and perhaps even to understand, something about Black Power."

In 1970 Hersey embarked for Rome on a year-long appointment as writer-in-residence at the Ameri-

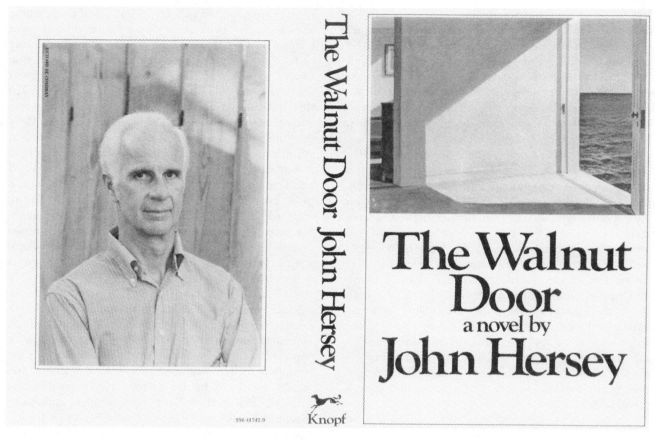

Dust jacket for Hersey's 1977 novel, a love story about two former hippies
(Richland County Public Library)

can Academy. There he began work on *The Conspiracy* (1972), a novel about proscribed Roman writers, most notably Seneca and his nephew, the poet Lucan of *The Pharsalia,* accused of joining Piso's conspiracy against Nero. This book takes the form of two sets of correspondence: reports exchanged between Tigellinus, commander of the Praetorian Guard; and Paenus, tribune of the Secret Police; and letters these officials have intercepted and copied between Lucan and Seneca. All that one learns of the poets comes from these presumably faithful copies and what Nero's operatives make of them. The conspiracy begins in the minds of Tigellinus, Paenus, and Nero, and it rises in the imaginations of Roman writers such as Lucan moved to tears or struck dumb by a Roman aristocracy given over to such sights as the footrace of dwarfs and hunchbacks at Nero's literary evenings.

"What can a writer do, what are his responsibilities in such a society?" Lucan asks of Seneca. "The responsibility of a writer is to avoid frenzy," Seneca replies from his rural retirement. Writers should follow the regimen of a philosopher, Seneca concludes after listing atrocities and orgies that his nephew must be wit-

nessing constantly in Rome. Lucan rejects this advice. "I am a poet . . . my anger is at the center of my sanity," he cries out to his uncle, who once tutored Nero. (Indeed, Tigellinus confides to Paenus that the emperor can still cower like an unprepared pupil when he thinks of Seneca.) Lucan eventually joins the conspiracy because he knows he cannot persuade his old friend Nero to stop feeding the madness in Rome.

The narrative describes the course toward the executions of the conspirators, their bloodletting at the hands of the police. With his "rehearsed and ready" demeanor before friends as his veins are opened, Seneca means his last moments to be reminiscent of the death of Socrates. Lucan dies with only Paenus and a court physician at hand, astonishing the operative by accusing the police of having invented the conspiracy because they wish to destroy Nero. "We Romans are all Nero's trained circus animals," he asserts in a fading voice, with tears streaming down his cheeks. His strength ebbing, he drifts into reciting passages from the unfinished *Pharsalia.* Paenus observes the poet becoming his poem and reports to his superior that he yearns to become a poet like Lucan because in his last state, "what did Lucan care about *conspiracy*. . . . The poem was all that was left alive in him."

The Conspiracy was reviewed with mixed praise. One critic called it "Alive" and "a delight to read" but stated that its moral (about a writer's responsibility) was uninspiring. Echoes of complaints about Hersey's objectivity in *Hiroshima* appeared in E. R. Lingeman's statement in the *New Republic* (10 June 1972) that while *The Conspiracy* was Hersey's "most distinguished novel in twenty years," the writer, like his Seneca, managed to "avoid frenzy."

Of two books Hersey published in 1974, the anthology he edited, *The Writer's Craft*, says more about his standards as a novelist than his slender dystopian fiction *My Petition for More Space* can demonstrate. For *The Writer's Craft* Hersey collected thirty-two pieces of testimony about writing, beginning with Joseph Conrad's preface to *The Nigger of the "Narcissus"* (1897) and ending with John Fowles's "Notes on an Unfinished Novel" (1969). His aim in these selections was to go beyond the writing process to show "the craft as a whole" in the belief that "the final test of a work of art is not whether it has beauty, but whether it has power."

My Petition for More Space, set in some unspecified future, begins with the narrator, Sam Poynter, standing for hours in a line that moves four abreast along a few blocks of downtown New Haven, hoping to reach a window where he may leave his petition for more space. Since long before first light he has moved forward in spurts of inches while jammed in tightly from all sides—the daily ritual of an overcrowded society. The narrator can recall no moment like his father's memory of having stood on a sand dune at Cape Cod seeing no one else in whichever direction he looked. Sam's allotted living space, marked out on the floor of an immense hall, is eleven feet by seven—whether he shares it with someone else or not, whether he pursues his aspirations as a writer at a desk or not. For Sam does aspire to write more than the reports he submits to his superiors.

Throughout his early morning ritual he strains at his perspectives, whether of his fellows in line whom he cannot see full face, the memories of his mother's kindnesses, or his father's aspirations, which have become "vaporous, indistinct." From the line, where his space is no space at all, he muses, "How big our room on Howe Street was by today's standards!" He enters the official building for the first time in six mornings of attempts and takes his place at a window where the light and the smudges keep him from making out anyone's face behind it. He can hear a dispassionate voice that breaks into his petition, especially when it senses any irrelevancy in Sam's recital of his hardships. "A writer needs—" Sam shouts; "nothing that a bus driver doesn't need," snaps the voice behind the window. Though angered by the way in which his petition has been denied, Sam turns away, struck by one statement he has made: if he had more space, he would gain more time. He would have more time to write reports that someone besides the computer might notice. "Yes," he concludes, "maybe I will come the day after tomorrow and present a petition for more time."

The tacit assumption in this novel—that the rest of the world is as crowded as New Haven—places a heavy burden on the single plot and setting of the "waitline," where there is no space between any two bodies and where the action is confined to the barely perceptible movement of these ranks and the fragmentary perceptions of the narrator. Considering the frustrations of the petitioners, there is a remarkable civility, let alone an absence of violence, until one recognizes that this scene is meant to show the immutable oppression that has come from unchecked population. The situation would appear to defeat the very thought of an existential approach beyond Sam Poynter's revising his petition. Hersey was more a worrier than a philosopher, said a hostile notice by R. K. Bryant in *The National Review* (6 December 1974). However, Granville Hicks, in *The New York Times* (22 September 1974), cited a "readable little novel" with a "lesson that will bear repetition."

The Walnut Door, Hersey's next novel, is about a pair of isolates who have dropped out from the remnant of their rebellious college generation. "In a burrowing frame of mind" Elaine moves into a lower-middle-class apartment in New Haven. Eddie is a carpenter and locksmith. Ominously, he picks Elaine's lock and scatters her belongings to create a need for his services. When she then hires him to install a new lock, he warns her that no lock can work with a flimsy door; and finally, after a fearful interval, he produces a walnut door, which, in his words, is "one perfect surface on which the statements of nature will fill the eye." The artist installs this immaculate artifact with its deadbolt lock reversed, keyhole outward, locking Elaine into her apartment. There the prisoner stays at the carpenter's mercy—not always alone because of extended conversations with her keeper about their hippie pasts and his munificence in providing take-out dinners—until one late night he raps at the door and she rushes to greet him. Hersey makes the situation an allegory of the creative process, with the flawless walnut door uniting beauty and power to bring the flawed lovers together. Peter Gardner in the *Saturday Review* (17 September 1977) called *The Walnut Door* "A love story that shimmers with vitality," while Gene Lyons in *The New York Times Book Review* (18 September 1977) found that "what these characters found compelling in each other will remain a mystery to most readers."

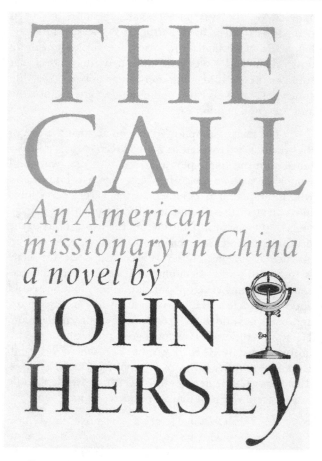

Dust jacket for Hersey's 1985 novel, inspired by his father's experiences (Richland County Public Library)

The Call (1985) began as Hersey's effort to imagine his father's world as a Protestant missionary in China. In the seven years he worked on it, the novel developed also into a questioning of what good one man can do on a mission alongside one of the massive revolutions of the twentieth century. Hersey had wondered for almost forty years whether he would ever be able to return to the land of his birth and was well into research in missionary library collections before he finally received permission in 1980 to visit Tientsin and other Chinese sites. He was looking for "evidence that his parents' lives had been worth living," he wrote in "The Homecoming" articles for *The New Yorker* in May 1982. That journey foreshadows his novel growing from a memorial to his father ("bookish . . . the gentlest of men" in his son's recollection) to the life of the fictional Treadup, who is all action and obsession, "a school fish . . . driven, moved."

Treadup is an Upstate New York farm boy who becomes converted to Christian service as a student at Syracuse University, then chooses to work in the YMCA overseas program rather than become an ordained minister and preach. "God crouching within" a classmate, he writes his parents from school, "told me that I must work the rest of my life not for my interests but in his vineyard"; yet, it becomes increasingly clear that Treadup follows the work that ideally serves his interests. How thoroughly these interests dictate his choice may be seen when he courts and marries a young woman, Emily, mainly because he is told that he must have a wife with him if he would undertake his overseas mission. Years after their wedding he notes his surprise in finding Emily so "delightful a companion," something he may not have paused to consider in their brief courtship. He arrives in China in 1905, when the conflict between evangelism and the social gospel was coming to a head in the Protestant mission. As eager as any of his countrymen to win souls for Christ, Treadup is struck by the idea of giving science demonstrations to his Chinese listeners, in effect converting them through the shows of the new century of progress. His superiors berate his "humanism," and they are accurate, because the godly Treadup works for approval by his fellow-men and sometimes even more for his own intense pleasure in doing so.

Treadup spends more than forty years in Japanese-occupied China, working in the villages and "living Chinese" while his family and most of his colleagues remain in city enclaves. There is no sign of any abatement of his spirit until in a remote village he faces a team of four Communists who are themselves missionaries of a sort, circuit riders, with their doctrines in the "patriotic" war against Japan. "On everything he records from then on," says the narrator, "there is a faint but permanent stain, a toxic trace, an imprint of some kind of foreboding." There may be a mission more powerful than his own, whether evangelical or humanistic, and this possibility may rest within a situation that can overturn any assumptions he has held.

When the Japanese intern all American missionaries after Pearl Harbor, Treadup's mission is terminated; his work is taken from him, and he is placed under house arrest in Tientsin. After he is transferred to an internment camp, he has one night when he is near hallucination that leaves him "out of touch with God" and considering that there is no God. Is it worse, one might ask, to doubt God's existence or to feel, as White Lotus did, that one is so "godlessly worthless" as to be abandoned by God? With enforced leisure Treadup begins to write "The Search," an essay accompanying his diaries, that he hopes will take him "through tangled nets of memory on a search for the inner frame on which the house of me stands." He is repatriated in 1943 and returns to China in 1946 to work uneventfully for the United Nations. Treadup dies at the beginning of formal retirement in the United States, a man who has lost his work and his faith, even the gyroscope that served him in place of a crucifix. In the view of Chinese scholar Jonathan Spence, *The Call* will be "perceived as the capstone to a writing career of enviable range and originality, big enough, subtle enough, and historically and emotionally convincing enough that we can lose ourselves in it" (*New Republic*, 13 May 1985).

The author's note in Hersey's last novel, *Antonietta* (1991), states that "This book was written for the fun of it," but the same could be said of *Blues* (1987) as well. This homage to one of his favorite pursuits—bluefish angling—takes the form of talks between Fisherman, the author, and Stranger, who may stand for all kinds of people who went fishing with Hersey over the years. Fisherman's often grim reflections on the future of the world's fisheries never come at the expense of his delight in fishing. Each day's trip ends with a recipe for catch in hand (never more than needed for the table) and a poem that Fisherman recalls out in the Sound and picks off his shelves after supper. While *Blues* celebrates the pleasures of fishing, it is also a solemn treatise on ecological systems that envelop bluefish and mankind.

The title character of *Antonietta* is a violin. As a boy of eight, Hersey had his first violin lessons in Tientsin from Paul Federovsky, a White Russian refugee who eventually played with the Boston Symphony and never forgave Hersey for giving up music in favor of writing, which "he said anybody could do." In 1986 Hersey claimed that he had never dared to touch the instrument once he had made his choice; it does not appear in his writings until *Antonietta*. The story of the talismanic violin begins with its making at the hands of Antonio Stradivari in the most fanciful scenes of the book. Hersey combined the little that he could learn about the life of Stradivari with the abundant details of a violinmaker's craft to form admitted "untruths" or "peppercorns of fiction," such as the conception of Antonietta at the instant that the maestro became aware of the glow on a young widow's face as she strode across the square beneath his balcony. As Stradivari works silently at his bench, he thinks: "repetition dries up the springs of one's energy, leads to sameness and dullness tends toward death. Thus, every violin must be an invention."

Familiar biographical sources support stories that place Antonietta in the lives of Wolfgang Amadeus Mozart, Hector Berlioz, and Igor Stravinsky. Hersey mimics the slyly deferential tone Mozart used in his letters from Paris to his father in Vienna. The violinist Pierre Baillot narrates the effect that Antonietta has on Berlioz, who weeps upon hearing it for the first time and summons it at other high emotional states while he composes *Symphonie fantastique* (1830). Antonietta arrives

Dust jacket for Hersey's last novel (1991), about a violin made by Antonio Stradivari and owned by a succession of well-known violinists (Richland County Public Library)

with the fictional violinist Federovsky at the Swiss-exile household of Stravinsky, whose rapture upon hearing his old friend play is broken only by a spark that will lead to something that could make money. The indulgent violinist knows that the secret of Stravinsky's genius is that he is a little boy. Stravinsky says of Federovsky that he is "like an old boot that perfectly fits my foot."

The last segment of *Antonietta* is written in the form of a treatment for a movie or television script in which the violin appears as the intended ornament in the career of a speculator and promoter who is about to complete his supreme coup of insider trading. Of course, he is led off in handcuffs from a reception at his Martha's Vineyard palace, and the bewildered guests get to hear the music of Arnold Schoenberg issuing from Antonietta in a manner that no one has heard before. "Who would have imagined that anything by Arnold Schoenberg could be *erotic*?" Hersey asks, and in a final moment of playfulness declares himself the present owner of the violin, bought at auction for $440,000 with funds advanced to him by his publisher for this book. So the last of his novels ends with the most personally humorous notion to be found in his work.

John Hersey spent the last several winters of his life in Key West. The locale inspired *Key West Tales* (1994), which includes a story about an AIDS victim and his caretakers that might have become a novella given the complexity of the household situation. Hersey continued working until the end of his life; Robert Brustein revealed in a eulogy that only a few weeks before his death Hersey had decided to give up his outsized, outmoded Lanier word processor for a smaller computer. Hersey suffered a stroke in 1992 and died of cancer in Key West on 24 March 1993. He was survived by his wife, Barbara, whom he married in 1958; their daughter, Brook; three sons and a daughter—Martin, John, Ann, and Baird—from his marriage to Frances Ann Cannon from 1940 to 1958; and six grandchildren. He is buried in the neighborhood cemetery in West Chop on Martha's Vineyard. "To be in his presence," said the columnist Anthony Lewis in an October 1983 *Yale Alumni Magazine* tribute, "was to be in an oasis of gentleness, good humor, kindness, quiet pleasure in others. And yet one sensed underneath, in John, a pain suffered; perhaps personal, or perhaps the pain of knowing so much about man's inhumanity to man."

Interviews:

Tom Spain, "PW Interviews John Hersey," *Publishers Weekly* (10 May 1985): 232–233;

Jonathan Dee, "The Art of Fiction XCII: John Hersey," *Paris Review*, 100 (Summer/Fall 1986): 211–249.

Bibliography:

Nancy Lyman Huse, *John Hersey and James Agee: A Reference Guide* (Boston: G. K. Hall, 1978), pp. 7–54.

References:

David Daiches, "Record and Statement," *Commentary*, 9 (April 1950): 385–388;

Maxwell Geismar, "John Hersey: The Revival of Conscience," in his *American Moderns: From Rebellion to Conformity* (New York: Hill & Wang, 1958), pp. 180–186;

Samuel B. Girgus, "Against the Grain: The Achievement of John Hersey," dissertation, University of New Mexico, 1972;

Robert N. Hudspeth, "A Definition of Modern Nihilism: Hersey's *The War Lover*," *University Review*, 35 (Summer 1969): 243–249;

Nancy Lyman Huse, *The Survival Tales of John Hersey* (Troy, N.Y.: Whitston, 1983);

Alfred Kazin, "John Hersey and Noach Levinson," *New Yorker* (4 March 1950): 96–100;

David Sanders, *John Hersey* (New York: Twayne, 1967);

Sanders, *John Hersey Revisited* (Boston: Twayne, 1991);

Michael J. Yavendetti, "John Hersey and the American Conscience: The Reception of *Hiroshima*," *Pacific Historical Review*, 43 (February 1974): 24–49;

Mas'ud Zavarzadeh, *The Mythopoeic Reality: The Postwar American Nonfiction Novel* (Urbana: University of Illinois Press, 1976), pp. 94–102.

Papers:

The major collection of John Hersey's papers is at the Beinecke Library, Yale University.

William Humphrey

(18 June 1924 – 20 August 1997)

John M. Grammer
University of the South

See also the Humphrey entries in *DLB 6: American Novelists Since World War II, Second Series; DLB 212: Twentieth-Century American Western Writers, Second Series;* and *DLB 234: American Short-Story Writers Since World War II, Third Series.*

BOOKS: *The Last Husband and Other Stories* (New York: Morrow, 1953; London: Chatto & Windus, 1953);

Home from the Hill (New York: Knopf, 1958; London: Chatto & Windus, 1958);

The Ordways (New York: Knopf, 1965; London: Chatto & Windus, 1965);

A Time and a Place: Stories (New York: Knopf, 1968); republished as *A Time and a Place: Stories of the Red River Country* (London: Chatto & Windus, 1969);

The Spawning Run (New York: Knopf, 1970; London: Chatto & Windus, 1970);

Proud Flesh (New York: Knopf, 1973; London: Chatto & Windus, 1973);

Ah, Wilderness! The Frontier in American Literature (El Paso: Texas Western Press, 1977);

Farther Off from Heaven (New York: Knopf, 1977; London: Chatto & Windus, 1977);

My Moby Dick (Garden City, N.Y.: Doubleday, 1978; London: Chatto & Windus, 1979);

Hostages to Fortune (New York: Delacorte/Seymour Lawrence, 1984; London: Secker & Warburg, 1985);

The Collected Stories of William Humphrey (New York: Delacorte/Seymour Lawrence, 1985; London: Secker & Warburg, 1986);

Open Season: Sporting Adventures of William Humphrey (New York: Delacorte/Seymour Lawrence, 1986);

No Resting Place (New York: Delacorte/Seymour Lawrence, 1989; London: Alison, 1989);

September Song (Boston: Houghton Mifflin/Seymour Lawrence, 1992).

After William Humphrey's critically acclaimed and popular first novel, *Home from the Hill,* was pub-

William Humphrey (photograph from the dust jacket for My Moby Dick, *1978)*

lished in 1958, the young author seemed as successful and full of promise as any serious writer of his generation. The book had been published by the prestigious house of Alfred A. Knopf, which had pursued him as an author after his short stories began to win recognition in the early 1950s. *Home from the Hill* was reviewed with considerable enthusiasm in the United States and in Britain: William Goyen in *The New York Times* (12 January 1958) called it "one of the most distinguished firsts by a young writer to appear in some years," while Elizabeth Bowen in the *Tatler* (12 March 1958) described it as "a tragic masterpiece" by "a writer of genius." It was a finalist for the National Book Award, and—the final seal of literary success—it was bought by Metro-Goldwyn-Mayer. The *Variety* headline describing the sale of the movie rights might not have seemed implausible: "Humphrey Sells Book for $750,000."

As Humphrey recalled later, however, *Variety* reported "one zero too many." And although it had a good cast and an accomplished director in Vincente Minnelli, the 1960 movie *Home from the Hill* (with screenplay by Harriet Frank Jr. and Irving Ravetch) turned Humphrey's Hardyesque rural tragedy into what one reviewer called a "glossy MGM soap opera." Humphrey was not particularly distressed: he avoided seeing the movie, and even the smaller check he actually received from Hollywood was enough to allow him to quit his teaching job and live abroad for several years. But the event was in some ways prophetic of greater disappointments. Though he worked steadily at his trade for the rest of his life and published fourteen books, several of them better than *Home from the Hill*, he never again enjoyed such critical or popular success. Nor was Minnelli the last reader to misunderstand his work: reviewers and academic critics did so consistently throughout his life, usually insisting on reading him in terms of a misleading comparison with an earlier Southern writer. "Once again the reviewers seem to have trouble spelling my name," he wrote to his agent in 1965, after his second novel was published; "it usually comes out F-a-u-l-k-n-e-r—but then how can you expect people to know how to spell who don't know how to read?" By the end of his life the rueful wit had become a real bitterness toward some critics, toward the publishing industry that he felt had failed him, and toward the readers who, since the 1970s, had paid less and less attention to his books. When he died in 1997, *The New York Times* obituary (21 August 1997) identified him as an "author of novels about rural Texas," which he had not been for more than twenty years, and said little about his distinguished later work.

The writings for which Humphrey was remembered in *The New York Times* all centered upon the northeast Texas town of Clarksville, where he was born William Joseph Humphrey on 18 June 1924. Clarksville was then a prosperous town, with an impressive "Texas Gothic" courthouse and a Confederate monument on the town square nearby. These are still the principal landmarks of the town and are both prominent symbols in much of Humphrey's fiction. The other important geographic feature in Humphrey's literary landscape, lying just south of town, was a large wilderness known as Sulphur Bottom, a destination for

hunters and a powerfully symbolic setting in his books. Though the author left Clarksville for Dallas in 1937, when he was thirteen years old, and never lived there again, his imagination continued to return there in search of settings and symbols, and much of his most memorable writing draws upon material gathered unconsciously as a Clarksville boy.

Though many Southern writers have tried to represent the lives of poor whites, Humphrey could claim a much closer acquaintance with that class than most. His father, Clarence Humphries, was the son of part–Native American sharecroppers; he taught himself to be a skilled automobile mechanic and eventually moved to town to follow that trade. The author's mother, Nell Varley, came from a family of cotton farmers also, but tenants, not sharecroppers: a distinction significant enough for her parents to oppose on grounds of social class the romance between their daughter and Clarence Humphries, and the reason Nell Varley changed the spelling of the family name to Humphrey, which she thought more genteel. Her father, Edward Varley, was an Englishman who had come to Texas as a boy; he is the original of Mr. Hardy in the early story "The Hardys" and of two different characters in Humphrey's second novel, *The Ordways* (1965).

Humphrey recalled his childhood in Clarksville as nearly idyllic. He was known by everyone and admired for his careful grooming and flawless manners (the products of his mother's wish that he occupy a higher social class than her own) and his equally flawless school report cards (an early story, "Report Cards," is based on these memories). He spent a good deal of time with his mother while recovering from a serious knee injury, and he idolized his father, particularly for his hunting skills. Clarence Humphrey was known locally as the most knowledgeable guide to Sulphur Bottom and was once called upon to track down an armed robber who had made his getaway into the Bottom—an episode Humphrey reconstructed vividly in his memoir *Farther Off from Heaven* (1977) and drew upon for the denouement of *Home from the Hill*. His father coached young William intensely in outdoor matters, giving him his first .22 rifle when he was only four years old and eventually allowing the boy to join him on expeditions into the Bottom. Hunting and fishing remained both personal and literary preoccupations throughout the author's life.

This comfortable childhood came to an abrupt end on 5 July 1937, when Clarence Humphrey was fatally injured in a car wreck. This accident is the central event in *Farther Off from Heaven* and in many ways the turning point that shaped Humphrey's identity as a writer. "I lost not only my father," he said in a 1988 interview with Ashby Bland Crowder, "I lost my life,

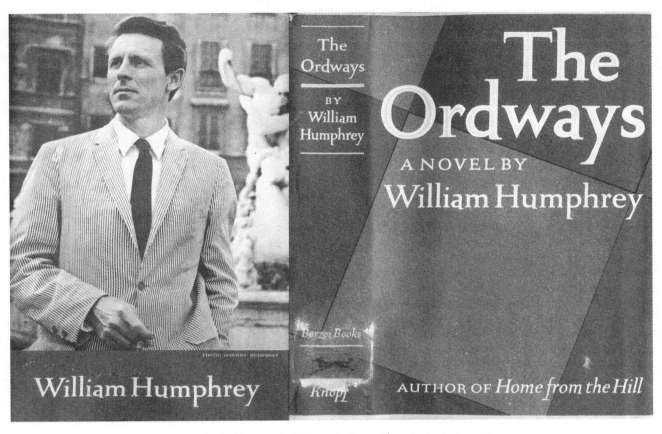

*Dust jacket for Humphrey's 1965 novel, about a Texas family that resembles
the author's own (Richland County Public Library)*

my whole *way* of life." Unable to support her son in
Clarksville, Nell Humphrey took William to Dallas,
where her sister lived. Though he proved a poor student at Adamson High School, he formed during these
years his first serious ambitions. He won a scholarship
to the Dallas Institute of Art and continued working
toward an artistic career until he discovered, while
attempting to enlist in the navy during World War II,
that he was color-blind. However, he had planted the
seeds of another, more feasible ambition when one day
in a bookstall on the streets of Dallas he impulsively
bought a copy of Miguel de Cervantes' *Don Quixote*
(1605, 1615), feeling the gesture to be a protest against
his heritage of poverty and illiteracy. This rebellion was
encouraged by a Dallas acquaintance, Jack Boss, an
insurance salesman and bookstore clerk, who converted Humphrey to both a love of literature—particularly Virginia Woolf and E. M. Forster—and to
socialism. The political commitment did not last ("I was
a Socialist at 14, a Communist at 17 in a college cell,
and an ex-Communist at 19," he told Herbert Mitgang
in 1985); but the love of literature never left him. In

1989 Humphrey dedicated his novel *No Resting Place* "to
the memory of Mr. Jack Boss, who shaped my life."

He studied at both the University of Texas, where
he took the premed curriculum and joined the Young
Communist League, and Southern Methodist University, where his writing was encouraged by the
well-known Texas man of letters Lon Tinkle. From his
college years Humphrey also took two lifelong intellectual influences: Sigmund Freud, who shaped his understanding of family conflict, and Thomas Hardy, whom
he consistently identified as his favorite novelist. But
these benefits were not sufficient to make him stay for a
degree; he left school, moved to Chicago to work in a
defense plant (having been turned down by the navy),
and somehow conceived the idea of writing a play
about the life of Benjamin Franklin. During this period
Humphrey also undertook the program of reading that,
besides honing his skills as a writer, made him a deeply
learned (and opinionated) student of the novel and its
history. He took his completed Franklin play to New
York, hoping to interest the Broadway producer Brook
Pemberton. This hope was disappointed—the play was

five acts long and required a cast of 340–but he did meet Dorothy Feinman Cantine, a native of Brooklyn, a painter, and, like Humphrey, a former "Young Communist." They were married in 1949, after Cantine obtained a divorce from her first husband. During this period Humphrey worked in a series of odd jobs, including tending a flock of sheep near Woodstock and clerking at the famous Gotham Book Mart. The apprentice author solicited advice from Randall Jarrell, who suggested that he read Katherine Anne Porter. Doing so was a revelation to Humphrey: from her he got the clear, direct, and elegant prose style that characterized his work and, more important, a recognition that the Texas world in which he had grown up could be the stuff of great fiction.

By the late 1940s and early 1950s Humphrey was placing short stories in such magazines as *Accent, The New Yorker,* and *The Sewanee Review.* These successes won him a teaching job at Bard College in New York, where he remained for nine years and became acquainted with Porter, who offered to help him if she could. She encouraged the young author and promoted his work generously, though in later years she sometimes spoke unkindly about him, claiming that he was too eager to please editors and readers. Those early stories also brought him to the attention of the publisher Alfred A. Knopf, who eventually signed Humphrey as an author and published five of his books. Humphrey's prickly relationship with Knopf disproves Porter's suspicions about his desire to please editors: his letters to the legendary publisher, perhaps the most powerful figure in the American literary world in his day, declared independence so forcefully as to be belligerent. From the beginning Humphrey maintained a serious sense of his calling as an artist ("I don't want to create a seasonal stir," he wrote Knopf; "I want to be remembered after I'm dead."). Though he enjoyed his popularity and was hurt when it began to fade, he remained independent of the pressures of the literary marketplace and loyal to his own artistic conscience.

Humphrey's first book, *The Last Husband and Other Stories,* was published by Morrow in 1953 (and by Chatto and Windus in London that same year: throughout his life Humphrey's works were prominently published both in England and France and were respectfully reviewed abroad). The stories included are uneven in quality, as might be expected of an apprentice collection; they show an author still in search of his true theme. The title story, for instance, concerns the adulterous habits of New York commuters, an odd subject for the fledgling "author of novels about rural Texas." The best of them, though, draw directly on the author's own experiences.

After the collection appeared, Humphrey began work on a novel set in northeast Texas and at least obliquely based on his own family. He worked at it for four and a half years and later wrote to Knopf that "with a little more time I might have made a pretty good book out of it." Yet, *Home from the Hill* was the breakthrough book of his career and remains the one for which he is best known. Its self-consciously mythic tone, particularly as applied to the hunting episodes in the first half of the novel, had a familiar ring for readers of William Faulkner, as did the Southernness of the setting, replete with Confederate monuments and stereotypical black servants. Humphrey's clear prose, however, is the opposite of Faulkner's dense lyricism: where Faulkner's prose is meant to mystify his subjects, to reveal the mythic depths of mundane or sordid situations, Humphrey's is meant to demystify, to expose myth and show the mundane or sordid reality.

The title of *Home from the Hill* comes from Robert Louis Stevenson's funereal poem "Requiem" (1879), and the novel begins when a mysterious hearse, marked only by "Dallas County license plates," enters town (plainly Clarksville, though its name is never mentioned). The opening is portentous: the hearse slowly circles the town square, where idle men whittle in the shade of the Confederate monument, then finally comes to a stop so its driver can ask directions to the cemetery. The car, the townsmen learn, carries the body of Hannah Hunnicutt, a local aristocrat last seen fifteen years earlier, when she was carried away to a Dallas insane asylum. The men readily point the way to Hannah's cemetery plot, where her headstone is already carved and her grave has been dug, at Hannah's instructions, fifteen years before. The reasons for her madness are suggested by the headstones on either side of hers: one for her son, Theron, and one for her husband, Wade; all three stones name the same date of death, 28 May 1939. The unidentified narrator begins telling the undertaker about the family tragedy represented by those headstones.

Home from the Hill is essentially two stories–indeed two kinds of stories–that converge in the end. The first, and the most memorable, is the story of a young man's education as a hunter–a masculine plot that aligns it with American works going back as far as James Fenimore Cooper's *The Deerslayer* (1841). Its setting, primarily, is Sulphur Bottom. Theron Hunnicutt is the admiring son of Captain Wade Hunnicutt, the largest landowner in the county, a formidable hunter whose greatest feat was to track down and kill a deadly wild boar, reputedly the last in East Texas. Theron, an admirable but humorless and earnest adolescent, has been given a thorough education in outdoor skills, and in the first significant episode of the novel he duplicates his father's feat by hunting down another wild boar, as large and dangerous as Wade's, in the Bottom.

The plot of this hunting story—moving from a chase to a view to a kill—is simple and linear, in contrast to the webbed intricacies of the other plot in *Home from the Hill,* a drama of love, betrayal, and revenge. Humphrey deliberately adopts, as Hardy often did, the tone of traditional ballads. The setting of this plot is not the wilderness but the town, with its complicated social system, its networks of gossip, and most significant, the presence of both sexes. Readers learn that Wade is as notable for his exploits in adultery as for those in the sporting field, a fact of which his wife has always been bitterly aware but of which the worshipful Theron is ignorant. The plot of this story turns on Humphrey's characteristic subject: misunderstanding. A townsman, Albert Halstead, mistakenly believing that Theron shares his father's libidinous bad habits, has forbidden the boy to date his daughter, Libby. The two see each other secretly, but Halstead's strange suspicion eventually leads Theron to discover what the town has always known about his father's profligacy, which in turn causes the disappointed idealist to reject Wade and, trying to right his father's wrongs, to marry a young girl he mistakenly believes his father has impregnated. Meanwhile he must reject Libby, who, though he does not know it, carries his own child. After she gives birth, her father, noticing the unmistakable Hunnicutt looks of Libby's baby, blames the wrong Hunnicutt and, in paternal rage, murders Wade and flees into Sulphur Bottom. Theron, suddenly finding a clear path through the tangled human situation, at last knows what to do; he pursues Halstead into the only place where the outdated masculine codes still make sense, takes lethal revenge, and then disappears forever. His tombstone, readers now learn, stands over an empty grave.

Though the immediate response to the book was overwhelmingly positive, subsequent assessments have been more mixed. Some readers have found it overplotted or uncritical of Wade Hunnicutt and his masculine, aristocratic ethic. But most of its detractors have been troubled in some way by its apparent relationship to the work of Faulkner, though disagreeing on the question of whether it was too Faulknerian or not Faulknerian enough. Some readers, often scholars of Southern literature, valued the book mainly for its hunting episodes and tended to find the love-and-betrayal plot superfluous; the critic Louis D. Rubin Jr., for instance, thought the book a misguided attempt "to carry the Faulknerian primitivistic style—field and stream, the mighty hunter, etc.—into modern urban experience." Minnelli, apparently agreeing that the two were incompatible, seemed to prefer the love-and-betrayal story line and made hunting a minor subplot in the movie. But a full reading

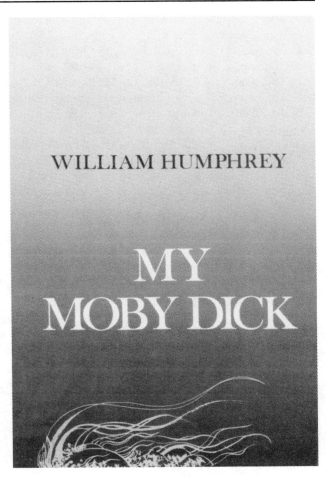

Dust jacket for Humphrey's 1978 book, a comic account of his attempts to master the art of fly-fishing (Richland County Public Library)

of the novel requires that readers recognize both plots and see that their interaction—the straightforward hunting story intersecting the social plot with its complications—is what generates Humphrey's theme. As in his short fiction, Humphrey is interested in the apparently doomed quality of human relations, the fated inevitability of misunderstanding, and in the limited and ultimately inadequate escape offered by nature.

The success of *Home from the Hill* gave Humphrey the financial freedom to leave his teaching post and live abroad. He and his wife settled in Rome for two years, where he began work on three separate projects: the novels that became *The Ordways* and *Proud Flesh* (1973), and the stories that were collected in *A Time and a Place* (1968). Eventually he focused his efforts on the first of these projects, and with the help of a grant from the National Institute of Arts and Letters and, later, an undemanding stint as Glasgow Professor at Washington and Lee University, he completed and published *The Ordways* in 1965. This novel is even more closely linked to Humphrey's own experience and family history than *Home from the Hill*. A multigenerational family saga, it concerns the migration of the Ordway family from Tennessee to northeast Texas during the Civil War and their lives there until the 1960s, when narrator Tom Ordway begins recounting his family's story. It is also an attempt to capture in a single novel much of the history and mythic identity of Texas. The setting is again Clarksville, in that frontier where the two principal historical myths of Texas, Southern and Western, collide, and—more significant—where two modes of American history, and of life, face one another. "The Civil War is one of the really truly great American tragedies," Humphrey told Crowder; "And the exploration of the West is a comedy; it's a farce. Indeed, it's how Americans forgot the Civil War, by getting away from the South and going West."

The Ordways is, as Humphrey admitted in the interview with Crowder, a "broken-backed" book, consisting of three parts of unequal size, with three different tones. The first section, "In a Country Churchyard," is emphatically Southern in tone, and its subject is essentially memory and the way the past bears upon the present. It begins with the narrator, Tom Ordway, recalling a ceremony of memory, a graveyard cleaning day in Clarksville in the 1930s, which leads him to begin telling the stories of the ancestors whose graves were tended that day. The most important of these is the story of Thomas Ordway, the badly wounded Confederate soldier who, in the waning days of the Civil War, brought the family from Tennessee to Texas. The migration westward is of course a major trope in American historical myth, one that usually signifies the leaving behind of a tragic past in favor of a hopeful future. But for the Ordways the significance is not so clear, for they have brought with them from Tennessee not only their hopes but also the bones, packed in barrels, of all their ancestors, along with the family tombstone: the metaphorical weight of the past, the "burden of Southern history," becomes literal. The climax of their journey is the crossing of the Red River, a mythically resonant event that Humphrey describes in powerful prose. The river itself is pointedly symbolic, combining the properties of the Red Sea in Exodus and Lethe in Roman myth and raising the question of whether, in crossing it, the Ordways have kept or forgotten their tribal identity. The ambiguity is underlined by the symbolic fact that the Ordway tombstone both sinks the wagon and keeps it from being carried away by the current. When the dangerous crossing is finally made, the Ordways settle near Clarksville, a defiantly Southern and backward-looking town, which at the first opportunity supplies itself with a Confederate monument. Thomas himself is similarly an aid to memory: blinded, crippled, with open wounds that stink and refuse to heal, he is a kind of walking memorial to the defining moment in Southern history and the shadow it casts on the present.

The next part of the novel, the "Western" part, is much longer. It focuses on Sam Ordway, Thomas's youngest son, a cotton farmer living near Clarksville in the 1890s. Like Humphrey's grandfather Varley, he has outlived one wife and married another, both women having borne him several children; this part of the novel concerns one of those children, Ned, who is kidnapped by a neighboring family and carried westward. This episode and its unexpected conclusion are based closely on an actual event in the Varley family. Though a deeply peaceable man, virtually incapable of anger, Sam Ordway grudgingly undertakes the mission that local custom imposes on him: he must pursue the kidnappers, recover his son, and take revenge. This mission is, as Humphrey has noted, "the plot of many a John Wayne film"; it is also the plot of one of the original Western narrative forms, the story of captivity and rescue. The section of the novel Humphrey called "Sam Ordway's Revenge" is, among other things, a parody of that old American trope. Sam, despite the mythic quality of his mission, is no John Wayne: he travels in a wagon, not on horseback, carrying not a shiny six-gun but an ancient Confederate pistol of doubtful reliability, and the errand of revenge is so foreign to his peaceful disposition that he must actually practice the words he will say to the culprit, Will Vinson, if he ever catches him. As it turns out, he never does; he searches for months, all over Texas, through ghost towns and abandoned frontier forts, through a landscape recognizable to any fan of John Ford movies; but his adventure never arrives at the violent denouement that such narratives require. Rather, Sam's quest is comic throughout, echoing not the romantic clichés of the Western but the antiromantic tropes of *Don Quixote*. Sam nearly becomes a political candidate, is pursued by a husband-hunting widow, joins the circus, and undergoes several other humiliations that John Wayne never faced, and at length he must simply give up and return home. Unable to recover his son, Sam must try to forget him; he is unable to sustain that covenant of memory that led his father to bring even the bones of his ancestors with him from Tennessee.

The first two sections of the novel offer two protagonists who personify the contrasting qualities of memory and forgetting; and they strike as well two contrasting narrative tones, tragic and comic. As biographer Bert Almon has argued, the final section, "Family Reunion," conforms to the genre that fuses comedy and tragedy: romance. Like William Shakespeare's *Cymbeline* (circa 1611) and *The Winter's Tale* (circa 1611), it involves the return of a lost child, for little Ned Ordway, long years after Sam gave him up, suddenly appears at his father's door. Now an adult, Ned has grown up believing himself to be Will Vinson's son, but Will, on his deathbed, confessed his crime and told Ned of his true parentage. Ned has traveled to Clarksville to claim his true kin, and there follows a joyous family reunion. Then Ned leads all his newfound relatives on a meandering trip down to his own home, a goat ranch in the Rio Grande valley. This leisurely caravan is a kind of modern parody of the two earlier journeys in the book, one that rescues the family from their place in a tragic history but that also deprives them even of such seriousness as Sam achieves in his mock-heroic quest for Ned.

The Ordways was quite well received when it appeared in February 1965; it was favorably reviewed by Elizabeth Janeway on the front page of *The New York Times Book Review* (31 January 1965) and in other important venues, many of them, as always, invoking the example of Faulkner. The novel won a prize from the Texas Institute of Letters but received no national literary awards. Columbia Pictures bought the rights, but no movie was ever made. Later commentators have been divided about the merits of the novel. Detractors have usually been troubled by its "broken-backed" nature, objecting particularly to the incongruity between the tragic Southern part, which they tended to like, and the comic Western portions, which they found aimless and obscure. Gary Davenport, however, writing in *The Southern Review* (1987), saw *The Ordways* as a distinct improvement over *Home from the Hill* and particularly praised the Western portions, likening their comic "hyper-reality" to work by Charles Dickens or even Gabriel García Márquez. Larry McMurtry, in his *In a Narrow Grave: Essays on Texas* (1968), has identified *The Ordways* as the best of Humphrey's works.

While working on *The Ordways,* Humphrey had continued to write the stories that were eventually collected as *A Time and a Place,* the strongest of his three collections of short fiction. "They're all on a related theme," he wrote to his agent about these stories: "the discovery of oil in my part of Texas-Oklahoma when I was a boy, and the effects (disastrous) that this sudden wealth had on the poor-whites and Indians whose land it was found on." The first of these appeared in *Esquire* in 1963; the last of them was completed and sent off to Knopf just a month and a half after the publication of *The Ordways* in 1965. The resulting collection was published in 1968, when it received good reviews. The best story of Humphrey's career may be "The Ballad of Jesse Neighbours," the first tale in the volume. *A Time and a Place* is a collection, like James Joyce's *Dubliners* (1914), that tries to capture a world—in this case a

1930s world of the Depression, dust-bowl poverty, and sudden oil wealth—by telling several of its stories. Also like *Dubliners,* it treats the protagonists of those stories as hopeless, trapped, and deluded souls, wishing for a way out of their oppressive lives but never finding it.

For the author there were two main escapes from such bleakness: humor, never absent for long even in the grimmest of his works, and sport. These two resources came together in Humphrey's next book, one that many readers have ranked as their favorite of his: *The Spawning Run* (1970), a brief account of the author's experiences salmon fishing in England and Wales. *The Spawning Run* differs from Humphrey's previous work not only in its setting but in almost all respects: in marked contrast to Humphrey's grim novels, the only tragedy possible in this work is failing to catch fish, which turns out to be actually the norm among the British gentlemen who fish for salmon. The point, for them, is the sport itself and the style with which one pursues it: Humphrey himself hooked only one fish during his British sojourn, and that one got away; but the author returned home with one of his most successful books.

During the late 1960s and early 1970s William and Dorothy Humphrey were often in Europe when not in residence at "High Meadows," the 1790s farmhouse near Hudson, New York, that they bought in 1965. The area around Hudson, in Duchess and Columbia Counties, was something of an artists' colony in those years; Humphrey's neighbors included Saul Bellow, Gore Vidal, and Mary Lee Settle. One of those neighbors, Hillary Masters, has written about the life of this community, which consisted of politically left-leaning, hard-drinking but also hard-working writers, of whom "the hardest worker of us all might have been William Humphrey." He presented the picture of a confidently successful writer, fully enjoying the fruits of success. But in fact, though Masters did not know it, during these years Humphrey was struggling as never before with his writing, suffering from what he himself called "a crack-up." In one of his notebooks, in February 1970, he unsparingly described his circumstances: "I am really disintegrating. God, even my handwriting shows it. Dead drunk every night. Sick, hungover. Shaky half the next day, recovering in time to start drinking again." The book that was giving him such trouble was *Proud Flesh,* originally conceived in 1961 as a short novel about another large Texas family, then reimagined several times over the course of twelve years, until it emerged as one of his longest and most perplexing.

Proud Flesh is a family chronicle like *The Ordways,* with a similarly large cast of characters; it is related to both of Humphrey's previous novels by its setting in a

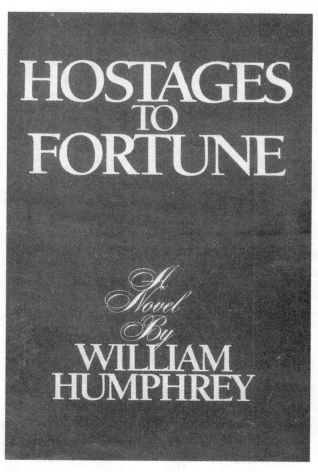

Dust jacket for the first of Humphrey's novels set in a location other than Texas (Richland County Public Library)

thinly disguised Clarksville. Set in the late 1960s, this novel carries Humphrey's informal chronicle of East Texas up to the present. But rather than stretching across several generations, *Proud Flesh* is focused tightly on a particular climactic moment: the final illness and death of Edwina Renshaw, the matriarch of a powerfully cohesive family. As her condition worsens, her children and grandchildren begin to converge on the family farm, and something of the dynamic of the large family is revealed. Edwina's husband, Lonzo, long dead, was apparently always a negligible figure in the family's life, his wife overshadowing him as she did all her children. All but one of them still live nearby and are ruled by Edwina, even giving their own children over to her for raising. None has managed a successful marriage, their devotion to "Ma" crowding aside all other attachments. As she subsides toward death, their lifelong eccentricities veer toward madness. They kidnap the town doctor and force him to keep vigil by her bedside and then to remain by her corpse for several days in case it displays any sign of life. Two of them, Lester and Ballard, set out for New York City in a hopeless effort to locate

Kyle, the only Renshaw ever to escape the pull of family; meanwhile, the others commandeer the local icehouse in order to preserve Ma's corpse until the prodigal is returned and a proper funeral can be held. Amy, who nursed her mother during the fatal illness, blames herself for Edwina's death and locks herself in the root cellar, determined to remain there forever. By the end of the novel the psychotic Amy has become a celebrity, the central figure of a quasi-religious cult whose members, along with television crews, curiosity seekers, and souvenir salesmen, now surround her root cellar.

The novel is full of bizarre incidents, but it actually conveys its effects principally through character rather than plot; readers follow the thoughts of one Renshaw after another. Yet, strangely, the characters never become truly vivid, seeming to have only a collective (and stereotypically Texan) identity. All of them, particularly the men, are submerged in the same "larger-than-life" regional cliché: Edwina's sons are unanimously aggressive, proud, and violent, but one has to keep reminding oneself which son runs the farm and keeps a black mistress, which one ignores the farm and keeps a pack of hunting dogs, and so on. Perversely, the family member who seems the most distinct is the one who never appears, Kyle. Some reviewers complained about the hazy and clichéd quality of the characters, but in fact these "flaws" convey a major theme of the work: the power of a community and its myths to smother independent selfhood. Edwina dressed her children identically and imposed the same haircut on all; as adults they think and act identically. A reader trying too hard to tell them apart would be missing the point.

The strange conclusion of the novel suggests that it is not only about the Renshaws but also about the world they inhabit, a demystified but also diminished world that cannot avoid staring, in speechless wonder, at the mad, "larger-than-life" family. The Renshaws seem not really to belong to their 1960s world of drugs and student demonstrations but to have been transported from some earlier moment of Southern history, an anachronism that has struck some readers as a flaw in the book. But again this "flaw" was essential to Humphrey's theme, for the other half of the equation the author is exploring is the family's remarkable ability to preserve their antiquated identities despite the inhospitable world they inhabit, and the power of those identities to confer a bizarre dignity on their disordered lives. Myths like the one lived out by the Renshaws are distortions and often generate tragedy; on the other hand, life without them seems colorless and small: thus, the crowd of awestruck, deracinated moderns that surrounds the Renshaw house at the end of the novel.

Proud Flesh received some positive reviews, but also several negative ones, particularly the influential one in *The New York Times* (4 April 1973) by Christopher Lehmann-Haupt, who published what Masters calls "the most viciously constructed condemnation of a writer's work in modern history." This attack on the book, though unfair and in places simply inaccurate, devastated Humphrey. Writing to his biographer, Almon, years later, he placed Lehmann-Haupt at the top of his private list of "bad critics," and in later interviews he insisted defiantly that *Proud Flesh* was actually "a far better book" than either of his previous novels. This judgment was affirmed by Davenport, who called the novel "brilliant" and found in it "gemlike concentrations of hyper-reality" which were "incredible and yet true to the point of inevitability." But the generally poor reception of the book marked a downturn in Humphrey's reputation from which it never fully recovered, despite the several excellent books he wrote afterward.

Despite his disappointments Humphrey quickly went back to work, turning again to those two refuges from despair, humor and the sporting life. Both were prominent in *My Moby Dick,* completed in 1975 and published in 1978. It is another fishing story, this time concerning Humphrey's slow acquisition of the art of fly-fishing and of the fish—an enormous, one-eyed brown trout—for whose sake he acquired it. It is also, as the title makes clear, a parody, an affectionate one not only of Herman Melville's 1851 novel ("Call me Bill," Humphrey begins, echoing the famous first sentence of *Moby-Dick*) but also of several lesser classics of fishing, and a gentle satire on the pretensions of fly-fishermen, a fraternity of which Humphrey was an enthusiastic member. It ends, like its inspiration, with the defeat of the angler and the escape of the fish, which, finally hooked on the last day of trout season, breaks the leader and disappears forever. Not quite the comic masterpiece that *The Spawning Run* was, *My Moby Dick* became nonetheless one of Humphrey's most popular books, reprinted at least eight times.

At the same time, the author was at work on a radically different sort of book, a political satire. Humphrey had participated in the 1971 march on the Pentagon to protest the Vietnam war (having been driven to Washington from Charlottesville, Virginia, and back again in time for dinner, in Porter's limousine). No longer the Young Communist of college days but only a "vague Social Democrat," he nonetheless felt a deep dissatisfaction with the political life of his country and a particular contempt for President Richard Nixon. "The Horse Latitudes," a novel centered upon an earthy and opinionated Texan named Cecil Smoot and set during the final summer of Nixon's presidency, became his vehicle for expressing that contempt. The novel had moments of both wit and insight, but Humphrey was never able to solve problems of plot and tone sufficiently to make the book publishable. It was rejected by two publishers, and he finally abandoned it.

In 1976, partly in response to a financial crisis caused by the failure of *Proud Flesh,* Humphrey accepted another teaching position, as Elizabeth Drew Professor at Smith College. At the same time he was signaling his recovery from this failure by writing what many consider his best book, the powerful and heartbreaking memoir *Farther Off from Heaven.* This work was an effort to set down truthfully his memories of childhood, including the painful ones that had haunted his life and his fiction, yet to give that truth "the shape of a novel." He eventually hit upon a method for doing that, creating his most intricately structured work by placing his father's fatal car wreck, and the three days between that event and the funeral, at the center of the narrative. He fills in prior events—including several that occurred before he was born—in a series of digressions that extend from that center like spokes from a hub; after each digression the sparse narrative of death and burial resumes.

As these recollections proceed, both of Humphrey's parents become vividly real and deeply sympathetic characters. Yet, as young William becomes aware of his parents' quarrels with one another, he begins to learn something of the hopelessness of human relations, as misunderstandings come between lovable people who care for one another. Loneliness and isolation are the major themes of the memoir. At the end, young William refuses to attend his father's funeral, to have his grief domesticated by a religion that he has already ceased to believe; his perverse refusal underlines both his aloneness and that of his beloved mother, now painfully conscious of having no husband to discipline her recalcitrant son. Such episodes alert young William to one of the central truths of the adult author's fiction: that "the grieving heart grieves all alone." The book is tragic, and one senses that Humphrey gets fully to the psychic bottom of the most painful event of his life. But the real power of *Farther Off from Heaven* arises from the recognition that it would be tragic even without the fatal accident at its center; his parents' separate dreams of transcendence and escape, and their shared dream of union, have already failed when Clarence Humphrey speeds down the highway for the last time.

The excellence of *Farther Off from Heaven* was immediately recognized when it appeared in 1977. Peter Shaw in the *Saturday Review* (28 May 1977) called the book "an incomparable portrait of small-farm and small town America, both as they looked on the outside and felt on the inside," while the novelist Reynolds Price, in *The New York Times Book Review* (22 May 1977), said that "with this sinewy story, William Humphrey has fathered new lives for his parents—lovely again and lasting now." In England *TLS: The Times Literary Supplement* (11 November 1977) called it "a rare and moving addition to American autobiography." But it sold poorly in both the United States and Britain. Humphrey was dismayed to see stacks of the book remaindered in New York only months after its publication. He felt that Knopf had failed to publicize the book adequately, and in 1981 he finally broke with the publisher, signing with Seymour Lawrence.

As always after his disappointments, Humphrey went immediately to work again. He had two ideas for novels: one, nursed for several years, concerned the removal of the Cherokee Indians from Georgia to Oklahoma in the 1830s; the other was a tightly focused psychological study of a middle-aged writer coming to terms with multiple tragedies. Though Seymour Lawrence was more interested in the former, Humphrey had begun work in 1977 on the latter, which was published in 1984 as *Hostages to Fortune*. During this period, between 1981 and 1982, he served as writer-in-residence at Princeton University, his last academic appointment. Princeton provided one of the settings of *Hostages to Fortune,* significantly the first of Humphrey's novels to be set anywhere except Texas. The protagonist, Ben Curtis, lives in Upstate New York in a house modeled on High Meadows, which is appropriate since, though his experiences are based on those of two of the author's friends, Ben is a thinly disguised Humphrey.

In *Hostages to Fortune*—which takes its title from a maxim of Francis Bacon, "He that hath wife and children hath given hostages to fortune"—Ben is the survivor of nearly unbearable catastrophes: the suicides of his son, his goddaughter, and his closest friend; the end of his marriage; and his own failed suicide attempt. When the novel opens, he is returning to his New York fishing club for the first time since these disasters. The novel begins, like *Home from the Hill,* with objects that are evidence of a catastrophe—in this case, two fishing licenses, dated just two years apart, both belonging to Ben: the first identifies a forty-eight-year-old-man, weight 205, hair black; the second a fifty-year-old man, weight 170, hair white. Readers discover the causes of this change through a series of retrospective digressions that depend on the slender, "present-tense" story of Ben's return to the club; because the club has been the scene of so many important moments in his marriage and in his closest friendship, the visit is the catalyst for the flashbacks through which the main story is told.

The subject of the book is announced in an early scene, when Ben buys his new fishing license from the twins who operate a sporting-goods store: "twins tickle something in us," says the narrator, "perhaps elating us with the feeling that for once nature has been tricked out of her stern rule that a person shall have but one lone self." The characters in *Hostages to Fortune* make several other attempts to trick nature by forming connections between lone selves: at one time Ben Curtis had a close friend in Tony Thayer; a wife, Cathy, with whom he was in love; and a son, Anthony, with whom

to share his love of fishing. But Tony, devastated by the suicide of his daughter, has withdrawn from Ben and finally takes his own life. Anthony hangs himself in his Princeton dormitory room without leaving a note. Ben and Cathy, rather than being united by grief for their son, are divided by it, finally divorcing. The suicides of the two young people have not exactly caused these ruptures among their elders; rather, they reveal previously invisible fault lines that were always there. Humphrey suggests this point through an elaborate metaphor: in an early scene Tony, drinking heavily to numb his grief, accidentally steers his antique wooden sailboat onto a reef; the impact, all the passengers realize, is such that "had the boat been a modern one its plastic hull would have split at the seam like a nut and gone down with all hands aboard." The friendships and marriages in *Hostages to Fortune* all turn out to have the defects of modern sailboats; the impact of disaster shatters them, and they sink, indeed, with all hands aboard.

Though *Hostages to Fortune* has no Texas connection, in other ways it displays strong continuities with Humphrey's earlier work. Ben and Cathy, for instance, share an extreme form of the problem that plagues other Humphrey characters, the failure of communication. After Anthony's suicide, Cathy withdraws completely from her husband, even refusing to hear from him how Anthony died so as to cling to her belief that his death was accidental. Thus is she trapped, alone, in her willed misunderstanding, and he in his solitary knowledge of how fiercely his son rejected life. The point of view of the novel traps readers entirely in Ben's consciousness: they see the other characters only through his memories of them, and therefore do not see any of them clearly—never even learning, for instance, what Cathy looks like. Humphrey's agent objected to this feature of the novel, but Humphrey made it clear to her that his subject was simply the mind of his main character. The isolation of that mind is the real point of the novel; the sharply limited point of view forces the reader to experience it firsthand. There is an added, bitter irony in Ben's failure to communicate with the people he loves, since he is a writer, vocationally committed to the idea that words do communicate and do offer, like friendship and marriage, a way of escaping isolation. But all these institutions fail in *Hostages to Fortune,* and in the end every character shares the fate of its ghostly central presence, the dead Anthony, who left no explanation for his action: every self is a hieroglyphic, inscrutable to all the others.

Ben comes to terms with this truth during the twenty-four-hour period that makes up the present action of the novel. He returns to his club, is eventually recognized despite his changed appearance, orders his usual drink, fishes his usual stretch of the river, and displays several times the club's signature "thumbs-up" sign to indicate his good spirits. In the final scene he successfully lands a big trout. Hesitating a moment about what to do, he elects not to release the fish but to kill it and bring it back to the club. By doing so he would send a message–false, but necessary–to his fellow members: that he had enjoyed his day, was again capable of taking pleasure in life, and had indeed "rejoined the club" of human life. It would be another version of the "thumbs-up" sign, which, readers finally realize, is not a philosophy of life but a disguise, a humane deception. And the rituals of sport, consolation to Humphrey's characters from Theron Hunnicutt onward, are valuable but painfully inadequate compensation for tragedy.

Hostages to Fortune was too bleak and cheerless to be a popular success, but its merit was recognized by most of the reviewers. Seymore Epstein in The New York Times (14 October 1984) praised the seriousness, dedication, and integrity of the novel, while Jonathan Yardley in the Washington Post Book World (23 March 1984) said it was "powerful . . . intelligent, compassionate, civilized; we could hardly ask for more" and called Humphrey "a marvelously accomplished writer, one of the best we have." Even Mark Royden Winchell, often a harsh critic of Humphrey's work, praised Hostages to Fortune in The Sewanee Review (1988) for its "honesty and conviction" and called it "Humphrey's most impressive book."

Almost immediately after the publication of Hostages to Fortune, Humphrey's new publisher, Seymour Lawrence, published The Collected Stories of William Humphrey (1985)–the contents of The Last Husband and A Time and a Place, along with two previously uncollected tales– and Open Season: Sporting Adventures of William Humphrey (1986), which gathered Humphrey's extensive body of outdoor writing, including The Spawning Run and My Moby Dick as well as shorter pieces that had appeared in such magazines as Sports Illustrated and Esquire. The former collection was reviewed respectfully, the latter enthusiastically. Robert Jones in the 8 December 1986 issue of Time magazine, for instance, referred to the author as "the best damn boot-in-the-mud nature essayist–piscine, avian or human–in the business."

Humphrey's final novel, No Resting Place, his long-contemplated work about the Cherokee Indians, was finally published in 1989. The book is dense with historical information, which Humphrey tries to integrate with a fictional story, framed once again with a Clarksville setting. Humphrey told Crowder that No Resting Place was his first historical novel, indicating apparently that he did not consider The Ordways, also set in the nineteenth century, to be one. In the strict sense he was right, for the form of the historical novel, estab-

Dust jacket for Humphrey's last novel (1989), about the forced migration of the Cherokee Indians from the southeastern states to Oklahoma during the late 1830s
(Richland County Public Library)

lished in English by Walter Scott and elaborated in the United States by Cooper, involves a fairly specific formula: the focus is on a single, climactic moment in history; the foreground is occupied by fictional characters who interact occasionally with the historical ones in the background; and there is often, though not always, a narrative frame that sets the historical moment against some later one in which the story is told. Humphrey honored most of these generic conventions: the removal of the Cherokee from their native lands was certainly a climactic moment in the history of white-Indian relations; the story includes both fictional and historical characters; and there is a frame narrative whereby the main story is accounted for and related to the present.

As he often did, Humphrey structures the novel by working backward, from present to past, effect to cause. It opens in 1936, the year of the Texas Centennial. The scene is a reenactment, on the junior-high football field, of the Battle of San Jacinto, fought exactly one hundred years before between Sam Houston's ragged and outnumbered Texans and the vast Mexican Army of General Antonio López de Santa Anna, fresh from their bloody victory at the Alamo. The narrator, Amos Smith, is recalling the event from his childhood. The evening before, he has proudly told his father that he has been chosen to play the part of one of the heroes of the battle, Mirabeau Lamar, commander of the Texan cavalry. "That sorry rascal!" his father replies. "Like hell you are!" The father soon takes the boy aside and tells him an episode of history and family lore of which his schoolbooks have left him ignorant; thus is the story of the Cherokees introduced.

At this point the story becomes that of an earlier Amos Smith, or as he is called at the time, Amos Ferguson, great-grandfather of the narrator. He is a Cherokee boy, also named Noquisi, living in Georgia in the 1830s. The large admixture of Scots blood in his veins is evidenced by the blonde hair, blue eyes, and thoroughly European mode of life. His father is a doctor, educated at William and Mary; the family lives in a farmhouse and raises the same crops as its white neighbors, and early in the novel Amos arranges to be baptized by the Presbyterian missionary who has taken up residence nearby. One of Humphrey's themes is the arbitrariness and fictionality of racial identity, the "constructedness of race," as social critics of a younger generation were putting it by the time the novel appeared. The narrative moves back and forth between the particular experiences of the Ferguson family and a political history of the Cherokee tribe in the 1830s, as the issue of migration westward is debated among real historical figures such as John Ross and Major Ridge. But eventually history, evidencing Humphrey's careful research, comes to outweigh fiction: readers learn much about Cherokee life and less about Amos and his relatives, who suffer with dignity but remain rather blurry as personalities, as does Humphrey's other chief fictional character, the Scottish missionary Malcolm McKenzie.

What comes into sharp focus is the atrocity of this episode in history: the massive injustice of the dispossession of the Cherokee, then the holocaust of the march west, during which thousands of Indians died of exposure, exhaustion, or cholera. The novel makes readers face these realities and thus unites two threads of Humphrey's thought that had been present since his adolescence: the grim literary naturalism he learned from Hardy and the political radicalism he learned from Jack Boss. The book is equally an indictment of the indifferent God who

permitted such horror and an exposé of the American nation that caused it. The story culminates in the Republic of Texas, near Clarksville, where a group of the dispossessed Cherokee have taken up residence, relying on President Sam Houston's guarantee of quiet enjoyment of their lands. But Lamar, Houston's successor as president of the republic, has demanded that the Cherokee leave those lands, and the Cherokee resolve this time to fight rather than move. The ensuing battle, a real but almost unknown episode of Texas history, ends as a bloody rout of the Indians, including Amos and his father.

Though a departure in many respects, *No Resting Place* actually picks up so many of Humphrey's characteristic themes and symbols that it seems like a summing up of the author's career. Humphrey's last novel ends with a handful of survivors of the battle, including Amos and his father, fleeing northward toward the Red River, reversing the progress of the Ordways in Humphrey's second novel, and reversing as well the meaning of that progress: a fugitive and defeated people, though they have migrated westward like the beaten Confederates of the earlier novel, find not a new life but death. And the novel ends where so many of Humphrey's fictions begin, with a misunderstanding: the white hunter who murders Amos Ferguson's father as he tries to swim the Red River also mistakes Amos for a white captive, believes he is rescuing him, and completes his good deed by adopting him and giving him a new name, Smith. Amos gratefully accepts, happy to claim a fictional identity that promises to release him from the nightmarish history in which his previous Cherokee identity, perhaps no less fictional, has involved him. Like so many of Humphrey's other characters, Amos and his descendants—down to Amos IV, who tells the story—live within the tension between memory and forgetting.

No Resting Place was respectfully reviewed, with nearly all the notices praising at least Humphrey's serious and sensitive treatment of a horrific episode of American history. Many found the book largely successful in rendering this material in fictional form. "The weight of such history would seem almost too oppressive for fiction to handle," commented one critic in *Time* (19 June 1989), "but Humphrey skillfully balances the misery with the detachment of ancient family legend." Negative assessments of the book dissented on precisely the issues of balance and control, tending to find the twentieth-century frame narrative awkward and distracting and to stress the inadequate integration of history and fiction. John Clute in *TLS* (1 December 1989), for instance, called the novel "pained, decent, and slightly fumble-footed," com-

DLB 278 — William Humphrey

plaining that Humphrey's use of the first-person frame narrative did nothing to sharpen his "control over difficult material." As with others of Humphrey's books, Hollywood was interested, but the movie version of *No Resting Place* that Home Box Office considered producing was never made.

By the time *No Resting Place* appeared, Humphrey was sixty-five years old and beginning to feel the effects of age: even the photograph of him on the dust jacket showed, for the first time, an old man looking vaguely at the camera, in place of the hearty, confident outdoorsman who smiled from the back cover of so many previous books. His most painful affliction was deafness, a condition that seemed to isolate the always reclusive author even from old and trusted friends. At the same time, he was settling into a real bitterness about the literary world, which had once treated him like young royalty and now seemed to have forgotten him. To Crowder's 1988 question about book publishing in the present day, Humphrey replied, "Oh, Lord, don't get me on that. You won't get out of here for another three days. And when you do, you'll want to jump off a bridge." When his publisher notified him that it would nominate *No Resting Place* for the Pulitzer Prize, Humphrey replied with a single word: "Hah!"

Humphrey published his last book, a collection of new short fiction called *September Song,* in 1992, to once again respectful but mostly unenthusiastic reviews. Yet, some of the stories in that collection, such as the poignant "Dead Languages" and "Buck Fever," display Humphrey's Hardyesque power undiminished; the former, indeed, makes of the protagonist's deafness a painfully literal instance of Humphrey's most characteristic theme, misunderstanding. Other stories, such as the whimsical "Portrait of the Artist as an Old Man" and "Dead Weight," are witty in the manner of *The Spawning Run.* Still others seem merely bitter, without any leavening of pathos or wit. The theme of the collection is, as the Winter 1992 *Virginia Quarterly Review* commented in a favorable notice, "advancing age, lost powers, encroaching death."

At about the time the book appeared Humphrey was diagnosed with cancer. He still lived at High Meadows, cared for eventually by a hospice team, while Dorothy, also seriously ill and in need of care, went to live with her daughter from her first marriage. His final years were cheered by the news that the Texas Institute of Letters had awarded him its lifetime achievement award, named after his old mentor Tinkle, as well as by the inquiries of Almon, who wanted his cooperation with an appreciative critical biography. Humphrey died at High Meadows on 20 August 1997. His passing was noted in obituaries all over the country, most of them following *The New York Times* in remembering him respectfully, but chiefly for his first three novels. In the *Dallas Morning News* (22 August 1997) critic Jerome Weeks compounded the insult by inadvertently revealing, in his clumsy summary of *Home from the Hill,* that he knew only the significantly altered plot of the movie. But Mel Gussow in *The New York Times* (21 August 1997) also quoted the poet Theodore Weiss, one of Humphrey's oldest friends, who characterized him as "a master craftsman and a man of authenticity." This judgment at least must stand; Humphrey was committed to a grim moral vision and to a prose style that emphasized clarity and precision rather than verbal pyrotechnics, and he stuck by these commitments even as they began to cost him fame, money, and readership—all of which he had relished.

Literary scholars paid only sporadic and superficial attention to William Humphrey during most of his life, but since the early 1990s a handful of significant articles have appeared in scholarly journals. Almon's *William Humphrey: Destroyer of Myths* was published in 1998 in the Texas Writers Series of the University of North Texas Press. For the foreseeable future Humphrey will likely continue to be viewed, as he usually has been, through the lens of regional literature. How large his achievement will look through that lens is still uncertain; oddly for a writer whose work began to be noticed more than fifty years ago, the jury is still out on his place in literary history.

Interviews:

Herbert Mitgang, "His Main Crop Is Words," *New York Times Book Review,* 18 August 1985, p. 3;

Ashby Bland Crowder, "History, Family, and William Humphrey," *Southern Review,* 24 (Autumn 1988): 825–839;

Crowder, "William Humphrey: Defining Southern Literature," *Mississippi Quarterly,* 41 (Fall 1988): 529–540;

Jose Yglesias, "*PW* Interviews William Humphrey," *Publishers Weekly,* 235 (2 June 1989): 64–65.

Bibliographies:

Stephen Cooper, "William Humphrey," *Contemporary Fiction Writers of the South: A Bio-Bibliographical Sourcebook,* edited by Joseph M. Flora and Robert Bain (Westport, Conn.: Greenwood Press, 1993), pp. 234–243;

Martin Kich, *Western American Novelists, Volume 1* (New York & London: Garland, 1995), pp. 708–802.

Biography:

Bert Almon, *William Humphrey: Destroyer of Myths* (Denton: University of North Texas Press, 1998).

171

References:

Dwight L. Chaney, "William Humphrey, Regionalist: Southern or Southwestern?" *Journal of the American Studies Association of Texas,* 19 (October 1988): 91–98;

Gary Davenport, "The Desertion of William Humphrey's Circus Animals," *Southern Review,* 23 (April 1987): 494–503;

John M. Grammer, "Where the South Draws Up to a Stop: The Fiction of William Humphrey," *Mississippi Quarterly,* 44 (Winter 1990–1991): 5–21;

Sylvia Grider and Elizabeth Tebeaux, "Blessings Into Curses: Sardonic Humor and Irony in 'A Job of the Plains,'" *Studies in Short Fiction,* 23 (Summer 1986): 297–306;

James W. Lee, *William Humphrey,* Southwest Writers Series, no. 7 (Austin, Tex.: Steck-Vaughn, 1967);

Hillary Masters, "Proud Flesh: William Humphrey Remembered," *Sewanee Review,* 108 (Spring 2000): 254–258;

Louis D. Rubin Jr., "The Experience of Difference: Southerners and Jews," in his *The Curious Death of the Novel: Essays in American Literature* (Baton Rouge: Louisiana State University Press, 1967), pp. 263–265;

Elizabeth Tebeaux, "Irony as Art: The Short Fiction of William Humphrey," *Studies in Short Fiction,* 26 (Summer 1989): 323–334;

Mark Royden Winchell, "Beyond Regionalism: The Growth of William Humphrey," *Sewanee Review,* 96 (Spring 1988): 287–292;

Winchell, *William Humphrey,* Boise State University Western Writers Series, no. 105 (Boise, Idaho: Boise State University, 1992).

Papers:

The major collection of William Humphrey's correspondence, manuscripts, and notebooks is at the Harry Ransom Humanities Research Center, University of Texas at Austin (William Humphrey and A. A. Knopf Collections). Letters are also at Princeton University (Theodore and Renée Weiss Collection); the University of Reading in England (Chatto and Windus Collection); the University of Sussex in England (Leonard Woolf Collection); the University of Mississippi (Seymour Lawrence Collection); University of Maryland at College Park (Katherine Anne Porter Collection); Southern Methodist University (William Humphrey Collection); Columbia University (Anne Laurie Williams and F. W. Dupee Collections); and Editions Gallimard, Paris, France (William Humphrey files). Jean Lambert of Souvigny, France, has a large collection of letters from the Humphreys.

John Irving

(2 March 1942 –   )

Todd F. Davis
Goshen College

and

Kenneth Womack
Pennsylvania State University, Altoona

See also the Irving entries in *DLB 6: American Novelists Since World War II, Second Series,* and *DLB Yearbook: 1982.*

BOOKS: *Setting Free the Bears* (New York: Random House, 1968);

The Water-Method Man (New York: Random House, 1972);

The 158-Pound Marriage (New York: Random House, 1974);

The World According to Garp (New York: Dutton, 1978; London: Gollancz, 1978);

3 by Irving (New York: Random House, 1980)–comprises *Setting Free the Bears, The Water-Method Man,* and *The 158-Pound Marriage;*

The Hotel New Hampshire (New York: Dutton, 1981; London: Cape, 1982);

The Cider House Rules (New York: Morrow, 1985; London: Cape, 1985);

A Prayer for Owen Meany (New York: Morrow, 1989; London: Bloomsbury, 1989);

Trying to Save Piggy Sneed (London: Bloomsbury, 1993; expanded, New York: Arcade, 1996);

A Son of the Circus (New York: Random House, 1994; London: Bloomsbury, 1994);

The Imaginary Girlfriend: A Memoir (New York: Random House, 1996; London: Bloomsbury, 1996);

A Widow for One Year (New York: Random House, 1998; London: Bloomsbury, 1998);

My Movie Business: A Memoir (New York: Random House, 1999; London: Bloomsbury, 1999);

The Cider House Rules: A Screenplay (New York: Hyperion, 1999; London: Bloomsbury, 2000);

The Fourth Hand (New York: Random House, 2001; London: Bloomsbury, 2001).

John Irving (photograph by Marion Ettlinger; from the dust jacket for A Prayer for Owen Meany, *1989)*

PRODUCED SCRIPT: *The Cider House Rules,* adapted by Irving from his novel, motion picture, Miramax, 1999.

John Irving enjoys a rare and prominent place among contemporary American writers not only for having published a string of best-sellers but also for having received accolades from critics in the popular and academic press alike. His status has been assured since the dizzying success of *The World According to Garp* in 1978. In addition to selling more than 120,000 hardcover copies and more than 3 million paperbacks, *The World According to Garp* established Irving as an American cultural icon—a phenomenon that R. Z. Sheppard subsequently referred to in *Time* magazine as "Garpomania" in the early 1980s. In 1979 Irving won the prestigious American Book Award. Since the publication of *The World According to Garp,* Irving's novels have been adapted into four motion pictures, including *The Cider House Rules* (1999), for which Irving received an Oscar for best screenplay in 2000. Originally published in 1985, *The Cider House Rules*—along with *The Hotel New Hampshire* (1981), *A Prayer for Owen Meany* (1989), and *A Widow for One Year* (1998)—has secured Irving's stature as one of America's most significant men of letters.

John Irving was born in Exeter, New Hampshire, on 2 March 1942. His birth name was John Wallace Blunt Jr., in honor of his biological father, a World War II flyer who was shot down over Burma. Irving's mother, Frances Winslow Irving, legally changed his name to John Winslow Irving when he was six years old after he had been adopted by her second husband, Colin F. N. Irving. Because his stepfather taught in the history department at Phillips Exeter Academy, Irving was granted admission, but his struggles as both an outsider (he was one of the few students at the academy who, like the other faculty children, was actually from Exeter) and as a floundering student who was later diagnosed as dyslexic became the backdrop for his journey as a writer. At Exeter, under the tutelage of his wrestling coach, Ted Seabrooke, and his writing teacher, Mr. Bennett, Irving began to cultivate his two lifelong passions: wrestling and writing. His writing process and his understanding of the act of writing were also influenced by the variety of coping strategies that he developed as a result of his learning disability. Because of his dyslexia, Irving understood that his writing process would be markedly distinct from other writers. Irving begins each novel knowing how it will end—even the very line it will end upon, in some instances—and he writes the first draft of each novel in the third person before working back through the manuscript in several drafts and revisions. "Good writing means *rewriting*, and good wrestling is a matter of *redoing*—repetition without cease is obligatory, until the moves become second nature," Irving writes in "The Imaginary Girlfriend," a memoir first collected in *Trying to Save Piggy Sneed* (1993).

As he explained in a 1978 interview with Thomas Williams, Irving's realization that he wished to become a writer led only to a sense of separation: "How lonely that was! There was nothing like majoring in French or going to law school or medical school to look forward to," Irving recounted; "I had a terrible sense of how different I was from all my friends, and I didn't want to be different at all. No kid wants to be different." After his first year of wrestling at the University of Pittsburgh—a source of athletic disappointment—Irving decided to travel to Vienna to study abroad, a choice that only heightened his sense of separation. He told Greil Marcus in a 1979 *Rolling Stone* interview that Vienna "was so new and strange—or so *old,* as it turns out, and strange—that it forced me to pay attention to every aspect of it." Irving's insight into the concept of difference—initially triggered by the stark contrasts between Vienna and the familiar New England landscape of his youth—serves as the basis for Irving's penchant for detail. His recognition that the visceral, material accretion of detail is what represents the singularity of a setting or character complements his devotion to the novelistic forms of Charles Dickens, another master of such techniques. Irving's work poses the aesthetic question of range, asking how a story may be told truthfully if the reader does not receive as full and descriptive a picture as possible.

After returning from Vienna, Irving received his B.A., cum laude, from the University of New Hampshire in 1965. In the same year, he published his first story, "A Winter Branch," in *Redbook* and traveled west to the University of Iowa Writers' Workshop, where he studied with Vance Bourjaily and Kurt Vonnegut. Irving's friendship with Vonnegut continues, and Vonnegut's own sense of discomfort with mainstream America and the literary establishment served as an example and encouragement to Irving. In fact, as a defender of Vonnegut's work in "Kurt Vonnegut and His Critics," published in *The New Republic* in 1979, Irving creates his own manifesto for writing. In the article, he damns the contemporary novels that seem obscure and philosophically obtuse, arguing against "the assumption that what is easy to read has been easy to write." Naming Thomas Pynchon in particular, Irving suggests that such writers have not "struggled hard enough" to make their work "more readable."

Although Irving's career is marked by a radical separation from both mainstream academic and popular fiction, the early arc of his writing life mirrors that of many contemporary American authors. With the rise of creative-writing programs and M.F.A. workshops, the vast majority of writers in the latter half of the twentieth century found themselves aligned in some fashion with the academy, often as writers in residence or tenured faculty members. Upon receiving an M.F.A. from the University of Iowa in 1967, Irving entered academe as a professor at the now defunct Windham College in Putney, Vermont. Putney was Irving's primary residence until his 1981 divorce from his first wife, painter Shyla Leary, whom he had married in 1964. Between 1967 and 1978, however, Irving traveled to various colleges and universities, hoping to find time to write while supporting his young and growing family. In 1969 Irving, his wife, and his first son, Colin, journeyed to Vienna so that Irving might work on the screenplay of his first novel, *Setting Free the Bears* (1968); Irving's second son, Brendan, was born in Vienna. Upon his return to the United States, Irving taught at the Iowa Writers' Workshop for three years, at Mount Holyoke College in South Hadley, Massachusetts, for two years, and at Brandeis University in Waltham, Massachusetts, for another year. The only exceptions to his teaching schedule during this eleven-year period came as the result of a grant from the Rockefeller Foundation in 1972 and later a Guggenheim Fellowship in 1976.

Although such a rigorous course load did not hamper Irving's productivity—he wrote and published four novels over eleven years—it did wear upon him. As he explained to Marcus, "I felt I'd *been* to Iowa. I'd gotten a lot out of it, I'd liked it fine. But now. . . . I was *sick of* teaching. I didn't want to *do it anymore.*" Of course, the success of *The World According to Garp* made it possible for Irving to forego a dual career as a teacher and a novelist. But his dedication to the sport of wrestling did not waver, and despite having no financial need to do so, he continued to coach wrestling until 1989. In 1987 he married literary agent Janet Turnbull, with whom he has a third son, Everett.

In his novels Irving has crafted a peculiar form of postmodernism in which he fashions immense Dickensian narratives that explore various aspects of postwar Americana—from the politics of sex and love to the often corrosive intersections between violence and the family in contemporary life. From his first novel, *Setting Free the Bears,* many of the motifs that characterize Irving's fictions—including his penchant for magical bears, moments of devastating violence, the netherworld of Vienna, and earthy doses of sexuality—exist, albeit in relatively primitive forms. With Vonnegut's guidance, Irving began composing *Setting Free the Bears* as his M.F.A. thesis at the University of Iowa Writers' Workshop. Clearly influenced by the fictions of Vonnegut and Günter Grass, Irving's first novel is divided into three discrete sections. In "Siggy," Irving traces the experiences of Siegfried "Siggy" Javotnik and Hannes Graff, who drop out of the University of Vienna in 1967 and travel rather indiscriminately around Austria on a 700cc British Royal Enfield motorcycle. A journey narrative of sorts, Siggy and Graff's story exists, on its

more simplistic levels, as a sentimental paean to the enduring human search for freedom. Siggy and Graff eventually plan to visit the Riviera, although their relationship with Gallen, a young woman also bent on enjoying the freedom of her youth, threatens to derail their friendship. After they visit the Vienna zoo, Siggy dreams of freeing the animals. Later, when he returns to Vienna in order to put his zoo plot into action, Siggy dies when the motorcycle crashes into a truck filled with beehives. Guilty over his friend's untimely death, Graff endures a lengthy recovery from the bee stings that he receives in the accident.

In the second part of the novel, "The Notebook," Graff reads his late companion's autobiographical journal, which includes Siggy's detailed plans for the zoo break. The notebook, which Siggy calls his "pre-history," tells the story of his family's experiences during the Anschluss, the German annexation of Austria in 1938. "The Notebook" deftly contrasts the power of the state with the rights of the individual, a motif that exerts a significant impact upon part 3 of *Setting Free the Bears,* "The Zoo Watch," in which Graff carries out Siggy's mission. His liberation of the Vienna zoo ends in violence and despair. Graff's relationship with Gallen concludes in a rather dismal and painful fashion as well. Alone in his grief and dismay, Graff embarks on a search for Siggy's mentor, Ernst Watzek-Trummer, in an effort to learn the "real" history of Siggy's past. Deliberately vague, the conclusion of *Setting Free the Bears* suggests possibilities of hope and reconciliation in Graff's future as he rides away on the motorcycle: "I didn't panic; I leaned to the curves; I held the crown of the road and drove faster and faster. I truly outdrove the wind. For sure—for the moment, at least—there was no gale hurrying me out of this world."

Setting Free the Bears sold scarcely more than six thousand hardcover copies and received somewhat lukewarm, albeit optimistic, notices in the popular and critical press. In retrospect, Carol C. Harter and James R. Thompson noted in their 1986 study that "*Setting Free the Bears* possesses the classic qualities of a first novel by a talented but underdeveloped writer: major weaknesses, signs of imitation and moments of unqualified literary success." Yet, "to the student of his later work," they add, "much that here both succeeds and fails points ahead to, and helps clarify, the mature fiction."

The Water-Method Man (1972) exhibits many of the stylistic idiosyncrasies of its predecessor. In terms of its narrative, though, Irving's second novel demonstrates the writer's evolution as a literary craftsman with a keen eye for character and plot. Explicitly intended as a comic novel, *The Water-Method Man* traces the story of the irresponsible and indecisive Fred "Bogus" Trumper, who discovers the value inherent in having a family and a

Dust jacket for Irving's 1981 novel, about a family whose motto is "keep passing the open windows"
(Richland County Public Library)

vocation. Shifting between first- and second-person points of view, the novel devotes particular attention to Trumper's experiences with a blocked urinary tract, for which he sees a urologist, Dr. Jean Claude Vigneron. The cure for his ailment—the "water-method" treatment—involves imbibing vast quantities of water both before and after sex. Separated from his family, Trumper pursues an extramarital affair in New York City with Tulpen, a twenty-eight-year-old German émigré. In addition to eschewing his family obligations back in Iowa, Trumper has abandoned his English doctoral dissertation. After impregnating Tulpen, Trumper escapes to Vienna in the throes of an early midlife crisis of sorts in which he searches for Merrill Overturf, his long-lost best friend from his undergraduate years. In Austria, Trumper finds himself involved in a bizarre drug-smuggling operation and is felled by a nervous breakdown. After he discovers that Overturf had died, rather senselessly, two years earlier, Trumper returns to the United States, where he travels to Maine in search of another friend from his youth, Cuthbert "Couth" Bennett.

When Trumper is finally reunited with Couth in Maine, he learns that Couth is now living with Trumper's estranged wife and son at the Pillsbury estate. This discovery triggers an epiphany in Trumper, who realizes his immaturity and inability to grow up. He subsequently returns to the University of Iowa, where he completes his dissertation, a translation of the Old Low Norse work *Akthelt and Gunnel*. In addition to completing his doctoral work, Trumper returns to Tulpen and their child. As the novel comes to a close, Trumper savors the possibility of a teaching position, and his new family enjoys a celebration—the festival of Throgshafen—at the Pillsbury estate as the guests of Couth, who has now married Trumper's former wife and fathered a child of his own. "In good company we can be brave. Mindful of his scars," Irving writes, "Bogus Trumper smiled cautiously at all the good flesh around him." In his review of the novel in *The New York Times* in 1972 Jan Carew wrote:

Irving's first novel, *Setting Free the Bears,* received the kind of critical praise that makes one approach his second, *The Water-Method Man,* with a certain amount of caution. But the first few chapters of this new work dispel any doubts about the sustained vigor of his talent. He quickly reasserts his inventiveness, wit and obvious ability to devour new experiences, digest them rapidly and convert them into imaginative symbols and lively literary episodes.

The novel typically received good reviews, but it sold less well than *Setting Free the Bears*.

Irving's third novel, *The 158-Pound Marriage* (1974), finds the writer at an authorial crossroads of sorts. In one sense, he seems ready to embark upon a novel of more depth and scope than his previous efforts; yet, in many ways, he appears confused about the larger direction that his narratives should take. In his interview with Marcus, Irving admitted that "*The 158-Pound Marriage* is about two couples—a sexual foursome—and it grew very specifically out of Ford Madox Ford's *The Good Soldier* [1915] and John Hawkes's *The Blood Oranges* [1971]." Although Irving's critics frequently deride *The 158-Pound Marriage* as his most poorly written and least significant work, the novel nevertheless demonstrates the emergence of the literary voice that found greater success in *The World According to Garp*. As his most extended analysis of wrestling, moreover, *The 158-Pound Marriage* compares the nature and duration of marriage to a wrestling match, a competition of sorts that challenges its players to understand the ebb and flow of the sport or of the rhythms inherent in an intimate interpersonal relationship.

The novel tells the story of two couples, the first of which includes Irving's unnamed narrator, a history professor, and his wife, Utch, an Austrian immigrant and a refugee from World War II, which claimed the lives of both of her parents. The other couple in *The 158-Pound Marriage* consists of Severin Winter, a German professor and wrestling coach at the same New England university as the narrator, and his wife, Edith, a budding writer of wealthy lineage. The two couples' social relationship soon develops into a consensual sexual one of nearly idealistic proportions: as a Viennese war refugee, Severin enjoys a natural affinity for Utch, while the narrator and Edith share a passion for literature and language. Their extramarital affair collapses after its participants—except Severin, who warns the others not to take their new erotic relationship too seriously—lose control of their emotions. When their "quaternion" begins to threaten the well-being of their marriage, Severin and Edith finally end the affair to the great chagrin of the narrator and Utch, who has fallen in love with Severin, her countryman. The narrator later discovers that their entire episode of wife-swapping had been deftly orchestrated by Edith as a punishment of sorts for Severin because of a previous infidelity. As the novel comes to a close, Utch leaves Irving's narrator and returns to Austria with their children. The demise of their marriage forces the narrator to confront his ethical failings

and to realize that "I knew once again that I knew nothing."

A variety of critics in the popular press were unimpressed with Irving's musings on the ethically fractious state of contemporary America. In *The New York Times Book Review,* in 1974, Anatole Broyard wrote that in *The 158-Pound Marriage*

> Irving seems to be saying that, unless we Americans start seriously grappling with our national and sexual history, we are lost. Though there is some truth in this, he exaggerates. In taking intellectuals as representative Americans, he flatters and slanders them at the same time. And his book, to borrow one of his own phrases, merely "stumbles toward profundity."

Perhaps more important, though, several readers questioned the overall construction of Irving's third novel, particularly in terms of the writer's attempt at fashioning an intertextual relationship with Ford's and Hawkes's novels. Kenneth Womack, for example, contended in *International Fiction Review* (1996) that the "real failure" of *The 158-Pound Marriage* "lies simply in the fact that it demonstrates nothing new about *The Good Soldier* and *The Blood Oranges*. Irving offers his readers no fresh nuances or revelations about the subjects and narrative forms previously broached by his primary texts. Instead," Womack added, Irving "merely borrows their ideas about character and plot design."

The publication of *The World According to Garp* in 1978 irrevocably altered the course of Irving's career. While the narrative draws upon terrain already familiar to his readers—including New Hampshire and Vienna as its well-trodden settings—Irving self-consciously re-envisions his approach to the novel as literary form. Eschewing traditional textual and temporal structures during the composition of *The World According to Garp,* Irving struggled with the new direction that his aesthetic was taking as the novel began to assume its now well-known shape:

> I had a shaky time in the early going with it—it was raggedly put together, and I feel about it a little like a tailor who sees somebody walking away in a suit that everybody else says looks like a good suit, but they can't see the seams, but he remembers how many times he had to cut the pant-leg, you know what I mean? . . . But *I* see the seams—I know that the *making* of that book was not a smooth and satisfying event.

In *The World According to Garp* Irving also begins to formulate his conception of the Dickensian novel as his principal writerly paradigm. In his 1986 essay on Dickens titled "The King of the Novel," Irving writes that the "intention of a novel by Charles Dickens is to move you emotionally, not intellectually, and it is by emotional means that Dickens intends to influence you socially." For Irving, the Dickensian novel implies a narrative superstructure that involves a morass of narrative and character detail, as well as overtly sentimentalized gestures designed to impact the reader in a highly personalized fashion. Irving adds that "Dickens was abundant and magnificent with description, with the atmosphere surrounding everything–and with the tactile, with every detail that was terrifying or viscerally felt." By purposefully creating a wide range of characters, each with his or her own peculiar sets of experiences and circumstances, Irving overwhelms the reader's senses with his characters' inherent particularity. In short, Irving's novels from *The World According to the Garp* onward demand that readers encounter his characters in all of the humanity, profundity, and absurdity that living in a postmodern world necessarily entails. Todd F. Davis and Womack describe this phenomenon in a 1998 *Style* article as Irving's desire to fashion "characterscapes." According to Davis and Womack, this aspect of Irving's fictive world involves "the description of specific incidents that reflect the inner life of a given character's personhood; fundamental elements of anatomy, dress, physical movements, professional habits, and the like must be foregrounded for readers."

In *The World According to Garp* Irving traces Garp's story from birth, his formative years, and his marriage through the growth of his family, his emergence as a writer of international standing, and his untimely death. Perhaps even more important, though, Irving attends to "Life after Garp" in the novel as well. In this way he establishes the characterscapes for many, if not all, of the characters and thus ensures that everyone in his fictive world enjoys a genuine sense of particularity. Characterized both by images of apocalyptic violence and moments of tender human accommodation, *The World According to Garp* is a complex meditation on what Irving perceives as the overarching interrelationship in contemporary culture between sex and violence.

The novel begins during the 1940s, when nurse Jenny Fields engineers her impregnation in Boston's Mercy Hospital by Technical Sergeant Garp, a mortally wounded ball-turret gunner. "I wanted a job and I wanted to live alone," Jenny explains in *The World According to Garp*. "Then I wanted a baby. But I didn't want to have to share my body or my life to have one." Her plans to raise Garp in a world of experience and uninhibited discovery begin with her son's youthful adventures at Steering Academy, where Jenny serves as the school nurse, and later in Vienna, where Jenny and Garp travel in order for him to find his authorial voice.

During his years at Steering Academy, Garp comes into the orbit of the Percy children, the copious offspring of a dysfunctional marriage that pointedly lacks love as its ethical firmament. After Garp's adolescent sexual initiation at the hands of Cushie Percy, the aspiring writer falls in love with Helen Holm, the daughter of his beloved wrestling coach. In Vienna, Garp makes little progress as a writer, while Jenny composes her massive autobiography, a feminist manifesto on gender and power dynamics. Titled *A Sexual Suspect,* Jenny's volume becomes an international best-seller and establishes her as one of the premier voices of the feminist movement. In her autobiography Jenny writes that "in this dirty-minded world, you are either somebody's wife or somebody's whore–or fast on your way to becoming one or the other." Jenny subsequently opens a women's shelter at her family's ancestral home at Dog's Head Harbor on the New Hampshire coast. Meanwhile, Garp marries Helen, with whom he has two children, Duncan and Walt.

As a frustrated writer in his mother's considerable shadow and a househusband of sorts, Garp engages in affairs with the children's babysitters, while Helen, now a university professor, develops an erotic relationship with Michael Milton, one of her graduate students. The tragic conclusion of Helen's affair with Michael is one of the most violent scenes in Irving's corpus, as well as a powerful exemplar of the manner in which Irving intermingles sex and death in the novel. The car accident that concludes their relationship takes place in the Garps' driveway as Helen accommodates her young lover with a farewell bout of oral sex. In the ensuing collision–as Helen's family literally crashes into her secret life with Michael–Walt dies; Garp and Helen sustain serious injuries; Duncan loses an eye; and Helen bites off three-quarters of her young lover's penis.

Garp and Helen's marriage survives only because of their deep and abiding love for one another; yet, the "Under Toad"–Walt's playful rendering of the ocean undertow and Garp's sinister metaphor for fate–plunges the family into grief yet again when an antifeminist assassinates Jenny. Although Garp finally enjoys commercial success with the publication of *The World According to Bensenhaver,* various moments of sorrow and the ominous "Under Toad" threaten the tranquility of his final years, when he returns to Steering Academy to coach wrestling. In addition to his increasingly public confrontations with the Ellen Jamesians–a radical feminist group whose members engage in self-mutilation in order to honor Ellen James, the victim of a childhood rape in which her assailants cut out her tongue–Garp's latter years are marked by the renewal of his family circle, an ever-widening ménage that includes young Jenny Garp (named after her slain grandmother), the transgendered former National Football League (NFL) linebacker Roberta Muldoon, and even Ellen James herself, who finally discovers a more fully realized sense of self in the Garps' regenerative, commune-like household. Garp's assassination–on the wrestling mat, no less–at the hands of demented Pooh Percy, who associates her sister Cushie's death in childbirth with Garp's raging adoles-

-12-

It took Nurse Angela and Nurse Edna about a year before Homer Wells stopped

waking up with a scream or letting out a wail whenever someone crossed his

field of vision, or whenever he heard a human sound, even a chair being dragged

across the floor, or even a bed creak, a window shut, a door open. Every sight

and sound connected with a human being who might possibly be headed in Homer's

direction produced a high, stammering shout and such tearful blubbering

that anyone visiting the boys' division would have thought that the orphanage

was (in fairy-tale fashion) a torture shop, a prison of child molestation and

abuse beyond imagining.

"Homer, Homer," Dr. Larch would say soothingly while the boy burned

scarlet and refilled his lungs. "Homer, you're going to get us investigated

for murder! You're going to get us shut down."

The family from Three Mile Falls (although Homer would finally not remember

them) must have made a strong impression.

"Sometimes I can't sleep because I see them so clearly," Nurse Angela

used to admit, although she'd never (as they say in Maine) laid eyes on

the family.

"Sometimes I don't dare to fall asleep, because that's where I find

them in my sleep, with me," Nurse Edna would confess; but she hadn't met them,

either.)

Nurse Edna and poor Nurse Angela

The poor women were probably more permanently scarred by the family from

Three Mile Falls than Homer Wells was, and the good and the great Saint Larch

never fully recovered from the incident. He had met the family, of course. He'd

he'd interviewed them all and been horribly wrong about them, and he'd seen them

all again on the day he went to Three Mile Falls to bring Homer Wells back

to St. Cloud's.

What Dr. Larch would always remember was the fright in all of their

expressions when he'd marched into their house and taken Homer up in his arms.

Page from the corrected typescript for The Cider House Rules, *Irving's 1985*
novel (Special Collections, Phillips Exeter Academy)

cent lust, brings Irving's dark musings on the interconnections between sex and death full circle. Irving's epilogue, "Life after Garp," traces the personal histories of the surviving characters. A unifying mechanism of sorts, "Life after Garp" suggests that Irving's readers, as with the characters in his novel, also share in the larger fate of humankind. "In the world according to Garp," Irving writes at the conclusion of the novel, "we are all terminal cases."

Irving could scarcely have begun to imagine the remarkable popular and critical response to *The World According to Garp,* which became an international phenomenon. The novel sold more than 100,000 copies in hardcover; by contrast, *The 158-Pound Marriage,* his commercially weakest novel, sold a mere 2,500 copies. The paperback edition of *The World According to Garp* later earned the American Book Award for the best paperback of 1979. Nominated for the National Book Award, the novel was the subject of a highly aggressive and effective advertising campaign that featured the slogan, "I Believe in Garp." Directed by George Roy Hill, scripted by Steve Tesich, and starring Robin Williams, the 1982 motion-picture adaptation of the novel enjoyed rave reviews as well. The critical response to the new direction in Irving's postmodern approach to narrative was overwhelmingly positive. In his analysis of the novel in *The New York Times Book Review,* Christopher Lehmann-Haupt observed in 1978 that "*The World According to Garp,* for all its realism, is not a realistic novel. It is a novel about a writer writing novels—or, more precisely, about the way a sensitive human being communicates his response to reality through the stories he makes up. . . . However you see it, between the imagined event and mundane reality that inspired its invention, there is room for laughter."

Literary critics continue to characterize *The World According to Garp* as the signal moment in Irving's evolution as a writer. Josie P. Campbell, for example, praises the novel in her 1998 study for the "richness of its many layers, the extraordinary flexibility and grace of its prose, and the fulfillment of Garp's—and Irving's—criteria for good fiction; the novel makes the reader wonder what will happen next, and what happens is not so much real but 'true.'" *The World According to Garp* obviously moves beyond Irving's more derivative, intertextual indulgences in *The 158-Pound Marriage.* Raymond J. Wilson III contends, moreover, that *The World According to Garp* "illustrates a key aspect of postmodernism, that of formal replenishment," as well as a tendency toward metafiction and a rejection of the high modernist pretensions of Irving's more immediate literary precursors.

In contrast, in his introduction to an anthology of critical essays devoted to Irving's work, Harold Bloom sees *The World According to Garp* as "essentially . . . a period piece, as all of Irving's novels and stories seem fated to become." He describes rereading *The World According to Garp* after more than two decades as a "mixed experience, since the novel itself is a rather eclectic mix. It starts out as a Joycean portrait of the artist as a young man, but turns into a Pynchonian 'Postmodernist' parody." Yet, Bloom's commentary hardly begins to account for the considerable role of *The World According to Garp* as a textual conduit of sorts between the grand narratives of the collective literary past and the often more experimental novels of the late twentieth century that challenge the boundaries of the novel as literary genre and attempt to address the vexing interpersonal contradictions and complexities inherent in contemporary life.

On the morning of his assassination, Garp writes a letter to his publisher about his plans for his next novel, *My Father's Illusions.* An exuberant Garp explains the plot as a story about "an idealistic father who has many children. He keeps establishing little utopias for his kids to grow up in." In many ways, Irving's fifth novel, *The Hotel New Hampshire,* explores this same quasi-utopian premise. A self-conscious rereading of the conclusion of F. Scott Fitzgerald's *The Great Gatsby* (1925), this novel is hardly derivative in the same fashion as *The 158-Pound Marriage* and its overt intertextual pandering. Rather, *The Hotel New Hampshire* succeeds because of the manner in which Irving employs the same kind of Dickensian scope evident in *The World According to Garp.* Irving's notion of utopia in *The Hotel New Hampshire* finds its origins in his characters' search for ways in which to emerge from the conflicts and compromises of life in order to create brave new worlds of existence.

The Hotel New Hampshire traces several years in the life of the Berry family of Dairy, New Hampshire. At times the stuff of fairy tales, while at others a narrative of genuine sorrow and disdain, *The Hotel New Hampshire* begins with the initial meeting and later marriage of Winslow Berry and Mary Bates, whose romantic courtship comprises the core of the Berry family's existence. After serving in World War II and after graduating from Harvard in 1946, Win opens the first Hotel New Hampshire in a former girls' school in Dairy. Win and Mary raise five children: Frank, Franny, John (the intentionally sentimental narrator of the novel), Lilly, and Egg. During their years in Dairy, the Berry children discover sex, which functions, as in *The World According to Garp,* as a simultaneously thrilling and harrowing adventure that defines the nature of their existence. Frank, for example, learns that he is homosexual, an aspect of his persona that separates him from his condescending peers. Franny's gang rape by high-school quar-

*Dust jacket for Irving's 1989 novel, about the narrator's friendship with a boy who believes himself
to be "God's instrument" (Richland County Public Library)*

terback Chipper Dove and his cohorts on Halloween leaves her spiritually scarred. John engages in a sexually unfulfilling relationship with Ronda Ray, an employee at the unsuccessful first Hotel New Hampshire.

Win and Mary decide to open the second Hotel New Hampshire in Vienna as a favor to the gnome-like character Freud, who, with a bear called State o' Maine, helped create the magic of their youthful, prewar courtship days in Maine. After Mary and Egg die in a plane crash on their way to Europe, the surviving members of the Berry family discover that the hotel in Vienna, the Gasthaus Freud, is nothing more than the home of a coterie of prostitutes and revolutionaries. During their stay in Vienna, the children, particularly John and Franny, become increasingly isolated. The mantra "keep passing the open windows" functions as the maxim that the Berry family repeats in order to ensure their mutual psychological and physical survival. After subverting the revolutionaries' plot to blow up the State Opera in Vienna, the Berry family relocates to New York City, where they live in a pair of hotels. During this period John and Franny confront their growing

incestuous attraction for one another; Frank becomes a successful literary agent; and the dwarf-like Lilly finds her voice as an author and enjoys a lucrative writing career. John and Franny subsequently "cure" themselves of their erotic desires by engaging in an exhausting sexual encounter in Franny's hotel room. Working on the family biography, *Trying to Grow,* Lilly finds herself unable to proceed beyond the scene of the plane crash that claims Mary and Egg's lives. Despondent and unable to keep passing the open windows, Lilly leaps to her death from her room in the Stanhope Hotel. The family subsequently opens the third Hotel New Hampshire, formerly the Arbuthnot-by-the-Sea, in order to satisfy Win's remaining illusions. Never truly a hotel, the last Hotel New Hampshire functions as a rape-crisis center.

As the novel comes to a close, John celebrates the family's life together through his dream-like parody of Fitzgerald's final words in *The Great Gatsby:*

So we dream on. Thus we invent our lives. We give ourselves a sainted mother, we make our father a hero, and someone's older brother, and someone's older sister–they become our heroes, too. . . . We dream on and on: the best hotel, the perfect family, the resort life. And our dreams escape us almost as vividly as we can imagine them.

Published in 1981 with a massive commercial run of 175,000 hardcover copies–followed by a second printing of 100,000 additional copies shortly thereafter– *The Hotel New Hampshire* was a popular success. Critically, the novel received mixed reviews. In *The New York Times* in 1981, for example, James Atlas wrote that Irving, being "unwilling to entrust himself to the tragedy inherent in our common lot, brings in doom with all the subtlety of a set change on an opera stage. His obsession with grotesque and violent death is so persistent that after a while it begins to seem hostile, punitive–another form of authorial aggression." Yet, in 1981 in the *Village Voice,* Eliot Fremont-Smith praised the novel for "its sheer energy" and for its "magnetic characters, scenic wonders, horrendous happenings, and raffish, boffo jokes on every page." Ultimately, Fremont-Smith writes, *The Hotel New Hampshire* "alerts concern" about postmodern morality and the significance of the family.

In his sixth novel, *The Cider House Rules* (1985), Irving tackles the issue of abortion and its bifurcating impact upon contemporary American life. The most Dickensian of his novels in terms of its textual scope, wide range of characters, and expansive ideological vision, *The Cider House Rules* traces the story of Homer Wells's formative years at an orphanage in St. Cloud's, Maine, where he becomes the protégé of Dr. Wilbur Larch, St. Cloud's resident obstetrician and covert abortionist. An ether addict, Larch begins performing abortions after his experiences at pre–World War I Boston's Lying-In Hospital, where he witnesses the nightmarish consequences of illegal abortions. At the orphanage in St. Cloud's, Larch's moral philosophy regarding the ethics of abortion is founded upon an exceedingly pragmatic principle: as obstetrician, he delivers babies; as abortionist, he "delivers mothers." In the evenings, he pointedly reads aloud to his young charges from Dickensian novels about orphans–including *David Copperfield* (1849–1850) and *Great Expectations* (1860–1861). His nightly salute–"Good night, you Princes of Maine, you Kings of New England!"–underscores Larch's ethical desire to "treat orphans as if they came from royal families."

A surrogate son of sorts to Larch, Homer soon learns how to function as a midwife, although he pointedly refuses to become schooled in the medical art of performing abortions. While Larch considers a fetus the "product of conception," Homer believes that a fetus possesses a soul. Quite obviously, their debate

over the morality of abortion exists as a microcosm for the much larger, although equally disjunctive, dispute that occurs across the globe.

Much to Larch's dismay, Homer finally leaves St. Cloud's after meeting Wally Worthington and Candy Kendall, a young couple from Ocean View, Maine, who have come to the orphanage to avail themselves of Larch's services as abortionist. In Ocean View, Homer joins the Worthington household, for whom he works in the family's apple orchard. Homer feels a brotherly affection for Wally and harbors a thinly veiled attraction for Candy. After Wally's plane is lost over Burma during World War II, Homer and Candy conceive a child, Angel, who is born in secret at St. Cloud's. When a paralyzed Wally is discovered alive, Homer and Candy return to Ocean View with Angel, whom they claim to be their adopted son. Wally, Candy, and Homer subsequently raise Angel together in the Worthington homestead. The novel reaches its moral crisis when Homer learns, via the now-adolescent Angel, that Mr. Rose, the de facto supervisor of the coterie of migrant orchard workers, has impregnated his own daughter, Rose Rose. Finally forced to choose between the ethical dilemmas inherent in the tragedy of incest versus the moral implications of abortion, Homer opts to perform an abortion for Rose Rose. After Larch overdoses on ether, Homer returns to St. Cloud's, where he assumes Larch's work as the deliverer of babies and of mothers.

Irving's pro-choice manifesto in *The Cider House Rules* was a significant popular success. Critically, *The Cider House Rules* enjoyed rave reviews in the popular and scholarly press alike. In his review of the novel in 1985 in *The New York Times,* Benjamin DeMott wrote that "what is felt in the grain of *The Cider House Rules*–in its study of rule-givers and rule-breakers–is that the history of compassion cannot have a stop and must perpetually demand larger generosities than those hitherto conceived. By responding to that demand we may, tomorrow, invent ways to abolish nightmare choices between born and unborn." In *Understanding John Irving* (1991), moreover, Edward C. Reilly astutely lauds the novel and its place in Irving's fictive canon as "a definite maturing in Irving's talents."

In many ways Irving's seventh novel, *A Prayer for Owen Meany* (1989), has emerged as his most popular narrative. Despite a mixed critical response, the novel continues to enjoy a tremendous following among Irving's substantial readership. *A Prayer for Owen Meany* tells the dramatic story of narrator Johnny Wheelwright's peculiar religious apotheosis via his friendship with Owen Meany. A bildungsroman of sorts, Johnny's narrative deftly merges the past with the present as he sifts through his memories in a painstaking effort to understand Owen's remarkable impact upon his life. "I am doomed to remember a boy with a wrecked voice," Johnny writes, "not because of his voice, or because he was the smallest person I ever knew, or even because he was the instrument of my mother's death, but because he is the reason I believe in God; I am a Christian because of Owen Meany." As a diminutive child with a shrill and awkward voice–so awkward, in fact, that Irving opts to represent it throughout the novel with capital letters–Owen indeed believes that he is "God's instrument," a role for which he prepares throughout his life. In their childhood years, for example, Johnny and Owen effect a basketball maneuver in which Owen slam-dunks the ball after being boosted by Johnny. Owen pointedly insists upon perfecting the shot until he can perform it in three seconds flat. Much of the novel concerns Johnny's search for his elusive father, as well as Owen's quasi-religious destiny and its ethical interrelationship with the social and cultural chaos surrounding the Vietnam War during the late 1960s.

Structurally, the narrative of *A Prayer for Owen Meany* involves two significant plot elements: the peculiar death of Johnny's mother, and Owen's heroic moment of personal sacrifice in 1968, the year that Johnny flees the United States and the specter of the Vietnam War for Canada. In the first chapter of the novel Johnny's mother, Tabby, is felled by a foul ball hit by Owen in a Little League game. The event is filled with tragicomic absurdity; years later, Johnny's Little League coach, Mr. Chickering, despite his progressing Alzheimer's disease, still remembers Tabby's bizarre demise. Johnny and Owen's careful, exacting search for the narrator's father ends in utter disappointment, when they discover that his father is Reverend Merrill, the pleasant but ineffectual minister of the local Congregational church. In the interim, Owen's own search for identity involves his performance in two Christmas pageants, the church Christmas play and a production of Dickens's *A Christmas Carol*. In the latter, Owen takes the part of the Ghost of Christmas Yet to Come, while he plays the Christ child in the former production. The narrator astutely recognizes in Owen a "deity to be reckoned with" and a "special Christ." Owen's destiny finally comes to fruition in a restroom in the Phoenix airport in 1968 when he sacrifices his own life to save a group of Vietnamese children. In a single, dramatic scene, Irving merges the moral tragedy of the Vietnam War with Owen's self-sacrifice and the vague promise of a more hopeful and ethical future to come.

The novel originated in Irving's own confusion about the mystery of faith and miracles. As he told Richard Bernstein in a 1989 interview, "I've always asked myself what would be the magnitude of the mira-

cle that could convince me of religious faith." *A Prayer for Owen Meany* enjoyed a massive commercial response upon its publication in 1989. In his 1989 *New York Times Book Review* analysis of the novel, Alfred Kazin challenged the serious pretensions of *A Prayer for Owen Meany*: "Irving is terribly in earnest most of the time, politically and sacramentally, with the same easy sense of virtue. The book is as cunningly contrived as the most skillful mystery story–that is the best of it. But there is absolutely no irony." Yet, other critics praise the deliberate lack of irony and deceivingly simple structural design. Philip Page, for example, argues that in *A Prayer for Owen Meany* "Irving plays with the hermeneutical dialectic. He sets up an apparent dichotomy between the two traditional ways of knowing, but simultaneously he parodies each approach, unravels the distinction between them, and half-mockingly offers common sense as a third alternative." In her critique of the novel, Debra Shostak valorizes Irving's intentionally "earnest" narration of Owen's act of self-sacrifice. Owen's miracle, she writes, "is an ambiguous discovery" for Johnny, since it leaves him "drifting in the human world, emotionally sterile and sexually neutered. His recovery of origin does not grant him the power in the worlds of matter or spirit that we have come to expect from the conventions of such a narrative quest."

Written as a sentimental paean to Graham Greene, *A Son of the Circus* (1994) is, at least in North America, Irving's most poorly received novel since his tremendous post–*World According to Garp* success. A convoluted admixture of genres–including the murder mystery, the thriller, and the author's regular forays into the Dickensian form–*A Son of the Circus* presents the life and work of Farrokh Daruwalla, an eminent, albeit unsettled and awkwardly isolated, Indian surgeon who, as a hobby of sorts, studies the origins of achondroplasia, commonly known as dwarfism. For this reason, he extracts blood from circus dwarfs in order to analyze genetic markers of achondroplasia. In his spare time Daruwalla relaxes at Bombay's Duckworth Club and writes screenplays, including the fictive Inspector Dhar series. "Because his medical practice was an exercise of almost pure goodness," Irving writes, Daruwalla "was ill prepared for the real world. Mostly he saw malformations and deformities and injuries to children; he tried to restore their little joints to their intended perfection. The real world had no purpose as clear as that." The plot concerns the murder of Dr. Lal, a distinguished member of the Duckworth Club, and the parallel narrative of Vinod and his family of circus dwarfs. In addition to a subplot involving Daruwalla's adopted younger brother, John D., who was separated from his own twin brother at

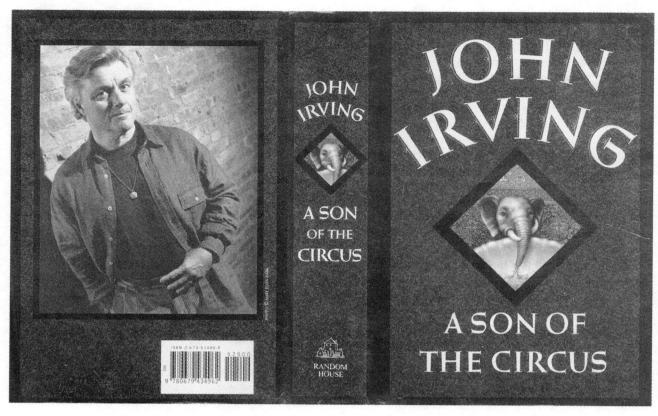

*Dust jacket for Irving's 1994 novel, the adventures of an Indian surgeon who solves the murder of a colleague
and reunites his adopted brother with a lost twin (Richland County Public Library)*

birth, the novel traces the ensuing high jinks of Lal's suspected murderer, a compulsive note writer and cartoonist of sorts who has assumed the persona of Inspector Dhar and may also, in fact, be the serial killer of several of Bombay's "cage-girl" prostitutes.

Daruwalla and John D. are ultimately called into action as de facto detectives at the behest of Inspector Patel, himself a form of homage to the detectives who inevitably appear in novels by Greene and Dickens. Much of the labyrinthine, multifarious plot centers on the machinations of Nancy, a young American hippie who witnesses yet another murder and carries an enormous cash-filled dildo with her. Her subsequent marriage to Inspector Patel, and Vinod's increasingly significant role in the crime narrative, allow Irving to begin merging the seemingly disparate threads and subplots in order to unmask the killer, reunite John D. with his long-lost twin, and provide the displaced Daruwalla with a new vocation involving AIDS research at a Canadian hospice. After capturing Lal's killer and engineering John D.'s reunion with his identical twin, Martin Mills, Daruwalla leaves for Toronto. In an epilogue in the tradition of *The World According to Garp,* Irving recounts the postnarrative experiences of Daruwalla, John D., Inspector Patel, Nancy, and Vinod. The syn-

ergy of their lives in Irving's novel clearly functions as a loosely veiled metaphor for the inevitable interrelationships that people share in the real world. This theme exists at the heart of many of Irving's narratives, with their fairly explicit interpersonal ethics.

After its publication in September 1994, *A Son of the Circus* met with a decidedly mixed response. Several critics strongly objected to what they perceived to be the overly circuitous and perplexing narrative structure. Robert Towers, for instance, contended in 1994 in *The New York Times Book Review* that Irving's many "thematic excursions . . . tend to be superficial, insufficiently grounded in the characters and inadequately dramatized in the novel's action. I found them a little boring, interruptions rather than enhancements of my pleasure in the lively progression of events. More seriously, the characters themselves, while often striking in their conception, do not really cohere." In addition to echoing Towers's remarks about the tortuous plot, Earl L. Dachslager, in his 1994 review of *A Son of the Circus* in the *Houston Chronicle,* wrote: "Whether intended or not, the novel, as a sort of postmodern parody, resembles nothing less than a three-ring circus. A lot of strange stuff goes on, some of it meant to be amusing, some of it exciting and scary, some of it simply weird. In the end, very little of it proves rewarding or memorable." Yet, in *John Irving: A Critical Companion* Campbell defends *A Son of the Circus,* arguing that the novel "has been misread and undervalued by most reviewers, who fail to see his experimentation with such forms as the crime novel and the thriller. . . . Irving has written his own allegory for our time."

Irving's ninth novel, *A Widow for One Year* (1998), is a much more fully realized entry in his fictive canon–particularly in comparison to the flawed *A Son of the Circus.* While it hardly reaches the narrative heights of *The World According to Garp, The Hotel New Hampshire,* and *The Cider House Rules,* the novel is a stylistic triumph. As the title *A Widow for One Year* suggests, the novel concerns itself with the passage of time and the manner in which temporal continuity and discontinuity impact the rhythms of human lives. The narrative traces the story of Ruth Cole during three substantial phases in her life: as a four-year-old in, for her, the idyllic summer of 1958; as a thirty-six-year-old writer in the fall of 1990; and as a widow in 1995 at the age of forty-one. For Ruth's family, time figuratively stops when the teenage brothers that Ruth never knew, Thomas and Timothy, die in an automobile accident. Their memory and their awful demise haunt the family, especially their grieving mother, Marion, who hangs photographs of the boys throughout the house on Long Island that she shares with her husband, Ted, and Ruth, the daughter that the couple conceived in a rash attempt to assuage their pain over Thomas and Timothy's untimely deaths.

A children's book illustrator and an alcoholic adulterer, Ted hires Eddie O'Hare, a fledgling writer from Exeter Academy, to work as the family's driver and as his assistant. An inveterate plotter, Ted chooses the youthful Eddie for the job because of his uncanny resemblance to Thomas. Ted hopes that Marion will engage in a love affair with Eddie and thus provide him with the necessary grounds for divorce. Although Marion indeed falls passionately in love with Eddie, readers soon learn that she was planning to divorce Ted anyway and move to Canada, leaving her daughter to be raised by her estranged husband. In Toronto, Marion writes a series of successful detective novels as Alice Somerset. Before leaving Long Island, however, Marion removes all of the boys' photographs from the house, leaving empty hooks in their places in the walls. In the ensuing years, Ruth will fashion stories for each of the hooks and thus create new narratives about the lives of her unknown brothers. By the age of thirty-six, Ruth has emerged as a successful novelist. When she travels to Amsterdam for a book tour, she begins writing her latest novel, *My Last Bad Boyfriend,* after observing the seamy underworld of the city's famous red-light district.

In one of the most important scenes of the novel, Ruth pays a prostitute, Rooie, so that she can covertly watch Rooie with a customer. Instead of witnessing the planned sexual transaction, Ruth watches in horror as the customer breaks Rooie's neck. Ruth's subsequent guilt over her inaction and Rooie's death serve as the catalysts for several key events in her life, including her secret role in the capture of Rooie's murderer, her hasty marriage to her editor, Allan Albright (who dies of a heart attack shortly thereafter), and the birth of her son, Graham (named in honor of Graham Greene). After the publication of *My Last Bad Boyfriend,* Dutch detective Harry Hoekstra recognizes the details of Rooie's murder and arranges to meet Ruth, whom he loves and eventually marries. In the tradition of the Romance, the novel concludes with a series of marriages, reunions, and reconciliations. Marion and Ruth are reunited on Thanksgiving weekend, as are Marion and Eddie, who have maintained a tender and enduring love for one another. As the novel comes to a close, the words "time doesn't stop" pointedly echo in Eddie's mind.

A Widow for One Year, like its predecessor, received generally poor reviews, although it sold an astounding three hundred thousand hardcover copies in the United States alone. Irving's critics largely derided *A Widow for One Year* for lacking a significant plot in the tradition of his earlier novels. Lewis A. Turlish, in his 1998 review in *America,* wrote that "while Irving has written a compelling murder mystery, he seems to fear a lapse in intensity. The book abounds in italicized words, creating a style that is hyperactive, hectoring and insistent–like listening to an adolescent's account of his trip to the mall, suffused with an anxiety signaling that you failed to sense the urgency or that you don't get the point. I would have enjoyed the book more without all the shouting." Writing in *The Christian Century* in 1998, Christopher Bush observed that "Irving's greatest strength always has been creating fascinating, flawed people with whom the reader can identify and sympathize, even when they behave destructively. In this novel, his characters are vibrant, but they stand in need of a compelling theme or plot." Finally, in his 1999 acerbic review on the Canadian television program *Hot Type,* Tom Wolfe mocked what he perceived to be the overarching inaction in the novel. "At one point" in *A Widow for One Year,* Wolfe said, Irving's protagonists "leave the house! They get in a car! They're driving through a nearby hamlet . . . and I'm begging them to please stop–park next to the SUVs and German sedans and have a soda at the general store . . . do something–anything."

Irving's next novel, *The Fourth Hand* (2001), continues to work through the earlier terrain of his career: the dysfunction of human relationships, the tragic and

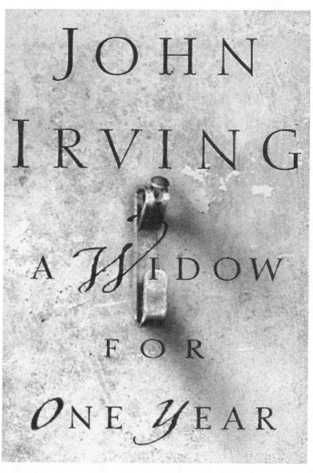

Dust jacket for Irving's 1998 novel, about the passing of time and its capacity to heal (Richland County Public Library)

dox insistence that she be allowed visitation rights with her deceased husband's hand. As in much of Irving's fiction, where death intervenes, sex cannot be far behind, and to that end, Doris, who tried unsuccessfully to begin a family with Otto, seduces Patrick before his surgery—a move reminiscent of Jenny Field's seduction of Technical Sergeant Garp in *The World According to Garp*. Despite the fact that Patrick's body ultimately rejects Otto's hand, Patrick and Doris find in each other an unexpected bond that remains long after the hand is removed. Ultimately, the fourth hand to which the title refers is a hand that does not exist physically. Unlike Otto's transplanted hand, which is rather lifeless, the hand that begins to exist for Patrick after the rejected hand is removed is much more mystical. While not made of corporeal flesh, the hand metaphorically allows Patrick to believe that he may actually touch Doris—a sensation and an intimacy that had eluded Patrick throughout his entire life.

Whether one believes that John Irving's later fiction represents a downward turn in his career, few can doubt that the novelist will continue to refine his craft. Irving's endurance—signaled not just by the volume of his corpus but by the weight of the emotional and philosophical subject matter with which it deals—suggests that his best work may yet lie ahead. As Irving explains in his memoir *My Movie Business* (1999), "When I feel like being a director, I write a novel. . . . A novelist controls the pace of the book," he continues. "In part, pace is also a function of language, but pace in a novel *and* in a film can be aided by the emotional investment the reader (or the audience) has in the characters." As Peter Matthiessen notes, Irving's work "has a sense of myth and time and weight and resonance. He's certainly not just 'a good plot man.' He's probably the great storyteller of American literature today."

catastropic mishaps all too often born out of such dysfunction, and the ghosts of the past that hover over the lives of those who live in the present. While many reviewers criticized the light tone of the work, this criticism may say more about their expectations for what an Irving novel ought to do than the quality of the work Irving actually produced. *The Fourth Hand* is undeniably light at times, moving quickly from one grotesquely comic scene to another. But at its heart, the novel is a serious love story about a journalist, Patrick Wallingford, who while in India loses his hand to a lion during a live broadcast, and Doris Clausen, an assistant in ticket sales for the Green Bay Packers, who loses her beer-delivery husband, Otto, when he accidentally shoots himself after the Packers' loss in the Super Bowl. The two are brought together when Patrick opts to become the first American to receive a hand transplant. As the recipient of Otto's hand, Patrick is thrust into a relationship with Doris because of her rather unortho-

Interviews:

Thomas Williams, "Talk with John Irving," *New York Times Book Review*, 23 April 1978, p. 6;

Barbara Bannon, "*PW* Interviews John Irving," *Publishers Weekly*, 213 (24 April 1978): 6–7;

Michael Priestley, "An Interview with John Irving," *New England Review* (Summer 1979): 489–504;

Greil Marcus, "John Irving: The World of *The World According to Garp*," *Rolling Stone* (13 December 1979): 68–75;

Alvin P. Sanoff, "A Conversation with John Irving: Humans Are a Violent Species—We Always Have Been," *U.S. News and World Report* (26 April 1981): 70–71;

Richard West, "John Irving's World After Garp," *New York* (17 August 1981): 29–32;

Laura de Coppet, "An Interview with John Irving," *Interview,* 11 (October 1981): 42–44;

James Feron, "All About Writing: According to Irving," *New York Times,* 29 November 1981, section 2, p. 4;

Joyce Renwick, "John Irving: An Interview," *Fiction International,* 14 (1982): 5–18;

Larry McCaffery, "An Interview with John Irving," *Contemporary Literature,* 23 (Winter 1982): 1–18;

Corby Kummer, "John Irving: Fascinated by Orphans," *Book-of-the-Month Club News* (Summer 1985): 5;

Ron Hansen, "The Art of Fiction XCIII: John Irving," *Paris Review,* 28 (1986): 74–103;

Michael Anderson, "Casting Doubts on Atheism," *New York Times Book Review,* 12 March 1989, p. 30;

Phyllis Robinson, "A Talk with John Irving," *Book-of-the-Month Club News* (April 1989): 3;

Richard Bernstein, "John Irving: Nineteenth-Century Novelist for These Times," *New York Times,* 25 April 1989, pp. C13, C17;

Gregory Wolfe, "A Conversation with John Irving," *Image: A Journal of the Arts and Religion,* 2 (Summer 1992): 45–57;

Alexander Neubauer, "John Irving," in his *Conversations on Writing Fiction: Interviews with Thirteen Distinguished Teachers of Fiction Writing in America* (New York: HarperPerennial, 1994), pp. 141–152;

Suzanne Herel, "John Irving," *Mother Jones* (1 May 1997): 64;

Alison Freeland, "A Conversation with John Irving," *New England Review,* 18 (1997): 135–142.

Bibliography:
Edward C. Reilly, "A John Irving Bibliography," *Bulletin of Bibliography,* 42 (March 1985): 12–18.

References:
Bruce Bawer, "*The World According to Garp:* Novel to Film," in *Take Two: Adapting the Contemporary American Novel to Film,* edited by Barbara Tepa Lupack (Bowling Green: Bowling Green State University Popular Press, 1994), pp. 77–90;

Harold Bloom, ed., *John Irving: Modern Critical Views* (Philadelphia: Chelsea House, 2001);

John Budd, "The Inadequacy of Brevity: John Irving's Short Fiction," *Round Table,* 26 (Spring 1985): 4–6;

Josie P. Campbell, *John Irving: A Critical Companion* (Westport, Conn.: Greenwood Press, 1998);

Evan Carton, "The Politics of Selfhood: Bob Slocum, T. S. Garp, and Auto-American-Biography," *The Novel: A Forum on Fiction,* 20 (Fall 1986): 46–61;

William Cosgrove, "*The World According to Garp* as Fabulation," *South Carolina Review,* 19 (Spring 1987): 52–58;

Wulf Cude, "Beyond Coincidence: Comedic Interplay between Irving and Davies," *Antigonish Review,* 100 (1995): 135–147;

Todd F. Davis and Kenneth Womack, "Saints, Sinners, and the Dickensian Novel: The Ethics of Storytelling in John Irving's *The Cider House Rules,*" *Style,* 32, no. 2 (1998): 298–317;

Morris Dickstein, "The World as Mirror," *Sewanee Review,* 89 (Summer 1981): 386–400;

Janice Doane and Devon Hedges, "Women and the *World According to Garp,*" in their *Nostalgia and Sexual Difference: The Resistance to Contemporary Feminism* (New York: Methuen, 1987), pp. 65–76;

Margaret Drabble, "Muck, Memory, and Imagination," *Harper's,* 257 (July 1978): 82–84;

Joseph Epstein, "Why Is John Irving So Popular?" *Commentary,* 73 (June 1982): 59–63;

Marilyn French, "The *Garp* Phenomenon," *Ms* (September 1982): 14–16;

Susan Gilbert, "Children of the 70s: The American Family in Recent Fiction," *Soundings,* 63 (Summer 1980): 199–213;

Donald J. Greiner, "Pynchon, Hawkes, and Updike: Readers and the Paradox of Accessibility," *South Carolina Review,* 16 (Fall 1983): 45–51;

Scott Haller, "John Irving's Bizarre World," *Saturday Review,* 9 (September 1981): 30–32, 34;

Carol C. Harter and James R. Thompson, *John Irving* (Boston: Twayne, 1986);

Jane Bowers Hill, "John Irving's Aesthetics of Accessibility: Setting Free the Novel," *South Carolina Review,* 16 (Fall 1983): 38–44;

Andrew Horton, "Comic Triumph in George Roy Hill's Adaptation of John Irving's *The World According to Garp,*" *Studies in American Humor,* 4 (1985): 173–182;

Edward T. Jones, "Checking into While Others Check Out of Tony Richardson's *The Hotel New Hampshire,*" *Literature/Film Quarterly,* 13 (1985): 66–69;

Jones, "Revisiting and Re-Visioning: *A Delicate Balance* (1973) and *The Hotel New Hampshire* (1984)," in *The Cinema of Tony Richardson: Essays and Interviews,* edited by James M. Welsh (Albany: State University of New York Press, 1999), pp. 237–249;

Augustus M. Kolich, "Does Fiction Have to Be Made Better than Life?" *Modern Fiction Studies,* 29 (1983): 159–174;

Barbara Lounsberry, "The Terrible Under Toad: Violence as Excessive Imagination in *The World According to Garp,*" *Thalia,* 5 (1982–1983): 30–35;

Kim McKay, "Double Discourse in John Irving's *The World According to Garp*," *Twentieth-Century Literature*, 38 (1992): 457–475;

Gabriel Miller, *John Irving* (New York: Ungar, 1982);

Don Morrow, "Wrestling John Irving," *Aethlon*, 14 (1997): 41–51;

Renfreu Neff, "John Irving on Screenwriting," *Creative Screenwriting*, 7 (2000): 6–11;

William Nelson, "The Comic Grotesque in Recent Fiction," *Thalia*, 5 (1982–1983): 36–40;

Nelson, "Unlikely Heroes: The Central Figures in *The World According to Garp, Even Cowgirls Get the Blues*, and *A Confederacy of Dunces*," in *The Hero in Transition*, edited by Ray B. Brown (Bowling Green: Bowling Green State University Popular Press, 1983), pp. 163–170;

Lawrence O'Toole, "John Irving Adjusts: Is There Life After *Garp?*" *Macleans*, 92 (11 June 1979): 46;

Philip Page, "Hero Worship and Hermeneutic Dialectics: John Irving's *A Prayer for Owen Meany*," *Mosaic*, 28 (September 1995): 137–156;

Michael Priestley, "Structure in the Worlds of John Irving," *Critique*, 23 (1981): 82–96;

Edward C. Reilly, "The *Anschluss* and the World According to Irving," *Research Studies*, 51 (June 1983): 98–110;

Reilly, "John Irving's *The Hotel New Hampshire* and the Allegory of Sorrow," *Publications of the Arkansas Philological Association*, 9 (Spring 1983): 78–83;

Reilly, *Understanding John Irving* (Columbia: University of South Carolina Press, 1991);

John Rickard, "Wrestling with the Text: The World According to John Irving," *Meanjin*, 56 (1997): 714–722;

Bruce L. Rockwood, "Abortion Stories: Uncivil Discourse and 'Cider House Rules,'" in *Law and Literature Perspectives*, edited by Rockwood and Roberta Kevelson (New York: Peter Lang, 1996), pp. 289–340;

Randolph Runyon, *Fowles/Irving/Barthes: Canonical Variations on an Apocryphal Theme* (Columbus: Ohio State University Press, 1981);

Runyon, "Of Fishie Fumes and Other Critical Strategies in the Hotel of the Text," *Cream City Review*, 8 (1983): 18–28;

R. Z. Sheppard, "Life into Art: *Garp* Creator Strikes Again," *Time*, 118 (31 August 1981): 46–51;

Debra Shostak, "The Family Romances of John Irving," *Essays in Literature*, 21 (1994): 129–145;

Shostak, "Plot as Repetition: John Irving's Narrative Experiments," *Critique*, 37 (1995): 51–70;

John Sykes, "Christian Apologetic Uses of the Grotesque in John Irving and Flannery O'Connor," *Literature and Theology*, 10 (1996): 58–67;

Raymond J. Wilson III, "The Postmodern Novel: The Example of John Irving's *The World According to Garp*," *Critique*, 34 (Fall 1992): 49–62;

Kenneth Womack, "Lumbering through Illyria: John Irving's 'Literary Debate' with Ford Madox Ford and John Hawkes," *International Fiction Review*, 23 (1996): 50–58;

Eleanor B. Wymard, "New Visions of the Midas Touch: *Daniel Martin* and *The World According to Garp*," *Modern Fiction Studies*, 27 (Summer 1981): 284–286.

Papers:

John Irving's papers are deposited in the library at Phillips Exeter Academy, in Exeter, New Hampshire.

John Jakes

(31 March 1932 –   )

Mary Ellen Jones
Wittenberg University

See also the Jakes entry in *DLB Yearbook: 1983*.

BOOKS: *The Texans Ride North: The Story of the Cattle Trails* (Philadelphia: Winston, 1952);

A Night for Treason (New York: Bouregy & Curl, 1956);

Wear a Fast Gun (New York: Arcadia House, 1956; London: Ward, Lock, 1957);

The Devil Has Four Faces (New York: Mystery House, 1958);

The Seventh Man, as Jay Scotland (New York: Mystery House, 1958);

This'll Slay You, as Alan Payne (New York: Ace, 1958);

I, Barbarian, as Scotland (New York: Avon, 1959); revised, as Jakes (New York: Pinnacle, 1976);

The Imposter (New York: Thomas Bouregy, 1959);

Johnny Havoc (New York: Belmont Books, 1960; New York: Armchair Detective Library, 1990);

Strike the Black Flag, as Scotland (New York: Ace, 1961);

Johnny Havoc Meets Zelda (New York: Belmont Books, 1962); republished as *Havoc for Sale* (New York: Armchair Detective Library, 1990);

Sir Scoundrel, as Scotland (New York: Ace, 1962); revised as *King's Crusader,* as Jakes (New York: Pinnacle, 1977);

The Veils of Salome, as Scotland (New York: Avon, 1962);

Arena, as Scotland (New York: Ace, 1963);

G. I. Girls (Derby, Conn.: Monarch, 1963);

Johnny Havoc and the Doll Who Had "It" (New York: Belmont Books, 1963); republished as *Holiday for Havoc* (New York: Armchair Detective Library, 1991);

Traitor's Legion, as Scotland (New York: Ace, 1963); revised as *The Man from Cannae,* as Jakes (New York: Pinnacle, 1977);

Ghostwind, as Rachel Ann Payne (New York: Paperback Library, 1966);

Tiros: Weather Eye in Space (New York: Messner, 1966);

Famous Firsts in Sports (New York: Putnam, 1967);

When the Star Kings Die (New York: Ace, 1967);

John Jakes, 2002 (photograph by Rob Kaufman; courtesy of the author)

Brak the Barbarian (New York: Avon, 1968; London: Tandem, 1970);

Great War Correspondents (New York: Putnam, 1968);

Making It Big (New York: Belmont Books, 1968); republished as *Johnny Havoc and the Siren in Red* (New York: Armchair Detective Library, 1991);

The Asylum World (New York: Paperback Library, 1969; London: New English Library, 1978);

Brak the Barbarian vs. The Mark of the Demons (New York: Paperback Library, 1969; London: Tandem, 1970);

Brak the Barbarian vs. The Sorceress (New York: Paperback Library, 1969; London: Tandem, 1970);

Great Women Reporters (New York: Putnam, 1969);

The Hybrid (New York: Paperback Library, 1969);

The Last Magicians (New York: New American Library, 1969);

Mohawk: The Life of Joseph Brant (New York: Crowell-Collier, 1969);

The Planet Wizard (New York: Ace, 1969);

The Secrets of Stardeep (Philadelphia: Westminster Press, 1969);

Tonight We Steal the Stars (New York: Ace, 1969);

Black in Time (New York: Paperback Library, 1970);

Dracula, Baby, lyrics and book revision by Jakes, uncredited (Chicago: Dramatic Publishing, 1970);

Mask of Chaos (New York: Ace, 1970);

Master of the Dark Gate (New York: Lancer, 1970);

Monte Cristo #99 (New York: Curtis, 1970);

Six-Gun Planet (New York: Paperback Library, 1970; London: New English Library, 1978);

Conquest of the Planet of the Apes (New York: Award, 1972);

Mention My Name in Atlantis (New York: DAW, 1972);

A Spell of Evil (Chicago: Performance Publishing, 1972);

Stranger with Roses (Chicago: Dramatic Publishing, 1972);

Time Gate (Philadelphia: Westminster Press, 1972);

Violence (Elgin, Ill.: Performance Publishing, 1972);

Wind in the Willows, music by Claire Strauch (Elgin, Ill.: Performance Publishing, 1972);

Witch of the Dark Gate (New York: Lancer, 1972);

Doctor, Doctor! book and lyrics adapted by Jakes and others from Molière's *Physician in Spite of Himself,* music by Gilbert M. Martin (New York: McAfee Music, 1973; Chicago: Dramatic Publishing, 2000);

Gaslight Girl, music by Strauch (Chicago: Dramatic Publishing, 1973);

On Wheels (New York: Paperback Library, 1973);

Pardon Me, Is This Planet Taken? music by Martin (Chicago: Dramatic Publishing, 1973);

Shepherd Song, music by Martin (New York: McAfee Music, 1974);

The Bastard (New York: Pyramid, 1974); republished in two volumes as *Fortune's Whirlwind* and *To an Unknown Shore* (London: Corgi, 1975);

The Rebels (New York: Pyramid, 1975; London: Corgi, 1979);

The Seekers (New York: Pyramid, 1975; London: Corgi, 1979);

The Furies (New York: Pyramid, 1976; London: Corgi, 1979);

The Titans (New York: Pyramid, 1976; London: Corgi, 1979);

The Best of John Jakes, edited by Martin H. Greenberg and Joseph D. Olander (New York: DAW, 1977);

The Warriors (New York: Pyramid, 1977; London: Corgi, 1979);

Brak the Barbarian: When the Idols Walked (New York: Pocket Books, 1978);

The Lawless (New York: Jove, 1978; London: Corgi, 1979);

The Americans (New York: Jove, 1980);

The Fortunes of Brak (New York: Dell, 1980);

North and South (New York: Harcourt Brace Jovanovich, 1982; London: Collins, 1982);

Love and War (San Diego: Harcourt Brace Jovanovich, 1984; London: Collins, 1985);

Susanna of the Alamo: A True Story (San Diego: Gulliver Books, 1986);

Heaven and Hell (San Diego: Harcourt Brace Jovanovich, 1987; London: Collins, 1987);

California Gold (New York: Random House, 1989; London: Collins, 1990);

The Best Western Short Stories of John Jakes, edited by Bill Pronzini and Greenberg (Athens: Ohio University Press, 1991); expanded as *In the Big Country* (New York: Bantam, 1993); expanded again as *The Bold Frontier* (New York: New American Library, 2000);

Homeland (New York: Doubleday, 1993; London: Little, Brown, 1993);

American Dreams (New York: Dutton, 1998; London: Little, Brown, 1998);

On Secret Service (New York: Dutton, 2000; London: Little, Brown, 2000);

Crime Time: Mystery and Suspense Stories (Waterville, Me.: Five Star, 2001);

Charleston (New York: Dutton, 2002).

PLAY PRODUCTIONS: *A Christmas Carol,* adapted by Jakes from Charles Dickens's novel, Montgomery, Alabama Shakespeare Festival, 1989;

Great Expectations, book and lyrics adapted by Jakes from Dickens's novel, Chester, Connecticut, Goodspeed Musicals, 2001.

OTHER: *New Trails: Twenty-three Original Stories of the West from Western Writers of America,* edited by Jakes and Martin H. Greenberg (New York: Doubleday, 1994);

A Century of Great Western Stories, edited by Jakes (New York: Forge, 2000).

SELECTED PERIODICAL PUBLICATIONS–
UNCOLLECTED: "The Historical Family Saga,"
    Writer, 92 (November 1979): 9–12;
"Three Essentials for a Writing Career," *Writer,* 94
    (July 1981);
"What? A Successful Media Campaign Without TV
    Spots and Phil Donahue?" *TV Guide* (2 November 1985): 12–15;
"To Be a Writer: What Does It Take?" *Writer,* 100
    (January 1987): 9–11;
"If I Don't Like It, I Don't Blurb It," *Wall Street Journal,*
    20 February 1991, p. A15;
"There's Always a Book–Or Is There?" *Parade Magazine* (13 March 1994): 12–13;
"Cultivating the Literary Habit," *Writer,* 107 (July
    1994): 5–6.

John Jakes, variously called the "godfather of the historical novel," "the people's author," and "America's history teacher," is the acknowledged contemporary master of the family saga. Best known as the creator of the Kent Family Chronicles (1974–1980), the Main and Hazard families of the *North and South* trilogy (1982–1987), James and Nellie Chance of *California Gold* (1989), the Crown family of *Homeland* (1993) and *American Dreams* (1998), and the Bells of *Charleston* (2002), Jakes has achieved sales figures of more than sixty million copies. Six of these sagas have been adapted for television; the 1985 ABC/David Wolper *North and South* was among the ten highest Nielsen-rated miniseries. While this popular success may cause some academic critics to disparage Jakes's novels, Nick Salvatore and Ann Sullivan, writing in the *Radical History Review* (1982), suggest that "the themes Jakes presents constitute an important and influential source of public history in modern American culture." Though Jakes never glosses over America's flaws–dealing honestly with, for example, slavery, the usurpation of Indian lands, government corruption, and the excesses of the Gilded Age–the body of his work is an optimistic affirmation of American values.

John William Jakes was born on 31 March 1932 in Chicago, the son of John Adrian and Bertha Retz Jakes. The only child of parents in their forties when he was born, Jakes early shared many of their pastimes, especially reading, the movies, and theater. Originally hoping to be an actor, he committed to writing when he sold his first science-fiction story at eighteen, while a freshman at Northwestern University. Following a transfer to DePauw in his sophomore year, Jakes moved out of his college fraternity house for the quiet he needed to write fiction while carrying a full academic load. In June of 1951 he and Rachel Ann Payne, who had been his zoology lab instructor, married. Jakes graduated from the creative-writing program at DePauw in 1953; he then earned an M.A. in

William Shatner as Paul Revere and Andrew Stevens as Philip Kent in the 1978 television miniseries of Jakes's 1974 novel, The Bastard, *the first of the Kent Family Chronicles (Everett Collection)*

American literature at Ohio State University in 1954 but left the Ph.D. program to meet the demands of a growing family. He and his wife have four children: Andrea, Ellen, John Michael, and Victoria. Jakes's first job was with Abbott Laboratories in North Chicago (1954–1960), where he began as a copywriter and became product promotion manager. From then until 1971 he worked at advertising agencies in Rochester, New York, and Dayton, Ohio. In 1978 the Jakes family moved to Hilton Head Island, South Carolina.

During his advertising years Jakes wrote at least sixty books, probably more: "At 78, I lost track," he told an interviewer in 1994. Most of these were published as ephemeral and are therefore difficult to find in libraries; some have disappeared. Many were written under pseudonyms–Alan Payne, Rachel Ann Payne, and Jay Scotland. Don Wollheim, the editor of Jakes's historical novel *Strike the Black Flag* (1961), was adamantly opposed to the name "John Jakes" on the cover: "Sounds like a piece of faulty machinery," he argued. Only with the Kent Family Chronicles did Jakes reclaim his own name as a writer of historical fiction. But in the meantime, "'John Jakes' wrote a good deal of science fiction," Jakes observed in his foreword to the 1976 Pinnacle edition of *I, Barbarian* (1959).

Even during this early period Jakes wanted to write historical novels with American themes, but his publishers told him that "those guys in three-cornered hats don't sell." And in those days, Jakes wrote to sell, writing at night and earmarking his earnings for his children's education.

Although he met that goal "in fine style," Jakes observed in an unpublished 1995 interview, "I have a certain amount of regret about the hasty writing during this period. 'More,' not 'better' was the watchword for too long." During this early period Jakes wrote in a variety of genres: science fiction, mystery/suspense, fantasy, a detective series; short stories, novels, and the books to musical comedies; and children's fiction and nonfiction. This versatility may have contributed to an unevenness in the quality of his writing. He observed in Kirk Polking's 1977 *Writer's Digest* article, "I like to do too many kinds of things, and I think that's always been one of my troubles. I never really specialized enough."

In many of his early works Jakes was experimenting with techniques and themes he later refined: combining a compelling plotline with descriptive detail, often from nature, to suggest characters' emotions; juxtaposition of simultaneous events from different plotlines to heighten the contrast between good and evil; frequent use of literary allusions, which, in his major novels, becomes more integral as he utilizes the epigraph to introduce his central theme; and dividing the novel into distinct sections to achieve economy.

Throughout his career Jakes has been concerned with accuracy, engaging in intensive research as preparation for writing and sometimes utilizing this knowledge in multiple works. In his major novels, from the Kent Family Chronicles on, he frequently intermingles the lives of actual and created characters. For instance, Stephen Crane and Richard Harding Davis, profiled in *Great War Correspondents* (1968), later appear in *Homeland*, covering the Spanish-American War. Susanna Dickinson, a survivor of the Alamo and the title figure of a children's book by Jakes in 1986, had appeared earlier in *The Furies* (1976).

Finally, in his "lesser" works, Jakes addresses for the first time some of his ongoing themes: the theme of the Other, the alien, including the conflict between cultures; the necessity of ethical behavior, decency, morality, and love; the recognition that science and technology may be perverted in the pursuit of wealth and power rather than used to benefit society; and the concern that the American dream of upward mobility may turn to nightmare when society fragments into the haves and the have-nots. Chief among his themes is the belief that the United States and the principles upon which it was founded are unique and precious. He does not, however, subscribe to the belief that any means are acceptable to preserve the nation, arguing instead that Americans must be on guard against those who emphasize order over freedom and, in the name of

protecting society, undermine its principles. Jakes has also developed a conviction that "absolute evil (in human form) does exist—with no redeeming 'causes,' excuses or other ameliorating aspects." He commented in 1995 that "It may be relatively rare, but I believe it's with us. Look at the pathological Nazis, for an obvious example." There is, thus, a darker undertone present in many of Jakes's works, despite their fundamental optimism.

Jakes himself recognizes two distinct periods in his writing. During the first, into the 1970s, his books were plot-driven, and his purpose was "solely to entertain." Though he still believes that "without hooking . . . the reader *first,* you can't accomplish any other goals," he feels he "fell short." He added, in an unpublished 1995 letter, "My success came in the second period, when I fused my dedication to entertaining a reader with a desire to provide solid historical context—I guess you could say 'teach' if that isn't too pretentious." The nadir of his writing career came in 1972, when he agreed to write the novel version of the movie *Conquest of the Planet of the Apes.* In a 1984 interview with Robert Dahlin for *Publishers Weekly,* Jakes remembered that low point, when he thought he had been "wasting the last 20 years" and "couldn't cut it as a writer."

His breakthrough came when he was approached by Lyle Kenyon Engel, who with paperback publisher Pyramid Books had conceived the frankly commercial idea of producing a series of historical novels, timed to coincide with the American Bicentennial. The result was the Kent Family Chronicles. Initially planned as five novels that would bring the fictional family to 1976, the series grew to eight volumes with some ninety years to go when Jakes brought them to a halt. Eight big novels in six years had been exhausting, but, more important, as he explained to Dahlin, Jakes believes in the theater principle of "leaving the audience wanting more, rather than the television route where the story drags on week after week."

With the Kent Family Chronicles was born what Dale Walker, in the introduction to *In the Big Country* (1993), called "a new and sustaining form of popular fiction—the paperback original, multi-volumed, continuing-character, generation-spanning, romantic-historical family saga." Jakes shortened the term to "historical family saga" and discussed the genre in a November 1979 article in *Writer.* Because such novels inevitably involve characters in specific historical events, one of the goals is to evoke a past era; thus, research is imperative to "set up story lines, to decorate the stage and clothe the characters, to give texture to the scene." Sometimes criticized for the violence in these novels, Jakes argues that though he enjoys writing action stories, he would not trivialize violence; he recognizes it as an element in the American character, and moreover, he believes that violence can be a powerful catalyst for character change. In contrast to his

Dust jacket for the first volume of the Civil War series in which Jakes traces the intertwined lives of a Pennsylvania family and a South Carolina family (Richland County Public Library)

earlier works, in his historical family sagas Jakes makes use of multiple points of view to gain narrative scope and freedom. Analyzing the success of the genre, Jakes believes the historical family saga is popular because it meets societal needs. Searching the past for "values and a sense of continuity" helps lessen anxieties about the present. Further, in an age of family fragmentation, sagas about "idealized families that manage to survive . . . harrowing test[s]" are, Jakes believes, reassuring.

Central to establishing such a family is introducing a character about whom the public cares enough to continue reading multiple volumes. *The Bastard* (1974) begins in 1770 and follows Phillipe Charboneau, the illegitimate son of a French actress and an English duke, from his late adolescence in rural France to Concord, Massachusetts, where he, along with other American patriots, marches against the British to establish a new nation. Twin influences shape his early life: his mother's obsession that he be publicly recognized as James Amberly's heir, and the revolutionary writings of Voltaire, Jean-Jacques Rousseau, Denis Diderot, and Montesquieu. In the epigraph from a 1776 speech by William Pitt to Parliament, Jakes links these catalysts and establishes the father-son motif

crucial to the novel. The colonists, Pitt argues, must be granted "all the natural rights of mankind" and equal treatment under the English constitution: "The Americans are the sons, not the bastards, of England."

With the bastard motif, Jakes links the fate of his protagonist to the fate of the colonies. The legitimacy that Phillipe's mother desires for her son, and that Pitt is willing to grant the colonies, is opposed by Lady Jane Amberly for the sake of her own son, Phillipe's half brother. She represents an England unable or unwilling to change, a decadent England in which the church can be suborned by the aristocracy and in which corruption, both social and political, demands revolution.

Abandoning his mother's dream, Phillipe flees to London, where he learns the printer's trade; meets Benjamin Franklin, a father-surrogate; and decides to start afresh in the colonies. Symbolic of his rebirth as a new man, he rechristens himself Philip Kent in the final stages of the Atlantic passage.

Though he has rejected England, Philip is not yet an American. As a printer of political pamphlets, he meets many of the Sons of Liberty, among them Paul Revere, John Hancock, and Samuel Adams. Through

Philip's eyes the reader sees the colonists' response to the Boston Tea Party, the increased number of British troops under General Thomas Gage, and the virtual dismantling of the Massachusetts provincial government. Gradually, Philip shifts from an observer to a participant, but he is not wholly committed until he rescues Anne Ware, the woman he loves, from his half brother Roger, now a colonel in a proprietary regiment. Anne, like Philip, has read the revolutionary philosophers; she has incorporated them into her personal philosophy, linking the political freedoms of the colonies to her own freedom as a woman. Though she arouses Philip physically, she is not manipulative, refusing to trap Philip by sex. Instead, she demands commitment to her person and to her cause if their relationship is to develop: choosing to love Anne is analogous to choosing to fight for the Revolution. Just as the battles of Lexington and Concord announce a new world, Philip Kent becomes, on two levels, a founding father—of the Kent family ("I think the Kents will turn out to be a very fine family indeed") and of the nation, which Jakes unabashedly feels is "very fine indeed."

The Rebels (1975) begins two months after the conclusion of The Bastard and focuses completely on the period of the Revolutionary War. Unlike the generally hopeful tone of The Bastard, the tone of The Rebels reflects the desperation of a ragtag army taking on one far greater. Jakes repeatedly lets the reader see how close to defeat the Americans were and thus gives added meaning to their ultimate victory.

Jakes's patriots, from New England, the South, and the Middle Atlantic, collectively personify the national motto E pluribus unum. Jakes also introduces the frontier as a place of personal opportunity, hope, and renewal, a fresh start, thus preparing for the next two volumes of the series. He does not, however, ignore the consequences to the Native Americans of what will ultimately be termed Manifest Destiny.

Jakes's multiple plotlines also contribute to this forging of one from many and to the establishing of the Kent family as metaphor for the nation. The first plotline continues the Philip Kent–Anne Ware story begun in The Bastard. Now the parents of a young son, Abraham, they sacrifice the comfort of family to duty toward country. Philip fights through most of the war, returning home seriously wounded to care for the boy and to establish the printing firm Kent & Son. Anne, in the meantime, meets a violent death at the hands of a villainous sea captain. The second plotline focuses on the Fletcher family of Virginia, plantation owners. Thus Jakes creates an ironic contrast—while thirteen colonies are fighting a rebellion for the rights of men, half of them fear a slave rebellion. Judson Fletcher is disowned by his father for having an affair with Peggy Ashford McLean, the only woman Judson ever loved and the wife of

another planter. He seeks personal redemption on the Pittsburgh frontier, where he dies saving the life of George Rogers Clark. When Philip and Peggy meet and marry (her first husband, Seth, having been killed in a slave rebellion), the Kent family—including his son, Abraham; her daughter, Elizabeth; and their son, Gilbert—becomes representatively American with French, New England, and Virginia blood. Through Judson, Elizabeth's father, it has also acquired the "tainted blood"—a self-destructive wild streak and rejection of social and religious norms—that haunts future generations.

The Seekers (1975) and The Furies are so closely linked that a critic once asked Jakes whether he had originally intended them to be one novel. "Yes," he replied, "but the characters ran away with it." As a cohesive unit covering more than six decades of American history, in sharp contrast to the tight focus of The Rebels, these books take the reader, the Kent family, and the nation from their first tests on the borders of the Old Northwest to the brink of the Civil War. Covering, respectively, the years from 1794 to 1814 and 1836 to 1852, they treat almost impressionistically the Battle of Fallen Timbers, the sea battle between the Constitution and the Guerriere, the end of the fur frontier, the fall of the Alamo, and the California gold rush. By the end of The Seekers the first generation of the Kents are dead; the house of Kent—the home and the publishing house—has fallen to an unscrupulous villain consumed by a desire for revenge against the family. The two novels focus on Jared, son of Abraham and Elizabeth, and Amanda, daughter of Gilbert and Harriet LeBow; Jared and Amanda flee west to refuge, believing they have murdered the usurper.

Near Nashville they are accosted by the "Reverend" William Blackthorn, one of Jakes's basest villains, who beats Jared senseless and rapes the ten-year-old Amanda, abducting her to sell as a whore to fur traders. For years the cousins' paths are separate. The Seekers, mainly Jared's story, has as its themes guilt (for not protecting Amanda), redemption, and the search for self; The Furies, mostly Amanda's story, explores themes of survival, vengeance, and what it means to be a Kent. Both cousins had been instructed in the family motto: Carpe locum et fac vestigium, "Take a stand and make a mark," which serves as a touchstone for assessing their lives. For Amanda, one of Jakes's strongest women, the motto and the corollary goal—to be worthy of the name Kent and to regain its honor—become a near obsession. Both live awhile with Native Americans, deriving peace and strength from the culture; Jared marries Grass Singing and fathers Jephtha, a wholly upright man ruled by conscience. Amanda gives birth to Louis, son of an honorable Mexican officer who rescues her at the Alamo. Thus both cousins, separated for years and thinking themselves likely the last of the Kents, introduce new

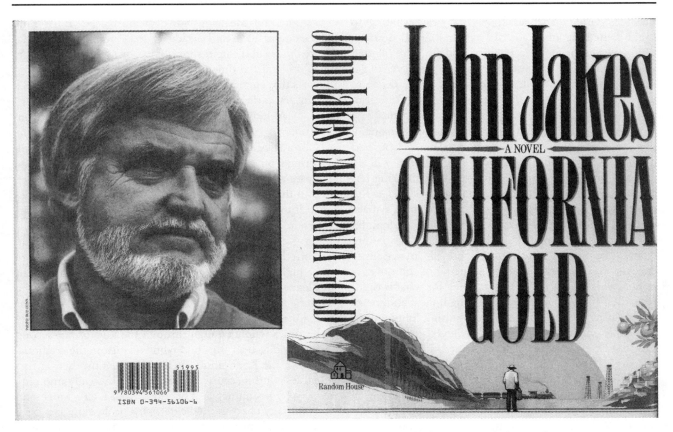

Dust jacket for Jakes's 1989 novel, in which the protagonist seeks his fortune in the oil, citrus, and railroad industries at the turn of the twentieth century (Richland County Public Library)

blood to the family. Jared and Amanda are briefly reunited in California. After he is shot, he leaves her his share of a gold mine in trust for Jephtha. Amanda returns to the East, where she further expands the "family" by gathering around her a coterie of advisers—including Michael Boyle, a quintessential Irish immigrant—who, though not related, are loyal to Kent family principles. Amanda, in many ways, reminds one of Philip: as he dared to break British law during the Revolution, she puts principle above the law, becoming an abolitionist and helping slaves escape, in direct violation of the Fugitive Slave Law. Jakes makes conscious allusion to the Furies of Greek mythology. Amanda's death is almost archetypally sacrificial; she dies upholding Kent values and sacrificing herself for a slave's freedom, her son's life and future, and the family icons.

With *The Titans* (1976) Jakes experimented with structure, dovetailing a "Prologue," "Interlude," and "Epilogue" with two books, "Black April" and "Red July," their titles suggesting the bleak, black despair of Americans on both sides at the seemingly inevitable dissolution of the Union and the battlefield carnage that follows. The bulk of the novel is bracketed by the attack on Fort Sumter and the Battle of Manassas, thus emphasiz-

ing the irony of the belief that the war would be over in ninety days. The focus is on three Kents: Jephtha, now a minister defrocked for his abolitionist views; his son Gideon, fighting for the Confederacy; and Amanda's son, Louis, amoral and venal, who believes the war is an opportunity for profit. As in the four previous novels, Jakes again lets the Kents symbolize the nation—now a house divided against itself. The book explores the complex relationships between freedom, personal responsibility, and public order, condemning unprincipled materialism as well as hypocritical repression of individual rights in the name of state security.

In contrast to the tight focus of *The Titans, The Warriors* (1977) encompasses half of the Civil War, the start of Reconstruction, and the postwar movement west, including the construction of the transcontinental railroad. Jakes focuses on Jephtha's sons Gideon and Jeremiah and on Michael Boyle, all of whom fought in the Civil War, and briefly on Jephtha and Louis. Jeremiah, who witnessed the worst of Sherman's March to the Sea, became disillusioned with conflict, declared his old self dead, and went west to reinvent himself; there, with his Sioux friend Kola, he remains a killer, a twisted knight, meting out justice according to his own standards of virtue. Michael, too, goes west, wanting to build something (the railroad) rather than to destroy; ultimately he becomes a pacifist. Gideon, half-blinded in prison camp by a sadistic sergeant, vows never to get involved in any more lost causes; but as he becomes increasingly aware of the exploitation of American workers, he takes up the cause of labor unionism.

All three men adhere to a rigid, though personally defined, code of honor. In contrast, Louis, who had bought an exemption from service in the war, will do anything to multiply his millions. Jephtha, thinking Jeremiah dead, rewrites his will, making Michael a full member of the family and giving him Jeremiah's share of the California gold acquired by Amanda. Jephtha purchases Louis's mansion, recovers the Kent family icons, and orders the house and its materialistic excesses torn down. The central theme of the novel is honor, which Jakes defines as standing for what is right, regardless of personal cost; remaining honest and maintaining personal integrity; and recognizing humanity in all people and treating them accordingly. Jephtha realizes that Louis has "no regard for the traditions or ideals" of the Kent family, while Michael does. Honorable behavior, thus, rather than blood, defines a Kent.

Though the Battle of the Little Big Horn is treated briefly in *The Lawless* (1978), its ironic juxtaposition to the Philadelphia Centennial Exposition sets the tone for the novel: dark, bleak, and often pessimistic rather than celebratory. Though the Civil War is now memory, conflict polarizes America. Its battles, no longer military, are wars of economics and ideology, of class, race, and gender. Workers—native-born and immigrants—are cruelly exploited by capitalists so consumed by profits at any cost that they call in private police forces such as the Pinkertons to suppress unrest. In the West, the land and cultural identity of the Native Americans have nearly vanished, despite the voices of reformers, quickly stilled, and the victory against General George Armstrong Custer can bring only retribution. Women, struggling to achieve personal and political parity, face powerful opposition.

The fifth and sixth generations of the Kents respond to this America. Jeremiah, a disillusioned hired gun, rouses himself from his alcoholic haze only to save Gideon's life. Jephtha's third son, Matthew, no longer able to accept those people in power who destroyed a generation of young men in war and who now, as robber barons, grow rich from others' labor, rejects America and chooses life in Europe as an expatriate artist. Gideon, maintaining some of the Kent idealism, sees America's wrongs and tries to right them with Julia Sedgwick, a staunch advocate of women's suffrage, at his side. Their struggle, however, will be difficult. The nation that had plunged into the Civil War out of con-

viction and idealism, however misplaced, must now reexamine itself and decide its goals: to pursue material wealth, to abdicate responsibility, or to fight for change. Writing at the time of the second centenary, Jakes suggests that such reexamination is as important as it was a century earlier.

Although Jakes had not yet brought the Kent family to 1976, he felt it was time to draw a halt to the Chronicles. *The Americans* (1980) opens as Gideon, suffering from chest pains and aware of his own mortality, poses the central question: after I am gone, who will lead the family? Carter, Julia's son by Louis Kent, goes west to escape family responsibility; although he is successful in California politics, he views it not as public service but as a "game" in which you "get all you can from the trough while convincing the rest of the hogs to be high-minded instead of hungry." Gideon's daughter, Eleanor, an actress, becomes a victim of anti-Semitism after marriage to Leo Goldman. Plunged into near madness when he is killed by a bigot, she eventually becomes whole enough through the love of her second husband to bear the child who will ensure the continuation of the Kent family. Will, Eleanor's brother, at first aimless and insecure, is challenged physically and ethically by a summer at Theodore Roosevelt's ranch and eventually chooses medicine as his profession. His goal, however, is not yet clear—to use medicine to serve society or as a means to wealth and social prominence. When Will takes to heart the lines on the Statue of Liberty—"give me your tired, your poor, your huddled masses"—and chooses to practice where he is needed, among the immigrant poor, Gideon is reassured. Eleanor continues the bloodline begun by Philip Kent, while Will continues its values. Despite America's problems—its social stratification, its apparent loss of idealism, its "drift to materialism"—the wonder of America as fresh start and haven infuses *The Americans* as it did earlier novels in the series.

In the *North and South* trilogy (*North and South*, 1982; *Love and War*, 1984; and *Heaven and Hell*, 1987) Jakes returns to material he had explored earlier. The massive trilogy, covering the years from 1841 to 1883, is unified by the seemingly endless military campaigns before, during, and after the Civil War, which Jakes in the epilogue to *Love and War* called the "greatest redefinition of America, in the shortest time, that we have experienced."

Originally he had planned to write one novel about a single military family during the Civil War, but as he did research at the library of the United States Military Academy at West Point, he encountered case after case of cadets—brothers in arms at the academy—who faced each other across battle lines after the war began. This historical reality led him to create two families, the Mains of South Carolina and the Hazards of Pennsylva-

pictures. They worked wonderfully as chasers. And their
novelty drove audiences wild. That was evident the first
night they showed "The Wabash Cannonball," which Pflaum
introduced personally, stepping before the curtain in a suit
of tails to warn that any person with a feeble constitution
should hold tightly to the seat or, alternatively, leave the
hall.

No one took the warning. When the Cannonball
loomed in the center of the screen, Shadow and Jimmy, and
Paul and Mary were nearly trampled in the cross-aisle at the
rear. Men kicked and pushed as they fled; women shrieked
and sobbed. Several were unable to leave their seats
because they fainted; Pflaum had to revive them with sal
ammonia.

Never mind; those were the kind of problems that
meant revenue. Ever after that summer night when the Music
Hall first showed the Cannonball, Pflaum wanted films and
more films.

Riding the tide of opportunity, Colonel Sid Shadow
flogged himself and his employees to unprecedented effort.
There weren't enough hours to travel to locations to shoot
one-minute actualities, as the colonel had taken to calling
them, and process the film, and build a new projector, and
train another operator for another theater, and attend to
the arcade. Shadow transferred operation of the arcade to a
couple of middle-aged men. He pulled all the cards from the

TC-821

Page from the revised typescript for Jakes's 1993 novel, Homeland, *with additions by Jakes and queries
from editor Herman Gollub (Special Collections, Thomas Cooper Library, University of South Carolina)*

nia, friends who became opponents but never quite enemies. Asked which side of the war he supports, Jakes noted in the epilogue of *North and South*, "the side of those who suffered . . . who lost their lives in battle, and those who lost their lives more slowly but no less surely, in bondage." The novels are linked, examining life during the Mexican War, the Civil War, and the Plains Indian wars; their themes, respectively, are dissolution and separation, change and slaughter, and reconstruction and possible reconciliation. Writing of the Civil War, Jakes observes in the epilogue to *Love and War:* "As a people we all tend to be myth makers as the generations pass. . . . We mythologize not only individuals [such as Abraham Lincoln and Robert E. Lee] but also the war itself." He adds that perhaps the "quite natural human tendency to prefer the glamorous to the gory" has "put a patina on the war. To render it romantic. It was–for about ninety days. After that came horror. And the horror grew." Though Jakes is neither a revisionist historian nor a pacifist, one of the effects of his inclusion in this trilogy of Chapultepec and Washita as well as Manassas and Chancellorsville–and the analogies he draws between Charles Main and those who served in Vietnam–is to suggest that the "horror" is universal and that healing will occur, though it may be a long time coming.

California Gold is Jakes's first major novel that is not part of a family saga. Its protagonist, James Macklin "Mack" Chance, son of a failed forty-niner, searches for the new California gold–in land, oil, and the movies. Though Mack achieves immense wealth, Jakes is careful to distance him from the exploiters of environment or labor. Jakes argues in this book that society and individuals must somehow maintain a balance between ambition and moral responsibility.

With *Homeland*, Jakes began his third family saga, focusing on the Crown (née Kröner) family of German immigrants. Set in the last decade of the nineteenth century, the novel, according to Jakes's "Author's Note," portrays "a decade in which a naive young giant flexed its muscles and began to understand and use its enormous strength." The adolescent America coming of age among the family of nations is contrasted with European powers, specifically Germany. Jakes's portrayal of an increasingly sinister and militaristic Germany under the First Reich provides the young Pauli Kröner a motive for immigration and foreshadows conflicts of subsequent books when the saga moves into the twentieth century.

Like Philip Kent, Pauli is the immigrant founder of a new American family; like Philip, he renames himself–as Paul Crown–to underscore his Americanization. Though this America is not utopia–Jakes shows the sordid underside of the American dream, including racial prejudice and economic inequity–it is a land in which one is free, to do good or evil, but most importantly to make his or her own choice. Jakes notes in his afterword that, despite polls in the spring of 1992 that indicated 60 percent of respondents felt the United States was a nation in decline, he chose to write of a time when "America symbolized virtually limitless opportunity" and "hope was in the air." In this novel, one of his most personal and most polished, Jakes reaffirms his fundamental optimism about America and her future.

The second volume of the Crown family saga, *American Dreams,* was published in July 1998. Jakes initially wanted to explore the lives of the Crown family during World War I. However, reminiscent of earlier experts' comments that "no one wanted to read about guys in three cornered hats," editorial opinion held that late-twentieth-century readers were not interested in World War I. Contemporary publishing trends also dictated that novels should be short; so Jakes was instructed to cut the original manuscript by almost a quarter, as a condition of publication. Thus, although *American Dreams* follows the Crowns into new ventures in acting, racing, and flying, the book lacks the depth, both of character and theme, the reader has come to expect.

With *On Secret Service* (2000) Jakes returns to the Civil War, the last of the great old-fashioned wars, the first of the great modern wars. Among its innovations was "the first organized espionage that the country ever knew." The novel spans the period from January 1861 to May 1865 and is set primarily in the Washington/Baltimore/Richmond nexus of power. Although there are battle scenes as explicitly powerful as any in the *North and South* series, the emphasis is on political machinations and their impact on both military and civilian destinies. Jakes delves deeply into all sorts of intelligence gathering. The most overt are the military reconnaissance operations of both armies. But the reader also learns much about nineteenth-century intelligence tradecraft: passwords and countersigns, safe houses and drops, assumed names, disguises, fake documents, and the use of informants.

However, Jakes humanizes what might otherwise be an arcane discussion by juxtaposing two pairs of unlikely lovers. Lon Price, a Northern operative, loves Margaret Miller, close friend of the Confederate spy Rose Greenhow. Fred Dasher, a Confederate cavalry officer turned spy, becomes involved with Hanna Siegel, whose father works at the United States War Department. Not only do their loves seem impossible, but they also become a metaphor for the nation, split asunder by conflicting allegiances.

While Civil War intelligence services began of necessity and with good intentions, they succumbed on occasion to excess. Jakes writes of agents "charged with the investigation and discovery of disloyal citizens," of arrests without warrants, of "enemies of the government . . . kept in prison for years, without cause, without recourse to the legal system, or any hope of pardon." In the afterword, Jakes notes that at the outset of the Civil War, spying was "a game for genteel men and women" but quickly became "a savage battle without rules."

With *Charleston* (2002) Jakes returns once again to his signature genre, the continuing family saga, but with innovations suggesting an author still evolving and experimenting. The novel is a sweeping narrative of six generations of the fictional Bell family of Charleston, South Carolina, from before the American Revolution to Reconstruction. But in contrast to the multivolume Kent Family Chronicles and *North and South* series, Jakes tells this tale in a single volume divided into three books: "City at War, 1779–1793," "City on Fire, 1822–1842," and "City of Ashes, 1863–1866."

As he did in the Kent Family Chronicles, Jakes introduces a particularly American theme—the freedom to start anew, to re-create oneself. Sydney Greech, a former pirate turned trader, and his pregnant lover Bess travel to Charles Town in search of a better life. He proposes marriage; she agrees, subject to his changing his name— "Greech" is too ugly. Thus, in 1720, the Bell family is founded, the first of six generations of Bells to populate the novel and the city.

Charleston itself becomes a complex, contradictory character in the novel. Jakes depicts it as the hub of international trade, an urbane and genteel city with rich intellectual and political traditions—and excruciating poverty. To illustrate such complexity, Jakes links the Bell family story with those of the Strongs (née Poorly), once slaves, now freedmen; the Larks, who through generations— from poor whites to a congressman—maintain a vendetta against the Bells with its roots in the Revolution; and the Marburgs, German Jews who rise to become leaders of the intellectual and financial community.

Yet, just as Charleston is cosmopolitan, the novel is far more than local-color fiction. It presents the American Revolution, so familiar from *The Bastard* and *The Rebels,* from the Southern perspective. And Charleston is portrayed during the Civil War as part of a nation riven. Cal Bell Hayward fights not for the perpetuation of slavery but for political freedoms. Alexandra Bell, despised by some in her hometown for her belief in racial equality, travels north to work for the abolition of slavery, only to discover violent opposition to her ideas from bigots there.

The cast of characters includes patriots and partisans, Americans and Anglophiles of the Revolution; the Nullifiers and Unionists of the years before the Civil War; Confederate soldiers who had held no slaves but who are detained in Union military prison hellholes; and Southern lawyers who defend imprisoned black survivors of the Massachusetts 54th's assault on Fort Wagner. While this

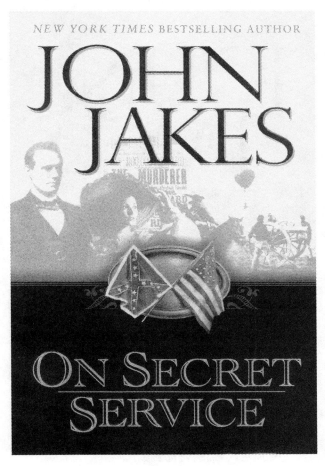

Dust jacket for Jakes's 2000 novel, about espionage and intelligence-gathering during the Civil War
(Richland County Public Library)

kaleidoscopic diversity of characters creates a rich portrait of Charleston, and America, it also underscores one of Jakes's important themes: the insidious danger of prejudice, its corrosive impact on society and one's soul.

Like earlier family sagas, *Charleston* reveals Jakes as "America's history teacher." Readers learn how blacks replaced Indian slaves in South Carolina's labor-intensive agriculture; they learn that some British units wore green coats rather than red. Jakes depicts South Carolina's flourishing Jewish community and Francis Marion's Huguenot ancestors. Other tidbits of information include the facts that oleander tea can poison an enemy; that bullets partially halved or quartered were the Revolutionary War precursor of modern "cop-killer" bullets; that wealthy South Carolinians fled to Newport, "Carolina's hospital," to escape yellow fever; and that antebellum condoms were made of sheep or pig intestines.

Jakes's details lead the reader ultimately to major themes. Early in the novel Tom Bell observes that Loyalist partisans operating inland "are not honorable men." Honor, as opposed to mere reputation, is thus established

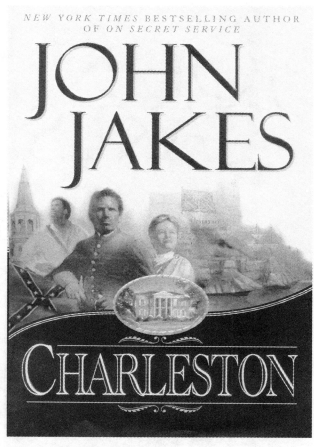

Dust jacket for Jakes's 2002 novel, about six generations of a South Carolina family from the American Revolution to Reconstruction (Richland County Public Library)

as the touchstone of character. Those who are motivated by personal gain—economic, political, social, or sexual—are the villains of the novel, in contrast to those who adhere to principle. The Marburgs staunchly defend First Amendment rights and intellectual freedom: "The right of every opinion to be aired, even the frivolous or mischievous, is essential. . . . the circulation of ideas is usually suppressed to protect the interests of those in authority." Alexandra, in her abolitionist speeches, links racial and gender equality: "How can we care about the freedom of Negroes and ignore the bondage of women?"

Certainly Jakes had espoused such values before *Charleston,* but his methods of conveying them in this novel are more daring than before. Unlike earlier heroines with Native American or Hispanic lovers, Alexandra, in her love for Henry Strong, an African American whose

forebears had been freed by her grandfather, impinges on a taboo that still lingers in parts of twenty-first-century America. Similarly, Jakes's attacks on anti-Semitism go beyond letting the villains scorn Jews as a group. In his descriptions of the book burnings in the chapters "Omens" and "Fanning the Flames" the image of broken shop windows is a direct allusion to *Kristallnacht* and the totalitarian assaults on freedoms during the Third Reich.

John Jakes continues to work on new projects and to revisit earlier material in new ways; one such endeavor is a collaboration with two Broadway writers on a musical based on *North and South.* In recognition of his work, Jakes has received honorary degrees from Wright State University (1976), DePauw University (1977), Winthrop College (1993), the University of South Carolina (1993), and Ohio State University (1996). These honors reflect his status as an historical novelist who is both best-selling and respected.

Interviews:

Robert Dahlin, "John Jakes," *Publishers Weekly,* 226 (30 November 1984): 99–100;

Gwen Czura, "Up Close and Personal with John Jakes," *Island Events* (December 1994): 12.

References:

Barbara Brannon and Vanessa Farr, *John Jakes: The People's Author,* exhibition catalogue (Columbia: University of South Carolina, 1993);

Robert Hawkins, *The Kent Family Chronicles Encyclopedia* (New York: Bantam, 1979);

Mary Ellen Jones, *John Jakes: A Critical Companion* (Westport, Conn.: Greenwood Press, 1996);

Kirk Polking, "John Jakes Has a Fever. A Writing Fever," *Writer's Digest,* 57 (January 1977): 22–23;

Nick Salvatore and Ann Sullivan, "From Bastard to American: The Legitimization of a Fictional Family," *Radical History Review,* 26 (1982): 140–150.

Papers:

The major collection of John Jakes's papers is the John Jakes Archive at Thomas Cooper Library, University of South Carolina, which includes manuscripts, correspondence, and promotional materials. The DePauw University Library, Greencastle, Indiana, holds final typescripts of the eight Kent Family Chronicles novels. The Archive of Contemporary History, University of Wyoming, Laramie, has a miscellaneous collection, including some pre-Kent novels. Some early science-fiction and fantasy materials are housed at the Archive of Popular Culture, Bowling Green State University, Ohio.

Charles Johnson

(23 April 1948 –   )

John Whalen-Bridge
National University of Singapore

See also the Johnson entry in *DLB 33: Afro-American Fiction Writers After 1955.*

BOOKS: *Black Humor* (Chicago: Johnson, 1970);

Half-Past Nation Time (Westlake Village, Cal.: Aware Press, 1972);

Faith and the Good Thing (New York: Viking, 1974);

Oxherding Tale (Bloomington: Indiana University Press, 1982; London: Blond & Briggs, 1983);

The Sorcerer's Apprentice: Tales and Conjurations (New York: Atheneum, 1986; London: Serpent's Tail, 1988);

Being & Race: Black Writing Since 1970 (Bloomington: Indiana University Press, 1988; London: Serpent's Tail, 1988);

Middle Passage (New York: Atheneum, 1990; London: Picador, 1991);

In Search of a Voice, by Johnson and Ron Chernow, National Book Week Lectures (Washington, D.C.: Library of Congress, 1991);

Africans in America: America's Journey through Slavery, by Johnson and Patricia Smith (New York: Harcourt Brace, 1998);

Dreamer: A Novel (New York: Scribner, 1998; Edinburgh: Canongate, 1998);

Soulcatcher and Other Stories (San Diego: Harcourt, 2001);

Turning the Wheel: Essays on Buddhism and Writing (New York: Scribner, 2003).

PRODUCED SCRIPTS: *Charlie's Pad,* television, 52 episodes, PBS, 1970–1980;

Charlie Smith and the Fritter-Tree, television, PBS, fall 1978;

"Bad Business," *Up and Coming,* television, PBS, 18 April 1981;

"Booker," *Wonderworks,* television, PBS, October 1984.

OTHER: Mark Twain, *What Is Man?* introduction by Johnson (New York: Oxford University Press, 1996);

Charles Johnson (courtesy of the author)

Black Men Speaking, edited by Johnson and John McCluskey Jr. (Bloomington: Indiana University Press, 1997);

"Executive Decision," in *Outside the Law: Narratives on Justice in America,* edited by Susan Richards Shreve and Porter Shreve (Boston: Beacon, 1997);

Ralph Ellison, *Juneteenth: A Novel,* edited by John F. Callahan, introduction by Johnson (New York: Random House, 1999);

King: The Photobiography of Martin Luther King Jr., text by Johnson and Bob Adelman (New York: Viking Studio, 2000);

Harriet Beecher Stowe, *Uncle Tom's Cabin,* introduction by Johnson (New York: Oxford University Press, 2002).

Author of four highly acclaimed novels, two volumes of short stories, two works of nonfiction, and two published collections of political cartoons, Charles Johnson has produced a wide-ranging body of work. His fiction combines the myths and texts of Asian and African religion, philosophy, and folklore with the canonical writings and mystical counterculture of European civilization. He is often discussed as a practitioner and theoretician of what he calls "a genuinely philosophical black fiction," and he has written key essays and extended philosophical works to develop this tradition. As Jonathan Little has demonstrated in *Charles Johnson's Spiritual Imagination* (1997), neither the raceless and classless "integrationist poetics" of the 1950s and 1960s limned by Houston Baker, nor the Black Aesthetic articulated by Amiri Baraka in 1975, properly describe Johnson's Hegelian synthesis of African American cultural pride and an American-centered, Buddhist humanism: "Johnson inverts the neat chronology of African American poetics that Baker constructs, reviving integrationist poetics with a difference. Through a well-thought-out and philosophically grounded aesthetic methodology, Johnson uses the particulars of racial experience to limn the universal and to emphasize the ties that bind." Johnson has paid a price with the most influential critics of African American literature, as Little notes: "Johnson's often-repeated denials of distinct racial difference help to explain [Henry Louis] Gates's gatekeeping exclusion of Johnson in lists of significant contemporary African American writers." Johnson's black philosophical fiction could well be considered as a development of novelist John Gardner's proposed "moral fiction" but with African American experience as its central subject matter.

Johnson extracts humor from the most painful patterns of life in order to promote eventual health and happiness. To this end, he freely shifts modes (he ranges between naturalism, allegory, satire, and even mysticism) in order to envision freedom and happiness in a world of constraint and pain. Critics of Johnson's gumbo of fictional modes have argued that his work, like cartoon drawings, are free to be so various only because they are unfaithful to the texture of felt life, but Johnson defenders praise him as a literary trickster or, to use his own word, "conjurer."

Johnson has written about his life in some detail, but he invariably begins by defining himself in terms of his relationships with others, such as his parents or his great-uncle Will, who was the first member of Johnson's family to make the migration from the South to the industrializing North, where he started two businesses. Positive role models and other beneficent aspects of Johnson's upbringing left Johnson with feelings of familial, ethnic, and national pride, as he wrote in the essay "An American Milk Bottle" (included in *Turning the Wheel: Essays on Buddhism and Writing,* 2003): "I never doubted—not *once*—the crucial role my people have played since the 17th century colonies in the building of America on *all* levels—the physical, cultural, economic and political." Because Great-Uncle Will was able to offer jobs to his nieces and nephews, Johnson's father came north to Evanston, Illinois, shortly after World War II. On 23 April 1948 Charles Richard Johnson was born to Benny Lee and Ruby Elizabeth (née Jackson) Johnson at an all-black facility called Community Hospital. Johnson's father sometimes worked three jobs, and his mother took various jobs as well, including work as a cleaning woman for Gamma Phi Beta sorority at Northwestern University, where Johnson's grandmother also worked as a cook. This sorority claimed that it would never admit blacks, and Johnson relishes the irony not only that his mother was "admitted" under such conditions but also that this attempt at oppression, in Johnson's own mind, became an early causal link in his education: "my mother brought home books thrown away by sorority girls when classes ended, and in those boxes I found my first copies of Shakespeare's tragedies." From his mother's bookcases Johnson also drew other works that inspired his later braiding of fantasy and history, such as James T. Farrell's Studs Lonigan trilogy, various works by Jack London, *The Swiss Family Robinson* (1812–1813), Richard Wright's *Black Boy* (1945), Plutarch's *Lives of the Noble Grecians,* the poetry of Rainer Maria Rilke, and popular works such as Ian Fleming's James Bond novels, comic books, and works of science fiction. His mother also gave Johnson a blank book, a diary in which he began the lifelong habit of critically transcribing his experiences.

One particular book from his mother's library proved especially influential on Johnson: when he was fourteen he found a manual of hatha yoga practices that included a short section on meditation, which he proceeded to try. He recalled in *"I Call Myself an Artist": Writings By and About Charles Johnson* (1999), "After half an hour of this—the most tranquil thirty minutes I'd ever known," the experience "radically slowed my sense of time and divested me of desire"; but he also reported a fear of this practice, "as if I'd been playing with a loaded pistol." Johnson decided to set aside this form of experience for a later period in his life, when he returned to meditation via the practice of Asian martial arts.

While Johnson's mother encouraged his spiritual, intellectual, and artistic inclinations, his father urged a much more practical view upon him, refusing to allow Johnson to consider a career as an artist. Citing famous cartoon artists George Cruikshank, Thomas Rolandson, Honoré Daumier, and Thomas Nast as influences, Johnson in *"I Call Myself an Artist"* recalled his growing obsession with drawing: "I was determined to be nothing *but* a commercial artist." Johnson's father, who knew no black artists, prohibited this career plan, saying "They don't let black people do that. You should think about something else." Johnson was dejected for a short period but soon wrote to Lawrence Lariar, a cartoonist profiled in *Writer's Digest* who offered correspondence courses, explaining his predicament. "Lariar, a true liberal—a Jewish man . . . who once took gleeful pleasure in his neighbor's anger when he invited a group of black artists to his Long Island home to give them instruction—fired back a letter to me within a week: 'Your father is wrong. . . . You can do whatever you want with your life. All you need is a good drawing teacher.'" Benny Lee Johnson agreed and paid for the two-year correspondence course. Johnson thus began a career as a cartoonist; he sold his first pen-and-ink illustrations to a magic-company catalogue in Chicago in 1965.

Still, he was not unmindful of his father's concern that artists—whether black or white—have difficulty earning enough money to raise a family. On the advice of his high-school art teacher and guidance counselor, Johnson applied to and was accepted by Southern Illinois University in Carbondale, where he began his studies in 1966. Johnson immersed himself in the works of the pre-Socratic philosophers, the novels of Jean-Paul Sartre and Hermann Hesse, and the writings of Karl Marx and Friedrich Engels, as well as the popular culture of the moment: "we'd sit together, smoking and drinking beer, through each and every episode of 'Star Trek's' first season on the dorm's TV." Besides the crew of the *Enterprise,* other heroes included Plato, Kurt Vonnegut, and Richard Brautigan, as well as Jimi Hendrix and the Rolling Stones. The easy mixture of popular culture, collegiate banter, and a variety of philosophical argumentative gambits continues to characterize Johnson's best work.

Johnson's first summer job was to collect garbage on a route in Evanston, a job his father selected for him. In the evenings he began to study a Chinese martial arts style at the Chi Tao Chuan of the Monastery "kwoon" (martial-arts training club). This training hall contained a Buddhist shrine at which students were expected to say a prayer. Johnson recalled in *"I Call Myself an Artist"* that "The *feel* of this place, so meditative, so simple in its stark furnishings, struck me as exactly right for what I needed at this juncture in my life: a discipline of the body that also required an ongoing testing of the spirit."

Dust jacket for Johnson's first novel, about a "brown-sugared soul sister" on a spiritual quest (Bruccoli Clark Layman Archives)

Johnson came to Buddhism through his interest in martial arts, and these elements figure in key ways in his work. He continues to teach a form of kung fu in the Seattle area. Essays about Johnson's philosophical engagement with the interrelations between Buddhism, postmodern thought, and literature have been published in *Turning the Wheel,* and Johnson is a contributing editor to the Buddhist review *Tricycle.* His early interest in Asian philosophy and disciplines has had a steadily productive influence on his writing.

Halfway through his studies at Southern Illinois, Johnson met Joan New, a student at the National College of Education in Evanston. They were married in 1970 in the Ebenezer AME Church; they have two children, Malik (born in 1975) and Elizabeth (born in 1981), named after Johnson's mother, who passed away the same year.

Two other people have had a profound effect on Johnson's development: the poet Amiri Baraka, whom Johnson saw at a poetry reading in 1969, and the novelist John Gardner, with whom Johnson studied creative writing at Southern Illinois University. At Baraka's appearance, as the poet told his listeners to take their talent "back into the black community," Johnson felt personally inspired; within a week he had created the political cartoons that compose *Black Humor,* which appeared in 1970 under the imprint of John H. Johnson, publisher of *Ebony* and *Black World* (formerly called *Negro Digest*). Johnson then parlayed his talent as an artist into a "how to draw" television show for PBS (Public Broadcasting Service) called *Charlie's Pad,* a fifty-two-part series that was first aired in the spring of 1970 and was later nationally distributed by PBS. Two years later, in 1972, he published his second collection of cartoons, *Half-Past Nation Time.*

At this point, Johnson started writing novels, though he says his first efforts were "not good." After six forays into this art form and several thousand pages of manuscript, Johnson moved away from the naturalistic style of writers he had admired, such as Richard Wright and James Baldwin, and he began to write the sort of novel for which he has earned fame, the "philosophical novel." Johnson knew he needed a good teacher to develop as a writer, and so he called upon Gardner. Johnson showed up at Gardner's house with his manuscripts under his arm and attended only one creative-writing seminar; Gardner agreed to meet with Johnson separately each week to discuss Johnson's drafts. Johnson also attended Gardner's class on epic literature (while Gardner was completing *Jason and Medeia,* 1973). Though Johnson continued to publish cartoons and had begun to work toward his Ph.D. in philosophy at the State University of New York–Stony Brook, his real career as a successful novelist had begun: "With Gardner looking over my shoulder and scolding me whenever I started to go wrong, and after reading eighty books on magic and folklore, I wrote *Faith and the Good Thing* in nine months, which I thought was an incredibly long incubation period." Gardner taught Johnson to slow down, to put more value on revision, and to realize that "Any sentence that can come out *should* come out." After generating 2,400 pages of manuscript, Johnson winnowed the narrative to 250 pages, and Viking Press published *Faith and the Good Thing* in 1974.

The heroine of *Faith and the Good Thing* is the eponymous orphan Faith Cross, and the novel is an allegorical examination of the place of "faith" in the contemporary world. As John McCumber points out in his essay in *"I Call Myself an Artist,"* Faith, as the "uncomplicated whore and plaything of every man she meets," is at first blush an unlikely personification of philosophy, but this counterintuitive characterization is a central strategy in Johnson's mode of comic defamiliarization.

Prior to the beginning of the novel, Faith's father, Todd Cross, known for a carpe diem approach to life and for his storytelling, is lynched. In the first chapter Faith's mother, Lavidia, dies twice: after being resuscitated through heart massage the first time, she returns from her near-death experience with a look of great fear and insists to Faith that she must settle for nothing less than "a good thing." After her mother dies Faith sets out on a picaresque adventure involving the extremes of prostitution and middle-class life, spiritual despair and enlightenment.

The narrative is presented by a storyteller who suggests he or she is part of a mysterious, marginal lineage:

> It is time to tell you of Faith and the Good Thing. People tell her tale in many ways—conjure men and old gimped grandmothers whisper it to make you smile—but always Faith Cross is a beauty, a brown-sugared soul sister seeking the Good Thing in the dark days when the Good Thing was lost or, if the bog-dwelling Swamp Woman did not lie, was hidden by the gods to torment mankind for sins long forgotten.
> Listen.

Johnson maintains a tension in this work between the fast-talking comic tone of "brown-sugared soul sister seeking the Good Thing" and the measured, careful philosophical gravity of the perennial questions shaping his stories. William R. Nash points out that, in deploying folk literature within avant-garde experimental literature, Johnson is part of a long tradition in African American letters: "he tells a story as a folktale and incorporates elements of the oral tradition into the narrative. This choice of form places him in a lineage of African-American writers that includes Charles Chesnutt, Jean Toomer, Langston Hughes, Ralph Ellison, John Oliver Killens, and Toni Morrison."

When Johnson began to write *Faith and the Good Thing,* he had just completed his master's-level qualifying examinations and had memorized the main positions of eighty philosophers, and so the novel is rich in references to philosophers from Plato to Sartre. Johnson refers to this book as his "pre-phenomenological novel." He is worldly in his field of reference, and his repetitions and ironic conjunctions demonstrate a lively appreciation of the clash of ideas, East and West, European and African, idealistic and materialistic. Nash rightly acknowledges the syncretism of Johnson's vision in bringing together Christian theology and Buddhist doctrine with Africanist folklore. Asceticism, hedonism, and materialism are three of the main pathways to the Good in this novel that are examined and found wanting.

After Lavidia's death, Faith departs from rural Georgia and, at the urging of the Swamp Woman, a one-eyed hag with magical powers, begins her quest. This mythic, folk element combines with an imaginative representation of the African American northern migration of the first half of the twentieth century—an historical movement that is essential, as well, to the shape of Ellison's *Invisible Man* (1952). As with Ellison's protagonist, Faith is a naive figure who learns everything the hard way. In Chicago she meets Arnold Tyler Tippis, who buys her a drink, rapes her, and then gives her money, which is how Faith becomes a prostitute. Another male character appears to be the Good Thing but is again a doorway to suffering: Alpha Omega Holmes, who courted Faith in high school until her mother chased him away and who now wishes to be an artist, has an affair with Faith but abandons her when she reveals that she is pregnant. Faith has married Isaac Maxwell, for whom money is the Good Thing. He throws her out when he learns that she is not sexually innocent by bourgeois standards and that she is pregnant. She also meets Dr. Richard M. Barrett in Chicago, who robs her, later repents and returns possessions to her, and gives her his book of wisdom, called a "Domesday Book." But this volume turns out to be empty—every page is blank.

As Nash points out, Faith's journey has a structure that reveals not blind faith but rather deliberate choice and a commitment to what Johnson has called "whole sight." Nash writes, "Throughout her journey, Faith encounters individuals damaged by the objects or ideals that they use to define themselves: Reverend Brown adheres to conventional religious doctrine, Doctor Lynch to empirical science, Richard Barrett to abstract philosophy, and Alpha Omega Holmes to a romantic conception of art. Faith experiments unsuccessfully with each belief system. When the last bad faith object fails her, she returns to the Swamp Woman, who combines elements of all these separate paths." Faith does not finally achieve knowledge of the Good Thing, but after she is fatally burned in the final chapter, she steps out of her skin and into that of the Swamp Woman, as if to say that dedication to the path toward the Good Thing is the goal as well.

At the time *Faith and the Good Thing* appeared, jobs were becoming increasingly scarce in philosophy. Members of the English department of the University of Washington, who read and liked *Faith and the Good Thing,* invited Johnson to apply for a position as assistant professor of creative writing; so in 1976 Johnson left Stony Brook for Seattle with his wife, baby son, and new novel, but without his dissertation. Although Johnson had submitted two drafts of his dissertation, he was gaining popularity as a PBS scriptwriter and was beginning to write the book that became *Oxherding Tale* (1982), and so he did not complete his degree in the allotted time. However, Johnson was awarded both an honorary and an earned doctorate from SUNY–Stony Brook in 1999, but the awarding committee backdated

Dust jacket for Johnson's 1982 tale about the son of a slave and the mistress of a plantation (Bruccoli Clark Layman Archives)

the Ph.D. to 1988, the year his philosophical study *Being & Race: Black Writing Since 1970* was published.

At the University of Washington (where he received early tenure and became S. Wilson and Grace M. Pollack Distinguished Professor of Creative Writing in 1990), Johnson composed the stories that form *The Sorcerer's Apprentice: Tales and Conjurations* (1986) while working on *Oxherding Tale*. The late 1970s may have been the busiest period in Johnson's life: he was also writing essays such as the frequently reprinted "Primeval Mitosis: A Phenomenology of the Black Body" and, the following year, the short story "The Education of Mingo," which was first published in *Mother Jones* in 1977. Dozens of essays and short stories appeared within the next three years, and he wrote the script for *Charlie Smith and the Fritter-Tree,* a ninety-minute fictionalized biography of Charlie Smith, the former slave and black cowboy who was then the oldest living American. This show was televised on PBS in 1978. During these years Johnson was also a regular book reviewer for *The New York Times Book Review* and *The Los Angeles Times*

Book Review. His work began to earn awards and other signs of public recognition: he received the Friends of the Delta Award from Southern Illinois University in 1977, a Rockefeller Foundation grant for 1977–1978, and a Creative Writing Fellowship from the National Endowment for the Arts in 1979. He has averaged, since then, about one major award per year, including a Guggenheim Fellowship in 1988, several international literary prizes, a National Book Award (1990), and a MacArthur Fellowship (also known as a "genius grant") in 1998.

In 1986 Johnson published his first collection of short stories, *The Sorcerer's Apprentice: Tales and Conjurations*. The subtitle signals a link to the "conjure men" who may be imagined to speak in the first paragraph of *Faith and the Good Thing*. The main title pays homage to Johnson's mentor Gardner, whom Johnson mentions explicitly in the acknowledgements: "I am deeply indebted to the late John Gardner for microscopically analyzing three of these stories and generally scolding for my mistakes." Nash writes that the stories apply lessons from Gardner in ways that forced Johnson "to push beyond Gardner's definition of moral fiction." Nash's chapter on this volume presents the stories as "Lumber for the Platform," meaning that, although *The Sorcerer's Apprentice* was published four years after *Oxherding Tale*, the stories—most of which were composed before the publication of that novel—work out solutions to problems that occupied Johnson in his second (and most successful) novel. The stories in the collection vary widely, including historical fiction, science fiction, nonnaturalistic social realism, and even a beast fable.

Johnson's stories are praised for their wit, for intellectual adventurousness, and for advancing the range of what might be done in the contemporary short story. "The Education of Mingo," "Exchange Value," "China," "Popper's Disease," "Alethia," and "The Sorcerer's Apprentice" have each won scholarly attention; many critics have discussed Johnson's use of Eastern philosophical traditions, but Gary Storhoff argues persuasively that Johnson also makes effective use of Western philosophers. Linda Ferguson Selzer has explicated the interrelations between Marxism and sorcery in "Charles Johnson's 'Exchange Value': Signifyin(g) on Marx" (2001). "Exchange Value" was also selected for inclusion in *Best American Short Stories 1982*, edited by Gardner and Shannon Ravenel.

Johnson also has his critics. "China" is about Rudolph, an aging black postal worker whose life is on autopilot until one day when he watches a kung-fu movie and is inspired to join a "kwoon," where he begins to remake himself. Bill Brown, in his essay "Global Bodies/Postnationalities: Charles Johnson's Consumer Culture" (1997), attacks Johnson's presentation of this theme, accusing him of uncritically celebrating the American self-development marketplace, making the implicit claim that American culture is really world culture, and presenting female characters merely as foils to prop up masculine identity.

"Popper's Disease" is a parodic science-fiction story in which a dying alien is quarantined from his world because he suffers from an "incurable" disease: selfhood. Many of the stories in this volume are essentially Buddhist parables. Johnson often disparages didactic fiction or writing that clumsily (rather than artfully) foregrounds a political message, but he skillfully presents the politics of presumption—the ways in which stereotypes take on a delusory appearance of permanent reality, often with disastrous effects.

"Alethia" is narrated by a highly intellectual philosophy professor who is no match for his femme fatale, an Equal Opportunity student: "Wendy was nobody's fool—she used Niggerese playfully, like a toy, to bait, to draw me out. She was a witch, yes." This story especially dramatizes the dilemma of the black middle class, for Wendy powerfully exploits the professor's fear that his own intellectualizations and idealism are inherently unreal, at least in relation to her streetwise banter. After announcing that she requires a good grade to stay in school, she lets the professor know that she will say they slept together if he does not play along with her "'A' for a lay" scheme. Johnson's presentations of stereotypical situations almost always depend on some sort of reversal, and in this case the typical power relations between teacher and student are clearly reversed: "She was armed with endless tricks and strategies, this black girl."

Johnson has referred to his next novel, *Oxherding Tale*, as his "platform novel," which is a reference to the Platform Sutra of the Sixth Patriarch of Zen Buddhism, the Chinese Zen master Hui Neng. Rudolph P. Byrd writes that *Oxherding Tale* is "perhaps the most widely taught and admired of Johnson's novels," the "pivotal work of fiction that constituted the greatest challenge in intellectual and artistic terms." *Oxherding Tale* is a road novel, a picaresque adventure relating various regions of the United States, different classes and the experiences associated with them, and life on both sides of what W. E. B. Du Bois called America's central problem, "the color line." The novel falls into two parts, "House and Field" (six chapters) and "The White World" (seven chapters), and it ranges from the Cripplegate Plantation in South Carolina to Chicago, Illinois.

The novel also organizes at least four plotlines. First, there is the bildungsroman story, in which the protagonist, Andrew, is comically conceived and educated. Second, there is the romance plot, in which Andrew initially seeks manumission that he might free his beloved Minty; later, while passing as a white man, he attempts to build a life with the witty bluestocking Peggy Undercliff. Third, there is the picaresque "road" plot, in which Andrew, after being sent to the plantation of femme fatale Flo Hatfield, flees for his life with the equivalent of a Zen master, the coffin maker Reb, and then later must flee the escaped-slave hunter and "soulcatcher" Horace Bannon. Finally, there is the escaped slave narrative, in the mode of the *Narrative of the Life of Frederick Douglass* (1845), which gives the basic shape to *Oxherding Tale* but in no way limits it.

Two elements make the bildungsroman plot one of the funniest books of postwar American literature. First, Johnson reverses the narrative in which a white man, through violence and coercion, fathers children with a slave woman and then disowns them (as occurs in *Narrative of the Life of Frederick Douglass*). In the opening chapter of *Oxherding Tale* the plantation owner Jonathan Polkinghorne and his slave George Hawkins are drinking together and complaining about the boredom of marital regularity, as if they considered themselves equals. This presentation of the master-slave relationship cannot be construed as a denial of the dehumanizing effects of slavery, as Johnson obviously both recognizes the worst of slavery and refuses to surrender his artistic freedom to a pious presentation of historical materials. When Jonathan and George decide to exchange marital beds one evening, Jonathan is thrown out on his ear by the slave Mattie, whereas George has an athletic experience with Anna Polkinghorne–who will become Andrew Hawkins's mother. Relations between Mattie and George and between Jonathan and Anna are spoiled by the birth of Andrew, who is considered a slave, and so George is demoted from "house" to "field." Consequently, in Johnson's satire, George becomes the original separatist revolutionary.

Continuing in this cartoonish vein, Jonathan feels guilty about the confusion he has wrought and arranges to have Andrew tutored. The instructor, Ezekiel William Sykes-Withers, can see the interior of objects as well as any Tibetan lama, is a correspondent with Karl Marx, knows more about the *Mahàbhárata* than anyone else in America, and comes with a reference letter that concludes, "you must never leave him alone for long in a room with a little girl." He "has a splendid future as an Orientalist ordained for him provided he isn't hanged, say, for high treason, or heresy." Through Sykes-Withers, Andrew comes to learn Greek, Sanskrit, and some Chinese, thus enabling the unlikely but highly entertaining philosophical dimension of the novel.

Because he loves the enslaved seamstress Minty, Andrew demands his own freedom, but although Jonathan signs the deed of manumission, he sends Andrew to Flo Hatfield's plantation to earn enough

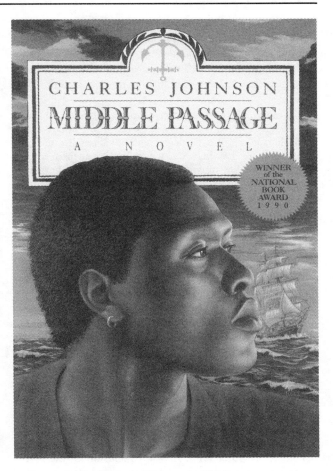

Dust jacket for Johnson's 1990 novel, which features a character from Johnson's invented African tribe, the philosophical Allmuseri (Richland County Public Library)

money to buy his freedom. The political fact of freedom is delayed by the drawn-out metaphoric enslavement to the senses: Flo is, it turns out, a vampiric embodiment of the hedonistic, carnal path in life, and her practice is to select a handsome young slave and drain the life out of him through endless sex. She represents, in highly comic terms, the Buddhist equation between desire and death. At her plantation Andrew meets the wisecracking black coffin maker Reb. When a man points a gun at Reb and boasts of being the sort of man who might shoot a slave without giving the matter a second thought, Reb replies with no hesitation that he himself could get shot without giving the matter a second thought; Reb's Zen-caliber freedom so startles the man that Reb is able simply to walk away.

Even the awful Bannon, the incarnation of Death whom no character (except Reb) can escape and who tracks down escaped slaves by adopting their mannerisms and shadowing them until they are spiritually exhausted, is comically and redemptively presented in relation to a thoroughly interdependent Wholeness.

When Bannon tells Andrew that he will not murder him (because Reb escaped and because Bannon promised to retire if anyone ever eluded him), Andrew asks about his father, George, at which point Bannon reveals his magical tattoos in which each of his victims is depicted:

> the intricately woven brown tattooes presented, in the brilliance of a silver-gray sky at dawn, an impossible flesh tapestry of a thousand individualities no longer static, mere drawings, but if you looked at them long enough, bodies moving like Lilliputians over the surface of his skin. Not tattooes at all, I saw, but forms sardined in his contour, creatures Bannon had killed since childhood: spineless insects, flies he'd dewinged; yet even the tiniest of these thrashing within the body mosaic was, clearly, a society as complex as the higher forms, a concrescence of molecules cells atoms in concert, for nothing in the necropolis he'd filled stood alone, wished to stand alone, had to stand alone, and the commonwealth of the dead shape-shifted on his chest.

All individual beings become tattoos on the body of Bannon, but, in the understanding of this condition, one overcomes not only loneliness but also, at least in the metaphorical extension of self beyond the individual's epidermis, Death: "all were conserved in this process of doubling, nothing was lost in the masquerade"—including George. In this passage Johnson daringly takes his comedic chiaroscuro of heavenly detachment and hellish delight to its outer limit. At the conclusion of the novel, Andrew (now passing as a white man under the name of William Harris) has freed Minty, who succumbs to a wasting illness; he then settles in Spartanburg, South Carolina, with his wife, Peggy Undercliff, and tells his tale, which ends in 1865, the year in which "Reb built his finest coffin, the one in which they laid Abraham Lincoln to rest."

Through the mid 1980s and early 1990s Johnson's prestige continued to grow. In the fall of 1985 he served as Visiting Minority Professor at the University of Delaware; he received a "Lifting Up the World" award from Sri Chinmoy in 1988; and he received the "First Citizen Award" from Seattle mayor Norman Rice in 1990. He has even been credited for writing plays during this period, but the Charles R. Johnson—though also born in 1948—who wrote the "farce in three acts" *Olly Olly Oxen Free* (1988) and *All This and Moonlight* (1990) is not the same Charles Johnson who wrote *Oxherding Tale,* as Barbara Z. Thaden claims. Johnson has worked in movies and television but has not written any strictly dramatic works, although *Faith and the Good Thing* was adapted for the stage by Keli Garrett and performed at the City Lit Theatre in Chicago in 1994.

In 1990 Johnson's novel *Middle Passage* received the National Book Award and the Northwest Booksellers' Award. His books began to appear regularly on contemporary American literature syllabi, and *Middle Passage* was required reading for all freshman students at Stanford and Washington & Lee universities in 1998.

Johnson actually began to compose *Middle Passage* as one of his earlier "apprentice" novels, but he set it aside to work on *Oxherding Tale.* Both novels combine transformations of conventional plots to arrange a comic encounter with the most brutal realities. The cavalier protagonist of *Middle Passage* believes, having attained manumission and living as he does in New Orleans, that he has died and gone to heaven. The protagonist is named Rutherford Calhoun, which, Francine Dempsey suggests, recalls both Rutherford Hayes (the president who ended Reconstruction) and John Calhoun (an ardent defender of American slavery). Ashraf H. A. Rushdy points out that Calhoun has three separate but interrelated careers: he is a thief, a lover, and a writer. Rushdy adds that "What is interesting about Rutherford's three careers is that he seems to wish to work at each in order both to create an identity for himself and to criticize a capitalist economic system." As a thief he is vulnerable to blackmail and is about to be "shot-gunned" into a wedding when, like Ishmael in the first chapter of *Moby-Dick* (1851), he takes to the sea: "Of all the things that drive men to sea, the most common disaster, I've come to learn, is women." The comically disgruntled masculine complaint, clearly exaggerated in the way it falls short of Ishmael's suicidal despair, sets the plot in motion.

The rakish flight-from-marriage plot figures prominently in most of Johnson's novels. Elizabeth Muther argues in "Isadora at Sea: Misogyny as Comic Capital in Charles Johnson's *Middle Passage*" that Johnson's attitudes toward women, at least as expressed in his creation of female characters, is "contemptuous": Rutherford flees from Isadora, who is, according to Muther, "a singularly unlikable character. Johnson creates her under a consistent mask of misogyny, though it is arguably Calhoun's and not his own." At the conclusion of the novel, however, Rutherford has fallen genuinely in love with Isadora, having matured through his endurance of the Middle Passage (the crossing of the Atlantic Ocean in a slave ship) and through a pivotal encounter with a man from a tribe Johnson invented: the Allmuseri.

Johnson's Allmuseri are a magical tribe possessed of an uninterrupted sense of Being, at least until the slave traders capture them and disrupt their way of life. They are the economic heart of this novel, and they are also the philosophical center of Johnson's universe. He began to connect some of his African American characters to this lost tribe in the stories of *Sorcerer's Apprentice,* such as "The Gift of Osua," "The Education of Mingo," and "The Sorcerer's Apprentice." Mingo is "the youngest son of the reigning king of the Allmuseri, a tribe of wizards," when he is purchased by an ignorant farmer named Moses Green who wishes to teach Mingo everything he knows.

The Allmuseri connection invariably signifies both lost promise and inherent potential: the spiritually advanced Reb in *Oxherding Tale* is descended from the Allmuseri. In *Middle Passage* Johnson gives this tribe their most extended treatment.

The Allmuseri connection serves several purposes in Johnson's fictional universe: it allows Johnson to bridge his Asian philosophical connection to ancestral Africa, and it also historicizes an ideal period in human history before man fell from enlightenment. This previous golden age is an explicit theme in *Faith and the Good Thing,* and, with reference to the Allmuseri, Johnson develops this theme in all of his subsequent major works. The Allmuseri represent the possibility of human wholeness, of "beloved community," and Rutherford Calhoun comes to see them as "less a biological tribe than a clan held together by values."

Like Johnson's previous three novels, *Dreamer* (1998) orchestrates several plotlines simultaneously. As human ideal possibilities are incarnated in the Allmuseri of *Middle Passage* and the detached-yet-worldly-wise Reb of *Oxherding Tale,* Martin Luther King Jr. in *Dreamer* is a more-or-less perfected human being. This motif might be called the "avatar plot" in Johnson's fiction. The romance plot is much less important in this novel, though the narrator, Matthew Bishop, does fall in love with a young woman named Amy Griffith, and the consummation of this romance does mark a shift in Matthew from a geekishly cerebral to a more humane, well-rounded young man. As in the previous novels, there is a road trip that involves encounters with fallen humanity: in this case, the earthy, crude, and even violent Chaym Smith.

In "A Sangha by Another Name" (1999), an essay on African Americans in relation to Buddhism, Johnson interprets King as a kind of Buddhist exemplar. Johnson's King is dedicated to the idea of healing through integration, and Johnson's artistic ambition has been to develop a poetics of integration that cultivates political, aesthetic, philosophical, and spiritual forms of integration.

In the opening pages of *Dreamer,* King is a frustrated man grappling with an intractably divided world, a world seemingly cursed by "that mysterious dichotomy inscribed at the heart of things." Johnson has researched King's final years exhaustively; however, King's life is not really central to *Dreamer,* and Johnson only treats the negative aspects of King's life (such as the plagiarism of his doctoral dissertation and his philandering) indirectly. Johnson is concerned primarily with King's vision, not his life, and so the characters within the King camp who aid King, with the exception of King's double, Chaym Smith, treat King as an infallible holy man.

Johnson's narrative abruptly parts ways with the historical narrative of King's life with the introduction of Smith, a man who looks exactly like King but in many ways can be thought of as King's opposite. He has the same height, weight, and birthday as King, but he is a lower-class failure instead of a paragon of black middle-class aspirations. Matthew, who is, figuratively, an apostle writing the first Gospel of Martin Luther King, recognizes Smith as something of a Judas figure, but Matthew also recognizes the ways in which Smith, despite his undeniable flaws, is bettered by his confrontation with King's vision.

At the end of the novel King is assassinated; Smith (and the FBI) may or may not have been involved in the killing; and King's followers are left with huge questions and an uncertain sense of how to proceed. The drama of *Dreamer* centers on Matthew's realization that King and Smith are not opposites; the breakdown of rigid binaries is implicit from the beginning of the novel, since King, the Western/Christian minister, is the relatively selfless man, whereas Smith, the avowed Buddhist, is a latter-day Cain figure who is given to intense bouts of self-consciousness and envy. Matthew's response at the end of the novel, however, is not to point a finger at Smith's failings but to move from criticism to identification. As Amy and Matthew see King's bier begin its journey from downtown Atlanta to Morehouse College, Matthew ponders the loss:

> We'd killed him—all of us, black and white—because we didn't listen when he was alive, though this was, of course, the way of things: no prophet was accepted in his own country. Even before his death, we were looking for other, more "radical" black spokesmen. The Way of agapic love, with its bottomless demands, had proven too hard for this nation. Hatred and competition were easier. Exalting the ethnic ego proved far less challenging than King's belief in the beloved community. We loved violence—verbal and physical—too dearly.

Matthew's final recognition is not that there is no difference between King and Smith—the novel is all about their differences—but rather that the love of one (the Christ figure) must, if the message of love is truly understood, extend to the other (though he is the Judas figure). Matthew realizes that Smith's—and by extension America's—possible betrayal of King does not rule out the beneficent potential and achievements of this fallen self. When asked where Smith is, Matthew responds "Everywhere," suggesting that humans are all interdependent with the worst as well as the best among them.

Since *Dreamer,* Johnson has published another collection of short stories, *Soulcatcher* (2001), which consists of stories Johnson wrote to accompany the PBS series *Africans in America: America's Journey through Slavery.* Intended as they are to illustrate a documentary history of Africans in America, these stories are not as multivalent as

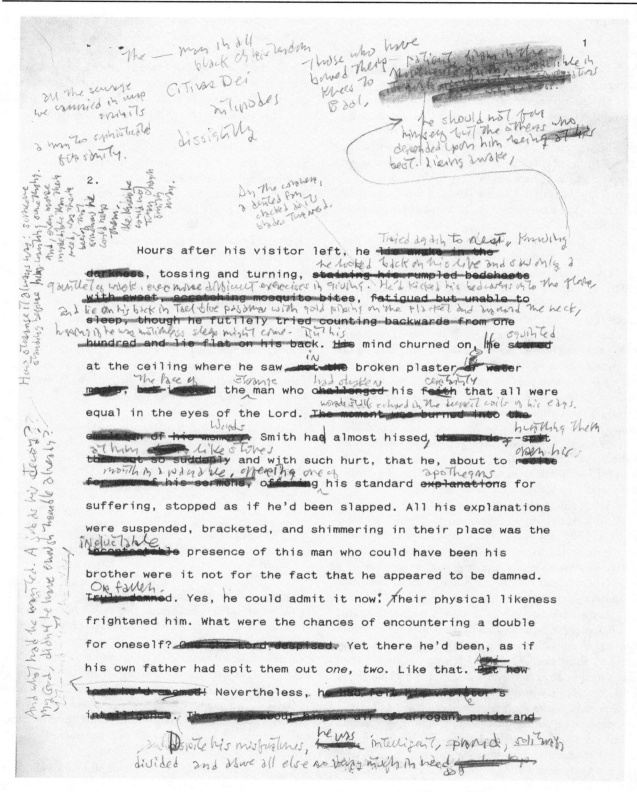

The typescript shows heavy handwritten revisions. The printed (typed) text reads:

Hours after his visitor left, he ~~lie awake in the~~ ~~darkness,~~ tossing and turning, ~~staining his rumpled bedsheets~~ ~~with sweat, scratching mosquito bites,~~ fatigued but unable to ~~sleep, though he futilely tried counting backwards from one~~ ~~hundred and lie flat on his back. His~~ mind churned on, ~~he stared~~ at the ceiling where he saw ~~not the~~ broken plaster ~~of water~~ ~~marks, but imagined~~ the man who ~~challenged~~ his ~~faith~~ that all were equal in the eyes of the Lord. ~~The moment was burned into the~~ ~~emulsion of his memory.~~ Smith had almost hissed, ~~the words spit~~ ~~them out so suddenly~~ and with such hurt, that he, about to ~~recite~~ ~~for one of his sermons, offering~~ his standard ~~explanations~~ for suffering, stopped as if he'd been slapped. All his explanations were suspended, bracketed, and shimmering in their place was the ~~incontestable~~ presence of this man who could have been his brother were it not for the fact that he appeared to be damned. ~~Truly damned.~~ Yes, he could admit it now: Their physical likeness frightened him. What were the chances of encountering a double for oneself? ~~One the Lord despised.~~ Yet there he'd been, as if his own father had spit them out *one*, *two*. Like that. ~~But how~~ ~~loathsome seemed!~~ Nevertheless, ~~he doubted his visitor's~~ ~~intelligence. There was about him an air of arrogant pride and~~

those in *The Sorcerer's Apprentice,* but they bring together key figures in American history such as Phillis Wheatley, George and Martha Washington, Frederick Douglass, and John Brown. In addition to these stories, Johnson has written many essays and introductions for books. Essays such as "The Elusive Art of Mindfulness," "A Sangha by Another Name," and "Reading the Eightfold Path" form part of his collection of philosophical writings, *Turning the Wheel.* In addition to these and several dozen other essays, prefaces, and reviews, Johnson has produced a half-dozen highly regarded stories ("Kwoon" was selected for the O. Henry Prize Stories in 1993). He has also found time to complete other projects, such as *Black Men Speaking* (1997), edited with John McCluskey Jr., and the biographical text for *King: The Photobiography of Martin Luther King Jr.* (2000), written with Bob Adelman. Johnson is also a lecturer; in the year 2001 he gave some two dozen talks, thus continuing to prove himself one of the hardest-working American writers.

In his review of *Middle Passage,* quoted on the dust jacket, critic Stanley Crouch claimed that this novel "firmly" places Johnson "within the universal minority whose will to mastery is made manifest by the quality of their creations." On 15 May 2002 Johnson received an American Academy of Arts and Letters Award for Literature. The citation accompanying this award provides a succinct introduction to Johnson's achievement so far: "Charles Johnson is a storyteller with a philosopher's intellect and a historian's belief in the power of the past to shape the present. But he is before all else a true storyteller."

References:

Houston Baker, *Blues, Ideology, and Afro-American Literature* (Chicago: University of Chicago Press, 1984), pp. 65–79;

Amiri Baraka, "Why I Changed My Ideology: Black Nationalism and Social Revolution," *Black World,* 9 (July 1975): 30–42;

Bill Brown, "Global Bodies/Postnationalities: Charles Johnson's Consumer Culture," *Representations,* no. 58 (Spring 1997): 24–48;

Rudolph P. Byrd, ed., *"I Call Myself an Artist": Writings By and About Charles Johnson* (Bloomington: Indiana University Press, 1999);

Francine Dempsey, "Middle Passage," in *Masterpieces of African-American Literature,* edited by Frank N. Magill (New York: HarperCollins, 1992), pp. 305–308;

Henry Louis Gates Jr., *The Signifying Monkey: A Theory of Afro-American Literary Criticism* (New York: Oxford University Press, 1988);

Frederick T. Griffiths, "'Sorcery Is Dialectical': Plato and Jean Toomer in Charles Johnson's *The Sorcerer's Apprentice,*" *African American Review,* 30, no. 4 (1996): 527–538;

Linda Hutcheon, "Historiographic Metafiction: Parody and Intertextuality of History," in *Intertextuality and Contemporary American Fiction,* edited by Patrick O'Donnell and Robert Con Davis (Baltimore: Johns Hopkins University Press, 1989), pp. 3–32;

Jonathan Little, *Charles Johnson's Spiritual Imagination* (Columbia: University of Missouri Press, 1997);

Albert Murray, "Something Different, Something More," in *Anger and Beyond: The Negro Writer in the United States,* edited by Herbert Hill (New York: Harper & Row, 1966);

Elizabeth Muther, "Isadora at Sea: Misogyny as Comic Capital in Charles Johnson's *Middle Passage,*" *African American Review,* 30 (Winter 1996): 649–658;

William R. Nash, *Charles Johnson's Fiction* (Urbana: University of Illinois Press, 2002);

Nedra Floyd Pautler, "He's Officially *Dr. Johnson,*" *University Week* [Seattle, Wash.], 27 May 1999, pp. 2–3;

Rosemary M. Canfield Reisman, "Faith and the Good Thing," in *Masterpieces of African-American Literature,* edited by Magill (New York: HarperCollins, 1992), pp. 157–160;

Ashraf H. A. Rushdy, "The Properties of Desire: Forms of Slave Identity in Charles Johnson's *Middle Passage,*" *Arizona Quarterly,* 50 (Summer 1994): 73–108;

Linda Ferguson Selzer, "Charles Johnson's 'Exchange Value': Signifyin(g) on Marx," *Massachusetts Review,* 42 (Summer 2001): 253–268;

Gary Storhoff, "The Artist as Universal Mind: Berkeley's Influence on Charles Johnson," *African American Review,* 30, no. 4 (1996): 539–548;

Barbara Z. Thaden, "Charles Johnson's *Middle Passage* as Historiographic Metafiction," *College English,* 59 (November 1997): 753–766;

John Whalen-Bridge, "Waking Cain: The Poetics of Integration in Charles Johnson's *Dreamer,*" *Callaloo,* 26 (Spring 2003).

Gayl Jones
(23 November 1949 –)

Kathryn A. Brewer
Stillman College

See also the Jones entry in *DLB 33: Afro-American Fiction Writers After 1955.*

BOOKS: *Corregidora* (New York: Random House, 1975);
Eva's Man (New York: Random House, 1976);
White Rat: Short Stories (New York: Random House, 1977);
Song for Anninho (Detroit: Lotus Press, 1981);
The Hermit-Woman: Poems (Detroit: Lotus Press, 1983);
Xarque and Other Poems (Detroit: Lotus Press, 1985);
Liberating Voices: Oral Tradition in African American Literature (Cambridge, Mass.: Harvard University Press, 1991);
The Healing (Boston: Beacon, 1998);
Mosquito (Boston: Beacon, 1999).

Gayl Jones, a contemporary African American writer, explores in her novels the effects that racism and sexual abuse have on successive generations of black women. She says of her own writing, "I am interested principally in the psychology of characters—and the way(s) in which they order their stories—their myths, dreams, nightmares, secret worlds, ambiguities, contradictions, ambivalences, memories, imaginations, their 'puzzles'." Her command of language, speech, dialogue, and nonlinear structure in her novels virtually place the reader alongside the characters. All of her novels blend the qualities of oral storytelling with the blues and dialogue that expresses the journey of African American women from slavery to the present.

Born on 23 November 1949 in Lexington, Kentucky, Gayl Jones has lived a life that reads much like that of one of the characters in her novels. The daughter of Franklin Jones, a cook, and Lucille Wilson Jones, a housewife and writer, Jones learned to write by watching her mother compose at home. In the oral tradition, Lucille Jones would read aloud the stories she had written to Jones and her brother. Jones, who began writing at age seven, says that the individuals who influenced her the most in her writing were her mother,

creative-writing teachers Michael Harper and William Meredith, and her high-school Spanish teacher, Anna Dodd.

After graduating from Connecticut College in 1971 with a B.A. in English, Jones was accepted into the creative-writing program at Brown University, where she received an M.A. in 1973 and a D.A. in 1975. While at Brown, she published many stories and produced a play. After graduating from Brown, she became a tenured professor in the English program at the University of Michigan, where she gained the reputation of a recluse. She also published her first two novels, *Corregidora* (1975) and *Eva's Man* (1976). Toni Morrison, her editor at the time, praised Jones's work highly, but Jones was so reclusive that she never met with Morrison. Morrison later resigned as her editor, stating that Jones needed to find someone she could trust to edit her manuscripts. While at the University of Michigan, Jones met her future partner, Bob Higgins, who later took her last name. He was a student at the university, and her relationship with him started her descent into a difficult time in her life.

In 1983 Bob Higgins Jones appeared at a gay-rights rally in Ann Arbor, Michigan, carrying a shotgun. He was arrested on a weapons charge and posted bail. Before his trial, he and Jones fled to Europe. Jones sent a letter to the University of Michigan announcing her resignation from the university, saying, "I will not continue at this university. I reject your lying racist s—t and I call upon God. Do what you want. God is with Bob and I'm with him." She also sent a letter to President Ronald Reagan denouncing the American system of justice. She and Bob Jones lived in Europe for fifteen years before returning to Kentucky to take care of Jones's ill mother. In February 1998 the Lexington police tried to serve the existing warrant on Bob Jones. The couple barricaded themselves in their house; when police smelled natural gas coming from it, they rushed in. They managed to save Jones's life, but Bob Jones had already slit his throat with a knife. As a result of this incident, Jones was taken to a mental

212

Gayl Jones (photograph © by Jill Krementz; from the dust jacket for White Rat: Short Stories, *1977)*

hospital, where she was treated for depression. However, at the same time, her third novel, *The Healing* (1998), was published. In keeping with her intensely private nature, she e-mailed the manuscript for this novel and her next novel, *Mosquito* (1999), to her editor, who has never met her in person. Her own life, then, is as full of myths, nightmares, ambivalences, contradictions, and memories as is her writing.

Her first novel, *Corregidora,* published in 1975, is a nonlinear narrative in which Jones explores the themes of African American women entrenched in the historical abuses of slavery that produce psychological factors so devastating that they are passed from generation to generation. Claudia Tate has described *Corregidora* as "a bizarre, romantic story." Amy S. Gottfried says, "the novel challenges the reader to think about how the system of slavery reifies a concept of black women as hypersexual by regarding them as property." Not until Ursa, the main character and the last of the Corregidora women, can express the unspeakable acts of violence and incest perpetrated against her great-grandmother, grandmother, and mother can she create a new voice not ensconced in violence. Until that time, though, she continues to suffer the physical and sexual abuse, immortalizing the slave owner who began it.

"Corregidora" in Portuguese means "judicial magistrate." Ursa Corregidora becomes the judge in her family to correct the historical invisibility the women have suffered. Ursa must learn the history of this exploitation as a defense against future abuse. As she learns of her family's past, the reader discovers that her name, Corregidora, came from the Brazilian coffee plantation owner who exploited black slave women, treating them as concubines and thus starting the pattern of abuse and silencing of the Corregidora women. Because Corregidora, the plantation owner, burned all documents proving the women were slaves, the Corregidora women could not prove their existence. Thus, these women pledged that they would "make generations" to prove and maintain their existence.

When slavery was abolished, there was no written record of the maternal side of Ursa's family. Ursa's great-grandmother, Great-gram, and grandmother, Gram, created an oral history to pass down to future generations that would document their lives. Ursa's mother, Mamma, in turn, married Ursa's father, Martin, and copulated with him only for the purpose of following Gram's directive to procreate, thus continuing the abusive pattern. When Martin learns this motivation, he parades Ursa's mother down Main Street like a concubine. Content, though, that she has fulfilled her role in making generations when Ursa is born, Mamma leaves her husband, takes back her maiden name, and returns to celibacy. She has continued the Corregidora female oral history, in which a woman never owns her body, her sexuality, or her soul. She is only an object for the sexual gratification of male owners or family members.

As Melvin Dixon indicates, "Ursa's sexuality has been silenced by her family's outrageous history." Like the women before her, Ursa identifies herself only through her ability to reproduce. She also continues the family pattern of tolerating abuse: her husband, Mutt, throws her down a flight of stairs in a jealous rage. Pregnant with her first child, Ursa is rushed to the hospital, where she loses the baby and has a hysterectomy. The loss of her womb means she is unable to fulfill the pledge passed down by her mother to "make generations." Ursa thus becomes the first woman in her family to break the cycle of incest and sexual violence. Her inability to bear children leads her to find an identity outside the abuse of men, family, and history.

To break the cycle of abuse, Ursa learns to understand her own past. A performer, Ursa sings her way to spiritual, mental, physical, and sexual health. After she leaves Mutt, she moves in with Tadpole, the owner of the club she sings in, and eventually marries him. She cannot respond sexually to him, however, and he looks for sex elsewhere. Leaving him, she goes across town to sing in another club, where she meets Mutt again and, through his questioning of her family heritage, begins to explore her past to find out why the Corregidora women felt they had to "make generations." When Ursa goes beyond this pattern created by the women before her and their abusers, she learns to respond to and communicate with Mutt on both a spiritual and sexual level that allows her to move forward. She thus creates a new oral narrative for herself and all other black women who share her historical past.

Eva Medina Canada, the main character in Jones's second novel, *Eva's Man,* published in 1976, cannot break the cycle of sexual and racial abuses. She cannot create a voice or an identity separate from the violent patterns she has learned from her familial and historical pasts. As Dixon indicates, "the unrelenting violence, emotional silence, and passive disharmony in *Eva's Man* are the undersides of the blues reconciliation and active lovemaking in *Corregidora.*" In a series of flashbacks, Eva relates the events in her life that led to the act of violence that has landed her in the psychiatric ward of a prison. Eva grows up in the projects in a household where her mother actively flaunts her affair with another man, a musician, while still living with Eva's father. This musician not only has sex with Ursa's mother but also tries to have sex with Eva. Eva's

introduction to sex, though, is with a neighborhood boy, Freddy Smoot, who uses a dirty Popsicle stick. She accepts this vulgarity and abuse. Whereas Ursa creates and sings her own blues, leading to healing and communication, Eva can only hear the blues, not create them, sing them, or resolve them. Thus, when she meets a man named Davis in a bar and goes to a hotel room with him, she repeats the cycle of violence she has been taught by family and society. In a violent rage, she poisons Davis; then she castrates him by biting him. The real significance, however, is in how she got to this point in her life. The environment in which she has been raised has taught her to devalue herself not only as a person but also as a woman.

Even her vulgar, violent, lewd language reveals her low self-concept. Her world is one in which women are meant to be objects of men's pleasure. Imprisoned in a psychiatric ward, Eva cannot express the abuse that led to her violent act, nor can she understand what led her to it. Incapable of communication, she sinks deeper into despair. In an interview with Mari Evans for *Black Women Writers (1950–1980): A Critical Evaluation* (1984), Jones said that she does not make moral or political judgments of her character: "my disapproval of Eva's action/choice in *Eva's Man* does not enter the work at all. She simply tells her story. I allow her to tell it, as much as she will tell. Eva Canada stands for no one but Eva Canada."

Both *Corregidora* and *Eva's Man* weave together flashbacks, the blues, and the oral storytelling tradition to create brutally honest, accurate, and believable voices of African American women. Dixon and Jerry W. Ward Jr. have commented on the ways in which these two novels invite the reader to enter the minds of the characters, who think and speak in the street language of their environments. These works paved the way for such later novels as Octavia E. Butler's *Kindred* (1979), Alice Walker's *The Color Purple* (1983), and Toni Morrison's *Beloved* (1987).

While in exile in Europe, Jones published *The Hermit-Woman: Poems* (1983) and *Xarque and Other Poems* (1985) and started writing *Liberating Voices: Oral Tradition in African American Literature* (1991). After a twenty-two-year break from publishing novels in the United States, Jones returned to the literary scene in 1998 with her third novel, *The Healing,* which was nominated for a National Book Award. This novel, along with the 1999 *Mosquito,* brought her back into public awareness. Still interested in how women mistreat and are mistreated, Jones explores a way to break the pattern of sexual violence in these novels. *The Healing* begins a cycle of recovery not fully treated or resolved in her first two novels. Jones again explores through language the ways in which abuse leads to psychological ramifications;

however, she calls her third novel a rejection of her earlier books that only emphasized the "man-done-her-wrong-type blues." Both *The Healing* and *Mosquito* focus on women who learn how to heal themselves from within, not letting the outside environment affect their senses of self or womanhood.

The main character of *The Healing,* Harlan Jane Eagleton, is a beautician turned manager of rock star Joan Savage. The narrative moves backward through time; Harlan's story is depicted in reverse, until the reader has arrived at the beginning of her transformation into a faith healer. Harlan says that a person cannot be a faith healer of others until she heals herself first. The focus of *The Healing,* as Jill Nelson says in *The Nation* (25 May 1998), is on "reconciliation and forgiveness, our ability to escape the violence that is visited upon us, to heal first ourselves and like Jane Eagleton, those around us."

The story moves from Saratoga to Louisville to Africa, and the reader meets many characters who become experts about history, politics, and music: Harlan's grandmother, a turtle woman in a carnival who wears a shell on her back every day to indicate her freakishness; Josef, a paranoid African German businessman whom Harlan dates; Josef's bodyguard; Harlan's former husband, Novelle, whom she left behind on their honeymoon in Africa to follow a medicine woman; and Joan Savage, whose violence brings Harlan to her healing powers. The reader first meets Harlan as she is returning to the United States after leaving her husband in Africa. Learning that he has cheated on her, she dissolves the marriage. She then meets Josef, who owns a horse farm in Kentucky. He becomes the symbol for self-doubt fueled by racism. Next the reader hears about the women in Harlan's past, particularly her grandmother, the turtle woman in the carnival sideshow. Appearing opposite her is the unicorn woman, who is usually portrayed as the ideal of white womanhood in fiction, while the turtle woman is a freak. However, both of these women symbolize the way black women are viewed. Even though the unicorn woman is supposedly the ideal, she is still a freakish or fake woman because she is black. She does not fit the conventional norms of physical beauty any more than the turtle woman. The unicorn woman thus leaves the carnival for the first man who sees her as a real woman, not as the amusement for a freak sideshow. The black woman still has no self-identity apart from the larger dominant society. Harlan teaches that she must create that identity from within.

Jones's fourth novel, *Mosquito,* continues a view of world politics, music, history, and culture to indicate how difficult solving world problems is until people heal themselves first. Eleanor J. Bader says that *Mosquito* is a

Dust jacket for Jones's first novel (1975), about a singer whose family name comes from the plantation owner who abused her female ancestors (Richland County Public Library)

"stunning glimpse into one woman's search for her place in the cosmos," while Tamala M. Edwards says in *Black Women Writers at Work* (1985) that *Mosquito* is "a carnival of digression and free association" that allows the reader to take a look into the minds of the characters without moral or political judgment. Mosquito, the main character, like Harlan in *The Healing,* is a politically savvy and sexually liberated woman who creates her own soul and identity. Mosquito (whose full name is Sojourner Jane Nadine Johnson) is a truck driver in southern Texas who takes the readers across the boundaries of time with her stories from the Underground Railroad of the American 1800s to the present-day underground railroad that brings Mexican laborers into the United States. Told through Mosquito's dreams, the books she has read, and a play by Jones's mother, Lucille Jones, *Mosquito* introduces the reader to a world of possibilities and theories about family, gender, race, love, and platonic relationships. These avenues of dis-

*Dust jacket for Jones's 1998 novel, about a woman who becomes
a faith healer (Richland County Public Library)*

course allow Mosquito and the reader to learn ways of
coping with abuse from the outside environment.

　　While driving her route along the Texas/Mexican
border, Mosquito finds a pregnant Mexican woman,
Maria, hiding in her truck. This incident starts her journey into the underground movement. Through it, she
learns a new independence in her relationships with
men, her connections to her female friends, and most of
all, her connection to her own self and soul. She learns
primarily from her Chicano bartender friend, Delgadina,
who not only tends bar but also writes stories and wants
to be a detective. Her childhood friend, Monkey Bread,
the assistant to a blonde Hollywood movie star, introduces her to "The Daughters of Nzingha." Finally, her
relationship with Ray, a revolutionary and a philosopher, makes Mosquito connect to herself both sexually
and intellectually. Jones said that Mosquito's journey is
"about self-definition, self-identification, the need to be
not afraid of who you are—to be yourself, even in a mul-
ticultural and multiracial society—the need everyone has
to define themselves and not be defined by others and to

tell his or her own stories." That is what Mosquito does,
through long, cumbersome narratives, in poetry, in song,
and in play form.

　　Sometimes condemned for her use of profanity
and violence, Jones writes novels that are, as Tate says,
"carefully wrought narratives developed from her
determination to relay a story entirely in terms of the
mental processes of the main character." Readers are
challenged to explore the interiors of caged personalities, men and women driven to extremes. Dixon adds
that Jones's use of black speech, incorporating the
rhythm and structure of the spoken language, creates
authentic characters and establishes possibilities for dramatic conflict between the reader and the text. There
are three levels of speech in her work: the language
itself, the rhythm of the people talking, and the rhythm
between the people talking. Her use of vulgar and raw
language allows the reader to experience the world and
environments the characters are forced to dwell within.
Her use of storytelling, according to Ward, also reflects
the psychosexual abuse of women and particularly African American women. Jones said she has to bring
things into an oral mode before she can respond to
them, and she has done so in all of her novels to date.
She says, in the interview with Evans, that she notices
voices and people, not things and landscape. She also
says that she is interested in relationships among history, society, morality, and personality.

　　The unpredictable structures of all of Gayl
Jones's fictions challenge the reader to construct meaning from the blues, oral storytelling, narrative structure,
and language in order to explore the social issues and
the physical and psychological environments confronting African American women in modern society. With
Morrison and Walker, Jones represents an early generation of contemporary African American novelists, and
with them and others, she continues to create an evolving, distinctly personal literature.

References:

Melvin Dixon, "Singing a Deep Song: Language as Evi-
　　dence in the Novels of Gayl Jones," in *Black
　　Women Writers (1950–1980): A Critical Evaluation,*
　　edited by Mari Evans (New York: Anchor, 1984),
　　pp. 236–248;

Amy S. Gottfried, "Angry Arts: Silence, Speech, and
　　Song in Gayl Jones's *Corregidora," African American
　　Review* (Winter 1994): 559–571;

Claudia Tate, *Black Women Writers at Work* (New York:
　　Continuum, 1985);

Jerry W. Ward Jr., "Escape from Trublum: The Fiction
　　of Gayl Jones," in *Black Women Writers (1950–
　　1980): A Critical Evaluation,* edited by Evans (New
　　York: Anchor, 1984), pp. 249–258.

Norman Mailer

(31 January 1923 –   )

John Whalen-Bridge
National University of Singapore

See also the Mailer entries in *DLB 2: American Novelists Since World War II; DLB 16: The Beats: Literary Bohemians in Postwar America; DLB 28: Twentieth-Century American-Jewish Fiction Writers; DLB 185: American Literary Journalists, 1945–1995, First Series; DLB Yearbook: 1980; DLB Yearbook: 1983; and DLB Yearbook: 1997.*

BOOKS: *The Naked and the Dead* (New York: Rinehart, 1948; London: Wingate, 1949);

Barbary Shore (New York: Rinehart, 1951; London: Cape, 1952);

The Deer Park (New York: Putnam, 1955; London: Wingate, 1957);

The White Negro: Superficial Reflections on the Hipster (San Francisco: City Lights Books, 1958);

Advertisements for Myself (New York: Putnam, 1959; London: Deutsch, 1961);

Deaths for the Ladies (and Other Disasters) (New York: Putnam, 1962; London: Deutsch, 1962);

The Presidential Papers (New York: Putnam, 1963; London: Deutsch, 1964);

An American Dream (New York: Dial, 1965; London: Deutsch, 1965);

Cannibals and Christians (New York: Dial, 1966; London: Deutsch, 1967);

The Bullfight: A Photographic Narrative with Text by Norman Mailer (New York: Macmillan, 1967);

The Deer Park: A Play (New York: Dial, 1967; London: Weidenfeld & Nicolson, 1970);

Why Are We in Vietnam? (New York: Putnam, 1967; London: Weidenfeld & Nicolson, 1969);

The Short Fiction of Norman Mailer (New York: Dell, 1967); republished in *The Essential Mailer* (Sevenoaks, U.K.: New English Library, 1982);

The Idol and the Octopus: Political Writings on the Kennedy and Johnson Administrations (New York: Dell, 1968);

The Armies of the Night: History as a Novel, The Novel as History (New York: New American Library, 1968; London: Weidenfeld & Nicolson, 1968);

Miami and the Siege of Chicago: An Informal History of the American Political Conventions of 1968 (New York:

Norman Mailer (photograph © 1991 Nancy Crampton; from the dust jacket for Harlot's Ghost, *1991)*

New American Library, 1968; London: Weidenfeld & Nicolson, 1968);

Of a Fire on the Moon (Boston: Little, Brown, 1971 [i.e., 1970]); republished as *A Fire on the Moon* (London: Weidenfeld & Nicolson, 1971 [i.e., 1970]);

Maidstone: A Mystery (New York: New American Library, 1971);

King of the Hill: On the Fight of the Century (New York: New American Library, 1971);

The Prisoner of Sex (Boston: Little, Brown, 1971; London: Weidenfeld & Nicolson, 1971);

The Long Patrol: 25 Years of Writing from the Work of Norman Mailer, edited by Robert F. Lucid (New York: World, 1971);

Existential Errands (Boston: Little, Brown, 1972); republished in *The Essential Mailer;*

St. George and the Godfather (New York: New American Library, 1972);

Marilyn: A Biography (New York: Grosset & Dunlap, 1973; London: Hodder & Stoughton, 1973);

The Faith of Graffiti (New York: Praeger, 1974); republished as *Watching My Name Go By* (London: Matthews, Miller, Dunbar, 1974);

The Fight (Boston: Little, Brown, 1975; London: Hart-Davis, 1976);

Some Honorable Men: Political Conventions, 1960–1972 (Boston: Little, Brown, 1976);

A Transit to Narcissus (New York: Fertig, 1978);

The Executioner's Song (Boston: Little, Brown, 1979; London: Hutchinson, 1979);

Of a Small and Modest Malignancy, Wicked and Bristling with Dots (Northridge, Cal.: Lord John Press, 1980);

Of Women and Their Elegance (New York: Simon & Schuster, 1980; London: Hodder & Stoughton, 1980);

Pieces and Pontifications (Boston: Little, Brown, 1982; Sevenoaks, U.K.: New English Library, 1983);

Ancient Evenings (Boston: Little, Brown, 1983; London: Macmillan, 1983);

Tough Guys Don't Dance (New York: Random House, 1984; London: Joseph, 1984);

Harlot's Ghost: A Novel of the CIA (New York: Random House, 1991; London: Joseph, 1991);

Oswald's Tale: An American Mystery (New York: Random House, 1995; London: Little, Brown, 1995);

Portrait of Picasso as a Young Man: An Interpretive Biography (New York: Atlantic Monthly Press, 1995; London: Little, Brown, 1995);

The Gospel According to the Son (New York: Random House, 1997; London: Little, Brown, 1997);

The Time of Our Time (New York: Random House, 1998; London: Little, Brown, 1998);

The Spooky Art: Thoughts on Writing (New York: Random House, 2003).

PRODUCED SCRIPTS: *Wild 90,* motion picture, Supreme Mix, 1968;

Beyond the Law, motion picture, Supreme Mix/Evergreen Films, 1968;

Maidstone, motion picture, Supreme Mix, 1969;

The Executioner's Song, television, NBC, 28 November 1982;

Tough Guys Don't Dance, by Mailer and Robert Towne, motion picture, Cannon Films, 1987;

American Tragedy, adapted by Mailer from Lawrence Schiller and James Willwerth's book, television, CBS/Fox, 12 November 2000;

Master Spy: The Robert Hanssen Story, television, CBS/Fox, 10 November 2002.

OTHER: Henry Miller, *Genius and Lust: A Journey through the Major Writings of Henry Miller,* edited by Mailer (New York: Grove, 1976).

Since his first novel, *The Naked and the Dead,* was published in 1948, Norman Mailer has written some forty books, including novels, essays, political journalism, poetry, drama, and screenplays. References to his writing appear in discussions of the sexual revolution in twentieth-century writing, of writers who challenge the border between literature and politics, and of postwar countercultural movements. His most important achievement has been the bridging of the novelistic imagination and nonfictional writing in a movement known as the New Journalism, which includes writers such as Truman Capote, Tom Wolfe, Joan Didion, Hunter S. Thompson, and Gay Talese. Few American writers have mixed fictional and nonfictional modes in such a range of ways.

Mailer's personal life, like his literary career, has been dramatic and various. Some critics complain that concern with the life of the author has eclipsed his actual artistic achievement. Mailer the personality became famous for such incidents as stabbing his second wife, Adele Morales, at a party; head-butting novelist Gore Vidal just before an appearance on Dick Cavett's television talk show in 1971; and championing the prison writer Jack Henry Abbott, who, soon after Mailer helped him get paroled, murdered waiter Richard Adan in 1981. Mailer the writer, however, has matured more certainly, and scholars such as Robert F. Lucid believe that Mailer's writing from *The Executioner's Song* (1979) onward is his best work, and, Didion has argued, that his stylistic mastery has been increasing rather than waning (*The New York Times Book Review,* 7 October 1979). Mailer was a touchstone figure in critical discussions such as Morris Dickstein's *Gates of Eden: American Culture in the Sixties* (1977), and he has been, as David Van Leer argues in the *Columbia Literary History of the United States* (1988), the paradigmatic rebel artist for the United States in the postwar period.

Norman Kingsley Mailer was born in Long Branch, New Jersey, on 31 January 1923, to Isaac Barnett Mailer, an accountant, and Fanny Schneider Mailer, who ran a nursing and housekeeping service. Mailer and his younger sister, Barbara, were raised in Brooklyn. According to biographer Carl Rollyson, Mailer's parents often called him a genius. At sixteen he entered Harvard University to study aeronautical engineering. Mailer's engineering degree was of no direct value until, twenty-five years later, he wrote an insightful critical study of the Apollo moon landing, titled *Of a Fire on the Moon* (1971); but his college years were nonetheless important to his developing ambition to be a writer. At Harvard, Mailer began to read writers such as James T. Farrell, Ernest Hemingway, and John Dos Passos, and he also wrote two novels and scores of short stories. His early writing indicates not only Mailer's tremendous energy as a writer (he made himself write three thousand words a day) but also his emerging talent. "The Greatest Thing in the World," a story he wrote in his sophomore year, won first prize in a *Story Magazine* contest in June 1941.

Mailer graduated from Harvard with honors in 1943, and the following year, shortly after his marriage to Beatrice Silverman, he was drafted into the United States Army for service in the Pacific theater of operation during World War II. He started out as a telephone lineman and clerk and then fought in the Philippines as a rifleman in a reconaissance patrol. After the Japanese surrender, he served in Occupied Japan until his discharge in 1946.

Some journalistic accounts of Mailer's life confine themselves entirely to his marital history. His first marriage, to Beatrice Silverman (1944–1951), produced Mailer's first daughter, Susan, born in 1949. Mailer married Adele Morales in 1954, and they divorced in 1962; from this union came two daughters, Danielle (born in 1957) and Elizabeth Anne (born in 1959). In 1962 Mailer married Lady Jeanne Campbell, mother of his fourth child, Kate, and this marriage ended in 1963. Mailer and Beverly Bentley married in 1963 and separated in 1970 after the births of sons Michael Burks in 1964 and Stephen McLeod in 1966; Mailer and Bentley divorced in 1980. In November 1980 Mailer was married twice: first to Carol Stevens to legitimize their daughter, Maggie Alexandra, who was born in 1971; then, after divorcing Stevens, Mailer married Norris Church, twenty-six years his junior. Their son, John Buffalo, was born in 1978. Critics occasionally mention high alimony bills as a motivation for Mailer's immense literary productivity.

At age twenty-five, Mailer shot to fame with his best-selling first novel, *The Naked and the Dead,* which Alfred Kazin claimed in 1973 was "probably still . . . the best novel about Americans at war." For this novel Mailer coined the verb "to fug" rather than challenge the still-strict censorship rules of 1948; nonetheless, his characters talk about sex with unusual candor. Set on the fictional island of Anopopei, *The Naked and the Dead* presents a complete sociological picture of the United States military as it battled the Japanese, island by island, for control of the South Pacific. Two story lines, one about officers and one about enlisted men, dovetail in the final third of the book. Mailer reworks the "Camera

Mailer as a private in the U.S. Army during World War II (Mailer family photograph)

Eye" device from Dos Passos's *U.S.A.* trilogy (1930–1936), interrupting the main plot lines of his story with the more poetic "Time Machine" sections, which present detailed psychological portraits of ten key characters.

The "enlisted" plot concerns a reconnaissance platoon headed by the authoritarian Sergeant Croft. Included in his platoon are characters drawn from different regions of the United States and representing the middle and lower classes. *The Naked and the Dead* reflects the way in which World War II blended social groups that might otherwise have remained distinct. In this novel Mailer attempts to fashion a complex vision of national identity, and *The Naked and the Dead* earned critical respect because it was so adept at blending the sociological particulars of life in the United States with an array of American literary voices. The historical/sociological mixture includes Wilson, a picaresque Southerner; Red, an angry outsider who seems to wander in from a proletarian novel; Gallagher, the bitter anti-Semite from Boston; and Goldstein and Roth, two Jews (one of whom is stereotypically gentle and thoughtful, the other of whom resists this stereotype by behaving aggressively). The literary mixture includes stylistic and thematic connections to such writers as Dos Passos, Hemingway, and Herman Melville.

Mailer's interest in middle- and upper-class social relations increased with each subsequent novel, but his notions about the ways in which, in F. Scott Fitzgerald's phrase, "the rich are different" are reflected in the officer sections of the novel. The officers are commanded by the cold and calculating General Cummings, who seems warm and ebullient to most soldiers but who presents his Machiavellian worldview to his aide, Lieutenant Hearn. While the soldiers in this war must confront an enemy Japanese force called the Toyaku Line, most of the drama centers on power struggles between officers jockeying for power or enlisted men who present subtle resistance to the officers. The personal struggle between Hearn and Cummings does not reflect a simple class struggle between upper-class and proletarian interests, since Hearn fits in with "the men" quite poorly, however much he fancies himself a rebel. The struggle between Hearn and Cummings, rather, reflects the struggle between highly educated members of the elite who affiliate themselves, contrastively, with upper- and lower-class interests. The class themes come together when General Cummings punishes Hearn by assigning him the command of a reconnaissance platoon; because of class-related tensions and intentional miscommunication between Hearn and subordinates, Hearn is killed by sniper fire early in this patrol.

All Mailer novels foreground highly sexualized struggles between men and women, but most of his novels are especially concerned with power struggles between men. Mailer has long been attracted to the notion that the victors in a struggle take on qualities of the vanquished, and these struggles blur conventional boundaries between personal and political levels of reality. The dialogue between Cummings and Hearn, as the general presents his hypothesis directly to the liberal and sometimes cynical lieutenant, represents the first in a series of highly personal Oedipal struggles in Mailer's work between an empowered and usually corrupt father figure and a naive or weak son figure. Typically in his fiction, sons resist fathers but take on the qualities of the fathers in order to survive. The personal struggle is a reflection of the transmission of power and authority between larger political identities. In *The Naked and the*

Dead, as in many of Mailer's subsequent works, the United States government risks becoming the fascist phoenix that rises from the ashes of Nazi Germany.

Mailer excels at giving political power struggles both microcosmic and macrocosmic levels within his fiction. Cummings, the evil genius of the novel, represents the danger of an overall militarization of society as a result of wartime organization, but at the microcosmic level these ideas are tested in the relationship between Cummings and Hearn. The two play out an Oedipal drama in which Hearn attempts to demonstrate to Cummings that his Machiavellian worldview will run up against overpowering resistance, while Cummings attempts to show Hearn that resistance is futile. As Stanley T. Gutman points out, Hearn's "integrity . . . is no match for Cummings' power." Mailer's general theme is that liberal softheartedness, even when it stems from genuinely admirable characteristics such as Hearn's refusal to be impressed by class rituals and other shallow value systems, faces a severe survival disadvantage in the world. While Mailer energetically disassociated himself from liberalism over the next decade, he actually developed, as Thomas H. Schaub argues, a "revisionist liberalism" suitable for postwar intellectual discourse.

The Naked and the Dead was a best-seller that earned Mailer much praise. Sinclair Lewis declared Mailer "the greatest writer to come out of his generation." The novel was nominated for the Pulitzer Prize and the Gutenberg Award, and the Associated Press named Mailer the Man of the Year in literature. Beginning his long career as a public intellectual, Mailer attended the Cultural and Scientific Conference for World Peace (the Waldorf Conference) in 1949 and campaigned for the Progressive Party's presidential candidate, Henry Wallace. At the same time, he began work on his second novel, *Barbary Shore* (1951).

This novel met with an especially harsh reception. Even sympathetic critics dismissed *Barbary Shore,* especially its last third, as a political tract. The novel received many poor reviews, and Robert Merrill skips the book completely in his study, except to note that it is a "miserable failure." Robert Solotaroff describes it as choked and claustral. The critical consensus is that the book fails; yet, *Barbary Shore* is an interesting reflection not only on Cold War suspicion but also on the reinvention of masculinity in postwar literature.

Barbary Shore is Mailer's most overtly political novel, and he comments in *Conversations with Norman Mailer* (1988) on the ways in which his own rapid political metamorphosis affected the composition of the novel: "I started *Barbary Shore* as some sort of fellow traveler, and finished with a political position which was a far-flung mutation of Trotskyism. And the drafts of the book reflected these ideological changes so drastically that the last draft . . . is a different novel altogether." Mailer has described *Barbary Shore* as his most autobiographical novel, although readers such as Judith Fetterley have found *An American Dream* (1965) to be more so.

The protagonist, Mikey Lovett, begins his quest with literal amnesia, opening the narration with: "Probably I was in a war." This degree of radical uncertainty is the result of a war wound, and Lovett tries to imagine how he received the wound and whether he was in the army or in another branch of the military. Since he is cut off from any certain history, his own experience of life is a surreal variation of most lives. People approach him with all sorts of presumptions about him, but these he can neither confirm nor deny. In the rooming house in Brooklyn in which this entire novel takes place, he meets McLeod, the unusual husband of his landlady, Guinevere. McLeod's assumed Irish name disguises a vague East European past, and much of the novel develops his shady history as a political functionary in Stalinist regimes. Many characters interact and attempt to attain their own ends in this novel, but the primary symbolic action unifying *Barbary Shore* is the transmission of leftist hope from McLeod to the amnesiac Lovett.

In *Barbary Shore* Mailer extends the father-son struggle with the addition of two female characters. Guinevere is initially described to Lovett as "a nymphomaniac," but when he meets her he decides that she is a jewel "set in brass." The Trotskyite Lannie is a psychologically and emotionally mad lesbian. Philip H. Bufithis finds Guinevere to be a more interesting character than either McLeod or Lovett, as she has a "Falstaffian vigor."

The romantic plot of *Barbary Shore* is somewhat strained. For example, the marriage between former apparatchik McLeod and a middle-class woman with no intellectual aspirations often seems more than unlikely. The novel has an allegorical level, and Guinevere, like her Camelot counterpart, is a tempting Eve figure: middle-class comfort is the forbidden fruit in this Marxist parable. Before turning his full attention to McLeod's apocalyptic political analysis, Lovett has affairs with both Guinevere and Lannie. Through the creation of these bizarre characters, Mailer attempts to suggest that a politically and psychologically volatile brew of possibilities is developing beneath the semblance of 1950s normality.

Mailer extends the urgency of many of the best sections of *The Naked and the Dead* in his second novel. The opening and closing sentences of *Barbary Shore* are stylistic homages to Franz Kafka, but the central sections are more realistic in manner. At the end of the novel, the secret police come crashing in; McLeod is murdered; and the small secret object that McLeod has been safeguarding has been passed on to the (rather clueless) Lovett, who takes up the role of guardian of revolutionary desire. Lovett, the amnesiac would-be novelist, is last

Dust jacket for Mailer's first novel (1948), for which he drew on his wartime experiences in the South Pacific (Ken Lopez catalogue, number 122)

seen running down an alley. Like Ralph Ellison's *Invisible Man* (1951), this entire novel is not so much a political action as the preparation for a future political action.

Politics remains an important background but a less specific motivation to action in Mailer's Hollywood novel *The Deer Park* (1955). Mailer's title alludes to the deer park of Louis XV, which is identified in the epigraph from Mouffle D'Angerville as "that gorge of innocence and virtue." The novel is a satirical anatomy of the forces checking creativity, but at the same time it fashions a romantic counterstatement to these forces, arguing that "There's a law in life so cruel and so just which demanded that one grow or pay for remaining the same." Growth and creativity are endangered species in a Darwinian world that preys on these qualities; yet, for Mailer, one of the largest mistakes is to conform to social conventions for the sake of short-term security.

Mailer wrote in *Advertisements for Myself* (1959) concerning the last draft of *The Deer Park* that "The most powerful leverage in fiction comes from point of view." In his third novel Mailer shows awareness of some of the weaknesses of *Barbary Shore* and tries to improve upon them by making his protagonist, Sergius O'Shaughnessy, tougher than Lovett, but Mailer is still at this point working with basically weak characters in search of personal resources. Like Hearn and Lovett, O'Shaughnessy fears that he is overmanned by the world. Mailer's most interesting protagonists confront a hollowness within themselves, an emptiness or lack that could be exposed. The hunger for power (narrative or political) in Mailer's works reveals a horror of powerlessness.

O'Shaughnessy does not suffer from amnesia like Lovett, but he is an orphan with a psychological war wound (sexual impotence) at the beginning of the novel. He is, like the protagonist of *Barbary Shore,* a narrator who depends on others to generate personal history from spiritual emptiness. That he is meant to suggest the mythic American who exists beyond history or in a kind of historical amnesia is comically suggested when Hollywood movie mogul Herman Teppis, head of the movie studio that figures centrally in the novel, refers to him as "Shamus Something-or-Other." O'Shaughnessy tells the story of his relationship with Eitel, a sympathetic but ultimately fallen character who wishes to direct and write his own movies but compromises on issues of artistic integrity to avoid censorship or blacklisting. Merrill found that Mailer strove to "regain his artistic equilibrium" in *The Deer Park* and produced one of his most important works; Didion, in her assessment of *The Executioner's Song* for *The New York Times Book Review* (7 October 1979), listed *The Deer Park* as one of Mailer's several "Great American Novels." Nonetheless, in *Advertisements for Myself* Mailer expressed dissatisfaction with his protagonists throughout the 1950s, complaining that "I seemed unable to create a narrator in the first person who was not overdelicate, over sensitive, and painfully tender."

The novel continues to claim attention for its trenchant attack on what Theodor W. Adorno called "the Culture Industry," but Mailer's construction of a writer manqué for his protagonist suggests at once the possibility that Hollywood produces bad writers and the contrasting possibility that Mailer could not successfully imagine a good writer. The protagonist-narrator introduces himself as a strong, silent type:

> In the cactus wild of Southern California, a distance of two hundred miles from the capital of cinema as I choose to call it, is the town of Desert D'Or. There I went from the Air Force to look for a good time. Some time ago.

It is not clear whether O'Shaughnessy is meant as an imitation of Hollywood formula heroes or as a parody of those heroes. He continues:

> Almost everybody I knew in Desert D'Or had had an unusual career, and it was the same for me. I grew up in a home for orphans. Still intact at the age of twenty-three, wearing my flying wings and a First Lieutenant's uniform, I arrived at the resort with fourteen thousand dollars, a sum I picked up via a poker game in a Tokyo hotel room while waiting with other fliers for our plane home. The curiosity is that I was never a gambler, I did not even like the game, but I had nothing to lose that night, and maybe for such a reason I accepted the luck of the cards. Let me leave it at that. I came out of the Air Force with no place to go, no family to visit, and I wandered down to Desert D'Or.

"Let me leave it at that," O'Shaughnessy offers, but his apparent overconfidence arouses suspicions.

Though he is supposed to be a witness of the real world of war, he asserts his toughness through the clichés of the not truly tough. He is impressed with the way Marion Faye, an evil genius/pimp, drives: "I drove with him once and tried to avoid it thereafter. I was pretty good with a car myself, but he drove like nobody I ever knew." O'Shaughnessy exists between the real world of war and the mummery of reality that predominates in Desert D'Or. But his claim that he is fit to report the falsehoods of Desert D'Or is evident in his presumptuous tone throughout the book. There is an adolescent aspect to some passages in this novel, a sense of a writer not yet in complete control of his material.

While reviews for *The Deer Park* were not quite as harsh as those Mailer received for *Barbary Shore,* this publication put Mailer into the critical pigeonhole of "author in decline" or "rebellious artist who squandered his gifts." Mailer could have chosen to follow his first novel with the guaranteed success of a World War II–based sequel, but he has consistently chosen the riskier artistic path over the demands of the marketplace.

The Deer Park begins Mailer's investigation of America's "Faustian" bargains, meaning situations in which one risks corruption by coming to terms with corrupt parties. In this novel the director Eitel, the older man whom O'Shaughnessy studies, wants to make truly worthwhile movies; but in order to get work, he must (because he has been associated with the Communist Party) make deals with Hollywood producers who care nothing for artistic integrity. Eitel cooperates with grandstanding politicians and movie moguls to gain his artistic freedom but loses his respectability in the process.

The most successful aspect of Mailer's pivotal third novel is probably the creation of a satirical backdrop. Mailer is fascinated by the existential struggle to achieve authentic being, but this aspect of his work should not overshadow his skill at portraying interlinking webs of social relations. In this novel characters betray one another sexually and professionally with some regular-

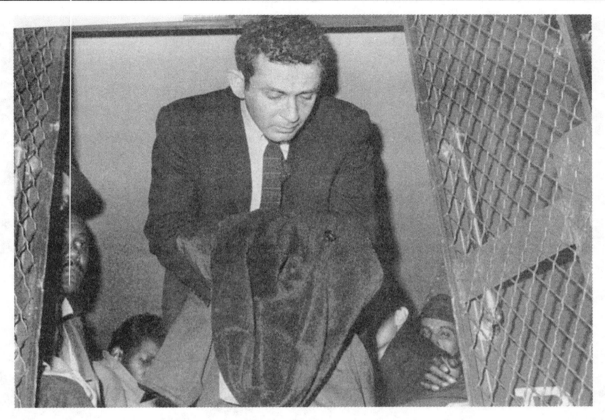

*Mailer being released from Bellevue psychiatric hospital in New York City, where he was committed for two weeks
in 1960 after wounding his second wife, Adele Morales, with a penknife (photograph © Corbis/Bettmann)*

ity; Mailer does not settle for easy disgust with the culture industry but rather takes this initial disgust as a starting point and examines how these characters struggle between what might be called caricature and being. The moneyed Hollywood interests falsify and shape lives for the sake of simple profits; for example, to preserve appearances, a homosexual actor (who is adored by heterosexual female fans) is to be forced into a marriage with Lulu Meyers, the starlet with whom O'Shaughnessy is in love. *The Deer Park* presents several sham relationships, but it also shows how characters such as Lulu do not always surrender to such forces but attempt, occasionally with success, to outflank them. None of these characters is particularly admirable in and of themselves, but in their struggle to survive as free individuals rather than pawns in someone else's game, they warrant deepening interest.

At the end of this novel O'Shaughnessy has a completely imaginary dialogue with the absent Eitel, who confessionally says, "I have lost the final desire of the artist, the desire which tells us that when all else is lost, when love is lost and adventure, pride of self, and pity, there still remains that world we may create, more real to us, more real to others, than the mummeries of what

happens, passes, and is gone." The imagined Eitel first counsels O'Shaughnessy to "blow against the walls of every power that exists" with "the small trumpet of your defiance" and then expands into God Himself, as O'Shaughnessy imagines how a conversation with the Creator might go. In the closing scene of the novel, God encourages O'Shaughnessy, saying, "'Go on, my boy. I don't know that I can help you, but we wouldn't want all *those* people to tell you what to do.'"

In his fiction and nonfiction writing from the mid 1950s through the early 1960s, Mailer explores bizarrely comic or even surrealistic situations in order to give such impossible dialogues some sort of imaginative foundation. Since these dialogues have frequently been dismissed as resulting from Mailer's overheated imagination, Mailer has developed two primary strategies for protecting his inventions against this sort of dismissal. Mailer's comic imagination plays on the incongruous coupling of intellectuality and obscenity: the existence of the obscene motive or representation exposes intellectual pretensions to a sudden comic deflation. Mailer's essayistic novella "The Man Who Studied Yoga" (included in *Advertisements for Myself*), which was intended as one section of a grand eight-part novel of which *The Deer Park* was supposed to

Dust jacket for Mailer's 1965 novel, about a war hero who becomes a congressman
(Richland County Public Library)

have been the first installment, concerns a group of intellectuals who view a pornographic movie and who rationalize their interest as best they can. Such deflation, which Mailer considers comedy of manners, can be found in all of his novels since *The Deer Park*.

Mailer collected his early essays, journalism, and short fiction in *Advertisements for Myself*. Much of his best short fiction was collected in *The Short Fiction of Norman Mailer* in 1967, along with a preface in which Mailer disparaged his talents as a short-story writer. But "The Man Who Studied Yoga" achieves impressive effects, and as Frederick Busch has argued, it makes a connection, at once resonant and mocking, between the quotidian reality of the United States in the 1950s and America's mythic past.

Insofar as it collected and organized a desire to outrage, *Advertisements for Myself* was a springboard for Mailer's work in the 1960s, when he became even more controversial. During the November 1960 party at which he meant to rally support for his campaign to become mayor of New York City, Mailer verbally abused and offered to box several of his guests; it was also the event at which he stabbed his second wife. Counseled to plead temporary insanity, Mailer refused

on the grounds that such a plea would injure his reputation as a writer. This surreal concern with literary reputation after just missing his wife's heart with a penknife is proof enough for some that Mailer was at least temporarily out of his senses, but the fiction that came out of this event was at once a quasi-political defense of such violence and an admission of madness. Mailer's *An American Dream* (1965), his first novel in ten years, was written initially in installments that were published in the magazine *Esquire* from January through August 1964; Mailer then revised his chapters for book publication the following year.

The novel recounts thirty-two hours in the life of Stephen Richards Rojack. This character tells readers in the first paragraph of the novel that, like Jack Kennedy, he was a war hero who became a congressman. Rojack claims that he seduced a girl (later his wife) "who would have been bored by a diamond as big as the Ritz." As the reference to Fitzgerald's comic and fantastic short story suggests, the narrative is realistic in manner but hyperbolic in its implications. Rojack murders his wife, Deborah Kelly; undergoes a series of existential tests and temptations; and finally travels west after the murder of his new love (a woman named Cherry, whom he meets just hours after killing his wife). Rojack literally gets away with murder, and the novel suggests that he does so in part because of the machinations of his evil father-in-law, Barney Kelly, who is the reincarnation in this novel of previous evil-genius characters such as General Cummings. But the novel also suggests that Rojack is a hero who must fight for his life against an adversary—his wife—who is, as General Cummings put it in *The Naked and the Dead,* a "great Bitch." Deborah "was an artist at sucking the marrow from a broken bone," and Rojack sees himself as a man in mortal danger because of her power over him: "At moments like that I would feel as if I had committed hari-kari and was walking about with my chest separated from my groin." Rojack and his wife are in the process of a painful separation when the novel begins, but when he feels helpless and lovelorn, she insults him, and he slaps her face. She then charges him and attempts, Rojack says, "to find my root and mangle me." Rojack thus presents the murder as partial self-defense.

The novel is artistically thrilling and stylistically exact, and its plotlines are clear. The title *An American Dream* suggests that this fantasy represents the American dream taken to its pathological extreme, but Rojack is the hero of the book, not an "anti-hero." Mary V. Dearborn writes that Rojack is Mailer's most successful character, in part because Rojack is "a strange fictionalization of the author." Mailer and Rojack share a risk-taking, macho, public persona; a rakish wit designed to outrage modesty; and a view of a large, magical struggle between good and evil in the universe. Mailer had begun to explore the possibilities of a redemptive violence in his 1958 essay "The White Negro" and in *The Presidential Papers* (1963), but the fact that a man who had stabbed his wife without being criminally charged had then written a novel about an existential hero who murders his wife and more or less becomes a better, happier person because of it was outrageous to many critics. As Barry Leeds has written in his 2002 essay "Mailer and Me," "In 1965, when *An American Dream* was published, any critic could get a license for Mailer-bashing out of a vending machine on any street corner." Leeds also points out that the same novel was redefined as a "contemporary classic" three years later, after Mailer won the Pulitzer Prize and the National Book Award for *The Armies of the Night: History as a Novel, The Novel as History* (1968).

With the publication of *An American Dream,* Mailer became more than just a literary "bad boy." Kate Millett, in her *Sexual Politics* (1970), attacked Mailer as one of the three most important sexual counterrevolutionaries (Henry Miller and D. H. Lawrence were the other two); he answered charges of misogyny in his polemical counterattack *The Prisoner of Sex* (1971), in which he defended his notions of masculine honor and warned of the "left total-itarianism" of feminism. Rival novelist Gore Vidal in 1971 lumped Miller, Mailer, and Charles Manson together as "M3." Mailer was perfectly happy to be associated with Miller (and in 1976 he edited a warmly appreciative combination of criticism and selections of Miller's best writings, *Genius and Lust*), but he was offended at the way Vidal equated Mailer's interest in psychic outlaws with Manson's murderous violence.

After *An American Dream,* Mailer published *Cannibals and Christians* (1966), another miscellany of nonfiction reviews, self-interviews, and political journalism. The most important essay in the collection is a description of the 1964 Republic National Convention, at which the conservative politician Barry Goldwater was selected as the presidential candidate to oppose Lyndon Baines Johnson. "Into the Red Light" argues that Goldwater was more of a radical than a conservative. Mailer begins in this essay to define his own paradoxical political position, "left conservatism," which he developed further in *The Armies of the Night.*

Mailer's next full-fledged novel was *Why Are We in Vietnam?* (1967). The primary character is a young man named D.J. who is having a going-away dinner at his parents' Dallas mansion on the night before he goes off to fight in Vietnam. There is an Oedipal dimension to this story, as the parents are only too happy to send off this difficult and perhaps even dangerous young man. The novel is Mailer's meditation on the character of American rebellion during the Vietnam era, a story in which Huckleberry Finn is crossbred with the Marquis de Sade—or, one could argue that this novel actually has little or nothing to do with character, since D.J. is a narrative pretext for Mailer to experiment with a baroque range of voices.

D.J. suggests that he is not really an angry young man but is, rather, a black man in Harlem. Or, he argues, he might even be a tape recorder that God is replaying: "the Lord hears your beep, the total of all of you, good and bad, sharp and flat, disharmonies and minor twelfths—wheeze!" Or, D.J. is really Norman Mailer, as Mailer's critical claim in his 1991 review "Children of the Pied Piper" strongly suggests: "To create a character intimately, particularly in the first person, is to convince the reader that the author is the character." D.J. has a consistent and developing personal disposition, but Mailer uses the idea of magical narrative channels between beings in ways that violate conventional notions of character, and so one frequently remembers that the author is speaking, albeit hyperbolically, through a mask.

If conventional ways of developing character are sublimated into style in this novel, the same could be said for politics. No one could possibly attack *Why Are We in Vietnam?* as a conventional political novel or say that, like *Barbary Shore,* it degrades into a tract at any point. Other

Mailer and his sixth wife, Norris Church, whom he married in 1980
(photograph © Corbis/Bettmann)

than the reference to Vietnam in the final pages of the novel, this country is never once directly mentioned, although the parallels to the American conflict in Vietnam, as understood by writers such as Mailer opposed to American involvement, are implicit throughout the text.

In the 1960s Mailer also produced, directed, and starred in three feature-length movies: *Wild 90* (1968), *Beyond the Law* (1968), and *Maidstone* (1969). None of these, however, were commercially released. Between *Why Are We in Vietnam?* and his next novel, Mailer wrote an astonishing variety of books. Works such as *The Armies of the Night; Miami and the Siege of Chicago: An Informal History of the Republican and Democratic Conventions of 1968* (1968); *Of a Fire on the Moon* (1971); *The Prisoner of Sex; St. George and the Godfather* (1972); *Marilyn: A Biography* (1973); and *The Fight* (1975) are nonfictional works that shape factual evidence that is the common property of author and readers. Each of these books, nonetheless, promotes the narrative voice to the level of fictional character, often taking on a shaping persona that is clearly not identical with the author. In talking about himself in the third person in *The Armies of the Night*, Mailer, like his predecessor Henry Adams, foregrounds the ways in which the shaping intelligence behind a work makes rather than finds history. Readers are invited to consider the novelistic imagination as the superior mode through which to consider moon launches, technology, and cultural politics. The radical intuitionist approach in *Marilyn*

is not an attempt to produce a scholarly interpretation of Marilyn Monroe's life; this work, and similar forays into the minds of Muhammad Ali, Henry Miller, and Gary Gilmore boldly argue that, to bend Wallace Stevens's phrase a little, "fiction is the supreme fiction," even when it is nonfiction.

During this period Mailer also wrote political journalism and reworked collections of shorter pieces. *Existential Errands* (1972) and *Pieces and Pontifications* (1982) show Mailer's maturing wit and increasing powers of observation. In *Existential Errands* Mailer expresses his fear that he gives in too much to distraction and so has not produced the "big book" that would prove to the world that he is a major rather than a minor talent. Mailer describes this period of his life as one in which "every thought of beginning a certain big novel which had been promised for a long time, the moot desire to have one's immediate say on contemporary matters kept diverting the novelistic impulse into journalism."

The Armies of the Night and *The Executioner's Song* each won several prizes and wide critical acclaim. Each of these books presents itself as a hybrid of fictional and nonfictional characteristics, and it is significant that Mailer won the Pulitzer Prize for *The Armies of the Night* in the category of nonfiction (1968), but he won the Pulitzer Prize in fiction for *The Executioner's Song* in 1980. Merrill approaches *The Armies of the Night* and *The Executioner's Song* as nonfiction and insists that Mailer's fiction is overshadowed by the celebration of his nonfiction. Mailer made this exact point in *The Armies of the Night* when recounting a discussion between himself and poet Robert Lowell in which Lowell tries to compliment Mailer on being the best journalist in America. Mailer is offended in this episode because of the tacit snub to his achievement as a novelist, as one who imagines rather than as one who merely reports.

In *The Executioner's Song,* which was advertised as a "true-life novel," Mailer did not include himself in the story in any direct way, though his style is often evident even in the documentary-realist language. Though the book won several awards for fiction, it is really a nonfictional account of the life of Gary Gilmore, a convict who spends most of his life in prison, is released, and commits two senseless murders. He does not warrant national attention until, having been sentenced to death, he refuses to appeal his sentence, which threatens to break the de facto moratorium on capital punishment in the United States. The first half of this thousand-page book is called "Western Voices," and it concerns the events of Gilmore's release from prison, his love affair with a woman named Nicole, his mystical ideas and violent temperament, and his murder of a hotel clerk and a gas-station employee during two robberies on consecutive nights. The second half of the book, "Eastern Voices," concerns the media circus that ensues after Gilmore refuses to appeal his death sentence and focuses in large part on Lawrence Schiller, Mailer's partner in previous journalistic ventures. Mailer achieved a complex portrait and claimed Gilmore as an important symbol of American identity; in a 1979 interview with *Publishers Weekly* Mailer said that Gilmore was "malignant at his worst and heroic at his best," and this simultaneity of apparently antithetical qualities accounts for the fascination of the book.

Mailer's next true novel, *Ancient Evenings,* was published to mixed reviews in 1983. This book, written over the course of eleven years, was to have been Mailer's "big book." While critics such as Anthony Burgess and Richard Poirier wrote glowing reviews, Christopher Lehmann-Haupt of *The New York Times* (4 April 1983) captured the ambivalence of many reviewers when, after praising the opening and closing sections, he suggested that the novel "lacks the pace and rhythm of good storytelling." The seven-hundred-page novel is basically the conversation of two ghosts in a tomb, Menenhetet I and his great-grandson Menenhetet II. The younger man has recently died, and he needs to learn from the older man before he can successfully make his way across the River Duad, hopefully to be reborn as a human being. The older man, like Mailer's previous father figures, is a complex blend of integrity and corruption, and the younger man hesitates over whether to place any trust in Menehetet I. This hesitation is evident in one of the main "ancient evenings" the two ghosts discuss at length: the one between Menenhetet I and Ramses IX, in which the pharoah considers making Menehetet I his chief vizier.

Reincarnation is the central metaphor of this novel, as Menenhetet I has the ability to reincarnate himself. Thus, he could be a good chief vizier, as his experience in past lives has been of an astounding variety: he has been a general, a harem master, a grave robber, and a priest. Many of these roles have connections to aspects of Mailer's own life. Menenhetet I dwells on his first life, in which he was an innovative general; Poirier wrote in his 1972 study that "Mailer has remained a war novelist." While J. Michael Lennon finds this statement too sweeping, arguing that "War is not sought for its own sake but only when it offers focus," and that Mailer was an early and severe critic of the war in Vietnam, there is a general consensus that war has been a major influence on Mailer's imagination, including Paul Fussell's discussion of Mailer and Thomas Pynchon in *The Great War and Modern Memory* (1975). Mailer's "first incarnation" as the author of *The Naked and the Dead* also has exerted a strong influence on all of his other "lives." The incarnation as a harem master has an analogue in the Mailer who challenged obscenity laws and wrote books such as *The Prisoner of Sex,* and the reincarnation as a grave robber recalls the charges of morbidity made by reviewers hostile to *Marilyn* and *The Executioner's Song.* In his final life, Menenhetet I hopes that he will finally be granted a leadership role. His hope meets disappointment; and Mailer, from the 1980s on, gave less of himself to public presentations, choosing instead to concentrate on fiction.

The most striking aspect of *Ancient Evenings* is its shocking mixture of styles. Reviewers were impressed by Mailer's gravid prose in "The Book of One Man Dead," although they found the sexually graphic discussion of the intrigues of Egyptian gods bewildering or even inappropriate. Mailer's intentional and playful violation of the notion that Egyptian royalty were as sanctimonious as their surviving art objects represent them to be challenges notions of direct realism; a quotation from Oscar Wilde, used as an epigraph for *Ancient Evenings,* reflects Mailer's efforts precisely: "To give an accurate description of what has never occurred is not merely the proper occupation of the historian, but the inalienable privilege of any man of parts and culture."

Ancient Evenings was originally intended as the first volume of a trilogy, with successive volumes set in the future and in the contemporary era. The second volume was to be "The Boat of Ra" and the third "Modern Times," but Mailer announced at a talk at Brown University in 1984 that he had scuttled this plan; *Ancient Evenings,* he said, "may have to stand alone."

In 1984 Mailer published, instead of a futuristic continuation of his epic novel, a detective novel titled

Dust jacket for Mailer's 1984 novel, whose theme is built on a line by Edwin Arlington Robinson: "There are mistakes too monstrous for remorse" (Richland County Public Library)

Tough Guys Don't Dance. This novel, one of Mailer's nine best-sellers, rose to number four on *The New York Times* best-seller list. Sharing structural and thematic similarities with previous Mailer novels, it begins with an amnesiac narrator and centers on extreme violence. It concerns especially the redefinition of life in the wake of a murder, for protagonist Tim Madden awakens one morning to find an arm tattoo that was not there before and a severed head in his Porsche.

In *Tough Guys Don't Dance* Mailer creates a protagonist similar to Rojack, his tough-guy narrator from *An American Dream,* although there are significant differences between these characters. Whereas Rojack presented himself as a success even if he felt hollow (war hero, congressman, intellectual, and television talk-show host are several of his achieved roles), Tim Madden is truly a failure. He has been to prison for three years on drug charges; his formidably tough father does not feel he is a "tough guy"; he is an unsuccessful writer; and he is in the process of being divorced by his wife, Patty Lareine. In the twenty-four days since his wife left him, he has

wanted to begin a book to be called "In Our Wild–Studies among the Sane," but he is not able to start.

Mailer had satirized glib jet-set dialogue in novels such as *The Deer Park* and stories such as "The Man Who Studied Yoga" from the 1950s and in several subsequent books and essays. What is strikingly different about *Tough Guys Don't Dance* is the degree to which Mailer clearly performs a role that some critics think quite close to Mailer; it is actually quite unlike the nonfictional Norman Mailer. He learned in *The Executioner's Song* to present his own interests and obsessions via other characters (historical beings, in that case) and thus to depersonalize the language that critics and reviewers typically assail for its egotism. The strategic use of fiction to present personal passions in ways that could not be dismissed as merely the author's own narcissistic indulgence is a concern in Mailer's work throughout the 1960s and 1970s. But in *Tough Guys Don't Dance* Mailer is clearly returning to a role he has played before, and one for which he has been criticized. *An American Dream,* written in the wake of Mailer's stabbing of his second wife, affirmed what Richard Slotkin has called, in a 1996 study, "regeneration through violence." Though fraught with risks, such an action is consistent with the amoral musings of Mailer's character Marion Faye in *The Deer Park* and of Mailer himself in "The White Negro." But in *Tough Guys Don't Dance* Mailer writes about a character who fears that he might have committed two murders (another severed head is found in Tim Madden's secret marijuana stash) but ultimately finds that he is not a killer. To consider *Tough Guys Don't Dance* in relation to *An American Dream* is to suggest that Mailer has changed his mind about violence, raising the question of why. Mailer expresses remorse and guilt about the stabbing in his only complete statement about the event, "The Shadow of the Crime": "Murder and its sibling, assault, are the most wanton of the crimes for they mangle the possibilities and expectations open to others."

One of the two epigraphs from *Tough Guys Don't Dance* is a line from Edwin Arlington Robinson: "There are mistakes too monstrous for remorse." While Mailer has said many times that his life went out of control on that day when he stabbed his wife, he consistently romanticizes the psychopathic outlaw in his work. He does not ignore the damage done by such people, but he argues, through a widening series of fictional meditations, that the reality *The Executioner's Song* supposedly documents is complex in ways that mock the presumption of historical comprehension. While Gilmore may look initially like a waste of human life, *The Executioner's Song* gives a thousand pages to the problem of evaluating Gilmore's life; while Mailer may not comment directly in the book on Gilmore's motivation, development, and psychic worth, the book shapes a growing series of sympathetic impressions, concluding with appreciation of the stoic way Gilmore died. For Mailer, as for Samuel Johnson, courage is necessarily the first virtue—and so Mailer celebrates it even in the life of someone such as Gilmore.

Mailer's evaluation of courage is constant from his first book to his most recent, but his defense of the human potential in violent figures such as Gilmore received a shock, perhaps even a fatal one, when Jack Henry Abbott murdered Richard Adan in 1981. Like Gilmore, Abbott was a hardened convict who also had a thoughtful quality with which Mailer could identify. When Mailer was doing research for *The Executioner's Song,* Abbott contacted him and told Mailer that he knew Gilmore and could explain prison life to Mailer. He and Mailer began to correspond, and the result of this exchange was Abbott's best-seller, *In the Belly of the Beast: Letters from Prison* (1981). On the day after winning the Pulitzer Prize for *The Executioner's Song,* Mailer wrote a letter to the parole board of the Utah state penitentiary to help Abbott get parole. Abbott, however, was nowhere

Dust jacket for Mailer's 1991 novel, about two double agents during the Cold War (Richland County Public Library)

near "reformed," and he stabbed Adan over a remark misunderstood as a challenge.

Mailer called a press conference to respond to charges of irresponsibility. Echoing the logic of "The White Negro," he told the press that it was worthwhile and necessary to risk the loss of innocent lives for the sake of great art. He also accepted partial responsibility for the death and called the murder "an absolute tragedy, a hideous waste and horror" (*The New York Times,* 19 January 1982). The *Chicago Tribune* (19 January 1982) quoted his statement that he had "never thought Abbott was close to killing, and that's why I have to sit in judgment on myself." When Abbott was sentenced to fifteen additional years in prison, Mailer commented, "The real question is when does a man expiate his crime." This question is answered by the Robinson epigraph to *Tough Guys Don't Dance:* some mistakes are too monstrous for remorse precisely because remorse, from the safety of retrospection, can only seem self-serving in the face of such huge mistakes. Clearly Mailer believes simple remorse, an after-the-fact expression of regret in conformity to a group's judgment, would be entirely suspect. In *Tough*

Guys Don't Dance Mailer wrote a book in opposition to the affirmations of violence of "The White Negro" and *An American Dream*. Mailer also wrote the screenplay for the 1987 cinematic version of *Tough Guys Don't Dance,* starring Ryan O'Neal and Isabella Rossellini, which Mailer directed.

Mailer wrote no books between *Tough Guys Don't Dance* and his next novel, *Harlot's Ghost: A Novel of the CIA* (1991). This novel draws its title from Mailer's 1976 *New York* magazine essay (later reprinted in *Pieces and Pontifications*) on the Watergate break-in and cover-up, "Of a Harlot High and Low," which itself draws from the title of an Honoré de Balzac novel. The book that flows from the *New York* essay is not nearly as condensed in its effects, although some passages rival the poetic intensity of anything else Mailer has written. The novel is long (more than 1,300 pages); it also takes formal risks, for example, by concluding with the words "TO BE CONTINUED." It is clear in this book, as it was in *Ancient Evenings,* that Mailer is not writing for his contemporary critics, whom he does not trust to evaluate him properly.

Harlot's Ghost falls structurally into two parts, the "Alpha" and the "Omega" manuscripts, and this structural division figuratively represents the idea of the dual personality developed by Harry Hubbard's lover (and then wife), Kittredge. Her theory is that each person is composed of warring elements, the Alpha and the Omega selves. This dual structure recurs at all levels: the book has two stylistically distinct parts; the story (at the level of individual characters) deals with the inner lives of double agents; and the novel represents (in geopolitical terms) the warring entities of the United States and the Soviet Union during the Cold War.

The first section, "Alpha," is, at 150 pages, far shorter than the second. This concise novella has the intensity of a well-written political thriller. At the end of this narrative, a mansion burns to the ground. The second section is 1,100 pages long, composed largely of a voluminous correspondence between Harry and Kittredge. While it includes sections of great interest, it does not display the same sort of dramatic compression. By making these sections structurally parallel and yet dramatically distinct, Mailer balances breadth and depth. In the "Alpha" manuscript he demonstrates that he can present an impressive amount of information in a rather confined space. But in interviews given since the publication of *Ancient Evenings,* Mailer rails against America's culture of interruption and impatience, arguing that profounder meditations such as the encyclopedic modernist novel have a poor chance against media such as the brief journalist article or the MTV video, which cater to the attention-deficit tendencies of the population. With "Alpha" Mailer proves that he could write short, punchy fiction if he wished, and he therefore has done what he

could to earn a hearing for longer novels such as *Ancient Evenings* and *Harlot's Ghost*. Mailer's mature work, however, has not found a broad readership. Novelists Burgess and Salman Rushdie praised *Harlot's Ghost,* but except for John Whalen-Bridge's "Adamic Purity as Double-Agent in *Harlot's Ghost*" (1998), there have been no sustained readings of this work.

Mailer chose, as the basis for his next fictional narrative, one of the most commented-upon texts in history. *The Gospel According to the Son* (1997) is the story of Jesus as presented in a first-person narrative. In an interview with Sean Abbott, Mailer explained that he was visiting his in-laws in Arkansas when he accepted an invitation to a Bible study group. Thinking that he might be resented as a Jew, he was charmed to be received as something more like an elder cousin, and this experience emboldened him to consider the Christian story from his own perspective. This book is completely unlike narratives that burlesque Christianity (such as Vidal's *Live from Golgotha,* 1992), for Mailer puts the necessary boldness of imagining such authority to good literary use. In an early passage Jesus explains why the authors of the Synoptic Gospels did not get it quite right:

> While I would not say that Mark's gospel is false, it has much exaggeration. And I would offer less for Matthew, and for Luke and John, who gave me words I never uttered and described me as gentle when I was pale with rage. Their words were written many years after I was gone and only repeat what old men told them. Very old men. Such tales are to be leaned upon no more than a bush that tears free from its roots and blows about in the wind.

The narrative brings together the revisionist thinking about the New Testament offered by scholars such as Elaine Pagels and by the broad range of scholars involved in the "Jesus Project," but it is also not the case that Mailer has offered a humanized, postmodern Jesus. In Mailer's novel miraculous events occur, and Jesus and some of his followers believe these events signify that he is the Son. Jesus knows the things people say about him, but he is not sure they are true until he wins a battle of minds with Satan, who tempts him with various offerings. Mailer's Jesus criticizes the authors of the Gospels for errors they committed through a weakness in belief: "not one had believed in the Son or in the Father sufficiently to say no more than the Truth."

Mailer's Satan says Mailerian things such as "a hint of disobedience and a whiff of treachery are a way to the joy of life," and in several instances Mailer's revision of the biblical text echoes his other writings. Satan's claims about God's misogyny turn on the discussion of the word "harlot" in Isaiah, presumably in reference to the moral decline of Israel. Satan's comments about the salutary effects of occasional disobedience recall Mailer's frequent promotions of romantic rebellion, but Satan's ideological analysis recalls the practices of modern literary critics. Dramatically, Mailer plays shades of identities against one another to highlight the difficulty of Jesus' position, thus presenting "temptation" in ways that reflect his own career.

Though *The Gospel According to the Son* may at first seem like a bizarre departure even for Mailer, many of its themes are consistent throughout his work. The shifts between the perspective of fathers and sons is perhaps the key unifying theme. Mailer's theological vision is Manichean in *The Gospel According to the Son,* as it has been in all of his books from *The Naked and the Dead* on: "God and Mammon still grapple for the hearts of all men and women. As yet, since the contest remains so equal, neither the Lord nor Satan can triumph. I remain on the right hand of God, and look for greater wisdom than I had before, and I think of many with love." God (and his Son) are not all-powerful in this Manichean cosmology, in which darkness can potentially win and overthrow the forces of light. But Mailer imagines a balance between the forces of good and evil that dignifies the struggle for good in uncertain, existentialist terms; this cosmological balance also has a strong element of "fortunate fall" theology, since by a Darwinian logic in which competition brings out excellence among all the competitors, the presence of evil in the universe enhances the powers of goodness. In the final chapter of this book, in which Jesus, with some uncertainty, recollects his death and ascension from the grave, Mailer maps his narrative of the time of Christ onto the twentieth century, explaining his fidelity to a Manichean cosmology: "Great battles have been lost. In the last century of this second millennium were holocausts, conflagrations, and plagues worse than any that had come before."

Mailer's broad-mindedness is demonstrated again in *The Time of Our Time* (1998), a collection of pieces arranged not according to when they were published but rather according to the historical moment that they treat. This collection, a monument to the range of Mailer's writing life, can also be read as a novel made up of pieces, of found parts artfully arranged. As such, it is a less self-reflexive novel than any of the others Mailer has written since *The Naked and the Dead,* since Mailer chose materials so as to de-emphasize the role of narrative self-creation and to emphasize the evolving story of the postwar United States.

Norman Mailer has developed his Manichean view of moral struggle in the universe into an astonishing variety of forms. This diversity has, as Jennifer Bailey argued in 1979, allowed many critics to claim simplistically that Mailer's forays into a wide range of

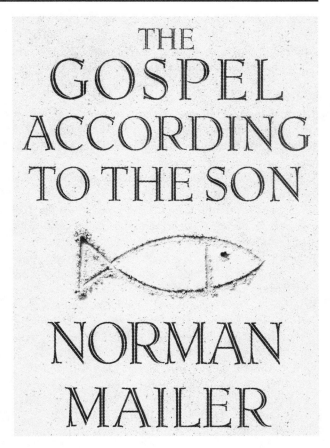

Dust jacket for Mailer's 1997 novel, a first-person narrative version of the life of Jesus (Richland County Public Library)

genres are merely "the amateur efforts of a versatile man." Bailey counters that attempts to pigeonhole Mailer as a novelist, poet, biographer, screenwriter, and so forth tend to "miss the essentially innovatory nature of Mailer's talent," which is perhaps one of the most diverse and underrated.

Interviews:
J. Michael Lennon, ed., *Conversations with Norman Mailer* (Jackson: University of Mississippi Press, 1988);
Sean Abbott, "Mailer Goes to the Mountain," *At Random* (Spring/Summer 1997): 48–55;
Malcolm Jones, "'You're in the Lap of History,'" *Newsweek* (27 January 2003).

Biographies:
Hilary Mills, *Mailer: A Biography* (New York: Empire Books, 1982);
Peter Manso, ed., *Mailer, His Life and Times* (New York: Simon & Schuster, 1985);
Carl Rollyson, *The Lives of Norman Mailer: A Biography* (New York: Paragon House, 1991);

Adele Mailer, *The Last Party: Scenes from My Life with Norman Mailer* (New York: Barricade Books, 1997);

Mary V. Dearborn, *Mailer: A Biography* (New York: Houghton Mifflin, 1999).

References:

Laura Adams, *Existential Battles: The Growth of Norman Mailer* (Athens: Ohio University Press, 1976);

Robert Alter, *Motives for Fiction* (Cambridge, Mass.: Harvard University Press, 1984);

Jennifer Bailey, *Norman Mailer, Quick-Change Artist* (New York: Barnes & Noble, 1979);

Peter Balbert, "From *Lady Chatterley's Lover* to *The Deer Park:* Lawrence, Mailer, and the Dialectics of Erotic Risk," *Studies in the Novel,* 22 (1990): 67–81;

Robert J. Begiebing, *Acts of Regeneration: Allegory and Archetype in the Words of Norman Mailer* (Columbia: University of Missouri Press, 1980);

Begiebing, "The Magician as Tragic Hero," in his *Toward a New Synthesis: John Fowles, John Gardner, Norman Mailer* (Ann Arbor, Mich.: UMI Research Press, 1989);

Harold Bloom, ed., *Norman Mailer: Modern Critical Views* (New York: Chelsea House, 1986);

Leo Braudy, ed., *Norman Mailer: A Collection of Critical Essays* (Englewood Cliffs, N.J.: Prentice-Hall, 1972);

Philip H. Bufithis, *Norman Mailer* (New York: Ungar, 1978);

Anthony Burgess, *99 Novels: The Best in English since 1939* (New York: Summit Books, 1984);

Frederick Busch, "The Whale as Shaggy Dog: Melville and 'The Man Who Studied Yoga,'" *Modern Fiction Studies,* 19 (1986): 193–206;

Samuel Chase Coale, "Melville to Mailer: Manichean Manacles," in his *In Hawthorne's Shadow: American Romance from Melville to Mailer* (Lexington: University Press of Kentucky, 1985), pp. 22–45;

Morris Dickstein, *Gates of Eden: American Culture in the Sixties* (Chicago: Basic Books, 1977);

Dickstein, *Leopards in the Temple: The Transformation of American Fiction, 1945–1970* (Cambridge: Harvard University Press, 2002), pp. 33–37, 150–162, 190–208;

Judith Fetterley, "*An American Dream:* 'Hula, Hula,' Said the Witches," in her *The Resisting Reader: A Feminist Approach to American Fiction* (Bloomington: Indiana University Press, 1978);

Leslie Fiedler, "Going for the Long Ball," *Psychology Today* (June 1983): 16–17;

Paul Fussell, *The Great War and Modern Memory* (New York: Oxford University Press, 1975);

Andrew Gordon, *An American Dreamer: A Psychoanalytic Study of the Fiction of Norman Mailer* (Rutherford, N.J.: Fairleigh Dickinson University Press, 1980);

Stanley T. Gutman, *Mankind in Barbary* (Hanover, N.H.: University Press of New England, 1975);

Bernard Horn, "Ahab and Ishmael at War: The Presence of *Moby-Dick* in *The Naked and the Dead,*" *American Quarterly,* 34 (1982): 379–385;

Kathryn Hume, *American Dream, American Nightmare: Fiction since 1960* (Urbana: University of Illinois, 2000);

Diane Johnson, "Death for Sale: Norman Mailer on Gary Gilmore," in her *Terrorists and Novelists* (New York: Knopf, 1982), pp. 87–96;

Alfred Kazin, *Bright Book of Life: American Novelists and Storytellers from Hemingway to Mailer* (Boston: Little, Brown, 1973);

Barry Leeds, *The Enduring Vision of Norman Mailer* (New York: Pleasure Boat Studio, 2002);

Leeds, *The Structured Vision of Norman Mailer* (New York: New York University Press, 1969);

Nigel Leigh, *Radical Fictions and the Novels of Norman Mailer* (New York: St. Martin's Press, 1990);

J. Michael Lennon, ed., *Critical Essays on Norman Mailer* (Boston: G. K. Hall, 1986);

Lennon, ed., *Works and Days* (Shavertown, Pa.: Sligo Press, 2000);

Robert F. Lucid, "Crow's Nest Cottages, North Truro, 1946," *Provincetown Arts,* 14 (1999): 32–33;

Robert Merrill, *Norman Mailer Revisited* (New York: Twayne, 1992);

Stacey Olster, "Norman Mailer: A New Frontier in Fiction," in her *Reminiscence and Re-creation in Contemporary American Fiction* (Cambridge & New York: Cambridge University Press, 1989);

Donald E. Pease, "Citizen Vidal and Mailer's America," *Raritan,* 11 (1992): 72–98;

Norman Podhoretz, *Ex-Friends: Falling Out with Allen Ginsberg, Lionel and Diana Trilling, Lillian Hellman, Hannah Arendt, and Norman Mailer* (New York: Free Press, 1999), pp. 178–220;

Richard Poirier, *Norman Mailer* (New York: Viking, 1972);

Jean Radford, *Norman Mailer: A Critical Study* (London: Macmillan, 1975);

Thomas H. Schaub, *American Fiction in the Cold War* (Madison: University of Wisconsin Press, 1990);

Robert Solotaroff, *Down Mailer's Way* (Urbana: University of Illinois, 1974);

Tony Tanner, "On the Parapet: A Study of the Novels of Norman Mailer," in his *City of Words: American Fiction, 1950–1970* (New York: Harper & Row, 1971);

Joseph Wenke, *Mailer's America* (Hanover, N.H.: University Press of New England, 1987);

John Whalen-Bridge, "Adamic Purity as Double-Agent in *Harlot's Ghost,*" in his *Political Fiction and the American Self* (Urbana: University of Illinois Press, 1998), pp. 103–130.

Armistead Maupin

(13 May 1944 –   )

Samuel Gaustad
Phillips Community College of the University of Arkansas

BOOKS: *Tales of the City* (New York: Harper & Row, 1978; London: Corgi, 1980);
More Tales of the City (New York: Harper & Row, 1980; London: Corgi, 1984);
Further Tales of the City (New York: Harper & Row, 1982; London: Corgi, 1984);
Babycakes (New York: Harper & Row, 1984; London: Corgi, 1986);
Significant Others (New York: Perennial Library, 1987; London: Chatto & Windus, 1988);
Sure of You (New York: Harper & Row, 1989; London: Chatto & Windus, 1990);
Tales of the City, More Tales of the City, Further Tales of the City: An Omnibus (London: Chatto & Windus, 1989); republished as *28 Barbary Lane: A Tales of the City Omnibus* (New York: HarperCollins, 1990);
Omnibus II (London: Chatto & Windus, 1990)—comprises *Babycakes, Significant Others,* and *Sure of You;* republished as *Back to Barbary Lane: The Tales of the City Omnibus* (New York: HarperCollins, 1991);
Maybe the Moon (New York: HarperCollins, 1992; London: Bantam, 1993);
The Night Listener (New York: HarperCollins, 2000; London: Bantam, 2000).

PRODUCED SCRIPT: *The Celluloid Closet,* narration by Maupin, story by Rob Epstein, Jeffrey Friedman, and Sharon Wood, from Vito Russo's book, motion picture, Home Box Office, 1996.

RECORDINGS: *Babycakes,* read by Maupin, Harper Audio, 1990;
Significant Others, read by Maupin, Harper Audio, 1990;
Sure of You, read by Maupin, Harper Audio, 1990;
Maybe the Moon, read by Maupin, Harper Audio, 1992;
Tales of the City Audio Collection, read by Maupin, Harper Audio, 2000—includes *Tales of the City, More Tales of the City, Further Tales of the City, Babycakes, Significant Others,* and *Sure of You.*

Armistead Maupin (photograph © Greg Gorman; from the dust jacket for Significant Others, *1987)*

OTHER: David Deitcher, ed., *The Question of Equality: Lesbian and Gay Politics in America since Stonewall,* foreword by Maupin (New York: Scribners, 1995);
Susan Stryker and Jim Van Buskirk, *Gay by the Bay: A History of Queer Culture in the San Francisco Bay Area,* foreword by Maupin (San Francisco: Chronicle Books, 1996);
James J. Berg and Chris Freeman, eds., *The Isherwood Century: Essays on the Life and Work of Christopher*

Isherwood, foreword by Maupin (Madison: University of Wisconsin Press, 2000);

Clive Barker, *The Essential Clive Barker: Selected Fiction,* foreword by Maupin (New York: HarperCollins, 2000).

Armistead Maupin has established himself as one of the best-known openly gay contemporary American writers. He creates realistic gay male characters who share the same fears and joys that are central to all human experience. While Maupin's work is informed by political issues in general and the gay-rights movement in particular, he avoids becoming overtly didactic and political through his use of humor, crisp dialogue, and witty repartee. In a 23 November 1992 interview for *Christopher Street* Maupin told Scott A. Hunt: "I think the greatest challenge of a writer is to be able to combine the serious issues and serious concerns with comedy." Maupin's characters, whom he consistently imbues with a sense of personal warmth, are multifaceted. Although Maupin is predominantly known as a gay writer, he does not limit himself to depicting the lifestyle of the gay male. As he stated in an interview with Jean W. Ross for *Contemporary Authors:* "My aim from the very beginning was to create a large framework of humanity and to place gay characters within that framework." By dealing with a wide variety of character types, including heterosexuals, gay men, lesbians, transsexuals, African Americans, and dwarfs, Maupin creates a world that is distinctly inclusive and encompassing, rather than exclusive and elite. As Walter Kendrick stated in the 10 October 1989 *Village Voice Literary Supplement:* "From the start, he has sought to portray a microcosm in which every sexual bent—homo-, hetero-, bi-, trans-, and undecided—coexists amid comprehensive love and respect." Even though Maupin's work is time- and place-specific, his creation of realistic characters engaged in everyday interactions gives his writing a universal appeal.

The oldest of three children, Armistead Jones Maupin Jr. was born on 13 May 1944 in Washington, D.C. to Armistead Jones Maupin Sr., a Southern aristocratic lawyer, and Diana Jane Barton Maupin, of English descent. His brother, Tony, and sister, Jane, were born four and five years later, respectively. "Teddy," the nickname by which Maupin was called throughout his childhood, was raised in a fairly conservative family in Raleigh, North Carolina. Until the age of twelve he attended Ravenscroft, an Episcopal parochial school in Raleigh, after which he matriculated at Josephus Daniels Junior High School. The social climate in the South during Maupin's youth was one of segregation and extreme conservatism, and his father maintained the status quo. As an adolescent secretly

harboring physical and romantic feelings for the same sex, Maupin experienced the pressures of such a society; he told biographer Patrick Gale, "I'd read somewhere that homosexuality was a mental illness, so I tried to work up the nerve to tell my parents before it was too late to fix me. But the thought of doing that was too frightening." After high school Maupin attended the University of North Carolina at Chapel Hill, graduating in 1966. He remained in Chapel Hill, entering law school there, but soon found that he had no taste for law. Following his departure from Chapel Hill, Maupin entered the United States Navy, served in the Vietnam War, and was ultimately awarded a Presidential Commendation by Richard Nixon for his work with Southeast Asian refugees.

Leaving the navy in 1970, he returned to the South and worked as a writer for the *Charleston News and Courier* in South Carolina. After a year there, Maupin landed a job as an agency writer in the San Francisco office of the Associated Press, staying only about a year. Following this stint, Maupin held several short-lived positions, including a job as a mail boy at the ad agency Hoefer, Dietrich, and Brown. His intent was to work his way up through the company, but his enthusiasm and creativity were not appreciated, and he was soon let go. In 1973 Maupin accepted a position as an account executive at Lowry Russom and Leeper, where he wrote copy for about a year.

Maupin ultimately drew on these experiences as source material. In 1974 Maupin's *Tales of the City* series was born as a weekly column, titled simply "The Serial," in the San Francisco edition of the *Pacific Sun.* However, after only five weeks the paper folded, so he took a position as a publicist for the San Francisco Opera, writing a regular column called "The Prompter's Box." Then the *San Francisco Chronicle* picked up the serial, and the first four volumes of the series—*Tales of the City* (1978), *More Tales of the City* (1980), *Further Tales of the City* (1982), and *Babycakes* (1984)—appeared initially in serial form in that paper. In 1986 the serial was continued at the *San Francisco Examiner,* and in 1989 *Sure of You,* the sixth and final volume of the series, was published as an independent novel.

Serialized fiction is most commonly associated with the nineteenth century and Charles Dickens, an author Maupin holds in high regard. After achieving its greatest popularity in the Victorian era through the writings of such authors as Dickens and Anthony Trollope, the serial as a form of fiction declined markedly in the early part of the twentieth century. Although the general appeal of this genre waned, it by no means disappeared completely. Shawn Crawford suggested in a 1998 essay that serialized fiction was kept at least somewhat active during the twentieth century through the serialization of children's literature and the more romantic serials published in mainstream magazines for women. In the broader scope, however, the idea of the serial was adopted, absorbed, and made popular by movies and television. Crawford credits Maupin with "leading the renaissance" of serialized fiction in mainstream literature. *Tales of the City* was followed by such works as Tom Wolfe's *The Bonfire of the Vanities,* first published as a serial in *Rolling Stone* in 1987, and Stephen King's *The Green Mile,* published in six monthly installments between April and September of 1996.

The serials of the Victorian era generally tended to present narrow and restrictive definitions of acceptable morality and family structure within the established society, which castigated and ostracized any who deviated from the accepted norm. Aberrant behavior was viewed inflexibly as abhorrent and deplorable. Maupin's use of the serial form becomes ironic in this context. He has used this form, widely associated with a society often characterized as morally conservative and exclusive, to call into question long-accepted values. Maupin creates gray areas as a means of expanding the limitations and broadening the spectrum of acceptable sexual identities and, at the same time, redefining an appropriate type of family center. In his *Tales of the City* series, Maupin embraces a world in which being gay, lesbian, or transsexual is far from deplorable and is, in fact, quite acceptable, indeed often the norm. Also within this world, the traditional definition of "family" is questioned; surrogate families are created according to individuals' needs rather than as a mere consequence of circumstance or biology. As Maupin told Ross, "The myth that America is composed solely of these classic nuclear families is just that, a myth."

In a 1999 essay Robyn R. Warhol argues that in *Tales of the City* "serial formal conventions enable the series to accomplish significant antihomophobic cultural work. In an ironic twist worthy of one of his own outrageous plots, Maupin appropriates serial form . . . to propagate a profoundly anti-'Victorian,' anticonventional vision of sexual life." Warhol suggests that because the serial form is inherently episodic and thus resists clear endings or a strong sense of closure, Maupin was able to use this structure as a means of creating a "queer plot that reconfigures families, couples, and coupling in antitraditional and unpredictable patterns."

Maupin's *Tales of the City* series incorporates the basic elements of episodic plot structure, including the extensive use of intertwined subplots and a proliferation of events, locales, and characters. Warhol explains that in addition to the plot structure, Maupin has appropriated other conventions generally associated with nineteenth-century serialized fiction: "wild coincidences, melodramatic events, open-ended plots, recur-

ring characters, and cliff-hanger action." These characteristics are useful, even necessary, in the serial form and are effective devices for drawing readers into the action, creating a sense of anticipation and a strong need for the audience to return for the next installment. As Crawford states: "Making readers wait gives them a stake in the novel in a way that no other form of publication does." While many of these conventions often hold negative connotations in the present, Maupin avoids a type of writing that could be considered trite or contrived. Through his use of contemporary settings and current events, characters, and language, Maupin makes the conventions of serialized fiction palatable for present-day audiences.

The *Tales of the City* series, centered in and around San Francisco, uses actual landmarks such as Fisherman's Wharf, Telegraph Hill, Golden Gate Park, and the Pacific Union Club. Five primary characters appear throughout all six volumes of the series: Anna Madrigal, Michael Tolliver, Mary Ann Singleton, Brian Hawkins, and Mona Ramsey. These characters, embodying the transsexual, homosexual, heterosexual, and bisexual, form the surrogate family in residence at 28 Barbary Lane, the central locale. Anna, the landlady of the property, serves as the matriarch of the family, consistently showing concern and compassion for her tenants, or, as she refers to them, her "children." The action, however, is not solely limited to San Francisco. Characters travel around America and abroad, adding a layer of geographic color and interest to the work. In *More Tales of the City* Mona travels to Winnemucca, Nevada, offering a major contrast to the cosmopolitan world of San Francisco. Mary Ann and Michael embark on a Mexican cruise in the same volume. In *Further Tales of the City* Michael tours with the San Francisco Gay Men's Chorus, stopping in several cities, including Dallas and Minneapolis. Continuing his escapades in *Babycakes,* Michael travels to London and exchanges apartments for a month with another man. And finally, in *Sure of You,* Mona and Anna search for love on the Greek Isle of Lesbos. In each location outside of San Francisco, Maupin infuses the scenes with such vivid description and detail that the reader can only assume he is writing from experience.

The list of characters presented in Maupin's *Tales of the City* series is immense; they appear, disappear, and reappear throughout the series, connecting and overlapping in surprising and complex configurations. Many are intelligent, articulate, and witty, such as Anna, who quotes F. Scott Fitzgerald and Alfred Tennyson, adding an element of sophistication to the writing. In many instances, Maupin supplies enough background information about each character to explain and often justify the environmental and inherited motivations for their

Maupin in 1969, during river-patrol service with the United States Navy in Vietnam (Armistead Maupin Collection)

actions in the present. Even though the reader is ultimately given all necessary information by the end of the series, the expository material is presented gradually. As a result, some of Maupin's characters maintain a certain air of mystery throughout much of the work. Maupin refrains from any overt moralizing through his characters, a quality often associated with serialized fiction; clear-cut delineations of good and evil are, for the most part, avoided. With few exceptions, Maupin allows readers to make their own judgments.

As an integral part of episodic plot structure, the *Tales of the City* series is presented in a third-person voice, offering the reader glimpses into the thoughts and feelings of multiple characters. This semi-omniscient point of view makes the work accessible to a wider audience. Two characters in particular, Anna and Michael, function as *raisonneurs* for Maupin. Through Anna's consolatory or reminiscent conversations with other characters, Maupin offers the reader glimpses of his view of the human condition. In *More Tales of the City* Anna imparts philosophical advice and wisdom to Mona: "Loosen up, dear! Don't be so afraid to cry . . . or laugh, for that matter. Laugh all you want and cry all you want and whistle at pretty men in the street and to *hell* with anybody who thinks you're a damned fool!" Likewise,

Michael is used to articulate Maupin's feelings about the joys and difficulties of being gay. Over the course of a decade, Michael gradually reaches higher levels of self-understanding, as well as the acceptance of his own sexuality, and he rarely, if ever, becomes self-pitying.

Although Maupin embraces the idea of created families, such as the one at 28 Barbary Lane, he does not dismiss the traditional family structure. Anna eventually confronts her past, heals the long-standing familial wounds, and reunites with her mother and daughter. From this point forward, the created and traditional families function synchronously. The most eclectic, eccentric, and mysterious of the characters, Anna is a free spirit, growing her own marijuana plants and naming them after famous women she admires. In fact, Maupin uses Anna's penchant for gardening as an external manifestation of her nurturing personality. The great mystery surrounding Anna is that she was, in actuality, Andy Ramsey, Mona's father. As the reader discovers in *More Tales of the City,* Andy, having become a "miserable, self-pitying creature who had botched his own life and the lives of people around him," underwent a sex-change operation at age forty-four and reemerged as Anna Madrigal. At the end of *More Tales of the City,* Anna reveals to Mona that her new name is actually an anagram for "A MAN AND A GIRL." Maupin's inspiration for this indomitable, positive-natured character was his maternal grandmother, Marguerite Smith Barton; she was not a transsexual, but as Maupin related to Gale, "the whole idea of Anna Madrigal, was based on her spirit."

Michael "Mouse" Tolliver, a San Francisco transplant originally from Orlando, Florida, first appeared as Michael Huxtable in the original five columns written for the *Pacific Sun.* When the *San Francisco Chronicle* picked up the serial, Michael did not appear until after the thirtieth installment. As Gale has stated: "Armistead had decided to downplay *Tales'* gay content until he knew he could feel securely wedged in the paper's pages." Michael is a gay man in his twenties, searching for the ideal mate. Of all the characters in the series, he is the one who most personifies the idea of quintessential romantic longing. Realistically for the time, Michael goes through a series of short-lived sexual encounters that he hopes will turn into affairs of the heart. Ultimately Michael, not the heterosexual couples, enters a relationship that most resembles a healthy, functioning marriage. In *Tales of the City* Maupin presents the reader with a classic scenario, but with a twist. Michael literally runs into Dr. Jon Fielding at the roller rink, and the resulting scenario is "boy meets boy, boy loses boy"; not until *More Tales of the City* is Michael reunited with Jon in a "boy-gets-boy" resolution. The relationship has dissolved by *Further Tales of the City,* and, after Jon's death between this volume and *Babycakes,* Michael is paired with Thack Sweeney in *Significant Others* (1987), the two forming a lasting partnership in *Sure of You.*

Mary Ann Singleton appears in the opening scene of *Tales of the City.* Of the five primary characters in the series, Mary Ann undergoes the most apparent change, both externally and internally. The key to Mary Ann's development lies in her openness and naiveté, which she loses by the end of the series. At the onset, she is an unsophisticated twenty-five-year-old from Cleveland, Ohio, characterized by a general state of bewilderment. She has come to San Francisco on vacation and decides to stay, much to her mother's chagrin. Maupin uses her gradual ascent up the employment ranks to plot her development as a character. At the beginning of *Tales of the City* she takes a job as a secretary for Halcyon Communications, an advertising agency; by the beginning of *Further Tales of the City* she becomes hostess of a local television program, *Bargain Matinee;* by the beginning of *Babycakes,* she has landed her own show on a local television station; in *Significant Others* she appears on *Entertainment Tonight* in a feature spot; and, finally, in *Sure of You,* she leaves her husband and daughter to become host of a syndicated talk show based in New York. Throughout the series, this naive character gradually becomes sophisticated and worldly but also cold, self-involved, and somewhat callous. Maupin uses Mary Ann to comment on the negative effects of becoming an upwardly mobile, career-minded individual in the 1980s. As Kendrick observed: "For Maupin, it seems, taking the '80's seriously means turning into a cold-hearted bitch."

Brian Hawkins, another inhabitant of 28 Barbary Lane, is a waiter at Perry's Restaurant, a job that he holds for more than six years. In keeping with the times, Maupin created Brian as a sexually promiscuous, albeit frustrated, young man in his twenties, maintaining the veneer of a womanizer. Not until well into *Tales of the City* does the reader discover the depth of Brian's persona, as Brian confesses to Mary Ann his previous employment in and disdain for the legal profession: "I *hated* law. It was the causes I loved . . . and . . . well, I ran out of them." Upon first meeting, Mary Ann reacts to Brian with extreme caution. By the beginning of *Further Tales of the City,* however, Maupin has coupled the two characters, and by the end of the volume they are married. Unable to conceive because of Brian's infertility, Mary Ann and Brian adopt a daughter at the end of *Babycakes,* and a traditional family unit is formed. The couple experience their share of conflict and, unable to come to any satisfactory resolution, they dissolve their marriage at the end of *Sure of You.*

In the world of Maupin's series, where gays, lesbians, bisexuals, and transsexuals abound, Brian becomes a marginal figure. Still, Maupin's sympathetic treatment of Brian is related to his view of heterosexual men, as he expressed to Elgy Gillespie in a 1989 interview for the *San Francisco Review of Books:* "straight men are the last oppressed minority because they're the last to have their lives explained to them. Straight men got sold a bill of goods, like women, and haven't been shown anything in its place yet." In contrast to Mary Ann, Brian is neither upwardly mobile nor career-minded; he holds only two different jobs throughout the series, neither of which is high-profile. His internal development as a character is almost the complete inverse of his wife's: Brian gradually becomes softer, more human, and fatherly in contrast to Mary Ann's hardening. Through this relationship, Maupin demonstrates that the "traditional" family is not always the most perfect or effective one.

Mona Ramsey is also one of Anna's "children," figuratively and literally. She is the resident bisexual of 28 Barbary Lane, and, like Anna, she is a free and independent spirit. Maupin told Gale that a copywriter from Hoefer, Dietrich, and Brown, known to her coworkers as the "Resident Freak," served as the inspiration for this unconventional character. Born and raised in Minneapolis, Mona was employed by Halcyon Communications, but as Maupin explains in *More Tales of the City:* "she had been relieved of that position following a brief, but satisfying, feminist tirade against the president of Adorable Pantyhose, the ad agency's biggest client." Mona does not reveal her sexuality until well into *Tales of the City.* She explains to Michael why she had not shared this information earlier: "It never really seemed important, I guess. I wasn't exactly . . . into that scene. I was a lousy dyke." D'orthea Wilson, Mona's former lover, returns from New York, and the two briefly rekindle their affair. Disillusioned by the relationship, Mona returns to Barbary Lane at the beginning of *More Tales of the City,* only to flee impetuously to Nevada. On the bus, Mona is offered and accepts a position as receptionist at the Blue Moon Lodge, Mother Mucca's brothel. Through a series of coincidences, the truth about Mona's lineage is revealed: she is actually Mother Mucca's granddaughter, the son of Andy Ramsey. Maupin complicates this situation even further at the end of *More Tales of the City:* in a showdown between Mona's mother, Betty Ramsey, and Anna, Maupin reveals that Andy Ramsey was not actually Mona's biological father. After making a brief connection with Brian, thanks to Anna's matchmaking efforts, Mona disappears completely from *Further Tales of the City.* At the opening of *Babycakes,* Mona is residing in Seattle; she later resurfaces in England, married to Lord Roughton and living as the lady of the manor. Throughout the series, the reader often senses that Mona, in contrast to Anna, has yet to come to terms with her own adventuresome spirit.

Secondary characters in the series are plentiful. Of particular interest are the Halcyons, a wealthy, dysfunctional traditional family. Maupin presents the distinctive emotional baggage of each family member as a means of explaining the overall dysfunction. Edgar Halcyon is the owner of Halcyon Communications and patriarch of the family. At the start of the novel, he is characterized as a typical advertising mogul, somewhat stodgy and uptight. Facing his impending death from cancer at the end of *Tales of the City,* Edgar enters into a liaison with Anna. Through his intimate connection with the free-spirited Anna, Edgar's perspective is altered, and he reverts to the warm, open person he had once been.

Frannie Halcyon, the matriarch of the family, begins the series as an active alcoholic who has shut herself off from any significant connection with the outside world. Sinking into an immobilizing depression after Edgar's death, she is inducted into "Pinus," an exclusive club for wealthy women aged sixty and over. The sexual implications of the club name prove to be a significant life-affirming experience for Frannie, and by *Significant Others* she has married Roger "Booter" Manigault. Although she maintains many of the reserved qualities of a matriarch throughout much of the series, she is able to rejoin society after Edgar's death and acquire a newfound sense of adventure.

DeDe Halcyon Day, daughter of Edgar and Frannie, undergoes one of the most complicated and profound metamorphoses in the series. Seemingly powerless at the beginning of the series, she steadily grows stronger and more self-assured as she sheds her vacuous socialite upbringing. At the beginning of *Tales of the City* DeDe has perfected the veneer considered appropriate for a high-society debutante. Maupin characterizes her as a miserable, emotionally and sexually frustrated young woman, who is plagued by bouts of compulsive overeating in response to her loveless marriage to Beauchamp Day. In a moment of desperation, DeDe orders yet more binge food to be delivered, seduces the Asian grocery boy, Lionel Wong, and becomes pregnant with twins. She decides to have the babies, despite the fact that their lineage will be obvious to the rest of the world. Unable to cope with her husband's ever-increasing detachment, DeDe returns home to her mother in *More Tales of the City,* meets D'orthea Wilson, and, in a blatant rejection of propriety, the women become lovers. They join forces to raise the twins and remain together throughout the rest of the series. Although the couple has their share of disagreements, this healthy, nontraditional family unit serves as a major contrast to the dysfunctional, traditional Halcyons.

In contrast to his wife, Beauchamp Day does not change during the two novels he inhabits. The reader is given the impression that he has married into the Halcyon family for its wealth, power, and prestige. Beauchamp is a handsome, self-absorbed young man whose life is based completely on pretension. Beauchamp values social success, viewing it as directly proportionate to the degree of illusion one is able to create. Always the smooth operator, he seduces the naive Mary Ann to join him for a weekend getaway in Mendocino. Beauchamp proves unable to perform, however, and the liaison is never successfully consummated. Maupin is foreshadowing the truth about Beauchamp's sexuality and offering the reader an insight into the loveless quality of the Days' marriage. At the end of *Tales of the City* Beauchamp appears at the gay baths, having just engaged in a sexual liaison with another man. In *More Tales of the City* Beauchamp succumbs to the impending social disgrace that the Asian American twins will cause and makes arrangements with a lowlife drug dealer to have his wife roughed up so that she will miscarry. The attack is averted, however, when Beauchamp is killed in a car crash toward the end of the novel. Through his depiction of Beauchamp Day, Maupin demonstrates his views on the destructive effects caused by the denial of one's sexuality, not only on the individual but also on those surrounding him.

Many other characters populate the series, each presented as an individual with particular eccentricities. Norman Neal Williams appears only in *Tales of the City;* he is a private investigator hired by Betty Ramsey to uncover the true identity of Anna Madrigal. He is also a child pornographer. By pairing Williams with the naive Mary Ann and using her as a foil, Maupin magnifies Williams's negative characteristics and helps Mary Ann to become worldlier.

Burke Andrew, an amnesiac, is introduced on the Mexican cruise in *More Tales of the City.* Drawing on his experience with the Associated Press, Maupin created Burke as a former AP reporter. Burke and Mary Ann are paired romantically until Burke leaves San Francisco to accept a position in New York. Burke disappears from the series until *Sure of You,* when he returns as an influential television producer to offer Mary Ann her own syndicated talk show after her marriage to Brian. Through their involvement and exhaustive search for the cause of Burke's amnesia, Maupin is able to accelerate Mary Ann's psychological development throughout the volume.

Prue Giroux, a society gossip columnist, plays a prominent role throughout *Further Tales of the City.* Also introduced in that volume is Father Paddy Starr, host of *Honest to God,* a religious program aired by the same local television station that employs Mary Ann. As a gossipy cohort of Prue's, he is involved in all aspects of San Franciscan society. Maupin often uses Prue and

Father Paddy as comic relief for the more serious moments of the volume.

Babycakes introduces three British characters: Simon Bardill, Lord Teddy Roughton, and Miss Treves. Simon is a British Brian Hawkins counterpart who deserts Her Majesty's Navy in San Francisco. Mary Ann befriends Simon and, since Brian is infertile, seduces Simon in hopes of becoming pregnant. Simon, however, has had a vasectomy. Lord Teddy Roughton marries Mona to preserve appearances, then heads for San Francisco to explore the gay life there. Miss Treves, described as "no taller than the doorknob," is a royal manicurist and Simon's mother. This character was based on Tamara De Treaux, an actress friend of Maupin's who requested he write a character that she could play when the series was filmed. All of these characters, because of their individual peculiarities, add tremendous color and depth to the tapestry of the series.

Maupin often uses minor characters to comment on contemporary society. The group he chooses to handle the most satirically is the elite society of San Francisco. Maupin demonstrates, particularly in *Tales of the City,* how the upper class tends to exploit minorities. Drawing on his experiences as a publicist for the San Francisco Opera, he created the "A-Gays," a group of wealthy, pretentious, and often vicious "opera queens." Dr. Jon Fielding belongs to this clique. At a dinner party Jon is questioned about his involvement with Michael. The guests at the party saw Michael dance in an underwear contest at The Endup, and have no qualms about haughtily pointing out Michael's inferior social status to Jon. His response is to reject the A-Gays' supercilious remarks as he exits the party.

Earlier in *Tales of the City,* DeDe Day attends her first luncheon at The Forum, satirically described by Maupin as "a rarefied gathering of concerned matrons who met monthly to discuss topics of Major Social Significance." The topic for this particular meeting is rape; earlier topics had been "alcoholism, lesbianism and the plight of female grape-pickers." The group's special guest is Velma Runningwater, "a Native American who successfully defended herself against an attempted gang rape by sixteen members of the Hell's Angels in Petaluma." Through his inclusion of detailed descriptions of the menu being served, Maupin creates a vivid image of the gathering. He contrasts these society women with Velma, who never actually speaks in the scene, making it clear that the women of The Forum have no intimate understanding of their guest whatsoever, nor any genuine desire to gain any. She is simply there to add a touch of "color" to the self-serving matrons' fatuous meeting. In these two brief scenes, Maupin is able to share his views on the prejudices with which he grew

Maupin and his sister, Jane, in the North Beach neighborhood of San Francisco, 1981 (Armistead Maupin Collection)

up and, at the same time, satirize the patronizing and exploitative behavior of the gentry.

D'orthea Wilson, although not a minor character, serves as Maupin's most complex statement on the exploitation of minorities. She enters the series initially as an African American supermodel. By the end of *Tales of the City,* however, D'orthea confesses to Mona that she is not actually African American. Born to white, working-class parents in Oakland, Dorothy Wilson moved to New York but was unable to obtain any substantial modeling jobs. After she was photographed in dark makeup, however, people started asking for the "foxy black chick." Keenly aware of the climate of the late 1970s, when being of color was a marketable commodity for advertisers, D'orthea simply reacted. Having naturally dark coloring, D'orthea took pills normally used to treat vitiligo, the partial or total loss of skin pigmentation. The pills, combined with periodic ultraviolet treatments, gave her the appearance of being black. Her plan proved successful, and D'orthea spent five years with the Eileen Ford Agency. Growing tired of constantly having to maintain the elaborate charade, she returned to San Francisco to change back to the real Dorothy. Her driving force for this elaborate deception is finally divulged to DeDe at the end of *More Tales of the City:* "I wanted money so bad I dyed my skin black to get it." Through D'orthea's dialogue, Maupin points to the commodification of minorities typical of Madison Avenue in the 1970s.

In *Tales of the City* Michael's parents decide to pay a visit at an inopportune time for Michael, who is still closeted as far as his parents are concerned. He wonders if he will be able to "protect their fragile, *Reader's Digest* sensibilities from The Love That Dares Not Speak Its Name." Although this visit is the only actual appearance Herb and Alice Tolliver make, Maupin continues the communication between mother and son through the use of letters in *More Tales of the City.* Early in the novel, Michael receives a letter from his mother in which she mentions that she has signed up as a supporter of Anita Bryant's homophobic Save Our Children Campaign. Later in the volume, Michael receives another letter from his mother while he is hospitalized. In this letter Alice, now an active supporter of Bryant, unknowingly denounces her son as she continues her tirade against homosexuals: "If homosexuals are allowed to teach in Miami, then it might happen in Orlando . . . the devil is a lot more powerful than we think he is." In response, Michael finally writes his coming-out letter to his mother, expressing "my responsibility to tell you the truth, that your own child is homosexual, and that I never needed saving from anything except the cruel and ignorant piety of people like Anita Bryant." This mother-son confrontation occurs while Michael is paralyzed as a result of Guillain-Barré syndrome, suggesting a physical manifestation of Michael's inner psychological and emotional conflict with his parents. After he finishes this coming-out letter, Michael's body slowly regains its vitality. The relationship between son and parents, however, is never completely healed.

According to Gale, Michael's letter was intended by Maupin as his own coming-out to his parents; he knew they subscribed to the *San Francisco Chronicle* at the time. Gale explains, however, that Maupin's parents actually "found out through *Newsweek,* when he agreed to be identified as a 'gay journalist' in a story on beauty-queen-turned-homophobe, Anita Bryant." Michael's letter had a major impact on the gay community. Gale reports that "hundreds of gay readers of the *Chronicle* . . . chose to cut out the second year's episode titled 'Letter to Mama' and mail it to unsuspecting folks back home with a 'me too' as a postscript." Serving as the paradigm of coming-out letters, this excerpt was subsequently published in *40 Contemporary Lesbian and Gay Short Stories* in 1994.

As an openly gay writer, Maupin expressed his views to Gillespie about the need for gay men to publicly acknowledge their sexuality: "I still feel very strongly that closet gays should be more or less blackmailed out of the closet. But the trick, of course, is to do it with joy in your heart and a smile on your face and never to actually name names literally." That is precisely how Maupin dealt with the issue in *Further Tales of the City.* Maupin's most poignant statement on the subject is his inclusion of Michael's involvement with a closeted Hollywood star, referred to only as _____, which runs throughout much of the volume. Written before Rock Hudson's death from AIDS in 1986, the volume never actually names him. Maupin did, however, base this subplot on his own experiences with Hudson and maintains that his intent was criticism of closeted Hollywood stars in general and not Hudson in particular. Maupin's views on the importance for gays to be open about their sexuality led to his writing the narration for the 1996 movie version of Vito Russo's 1981 chronicle of Hollywood portrayals of homosexuality, *The Celluloid Closet.*

Typical of serialized fiction, Maupin's *Tales of the City* series uses many subplots, which add a density to the texture, and several outrageous plot complications, which give the work a theatrical flair. Maupin's most daring creation is the cannibalism cult in *More Tales of the City.* Associated with the Episcopal Grace Cathedral on Nob Hill in San Francisco, a small group of believers take the concept of transubstantiation beyond the limit. In a gallery high above the altar, they consume the flesh from amputated human body parts concurrently with the celebration of the Holy Eucharist below. Maupin introduces the complication at the beginning of the volume through Mary Ann and Burke's attempts to solve the mystery of Burke's amnesia. The final piece of the puzzle is the strange key that Burke had with him at the time of his memory loss. The idea for this resolution came from the actual elevator in Grace Cathedral; Gale reports that when Maupin saw it, he "hit on its mysterious keyhole as the perfect solution to the Burke Andrew enigma." Allowing the reader to revel in the anticipation, Maupin manages to delay the resolution of this complication until the end of the volume.

Maupin draws on contemporary experience to create a strong sense of verisimilitude. His use of explicit detail, which is often brand-specific, serves three functions: as a catalogue of popular American culture from the late 1970s through the late 1980s; as a means to delineate class; and as an aid in character development. In the opening scene of *Tales of the City,* Maupin describes the color of Mary Ann's mood ring, a mid-1970s fad; and in the second scene, he lists *Jonathan Livingston Seagull* (1970) and *More Joy of Sex*

Dust jacket for the fifth novel (1987) in Maupin's Tales of the City *series*
(Richland County Public Library)

(1973) as two of the books in Connie Bradshaw's apartment. At the opening of *Babycakes,* Mary Ann and Brian have made plans to see the motion picture *Gandhi* (1982), and in the opening scene of *Significant Others,* Mary Ann and Brian's daughter, Shawna, has traded her Cabbage Patch Preemie doll for a toy tank. Throughout all six volumes, Maupin uses references to food, clothing, and other elements, resulting in an historical documentation of trendy American tastes for a decade. Food is often used as a tool to contrast and distinguish social status. The matrons of The Forum are served a luncheon of crab quiche and asparagus in *Tales of the City,* while Bruno, a drug-dealing hit man in *More Tales of the City,* chomps on a hamburger slathered with mayonnaise. Maupin also uses change in material possessions as a reflection of a character's changing social status. Mary Ann's gradual ascent up the employment ladder is reflected in the car she drives: she begins the series with no car, progresses to a Le Car in *Further Tales of the City,* and ends up in a Mercedes in *Sure of You.*

Warhol suggests that "Serialized domestic fiction bears the marks of historical changes that happen during the period of composition." Maupin uses significant

contemporary political and social events as source material for the series, creating the illusion that the fiction is occurring in what Warhol describes as "real time." For example, Maupin included Queen Elizabeth II's much-anticipated 1983 visit to San Francisco in *Babycakes;* Mary Ann, as host of her own local talk show, covers the visit. According to Gale, Steve Beery, a friend of Maupin's who was working as a San Francisco gossip columnist at the time, supplied much of the detail for this story line. The most profound incorporation of current events in the series is that of AIDS. Maupin was one of the first writers to deal with the subject in fiction. The series can be evenly divided into the pre-AIDS novels, *Tales of the City, More Tales of the City,* and *Further Tales of the City,* and the post-AIDS novels, *Babycakes, Significant Others,* and *Sure of You.* The reader discovers between *Further Tales of the City* and *Babycakes* that Jon Fielding has died of AIDS. Subsequently, it is also revealed that Michael has tested HIV-positive in *Significant Others.* Avoiding a fatalistic approach to the situation, Maupin chose not to have Michael die from AIDS by the end of the series; he is, instead, actively engaged in life, functioning happily as the life partner of Thack. While these two characters are not completely autobiographical, Maupin has indicated that he drew on aspects of his life with Terry Anderson, both his partner and manager at the time; however, as Gillespie states: "In their own lives it is Terry who has tested sero-positive, not Armistead."

In *Significant Others* Maupin articulates the climate of the gay subculture at the time:

> It [AIDS] wasn't just an epidemic anymore; it was a famine, a starvation of the spirit, which sooner or later afflicted everyone. Some people capitulated to the terror, turning inward in their panic, avoiding the gaze of strangers on the street. Others adopted a sort of earnest gay fraternalism, enacting the rituals of safe-sex orgies with all the clinical precision of Young Pioneers dismantling their automatic weapons.

AIDS was initially thought of as a gay disease; significantly, the first character in the series to actually go through an AIDS scare is Brian, a heterosexual. Maupin clearly makes the point that the virus is not selective. Maupin generally handles the subject in the most positive manner possible. Although characters throughout the final three volumes deal with the everyday concerns associated with AIDS, such as medications, physical complications, and the omnipresent grief over friends dying, they do not become maudlin or self-pitying. Maupin weaves these concerns into characters' conversations as a natural and logical part of daily existence, avoiding the sentimental. In fact, the characters often seemingly maintain a sense of cool detachment from the oppressive reality as a means of emotional survival. After three volumes of lighter subject material, the inclusion of such a grave topic as AIDS shocked some readers. As Maupin told Gillespie: "The outcry from my readers was tremendous when AIDS came up half-way through the series. . . . They accused me of spoiling their breakfasts."

The six volumes of the *Tales of the City* series have engaged readers across America and abroad, obtaining cult status and even engendering a website devoted to Maupin's work (http://www.literarybent.com). *Tales of the City* was adapted for television and aired on Britain's Channel 4 in 1993, followed by a PBS broadcast in the United States in 1994. *More Tales of the City* was adapted and shown in 1998 by Showtime, with *Further Tales of the City* released by Showtime in 2001. The short scenes and crisp, fast-paced dialogue of the series make Maupin's writing ideally suited for translation to the cinematic medium. These miniseries versions, adapted by other writers, remain faithful, with only a few scenes reordered and slight changes made in the dialogue. In the manner of Alfred Hitchcock, Maupin makes cameo appearances in these miniseries. He is shown for a few seconds in *Tales of the City* as a writer in a window,

observing the conversation of Michael and Brian in the courtyard below. In *More Tales of the City* he appears as the Episcopal priest performing the Holy Eucharist at Grace Cathedral during the resolution of the cannibalism subplot.

In 1992 Maupin moved away from the serialized form of the *Tales of the City* series with *Maybe the Moon*. This novel does, however, continue many of the themes of his previous work. Marginal characters and surrogate families are a focus as Maupin attacks Hollywood's refusal to deal with them in any meaningful, realistic fashion. The protagonist is Cadence "Cady" Roth, a Jewish, thirty-one-inch-tall dwarf. Set in Los Angeles, the novel is written as her diary and is divided into three main sections: "The Spiral Notebook," "The Leatherette Journal," and "The Three-Ring Notebook." These sections are followed by two addenda: "The Director's Letter" and "The Screenwriter's Reply." Cady's impetus for the diary is the strong hope that a movie version of her life will eventually be made. At the end of the novel, Maupin suggests to the reader that a movie will indeed be made, albeit posthumously. Because the novel is written as Cady's diary, Maupin uses the first-person voice. The reader views all other characters as filtered through Cady's viewpoint, which is inherently subjective.

Maupin's inspiration for Cady was his friend De Treaux, a dwarf actress who sweltered in an alien suit working on Steven Spielberg's 1982 movie, *E.T.* Wanting to keep the magic of the movie intact, the producers had insisted that the dwarf actors remain silent about their role in the filming and were subsequently furious when De Treaux interviewed with *People* magazine. Maupin saw De Treaux's story not only as an expression of Hollywood's dehumanization of dwarves but also as an extension of the way in which gay actors are used by Hollywood, yet forced to stay closeted for the sake of public appearances. For *Maybe the Moon* Maupin created the fictional movie *Mr. Woods,* a parody of *E.T.,* in which Cady appears disguised in a latex outfit. Like the dwarf actors of *E.T.,* she is expected to keep silent about her contribution. Articulating her feelings about playing the character, Maupin offers the reader a glimpse into Cady's inner thoughts: "to be there and yet not be there, to be the living heart of something but not the thing itself." The character of Mr. Woods becomes a metaphor for Cady's place in society. She is not viewed as a real person and is, in fact, figuratively and literally trodden underfoot because of her size. Francis King suggested in a review for *The Spectator* (20 February 1993) that Cady's plight serves as "an allegory of the process whereby Hollywood actors are rigidly imprisoned inside the personae manufactured for them by their studios and publicity agents."

While the character list of *Maybe the Moon* is much shorter than that of the *Tales of the City* series, it is as inclusive. Neil Riccarton is an African American man who is first Cady's boss, then her accompanist, and ultimately her lover. Maupin uses this romantic involvement to explore existing myths about both minorities. Cady is concerned that Neil is attracted to her because of the magical powers that "little people" are supposed to possess. Neil wonders if Cady is attracted to him for reasons of "Jewish guilt," her version of a "freedom ride." Upon meeting Cady, Neil's son, Danny, reacts negatively, calling her "weird" and saying she "grosses me out." Ultimately, the romantic relationship ends when Neil fails to pass the test of true love, unable to admit to his son that he and Cady are intimately involved.

Maupin includes three gay characters in the novel, each representative of different perspectives on being homosexual. Jeff Kassabian, a close friend of Cady's, is a writer and gay political activist. Callum Duff, the child star of *Mr. Woods,* has returned to Hollywood to resume his movie career. Afraid of damaging his chances for success, Callum is extremely closeted about his sexuality. Maupin pairs Jeff and Callum romantically, using the characters as foils for each other. Ned, Jeff's deceased lover, having been a former lover of Rock Hudson, had warned Jeff about the difficulties of being intimately involved with a closeted movie star, stating that because of the dishonesty "you always end up feeling like a mistress." The relationship ends as a result of Jeff's and Callum's conflicting views about being closeted. Through Jeff, Maupin expresses his disdain for Hollywood's long-standing portrayal and treatment of gays: "We're only visible when we're killers or objects of ridicule." Cady and Callum's agent, Leonard Lord, is described by Cady as "a pissy queen . . . who is paid to think exactly like someone from Iowa." Maupin uses Leonard's insistence that Callum remain secret about his sexual orientation to demonstrate Hollywood's perpetual denial of real sexual identity.

Renee Blalock is Cady's housemate, a not-too-bright *Mr. Woods* fan with a heart of gold. Maupin uses this lovable character as a foil for Cady, giving Cady's barbed wit a sharper edge by contrast. Like the other characters, Renee is unlucky in love, going through a series of unsuccessful romantic involvements. Maupin continues to celebrate the idea of surrogate or created families: Cady, whose parents are deceased, bonds with Jeff and Renee to form the nuclear family of *Maybe the Moon.* As Edmund White observed of Cady in a 5 February 1993 *TLS: The Times Literary Supplement* review: "She finds her real place only in her inner circle. Within that circle a great deal of love circulates." The bonds of these characters are as strong as those in any biological family, offering a haven of emotional safety to all three.

While Maupin deals with important human issues in *Maybe the Moon,* he avoids becoming overly sentimental or didactic by imbuing Cady with a sense of humor and a crisp, sardonic wit. Aware of the real, everyday problems that challenge dwarfs, Maupin begins chapter 8 with Cady's humorous account of "how I got my butt sniffed on Rodeo Drive" as she is assaulted by a large dog in front of a chic shop. In a more serious moment, Maupin articulates Cady's perception of coping with life as a marginal person: "you spend your life accommodating the sensibilities of 'normal' people. You learn to bury your own feelings and honor theirs in the hope that they'll meet you halfway. It becomes your job, and yours alone, to explain, to ignore, to forgive—over and over again. . . . You do it if you want to have a life and not spend it being corroded by your own anger. You do it if you want to belong to the human race."

Throughout the novel, Cady tries to establish a valid career beyond the anonymity of *Mr. Woods,* either as an actress or a singer, but is unable to do so because of her size and physical appearance. The reader is left to assume that a biographical movie will be made, but with most aspects of Cady's life altered to fit Hollywood's rigid definition of what is appropriate for mainstream audiences. A taller actress will be used, and as the screenwriter suggests in her addendum: "I'd think seriously about using a midget instead of a dwarf, someone perfectly proportioned but small, which is less off-putting." Callum will be eliminated altogether for fear of legal ramifications, although the writer may include "one scene with a gay friend," someone less "strident" than Jeff. The romantic pairing of Cady and Neil will be changed to Renee and Neil, with Cady "acting as a sort of witty mediator between the full-sized lovers." The assumption is that sex between Neil and Cady, which is interracial and involves partners of different sizes, is too distasteful for the general audience. Thus, most of the particulars of Cady's actual life will disappear altogether; it is no longer her life story, but a sanitized Hollywood version of it. In the eight years after *Maybe the Moon* Maupin published several articles and essays, contributed forewords to two books, and wrote the libretto for *Anna Madrigal Remembers,* a choral piece in which the landlady of the *Tales of the City* series looks back at her life at age eighty.

In his next novel, *The Night Listener* (2000), Maupin continues to deal with marginal characters in a realistic, sympathetic manner. This novel, perhaps Maupin's most openly gay work, presents homosexuality as a normal part of everyday life. Through the narrator, Gabriel Noone, Maupin articulates some of the

*Dust jacket for Maupin's 1992 novel, about a dwarf actress
trying to succeed in Hollywood (Richland
County Public Library)*

lay, has sent to him in the hope that he will write a publicity blurb. Although initially not wanting to read the manuscript, Gabriel picks it up for distraction and finds himself completely absorbed by it. Ultimately, Gabriel describes Pete as a "wise and battered old soul." Gabriel and Pete establish a relationship over the telephone and, although the two never meet in person, the relationship develops into that of father and son, fulfilling an emotional need for both characters. After he turned in his biological parents to the police, and they were arrested and imprisoned, Pete was adopted by Donna Lomax, a divorced doctor. The two have settled in Wysong, Wisconsin, and have forged a strong, healthy mother/son relationship. Maupin includes Gabriel's family members in the novel, particularly his father, sister, and brother. Also included is Anna, Gabriel's bookkeeper, a twenty-one-year-old Asian American who turns out to be the grown-up daughter of DeDe and D'orthea from the *Tales of the City* series.

The Night Listener is semi-autobiographical, incorporating many details from Maupin's own experience. Gabriel is from the South, in this case Charleston; he has a brother and sister and a mother of English descent; and he is a writer of serialized fiction who has his work subsequently published in book form. As Maupin told Dick Donahue in *Publishers Weekly* (11 September 2000): "I wanted to work much closer to home than ever before. And there were things in my own life that I felt I might never explain to myself if I didn't try to contain them in fiction." These elements include Gabriel's ten-year relationship with Jess and their recent breakup, and Gabriel's relationship with his father, a key character in the novel.

Through Gabriel's descriptions of his childhood and relationship with his father, Maupin gives the reader a clear sense of the racism, bigotry, class consciousness, and homophobia that he experienced growing up. Gabriel's father's obstinate denial about these topics is summarized in Gabriel's description of him: "No one in *his* family could ever be less than aristocratic, just as no one could really be gay. When the truth locked horns with my father's prejudices, it was always the truth that suffered." Throughout the course of the novel, Gabriel continues to question the effectiveness and intimacy of his relationship with his father: "Semaphore was just right for us, I thought, the perfect metaphor for how we'd managed to coexist all these years. Histrionic but mute, we had signaled our deepest feelings through broad strokes of pantomime, and always from a distance." By the conclusion of the novel, however, Gabriel has worked through much of this angst, at least fictionally. Maupin contrasts the relationships of Donna and Pete, Gabriel and Pete, and Gabriel

difficulties of being gay: "That age-old pain came roaring out of nowhere to remind me that I'd never be strong enough, never be handsome enough, never be young enough, to really be a man among men." Gabriel, a writer like Maupin, admits that he used a fictional character to come out to his parents. Maupin addresses many of the same topics as in his earlier works, including gay relationships, biological and extended families, AIDS, and, albeit briefly, Hollywood's refusal to be open and honest about homosexuality.

Gabriel lives in San Francisco, where he has become a national radio star reading his work on *Noone at Night* for National Public Radio. At the beginning of the novel, he has recently separated from Jess Carmody, his partner of ten years. Jess is HIV-positive and on protease inhibitors. Gabriel establishes a relationship with Pete Lomax, a thirteen-year-old who has survived overwhelming sexual abuse at the hands of his parents. As a means of therapy, Pete has written a book, *The Blacking Factory,* which Gabriel's publisher, Ashe Find-

and Jess with those in the Noone family, using the surrogate and biological families as foils for one another.

As with his earlier works, Maupin creates a sense of reality through the inclusion of current events and popular culture. He incorporates the 1998 murder of Matthew Shepard by gay-bashers in Wyoming and, through Jess, offers an account of the reaction in San Francisco to this incident. He refers to movies, such as *Fargo* (1996), and television, including *The Simpsons* and *The X-Files*. He also includes specific popular cultural references from his childhood, mentioning *The Big Show,* hosted by Tallulah Bankhead, and *The Bob Cummings Show*. Generally the critical response to *The Night Listener* was favorable. It was praised as an intense, engaging mystery; some critics considered it Maupin's best work.

Although Maupin is predominantly known as a gay writer, he deals more generally with marginal characters, treating them compassionately throughout his work. Basing much of his writing on real-life characters, observations, and experiences, he combines the serious and comic to create a sense of verisimilitude for the reader while offering his commentary on contemporary American society. As White observed: "Maupin's experience as a gay man is everywhere apparent, in his humanizing treatment of marginal characters, his understanding of duplicity and his appreciation for the liberating power of honesty."

Interviews:

Elgy Gillespie, "Armistead Maupin at Tale's End," *San Francisco Review of Books,* 14 (Winter 1989–1990): 18–20;

Jean W. Ross, "Interview with Armistead Maupin," *Contemporary Authors,* 130 (1990): 308–311;

Scott A. Hunt, "An Interview with Armistead Maupin," *Christopher Street,* 192 (23 November 1992): 8–12.

Biography:

Patrick Gale, *Armistead Maupin* (Bath, U.K.: Absolute Press, 1999).

References:

Jimmy D. Browning, *The Lost Tribalism of Years Gone By: Function and Variation in Gay Folklore in Armistead Maupin's 'Tales of the City' Novels* (Bowling Green: Western Kentucky University, 1992);

Shawn Crawford, "No Time to Be Idle: The Serial Novel and Popular Imagination," *World and I,* 13 (November 1998): 323–331;

Dick Donahue, "Armistead Maupin: Tales Worth Talking About," *Publishers Weekly,* 247 (11 September 2000): 63–64;

Robyn R. Warhol, "Making 'Gay' and 'Lesbian' into Household Words: How Serial Form Works in Armistead Maupin's Tales of the City," *Contemporary Literature,* 40 (Fall 1999): 378–395.

William Maxwell

(16 August 1908 – 31 July 2000)

Michael Steinman
Nassau Community College, State University of New York

See also the Maxwell entries in *DLB 218: American Short-Story Writers Since World War II, Second Series,* and *DLB Yearbook: 1980.*

BOOKS: *Bright Center of Heaven* (New York & London: Harper, 1934);

They Came Like Swallows (New York & London: Harper, 1937; London: Joseph, 1937; revised, New York: Vintage, 1960);

The Folded Leaf (New York & London: Harper, 1945; London: Faber & Faber, 1946; revised, New York: Vintage, 1959);

The Heavenly Tenants (New York & London: Harper, 1946);

Time Will Darken It (New York: Harper, 1948; London: Faber & Faber, 1949; revised, New York: Vintage, 1962);

The Château (New York: Knopf, 1961);

The Old Man at the Railroad Crossing and Other Tales (New York: Knopf, 1966);

Ancestors: A Family History (New York: Knopf, 1971);

Over by the River and Other Stories (New York: Knopf, 1977);

So Long, See You Tomorrow (New York: Knopf, 1980; London: Secker & Warburg, 1988);

Five Tales: Written for His Family on Special Occasions & Printed to Celebrate His Eightieth Birthday, 16 August 1988 (Omaha: Cummington Press, 1988);

The Outermost Dream: Essays and Reviews (New York: Knopf, 1989);

Billie Dyer and Other Stories (New York: Knopf, 1992);

All the Days and Nights: The Collected Stories of William Maxwell (New York: Knopf, 1995; London: Harvill, 1997);

Mrs. Donald's Dog Bun and His Home Away from Home (New York: Knopf, 1995).

Edition: *Time Will Darken It, The Château, So Long, See You Tomorrow,* with an introduction by Maxwell (New York: Quality Paperback Book Club, 1992).

William Maxwell (photograph by Brookie Maxwell; from the dust jacket for So Long, See You Tomorrow, *1980)*

RECORDINGS: *So Long, See You Tomorrow,* read by Maxwell, Columbia, Missouri, American Audio Prose Library, 1996;

Kay Bonetti, *An Interview with William Maxwell,* Columbia, Missouri, American Audio Prose Library, 1996.

OTHER: "The Trojan Women," "What Every Boy Should Know," and "The French Scarecrow," in *Stories,* by Maxwell, Jean Stafford, John Cheever, and Daniel Fuchs (New York: Farrar, Straus & Cudahy, 1956), pp. 265–275, 276–294, 295–309;

"Frank O'Connor and *The New Yorker,*" in *Michael/Frank: Studies on Frank O'Connor,* edited by Maurice Sheehy (New York: Knopf, 1969), pp. 140–147;

Self-portrait, in *Self-Portrait: Book People Picture Themselves,* collected by Burt Britton (New York: Random House, 1976), p. 23;

Charles Pratt, *The Garden and the Wilderness,* edited by Maxwell (New York: Horizon, 1980);

Sylvia Townsend Warner, *The Letters of Sylvia Townsend Warner,* edited by Maxwell (New York: Viking, 1982; London: Chatto & Windus, 1982);

"J. D. Salinger," in *The Book of the Month,* edited by Al Silverman (Boston: Little, Brown, 1986), pp. 128–130;

Warner, *Four in Hand: A Quartet of Novels by Sylvia Townsend Warner,* introduction by Maxwell (New York: Norton, 1986; London: Chatto & Windus, 1986);

Warner, *Selected Stories of Sylvia Townsend Warner,* edited by Maxwell and Susanna Pinney (New York: Viking, 1988);

"The Little Boudin Beach Scene," in *Transforming Vision: Writers on Art,* edited by Edward Hirsch (Boston: The Art Institute of Chicago / Boston: Little, Brown, 1994), pp. 26–28;

Eudora Welty, *One Time, One Place: Mississippi in the Depression: A Snapshot Album,* introduction by Maxwell (Jackson: University Press of Mississippi, 1996);

Maeve Brennan, *The Springs of Affection,* introduction by Maxwell (Boston: Houghton Mifflin, 1997);

Warner, *The Music At Long Verney: Twenty Stories,* edited by Michael Steinman, introduction by Maxwell (Washington, D.C.: Counterpoint, 2001).

SELECTED PERIODICAL PUBLICATIONS–UNCOLLECTED: "Zona Gale," *Yale Review,* 76 (Winter 1987): 221–225;

"Maeve Brennan," *Wigwag* (Summer 1988): 62–63;

"Three Fables Written to Please a Lady," *STORY,* 42 (Spring 1994): 25–33;

"Stevenson Revealed," *New Yorker* (26 December 1994 – 2 January 1995): 134–143;

"Nearing Ninety," *New York Times Magazine* (19 March 1997): 76;

"The Room Outside," *New Yorker* (28 December 1998 – 4 January 1999): 110;

"Recognition," *Doubletake* (Winter 1999): 110;

"Grape Bay (1941)," *New Yorker* (7 June 1999): 76–80;

"The Education of Her Majesty the Queen" and "Newton's Law," *Doubletake* (Fall 1999): 62–65.

For six decades William Maxwell's fiction took as its subject the vanished world of early-twentieth-century Midwestern life. He was no nostalgic archaeologist, however, unearthing sentimental relics for facile effect; his fiction is distinguished by an intuitive awareness of the subtle emotional currents of domestic life. Shattering events dominate Maxwell's novels–a mother's death, crippling accidents, a suicide attempt, adultery, and murder–but these catastrophes are never exploited for their potential to shock. His plain, spare prose style draws readers, and his novels delineate marital and familial affections with extraordinary accuracy. Although all of his novels except *The Château* (1961) depict the landscape of his childhood, they transcend autobiography. Maxwell always separated unadorned recollection from imagination ("the landscape in which the facts take place") and said that his novels do not "represent an intention to hand over the whole of my life. They are fragments in which I am a character along with all the others. They're written from a considerable distance" (*Writers at Work,* 1988). Each novel, he said in a 21 December 1996 letter to Michael Steinman, taught him little about how to write the next one, for he was guided by instinct, not theory: "I usually didn't know what I was doing until I had done it."

William Keepers Maxwell Jr. was born in Lincoln, Illinois, on 16 August 1908; he was the middle child of three sons born to William Keepers Maxwell, an insurance executive, and Eva Blossom (Blinn) Maxwell. Much of his fiction focuses on the disasters of his youth: his mother's death in the Spanish influenza epidemic of 1918 and the accident that caused his older brother to lose a leg. Maxwell had intended to study at the Art Institute in Chicago after high school but instead enrolled at the University of Illinois, where, he said in a 1996 interview, he had "a very persuasive English teacher, who said an artist's life is very uncertain and a professor's life is pleasant and guaranteed, and why don't you do that?" After graduating in 1930 with a bachelor's degree in English and a fellowship to Harvard, he received a master's degree in 1931 and taught freshman composition at the University of Illinois in Urbana for two years. Rather than complete a doctorate at Harvard, Maxwell resigned from teaching because jobs were scarce; instead, he returned to the Wisconsin farm where he had worked as a high-school student and began to write.

There he wrote his first novel, *Bright Center of Heaven* (1934). He acknowledged to interviewers John Seabrook and George Plimpton that "Some of the characters were derived from people living on the farm at

William and Emily Maxwell in the late 1940s (from Michael Steinman, ed.,
The Happiness of Getting It Down Right, *1996)*

the time. . . . I would come for lunch and they would make remarks I had put in their mouths that morning." The novel depicts a day at Meadowland, a Wisconsin farm. The protagonists are Mrs. Susan West, the farm owner and matriarch; her family; and their boarders, primarily eccentric artists. Virginia Woolf's *To the Lighthouse* (1927) is an obvious influence; in a 2 January 1997 letter to Steinman, Maxwell said he even unconsciously "stole a character, [Woolf's] homesick servant girl."

Bright Center of Heaven focuses on its idiosyncratic characters, glimpsed through interior monologues and brief conversations. At the end of the novel, several major conflicts are unresolved, as if a realistic novel would not arrange for neat conclusions at its end. Maxwell's "fairy godmother," novelist and playwright Zona Gale, read the unpublished novel at his request. As he told Seabrook and Plimpton, "When she gave it back to me she said that she had been unable to sleep and had read until four in the morning, and then gone downstairs to her study looking for the last chapter. I was too

thickheaded to understand what she was trying to tell me, and said, 'No, that's all there is.' Twenty years after it was published I reread the book and saw the chapter she went downstairs looking for." Maxwell never wrote that chapter, however.

One subject of the novel is race prejudice. Susan West has invited Jefferson Carter, "a leader of the Negro race," to visit, not caring that her Southern-born sister is horrified by the idea of dining with him. At dinner, a confrontation occurs when several boarders (including the most "progressive") attack Carter verbally. Wounded, he leaves hastily. As a comic novel with lyrical flourishes, *Bright Center of Heaven* succeeds, but Maxwell's attempts at social realism are incomplete, for neither Carter nor his tormentors are fully realized. Reviewers found the novel entertaining; in the 15 September 1934 *Saturday Review of Literature*, Theodore Purdy Jr. called it "admirable satiric comedy, bitter-sweet in flavor, yet always humorous. . . . Even the most brilliant contemporary European work of this sort presents little that is more engaging than the best parts of this book." Maxwell, however, never let this novel be reprinted; in 1995, when an interviewer said he could not find a copy, Maxwell was relieved.

Maxwell's second novel, *They Came Like Swallows* (1937), is one of his most admired, although he later thought it too lyrical and was surprised that readers find it moving. In a letter to his friend Frank O'Connor in 1965, Maxwell praised Joseph Conrad's novella "The End of the Tether" (1902), describing its subjects in *The Happiness of Getting It Down Right* (1996) as "loss, the gradual withdrawal of all the props of life, the unequal struggle that love puts up against disaster." *They Came Like Swallows* depicts that struggle as Maxwell himself experienced it: "After my first novel was published, I naturally wondered what else I could write about, and the 'what else' turned out to be my mother's death. . . . If you search in the background of any serious writer, it isn't very long before you come upon a major deprivation of one sort or another—which the writer through the exercise of imagination tries to overcome or compensate for, or even make not have happened" (*Poets & Writers Magazine,* May–June, 1994).

What was fragmentary or inconclusive in *Bright Center of Heaven* gained cohesiveness in this novel because of a controlling visual image. In an undated letter to Steinman, Maxwell wrote: "I knew what I wanted, which was for the book to be like a stone thrown into a pond, creating a widening circle, and then a second stone thrown into the pond, creating a circle inside the circle, and a third doing the same." *They Came Like Swallows,* its title taken from William Butler Yeats's "Coole Park, 1929" (in *The Winding Stair and Other Poems,* 1933), shows Elizabeth Morison as reflected in the eyes of her two sons and husband, each perspective allotted a section of the book, moving from the youngest to the eldest. Although Maxwell was recalling events of his youth, the novel was not easy to write, as he made clear in an undated letter to Steinman: "I did the first section seven times, the eighth time during a stay at the MacDowell colony, and that version stuck. The second section took me all winter. I was living in Urbana, Illinois, grading papers for a member of the English faculty in return for room and board. I wrote the last section in two weeks in the same house, a good deal of the time walking the floor and brushing the tears from my eyes so that I could see the typewriter keys."

The book begins on a Sunday morning and traces an irreversible three weeks that end with Elizabeth's death. "Whose Angel Child," the first section, depicts the world as seen by eight-year-old Peter Morison, "Bunny," fearful and precocious. Only when his mother is present is he secure, his imagination wholly free. His section is a measured re-creation of twenty-four hours, from his first stirrings of consciousness and breakfast on Monday, 11 November 1918, the end of World War I. In these pages Maxwell paints the family life that will be lost. The second and third sections incorporate Bunny's perspective into those of his brother, Robert, and father, James. Seeing Elizabeth in these contexts also enriches readers' first view of her. Robert Morison, five and a half years Bunny's senior, is gregarious and happily engaged in the world outside, even though one leg has been amputated. In his section, "Robert," foreshadowings of sickness, separation, and death come true: all four Morisons catch influenza, and Elizabeth dies. Deprivation and grief dominate the final section, "Upon a Compass-point." The final chapters return James and his sons to a house irrevocably changed by Elizabeth's absence, ending with Robert and James in front of her coffin in the living room.

V. S. Pritchett praised the novel in the 28 August 1937 *New Statesman and Nation* as a "sensitive, wistful reminiscence of family life, very intimate and pathetic and with some acute observation." Amy Loveman wrote in the 1 May 1937 *Saturday Review of Literature* that Maxwell had depicted "tragedy but not sentimentality." The novel was chosen as a selection by the Book-of-the-Month Club.

In 1936, before *They Came Like Swallows* was published, Maxwell had been hired by *The New Yorker,* first as Katharine S. White's assistant and soon after as a fiction editor, beginning a distinguished forty-year career. Although Gale thought that full-time editorial work would hinder Maxwell's writing, his collaborations with exceptional writers were inspiring. He was "influenced by *The New Yorker*'s dislike for unnecessary words or padding or slowness. Space was at a premium and in editing I was taught to go through the manuscript looking for whatever was unnecessary." When the Vintage Press wanted to reprint *They Came Like Swallows* in 1959, Maxwell chose to act as his own editor and revised it. He wrote O'Connor in August 1959: "I was moved helplessly by the material, which will only cease to move me when I am dead, I suppose, but also discouraged that it wasn't better. I wrote it when I was twenty-four or five, and all the judgments are so harsh and, as I eventually discovered, in many cases quite wrong. But there was nothing I could do short of rewriting it out of existence, except here and there to do the small detail work that pulls a character back into recognizable human focus."

His third novel, *The Folded Leaf* (1945), was first conceived in 1940 as a short story. When he showed it to the poet Louise Bogan, she encouraged him to develop it; she read four years of drafts and suggested the title. *The Folded Leaf* might seem a sequel to *They*

Maxwell reading to his daughters, Kate and Brookie, circa 1960 (from Steinman, ed.,
The Happiness of Getting It Down Right, *1996)*

Came Like Swallows, its main characters adolescent versions of Bunny and Robert Morison, friends rather than brothers. Yet, this novel is more ambitious formally, with extended meditations that add to and disrupt linear narrative.

In 1923 two high-school students—Lymie Peters, thin, intellectual, and lonely, and Spud Latham, athletic yet equally lonely—warily become friends and go to the same college. Although the absence of Lymie's mother is strongly felt, the subject of this novel is not bereavement but the interweaving of worshipful love and destructive hostility in a friendship. Spud, puzzled by Lymie's devoted loyalty and unable to conceive of such love as anything but a burden, grows to hate Lymie, rationalizing his feelings as jealousy because his girlfriend is fond of Lymie. Because Lymie cannot convince Spud that he is wrong, Lymie attempts suicide. At the end, Spud and Lymie are reconciled, leaving childhood behind.

Maxwell's analysis of the murderous kernel of a loving relationship reveals shadings of emotion that resist categorization. Roger Austen (in *Playing the Game: The Homosexual Novel in America,* 1977) and James Levin (in *The Gay Novel in America,* 1991) have classified Lymie and Spud's relationship as homoerotic, a view Maxwell rejected. Maxwell depicts American

adolescence as neither simple nor bucolic by adopting the perspective of a cultural anthropologist, observing, for example, a fraternity initiation rite as a fascinated, horrified outsider.

The narrative of *The Folded Leaf* is distinguished by multiple shifts in point of view as well as addresses to the reader—leisurely commentaries reminiscent of nineteenth-century Russian novels. As if its emotional content would overflow traditional narrative, the novel includes more than a dozen meditative digressions: reveries on travel, death, April, or a group of little Spanish boys in the desert, or musings on what characters have done or will do. Thirty years after the publication of the novel, Maxwell said that these discursive passages were merely attempts to keep it from being linear, but they are as meaningful as the events they accompany. When Lymie and his father visit the cemetery on the anniversary of Mrs. Peters's death, their literal journey becomes a meditation about the novel itself, the shared responsibilities connecting writer and reader:

The great, the universal problem is how to be always on a journey and yet see what you would see if it were only possible for you to stay home: a black cat in a garden, moving through iris blades behind a lilac bush. How to keep sufficiently detached and quiet inside so that when the cat in one spring reaches the top of the garden wall, turns down again, and disappears, you will see and remember it, and not be absorbed at that moment in the dryness of your hands.

If you missed that particular cat jumping over one out of so many garden walls, it ought not to matter, but it does apparently. The cat seems to be everything. Seeing clearly is everything. Being certain as to smells, being able to remember sounds and to distinguish by touch one object, one body, from another. And it is not enough to see the fishermen drawing in their wide circular net, the tropical villages lying against a shelf of palm trees, or the double rainbow over Fort-de-France. You must somehow contrive, if only for a week or only overnight, to live in the houses of people, so that at least you know the elementary things—which doors sometimes bang when a sudden wind springs up; where the telephone book is kept; and how their lungs feel when they waken in the night and reach blindly toward the foot of the bed for the extra cover.

You are in duty bound to go through all their possessions, to feel their curtains and look for the tradename on the bottom of their best dinner plates and stand below their pictures (especially the one they have been compelled to paint themselves, which is not a good painting but seems better if you stay long enough to know the country in more than one kind of light) and lift the lids off their cigarette boxes and sniff their pipe tobacco and open, one by one, their closet doors. You should test the sharpness and shape of their scissors. You may play their radio and try, with your fingernail, to open the locked door of the liquor cabinet. You may even read any letters that they have been so careless as to leave around. Through all of these things, through the attic and the cellar and the tool shed you must go searching until you find the people who live here or who used to live here but now are in London or Acapulco or Galesburg, Illinois. Or who now are dead.

In her review of *The Folded Leaf* in *Nation* (21 April 1945), Diana Trilling said of these episodes that Maxwell was "free to comment on [his characters'] fates in his own person, so that we have the advantage of his intellect as well as of his creativity." She called the novel an "important social document" based on Maxwell's "remarkable, if quiet, gift for observation." Edmund Wilson in *The New Yorker* (31 March 1945) found it "moving" and "absorbing," compared it to Stephen Crane's *Whilomville Stories* (1900), and was enthusiastic about this "drama of the immature, with no background more glamorous than middle-class apartments and student fraternity houses."

In May 1945 Maxwell married Emily Gilman Noyes; they had two daughters, Kate (born in 1954) and Brookie (born in 1956). *Time Will Darken It* (1948), although set in the Illinois of Maxwell's earliest childhood, is, perhaps because of his recent marriage, a novel of adult love. Maxwell recalls in his introduction

to *Time Will Darken It,* "I had had the feeling that, for someone as happy as I was, writing was not possible, but one day, habit reasserting itself, I sat down at the typewriter and began describing an evening party in the year 1912. It took place in the house I lived in as a child. I seemed to have no more choice about this than one has about the background of a dream. I also hadn't any idea about what was going to happen to the characters." He explained that "the story advanced by set conversations. A, who was late for work, had to stop and deal with the large wet tears of B, C tried unsuccessfully to reach out to D at the breakfast table, but E, who was older and wiser about people, managed to . . . as if I were writing a play. When I started a new chapter it was a matter of figuring out which of them hadn't talked to each other lately."

Time Will Darken It begins placidly with the young lawyer Austin King; his pregnant, often irritable wife, Martha; and their daughter, Abbey. The immediate action is a summer visit from Austin's Mississippi cousins, known only through letters. His young cousin Nora falls disastrously in love with him, although Austin remains faithful to Martha. Nora returns to Mississippi, her hands and face disfigured by burns, emblems of deeper wounds. Even in this apparently peaceful small-town world, misinterpretation and betrayal are pervasive: financial transactions tempt Austin's amiable relatives into duplicity. Politeness masks casual slander, and reputations are destroyed by "They say. . . ." Violence and cruelty are never far away: Rachel, the Kings' cook, frightened by the return of her abusive husband, runs away with her children; meanwhile, Abbey is terrified by her older cousin Randolph's sexual display. One character has a milk pitcher decorated with these lines: "For every evil under the sun / there is a remedy or there is none, / if there be one try and find it, / if there be none never mind it." The novel considers the struggle to find remedies, how they fail, and how the results must be endured.

Two celebrated writers commended *Time Will Darken It.* Eudora Welty was quoted by George Blixby in the *Eudora Welty Newsletter* (Summer 1979) as saying, "Mr. Maxwell's . . . sensitive prose is the good and careful tool of an artist who is always doing exactly what he means to do. The careful, meditative examination of unfolding relationships among people of several sorts and ages—all interesting—has Mr. Maxwell's expected integrity; and the story's quiet and accumulating power a dark and disturbing beauty that has some of its roots, at least, in fine restraint." In a 3 December 1948 letter to Maxwell, Sylvia Townsend Warner wrote that "by the time I'd finished it I had the admiring sensation that something had hit me—a very well contained and well delivered blow."

550

CHAPTER 19

~~Their breakfast was brought in to them by a cold, dull-bosomed woman of forty, with carrot-colored hair and a beautiful carriage. "Bonjour monsieur dame," she said, and raised the front wheels of the~~ teacart and then the back, so that ~~~~ they did not touch the telephone cord. When she had gone back to the kitchen, Harold said, "There are plates and cups for three, which can only mean that he is having breakfast with us."

"You think?" Barbara said.

"By his own choice," ~~Harold~~ Harold said, "since there is now someone to bring him a tray in his room."

They sat and waited. In due time, Eugene appeared and drew the armchair up to the tea cart.

It was a beautiful day. The window was wide open and the sunlight was streaming in from the balcony. Eugène inquired about their evening with Sabine, ~~and then~~ said, "It is possible that I may be going down to the country ~~tomorrow~~ on Friday. A cousin of Alix is marrying. ~~They live outside~~ ~~Paris~~. And if I do go---as I should, since it is a family affair--- it will be early in the morning, before you are up. And I may stay down for the weekend."

They tried not to look pleased.

~~Eugène~~ He accepted a second cup of coffee and then asked what they had done about getting gasoline coupons. "But we don't need them," ~~Barbara~~ Harold said, and so, innocently, obliged Eugene to admit that he did. "I seldom ~~can~~ enjoy the use of my car," he said plaintively, "and it would be pleasant to have the gasoline for short trips into the country now and then."

He reached into his bathrobe pocket and brought out a slip of paper ~~on which he had written~~ ~~with~~ the address of the place they were to go to for gasoline coupons, ~~written on it~~.

"How can we ask for gasoline coupons if we don't have a car?" ~~Barbara~~ Harold

and the telephone, like a spoiled child that cannot endure the conversation of the grownups, started ringing. Eugène left the room. When he came back, he

Page from the revised typescript for The Château, *Maxwell's 1961 novel (Estate of William Maxwell; from John Seabrook and George Plimpton,* Writers at Work: The Paris Review Interviews, Seventh Series, *1988)*

The Château, Maxwell's only novel that is not set in the Midwest, grew out of four months he and his wife spent in France in 1948: "I couldn't bear not to be there, and so I began to write a novel about it." At first, on his return, he was "afraid it was a travel diary" and later modestly declared it a novel "in which nothing more profound happened than hurt feelings" (*Missouri Review,* 1996). *The Château* records the travels of Harold and Barbara Rhodes, a young American couple, but its center is the mysterious alternations of unexpected affection and coldness they encounter in France.

After Mark Twain and Henry James, there might seem little to say about the misunderstandings of Americans in Europe, yet Maxwell's extensions and disruptions of linear narrative are vividly original. A novel founded on a day-by-day record might have been restricted to Harold and Barbara's visit to this city or that cathedral; its emotional development might have been equally constrained, painful or pleasing encounters alternating or succeeding one another. Aware of these limitations, Maxwell creates a narrative of speculative turns, interrogations, and explorations. When Harold and Barbara sit through a too-formal, unrewarding conversation, Maxwell creates the conversations that should or might have happened. In another scene the photograph of a boy, long dead, shares his inmost feelings. These hallucinatory imaginings show the possibilities of an affectionate openness often denied the Americans. Many of the narrative improvisations are unannounced dialogues. In italics, a narrative voice raises questions that curious readers might ask, and another voice, sometimes amused, with some but not all of the answers about events or characters, replies. These interrogations may seem violations of some imagined classical form, but the effect is expansive, never obtrusive. The brief second section of the novel, "Some Explanations," is entirely devoted to queries and responses, and begins, "Is that all?" Although the first response is "Yes, that's all," readers share in a discussion that partially explains mysteries of motive and causality, reminiscent of the introspective meditations of *The Folded Leaf.* These last forty-five pages of *The Château* are Maxwell's fulfillment of the unwritten last chapter of *Bright Center of Heaven.* He insisted on keeping "Some Explanations" when an editor objected to it: "if I were to pick up *The Château* and that epilogue wasn't there, I think I would shoot myself."

Another of Maxwell's extensions beyond traditional expectations is his delight in anthropomorphizing objects or animals. This element first emerged in *Time Will Darken It* and reappears later in a short story, "The Lily-White Boys" (1995), in which the furniture of a burglarized Manhattan apartment discourses on the catastrophe, long after the human occupants have fallen asleep. In *The Château,* fountains, stones, the French flag, a block of granite, swallows, the sky, a wet bathing suit, a house, and pieces of furniture carry on warm, personal, enlightening conversations.

Richard Gilman wrote in *Commonweal* (7 April 1961) how he saw the novel as "most interestingly unconventional," its substance "the fragile network of relationships that the couple establishes between themselves and the people they meet . . . and between themselves and Europe." He considered its purpose "to pursue and to arrest those relationships, to present them in mystery and ambiguity, never exerting any pressure to explain them, make them yield up secrets."

Maxwell's last novel, *So Long, See You Tomorrow* (1980), returns to his physical and emotional homeland, not to predictable yearnings for a departed time but to adultery and murder. Maxwell remembered Cletus Smith, a boy he had befriended in junior high school, whose father had murdered another tenant farmer, once his closest friend. After Maxwell had moved to Chicago, he saw Cletus in the corridor of the new school; they recognized one another, but Maxwell said nothing. Years later "something made me think of that boy I had failed to speak to, and thinking of him I winced. I saw myself wincing and I thought, 'That's very odd indeed that after all these years you should have a response so acute; maybe that's worth investigating.'" The novel is in part a "roundabout, futile way of making amends" by exploring the past; as Maxwell told John Seabrook and George Plimpton in a 1981 *Paris Review* interview, "if writers don't put down what they remember, all sorts of beautiful and moving experiences simply go down the drain forever." *So Long, See You Tomorrow* might seem less a novel than an investigation of local history, but Maxwell did not see this perspective as a failure of creativity. He told Edward Hirsch in a 1997 interview, "I have come to put more faith in what actually happened. . . . But, of course, sometimes when you think you are following the actual truth, it turns out you were inventing." What Maxwell could not find in contemporary newspaper reports he chose to create, addressing readers directly: "The unsupported word of a witness who was not present except in imagination would not be acceptable in a court of law, but, as it has been demonstrated over and over, the sworn testimony of the witness who was present is not trustworthy either." Writing in February 1960 to Warner, who had freely created her own historical fictions, Maxwell stated, "The way to find out what the past was really like is to invent it," an idea resonant in *So Long, See You Tomorrow.*

Although the novel is Maxwell's most brief, its concerns are familiar—friendship and rage intertwined; a relationship both lovers know will be disastrous; the impact of a single act on participants and observers; his mother's death; his brother's accident—all of them newly re-created and powerful. Robert Towers in *The New York Times Book Review* (13 January 1980) praised the "strength and poignancy" of the novel and its "beautifully controlled writing"; in the *New Republic* (26 January 1980) Jack Beatty placed Maxwell alongside Gustave Flaubert, Leo Tolstoy, and Anton Chekhov for his ability to reduce life to its "tragic essence."

In a 1995 interview Maxwell gently dismissed Leonard Lopate's inquiry about future novels and stories, saying "It's possible I may have written enough." A year later, at eighty-eight, he told Hirsch, "the energy that it requires to imagine a novel and then carry the idea through to the final page is simply not there anymore. When people ask me 'What are you writing?,' even though I know they have asked the question merely out of politeness, I want to pick up something and throw it at them." Yet, Maxwell's *All the Days and Nights: The Collected Stories of William Maxwell* (1995) offered previously unpublished work; beginning in 1992 he also wrote new introductions to all of his novels (except *Bright Center of Heaven*) and to *The Outermost Dream* (1989), a collection of essays and reviews. His introduction to a posthumous volume of Maeve Brennan's stories, *The Springs of Affection* (1997), and "Nearing Ninety," his 1997 essay on age and death, are essential reading. The elements of his fiction are evident in his other prose, whether family history such as *Ancestors* (1971) or reflections on Samuel Butler and George Gordon, Lord Byron, in *The Outermost Dream*. His talking birds and clouds appear again in his fables and improvisations in *The Old Man at the Railroad Crossing and Other Tales* (1966), *Five Tales* (1988), and his books for children, *The Heavenly Tenants* (1946) and *Mrs. Donald's Dog Bun and His Home Away from Home* (1995). Maxwell died at the age of ninety-one in New York City on 31 July 2000, just eight days after his wife succumbed to cancer.

Maxwell had long been recognized by his peers and had received the American Book Award, the Brandeis Creative Arts Medal, the Howells Medal and the Gold Medal for Fiction from the American Academy of Arts and Letters, and the PEN/Malamud Award. He was president of the National Institute of Arts and Letters from 1969 to 1972. Yet, much of the public attention he has received focuses on his *New Yorker* career, as editor and friend of such figures as J. D. Salinger, John Cheever, Frank O'Connor, John Updike, Eudora Welty, Vladimir Nabokov, John O'Hara, Delmore Schwartz, and James Thurber. Maxwell's recollections of famous figures have enlivened literary biographies, and he was interviewed frequently; yet, no excerpts from his work appear in academic anthologies of Amer-

Dust jacket for Maxwell's 1980 novel, set in the Midwest of his childhood (Richland County Public Library)

ican literature. This neglect results from unexamined misconceptions. Some may wrongly believe that Maxwell's quiet success was owing to his position of privilege at an established New York literary institution. The selection of *They Came Like Swallows* by the Book-of-the-Month Club might stigmatize it as popular "middlebrow" fiction. Having written of his childhood so affectionately might brand Maxwell a cultural reactionary idealizing the past. Those who insist that modern fiction must be visibly complex may misread his work as old-fashioned; others praise him as a "writer's writer," thus intimating that only writers fully appreciate his work. Yet, his writing is never artistically conservative or morally complacent. Those who ignore Maxwell's fiction or exclude it from the modern canon may not know that *Bright Center of Heaven* dramatizes an early sensitivity to racial injustice, consistent in his fiction; that *They Came Like Swallows* offers alternatives to William Faulkner's multiple perspectives; that *The Folded Leaf* and *The Château* extend narrative through dream-like excursions and interrogations; that *So Long,*

See You Tomorrow hallucinates a past before that activity became a literary commonplace.

The most appropriate tribute to William Maxwell's writing may be the recognition that its subtlety defies easy classification. In a 6 November 1956 letter to Maxwell, Warner touched on its character when she wrote of reading his latest story in *The New Yorker,* at first unaware that he had written it: "Styles and signatures are a queer business, Here's William, I said to myself, about halfway down the first column—and for the life of me I can't say what touched off the recognition—nothing verbal; more like the way one recognises a painter's work, a depth and play of textures, a warmth and stillness."

Letters:

The Happiness of Getting It Down Right: Letters of Frank O'Connor and William Maxwell, 1945–1966, edited by Michael Steinman (New York: Knopf, 1996);

Michael Steinman, "Easy Does It," *The Newsletter of the Friends of the Amherst College Library,* 26 (1999–2000), pp. 4–6;

The Element of Lavishness: Letters of Sylvia Townsend Warner and William Maxwell, 1938–1978, edited by Steinman (Washington, D.C.: Counterpoint, 2001).

Interviews:

Robert Dahlin, "*PW* Interviews William Maxwell," *Publishers Weekly* (10 December 1979): 8–9;

Jean W. Ross, "*CA* Interviews the Author [William Maxwell]," *Contemporary Authors,* volume 93–96 (Detroit: Gale, 1980), pp. 347–348;

Gerald C. Nemanic, "*GLR* Interview: William Maxwell," *Great Lakes Review,* 9–10 (Fall 1983–Spring 1984): 1–15;

David Willis McCullough, "Eye on Books," in *The Book of the Month,* edited by Al Silverman (Boston: Little, Brown, 1986), pp. 297–299;

John Seabrook and George Plimpton, "William Maxwell," *Writers at Work: The Paris Review Interviews, Seventh Series,* edited by Plimpton (New York: Penguin, 1988), pp. 39–70;

David Stanton, "An Interview with William Maxwell," *Poets & Writers Magazine,* 22 (May–June 1994): 36–47;

Harvey Ginsberg, "A Modest, Scrupulous, Happy Man," *New York Times Book Review,* 22 January 1995: 3, 20;

Linda Wertheimer, "A Conversation with Author William Maxwell," *All Things Considered,* National Public Radio, 8 February 1995;

Charlie Rose, "Interview with William Maxwell," PBS, 1 March 1995;

Leonard Lopate, "Interview with William Maxwell," *New York and Company,* WNYC-AM, 8 March 1995;

Kay Bonetti, "An Interview with William Maxwell," *Missouri Review,* 19, no. 1 (1996): 81–98; 19, no. 2 (1996): 85–95;

Edward Hirsch, "Edward Hirsch and William Maxwell," *Doubletake,* 3 (Summer 1997): 20–29.

Biography:

Barbara Burkhardt, "William Maxwell: A Selected Critical Biography," dissertation, University of Illinois, 1994.

References:

Richard Bausch, "Maxwell's Smarts," *The New Yorker* (25 December 1996);

Bruce Bawer, "States of Grace: The Novels of William Maxwell," *New Criterion,* 7 (May 1989): 26–38;

George Bixby, "Blurbs: Eudora Welty on William Maxwell," *Eudora Welty Newsletter,* 3, no. 2 (1972): 3;

Paul John Eakin, "The Referential Aesthetic of Autobiography," *Studies in the Literary Imagination,* 23 (Fall 1990): 129–144;

Elizabeth Frank, *Louise Bogan: A Portrait* (New York: Knopf, 1985);

Brendan Gill, *Here at "The New Yorker"* (New York: Random House, 1975);

Ruth Limmer, ed., *What the Woman Lived: Selected Letters of Louise Bogan, 1920–1970* (New York: Harcourt Brace Jovanovich, 1973);

James F. Maxfield, "The Child, the Adolescent, and the Adult: States of Consciousness in Three Early Novels of William Maxwell," *Midwest Quarterly,* 24 (Spring 1983): 315–335;

Maxfield, "Memory and Imagination in William Maxwell's *So Long, See You Tomorrow,*" *Critique,* 24 (Fall 1982): 21–37;

Richard Shereikis, "Breath of Life: William Maxwell's Midwestern Adolescents," *Mid-America,* 17 (1990): 34–43;

Shereikis, "William Maxwell's Lincoln, Illinois," *Mid-America,* 14 (1987): 101–112;

John Updike, "Maxwell's Touch," *The New Yorker* (14 August 2000): 29;

Alec Wilkinson, "An American Original," *New Yorker* (27 December 1999 – 3 January 2000): 68–75;

Wilkinson, *My Mentor: A Young Man's Friendship with William Maxwell* (Boston: Houghton Mifflin, 2002).

Papers:

William Maxwell's papers, manuscripts, and correspondence are in the University of Illinois Library at Urbana.

Vladimir Nabokov

(23 April 1899 – 2 July 1977)

Charles Nicol
Indiana State University

See also the Nabokov entries in *DLB 2: American Novelists Since World War II; DLB 244: American Short-Story Writers Since World War II, Fourth Series; DLB Yearbook: 1980;* and *DLB Yearbook: 1991.*

BOOKS: *Stikhi* (St. Petersburg: Privately printed, 1916);

Al'manakh. Dva puti, by Nabokov and Andrei Balashov (Petrograd: Privately printed, 1918);

Grozd'. Stikhi, as V. Sirin (Berlin: Gamaiun, 1923 [1922]);

Gornii put', as Vl. Sirin (Berlin: Grani, 1923);

Mashen'ka, as Vladimir Sirin (Berlin: Slovo, 1926); translated by Michael Glenny and Nabokov as *Mary,* as Nabokov (New York: McGraw-Hill, 1970; London: Weidenfeld & Nicolson, 1971);

Korol' dama valet, as Sirin (Berlin: Slovo, 1928); translated by Dmitri Nabokov and Nabokov as *King, Queen, Knave,* as Nabokov (New York: McGraw-Hill, 1968; London: Weidenfeld & Nicolson, 1968);

Zashchita Luzhina, as Sirin (Berlin: Slovo, 1930); translated by Michael Scammell and Nabokov as *The Defense,* as Nabokov (New York: Putnam, 1964; London: Weidenfeld & Nicolson, 1964);

Vozvrashchenie Chorba, as Sirin (Berlin: Slovo, 1930 [1929]);

Podvig, as Sirin (Paris: Sovremennye Zapiski, 1932); translated by Dmitri Nabokov and Nabokov as *Glory,* as Nabokov (New York: McGraw-Hill, 1971; London: Weidenfeld & Nicolson, 1972);

Kamera obskura, as Sirin (Paris: Sovremennye Zapiski, 1933); translated by Winifred Roy as *Camera Obscura,* as Vladimir Nabokoff-Sirin (London: John Long, 1935 [1936]); translated again by Nabokov as *Laughter in the Dark,* as Nabokoff (Indianapolis & New York: Bobbs-Merrill, 1938; London: Weidenfeld & Nicolson, 1961);

Otchaianie, as Sirin (Berlin: Petropolis, 1936); translated by Nabokov as *Despair,* as Nabokoff-Sirin (London: John Long, 1937); revised and retranslated

Vladimir Nabokov, 1964 (© Henry Grossman/TimePix)

by Nabokov, as Nabokov (New York: Putnam, 1966; London: Weidenfeld & Nicolson, 1966);

Sogliadatai, as Sirin (Paris: Russkiia Zapiski, 1938)—comprises the title novel and twelve short stories; title novel translated by Dmitri Nabokov and Nabokov as *The Eye,* as Nabokov (New York: Phaedra, 1965; London: Weidenfeld & Nicolson, 1966);

Priglashenie na kazn', as Sirin (Paris: Dom Knigi, 1938); translated by Dmitri Nabokov and Nabokov as *Invitation to a Beheading*, as Nabokov (New York: Putnam, 1959; London: Weidenfeld & Nicolson, 1960);

The Real Life of Sebastian Knight (Norfolk, Conn.: New Directions, 1941; London: Editions Poetry, 1945);

Nikolai Gogol (Norfolk, Conn.: New Directions, 1944; London: Editions Poetry, 1947);

Bend Sinister (New York: Holt, 1947; London: Weidenfeld & Nicolson, 1960);

Nine Stories (Norfolk, Conn.: New Directions, 1947);

Conclusive Evidence: A Memoir (New York: Harper, 1951); republished as *Speak, Memory: A Memoir* (London: Gollancz, 1951); revised and enlarged as *Speak, Memory: An Autobiography Revisited* (New York: Putnam, 1967; London: Weidenfeld & Nicolson, 1967);

Dar (New York: Chekhov Publishing House, 1952); translated by Scammell and Nabokov as *The Gift* (New York: Putnam, 1963; London: Weidenfeld & Nicolson, 1963);

Stikhotvoreniia 1929–1951 (Paris: Rifma, 1952);

Lolita (Paris: Olympia Press, 1955; New York: Putnam, 1958; London: Weidenfeld & Nicolson, 1959);

Vesna v Fial'te i drugie rasskazy (New York: Chekhov Publishing House, 1956);

Pnin (Garden City, N.Y.: Doubleday, 1957; London: Heinemann, 1957);

Nabokov's Dozen: A Collection of Thirteen Stories (Garden City, N.Y.: Doubleday, 1958; London: Heinemann, 1959);

Poems (Garden City, N.Y.: Doubleday, 1959; London: Weidenfeld & Nicolson, 1961);

Pale Fire (New York: Putnam, 1962; London: Weidenfeld & Nicolson, 1962);

Notes on Prosody: From the Commentary to His Translation of Pushkin's Eugene Onegin (New York: Bollingen Foundation, 1963 [offprint]; trade edition, 1964; London: Routledge & Kegan Paul, 1965);

The Waltz Invention, translated by Dmitri Nabokov (New York: Phaedra, 1966);

Nabokov's Quartet, translated by Dmitri Nabokov (New York: Phaedra, 1966; London: Weidenfeld & Nicolson, 1967);

Nabokov's Congeries, edited by Page Stegner (New York: Viking, 1968); republished as *The Portable Nabokov* (New York: Viking, 1971);

Ada or Ardor: A Family Chronicle (New York: McGraw-Hill, 1969; London: Weidenfeld & Nicolson, 1969);

Poems and Problems (New York: McGraw-Hill, 1970 [1971]; London: Weidenfeld & Nicolson, 1972);

Transparent Things (New York: McGraw-Hill, 1972; London: Weidenfeld & Nicolson, 1973);

A Russian Beauty and Other Stories, translated by Dmitri Nabokov, Nabokov, and Simon Karlinsky (New York: McGraw-Hill, 1973; London: Weidenfeld & Nicolson, 1973);

Strong Opinions (New York: McGraw-Hill, 1973; London: Weidenfeld & Nicolson, 1974);

Lolita: A Screenplay (New York: McGraw-Hill, 1974);

Look at the Harlequins! (New York: McGraw-Hill, 1974; London: Weidenfeld & Nicolson, 1975);

Tyrants Destroyed and Other Stories, translated by Dmitri Nabokov and Nabokov (New York: McGraw-Hill, 1975; London: Weidenfeld & Nicolson, 1975);

Details of a Sunset and Other Stories, translated by Dmitri Nabokov and Nabokov (New York: McGraw-Hill, 1976; London: Weidenfeld & Nicolson, 1976);

Stikhi (Ann Arbor, Mich.: Ardis, 1979);

Lectures on Literature, edited by Fredson Bowers (New York & London: Harcourt Brace Jovanovich/Bruccoli Clark, 1980; London: Weidenfeld & Nicolson, 1980);

Lectures on Ulysses: A Facsimile of the Manuscript (Bloomfield Hills, Mich. & Columbia, S.C.: Bruccoli Clark, 1980);

Lectures on Russian Literature, edited by Bowers (New York & London: Harcourt Brace Jovanovich/Bruccoli Clark, 1981; London: Weidenfeld & Nicolson, 1982);

Lectures on Don Quixote, edited by Bowers (San Diego, New York & London: Harcourt Brace Jovanovich/Bruccoli Clark, 1983; London: Weidenfeld & Nicolson, 1983);

The Man from the USSR and Other Plays, translated by Dmitri Nabokov (San Diego, New York & London: Bruccoli Clark/Harcourt Brace Jovanovich, 1984; London: Weidenfeld & Nicolson, 1985);

The Enchanter, translated by Dmitri Nabokov (New York: Putnam, 1986; London: Picador, 1987);

Carrousel; Laughter and Dreams; Painted Wood; The Russian Song (Aartswoud, The Netherlands: Spectatorpers, 1987);

The Stories of Vladimir Nabokov (New York: Knopf, 1995; London: Weidenfeld & Nicolson, 1996);

Nabokov's Butterflies: Unpublished and Uncollected Writings, edited by Brian Boyd and Robert Michael Pyle, translations by Dmitri Nabokov (Boston: Beacon, 2000).

PRODUCED SCRIPT: *Lolita*, by Nabokov and Stanley Kubrick, motion picture, M-G-M, 1962.

Vladimir and Sergei Nabokov in St. Petersburg, 1916 (from Andrew Field, Nabokov: His Life in Part, 1977; by permission of Dmitri Nabokov)

TRANSLATIONS: Romain Rolland, *Nikolka persik (Colas Breugnon),* translated as Vladimir Sirin (Berlin: Slovo, 1922);

Lewis Carroll, *Ania v strane chudes,* translated as V. Sirin (Berlin: Gamiun, 1923);

Three Russian Poets: Selections from Pushkin, Lermontov, and Tyutchev (Norfolk, Conn.: New Directions, 1944 [1945]); republished as *Pushkin Lermontov Tyutchev: Poems* (London: Lindsay Drummond, 1947);

Mikhail Iur'evich Lermontov, *A Hero of Our Time,* translated by Nabokov and Dmitri Nabokov (Garden City, N.Y.: Doubleday, 1958);

The Song of Igor's Campaign: An Epic of the Twelfth Century (New York: Vintage, 1960; London: Weidenfeld & Nicolson, 1961);

Aleksandr Sergeevich Pushkin, *Eugene Onegin: A Novel in Verse,* 4 volumes (New York: Bollingen Foundation, 1964; London: Routledge & Kegan Paul, 1964; revised edition, Princeton: Princeton University Press, 1975; London: Routledge & Kegan Paul, 1976).

Vladimir Nabokov is one of the most important novelists of the twentieth century—and a thoroughly international one whose work is as carefully read in France, Germany, Japan, and Finland as in his homelands of Russia and the United States. Nabokov was a serious man of letters, researching Russian literary history while writing American novels. In his fiction he claimed that his purpose was aesthetic rather than moral; yet, he had a didactic streak that came out in his lectures, his scholarship, and his interviews. He was known for the brilliance of his language and the intricate structure of his novels, and his work is filled with careful observations, flamboyant language, and an Olympian wit. The deliberately laid puzzles in his novels are still being debated, and he is much discussed in the literary world.

Born to a wealthy St. Petersburg family on 23 April 1899, Vladimir Vladimirovich Nabokov grew up surrounded by the high culture of Europe. His family had a history of government service. His father, Vladimir Dmitrievich Nabokov, was a liberal and an active member of the *duma* (the Russian parliament) until he was briefly jailed and stripped of his political rights in 1908 for signing a manifesto opposing conscription. His mother, Elena Ivanovna (née Rukavishnikov) Nabokov, closely observed her son's childhood, and her spiritual qualities were as important to her son as his father's cultural tastes. Both parents were avid readers. Nabokov's evocative memoir, *Speak, Memory* (1951), is primarily concerned with these formative years, describing St. Petersburg, the country estate where his family usually spent the summer, his passion for collecting moths and butterflies, his voracious reading, his girlfriends, trips to Europe with his parents and four siblings, playing chess, writing poetry, and developing his own unshakable code of conduct.

Nabokov was fluent in English, French, and Russian at an early age. Taught at home until he was ten, he then entered the Tenishev School in St. Petersburg but also continued with some tutoring at home, including art lessons; it was thought that he would grow up to be a painter. At the Tenishev School, Nabokov rebelled against all forms of organized activities (except soccer, at which he played goalie through college and into his thirties). This reticence proved embarrassing for the son of such a prominent activist as his father, but even as a young man Nabokov was unyielding in his decisions. Throughout his life he refused to join societies and organizations, even academic ones.

In 1917 the February Revolution led to the temporary installation of a democratic regime, with Nabokov's father again active in politics, first as chancellor in the provisional government and then as a member of the constituent assembly. But the February Revolution was followed eight months later by the Bolshevik coup, or October Revolution, and the Nabokov family fled to the Crimea. Nabokov's father remained behind to work with the constituent assembly, but after being briefly jailed by the Bolsheviks, he too escaped to the Black Sea, where he then served as minister of justice in the Crimean provisional regional government. During an unsettled year and a half in the Black Sea area, Nabokov wrote poetry and carried on several love affairs. As the Bolsheviks arrived in April of 1919, the Nabokov family fled Sebastopol by ship.

The family settled in England for a year, and Nabokov enrolled at Cambridge University along with his younger brother; his major course of study was in French and Russian. The rest of the family left England for Berlin, where Nabokov's father helped establish a Russian-language newspaper, *Rul'* (The Rudder). In Cambridge, Nabokov began to write copiously, primarily in verse, and much of his work appeared in *Rul'* under the pen name Sirin. On 28 March 1922 Nabokov's father was shot by ultraright extremists in Berlin. Nabokov's reverence for his father was strong and comes out clearly in his writings; he seems to have felt occasional intimations of his father's presence in his later life.

Nabokov left England for Berlin in June 1922 after graduating from Cambridge, doing odd jobs and writing verse plays. One of his assignments that summer was to translate *Alice's Adventures in Wonderland* (1865) into Russian; Nabokov's writing has some affinities with Lewis Carroll's, and occasional allusions to the earlier author's works appear in Nabokov's fiction. He became engaged, but the arrangement was soon broken off, apparently under pressure from his fiancée's parents, worried about his lack of a steady job.

A year later, partially in an attempt to overcome a bout of depression, Nabokov spent the summer as a farmworker in the south of France, his only such attempt at manual labor. On his return he began to focus his writing more on short fiction, and he began actively courting Véra Slonim, whom he married on 15 April 1925. She protected him from various outside worries, typing and retyping manuscripts endlessly, and serving as an ideal secretary for him while continuing her daytime secretarial job; later in America she learned to drive a car so that Nabokov would not have to. She remained dedicated to his work throughout her life, and without such a partner Nabokov might not have been the artist he was. Resolutely remaining outside the spotlight, Véra Nabokov nevertheless has been the subject of a Pulitzer Prize–winning biography by Stacy Schiff (1999).

By 1925 Nabokov had begun tutoring in various languages and even in tennis, while picking up occasional extra funds through translating, publishing short works, and participating in readings. Although the center of the Russian emigration soon moved to Paris, Nabokov stayed in Berlin until 1937—a particularly

Nabokov in 1923 (Nabokov Family Archive; by permission of Dmitri Nabokov)

risky decision, as Véra Nabokov was Jewish. Neither Nabokov nor his wife was interested in politics, and neither seemed aware of how dangerous Adolf Hitler's Germany could be.

Nabokov's fiction encompasses the whole range from brief sketches to long novels. He started by writing short works for Russian-language newspapers, was soon working on his first novels, and by the late 1920s he had begun to write some memorable works. The stories included everything from almost plotless sketches to parts of abandoned novels and even stories related to actual novels. Of the stories that appeared before his first novel, the most notable are "La Veneziana" (1924), "Christmas" (1924), "The Potato Elf" (1924), and the fascinating "The Return of Chorb" (1925).

In 1924 Nabokov began a novel, "Happiness," that was never completed; one fragment became the story "A Letter That Never Reached Russia," while other elements were revised into parts of his first novel, *Mashen'ka* (1926; translated as *Mary,* 1970), a year later. Nabokov's Russian novels might be divided into three kinds: the vaguely autobiographical ones, in which the main character has a Russian background and shares Nabokov's own memories; the carefully plotted ones, with coldly observed German characters and love triangles; and the case studies, in which the main characters owe something to the psychiatric works that Nabokov read for ideas.

Mary was begun in the spring of 1925, soon after Nabokov's marriage. Much of it was built on his experiences, and he even quoted from love letters sent to him by Valentina Shul'gina, with whom he had had his first love affair in 1915. In the novel the Russian émigré inhabitants of a Berlin boardinghouse live out a pointless existence, waiting for the return to Russia that never comes. The protagonist, Ganin, is presented as a normally active young man who is now the victim of ennui and enmeshed in a tiresome love affair as well. But when he learns that the wife of one of his neighbors is arriving on the train from Russia, and that she is Mary, his long-lost love from prerevolutionary days, he begins a week of living in his memories. At this point the book abruptly changes tone from drab to vivid. Ganin's memories of Mary, which closely resemble Nabokov's recollections of "Tamara" in the twelfth chapter of *Speak, Memory,* occupy a major portion of the book. Many years later, Nabokov found that these fictionalized memories seemed to represent that time period better than his own memoir. Once Ganin has exhausted his memories, however, he cancels his plan to confront Mary at the train station, realizing that the past can be revisited in memory but cannot be relived in the present. He abruptly leaves Berlin, having finally overcome his inertia and indifference.

Nabokov's second novel was *Korol' dama valet* (1928; translated as *King, Queen, Knave,* 1968). An arrangement between his publisher and a German firm led to immediate and profitable translations of his first two novels into German (in the 1960s, new paperbacks of these old translations were the only available editions of *Mary* and *King, Queen, Knave*). Nabokov created a German cast for his second novel, a high-spirited but unsuccessful version of the love triangle. He had already begun using well-worn plots as the excuse for virtuoso effects in stories such as "An Affair of Honor," in which the challenger runs away to avoid the duel he initiated. In *King, Queen, Knave* the first scene is presented through the unfocused eyes of a character who has lost his glasses. Other scenes are presented during someone's fever, or even upside down as a madman bends down to see the world through his legs. There are also references to the story line being made into a movie even as it happens—a device that recurs in several later works. Nabokov and his wife appear in thin disguise toward the end of the novel, another device that he used with some frequency. In *King, Queen, Knave* Martha Dreyer has an affair with her husband's nephew, and the two of them plot to drown her businessman husband (the wittiest and most artistic of the three characters) in a staged rowboat accident. The "accident" misfires, and unexpectedly, a different character dies. Nabokov frequently reminds readers that situations in the novel resemble those in other novels, and he uses clichés to prepare the reader for his deliberate reversal of the conventional expectation.

King, Queen, Knave is not entirely a successful novel. One problem is that the very shallowness of the characters, as emphasized by the author, leaves them of less interest than they would be otherwise, although in *Nabokov and the Novel* Ellen Pifer has demonstrated that their psychology is developed with care. The highly stylized wittiness occasionally reveals that the novel has little substance. In the English translation of 1968 Nabokov felt free to make many changes—not just in incidental details but in several major plot matters. His tinkering may serve to highlight the arbitrariness of the novel. A theatrical version was successfully performed in Russia in 1999.

During the 1920s Nabokov also frequently wrote book reviews, primarily on poetry collections and fiction but also on an art exhibition and on a study of the chess masters José Raúl Capablanca and Alexander Alekhine—of some relevance to his third novel, *Zashchita Luzhina* (1930; translated as *The Defense,* 1964). In 1929 Nabokov wrote and began to serially publish in the Paris journal *Sovremennye zapiski* (Notes of the Fatherland) this first major novel, a psychological study of a chess genius who goes insane. It immediately drew the attention of the émigré critics, prompting the poet Vladislav Khodasevich to write a major review on 11 October 1930 in *Vozrozhdenie* (The Renaissance) arguing that "the central subject of Nabokov's art was art itself." Luzhin, the protagonist of *The Defense,* is an extremely sympathetic character. As Nabokov noted, Luzhin has several things in common with Bachmann, the virtuoso/composer protagonist of his eponymous story of 1924. But in addition to the exploration of the mind of a deteriorating genius, the novel also displays the kind of originality that is singled out by Nabokov's admirers and detractors alike, such as the way that Luzhin's last name is given in the first sentence of the book but his first name and patronymic are not given until its last—Nabokov's first attempt to make his novels circular (or rather spiral) in structure. Although the chapters of *The Defense* are normally chronological, the reader is not prepared for a sudden unexplained jump of many years in the middle of the novel. A subtle comparison of chess and music also runs through it. In addition, one aspect of the brilliance of the novel is that Luzhin's chess abilities—and growing madness—make him sensitive to all the little patterns and coincidences in life, and the novel weaves such a fabric around him that the reader begins to feel that more and more careful reading is both necessary and desirable. In the end, Luzhin commits suicide to prevent what he feels to be his own checkmate. The novel was made into a movie, *The Luzhin Defence* (screenplay by Peter Berry), in 2000.

Nabokov's next publication of any length was the novella *Sogliadatai* (1938; translated as *The Eye,* 1965), another psychological study but one depending on a single trick of viewpoint: after attempting suicide, the protagonist sees himself in third person, dissociated, and attempts to find out who that unknown person is. Although its first Russian book publication was as the title work of a collection of stories, it was eventually published in English by itself; since it was not included in the 1995 omnibus *Stories of Vladimir Nabokov,* it remains an elusive title.

The Eye was followed by *Podvig* (1932; translated as *Glory,* 1971), serialized in *Sovremennye zapiski* in 1931 and translated last among Nabokov's novels (it was referred to in scholarship as *The Exploit* until Nabokov altered the title in its 1971 translation). *Glory* is another of the works in which the hero shares many of Nabokov's experiences, and readers of *Speak, Memory* will recognize scenes from both the childhood and the Cambridge activities of protagonist Martin Edelweiss. The novel includes a sort of love triangle between Martin, his fellow émigré Sonia, and his English college friend Darwin, but ultimately Sonia eludes a serious relationship with either one. Martin is a kind but almost directionless young man, who eventually imagines a satirical version of Soviet Russia ("Zoorland") and then, having decided to cross incognito into the real totalitarian state as a test of his self-resolve, is apparently shot at the border. In the last scene of the novel Darwin pauses in the forest to commune either with his own thoughts or with Martin's spirit. Although the question is a muted one, *Glory* is the first of Nabokov's novels that raises the possibility of communicating with the dead. The novel is both somewhat mystifying and somewhat self-indulgent.

As *Glory* was being serialized in 1931, Nabokov was writing *Kamera obscura* (1933; translated as *Laughter in the Dark,* 1938), which was serialized in *Sovremennye zapiski* between 1932 and 1933. Like *King, Queen, Knave* this novel had an all-German cast, a love triangle, a murder plot, carefully worked out cinematic imagery (apparently the novel is being shown at the local theater while it is taking place), a cool, distant feeling as though the author were putting his puppets through their paces, and extensive revisions when it was translated; but this novel is a far more skilled work. An older man leaves his wife for a young woman (an usher in a cinema) who only wants his money. A visually oriented art critic, the man loses his sight in an auto wreck and, in a chilling plot twist, slowly grows aware in his blind-

Paper cover for Nabokov's first novel, Mashen'ka, *published in Russian in 1926 and in English as* Mary *in 1970 (Simon Finch Rare Books catalogue 53, 2002)*

ness that his young girlfriend has a lover. The first English translation of *Kamera obscura,* done by others, appeared in 1936. Nabokov then rewrote, improved, and retitled the novel for its American publication in 1938 as *Laughter in the Dark.* A movie version was made in 1969.

The next novel, *Otchaianie* (1936; translated as *Despair,* 1937), was serialized in *Sovremennye zapiski* in 1934, the same year that the Nabokovs' only child, Dmitri Vladimirovich, was born. Again, Nabokov uses a well-worn plot for virtuoso effect: the protagonist, Hermann, apparently discovers his double, a tramp with an identical appearance; Hermann decides to murder the tramp and collect the insurance money for his own death. The Nabokov twist is what Hermann fails to understand: to other people, he does not particularly resemble the man he has murdered. Hermann is not observant, and he fails even to realize that his wife is carrying on an affair with an artist friend under his nose. *Despair* carries to an extreme Nabokov's frequent use of references to other authors and parodic displays of well-worn literary devices. The madman narrator is a standard figure going back to Edgar Allan Poe and especially to Fyodor Dostoevsky, and references to *Notes from Underground* (1864), *The Double* (1846), and *Crime and Punishment* (1867) recur. At some points this substratum of literary parallels seems the point of the novel; it also tends to be the focus of the critics. In spite of a confusing ending (in which events move so quickly that the narrator has trouble keeping up with them in his diary), the novel is elegantly realized. However, as Nabokov has little admiration for his unintelligent murderer, his obsessive narration may not be sufficient to maintain the reader's interest. Nabokov's 1937 English translation of *Despair* attracted little interest; it was considerably revised for republication in 1966.

By 1936 Nabokov was desperately trying to leave Germany and find a career elsewhere. After completing his translation of *Despair* into English, he wrote several pieces in French, including "Mademoiselle O" (1936), which later became a chapter in his autobiography, *Speak, Memory*. He also wrote the novella "Spring in Fialta" (1936) in Russian. "Spring in Fialta" details the final encounter of the unnamed narrator and Nina, a woman with whom he has had a fitful love affair over the years. In spite of signs and warnings of various kinds that the narrator fails to interpret at the time, he is unprepared when he learns that immediately after leaving Fialta, Nina has been killed in an auto accident. It is one of the Nabokov stories in which much of the action is hidden from the actors and only visible to the reader after re-reading.

Nabokov had been planning his most important Russian novel, *Dar* (1952; translated as *The Gift*, 1963) since 1932; it was first serialized in *Sovremennye zapiski* between 1937 and 1938. It describes the life of a young Russian émigré writer, Fyodor Godunov-Cherndynt-sev, not too far removed in age and talent from Nabokov himself. In 1934 Nabokov published "The Circle," a story that obliquely shows some of the characters from the novel but that does not impinge on its action. The story shows moments from earlier in Fyodor's childhood and later in his career than are covered in *The Gift*. Nabokov then embarked on writing the fourth of the five long chapters of the novel, out of sequence. It is a biography written by Fyodor: a highly irreverent life of Nikolai Gavrilovich Chernyshevsky, the prominent nineteenth-century Russian novelist and political writer who was claimed as an ancestor by both the Russian liberals and the Bolsheviks. Although this debunking biography is significant as Nabokov's dismissal of nineteenth-century Russian idealist political literature, contemporary American readers may find it hard going. The rest of the novel certainly supports the general claim that *The Gift* is Nabokov's Russian masterpiece.

Set in the Russian émigré community in Berlin in the mid 1920s, *The Gift* is a Proustian evocation of a vanished culture; it tells the story of Fyodor's development as a writer, with samples of his work throughout. It has other dimensions as well: each of the five long chapters is written in a different style, apparently intending to evoke the history of Russian literature. Everything is acutely observed and sharply delineated, from how women sit when they talk on the telephone to how the audience behaves at literary readings, or how Germans sun themselves in the park. The first chapter also includes poems written by Fyodor about his childhood. The second, after some imaginary reviews of Fyodor's book of poems, moves into an imagined trip through Asia with Fyodor's father, a famous naturalist and explorer; it is written in the heightened, romantic style of Aleksandr Sergeevich Pushkin's travel literature. The third chapter, as much a description of Fyodor's associates as Fyodor himself, is more comic, its language mimicking that of great Russian comic author Nikolai Gogol (on whom Nabokov later wrote a book). While the chapter focuses on the absurd intrigues of the Russian literary intelligentsia in exile, the situations are universal. The fourth chapter, about Chernyshevsky, tries to pinpoint the stage at which Russian literature began its decline. The last chapter, after some satiric examples of supposed reviews of Fyodor's work, shows Fyodor in love with Zina Mertz and deciding to write a novel much like *The Gift*.

The Gift received surprisingly little attention from its puzzled (or shocked) Russian readers, and later criticism has also been scant. Aside from a thorough discussion in Brian Boyd's biography of Nabokov, what little scholarship there is tends to focus on the view of Russian literature that can be deduced from the troublesome Chernyshevsky chapter.

In the middle of his work on *The Gift*, Nabokov was suddenly inspired with the idea for *Priglashenie na kazn'* (1938; translated as *Invitation to a Beheading*, 1959). This novel takes place in the distant future, when most people have succumbed to received ideas and have no inner life of their own, with the exception of the protagonist, Cincinnatus C., who is imprisoned and sentenced to death for "gnostical turpitude" because he is not "transparent" to his fellows. Some of the other characters in the novel are revealed as being interchangeable, and in their total lack of sensitivity they scold him when he refuses to become friends with his executioner. As the clumsy world around him falls apart at the end of this highly idealistic novel—idealistic in a somewhat Platonic sense—Cincinnatus walks away from his execu-

Paper covers for Nabokov's 1955 novel, published first in Paris because American publishers considered it too controversial (Ken Lopez catalogue number 124, 2002)

tion toward the voices of "beings akin to him." Nabokov wrote the first draft in three weeks, and the novel remained one of his favorites; it also has gained appreciation from modern readers who do not respond so well to Nabokov's other fictions. Originally, the novel was seen as an antitotalitarian allegory, and in translation it has been compared to Franz Kafka's *The Trial* (1925) in its treatment of the individual and the state. Later criticism has tended to focus on the meaning of "gnostical turpitude" and whether it indicates a strand of mysticism in Nabokov's thought.

At the beginning of 1937 Nabokov moved to France and went on a reading trip to London as well. Véra Nabokov remained behind in Berlin, and Nabokov had an affair with Irina Guadanini, who was said to resemble his wife. The stresses of the time were apparently responsible for the painful and distracting outbreak of a skin disease that he suffered from for several months. The affair ended stormily after Véra Nabokov left Berlin for a reunion in Prague, where

Nabokov's mother was ill. From 1937 through 1939 the Nabokovs lived at various locations in the French countryside and occasionally in Paris, continually looking for a new career, their finances desperate. During this time *The Gift* was completed, but *Sovremennye zapiski*, the journal in which his works had appeared for many years, refused to publish the controversial Chernyshevsky chapter; it did not appear in print until the 1950s, in America, by which time the Russian émigré audience to which the argument was addressed had scattered. Nabokov's mother died in Prague in 1939.

During this unsettled time, Nabokov's writing was equally unsettled. He began a novel in Russian, "Solus Rex," and then abandoned it; two long chapters, "Ultima Thule" and "Solus Rex," were published as stories in Russian and eventually translated into English. Some of the ideas from the unfinished novel and its imaginary country resurfaced in *Bend Sinister* (1947) and later still, more prominently, in *Pale Fire* (1962). Nabokov also wrote a novella in Russian, *The*

Enchanter, which ten years later began to evolve into *Lolita* (1955). Thought lost at the time of composition of *Lolita,* the story resurfaced and was published as a short novel in English in 1986. What *The Enchanter* shares with *Lolita* is a protagonist who lusts after preteenage girls and who marries a woman in order to have access to her daughter; however, in this version the unpleasant protagonist does not get to tell his story himself, and when he attempts to seduce the daughter in a hotel after her mother dies, he comes to disaster.

The Nabokovs arrived in New York on 28 May 1940. While preparing lectures for his stint at Stanford the next summer, he began to write reviews and to do lepidoptera research. He met Edmund Wilson on 8 October, beginning an important literary and personal friendship that ended in a series of quarrels many years later. The well-known Wilson was as complete a man of letters as Nabokov and wrote fiction, poetry, and assorted unclassifiable works as well as literary essays; he also had a passionate interest in Russian literature. The two men carried on an impressive correspondence (published in 1979) and planned several joint projects involving Russian and American literature, only a few of which were eventually completed. Wilson also helped Nabokov get grants and, equally important, introduced him to *The New Yorker.*

Laughter in the Dark, the revision of *Kamera obscura,* had been published in America in 1938. Nabokov's next novel published in America was *The Real Life of Sebastian Knight,* the first novel he had composed in English; completed in France by the beginning of 1939, it was published at the end of 1941. *The Real Life of Sebastian Knight* is presented as a biography of the half-English, half-Russian novelist Sebastian Knight written in English by his entirely Russian half brother. A fairly slight book, it is a minor masterpiece. The narrator, known only as "V," recalls Sebastian's life, his attachment to his glamorous but indifferent mother, and his affair with an equally glamorous and indifferent woman who wrecked his life. Part of V's quest is to find this mysterious woman—who nearly catches him instead. In the course of his highly impressionistic biography, V also summarizes the plots of his brother's several novels; gradually it becomes apparent that the current story seems influenced by or reflective of these works and that the course of V's quest seems to be out of his own control—perhaps directed by his dead brother. Around 1970 three different critical articles described these correspondences and debated the significance of the final words of the novel: "I am Sebastian, or Sebastian is I, or perhaps we both are someone whom neither of us knows." Critics then lost interest until the 1990s, when Nabokov's "otherworld" became a topic to investigate.

Following his first teaching position, a summer at Stanford, Nabokov taught at Wellesley. After Russia became America's ally, his anti-Soviet stance became embarrassing to the school administration. He continued to teach there sporadically, and for several years he spent more time on a research fellowship in entomology at the Harvard Museum of Comparative Zoology than he did on literature and writing, although he published several lepidopteral papers. In these few years Nabokov's scientific work was difficult, technical, and ahead of his time; only since the 1990s has his reclassification of a group of butterflies known popularly as the "blues" received significant scientific attention. During this deep plunge into entomological research, these first years in America were the lowest point in Nabokov's literary productivity. His first English-language story, "The Assistant Producer," was published in *The Atlantic* in 1943, and soon afterward he began writing short works for *The New Yorker.* At this time his stories focused on Russian émigré life, a subject he soon abandoned except for the later novel *Pnin* (1957). His eccentric literary study *Nikolai Gogol* was published in 1944, using some of the same distancing techniques he had developed for the Chernyshevsky biography in *The Gift,* such as beginning with Gogol's death and ending with his birth. Nabokov's next novel, *Bend Sinister,* did not appear until 1947.

Bend Sinister, which takes place in an imaginary European country where the language is a mixture of Russian and German, dramatizes the struggle between the philosopher Adam Krug and the country's totalitarian dictator, nicknamed The Toad, who had been Adam's classmate in school. Adam's refusal to endorse the new regime leads to the death of everyone around him, including his son, and eventually to Adam's madness and death. There are several brilliant set pieces, including a dizzying discussion of William Shakespeare's *Hamlet,* but the obvious goodness of Adam and his friends and the practically subhuman character of the totalitarians makes the novel as a whole melodramatic. Again, the ending is a striking surprise: after being immersed in the novel, the reader is abruptly face to face with its author, who, having finished his manuscript late at night, seems to have turned his interest to the moths outside his window. In 1964 Nabokov contributed an extremely long introduction to a special edition of *Bend Sinister,* and these comments, which have been included with later editions, have proved to be the most thorough glimpse Nabokov ever offered into his fictional workshop.

By 1948, when the Nabokovs moved to Ithaca, New York, for Nabokov to begin his professorship at Cornell University, he was working again on literature, although his entomological research continued in the summers in the Rocky Mountains—where in 1951 he caught the first female of *Lycaeides sublivens*, a butterfly that helped to inspire *Lolita*. That year *Speak, Memory* was published in book form; he had been publishing chapters of it in *The New Yorker*. This autobiography is one of his best and best-loved books and has always been a principal source of information about his life and views; it also offers, at times, close parallels to his fiction. Nabokov stated that it was an attempt to follow "thematic designs" in his life, but critics have tended to treat it as a sourcebook rather than a text to be analyzed. The seventh chapter of Nabokov's memoir, originally titled "Colette" for magazine publication, was also included in his English-language story collection *Nabokov's Dozen* (1958) under the title "First Love." It was a fairly straightforward piece of prose but has been frequently anthologized, probably because in age and appearance Colette bears some superficial resemblance to Lolita.

In 1950 Nabokov began teaching "Masterpieces of European Fiction," a popular course at Cornell. At this time he began to plan *Lolita*. He was also at work on a translation of Pushkin's *Eugene Onegin*, partially as an aid to his students, a project for which he received a Guggenheim Fellowship in 1952. *Pnin* was added to the list of projects, and he published individual chapters of that novel in *The New Yorker* while completing *Lolita*. After failing to find an American publisher because of its scandalous subject matter, Nabokov published *Lolita* in Paris in 1955, in English.

At the end of the twentieth century, when various groups drew up lists of the most significant novels of the century, *Lolita* was included at or near the top of every one. It remains controversial more than a half century after it was written. Censorship concerns delayed the release of the 1997 movie version for several years. The basic plot of a man marrying a widow in order to have access to her underage daughter occurs as far back as *The Gift*, in which the man is a highly offensive minor character. Apparently the idea of developing this plot into a novel came to Nabokov after he captured the female of the elusive *Lycaeides sublivens* butterfly near Dolores, Colorado, in 1951. He was then able to transfer his own passion for lepidoptera to Humbert Humbert's obsession with barely pubescent girls: in the novel, desirable young women are called "nymphets," a term that also applies to insects such as butterflies that undergo metamorphosis. Although Humbert suffers for his misdeeds and dies at the end of the novel, his compelling madman's voice and his powerful evocation of Lolita are what the reader remembers. By the time that Humbert realizes that he actually loves Lolita, he has ruined her childhood and she has escaped his control. He launches a search for the even

Nabokov with his wife, Véra, and son, Dmitri, in 1960
(AP/Wide World Photos)

less scrupulous and more brilliant madman Clare Quilty, killing him in one of the most unforgettable—and imitated—scenes in literature. The wit of the narration, together with the powerful emotions evoked (and often ignored by Humbert himself), make *Lolita* a tour de force. The first movie version of *Lolita*, directed by Stanley Kubrick from a screenplay written by Nabokov and Kubrick, appeared in 1962; the 1997 version was somewhat less successful. A 1971 musical, *Lolita, My Love*, by John Barry with lyrics by Alan Lerner, never reached Broadway; a 1981 theatrical version adapted by Edward Albee was also a critical disaster. Many critical pages have been devoted to *Lolita*, but the most reliable guide is *The Annotated Lolita*, edited by Alfred Appel Jr. in 1970.

Although Graham Greene had selected *Lolita* as one of the best novels of 1955, it was not published in the United States until 1958. In the meantime *Pnin* was published in 1957 and widely admired. Reflecting Nabokov's experiences at Cornell, *Pnin* is his academic novel, with a teacher of Russian as its main character. Pnin is a brilliant man, but his intelligence is obscured in America by his Russian accent and his comic difficulties with the English language. Only in one central chapter is he seen as he really is, vacationing with fellow émigrés among whom his witty observations and kindly attitudes shine. The rest of the time he is humiliated by mocking colleagues, unreliable train schedules, painful trips to the dentist, an exploitative former wife, and job insecurity caused by faculty politics. Gradually, because of his resilience, patience, and strength, as well as the relationship he establishes with his former wife's son, he becomes a more sympathetic than comic character. Cruelly fired from his college position, he faces a final humiliation when he is replaced in his job by someone who seems to be not only the narrator but also Nabokov himself. Some of Nabokov's other protagonists seem to come eventually to an awareness that they are invented characters; Pnin seems able instead to face his creator at a personal level, transcending the printed page. There are clues indicating that he is in some way protected by the spirit of Mira, a girlfriend of many years earlier who died in the Holocaust, but these are merely part of a complex yet unobtrusive network of interlocking references throughout the novel that unite Russian literature, émigré life, and small-town New England.

The American publication of *Lolita* in 1958 brought Nabokov fame and fortune. He quit teaching early in 1959. After a long trip to Europe, in 1960 the Nabokovs returned to the United States for a few months for Nabokov to work on the *Lolita* screenplay. Again in Europe, in 1962 they moved to a sixth-floor apartment in the Montreux Palace hotel in Switzerland that they kept for the rest of their lives. By this time Nabokov was a public figure, and his carefully controlled interviews were eagerly sought after. Photographs of him enthusiastically chasing butterflies in the mountains appeared in magazines. He spent much of his time translating his earlier Russian works into English; yet, in his sixties Nabokov produced two major novels that are still among his most discussed and debated, *Pale Fire* and *Ada or Ardor: A Family Chronicle* (1969).

The appearance and structure of *Pale Fire* are distinctive. The novel consists of a foreword by Charles Kinbote, the 999-line poem "Pale Fire" by John Shade, and a commentary on the poem by Kinbote that is far longer than the poem itself, followed by an index. Shade is a famous old poet, somewhat on the lines of Robert Frost, who is shot and killed in front of Kinbote's house just after completing "Pale Fire," a serious, meditative, autobiographical poem describing his life and philosophy, including his lifelong love for his wife and the suicide of their bright but unattractive daughter. Shade has tried to discover whether there is life beyond the grave; although he fails in his attempt, he finds consolation in the conclusion that the complexities of life are themselves the clue, "not text, but texture."

The commentary by Kinbote is anything but serious: soon the reader realizes that Kinbote is not merely Shade's next-door neighbor and a fellow professor (whose real name is Botkin), but a madman who believes that he is the King of Zembla, continually in danger from the Shadows, a sinister group of revolutionaries. The two men are contrasts in everything: Shade is old, heterosexual, agnostic, American; Kinbote is young, homosexual, High Church, foreign. What comic aspects are revealed in Shade's character are mild and sympathetic, usually his own ironic observations, while on the other hand, the comedy of Kinbote is broad and burlesque, the result of his own lack of perception of himself.

The murder is a doubly complicated tragedy of mistaken identity and typical of the many levels of the novel: the criminally insane Jack Grey shoots Shade because he mistakes the poet for his neighbor, the judge who sentenced Grey to jail; however, Kinbote, who tries to protect Shade from the assassin, believes that he, the King of Zembla, was the actual target of the killer. On a personal level for Nabokov, the scene reflects his father's assassination in Berlin forty years earlier as he tried to protect another speaker. Not only is *Pale Fire* unusual in form and appearance, it is an amazing set of Kinbote's word games laid on top of Shade's eloquence.

When *Pale Fire* was published, Mary McCarthy published a long review that revealed and explored several intricacies of the novel; this review has remained one foundation for later work. For years various critics argued that either of the two main characters, Shade or Kinbote, might have actually written the whole work, creating the other character, but this line of argument seems to have declined since Boyd, Nabokov's biographer, abandoned his position as one of the "Shadeans" to explore the possibility that the pattern of ghostly presences for which Shade searched in vain may actually exist within the novel; he has devoted an entire book, *Nabokov's Pale Fire* (1999), to exploring this issue.

In 1964 Nabokov published his translation of Pushkin's *Eugene Onegin*, the great Russian verse novel of 1832, in four volumes. Somewhat in the fashion of his own *Pale Fire*, Nabokov's notes (two volumes of them) dwarfed the poem in size. His insistence on a literal translation—and his own idea of how such a translation should be written—proved controversial. Much earlier, he had published rhymed versions of a few of Pushkin's verses; now he limited his attempts to distinguish his translation from prose to simply writing it in iambics—and in a second edition he somewhat abandoned even that. Along with other controversies involving *Eugene Onegin*, Nabokov fought a protracted battle with Edmund Wilson in the pages of the *New York Review of Books* after Wilson's antagonistic review

Two of the notecards on which Nabokov wrote his 1962 novel, Pale Fire
(Library of Congress; by permission of Dmitri Nabokov)

of the translation; the exchange ended their long friendship.

This exhausting achievement was followed in 1969 by *Ada,* Nabokov's longest and most difficult novel. Told by Van, with emendations by Ada and occasional notes by others, it is the story of the incestuous love affair of two extremely wealthy children of eccentric parents who find out that they are not first cousins, as they have been told, but brother and sister. Their affair begins as children; then they grow up, are separated for a long time, and after being reunited, live happy lives together until their nineties. Their lives are sometimes destructive to those around them; when Van refuses to bring their half sister, Lucette, into the relationship, Lucette commits suicide. They seem to live on an alternative Earth called Antiterra, which may be merely a metaphor for their solipsism and tendency to close themselves off from everyone else. Even aside from confusion caused by the alternative history, with wildly different groups inhabiting the differently named continents and countries (Americans live in Estoty; the barbarous land of Tartary occupies Russia's territory), Van and Ada often have to correct each other's memories, and the language of the novel is an English heavily larded with French and Russian. The plot is extremely discursive. The novel is divided into five parts, the first of which, covering only a few years of childhood, takes up more than half the novel; each succeeding section is shorter but encompasses a longer stretch of time (with the exception of the fourth, which is both a lecture about the nature of time and a description of Van and Ada's reunion after many years apart). Whether *Ada* is a masterpiece or an overrich, overindulgent novel is still not entirely decided.

In 1972 Nabokov published *Transparent Things.* This slight but pleasant novel is about Hugh Person, an otherwise inoffensive man who strangles his wife, Armande, in his sleep. Her death and Hugh's later death in a hotel fire seem strangely underplayed until the reader comprehends exactly what Nabokov means at the end when Hugh passes "from one state of being to another." Some peculiar descriptive passages and the title become clear in the last line of the book, when the observant reader realizes that *Transparent Things* has been narrated by the novelist Mr. R. after his own death. This novel strikingly reminded readers that Nabokov's characters frequently encounter what is now referred to in the criticism as "the otherworld." Although it helped change critics' views of Nabokov's metaphysics, this novel seems to have attracted little attention and only moderate praise.

A less successful novel and Nabokov's last, *Look at the Harlequins!* appeared in 1974. The narrator is a novelist whose life and works parody Nabokov's own.

The novel thumbs its nose at readers who look for an author's confessions in fiction—particularly scandalous fiction like *Lolita* and *Ada:* Vadim N. gets involved with little girls and with his own half sister. *Look at the Harlequins!* seems to have been inspired by Nabokov's exasperation with Andrew Field, with whom he had cooperated when Field had been writing a biography that turned out, in Nabokov's opinion, often to miss the mark. Earlier, Field had written a landmark study of Nabokov's Russian works, but his biography occasionally offered speculations that were both unsubstantiated and unpalatable to their subject. Later, Boyd took on the role of biographer more successfully, achieving a two-volume work that has proved invaluable to students and other researchers.

After *Look at the Harlequins!* Nabokov worked fitfully on another novel but was frequently interrupted by illness. The work, known as "The Original of Laura," remained in fragmentary form when Nabokov died on 2 July 1977 after two difficult years in and out of hospitals. It has not been published.

At the time of Nabokov's death, the International Vladimir Nabokov Society was already in its infant stages; it has now grown to hundreds of members and has subsidiaries in several countries. Its substantial newsletter, *The Nabokovian,* has now appeared twice a year for twenty-five years; in addition, *Nabokov Studies,* a scholarly annual, is preparing its seventh volume; there is a Nabokov discussion group on the Internet, Nabokov-L, and a scholarly website, Zembla. Nabokov has become a reference point for discussions of other writers in almost every issue of the *New York Times Book Review* and *The New Yorker.* Over the years, many younger authors have acknowledged their indebtedness to Nabokov's works; some have added their imitations as well. Novelists John Updike, Erica Jong, Bobbie Ann Mason, Susan Fromberg Shaeffer, Joyce Carol Oates, Kingsley Amis, and his son Martin Amis have all written extensively about him, while his influence seems to be found in the works of many other writers. Collected editions are being completed in Russian, French, and German. With the collapse of the Soviet Union, Russian interest has swelled, and many younger Russian authors have come under Nabokov's influence; there is also a Nabokov Museum in St. Petersburg. The Library of America has published all of his American novels in three volumes, indicating his status as a classic author. It must be concluded that Vladimir Nabokov has more admirers than ever.

Letters:

The Nabokov–Wilson Letters: Correspondence Between Vladimir Nabokov and Edmund Wilson, 1940–1971, edited by Simon Karlinsky (New York: Harper & Row, 1979; London: Weidenfeld & Nicolson, 1979); revised as *Dear Bunny, Dear Volodya* (Berkeley & London: University of California Press, 2001);

Perepiska s sestroi (Ann Arbor, Mich.: Ardis, 1985);

Vladimir Nabokov: Selected Letters, 1940–1977, edited by Dmitri Nabokov and Matthew J. Bruccoli (San Diego: Harcourt Brace Jovanovich, 1989).

Bibliographies:

Andrew Field, *Nabokov—A Bibliography* (New York: McGraw-Hill, 1973);

Samuel Schuman, *Vladimir Nabokov: A Reference Guide* (Boston: G. K. Hall, 1979);

Michael Juliar, *Vladimir Nabokov: A Descriptive Bibliography* (New York & London: Garland, 1986).

Biographies:

Andrew Field, *Nabokov: His Life in Part* (New York: Viking, 1977);

Field, *VN: The Life and Art of Vladimir Nabokov* (New York: Crown, 1986);

Brian Boyd, *Vladimir Nabokov: The Russian Years* (Princeton: Princeton University Press, 1990);

Boyd, *Vladimir Nabokov: The American Years* (Princeton: Princeton University Press, 1991).

References:

Vladimir Alexandrov, *Nabokov's Otherworld* (Princeton: Princeton University Press, 1991);

Alexandrov, ed., *The Garland Companion to Vladimir Nabokov* (New York: Garland, 1995);

Gennady Barabtarlo, *Phantom of Fact: A Guide to Nabokov's* Pnin (Ann Arbor, Mich.: Ardis, 1989);

Brian Boyd, *Nabokov's* Ada: *The Place of Consciousness* (Ann Arbor, Mich.: Ardis, 1985);

Boyd, *Nabokov's* Pale Fire: *The Magic of Artistic Discovery* (Princeton: Princeton University Press, 1999);

Diana Butler, "Lolita Lepidoptera," in *Critical Essays on Vladimir Nabokov,* edited by Phyllis Roth (Boston: G. K. Hall, 1984), pp. 59–74;

Galya Diment, *Pniniad: Vladimir Nabokov and Mark Szeftel* (Seattle: University of Washington Press, 1997);

D. Barton Johnson, "The Ambidextrous Universe of Nabokov's *Look at the Harlequins!"* in *Critical Essays on Vladimir Nabokov,* edited by Roth (Boston: G. K. Hall, 1984), pp. 202–215;

Kurt Johnson and Steve Coates, *Nabokov's Blues: The Scientific Odyssey of a Literary Genius* (Cambridge, Mass.: Zoland, 1999);

L. L. Lee, "Vladimir Nabokov's Great Spiral of Being," in *Critical Essays on Vladimir Nabokov,* edited by Roth (Boston: G. K. Hall, 1984), pp. 74–86;

Bobbie Ann Mason, *Nabokov's Garden: A Guide to* Ada (Ann Arbor, Mich.: Ardis, 1974);

Mary McCarthy, "A Bolt from the Blue," in *The Writing on the Wall and Other Literary Essays* (New York: Harcourt, Brace & World, 1970), pp. 15–34;

Charles Nicol, "Martin, Darwin, Malory, and Pushkin: The Anglo-Russian Culture of *Glory,"* in *Nabokov's World: Volume 1: The Shape of Nabokov's World,* edited by Jane Grayson, Arnold McMillin, and Priscilla Meyer (London: Palgrave, 2002), pp. 159–172;

Nicol, "Music in the Theater of the Mind: Opera and Vladimir Nabokov," in *Nabokov at the Limits: Redrawing Critical Boundaries,* edited by Lisa Zunshine (New York: Garland, 1999), pp. 22–42;

Nicol, "Pnin's History," in *Critical Essays on Vladimir Nabokov,* edited by Roth (Boston: G. K. Hall, 1984), pp. 93–105;

W. W. Rowe, *Nabokov's Spectral Dimension* (Ann Arbor, Mich.: Ardis, 1981);

Stacy Schiff, *Véra (Mrs. Vladimir Nabokov)* (New York: Random House, 1999).

Papers:

The two major repositories of Vladimir Nabokov's papers are the Library of Congress and the Vladimir Nabokov Archive in the Henry A. and Albert W. Berg Collection of the New York Public Library.

Reynolds Price

(1 February 1933 –   )

Barbara Bennett
Wake Forest University

See also the Price entries in *DLB 2: American Novelists Since World War II* and *DLB 218: American Short-Story Writers Since World War II, Second Series.*

BOOKS: *A Long and Happy Life* (New York: Atheneum, 1962; London: Chatto & Windus, 1962);

The Names and Faces of Heroes (New York: Atheneum, 1963; London: Chatto & Windus, 1963);

A Generous Man (New York: Atheneum, 1966; London: Chatto & Windus, 1967);

The Thing Itself (Durham, N.C.: Privately printed, 1966);

Love and Work (New York: Atheneum, 1968; London: Chatto & Windus, 1968);

Late Warning: Four Poems (New York: Albondocani Press, 1968);

Permanent Errors (New York: Atheneum, 1970; London: Chatto & Windus, 1971);

Things Themselves: Essays & Scenes (New York: Atheneum, 1972);

Presence and Absence: Versions from the Bible (Bloomfield Hills, Mich. & Columbia, S.C.: Bruccoli Clark, 1973);

The Surface of Earth (New York: Atheneum, 1975; London: Arlington Books, 1978);

The Good News According to Mark (Privately printed, 1976);

Early Dark: A Play (New York: Atheneum, 1977);

Oracles: Six Versions from the Bible (Durham, N.C.: Friends of the Duke University Library, 1977);

Lessons Learned: Seven Poems (New York: Albondocani Press, 1977);

A Palpable God: Thirty Stories Translated from the Bible with an Essay on the Origins and Life of Narrative (New York: Atheneum, 1978);

Question and Answer: The Second Archibald Yell Smith IV Lecture (Chattanooga, Tenn.: Baylor School, 1979);

Nine Mysteries (Four Joyful, Four Sorrowful, One Glorious) (Winston-Salem, N.C.: Palaemon, 1979);

The Annual Heron (New York: Albondocani Press, 1980);

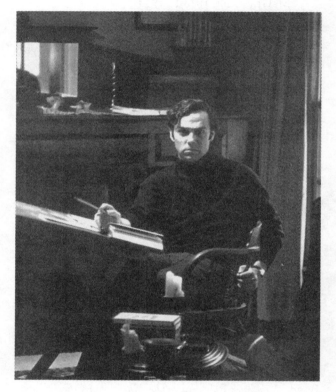

Reynolds Price (photograph by John Menapace; from the dust jacket for Learning a Trade, *1998)*

A Final Letter (Los Angeles: Sylvester & Orphanos, 1980);

The Source of Light (New York: Atheneum, 1981);

Country Mouse, City Mouse (Rocky Mount: Friends of the Library, North Carolina Wesleyan College, 1981);

A Start (Early Work) (Winston-Salem, N.C.: Palaemon, 1981);

Vital Provisions (New York: Atheneum, 1982);

Private Contentment: A Play (New York: Atheneum, 1984);

Kate Vaiden (New York: Atheneum, 1986; London: Chatto & Windus, 1987);

The Laws of Ice (New York: Atheneum, 1986);

A Common Room: Essays, 1954–1987 (New York: Atheneum, 1987);

House Snake: A Poem (Northridge, Cal.: Lord John Press, 1987);

Real Copies: Will Price, Crichton Davis, Phyllis Peacock, and More (Rocky Mount: North Carolina Wesleyan College Press, 1988);

Good Hearts (New York: Atheneum, 1988);

Back Before Day (Rocky Mount: North Carolina Wesleyan College Press, 1989);

Clear Pictures: First Loves, First Guides (New York: Atheneum, 1989);

Home Made (Rocky Mount: North Carolina Wesleyan College Press, 1990);

New Music: A Trilogy (New York: Theatre Communications Group, 1990)–includes *August Snow, Night Dance,* and *Better Days;*

The Use of Fire (New York: Atheneum, 1990);

The Tongues of Angels (New York: Atheneum, 1990);

The Foreseeable Future (New York: Atheneum, 1991)–includes *The Fare to the Moon, Back Before Day,* and *The Foreseeable Future;*

Blue Calhoun (New York: Atheneum, 1992);

An Early Christmas (Rocky Mount: North Carolina Wesleyan College Press, 1992);

The Collected Stories (New York: Atheneum, 1993);

Full Moon and Other Plays (New York: Theatre Communications Group, 1993)–includes *Early Dark, Private Contentment,* and *Full Moon;*

The Honest Account of a Memorable Life: An Apocryphal Gospel (Rocky Mount: North Carolina Wesleyan College Press, 1994);

A Whole New Life: An Illness and a Healing (New York: Atheneum, 1994);

The Promise of Rest (New York: Scribners, 1995);

The Three Gospels (New York: Scribners, 1996)–includes *The Good News According to Mark, The Good News According to John,* and *An Honest Account of a Memorable Life;*

The Collected Poems (New York: Scribners, 1997);

Roxanna Slade (New York: Scribners, 1998);

Learning a Trade: A Craftsman's Notebooks, 1955–1997 (Durham, N.C.: Duke University Press, 1998);

Letter to a Man in the Fire: Does God Exist and Does He Care? (New York: Scribner, 1999);

Feasting the Heart: Fifty-Two Commentaries for the Air (New York: Scribner, 2000);

A Perfect Friend (New York: Atheneum Books for Young Readers, 2000);

Noble Norfleet (New York: Scribner, 2002);

A Serious Way of Wondering: The Ethics of Jesus Imagined (New York: Scribner, 2003).

Editions: *Mustian: Two Novels and a Story Complete and Unabridged* (New York: Atheneum, 1983)–includes *A Generous Man,* "A Chain of Love," and *A Long and Happy Life;*

A Singular Family: Rosacoke and Her Kin (New York: Scribner, 1999)–includes *A Generous Man,* "A Chain of Love," *A Long and Happy Life,* and *Good Hearts;*

A Great Circle: The Mayfield Trilogy (New York: Scribner Classics, 2001)–includes *The Surface of Earth, The Source of Light,* and *The Promise of Rest.*

In the preface to her study of Reynolds Price's works, Constance Rooke claims that Price's vision is "darker than many of his readers have supposed." Perhaps one of the reasons for this dark vision is Price's philosophy about his life as a writer, specifically his belief that to be the artist he is, he must abandon many of the typical relationships that most people have. Price–much like Eudora Welty, one of his major influences and inspirations–has forgone marriage and family, finding purpose in his work. Rooke goes on to state that "at the heart of Reynolds Price's fiction is a dialogue between love and solitude," each of which is a blessing and a curse. Independence and the freedom it allows Price (and many of his characters) has a cost, most often the loss of love. Love of all kinds–familial, erotic, fraternal–plays an important role in the fiction of Price, who remarked in an interview with William Ray that "the two great forces in life" are "Eros and Thanatos, Love and Death." Both rewarding and terrifying in Price's work, love is seen finally as a betrayal: loved ones ultimately betray others by dying. Solitude, for Price's characters, can be interpreted as an attempt to minimize the chance of such hurt.

Much of Price's conflict about love, death, and family can be traced to his early life and the anxieties he felt as a small child. The birth of Edward Reynolds Price in the small rural town of Macon, North Carolina, on 1 February 1933, was a difficult one, and for a while it looked as if both he and his mother, Elizabeth Rodwell Price, might die in the struggle. Price recounts in his memoir *Clear Pictures: First Loves, First Guides* (1989) that in what has become a family legend, his father, William Solomon Price, "fled the house in the freezing dawn, went out to the woodshed; and there he sealed a bargain with God, as stark and unbreakable as any blood pact in Genesis–if Elizabeth lived, and the child, he'd never drink again." Later hearing about this dramatic event had an immense influence on young Reynolds. He remembers feeling like the "anchor in a triad of love," holding the family together, often playing the role of peacemaker and parent. Even after his younger brother was born eight years later, Reynolds continued to feel solely responsible for the welfare of both his parents.

Price sees the Great Depression as his generation's Civil War—the force that shaped personalities, created fears of ruin and desperation, and made adults of children. For most of his early childhood, he was surrounded by an extended family of relatives who spoke to him as a grown-up rather than as a child. His love for language came from these people who were not especially well read but who took great pleasure in storytelling, people who "treasured the *word* as the central means of continuance in human life . . . for the communication of past love, present and future obligation; above all, for consolation and delight." Because he was more interested in books and music than sports and children's games, he was rejected by many of his neighborhood peers. At school he made friends with the rural children who were bused to town, but when they returned home after class, he found himself alone. These rural children later served as models for many of the characters in his fiction, characters who emerge as noble and enduring, strong and virtuous.

By the time he was nine years old, Price had become comfortable with solitude, and he spent his hours reading, drawing, painting, watching movies, and creating his own outdoor dramas. All of these activities led Price to a life of writing fiction because, as he records in his notebooks, they were "alternate means for watching the world with close concentration." Price considered himself a writer from early in his teens, composing plays, movie scripts, short stories, poems, newspaper editorials, and autobiographical essays. In the eighth grade in Warrenton, Price's art teacher encouraged his interest in writing and sketching. Later, in his eleventh-grade English class in Raleigh, Phyllis Peacock—the same teacher who influenced Anne Tyler so significantly—helped perfect certain aspects of his writing style, encouraging him to pursue his creative talent when he attended Duke University. During the summer months between college semesters, when most young men were taking money-making jobs, Price remained in his parents' house, writing and waiting for inspiration to write more. In the preface to *A Singular Family: Rosacoke and Her Kin* (1999), he remembers spending "a good many vacant hours, prone in my locked room, gasping at the ceiling like a ravenous carp," confronting the fact that he had no "accessible subject for narrative prose," but sure that time would "furnish the food at its own wise rate."

While at Duke, Price met Welty, an experience that more than any other influenced him as a writer. Welty read and praised several of Price's early short stories, and she arranged for him to send his work to her agent, Diarmuid Russell. In a 1966 interview with

Wallace Kaufman, included in *Conversations with Reynolds Price* (1991), Price claims that Welty's stories "revealed to me what is most essential for any beginning novelist—which is that his world, the world he has known from birth, the world that has not seemed to him in any way extraordinary is, in fact, a perfectly possible world, base, subject for serious fiction."

After graduating from Duke with an A.B. in 1955, Price studied in England at Merton College, Oxford University, where he read the "great cornerstones of Western fiction"—John Milton, Leo Tolstoy, Ernest Hemingway, and especially the Bible—that influenced his style, themes, and plots even as he wrote about the rural life of the South. He earned a B.Litt. from Merton in 1958. When he returned to America, Price began teaching at Duke, where he has spent his professional life, with stints as writer in residence at the University of North Carolina at Chapel Hill (1965), the University of Kansas (1967, 1969, 1980), the University of North Carolina at Greensboro (1971), and as the Glasgow Professor at Washington and Lee University (1971). In 1977 he became the James B. Duke Professor of English. There he has served as mentor to other young writers—specifically Anne Tyler, Josephine Humphreys, Wallace Kaufman, David Guy, Fred Chappell, James Applewhite, and Charlie Smith—all of whom credit Price with positive influences on their own work.

One other major influence on Price's development was his creative-writing professor at Duke, William Blackburn. In the spring semester of 1955, Price found himself in Blackburn's narrative-writing course, faced with the need to produce a final short story. His inspiration came while he was visiting a sick friend at Duke Hospital. He encountered a trio of countrymen in the hallway, the same three men he remembered seeing the year before when he was a frequent visitor to the hospital while his father was dying. To his image of these three men, he added the memory of a young woman he had seen at a Howard Johnson's restaurant one Sunday, assigning to her the name of a classmate, Rosa Coke Boyle. This woman and the three kinsmen became the core of "A Chain of Love"—one of the short stories found in *The Names and Faces of Heroes* (1963)—and three novels about the Mustian family: *A Long and Happy Life* (1962), *A Generous Man* (1966), and *Good Hearts* (1988).

When "A Chain of Love" was reprinted in 1999 as part of *A Singular Family,* Price wrote in the preface that Rosacoke Mustian is based on "any one of a dozen girls" from his childhood bused to school from the rural areas. She is a character who, for Price, "stood up, live from her first paragraph . . . at once like a palpable creature, warm to the touch," and critics agree that Price's

*Price in 1961 (photograph by Wallace Kaufman; from the dust jacket for the 1987,
twenty-fifth anniversary edition of* A Long and Happy Life)

creation of Rosacoke was the beginning of his life as a writer and central to his whole career.

A Long and Happy Life received overwhelmingly positive reviews and earned the William Faulkner Award for a notable first novel. The predicament of Rosacoke Mustian was inspired in part by a Johannes Vermeer painting (*Woman in Blue Reading a Letter,* circa 1662), which depicts a pregnant girl wearing no wedding ring. Price's story chronicles the difficult courtship of Rosacoke and Wesley Beavers, the father of her child. The two struggle for control of their own lives and their relationship throughout the novel, ultimately resigning themselves to marriage and a life together. Price sees all his books as being "about human freedom—the limits thereof, the possibilities thereof, the impossibilities thereof," which is precisely the conflict that hovers over the troubled courtship of Wesley and Rosacoke. With their relationship, Price illustrates one of his common themes: that for each instance of giving and receiving love, there is a price to pay, usually individual freedom.

The title and the ending of this novel have greatly troubled critics. The title could be read ironically, for most of the people in this novel do not have an especially happy life, and many of those lives are not long; but there is hope, though tenuous, for happiness in the union of Rosacoke and Wesley. The ending can be read both optimistically and pessimistically. On one hand, Rosacoke relents and decides to marry Wesley because she is pregnant, and the novel ends on the word "love," an encouraging sign. The epigraph of the novel, from Dante, suggests that the marriage could thrive. On the other hand, the union is starting out on the rockiest of foundations, and the lines from "We Three Kings" heard in the final scene suggest bitterness, sorrow, and barrenness.

The next book in the Mustian saga, *A Generous Man,* takes place earlier in the family history. Rosacoke is only eleven years old, and although she is an important character in the book, her brother Milo, age fifteen, is the focus of this tale of a confident young man reaching a pivotal point in his maturation as he explores his newfound sexuality. This novel did not receive the uniform praise from critics that *A Long and Happy Life* did. John Wain, in *The New York Review of Books* (23 August 1968), called it "highly elaborate, complex in plot, mannered in style, booming with symbolic overtones" and remarked that it "smelled of the lamp." Other critics described it as absurdist, farcical, even ridiculous.

The basic plot is rather bizarre: the Mustian family takes their possibly rabid dog to the vet one morning; it escapes to chase a huge python (named Death) through the woods; and the dog's owner (Milo's brother Rato) chases the dog. A posse sets out to find all three runaways, with Milo getting separated and having many strange adventures on his journey. All three Mustian novels focus on and celebrate male sexuality, but this force is most keenly felt in *A Generous Man*. Milo is searching for the giant snake, a symbol of his manhood, which he equates solely with sexual activity; he sees himself as "a generous man" because he has been endowed with sexual gifts to give to women.

Some critics have seen this novel as a quest tale. James A. Schiff, in *Understanding Reynolds Price* (1996), described Milo as "the young knight on a quest, whose mission is to subdue the monster Death, rescue maidens in distress . . . and bring about a return to order and truth." In the end, however, Milo is unable to succeed in his mission; instead, he settles for less, deciding to live his life like everyone else: working at the mill, waiting for the next holiday, and living a long life with one woman.

In his next novel Price created the first in a series of similar characters: the artist/writer struggling to develop his craft and attempting to synthesize work with his personal life. *Love and Work* (1968) centers around Thomas Eborn, a married college professor whose writing has become more important to him than anything else. The novel, short and dense, is divided into four sections. In the first, Eborn is writing an essay about the significance of work in his life (an essay that is virtually word-for-word Price's own essay titled "Finding Work"), but he is interrupted by a phone call about his ailing mother, who has had a stroke that leads to her death before Eborn can get to the hospital. The second section takes place after the funeral as Eborn cleans out his mother's house; on his way home he comes on an auto accident and offers help too late to save a young man's life. Section three is a novel within a novel that Eborn writes about his parents' early lives together. Finally, the fourth section revolves around a break-in at his parents' house. During the walk-through after the burglary, Eborn is visited by the ghosts of his parents, who let him know they do not need his writing to justify and explain their possessive love of each other.

The reviews of this brief but complicated novel were generally positive—Marston LaFrance, in *Studies in Short Fiction* (1971), called it "soundly convincing, carefully constructed, well-written" —although many critics were disappointed by the turn Price's writing seemed to have taken from his earlier novels in its non-Southern

setting and its psychological focus. The biggest disappointment for reviewers seemed to be that Eborn is not a likable character. He is insensitive, selfish, and egocentric, and his writing and thinking are arrogant and pompous. These weaknesses, however, are what Price's novel seems to explore—the consequences of an inability to love, as Eborn finds it easier to write about love than to actually experience it.

A troubling aspect of the novel is the accident scene, a segment that some critics have seen as disconnected from the rest of the action, but which Gary M. Ciuba argues is a significant moment in Eborn's limited growth. Eborn hesitates before helping, and as a result, a young man dies. From this incident Eborn sees that "he can save neither in art nor in actuality if he does not work out of immediate love." Not until he experiences the vision of his parents in the final scene, however, does he seem to understand he cannot save others or their love in his fiction. The novel ends ambiguously, as readers are left to wonder whether this experience is sufficient to change Eborn.

After *Love and Work* Price turned temporarily from novels to other projects. His second book of short stories, *Permanent Errors* (1970), was followed by a book of essays, *Things Themselves* (1972). His work on one project—translations of biblical stories, *A Palpable God*, which was not published until 1978—was in some ways preparation for his next novel, particularly the stories about the rescue of Isaac and the sacrifice of Jephthah's daughter. This next novel, *The Surface of Earth* (1975), began for Price with an image he had been contemplating for nearly twelve years, that of a young boy traveling through eastern North Carolina with his alcoholic father, a situation that Price explored to a lesser degree in an earlier story, "The Names and Faces of Heroes."

The Surface of Earth is the first volume of Price's second trilogy, eventually titled *A Great Circle: The Mayfield Trilogy* (2001). The second and third parts are *The Source of Light* (1981) and *The Promise of Rest* (1995), and the series covers approximately ninety years in the history of the Mayfields. Although *A Singular Family* is also concerned with the workings of a Southern family, *A Great Circle* differs from Price's first trilogy in several ways. While *A Singular Family* functions more as separate stories about members of the Mustian family, the Mayfield novels are more closely connected in plot and theme. In addition, the Mustian novels (about a lower-class family) cover only one generation, while the Mayfield books cover six generations of a middle-class, relatively well-educated clan.

The Mayfield trilogy deals with fathers and their children (mainly sons) and the extremes to which children will go in order to cement their paternal bonds. A recurring plotline is that of fathers being separated from their children, either physically or emotionally, forcing the children to go on a sort of quest to find and make peace with the father figure. To save and then maintain the relationship with the father, children must often give up lives of their own, and the reader is left with the overwhelming feeling that love and families can be even more destructive than they are nurturing, a theme that Price repeats in other kinds of relationships in the novels. The title of the trilogy underscores the theme that history repeats itself, that the problems that plague one generation of parents and children return to torment the next as well.

The first novel of this trilogy, *The Surface of Earth,* is often considered Price's "big" novel, substantially longer than anything he had written before. The book received mixed reviews, and its merits were debated among scholars. The most notorious review came from Richard Gilman in *The New York Times Book Review,* in which he called the novel "a great lumbering archaic beast" with a "stiff queer presence of the representative of a species thought to be extinct." Gilman's review provoked the ire of many, including Welty, who wrote a letter in response to the negative review, defending Price's novel and style as well as Southern literature in general.

The three sections of *The Surface of Earth* revolve around the life of a Mayfield man as he seeks to be reunited with his father. "Absolute Pleasures" centers on Forrest Mayfield, whose wife, Eva, deserts him shortly after the birth of their son, Robinson. Forrest's quest to locate his own father (who deserted him as a child) contrasts with Forrest's forced separation from his son. The second section, "The Heart in Dreams," continues with Robinson, who as a young man journeys to find his father and tries to understand the family history that left him to grow up fatherless, but he ends up instead perpetuating the family curse by marrying, fathering a son, Hutchins, and then deserting his family. Finally, "Partial Amends" tells Hutchins's story of a forced reunion with his alcoholic father.

Family ties that both link and strangle add to the repeated conflict between love and independence in Price's work. Rooke notes that the "question of how much one can expect from marriage becomes pronounced" in this novel through each generation, and the theme that "any establishment of a new household damages a previous combination of human lives" bodes ominously for the entire institution of marriage. Price told Ray that his characters in this novel are "seeking rest; they're seeking surcease from pain; they're seeking the cessation of pain and struggle and unhappiness, as I fear all created beings are." The characters mistakenly believe that others have the power to give them that happiness and rest, but as they all discover, others only add to the pain. Each of the three sections of the novel concludes with a sort of reunion and forgiveness, but each character refuses to share that new knowledge and

understanding with the next generation, leading to a continuation of the circle of neglect and pain.

After publishing *Early Dark* (1977)—a dramatic version of *A Long and Happy Life*—and finishing his work on *A Palpable God,* Price returned to the Mayfield saga with *The Source of Light.* The novel picks up eleven years after *The Surface of Earth* concludes, focusing on Hutchins Mayfield, who has left his home to travel to Oxford to study and take his first steps toward being a poet. He is called home, however, in the middle of his first year because his father is dying of cancer. At the same time, Hutch is struggling with commitment, engaged to Ann Gatlin but exploring other options, including several intense homosexual experiences. These three issues—growth as a poet, the loss of a father, and the exploration of sexuality—make up the core of the novel. Although the novel was generally received well by critics, there was some dissension. Joyce Carol Oates, in *The New York Times Book Review,* complained that Price could have done more with his characters, that "it is disconcerting that Hutch remains so blurred to us and that Ann too lacks definition."

As a portrait of the artist, this novel is perhaps the closest so far to being autobiographical. Price, like Hutch, left the American South to study as a Rhodes scholar at Oxford University, and he dedicated this novel to his British friends and teachers, David Cecil and Stephen Spender. In addition, Price has expressed many times his own conflict between the necessity of solitude in work and the sacrifice it requires, as well as his own experience in losing his father. Finally, in his notebooks Price calls himself (and one of his characters) bisexual, a term that seems to fit Hutch.

In *The Source of Light* Price portrays homosexuality more explicitly than ever before in his career, although the third novel in this trilogy—*The Promise of Rest*—is even more candid. Unlike many contemporary authors, Price creates characters who approach homosexuality without anxiety, guilt, or shame, and in *The Promise of Rest* Price reveals that both of Hutch's parents, Rob and Rachel, had lovers of the same sex, supplying a kind of genetic precedent for Hutch that he never questions, analyzes, or explains.

Although sexuality is significant in the novel, the death of Hutch's father is the central issue. As Price discusses in his memoir *Clear Pictures,* the loss of the father is a paradox, both liberating and devastating, both an ending and a beginning, and Rob's death scene is perhaps the most powerful in the novel. Although critics have tended to see the ending of this novel as problematic because much of the action is unresolved and significant questions remain unanswered, Price felt the more important issues were tied to the loss of a parent who has been the center of strength for a child and how

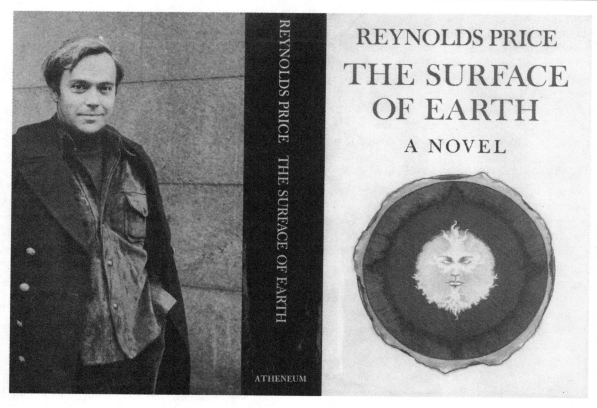

Dust jacket for Price's 1975 novel, the first in his Great Circle *trilogy
(Richland County Public Library)*

that child moves forward without the guide who has always been present before.

In early 1983, after completing a volume of poetry, *Vital Provisions* (1982), and working on a play, *Private Contentment* (1984), Price returned to prose with a particular goal in mind: the desire to write "an *emotional biography*" of his mother. He had previously written a poem called "A Heaven for Elizabeth Rodwell, My Mother" in which he described three difficult events his mother had endured; the novel *Kate Vaiden* (1986) was to be an expansion of this poem. Price told Jefferson Humphries that although the story "is by no means the story of the actual events of my mother's life," it seems to him "emotionally true to the interior voice of my mother."

Before he was able to complete this novel, however, Price's life changed in a dramatic and permanent way. In 1984, when he was about one-third finished with the new novel, a large tumor was discovered in Price's spinal cord. Surgery and radiation saved his life but left him a paraplegic. The experience—which Price recounts in his acclaimed memoir *A Whole New Life: An Illness and a Healing* (1994)—had an enormous impact on his creative energy and output. He wrote at a tremendous pace in the years following the detection of the

tumor. Managing pain became a reason to write, "the essential rehab," as one friend called it.

As soon as Price could, he returned to his work on *Kate Vaiden,* finding it an escape from his own problems and ultimately creating one of his most memorable characters, one that Rosellen Brown described in *The New York Times Book Review* (29 June 1986) as having a voice that "blows like fresh air across the page." The novel is written in the first person, from a female perspective. Price commented in *A Whole New Life* that with this book: "I was licensed to become a person as different from me as any I'd watched in thirty years of making up people—a woman with a fate that was harder than mine but who finally rounded on her torment, her own collusion in forty years of loss, desertion and pain, and cut her way clear with a skittish courage and a feisty tongue I could hide in at least." The novel became his most critically acclaimed since *A Long and Happy Life,* winning the National Book Critics Circle Award.

This memorable character is Kate Vaiden, orphaned at age eleven when her father murders her mother and then kills himself. By age eighteen she has lost two more people close to her—her first lover, Gaston, who commits suicide, and Daniel, the father of her illegitimate child, who shoots himself in the heart. Having learned early that people cannot be counted on, Kate decides to "leave people before they can plan to leave you," eventually abandoning her infant to the care of her aunt and embarking on a life filled with flight, return, and flight again. Forty years later, after a bout with cancer, Kate decides to tell her story, and the novel becomes her vehicle to explain her abandonment to her son and question whether she has a right to see him again.

Price's attempt to speak from a woman's point of view has generally been seen as successful and credible. However, Price's creation embodies more male stereotypical tendencies than female ones. Kate is autonomous rather than nurturing, a wanderer rather than patient waiter, the speaker rather than the listener. Price himself never saw the feat of writing from the opposite-sex point of view as daunting. He told Humphries: "I think our knowledge of one another is simply there, waiting. It's a common room where we inhabit, and it's waiting to be used by each of the genders."

Kate Vaiden is the beginning of a period in Price's career that tends toward the more personal, including more first-person narratives, and Kate is the first of what Schiff labels Price's "outlaw" characters—not outlaws in the legal sense, but characters whose behavior "is occasionally reckless or selfish" while they are still "basically thoughtful, considerate people who at some point simply refuse to continue to live in the style prescribed by society." Like Price himself at this point in his life, Kate comes to terms with her choices. Humphries writes that Price's works after the discovery of the tumor are in some ways the best of his career because "they show a voice which has fought great battles personal and physical, and which has achieved a firm, calm peace with its own gifts and limitations."

In the mid 1980s Price completed a book of poetry, *The Laws of Ice* (1986), and a volume of essays, *A Common Room* (1987). He then returned to the characters from his first short story and two novels, Wesley and Rosacoke (now called Rosa), to complete the *Singular Family* trilogy with *Good Hearts*. Because of Price's bout with cancer, he wanted to explore another life that, after years of "smooth sailing," had encountered a "shipwreck." Now living in Raleigh, Wesley walks out of his twenty-eight-year marriage to Rosa and begins life over with a younger woman named Wilson. Perhaps better than any other male writer of his generation, Price is able to understand and articulate both the male and female mind, and this ability is illustrated in Rosa and Wesley's relationship.

After so many years of marriage—and of what Price calls "benign neglect"—Wesley and Rosa exist as two separate beings, unsure what the other is thinking or feeling. As in most of Price's work, the main character in *Good Hearts* is conflicted by family responsibility versus personal freedom and exploration. Feeling trapped and "dead inside," Wesley, like many fictional American discontents, heads west, ending up in Nashville, looking for his lost youth and sexuality. Rosa feels nothing but confusion when Wesley leaves, and more important, she is left unprotected. In a somewhat strained cause-and-effect sequence, Rosa is raped at precisely the moment Wesley is consummating his new relationship with Wilson, leaving Rosa betrayed and violated on several levels. Eventually, Wesley's guilt about not being there to protect Rosa against the rapist brings him back home.

When Wesley returns out of guilt and responsibility, one wonders if these emotions are worthy as a base for their rebuilt marriage. What finally comes from this novel is a sense that for most people, life is ordinary. Wesley and Rosa, like nearly everyone, believed when they were young that their lives would be special. This misconception, Wesley admits, is "the lie that poisoned all the rest." Price leaves little room for optimism at the end of the novel, despite Wesley's return to Rosa. The final paragraph foresees a life together in their house with only "small calm pleasures" while they wait for death, which would "find them with ease."

In the summer of 1987 Price underwent hypnosis therapy to deal with the pain associated with his surgery and subsequent paralysis. One of the benefits of this process was that memories of his childhood were vividly enhanced. His memoir *Clear Pictures* and his next novel, *The Tongues of Angels* (1990), were direct results of his newly restored memory. According to Price, the books "tumbled" out of him at "a high clip of speed and pleasure."

One of Price's shortest novels, *The Tongues of Angels* is compact and rich. The plot is based on Price's experience at age twenty, in the summer of 1953, when he worked as a counselor at a boys' camp, Sequoyah, in the mountains of western North Carolina. It is part autobiography, tale of initiation, portrait of the artist, and elegy. Reviews were overwhelmingly favorable. The story is told in retrospective; like the speaker in *Kate Vaiden*, the narrator-protagonist—Bridge Boatner—is telling his story years later to his son, as explanation, confession, and expiation. Bridge's younger self is a camp counselor and landscape painter whose father has recently died. During the summer, Bridge comes to terms with the loss of his father and with his own mortality. The boys in his charge at Camp Juniper in essence become his "sons," just as the male members of the staff serve as new father figures for him. From this experience, he is able to understand love and duty in a new and significant way.

The title of the novel refers to the scripture from 1 Corinthians that argues that the greatest gift is charity, or as Price translates it, brotherly love. As in many of Price's novels, messages and lessons are brought to humans by angels, both of heaven and earth, and Bridge and Raphael Noren, a boy who dies at the end of the summer, are both angel figures. As an artist, Bridge translates the divine through his own creative vision, and Raphael brings Bridge a message about the importance of love and outward vision. While *The Tongues of Angels* includes some of Price's most moving scenes, it is also a novel of fun and laughter because of its youthful setting. The spiritual and emotional tension is nearly always tempered with adolescent high jinks.

After publishing a volume of poetry, *The Use of Fire* (1990), and a volume that included three long short stories, *The Foreseeable Future* (1991), Price published *Blue Calhoun* (1992), the story of Bluford Calhoun, a married man who fell in love with a sixteen-year-old girl, Luna Absher, when he was in his mid thirties. At the time Price was writing *Blue Calhoun,* he recorded in his notebooks that "the phenomenon of love and care across large decade-gaps is a natural concern of my own now and might well prove rewarding." The result is a novel that is, in many ways, similar to *Kate Vaiden* and *The Tongues of Angels:* all three are first-person narratives in which the speaker is explaining his/her life to a descendant in hopes of finding, if not forgiveness, at least understanding for the difficult and often destructive choices he/she has made. *Blue Calhoun* is written as one long letter from Blue to his fifteen-year-old granddaughter, Lyn, who, because of the deaths of her mother (from cancer) and father (suicide), has been put into Blue's care.

Blue Calhoun received mainly positive reviews, largely because the narrator, despite his obvious character flaws, is endearing and sympathetic. Some reviewers, however, questioned the credibility of the narrator's voice as well as criticized the actual content. Some questioned why a sixty-five-year-old man would explain to his emotionally fragile granddaughter the sordid details of the affair that nearly destroyed his marriage when it all took place long before she was born.

Criticism aside, the novel tells a compelling story about a man with an addictive personality. He is drawn to Luna in the same fierce way that he was drawn to alcohol and drugs when he was younger. He seems unable to stop himself even when he knows logically that his behavior could destroy the life he has worked so hard to rebuild, even when he sees it torturing the wife who has stood by him and the daughter, Mattie, he adores. On many levels, *Blue Calhoun* is a novel of lost innocence, about the violations people commit against the ones they claim to love most, and like *Kate*

Vaiden, it questions whether it is sometimes better for a person to turn away from loved ones—not to abandon them but to protect them.

In 1994 Price published a second memoir, *A Whole New Life,* focusing on his experience with cancer and recovery. The volume is a completely honest and explicit account of the suffering he endured both physically and psychologically, but it is also a story of larger concerns: the role of work in recovery, the importance of friendship and love, and the courage it takes to face a "whole new life" in a wheelchair. His new understanding of his illness perhaps led him to write his next novel, the third volume in the Mayfield trilogy and one of his most socially conscious novels, *The Promise of Rest.* The novel is set in the spring and summer of 1993, telling the story of Hutchins Mayfield and his son, Wade, who is dying of AIDS. Like *The Source of Light,* this novel focuses on how a father and son get through the death of one of them; this time, though, it is the son who is dying and leaving his father alone.

Many questions left open at the end of *The Source of Light* are answered early in the novel. Hutch has become a semi-well-known poet who teaches at Duke University. He did indeed deny his homosexual longings and marry Ann Gatlin, but they separated several months before the opening of the novel. Their son, Wade, has accepted his own homosexuality, moved to New York City, and found Wyatt Bondurant, a black gay man whose sister, Ivory, had earlier conceived a child with Wade. Wyatt contracts AIDS, passes it on to Wade, and then commits suicide when he realizes he has sentenced Wade to a painful death.

Wade represents the culmination of generations of Mayfield men because, as Schiff notes, "he is the first Mayfield to openly acknowledge and pursue, without guilt, shame, or fear, the two desires which so many of his ancestors have repressed or experienced only furtively: an attraction to blacks and to other men." And although the novel "serves to legitimize and normalize homosexuality," the open acknowledgment is ultimately destructive, leading to the suffering of Wade and Wyatt and everyone who knows and loves them. The passion of Wade and Wyatt leads to their early deaths, but the reader must also ask the question of whether it is better to die living a passionate and true life or die figuratively as Hutch had done by denying his true feelings in the pursuit of normalcy and social acceptance.

As in other Price novels, death is never an end: birth and death are linked. As Hutch loses his son to death, he also experiences various kinds of new beginnings: a new poem about love and hope in the newest of generations; a grandchild in whom Wade will live on; and the chance of repairing the damage done in his marriage to Ann. This grandson, Raven—a child of mixed race, mixed geography (North and South), the product of a homosexual man and a heterosexual woman—represents the possibility of a better future. He seems to have a bit of everyone in him, and Price, in his notebooks, calls the child a possible "savior" of the Mayfield line.

In his next novel, *Roxanna Slade* (1998), Price returned to a first-person narrative, the first from a female perspective since *Kate Vaiden,* and critics seem to agree that Price was once more successful in creating a woman's voice. The title character tells her story of life in a small North Carolina town from the distance of age: she is in her tenth decade. Her personal tragedies—the drowning of her first love in front of her, the loss of a child, depression, discovery of her husband's infidelity—are not so unbelievable that they put her in the realm of the unknowable, but they certainly make her life worth recounting.

Born in the year 1900, Roxanna emerges as a symbol of the twentieth century, and it is especially fitting that Price has chosen a woman to represent the times, considering that the next hundred years, in many ways, were focused on the progress of that sex. In her long life, Roxanna deals with all the things America dealt with in the twentieth century—death, depression, prejudice, loss, love, betrayal—but comes through a survivor with a philosophy that "the actual world is worth all your strength."

The strength of *Roxanna Slade,* like so many of Price's novels, is in the voice of the narrator, the feisty woman who has learned, as one reviewer remarked in *Kirkus Reviews* (1 April 1998), "to master her own anger, come to grips with her regrets, and who has drawn from the incidents of her life a hard-earned wisdom." In the first sentence of the book she denies that she is a saint, and as the novel progresses, the reader sees her story as a universal one: like most women of her generation, she spends her life taking care of others, trying to maintain a level of sanity, and attempting to be satisfied with a small world centered around her family and home. In the end, she lives true to her own philosophy and asks for no more, saying: "Life, in the world I occupy, is an adequate blessing."

Price's next publication was *Learning a Trade: A Craftsman's Notebooks, 1955–1997* (1998), a fascinating look at the writer in the process of creation. In it Price recorded his thoughts and plans for each of his works from the first idea to the last editing. Although it is not a book for the casual reader, it is a valuable record of the process of writing, from start to finish.

Price published two other books before his next novel. In 2000 he wrote a children's book, *A Perfect Friend,* and he compiled a book of personal essays written and recorded for the National Public Radio show

Dust jacket for Price's 1986 novel, which he has called "emotionally true to the interior voice of my mother" (Richland County Public Library)

All Things Considered called *Feasting the Heart: Fifty-Two Commentaries for the Air,* which also includes a Christmas story read on NPR's *Morning Edition.*

Noble Norfleet, released in 2002, is a novel exploring thirty years of a man's life. Noble, the protagonist, is just seventeen when his mother murders his younger brother and sister while they sleep, leaving Noble, for some reason he never understands, alive. Once his mother is sent to a prison for the criminally insane, Noble signs up as a medic in Vietnam, returning home after the war to become a nurse. He thus tries—in his own vague way—to make up for the harm his mother has done by healing and helping others, including the most dire cases in the pediatric burn unit. After thirty years in prison, his mother is released and returns home to Noble, making him confront the necessity of forgiving her and caring for her.

While not a totally satisfying story because of its many unresolved episodes and confusing sequences—

including several visionary experiences–the novel is important because it re-examines many of Price's ongoing concerns: definitions of sin, the results of guilt, the role of God in human lives, and the overwhelming but underanalyzed meaning of sex in the lives of humans. As he often does, Price leaves many of these subjects open-ended, preferring instead to ask the questions but not answer them.

Reynolds Price is an unusual author in the postmodern era because he is, at once, prolific, commercially successful, and critically acclaimed. It will be difficult for future scholars to decide what his most important contribution to American literature has been: his fiction, his memoirs, his poetry, or his tutelage of several generations of writers who have benefited from his presence. He is, perhaps, the closest thing this era has to a true Renaissance man.

Interviews:

William Ray, *Conversations: Reynolds Price & William Ray* (Memphis, Tenn.: Memphis State University, 1976);

Jefferson Humphries, ed., *Conversations with Reynolds Price* (Jackson: University Press of Mississippi, 1991).

Bibliography:

Stuart Wright and James L. W. West III, *Reynolds Price: A Bibliography, 1949–1984* (Charlottesville: University Press of Virginia, 1986).

References:

Barbara Bennett, "Outrage and Delight: Southern Scatological Humor in Reynolds Price's *The Tongues of Angels*," *Thalia: Studies in Literary Humor,* 14, no. 1–2 (1994): 30–39;

Gary M. Ciuba, "Price's *Love and Work:* Discovering the 'Perfect Story,'" *Renascence: Essays on the Value in Literature,* 44 (Fall 1991): 45–60;

Joseph Dewey, "A Time to Bolt: Suicide, Androgyny, and the Dislocation of the Self in Reynolds Price's

Kate Vaiden," *Mississippi Quarterly,* 45 (Winter 1991–1992): 9–28;

R. C. Fuller, "Lunging in the Dark: Blindness and Vision, Disappointment and Aspiration in Reynolds Price's Trilogy," *Southern Quarterly,* 33 (Winter–Spring 1995): 45–56;

Edith T. Hartin, "Reading as a Woman: Reynolds Price and Creative Androgyny in *Kate Vaiden*," *Southern Quarterly,* 29 (Spring 1991): 37–52;

Gloria G. Jones, "Reynolds Price's *A Long and Happy Life:* Style and the Dynamics of Power," *CEA Critic: An Official Journal of the College English Association,* 56 (Fall 1993): 77–85;

Sue Laslie Kimball and Lynn Veach Sadler, eds., *Reynolds Price: From* A Long and Happy Life *to* Good Hearts, *with a Bibliography* (Fayetteville, N.C.: Methodist College Press, 1989);

Michael Kreyling, "Motion and Rest in the Novels of Reynolds Price," *Southern Review,* 16 (1980): 853–868;

Tara Powell, "Fiction of Mercy: Suffering Delight in Reynolds Price's *The Promise of Rest*," *Mississippi Quarterly,* 53 (Spring 2000): 251–264;

Constance Rooke, *Reynolds Price* (Boston: Twayne, 1983);

Lynn Veach Sadler, "The 'Mystical Grotesque' in the Life and Works of Reynolds Price," *Southern Literary Journal,* 21 (Spring 1989): 27–40;

James A. Schiff, "Fathers and Sons in the Fiction of Reynolds Price: A Sense of Crucial Ambiguity," *Southern Review,* 29 (Winter 1993): 16–29;

Schiff, *Understanding Reynolds Price* (Columbia: University of South Carolina Press, 1996);

Schiff, ed., *Critical Essays on Reynolds Price* (New York: G. K. Hall, 1998).

Papers:

An archive of Reynolds Price's papers is at in the Perkins Library, Duke University.

John Rechy

(10 March 1931 –   )

Wanda H. Giles
Northern Illinois University

and

Ted Clontz
Northern Illinois University

See also the Rechy entries in *DLB 122: Chicano Writers, Second Series,* and *DLB Yearbook: 1982.*

BOOKS: *City of Night* (New York: Grove, 1963; London: MacGibbon & Kee, 1964);

Numbers (New York: Grove, 1967);

This Day's Death (New York: Grove, 1970; London: MacGibbon & Kee, 1970);

The Vampires (New York: Grove, 1971);

The Fourth Angel (New York: Viking, 1972; London: W. H. Allen, 1972);

The Sexual Outlaw: A Documentary. A Non-Fiction Account, with Commentaries, of Three Days and Nights in the Sexual Underground (New York: Grove, 1977; London: W. H. Allen, 1978; revised, New York: Grove, 1985);

Rushes (New York: Grove, 1979);

Bodies and Souls (New York: Carroll & Graf, 1983; London: W. H. Allen, 1985);

Marilyn's Daughter (New York: Carroll & Graf, 1988);

The Miraculous Day of Amalia Gómez (New York: Arcade, 1991);

Our Lady of Babylon (New York: Arcade, 1996);

The Coming of the Night (New York: Grove, 1999);

The Life and Adventures of Lyle Clemens (New York: Grove, 2003).

PLAY PRODUCTIONS: *Momma as She Became . . . But Not as She Was,* 1978;

The Fourth Angel, Los Angeles, 1985; produced as *Tigers Wild,* New York, Playhouse 91, 1986.

OTHER: "On Being a 'Grove Press Author'," *Review of Contemporary Fiction* (Fall 1990): 137–142;

Mysteries and Desire: Searching the Worlds of John Rechy, CD-ROM, Annenberg Center for Communications, 2000.

In 1963 a thirty-two-year-old west Texan, John Rechy, published his first novel, *City of Night.* In a time when other Texas writers alluded to homosexuality with euphemisms, if at all, Rechy opened the subject to honest portrayal. Writing from the highly marginal perspective of the gay hustler, Rechy defined the culture in a series of passionately and tenderly written novels. His books on the gay world are perhaps his best known, but he also writes about people in other unprivileged segments of American culture, particularly women and Latinos. *City of Night* opened the hidden worlds that became his subject matter as he crafted what Debra Castillo calls his "outlaw aesthetics" from naturalistic, romantic, and existential philosophies that were dominant in the post–World War II period.

Also influencing Rechy was his Catholic upbringing, with apocalypse underlying much of his work, often with the act of revelation leading to violence and destruction. The line that he planned to use in all of his books, "No substitute for salvation," captures the desperation of Rechy's characters, driven by their desire and need for a salvation he believes may be nonexistent. Sex, which for many of them represents a way to rebel, is always closely shadowed by death. Ben Satterfield sees Rechy's vision as hostile and indifferent, thus certainly capturing the hustler mentality of some of the characters, but he significantly views Rechy primarily as a moralist and sees in his nihilism a critique of society.

Rechy was born Juan Francisco Rechy in El Paso, Texas, on 10 March 1931, the youngest of six children born to Roberto Sixto Rechy and Guadalupe Flores Rechy. His parents' marriage is the basis for the fre-

*John Rechy (photograph by Tony Korody; from the dust jacket
for* Marilyn's Daughter, *1988)*

quently recurring figures of the artistic, raging, violent father and the oppressively loving mother in his novels. Growing up in a Spanish-speaking household, Rechy learned English only when he went to elementary school. His kindergarten teacher gave him the name John following a misunderstanding. In those years, Texas segregated blacks and Latinos, but Rechy had inherited light skin. Some of his family members had darker skin, and Rechy's ethnicity and his sexuality fostered in him a keen sympathy for those outside officially sanctioned society. Rechy's great love for his mother and his sisters led him to a warm appreciation for and understanding of women, and his father's theatricality and musical talents imbued in him a reverence for creative work. Roberto Rechy's feelings for his youngest child were mixed; sexual abuse was one of his expressions of approval. A more loving father figure was Rechy's brother Roberto, a compassionate man who Rechy feels sacrificed his own future to support and care for his siblings.

Rechy graduated from Texas Western College (now the University of Texas at El Paso) in 1952, majoring in his second language, English, and minoring in French. Before attending the New School of Social Research in New York, he joined the United States Army, serving in Kentucky and at Dachau in Germany. Returning from the army in 1954, he stayed in El Paso for a while before setting out to travel and discover himself. Virtually without sexual experience, he went to New York City and discovered the world of hustling. Four years later, writing a letter (never mailed) to a friend, he recognized that he had material for fiction. His first story, "Mardi Gras," appeared in the *Evergreen Review* in 1958, and more stories, including "The Fabulous Wedding of Miss Destiny" (*Big Table,* 1959), appeared soon after; these stories became part of *City of Night.* Even after he began writing novels, Rechy continued for years to work the streets, earning from the experience personal validation and awareness of the life of the sexual outlaw.

City of Night is generally regarded as Rechy's greatest achievement, a modern classic that is a fictionalized account of his wanderings in the gay underground of six American cities: El Paso, Chicago, New York, Los Angeles, San Francisco, and New Orleans. Along the way, he meets the people whose stories make up the book. Rechy presents a broad spectrum of the gay world, ranging from the controlling, sadomasochist Neil in San Francisco to the beautiful, vulnerable, dying Kathy in New Orleans. Many of the characters are written in voices that mirror Rechy's own in their wit and compassion, and the novel confronts the many lies and dissemblings on which gay life at that time had to be based. In one case, the unnamed narrator is offered genuine love; but following the hustler's code, which involves denial of participation in gay sex, the narrator flees the opportunity, though the tenderness of the scene between the narrator and Dave, another hustler, is as profound as the shock that follows the narrator's exit from the relationship.

The narrator takes on the role of the hustler, who provides sexual, but not emotional, connection. He toughens himself physically and emotionally, rejecting the loneliness that is his life. Yet, like Rechy, he thrives on human encounter, and characters such as Miss Destiny are as richly drawn as Rechy's less loving participants in what he calls "the sex hunt." It is noteworthy that the studied detachment of the narrator breaks at one significant sentence: "It's possible to hate the filthy world and love it with an abstract, pitying love."

The sexuality of this novel stunned most critics. Response to *City of Night* was emotional, with some reviewers questioning the existence of such a world as Rechy had portrayed; one critic, Alfred Chester, even questioned Rechy's own existence. In his essay "On Being a 'Grove Press Author'" (*Review of Contemporary Fiction,* Fall 1990) Rechy notes particularly the "shrieking review by Alfred Chester in the lofty *New York Review of Books*—and the equally malicious one by Richard Gilman in the *New Republic.*" Critics who managed to get past their outrage at the subject matter picked at literary conventions, complaining that the novel had no particular form, despite the fact that picaresque and road novels were hardly a novelty. Michael Denneny of the *Chicago Review* made perhaps the strongest critical point: "Very few books are dangerous. Very few books are actually threatening to the status quo of society, and *City of Night* was one of them. Which is why it is so important." Other critics noted on Rechy's website (<http://www.johnrechy.com>) are Herbert Gold, who called *City of Night* "one of the most remarkable novels to appear in years"; Larry McMurtry; and Christopher Isherwood, who noted Rechy's "great comic and tragic talent." The website also conveys the astonishment of

contemporary critics in a citation from *The New York Times:* "Mr. Rechy does a convincing job of showing the grubby, lonely, nearly psychotic underside of . . . life."

Driving with his mother from California to El Paso, Rechy began his second novel, *Numbers* (1967); Guadalupe Rechy held a notepad on the console of his Ford Mustang as Rechy wrote. Because of the explicitness of the sex hunt in this book—Johnny Rio sets out to have sex with thirty men in ten days in Los Angeles—the novel was at least as controversial as *City of Night.* The name Johnny Rio was one that Rechy had used on the streets; the author says, however, that he views the novelistic Johnny as a gay hustler's Everyman, not as a mirror image of himself. More than *City of Night, Numbers* emphasizes the harshness of the hustler's view of life—and the narcissism.

Johnny Rio is returning to Los Angeles after a three-year absence. In those years, he has been sexually abstinent, has worked out (Rechy himself is a well-known bodybuilder), and has lived a quiet, self-focused life, controlling his behavior. When the urge to return to the hunt overpowers him, he is drawn back to Los Angeles, choosing Griffith Park as his primary location. He exceeds his goal of thirty men (Rechy has said that numbness and the numbing quality of a controlled set of self-proving conquests is a major point of this book), obsessively losing himself in these meaningless encounters in which he rigorously abstains from emotion except to protect himself from rejection. Although Johnny is committed to the hustler's essential indifference, he feels in spite of himself an anxiety that rises to vulnerability, the thing he seeks to avoid by the control he exercises in much of his life. Sex is his outlet, but the desperate hunt is a form of the very death it is supposed to keep at bay.

Critics responded negatively to this book, failing to take interest in its existential despair and focusing instead on revulsion over the sexual content. Webster Schott, in *The New York Times Book Review* (14 June 1968), called the book part of a "siege" on American literature by gay novelists.

Rechy followed *Numbers* three years later with *This Day's Death* (1970), slowing the pace of his two earlier novels as he contemplated circumstances in his own life: an arrest in Los Angeles and the illness of his mother. *This Day's Death* is a realistic, plot-driven, politicized narrative. The protagonist, Jim Girard, struggles with legal and family problems: his arrest on sex-perversion charges for an alleged encounter in Griffith Park and the fact that his mother is slowly dying. The charges against him are trumped up, something of an irony in the hustling and cruising world of Griffith Park at that time. Girard is nevertheless convicted for what he has not done; the only good coming from the travesty is his own recognition and acceptance of his identity as a gay man. This revelation comes, however, as a result of blatant injustice and is accompanied by the added sorrows of the loss of his legal career and his mother's death. The mother's illness and the court case keep Girard on the road throughout the novel (as they did in Rechy's life); he travels alone, dealing with both situations singly. Girard and his mother's nurse are among the many strong Mexican American characters in Rechy's novels.

Despite his passionate indictment of the system of sexual injustice, Rechy came to dislike this novel, once stating that he wished he could "unpublish" it. Critics were predictably more open to *This Day's Death* than to the earlier books, as this novel is told from a sufficiently detached point of view and with enough social commentary that they could relate to it with more compassion for Girard than to the hustlers of the first two novels. Schott, however, commented in *The New York Times Book Review,* "If you don't know by now what homosexual life is like in the United States, don't blame John Rechy." Such remarks were not uncommon in early Rechy criticism.

Rechy moved to Los Angeles shortly after his mother's death in 1970. The book that followed, *The Vampires* (1971), came as a surprise to readers who read Rechy solely as a homosexual novelist. Based in part on the times Rechy had spent on a private island in a man-made lake near Mundelein, Illinois, *The Vampires* abandons the direct social commentary and realistic narration of *This Day's Death* for a private Caribbean island setting lorded over by a controlling host, Richard, who invites a group of men and women for an house party. The guests are an odd mélange, including Richard's son, his possible illegitimate son, a perfectly shaped midget, a gay hustler named Blue, a beautiful woman named Savannah, two actresses, and a priest. Their weekend of confession and sex unfolds with cinematic techniques, including jump cuts and flashbacks, a favored Rechy device. The characters, having consented to the peculiar torment that is their entertainment, tell all and form various alliances as the time flows. The book includes many of Rechy's traditional themes—beauty, control, the chimeric nature of truth—but the novel moves slowly and without the redeeming tenderness of the three that preceded it. The characters are assembled to confess their evil, only to learn that—while hoping to be refused in his perverse quest—the host collects exotic people who will reveal themselves. Richard proves to himself the weakness and banality of people, unmasks them. Even the searches for truth in the enmeshed group end in horror as a young woman, Valerie, kills her twin brother, Paul, in an effort to save

him from the evil of their lives (an incestuous relationship).

The critical response, by now fairly slim, was largely bewilderment, with shock at the move from Rechy's traditional urban grittiness and a consistent failure to accept the nontraditional exotic characters and setting. There were recognitions of the cinematic techniques and the stylistic innovations, but the book was not received with the kind of passion stimulated by the gay novels, and the response continues to be a disappointment to Rechy, who is particularly fond of this novel.

The Fourth Angel, the only Rechy novel to date set entirely in Texas, appeared in 1972. The Angels of the title are a group of teenagers led by a girl called Shell, who controls her three male companions with a studied hardness. The fourth Angel is Jerry, whose mother has recently died. The four live on the streets, preying on the weakness of others, brilliantly observing and feasting on it.

Rechy focuses in this book, as in *The Vampires,* on the workings of groups. As Shell tries to maintain the leadership of the Angels, all confess to and participate in a variety of cruelties and frivolities stemming from their brief, battered pasts. Shell was, as Cob cannily suspects, raped by her father when she was a child; Manny's mother hated him; Jerry's mother died and left him; Cob lived as a young gay man in a world that did not welcome him. They seem to unite to heal themselves from significant hurts, but their union is one of barely concealed tensions. Shell probes Cob, trying to uncover childhood molestation. Manny resents Jerry, who cannot bear the exposed emptiness of his dead mother's room. The boys' feelings for Shell are a mix of desire and fear, clouded further by the psychedelic drugs through which the group communes. The drugs, initially unifying, become controlling, and the Angels assault one another physically and emotionally, exposing painful truths. Jerry is perhaps the most invaded by the group, as they force their way into his mother's room, cruelly exposing his aloneness. Shell struggles to maintain the hard anger that is her imperfect protection, but Jerry, though devastated, begins to open himself to a salvation through compassion.

Again, critical response was scant; those commenting seemed to wish for a return to the clear sexual focus of his first two novels. Rechy responded generously to critics who seemed fair and sharply taunted the established journalists who scorned or ignored him.

Five years intervened between *The Fourth Angel* and *The Sexual Outlaw: A Documentary* (1977). In Rechy's life, these were years of recovery from his mother's death and of self-acceptance as a gay man, something that was for him a long process. In a chance encounter on the streets of Los Angeles, he met actor and later movie producer Michael Snyder. After a tumultuous early relationship, complicated by Rechy's commitment to the hustler's code of indifference and promiscuity, they eventually formed a committed and creative partnership. Having achieved security with his sexuality, Rechy turned toward a nonfiction novel or "prose documentary" that would document his views on gay life in the United States. (Rechy's website categorizes *The Sexual Outlaw* as a work of nonfiction.) The book has a protagonist named Jim, who spends a weekend of sex in Los Angeles. The most innovative parts of the book are "Voice Overs," in which Rechy comments on contemporary gay life, primarily upholding and celebrating it but criticizing the sadomasochistic subculture. Particularly striking are the verbal montages of Los Angeles, Rechy's home for thirty years and a major character in nearly all of his books. The book rejects the safety of certain gay groups among the middle class and college students and calls for a revolution based on the street sex he has depicted. *The Sexual Outlaw* is thus a codification of the outlaw aesthetics cited by Castillo.

The Sexual Outlaw received favorable reviews; Alix Nelson in *The New York Times Book Review* (3 April 1977) acknowledged its intelligence and persuasive quality, calling it a "heartbreaking manifesto." A *Los Angeles Times* reviewer called it an "intensely personal and courageous document." It was, at the time, Rechy's most openly political and philosophical statement (he continues to write on these themes, with the website as a point of access), and his criticism of the sadomasochistic gay society continued in his next novel. *Rushes* (1979) takes place in an unnamed city that is based on New York; the title is the name of a bar catering to masculine gays. Reflecting the views expressed in *The Sexual Outlaw* and the resistance to control prominent in most of Rechy's novels, the bar is a metaphor for the intolerance in gay society, in which masculine men have been valued over drag queens and femmes. Rushes is filled every night with middle-class gays masquerading as macho construction workers and soldiers, something one character notes as a new kind of drag.

One of Rechy's most formally structured works, *Rushes* takes the form of a mass, with the pornographic murals on the bar walls representing stations of the cross, and ritual plays an important role. Endore, who represents Rechy in this book, opposes his philosophical rival, Chas, an ironic Christ figure who seeks to convert the manly bar patrons to his sadomasochism. The two seem to centralize the vision of *The Sexual Outlaw*, with Endore, a columnist for a straight magazine (possibly reflecting Rechy's own long career with such journals as the *Nation*), criticizing the safe gay lifestyle, which is ghettoized, and equally rejecting sadomasochism, a sexuality that internalizes in its degrading vio-

Rechy and his mother, Guadalupe Flores Rechy, in the mid 1960s (from Charles Casillo, Outlaw: The Lives and Careers of John Rechy, *2002)*

lence the hatred of the straight world toward gays. Chas, too, rejects much that denigrates gay life, particularly the effeminate stereotypes, but he denies his rejection of those, such as drag queens, who do not fit into his hypermasculine worldview.

A character of key importance is Don, a man in his forties who has never been as attractive as the friends he relies on to get into Rushes. Knowing he has lost whatever sexual appeal he might have had, Don experiences desperation at his status and age, a central theme in Rechy's writing since *City of Night*. Although most of the Rushes patrons feel some empathy for Don, he is attacked outside and then, in a final gay bashing, is rejected by a Rushes habitué who is similar to him in age and looks but repulsed by both the similarities and the evidence of the beating on the docks. Don is a martyr to the artifice of the gay world, which rejects the natural process of aging, and he is a victim of the homophobia outside. Control is also an issue for Bill, another man presented as a loser in life. He complains of the loss of a lover who insisted that he do things he did not want to do; Endore accuses him of controlling the relationship through his passivity. Bill represents a major Rechy theme, the danger of the myth of love used to control. The entry of a woman, Lyndy, into the all-male bar culture also threatens the safety of Rushes, raising more questions as to who belongs.

Every encounter in Rushes underscores the self-hatred and rage of the men in this bar. The final competition between Chas and Endore revolves around a man in black leather. He never speaks, and Chas experiences the touch of his gloved hands as warm, whereas to Endore's touch he is cold. This man and one other, Michael, lead Chas and Endore to their final, desperate competition, in which faces merge in a violent scene that enacts all the self-loathing that has pervaded this novel. *Rushes* is one of Rechy's most despairing books. Rushes should have been a safe place for the men who go there, but it is instead a self-violating ghetto that reenacts the pain and punishment originated in the straight world. Don, who fails and is rejected most painfully, laments the old days, when to be gay "meant accepting being an outcast."

After such despair, *Bodies and Souls* (1983) turns toward a search for salvation, depicting a Los Angeles that is only in part gay underworld. A multifaceted novel, *Bodies and Souls* explores the claim of Sister Woman, a street preacher, that she can redeem lost souls, even those who have gone to hell. If she can prove she has redeemed the soul of one bitterly cynical, wealthy woman, she and her followers will receive a large sum of money from the woman's estate. Characters cross over, making cameo appearances in the lives of other characters. Images of snipers and intersections recur throughout the novel, giving the book cohesion beyond the linking concept of intersecting fates. Orin, a young man who drives around Los Angeles with friends named Lisa and Jesse James, must judge the success of Sister Woman's mission and determine whether the cynical woman, who is possibly Orin's mother, has been rescued from hell. On their way to test this salvation, the three young people encounter a variety of people, depicted with Rechy's characteristic passion and wit. As in *City of Night,* Rechy visits every level of society, offering such portraits as a judge who attempts to control both his family and society; a bag lady barely surviving on the city streets; a black cleaning woman

from Watts; a young Chicano with a tattoo of a naked Christ; and an aging gay man who no longer finds any comfort in his own life. Rechy's chapter about the man who lectures "On Nothing," a famous segment of the book, holds out a mystifying hope that is always present, even if inexplicable, in Rechy's writings. Many of the characters, however, including Orin and Jesse, end up dead or wounded in the banal violence on the freeways. Reviewers responded favorably to this book, the *Los Angeles Times* (17 July 1983) calling it a "memorable feast" and *The New York Times Book Review* (17 March 1983) noting its "scarred beauty."

The book that followed, *Marilyn's Daughter* (1988), surprised many readers; it departs once again from the gay scene they insisted was Rechy's topic and presents a young woman's search for her personal origins. Normalyn Morgan, a California girl now living in Texas, believes she may be the unacknowledged daughter of Marilyn Monroe and Robert F. Kennedy. In her search for identity, a theme carried through every Rechy novel, Normalyn moves between Texas and California, seeking to know her putative mother and to learn the truth of her parentage. She has a dominant mother figure, Enid Morgan, who knew Monroe as a child in a southern California orphanage. After the death of the movie goddess, Enid fled California, taking with her Normalyn, whose name is a combination of Monroe's real name, Norma Jean, and her screen name. Enid's suicide some years later in Texas leads Normalyn back to California in a quest for the truth. The search plot is elaborate, involving J. Edgar Hoover, Robert Kennedy, John F. Kennedy, and a left-wing adviser to the stars, Alberta Holland.

The question of Normalyn's identity is difficult to resolve because in death Monroe has become an untouchable, ruling legend. Stardom and image are themes that fascinate Rechy, raising issues of identity that transcend history and biology; his real focus is on Monroe as the perfect creation of Norma Jean, who preceded her and coexisted in her body. Two characters from the Los Angeles sexual underground befriend Normalyn and expand upon the theme of self-creation: Troja is a black transsexual who does a Monroe impersonation, and Kirk is a body-sculpted Mr. Universe contestant afraid of aging and hooked on cocaine.

Rechy unites the worlds of image and identity through a flashback pastiche depicting the Dead Movie Stars, a Los Angeles cult who live as the dead actors they impersonate. To take on these lives, the Dead Movie Stars must sully the real people they represent by finding out the truth behind their scandals, and they, along with Troja, end up living hollow, untenable imitations of life. Normalyn lives, almost because she decides she must leave the past, even if it is hers; she becomes one hopeful young woman who enters—and leaves—Hollywood on a bus, her departure a tribute to her own beauty and self-creation.

Marilyn's Daughter, which Rechy has said was perhaps the most difficult of his books, received a somewhat confused and frustrated critical response from those who would not allow Rechy fictional space off the urban gay streets; but a critic for the *San Francisco Chronicle,* noting the complex, ambitious structure of the novel, called it a "masterpiece of narrative engineering" by a "major American novelist." On the other coast, a reviewer for the *Village Voice* appreciated Rechy's sense of "the innocent trashiness, the vulnerable screw-loose fascination of Monroe herself."

In *The Miraculous Day of Amalia Gómez* (1991) Rechy turned more directly to his Hispanic roots than he had done previously, though there is always at least one Latino character in all his novels, and he has consistently appreciated his heritage. The focus on a Mexican American woman, however, fulfilled a longtime critical desire.

Rechy's Los Angeles in this novel is peopled in part by characters from earlier novels. Sister Woman, who also appeared in *Marilyn's Daughter,* resurfaces in *The Miraculous Day of Amalia Gómez,* as does Mandy Lang-Jones, the journalist from *Bodies and Souls.* A major event of this novel, in fact, originates in *Bodies and Souls,* as Manny Gómez, Amalia's son, is jailed after the freeway slaughter. In this book Rechy continues his focus on women, begun in *Marilyn's Daughter,* and particularly on the maternal experience, heretofore examined from outside in such novels as *City of Night* and *This Day's Death.*

Amalia Gómez, whose relationship with her three children is central to her self-perception, undergoes brutal torment in this novel, including Manny's suicide in prison. She also has been the victim of rape and a resultant pregnancy, religious guilt, two divorces, violence from a lover, drug addiction on the part of a son, and a daughter clearly headed for trouble. She has idolized her children and is in the course of this day stripped of her illusions. As Rechy unfolds these elements (the cataclysmic violence of Amalia's miraculous day is nearly surreal), he exposes also his much-loved streets of Los Angeles. (He had walked or driven to all of the locations in Amalia's life, choosing her precise bungalow off Hollywood Boulevard, for example.) He contrasts the reality of the streets with the sustaining daily reality of the lives of women who rely on *telenovelas* (soap operas); the televised melodramas pale beside the harsher and much more fascinating realities of the day-to-day lives of their devotees.

The miraculous day begins with Amalia's vision of a silver cross in the sky. The pious woman takes this vision as a miracle, a sign from heaven; Rechy contrasts

Rechy in 1967 (photograph from the dust jacket for Numbers*)*

it ironically with the miraculous event that concludes the novel. Despite the many heartbreaks of her life, Amalia has until now lived without regret, moving from crisis to crisis without resentment or rage. Like many of the women in the sweatshop where she works, she uses her *telenovelas* as an escape and as a mirror to the tragedies and hopes in their lives; she also listens there to Rosario, her friend who is a politically committed worker. The workplace offers more torment than her personal life, with sexual harassment by the employer and Immigration and Naturalization Service agents daily accompanying economic exploitation. Nor has the church been a consistent solace: a priest masturbates during her confession. The Chicano movement, where she might have found political support, instead has marginalized women in a reenactment of machismo. In her near seduction by a coyote (a procurer of illegal migrant workers) she is again exploited by a man of her culture. All this hardship she has borne without complaint.

The novel turns when Amalia, watching a *tele-novela* and identifying with a character's lack of choice, recognizes the horror of her own life. She has been rejected and disregarded increasingly by her family, and her society is even less aware of her, though dependent on her usefulness. She has coped by denying what she could not change, for example, her son Juan's homosexuality and her lover's advances toward her daughter. In a hallucinatory final sequence she moves from confessing all to a statue of the Virgin to demanding a miracle. She then hears the voice of Rosario in her memory, saying, *"Find your own strength."* In the climax of the novel, Amalia acts on this advice. Captured by a gunman fighting with police, she resists, shouting "No more," a motto taken from the "¡No Mas!" of the Chicano liberation movement. As she nonetheless blesses the man who has held her hostage, she sees the Virgin before her; and she understands her miracle to be real because of her own reality and strength.

The critical response to *The Miraculous Day of Amalia Gómez* varied; a reviewer for *The New York Times* said the book was "not so miraculous," but a critic for the *Washington Post* praised the novel as one "with more truth in it than a carload of best-sellers." *Newsday* saw the book as a triumph, "a sad, beautiful and loving book," and in *The Naturalistic Inner-City Novel in America: Encounters with the Fat Man* (1996) James R. Giles argues that this book is the first of Rechy's novels in which an individual takes power over the dominant ethnic and economic cultures, therein finding a substitute for salvation.

Our Lady of Babylon (1996) continued Rechy's fictional study of women. In this novel a Lady moves throughout heaven and hell and much of Earth. This Lady and her mentor, the spiritual guide Madame Bernice, speak with asperity, displaying a characteristic wit that nevertheless may surprise readers in this sustained comic performance. The woman of the title is Lady du Muir, a French noblewoman who represents women who, from Eve and Mary Magdalene onward, have borne the label of whore and the unjust blame for most of the problems in the world. Rechy writes in first person in this novel for the first time since *City of Night*. The Lady is central in a plot by her brother and sister-in-law to murder her husband and blame it on the Lady, so that she will be unable to inherit. All the power structures in the Lady's world are brought to bear against her; even the Pope proves in the end to be the inspiration for the plot, as he is bent on silencing the memories that the Lady speaks. Rechy has never before gone so far from his modern settings to depict the repression of individual wit and sexuality as he does in this novel with dialogue between the Lady and Madame Bernice in preparation for the Lady's appearance before the inquisitor.

The Lady relates stories of Adam, Mary, Judas and Jesus, Mary Magdalene, the war in heaven (with an angel named Cassandra as Lucifer's sister), and St. John the Divine. In this novel God is the image of the vain, controlling, and destructive men he has created, reminiscent of the father figures in earlier Rechy novels. Until convinced otherwise, the Jesus of this book is an earthy, sensual revolutionary who has taken Mary Magdalene and Judas as childhood lovers. His mother, however, convinces Jesus that he is the Son of God and that nothing will happen to him—certainly not a truthful presentation, but one that the Lady explains as necessary so that Mary will not suffer for her out-of-wedlock pregnancy.

The visions of the Jesus in this novel are mushroom induced, and he believes his healing power results from the positive belief he instills. He goes to the execution on the cross believing, along with Mary, that God will intercede to free him. Judas hangs himself in response to the death of a beloved friend. The war in heaven results from God's attempt to control his angels, an old Rechy theme, and the angels are damned by their desire for freedom. In the theology of this novel, Eve does commit the original sin, but it is the sin of free will, not of carnal knowledge. Woman's sin, in fact, is that Adam chose Eve over God; and St. John's vision of the whore of Babylon becomes in Rechy's version the historical metaphor for all women who have resisted or been crushed by dominant forces. In an inversion of his earlier vision, however, death is the only way to avoid these controlling forces. Rechy has remarked that readers have enjoyed the audacious originality and wit of this book but seem to have overlooked the foreshadowing of a terrible modern despair. The Lady has not yet met her inquisitor nor triumphed outside her small, safe circle. In her challenge to received wisdom and conventional, male-dominated authority, she is as vulnerable as any street angel in any of Rechy's early books.

In *The Coming of the Night* (1999) Rechy returns to the subject of gay society in Los Angeles. Set in 1982, roughly the same time as *Bodies and Souls,* this book depicts a time when the gay community lived on the brink of the knowledge of AIDS. The novel follows several men, including a gang of gay-bashers, as they make their way through a Saturday. Much as in *Bodies and Souls,* the men move along, sometimes crossing paths, until most gather late at night in a park for a celebration of sexual excess. The Santa Ana winds bring in a damaging, intense heat, symbolizing the fear and knowledge spreading through the community. The novel concludes in an apocalyptic, symbolic sacrifice to a life of sex, with a man celebrating his twenty-second birthday by narcissistically offering himself to a lengthy sequence of anonymous sex partners who use him and abandon him as he sprawls against a toolshed. Rechy witnessed such an event in Los Angeles and then talked with a friend about the rumored new illness, unnamed in this book.

The story lines involve a broad spectrum of men and interests. In a rehearsal for a porn-movie shoot involving a drag queen named Za-Za La Grande, Rechy uses humor. A priest searches for a hustler with a naked Christ tattooed on his back—a figure from *Bodies and Souls*. One man from New York, Clint, enters the city clearly sick. Thomas represents those who have grown older and are rejected by the temporarily strong and ruling class of young men. Sex and death are melded in a new way in this novel: sex is no longer the thing that obliterates death but that which delivers it.

Pamela Warrick wrote in the *Los Angeles Times* that *The Coming of the Night* is "as exciting as it is chilling," but Gary Indiana's later review in the book section of the same newspaper denigrated the novel, comparing it to a Jackie Collins tale and saying that "Rechy may be more shocking to the still-shockable." In a review for *Salon*, however, Frank Browning praised Rechy as someone who "touches greatness" and noted that the focus of the novel is the exquisite moment when ecstasy and abyss collide.

Rechy's 2003 novel, *The Life and Adventures of Lyle Clemens,* is inspired by Henry Fielding's 1749 classic *Tom Jones.* It is illustrated and presented in the format of eighteenth-century novels, but with a modern cast. Rechy's protagonist wanders from Texas to Las Vegas and Los Angeles. Rechy also continues to work on a project that has attracted him for years, "Autobiography: A Novel," and he has drafted a short novel, "In the Blue Hour." *Mysteries and Desire: Searching the Worlds of John Rechy* (2000) is a multimedia presentation on CD-ROM combining excerpts from "Autobiography" and Rechy's other works with photographs, archival footage, sound clips, drawings, and other materials, grouped in three sections: "Memories," "Bodies," and "Cruising." Rechy also has taught and lectured at several universities and runs a writing workshop that has included some forty published writers.

In the late 1990s Rechy began a rise in critical esteem. He received the PEN-USA-West lifetime achievement award in 1997, the first novelist to be so honored. In 1999, when he received the William Whitehead Lifetime Achievement Award from Publishing Triangle, the announcement of the award quoted Edmund White's assessment of Rechy as a "heroic American life" and a "touchstone of moral integrity and artistic innovation." These awards have been accompanied by some revisions of critical opinion, including that of Gore Vidal, not always an admirer, who calls Rechy, in a jacket blurb for Charles Casillo's 2002 biography, "in retrospect one of the few original writers of the last

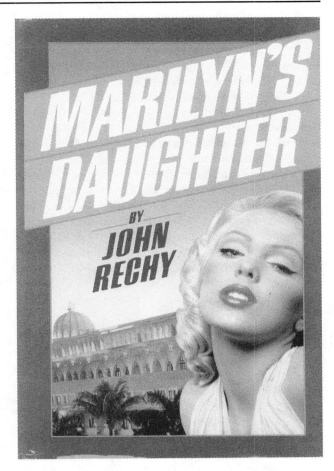

Dust jacket for Rechy's 1988 novel, about a young woman who believes she is the illegitimate daughter of Marilyn Monroe and Robert F. Kennedy (Richland County Public Library)

century." At the Whitehead award ceremony, Michael Bronski summarized Rechy's impact on gay literature, saying that John Rechy "super-radically and forever altered how mainstream American culture wrote about, saw, experienced and conceptualized homosexuality." Rechy's vision, of course, is not limited to the gay world, but he allies himself with the vulnerable beauty of struggling people and vibrant language.

Interviews:

James R. Giles and Wanda H. Giles, "An Interview with John Rechy," *Chicago Review,* 25 (Summer 1972): 19–31;

William Leyland, "John Rechy," in *Gay Sunshine Interviews,* volume 2, edited by Leyland (San Francisco: Gay Sunshine, 1978), pp. 251–268;

Charles Ortleb, "Interview: John Rechy," *Christopher Street* (December 1979): 59–62;

Debra Castillo, "John Rechy," *Diacritics: A Review of Contemporary Criticism,* 25 (Spring 1995): 113–125.

Biography:

Charles Casillo, *Outlaw: The Lives and Careers of John Rechy* (Los Angeles: Advocate Books, 2002).

References:

Stephen D. Adam, "Terminal Sex: John Rechy and William Burroughs," in his *The Homosexual as Hero in Contemporary Fiction* (Totowa, N.J.: Barnes & Noble, 1980), pp. 83–105;

Lawrence Birken, "Desire and Death: The Early Fiction of John Rechy," *Western Humanities Review,* 51 (Summer 1997): 236–245;

Juan Bruce-Novoa, "In Search of the Honest Outlaw: John Rechy," *Minority Voices,* 3, no. 1 (1979): 37–45;

Alfred Chester, "Fruit Salad," *New York Review of Books,* 1 (May 1963);

James R. Giles, "Larry McMurtry's *Leaving Cheyenne* and the Novels of John Rechy: Four Trips along 'the Mythical Pecos'," *Forum,* 10 (Summer–Fall 1972): 34–40;

Giles, *The Naturalistic Inner-City Novel in America: Encounters with the Fat Man* (Columbia: University of South Carolina Press, 1996), pp. 113–128;

Giles, "Religious Alienation and 'Homosexual Consciousness' in *City of Night* and *Go Tell It on the Mountain,*" *College English,* 36 (1974): 369–380;

Richard Gilman, "John Rechy," in his *The Confusion of the Realms* (New York: Random House, 1963), pp. 53–61;

Stanton Hoffman, "The Cities of Night: John Rechy's *City of Night* and the American Literature of Homosexuality," *Chicago Review,* 17, nos. 2–3 (1964): 195–206;

Lee T. Lemon, "You May Have Missed These," *Prairie Schooner,* 45 (Fall 1971): 270–272;

Honorah Moore Lynch, "Patterns of Anarchy and Order in the Works of John Rechy," *DAI,* 37 (1976): 158A;

Emmanuel S. Nelson, "John Rechy, James Baldwin, and the American Double Minority Literature," *Journal of American Culture,* 6 (Summer 1983): 70–74;

Ricardo L. Ortiz, "Sexuality Degree Zero: Pleasure and Power in the Novels of John Rechy, Arturo Islas, and Michael Nava," *Journal of Homosexuality,* 26, nos. 2–3 (1993): 111–126;

Rafael Pérez-Torres, "The Ambiguous Outlaw: John Rechy and Complicitous Homotextuality," in *Fictions of Masculinity, Crossing Cultures, Crossing Sexualities,* edited by Peter F. Murphy (New York: New York University Press, 1994), pp. 204–225;

José R. Santana, "Fictions of Masculinity in the Novels of John Rechy and Michael Nava" <http://www.aad.berkeley.edu/96journal/santana.html>;

Ben Satterfield, "John Rechy's Tormented World," *Southwest Review,* 67 (Winter 1982): 78–85;

Terry Southern, "Rechy and Gover," in *Contemporary American Novelists,* edited by Harry T. Moore (Carbondale & Edwardsville: Southern Illinois University Press, 1964), pp. 222–227;

Trudy Steuernagel, "Contemporary Homosexual Fiction and the Gay Rights Movement," *Journal of Popular Culture,* 20 (Winter 1986): 125–134;

Charles M. Tatum, "The Sexual Underworlds of John Rechy," *Minority Voices,* 3 (1979): 47–52;

Carlos Zamora, "Odysseus in John Rechy's *City of Night:* The Epistemological Journey," *Minority Voices,* 3 (1979): 53–62.

Papers:

The papers of John Rechy are collected at Boston University.

Isaac Bashevis Singer

(14 July 1904 – 24 July 1991)

Joseph Sherman
Oxford Centre for Hebrew and Jewish Studies

See also the Singer entries in *DLB 6: American Novelists Since World War II, Second Series; DLB 28: Twentieth-Century American-Jewish Fiction Writers; DLB 52: American Writers for Children Since 1960: Fiction;* and *DLB Yearbook: 1991.*

BOOKS IN ENGLISH: *The Family Moskat,* translated by A. H. Gross (New York: Knopf, 1950; London: Secker & Warburg, 1966);

Satan in Goray, translated by Jacob Sloan (New York: Noonday, 1955; London: Owen, 1958);

Gimpel the Fool and Other Stories, translated by Saul Bellow and others (New York: Noonday, 1957; London: Owen, 1958);

The Magician of Lublin, translated by Elaine Gottlieb and Joseph Singer (New York: Noonday, 1960; London: Secker & Warburg, 1961);

The Spinoza of Market Street and Other Stories, translated by Martha Glicklich, Cecil Hemley, and others (New York: Farrar, Straus & Cudahy, 1961; London: Secker & Warburg, 1962);

The Slave, translated by Isaac Bashevis Singer and Hemley (New York: Farrar, Straus & Cudahy, 1962; London: Secker & Warburg, 1963);

Short Friday, and Other Stories, translated by Joseph Singer, Roger H. Klein, and others (New York: Farrar, Straus & Giroux, 1964; London: Secker & Warburg, 1967);

In My Father's Court, translated by Channah Kleinerman-Goldstein, Gottlieb, and Joseph Singer (New York: Farrar, Straus & Giroux, 1966; London: Secker & Warburg, 1967);

Zlateh the Goat and Other Stories, translated by Elizabeth Shub and Isaac Bashevis Singer (New York: Harper & Row, 1966; Harmondsworth, U.K.: Longman/Young, 1970);

Selected Short Stories of Isaac Bashevis Singer, edited by Irving Howe (New York: Modern Library, 1966);

Mazel and Shlimazel; or, The Milk of a Lioness, translated by Shub and Isaac Bashevis Singer (New York: Farrar, Straus & Giroux, 1967; London: Cape, 1979);

Isaac Bashevis Singer (photograph by Jerry Bauer; from the dust jacket for The Collected Stories of Isaac Bashevis Singer, *1982)*

The Manor, translated by Joseph Singer and Gottlieb (New York: Farrar, Straus & Giroux, 1967; London: Secker & Warburg, 1968);

The Fearsome Inn, translated by Shub and Isaac Bashevis Singer (New York: Scribners, 1967; London: Collins, 1970);

When Shlemiel Went to Warsaw and Other Stories, translated by Isaac Bashevis Singer and Shub (New York: Farrar, Straus & Giroux, 1968; Harmondsworth, U.K.: Longman/Young, 1974);

The Séance and Other Stories, translated by Roger H. Klein, Hemley, and others (New York: Farrar, Straus & Giroux, 1968; London: Cape, 1970);

A Day of Pleasure: Stories of a Boy Growing Up in Warsaw, translated by Kleinerman-Goldstein and others (New York: Farrar, Straus & Giroux, 1969; London: MacRae, 1980);

The Estate, translated by Joseph Singer, Gottlieb, and Shub (New York: Farrar, Straus & Giroux, 1969; London: Cape, 1970);

Joseph and Koza; or, The Sacrifice to the Vistula, translated by Isaac Bashevis Singer and Shub (New York: Farrar, Straus & Giroux, 1970; London: Hamilton, 1984);

Elijah the Slave: A Hebrew Legend Retold, translated by Isaac Bashevis Singer and Shub (New York: Farrar, Straus & Giroux, 1970);

A Friend of Kafka and Other Stories, translated by Isaac Bashevis Singer, Shub, and others (New York: Farrar, Straus & Giroux, 1970; London: Cape, 1972);

An Isaac Bashevis Singer Reader (New York: Farrar, Straus & Giroux, 1971);

Alone in the Wild Forest, translated by Isaac Bashevis Singer and Shub (New York: Farrar, Straus & Giroux, 1971);

The Topsy-Turvy Emperor of China, translated by Isaac Bashevis Singer and Shub (New York & London: Harper & Row, 1971);

Enemies, A Love Story, translated by Aliza Shevrin and Shub (New York: Farrar, Straus & Giroux, 1972; London: Cape, 1972);

The Wicked City, translated by Isaac Bashevis Singer and Shub (New York: Farrar, Straus & Giroux, 1972);

A Crown of Feathers and Other Stories, translated by Isaac Bashevis Singer, Laurie Colwin, and others (New York: Farrar, Straus & Giroux, 1973; London: Cape, 1974);

The Hasidim, by Singer and Ira Moskowitz (New York: Crown, 1973);

The Fools of Chelm and Their History, translated by Isaac Bashevis Singer and Shub (New York: Farrar, Straus & Giroux, 1973);

Why Noah Chose the Dove, translated by Shub (New York: Farrar, Straus & Giroux, 1974);

Passions and Other Stories, translated by Isaac Bashevis Singer, Blanche Nevel, Joseph Nevel, and others (New York: Farrar, Straus & Giroux, 1975; London: Cape, 1976);

A Tale of Three Wishes (New York: Farrar, Straus & Giroux, 1975);

A Little Boy in Search of God; or, Mysticism in a Personal Light, translated by Joseph Singer (Garden City, N.Y.: Doubleday, 1976);

Naftali the Storyteller and His Horse, Sus, and Other Stories, translated by Joseph Singer, Isaac Bashevis Singer, and others (New York: Farrar, Straus & Giroux, 1976; Oxford: Oxford University Press, 1977);

Yentl: A Play, by Singer and Leah Napolin (New York: S. French, 1977);

A Young Man in Search of Love, translated by Joseph Singer (Garden City, N.Y.: Doubleday, 1978);

Shosha, translated by Joseph Singer and Isaac Bashevis Singer (New York: Farrar, Straus & Giroux, 1978; London: Cape, 1979);

Old Love, translated by Joseph Singer, Isaac Bashevis Singer, and others (New York: Farrar, Straus & Giroux, 1979; London: Cape, 1980);

Nobel Lecture (New York: Farrar, Straus & Giroux, 1979; London: Cape, 1979);

Reaches of Heaven: A Story of the Baal Shem Tov (New York: Farrar, Straus & Giroux, 1980);

The Power of Light: Eight Stories for Hanukkah (New York: Farrar, Straus & Giroux, 1980);

Lost in America, translated by Joseph Singer (Garden City, N.Y.: Doubleday, 1981);

The Collected Stories of Isaac Bashevis Singer (New York: Farrar, Straus & Giroux, 1982; London: Cape, 1982);

Isaac Bashevis Singer, Three Complete Novels, translated by Isaac Bashevis Singer and Hemley (New York: Avenel Books, 1982)—comprises *The Slave; Enemies, A Love Story;* and *Shosha;*

The Golem (New York: Farrar, Straus & Giroux, 1982; London: Deutsch, 1983);

Yentl the Yeshiva Boy, translated by Marion Magid and Elizabeth Pollet (New York: Farrar, Straus & Giroux, 1983);

The Penitent, translated by Joseph Singer (New York: Farrar, Straus & Giroux, 1983; London: Cape, 1984);

Love and Exile (Garden City, N.Y.: Doubleday, 1984; London: Cape, 1985)—comprises *A Little Boy in Search of God; or, Mysticism in a Personal Light; A Young Man in Search of Love;* and *Lost in America;*

Stories for Children (New York: Farrar, Straus & Giroux, 1984);

Teibele and Her Demon, by Singer and Eve Friedman (New York: S. French, 1984);

The Image and Other Stories, translated by Isaac Bashevis Singer, Pollet, and others (New York: Farrar, Straus & Giroux, 1985; London: Cape, 1986);

Gifts (Philadelphia: Jewish Publication Society, 1985);

The Death of Methuselah and Other Stories, translated by Isaac Bashevis Singer, Lester Goran, and others (Franklin Center, Pa.: Franklin Library, 1988; New York: Farrar, Straus & Giroux, 1988; London: Cape, 1988);

The King of Fields, translated by Isaac Bashevis Singer (New York: Farrar, Straus & Giroux, 1988; London: Cape, 1988);

Scum, translated by Rosaline Dukalsky Schwartz (New York: Farrar, Straus & Giroux, 1991; London: Cape, 1991);

My Love Affair with Miami Beach, text by Singer, photographs by Richard Nagler (New York: Simon & Schuster, 1991);

The Certificate, translated by Leonard Wolf (New York: Farrar, Straus & Giroux, 1992; London: Cape, 1993);

Meshugah, translated by Isaac Bashevis Singer and Nili Wachtel (New York: Farrar, Straus & Giroux, 1994; London: Cape, 1995);

Shrewd Todie and Lyzer the Miser & Other Children's Stories (Boston: Barefoot Books, 1994);

Shadows on the Hudson, translated by Joseph Sherman (New York: Farrar, Straus & Giroux, 1998; London: Cape, 1999);

More Stories from My Father's Court, translated by Curt Leviant (New York: Farrar, Straus & Giroux, 2000).

BOOKS IN YIDDISH: *Der sotn in goray* (Warsaw: Yiddish PEN-Klub, 1935; New York: Matones, 1943);

Di familye moshkat, 2 volumes (New York: Sklarsky, 1950);

Mayn tatns bes-din shtub (New York: Der Kval, 1956; Tel Aviv: Y. L. Perets, 1979);

Gimpel tam un andere dertseylungen (New York: Tsiko, 1963);

Der knekht (New York: Tsiko, 1967; Tel Aviv: Y. L. Perets, 1980);

Der kuntsnmakher fun lublin (Tel Aviv: Hamenorah, 1971);

Mayses fun hintern oyvn (Tel Aviv: Y. L. Perets, 1971);

Der bal-tshuve (Tel Aviv: Y. L. Perets, 1974);

Der shpigl un andere dertseylungen (Jerusalem: Magnes, 1975);

Mayn tatns bes-din shtub [hemsheykhim-zamlung] (Jerusalem: Magnes, 1996).

OTHER: "I See the Child as a Last Refuge," *New York Times Book Review,* 9 November 1969, VII: 1, 66;

"Hasidism and Its Origins," in *Tully Filmus: Selected Drawings* (Philadelphia: Jewish Publication Society, 1971), pp. xi–xx;

"I. B. Singer Talks to I. B. Singer About the Movie 'Yentl'," *New York Times,* 29 January 1984.

TRANSLATIONS: Knut Hamsun, *Pan; fun leytenant Tomas Glans ksovim* (Vilna: Kletskin, 1928);

Hamsun, *Di vogler* (Vilna: Kletskin, 1928);

Gabriele D'Annunzio, *In opgrunt fun tayve* (Warsaw: Goldfarb, 1929);

Karin Michaëlis, *Mete Trap: di moderne froy* (Warsaw: Goldfarb, 1929);

Stefan Zweig, *Roman Rolan* (Warsaw: Bikher, 1929);

Hamsun, *Viktorya* (Vilna: Kletskin, 1929);

Erich Maria Remarque, *Oyfn mayrev-front keyn nayes* (Vilna: Kletskin, 1930);

Thomas Mann, *Der tsoyberbarg,* 4 volumes (Vilna: Kletskin, 1930);

Remarque, *Der veg oyf tsurik* (Vilna: Kletskin, 1931);

Moshe Smilansky, *Araber: folkstimlekhe geshikhtn* (Warsaw: Yidishe bibliotek farn folk, 1932).

Isaac Bashevis Singer, the only Yiddish writer ever to be awarded the Nobel Prize in literature, was among the most popular and widely read authors of the twentieth century. By the time of his death at the age of eighty-seven, Singer had received a lion's share of the world's foremost literary prizes, including the Louis Lamed Prize (1950, 1956), the American Academy Grant (1959), the Epstein Fiction Award (1963), the Daroff Memorial Award (1963), the Foreign Book Prize (France, 1965), two National Endowment for the Arts grants (1966), the Bancarella Prize (Italy, 1967), two Newbery Honor Book Awards (1968, 1969), two National Book Awards (1970, 1974), the S. Y. Agnon Gold Medal (Israel, 1975), and the Nobel Prize in 1978. In addition, he had been awarded eighteen honorary doctorates and had been elected to both the American Academy and the American Institute of Arts and Letters, from which he had received the high honor of the Gold Medal.

Singer's extensive body of work is preoccupied with the destruction of the lost Orthodox Jewish world of Eastern Europe. For Singer, the faith that characterized this world was eroded for Jews by two forces: secular rationalism, coupled with the temptation to acculturate to Western norms; and the physical destruction of the Jews of Europe. The tension in Singer's fiction is always generated by the conflict between the old ways and the new, between faith and rationalism, between the sacred and the profane. His typical protagonist is a man like himself who abandons the regimen of strict, devout Orthodox Jewish observance in which he was raised and embraces the secular, modern world but is unable to find contentment there. The irreconcilable demands of the world of skeptical rationalism and the world of unquestioning faith generate the kind of anxiety and disillusionment that link Singer's fiction, in content if not in form, with the thematic preoccupations of modernism, the challenge to human existence in the twentieth century.

how the physical world operated, aggravated by the family's bitter poverty, led to parental conflicts that made a lasting impression on the young Isaac and later found encoded expression in much of his fiction.

Singer was the third of his parents' surviving four children. His two elder siblings were his sister, Hinde Esther, and his brother Israel Joshua, both of whom became respected Yiddish writers and who, in different ways, exercised enormous influence on him—his sister through her highly volatile temperament and radical mood changes, to which Isaac was exposed when he was only a boy, and his brother through the force of his personality and his subsequent professional success and prestige. The fourth and youngest child, a son named Moshe, became a rabbi and perished together with his mother in a Soviet work camp during World War II. Other influences of his childhood, which Singer felt throughout his life, came from his maternal grandfather, Yankev-Mordkhe Zylberman, and the rabbinical household he dominated. In 1914, at the outbreak of World War I, Isaac's mother sought safety for her children by returning to her birthplace, the Polish village of Bilgoray, where her father ruled his strictly observant community with an iron discipline, uncompromisingly setting his face against all manifestations of modernity. In Bilgoray, a town with a long-established scholarly reputation, young Isaac acquired an intimate knowledge of the minutest observances of Jewish Orthodoxy, of ancient Jewish folk customs and superstitions, and of a rich range of Yiddish idioms. As Singer often acknowledged, all this learning formed the raw material from which he shaped his fiction. In a 1963 interview (republished in *Isaac Bashevis Singer: Conversations,* 1992), for instance, he remarked of Bilgoray: "Not much had changed there in many generations. In this town the traditions of hundreds of years ago still lived. There was no railroad nearby. It was stuck in the forest and it was pretty much the same as it must have been during the time of Chmielnicki. . . . I could never have written *Satan in Goray* or some of my other stories without having been there."

Like all Orthodox Jewish boys of his time, Singer received his early education in traditional religious schools, where he studied the Bible and Talmud. The sheltered world of traditional Jewish learning was designed to insulate Jewish boys from the contaminations of the secular Gentile world, but it failed to do so for the adolescent Isaac in the aftermath of the upheavals wrought by World War I.

Since his parents expected him to enter the rabbinate, at the age of seventeen Singer enrolled in the Tachkemoni Rabbinical Seminary in Warsaw. However, he was unable to find his vocation there and remained a student for only one year, between 1921

Singer in Warsaw, circa 1922 (from Paul Kresh, Isaac Bashevis Singer: The Magician of West 86th Street, *1979)*

The son and grandson of rabbis on both sides of his family, Singer was born Icek-Hersz Zynger, the second son of strictly observant Orthodox Jewish parents, on 14 July 1904 in the village of Leoncin, a provincial town northeast of Warsaw in Poland, where his father, Pinkhos-Menakhem Zynger, was the resident rabbi. When Isaac was four years old, his father moved the family to Warsaw in search of a better livelihood. There Pinkhos-Menakhem Zynger became a rabbinical judge on poverty-stricken Krochmalna Street, where his meager earnings were wholly dependent upon donations given by those whose affairs he arbitrated. Singer's father was a learned and devout Hasid with a strong emotional bent that was sharply counterbalanced by the uncompromising rationalism of his wife. Singer's mother, Basheve (born Zylberman), was herself the daughter and granddaughter of distinguished rabbis, but they were *misnagdim,* unbending opponents of Hasidism and its ecstatic, mystical, and hierarchical traditions. Moreover, while Pinkhos-Menakhem Zynger was deeply learned only in traditional Jewish holy lore, Basheve Zynger had from an early age immersed herself not only in sacred learning but also, through the Hebrew newspapers she read, in contemporary politics and literature. Isaac's parents' opposed conceptions of

and 1922. The contrast between his brother's secular materialism and his father's spiritual unworldliness made a profound impression on the young Singer and provided the moral tension that informed most of his mature work. Having come early into contact with the great classics of Western literature in Yiddish translations, and lured by the artistic world of writers and journalists, Singer was nevertheless unable to gain entrée into the world of Warsaw Yiddish letters and turned for help to his brother, who had returned from revolutionary Russia disillusioned but with an established and growing reputation as a journalist. In the summer of 1923 Israel Singer introduced his brother to the Warsaw Yiddish Writers' Club situated at No. 13 Tlomackie Street, where Singer found a welcoming home and set about establishing a sense of direction for his life.

Like his brother, Singer was determined to be a writer, and he served a kind of literary apprenticeship by working as proofreader for the distinguished Warsaw Yiddish journal *Literarishe bleter* (Literary Pages) between 1923 and 1933. He augmented his paltry income by translating several mainstream European novels into Yiddish, mainly for the well-known Yiddish publisher Boris Kletskin. Among the distinguished works he rendered, working solely from German or Hebrew texts, between 1928 and 1932 were *Pan, Under høststæjrnen* (The Wanderers) and *Viktoria* by Knut Hamsun; *Il fuoco* (The Flame) by Gabriele D'Annunzio; *Im Westen nichts Neues* (All Quiet on the Western Front) and *Der Weg zurück* (The Way Back) by Erich Maria Remarque; and *Zauberberg* (The Magic Mountain) by Thomas Mann. The style, subject matter, and construction of these novels, all modern and innovative for their time, would certainly have provided useful lessons to a budding writer.

At the same time, Singer began work on his own writing in Yiddish, which appeared in Warsaw to some acclaim. In 1925 his first published work of fiction, a short story titled "Oyf der elter" (In Old Age), won a high-status prize offered by *Literarishe bleter*. This debut story was also the first to be signed Yitskhok Bashevis, the pseudonym by which Singer elected to be known to his Yiddish readers. His choice of this name expressed his determination to establish an independent identity, and a distinct persona, as a Yiddish writer. At the same time it signaled several other intentions. He was dissociating himself from the family name under which his brother had become famous and admired, partly in an attempt to cut himself free from the debts owed to the influence and generosity of his brother, with whom he felt an intense sibling rivalry. Moreover, the name he chose publicly declared his intellectual kinship with his rationalistic mother. In Yiddish usage, the name Bashe-

vis is the possessive form of the name Basheve, so Singer became, as a Yiddish writer, "the one belonging to Basheve." From this name he never departed in signing his fiction in Yiddish. The various ways he chose to sign different genres of his writing remained a matter of great importance to him all his creative life.

Between 1926 and 1935 Singer lived with, but never married, Rokhl (Ronye) Shapira, by whom he had one son, Israel Zamir, born in 1929. Singer did not neglect his literary work, however, and with his lifelong friend Arn Tseytlin became the joint founder and editor of a new Warsaw Yiddish literary journal titled *Globus,* which appeared between 1933 and 1935 and in which he serialized his first novel, *Der sotn in goray* (translated as *Satan in Goray,* 1955), in 1933.

By this time, although Singer seemed well on the way to literary success—Warsaw's eminent Yiddish Pen Club had published *Der sotn in goray* in book form—the complications of Singer's personal life had merged with the deepening crisis in world affairs to make Warsaw a frighteningly uncongenial place in which to live. Singer's family had irrevocably split up with the death of his father in 1929; the mother of his son was a fervent Communist, an ideology Singer detested; Adolf Hitler's rise to power in Germany had led to an intensification of Jew hatred in Poland; and Singer felt trapped in a dead end. Israel Singer had immigrated to the United States in 1934, where his reputation and ability had established him as a senior member of the staff of New York's leading Yiddish daily, *Forverts* (Forward). Singer turned once again to his brother for help, and through Israel Singer's influence, Singer was also able to immigrate to the United States in 1935. His son and Ronye Shapira made a difficult journey through Russia and Turkey to settle in what was then Mandate Palestine, while Singer began carving out a literary livelihood for himself in New York, working first as a proofreader and then as a columnist at *Forverts.* To this newspaper, Singer remained loyal for the rest of his life, and in it he published the greatest part of all his work in Yiddish. In 1940 Singer married Alma Wassermann (born Haimann), a German Jewish immigrant, and became a naturalized United States citizen in 1943.

Although Singer was aware all his life that, as a writer, he could work genuinely only in Yiddish, which he called "my mother language and the language of the people I wanted to write about," soon after his arrival in America he realized that he would have a limited future if his work were published only in Yiddish, a language with a steadily diminishing readership. Determined to follow the example of Sholem Asch, the first Yiddish writer to gain international recognition and a mass readership in English translation, Singer began

Singer's common-law wife, Ronye Shapira, and their son, Israel Zamir, during the 1930s
(Archives of the YIVO Institute for Jewish Research)

encouraging English translations of his work, through which he steadily achieved worldwide celebrity.

The first of Singer's translated novels to reach an English readership was *The Family Moskat* (1950), a chronicle of the changing fortunes of the wealthy Polish Jewish Moskat family across four generations. It had first been serialized in Yiddish as *Di familye moshkat* in *Forverts* between 17 November 1945 and 1 May 1948 and appeared in book form in Yiddish in 1950. In choosing to write an extended family chronicle, a form richly exploited by major European writers in the first half of the twentieth century, Singer was not so much following popular taste as writing under the influence of Israel Singer, two of whose major novels, *The Brothers Ashkenazi* (1936) and *The Family Carnovsky* (1943), had been cast in this saga form. Singer made his professional rivalry with his brother—and his guilt over it—explicit by dedicating the English translation of *The Family Moskat* to "the memory of my late brother I. J. Singer. . . . To me he was not only the older brother, but a spiritual father and master as well."

By the time Singer published *The Family Moskat,* his brother had been dead for six years. Since several of Israel Singer's novels had been translated and published in English by Knopf to generally favorable notices, Singer needed a pen name that would set him apart in the minds of his English readers. In his extensive body

of writing in Yiddish, he always strictly maintained a separate name and a discrete persona for the different genres of work he contributed to *Forverts*. He always signed what he regarded as his most accomplished artistic efforts with the name Yitskhok Bashevis. For work of a more popular kind, he used the pseudonyms Y. Varshavsky ("the man from Warsaw") for feuilletons; G. Kuper (the maiden name of his sister-in-law) for gossip and "agony-aunt" columns; and Y. Segal—among others—for subjects such as political and social commentary and the imparting of arcane information to curiosity-seeking readers. For his English readers, he now signed himself Isaac Bashevis Singer. By retaining the name Bashevis he subtly called attention to the fact that he was, and would remain, a writer who wrote primarily in Yiddish. By rendering his first name in its English form of Isaac, he signified his readiness to address a readership that knew little or nothing about Yiddish or its literature. And by reclaiming his family name, he felt able at last to signal both his kinship and his rivalry with his brother.

His first novel in English translation was a major achievement. The Moskat family's varied interrelationships, transmutations, and final dissolution come to represent the mutations undergone by the whole of Eastern European Jewry during the first forty years of the twentieth century. As Singer depicts them, the crises faced by individuals, and the sociopolitical and personal tensions that divide and destroy them, delineate complex shifts in the ways Jews are forced to redefine who and what they are in a rapidly changing world. Inevitably, the novel also questions whether the Jewish people can survive the genocide visited on them by the Nazis. Nathan Rothman, the earliest reviewer of the novel, immediately recognized the despondency implicit in this fictional reconstruction, noting in the 25 November 1950 *Saturday Review* that "those readers who can plow through the thick and moody substance of this novel will find themselves haunted by an after-image not easily blinked away."

The Family Moskat bleakly recognizes that, just as all worldly "progress" is powerless to prevent Nazism, so too are faith and piety defenseless against rampant evil. Though all European Jews, pious or "enlightened," are shown to face the same kind of death in the Holocaust, the novel attempts to assess the relative value of different ways of Jewish life. The worldly unbeliever Hertz Yanovar and the devoutly Orthodox Manasseh David may both perish in the same extermination camp, as the narrative relates, but the novel weighs the disparity in meaning that each of these characters can attach to his death. For the believer, confident in Divine determinism, the coming of Hitler means that "The Messiah is at our heels." For the secular Jew, bereft of faith, life is devoid of meaning. Since the novel speaks to a predominantly secular readership, the last sentence of the English version is the despairing cry of Hertz Yanovar, who shouts out above the sound of Nazi bombs destroying Warsaw: "Death is the only Messiah. That's the real truth."

In this novel Singer expresses for the first time his abiding conviction that Jewishness, being a transcendent as well as an earthly condition, endures its greatest threat to survival not in physical but in spiritual terms. The Jews of *The Family Moskat,* having lost a recognizably common identity, are shown to have a shared identity violently thrust upon them by the Nazis. Though they cannot share the same way of life, they are forced into a shared way of dying to which, the narrative of *The Family Moskat* makes clear, only a sense of individual moral responsibility can give meaning.

Though it sold moderately well, *The Family Moskat* did not become a best-seller. The work that brought Singer to the forefront of American literary critical attention was "Gimpel the Fool," sensitively translated by Saul Bellow and published in the *Partisan Review* in May 1953. This short story was the piece by which Singer became best known, and two years after its appearance it was hailed by the *Saturday Review* as "a classic of Yiddish literature" (14 December 1955). Its central character, the seemingly naive water carrier

Gimpel, is among the most vividly drawn of a long line of saintly innocents who appear throughout Yiddish literature. Through his subtly nuanced re-creation of the archetypal Jewish folk figure of the schlemiel or bumbling, unworldly incompetent, Singer poses profound questions about the nature of truth and lies, through which he points to the difference between this world and the world to come. As Gimpel remarks at the end of the story: "No doubt the world is entirely an imaginary world, but it is only once removed from the true world. . . . When the time comes I will go joyfully. Whatever may be there, it will be real, without complication, without ridicule, without deception. God be praised: there even Gimpel cannot be deceived." During the rest of the 1950s and until the end of his life, Singer found his short stories in great demand; they appeared prominently in such high-profile magazines as *Commentary, The New Yorker, Harper's,* and *Esquire.*

In 1955 *Satan in Goray* appeared in Jacob Sloan's much admired translation, becoming Singer's second novel to reach an English readership. A critic for *The New York Times Book Review* (13 November 1955) praised it as being "beautifully written by one of the masters of Yiddish prose, and beautifully translated . . . folk material transmuted into literature." Through a painstaking re-creation of seventeenth-century Jewish Poland in the aftermath of the savage anti-Jewish massacres in 1648 by the Cossacks under the leadership of Bogdan Chmielnicki, *Satan in Goray* scrutinizes the shattered faith of persecuted Jews who desperately seek to force the coming of that Messiah for whose redemption they have waited so long. Focusing with near-psychotic intensity on the hysteria provoked among the devastated Jewish communities of Poland by the claims of the false messiah, Sabbatai Zevi, this novel has been interpreted, notably by Seth L. Wolitz in a 1989 article, as a paradigm expressing Singer's uncompromising dismissal of the messianic expectations awakened by the Russian Revolution. Ruth R. Wisse asserted in *The Modern Jewish Canon* (2000) that the book "looms as one of the finest political novels in the Western canon." There is no question that, in its unsparing depiction of the spiritual self-evisceration of a desperate people, *Satan in Goray* makes a radically conservative statement of convictions Singer consistently held and restated throughout his work.

Gimpel the Fool and Other Stories, Singer's first book-length collection of short fiction, appeared in 1957 and was received with great admiration. One critic for *The New York Times Book Review* (29 December 1957) declared that with this volume, "Singer takes his place with the epic storytellers, transcending geographical and chronological boundaries." Among the tales that appeared for the first time and have been most often

The 1932 passport Singer used when he emigrated from Poland in 1935 (from Kresh,
Isaac Bashevis Singer: The Magician of West 86th Street, *1979)*

republished since are "The Little Shoemakers" and "Joy." Singer replayed the theme of *Satan in Goray* with "The Gentleman from Cracow" and introduced English readers to the demon-narrator, one of the hallmarks of many subsequent short stories, with "The Mirror" and "The Unseen."

Singer's growing popularity with English readers was clearly demonstrated by the speed with which his next novel was made available in English. Whereas twenty years had elapsed between the publication in Yiddish of *Der sotn in goray* in Warsaw in 1935 and its English version in 1955, *The Magician of Lublin* was serialized in Yiddish in *Forverts* in 1959 and published in English in 1960. The reviewer in the *New Statesman* (15 September 1961), acknowledging the meticulous care with which Singer had re-created nineteenth-century Poland in this novel, also called attention to the way in which "this realistic picture is, as it were, gently stretched outwards until it achieves a grotesque or menacing distortion." Grotesque elements became increasingly evident in Singer's ensuing work.

In *The Magician of Lublin* Singer moved from depicting a community shattered by sociopolitical turbulence to an individual in psychological turmoil. Humiliatingly confronted by the extent of his own limi-

tations, the central character, Yasha Mazur, a celebrated Jewish circus artist, is obliged to seek a way of surviving in a world that resists his arrogant attempts to dominate it. He tries to balance the conflicting demands of his personal life on a figurative tightrope that parallels the literal tightrope on which he performs his acclaimed acrobatic tricks. Yasha seeks to straddle the mutually exclusive worlds of Orthodox Jewish piety, embodied in his loyal Jewish wife, Esther, and Western secular culture, typified by his Polish Catholic mistress, Emilia. Steadily, Yasha discovers that every avenue of advancement into the secular Gentile world he longs to join is closed to him, so that at the end of the novel he returns to a rigorous observance of Jewish Orthodoxy. To enforce the discipline of his penitential return, he bricks himself up in a specially constructed cell.

Singer was adamant about this coercive manner of denying the material world in order to pursue the spiritual; he restated it several times more in his subsequent work. The first critic tentatively to question the validity of this drastic expedient was Irving Howe, in his review for *Commentary* (October 1960): "While there is no difficulty in making out what happens . . . there is a real question as to what it all signifies." Later critics have more boldly challenged Singer's seemingly simplistic solution to an enormous existential problem. They suggest that if a life of Orthodox Jewish observance can be lived only within the confines of a prison—whether a monastic cell or a hermetically sealed-off ultra-Orthodox community—then Orthodox Judaism is incapable of speaking to modern people. For Singer, however, there is no moral middle ground between wantonness and the discipline of religion, as Wisse points out: he "insisted, as his parents had done, on the ontological reality of good and evil, but he could not reconstruct the religious discipline that alone could uphold these distinctions. He did not think that what was morally necessary was possible." This binary opposition informed Singer's personal and artistic conflict all his life.

In 1961 Singer's second collection of short fiction, *The Spinoza of Market Street and Other Stories,* was published to a generally favorable reception. Irving Howe, writing in the *New Republic* (13 November 1961), was one of the few critics to voice reservations: "Singer seems almost perfect within his stringent limits, but it is perfection of stasis . . . he seems to be mired in his own originality." In the Fall 1962 *Jewish Heritage,* Milton Hindus disagreed: "What Howe calls Singer's 'narrow', 'stringent' limitations are precisely the source of his power. . . . Singer never loses sight of the fact that his forte is the imaginative transportation of reality." The title story poignantly dramatizes Singer's long-standing contempt for barren intellectualism and its impotence to validate human life. The chief character, the aged and infirm Dr. Nahum Fischelson, who has devoted his entire life to the study of Benedict de Spinoza, is granted a meaningful perspective on what it means to be human only when he marries the illiterate cleaning woman, Dobbe. He recognizes the true reality "of that infinite extension which is, according to Spinoza, one of God's attributes" for the first time in his life when he rises from his marriage bed: "In his long nightshirt he approached the window, walked up the steps and looked out in wonder. . . . Yes, the divine substance was extended and had neither beginning nor end; it was absolute, indivisible, eternal, without duration, infinite in its attributes . . . and he, Dr. Fischelson, with his unavoidable fate, was part of this."

The other stories in this collection reiterated some of the chief moral concerns expressed in Singer's novels and gave American readers more of the kind of demonism they had earlier enjoyed. "The Black Wedding" and "The Destruction of Kreshev," stories originally published in Yiddish years earlier, are small-scale reworkings of the material in *Satan in Goray,* while "Shiddah and Kuziba," set in the netherworld, presents a mother demon teaching her child that humans are the beings most greatly to be feared.

Critical acclaim was unanimous for the English translation of *The Slave,* which appeared in 1962. It had first been published in Yiddish as *Der knecht* in *Forverts* between 14 October 1960 and 18 March 1961; the English translation was from this serialization. A critic for *The Saturday Review* (16 June 1962) noted that "few writers since Shakespeare have been able to evoke so harrowingly the nightmare world of savage animals . . . and of man's kinship with them." Many of the earliest readers of the book regarded *The Slave* as Singer's most lyrical and perfectly constructed novel. Three years after its debut, the British poet Ted Hughes called it "a burningly radiant, intensely beautiful book," and Hughes implicitly disagreed with Howe about the supposed lack of development in Singer's work: "Looking over his novels in their chronological order, the first apparent thing is the enormous and one might say successful development of his vision" (*New York Review of Books,* 22 April 1965).

In *The Slave* Singer reverses the situation of Yasha Mazur, returning for this purpose to the historical period immediately following Chmielnicki's pogroms. Jacob, the pious Jew who is the slave of the title, is doubly in exile. He is a Polish Jew, driven with his people from Jerusalem and his homeland, and he is cut off, through enslavement to a Polish peasant, from his native village and the Jewish communal life central to his spiritual practice. By name and nature, Jacob is a paradigm of his biblical namesake, reenacting the age-old struggle of the Jewish people to retain their identity in a hostile environment. He too is a survivor, but unlike those who survive the massacres in *Satan in Goray,* he follows a strict regimen of prescribed religious observance. As constant as evil may be in the cycle of history, the novel suggests, so too is the power of individual freedom.

Jacob loves and is passionately loved in return by Wanda, the semipagan daughter of his master, and for love of Jacob, Wanda converts to Judaism and dies giving birth to Jacob's son. This child, the fruit of the union between a passionately believing Jew and a pious convert, introduces for the first time in Singer's work a theme to which he returns several times later—the suggestion that the decimated and demoralized Jews of Eastern Europe can hope to renew the vitality of their people only through the infusion of the new blood of devout converts. Singer invokes the biblical paradigm of Ruth the Moabitess, who follows her mother-in-law, Naomi, back to the land of Judah, where she embraces the faith of Israel, a decision so favored by God that Ruth is found worthy to become the great-grandmother of King David.

Trained in the exegesis of sacred texts, Singer found it natural to use biblical quotation, paradigm, and

Brothers Israel Joshua and Isaac Bashevis Singer in the United States, 1935
(Archives of the YIVO Institute for Jewish Research)

allegory to universalize the particular lives and events that are the subjects of his fiction. His descriptions of the physical world are developed as symbolic extensions of his themes. The order imposed on the events described, their selection, juxtaposition, and emphases, like those of biblical narratives, are all determined by the moral viewpoint of the teller of the tale. Moreover, the interviews Singer gave throughout a period of more than forty years reveal the extent to which he himself is present in much of his fiction. Often characters in his later novels and short stories speak words almost identical to those uttered by Singer on one or another public occasion. The cumulative effect of this blurring of reportage with fiction is to create fictionalized extensions of the author, through which he debates the ambiguities of modern Jewish identity.

By this time, appearing as they did in leading magazines, Singer's short stories were becoming widely known, and literary critics initiated a debate about whether Singer was better at writing short stories than novels. Interviewers who asked the author which of the two forms he preferred were given an answer that remained unchanged; as he said in a 1984 interview with Joseph Sherman: "I like both the novel and the short story. Of course, I would say it's more difficult to write a good short story than a good novel, because

your time, your space is so limited. . . . To make it short and still good is a great challenge. But actually, we cannot really interchange them."

Singer's next collection of short stories, published in 1964 under the title *Short Friday, and Other Stories,* was also dedicated to Israel Singer, "who helped me to come to this country and was my teacher and master in literature." Some critics greeted the volume patronizingly: a review in the *Nation* (4 January 1965), for instance, suggested that "For those who suffer nostalgia for what they've never known, Singer is a little genre painter offering heartwarming portraits." The reviewer for *The New York Times* (14 December 1964) suggested that "the peculiar quality" of Singer's work "is probably too special for most tastes." In *The New Leader* (21 December 1964), however, Stanley Edgar Hyman asserted that with this collection, "it becomes obvious that Singer is more than a writer; he is a literature." The volume was extremely varied in content and included several stories that were soon recognized as among Singer's best work, such as "Taibele and Her Demon" and "Yentl the Yeshiva Boy." The different kinds of sexual ambiguity presented in these two tales made them immensely intriguing, and both were later adapted for the stage. "The Last Demon" is among Singer's most powerful evocations of the Holocaust. With an excoriating wit, its narrator sets the chilling tone in his opening remark: "I, a demon, bear witness that there are no more demons left. Why demons, when man himself is a demon?"

The moral universe Singer evokes in this collection is once again starkly divided between piety and wickedness. The simplicity of Shmuel-Leibele and his wife, Shoshe—the devout, accidentally suffocated couple in the title story, "Short Friday"—is set in jarring contrast to the headlong moral descent of the lustful Risha in "Blood." Her insatiable desire to witness the shedding of animal blood in the slaughterhouse leads inevitably to the indulgence of her voracious sexual appetite, her conversion to Christianity, and her eventual transmogrification into a werewolf, a physical manifestation of her total dehumanization. Similarly, in "Zeidlus the Pope" the genius Zeidel, a desiccated, small-town scholar hungry for worldly glory, converts to Christianity in hopes of becoming pope but is instead reduced to blindness and destitution before being dragged off to the netherworld by gloating demons. Noteworthy in stories such as these is the extent to which Singer, even in English translation, makes an uncompromising equation between Christianity and the temptations of the world, the flesh and the devil. For those of his characters who abandon the rigors of Orthodox Jewish observance, there is absolutely no worldly reward; there is merely the shattering of grandiose illusions.

For the first time, in this seminal collection Singer also published two stories set wholly in the United States: "Alone" and "A Wedding in Brownsville." In both, supernatural phenomena are placed in a modern setting. The stories in this collection define the range of Singer's themes in the work that followed.

The second half of the 1960s was a productive period in Singer's creative life and brought him praise and remuneration. *The Family Moskat* was republished in 1965 and was even more warmly received. In 1966, in response to the urging of editor Elizabeth Shub, Singer produced *Zlateh the Goat and Other Stories,* the first of his many books for children. Wittily illustrated by Maurice Sendak, this book was well received and won Singer his first Newbery Honor Book Award. Based in part on old Jewish folktales, these stories, recast for young readers, enabled Singer to be openly didactic; he offered unambiguous wish-fulfillment tales in which the good are rewarded and the wicked punished. In "I See the Child as a Last Refuge," a piece written for *The New York Times Book Review* (9 November 1969), Singer praised the world of children, noting that "their literature is still preoccupied with kings, princesses, devils, demons, imps, werewolves and other old-fashioned creatures." His work for children also allowed him to express, for the first time in English, a poignant, personal nostalgia

for his own childhood and the Poland in which it had been spent.

In 1966 Howe edited and introduced his own selection of Singer's short stories, and in the same year, Singer published an English version of his first collection of semi-autobiographical memoirs, titled *In My Father's Court.* This book, which had originally appeared in Yiddish in 1956 as *Mayn tatns bes-din shtub,* became one of the most popular of all Singer's writings. Through his vignettes of the way his father carried out his duties as a Jewish rabbinical judge, Singer presents an elegiac portrait of a vanished world of Orthodox religious observance. Some critics later came to feel that these sketches were romanticized. Following the lead given by the distinguished Yiddish poet Jacob Glatstein, they rebuked the book for feeding into sentimental mythmaking about destroyed Eastern European Jewish life. In his review of the Yiddish serialization of *In My Father's Court* the year before it was published in English, Glatstein, always one of Singer's harshest critics, asserted in *Congress Bi-Weekly* (27 December 1965) that "Rarely has a writer committed to publication such trivial, commonplace and egocentric effusions." Jules Chametzky, however, disagreed in the *Nation* (17 October 1966), emphasizing that "The last word in the book is 'love', and it is with love, dignity and restraint that Singer walks his difficult tightrope and achieves the miracle of art." The leading American literary critics concurred with this judgment. The overall impact of this memoir on the English-reading public remained profound in its assertion of the potential for virtuous human conduct held out by the precepts of religion to those capable of faith.

The following year, in 1967, Singer published *The Manor,* the first of two volumes of the English version of another saga novel that traces the history of Polish Jewry from the failed Polish rebellion of 1863 to the outbreak of World War I. The second and concluding volume, *The Estate,* appeared two years later, in 1969. The one-volume Yiddish version, titled *Der hoyf,* had been serialized in *Forverts* between 1952 and 1955 but not published in book form. *The Manor* and *The Estate* complete the historical sweep of those decisive events through which Singer, at this period of his artistic life, explored the crisis of modern Jewish survival. With a huge cast of characters and a mass of precise detail, this epic novel examines the radical mutations within the family of Calman Jacoby, a wealthy and pious Polish Jew who lives to witness the destruction of everything he has believed in.

Throughout the novel, Singer shows that all human endeavor yields painful ambivalences. While modern technological progress condemns to scientific ignorance those Jews immersed exclusively in their

Singer and Elizabeth Shub, with whom he began collaborating on children's books in the 1960s (from Kresh, Isaac Bashevis Singer: The Magician of West 86th Street, *1979)*

ancient holy writings, its insistence on moral relativism raises with equal force the question of what Jews can possibly be without their ancient law and liturgy. By drawing a rigid distinction between spiritual and material life, the narrative suggests that what is arrogantly called "progress" can also be viewed as moral regression. Chametzky, writing in the *Nation* (30 October 1967), pointed out that Singer was offering a vision "of the contemporary void . . . and a bodying forth of the knowledge that its negotiation requires the most delicate, and perilous, balance between worlds lost and found, known and unknown." *The Manor* was nominated for the National Book Award.

In 1968 the appearance of Singer's fourth collection of short fiction in English translation, *The Séance and Other Stories,* was greeted with mixed reviews, and for the first time Singer's work was accused of losing its thematic substance and becoming shallow, anecdotal, and repetitive. One critic for *The New York Times Book Review* (20 October 1968) suggested that in this newest collection, "too often" Singer's stories are "merely interested in describing a kind of fiddler-on-the-roof Poland." Dedicated to the "memory of my beloved sister Hinde Esther," this collection did break some new ground for Singer and offered some reworkings of old themes. The title story dramatizes, with wit and irony,

Singer's abiding interest in spiritualism. "The Lecture" transforms a personal experience into a frightening tale of death and dissolution; "The Needle" introduces English readers to the monologue tale narrated by Aunt Yentl, a superstitious village gossip; and "Zeitel and Rickel," depicting the doomed love between two lesbians, develops Singer's exploration–begun with "Yentl the Yeshiva Boy"–of alternative sexualities.

By the 1970s, the decade in which he was most prolific in publishing the English translations of his work, Singer had reached the pinnacle of his fame and success. He won a 1970 National Book Award with the publication of *A Day of Pleasure* (1969), a collection of nineteen memoiristic sketches depicting the first fourteen years of his life. Fourteen of these stories had previously appeared in slightly different versions in *In My Father's Court,* while five were published in English for the first time. The volume was illustrated with intensely evocative photographs of pre–World War II Poland taken by Roman Vishniac, augmented by photographs from Singer's personal album.

Later in 1970, Singer published his fifth collection, *A Friend of Kafka and Other Stories,* and while one review in *The New York Times* (20 September 1970) suggested that too much Singer in one volume could lead to "the possible dilution of magic performed in quantity," *Time* magazine (21 September 1970) hailed these stories as "miraculous creations . . . in the highest artistic tradition." Monologue stories told by unreliable narrators are prominent in this collection: Aunt Yentl reappears to relate the events in "The Blasphemer," while a trio that resurfaces in later work–Zalman the glazier, Levi Yitskhok in his blue-tinted spectacles, and Meier the eunuch–make their debut in English in "Stories from Behind the Stove." The operation of supernatural forces, even in the streets of contemporary Manhattan, is demonstrated in "The Key" and "Powers," and the Warsaw Writers' Club is satirically recalled in the title story and in "Dr. Beeber." One powerful tale, "The Cafeteria," evokes the horror of the Holocaust through the experiences of a survivor in modern New York, and in "The Son" Singer relates a fictionalized version of his meeting with his son after an estrangement of twenty years. "The Mentor," the first of Singer's stories to be set in the State of Israel, permitted him to express some ambivalent, personal views about its significance to Jews of his generation and background.

In 1970 Singer also published two long tales for children: *Joseph and Koza; or, The Sacrifice to the Vistula,* and *Elijah the Slave: A Hebrew Legend Retold.* More children's stories followed in book form: *Alone in the Wild Forest* and *The Topsy-Turvy Emperor of China* in 1971; *The Wicked City* in 1972; *The Fools of Chelm and Their History* in 1973; *Why Noah Chose the Dove* in 1974; *A Tale of Three*

Wishes in 1975; and *Naftali the Storyteller and His Horse, Sus, and Other Stories* in 1976. All these stories, retellings of well-known Jewish folktales, were published in beautifully designed large-print books; they reached a wide readership and were much praised. For adult readers, Singer wrote the text for a special limited-edition volume in 1973 titled *The Hasidim.* Lavishly illustrated by Ira Moskowitz, this book offers a vibrant and respectful celebration of Hasidism, stressing the spiritual significance of the faith-through-joy movement.

Singer's mature work appeared steadily during the 1970s. In 1972 came the English version of *Enemies, A Love Story,* the first of his novels to focus entirely on survivors, to deal directly with the physical, psychological, and spiritual devastation wrought on them by the Holocaust, and to be set in the United States. The original Yiddish version, titled *Sonim: di geshikhte fun a libe,* had been serialized in *Forverts* between 11 February and 13 August 1966 but not published in book form. A reviewer for *The New York Times* (25 June 1972) characterized it as "bleak" and "obsessive," while a critic for the *New York Review of Books* (20 July 1972), noting its grotesquely comic elements, nevertheless maintained that Singer "elevates this farce situation into tragicomedy."

All the survivors in this novel are depicted as simultaneously alive and dead: because they cannot forget their destroyed European past, they are alienated from their re-created present. They feel this disjunction most keenly in the loss of their mother tongue, and in this novel, as elsewhere in his work, Singer exploits the symbolic correspondence between the destruction of the Yiddish world and the Yiddish word, a culturally annihilating perception he also expressed in an important essay, "Problems of Yiddish Prose in America," first published in Yiddish in 1943.

Several critics have noted that, despite its grim comedy, what gives *Enemies, A Love Story* its strength is the fact that its chief character, a dislocated moral coward and cheat named Herman Broder, is not the sole, nor even the dominant, voice in the novel. He is classed among "those without courage to make an end to their existence," hopeless people who "have only one other way out: to deaden their consciousness, choke their memory, extinguish the last vestige of hope." By contrast, Herman's first wife, Tamara, a survivor of a death camp, has grown through suffering to a recognition that life makes demands on the living, an acknowledgment that makes her insist on distinguishing between self-indulgence in a godless universe—the escape route seized by Herman—and the duty to exercise the power of positive choice.

The publication in 1973 of his collection of short stories *A Crown of Feathers* won for Singer his second National Book Award (given in 1974), and high praise

from a critic for *The New York Review of Books* (7 February 1974), who remarked on the writer's ability to depict, in "a remarkable range of styles and tones," the "moral and cultural space" that divides people. In his speech accepting this award, Singer made a point of stressing that "Only in such a lavish and giving country as the United States is it possible for a writer who writes in a foreign language to get a national award. No man who lives here remains a stranger." For the most part, the collection offers few surprises either in form or in content. Only in "The Captive," a bizarre tale of how a living writer's identity is subsumed by the posthumous life of a dead painter, does Singer develop further his own response to some of the demands on Jewish life made by the State of Israel. In the majority of the other tales in this collection, Singer restates some of his favorite themes, such as the way mysterious otherworldly forces operate in the lives of contemporary people (in "The Briefcase," a tale drawn from the writer's personal experiences on the American lecture circuit) and the way the living can be possessed by the spirits of the dead (in "A Dance and a Hop").

The story "The Beard" from this collection formed the basis of a short documentary/fantasy movie about Singer's working life made in 1972 and titled *Singer's Nightmare and Mrs. Pupko's Beard.* Directed by Bruce Davidson, with the aid of a grant from the American Film Institute, the movie was aired on public television and won a prize at the 1972 American Film Festival. By the mid 1970s other Singer works were adapted for the stage, television, and the cinema. On 23 October 1975 a stage version of "Yentl the Yeshiva Boy," written in collaboration with Leah Napolin, opened on Broadway at the Eugene O'Neill Theater. Despite praise for the leading actress, Tovah Feldshuh, the play was poorly received. Indifferent, and sometimes hostile, reception of his stage adaptations had started as early as 1963, when "Gimpel the Fool" premiered as a one-act play at the Mermaid Theater in New York. The Yale Repertory Theater adaptation of "The Mirror" ten years later in 1973 was equally poorly regarded, and condemnation climaxed in the reviews that greeted the 16 December 1979 opening, at the Brooks Atkinson Theater, of the stage version of "Teibele and Her Demon" that Singer wrote with Eve Friedman. The common objection in the consistently negative reviews of all of these adaptations was that the ambiguities and subtleties of Singer's prose fiction were wholly incapable of being transmitted through the medium of the theater.

Singer's seventh collection of short stories in English, *Passions and Other Stories* (1975), renewed critical objection to what was now perceived as Singer's repetitiveness and also to his absorption with the events of his

Singer autographing copies of Shosha *(1978) in Miami
(photograph © The Miami Herald/Battle Vaughan)*

own life. A reviewer for *The Village Voice* (2 February 1976), for example, maintained that *Passions and Other Stories* "is a recapitulation of all that precedes it" and that Singer's stories "are a long biography of himself, the good, famous Yiddish writer." In his "Author's Note" to this collection, Singer explicitly stressed that his work was a memorial to the destroyed world of Eastern Europe, specifically to "the Yiddish-speaking Jews who perished in Poland and those who emigrated to the U.S.A." The story that most clearly fulfills this aim is "Sam Palka and David Vishkover," in which a Jewish immigrant, grown rich and successful in America, nevertheless longs greatly for the impoverished life of the old *shtetl,* the small market town in Poland in which he grew up. He is even prepared to assume another identity in order to relive some of his past with Channah Basha, a newcomer who rents one of his seedy apartments in Brownsville, where she lovingly maintains all the values, customs, and behavior patterns of old-world Jews. Seven of the twenty stories in this collection are fictional reworkings of autobiographical materials, covering

events in Singer's life both before he left Poland and after he became famous in America. Monologue pieces set in pre-Holocaust Poland are also prominent: the character of Aunt Yentl reappears as the narrator of "The Gravedigger" and "The Sorcerer," while the entertaining trio of Zalman, Levi Yitskhok, and Meier all contribute to the telling of "Errors." More than any other, this collection unambiguously articulates Singer's determination to commemorate the lost past.

The appearance in 1976 of a memoir titled *A Little Boy in Search of God; or, Mysticism in a Personal Light* seemed to some critics to prove Singer's intensifying solipsism. Even the format of this book caused puzzlement, particularly about its genre. It appeared under the imprint of Doubleday, rather than of Singer's long-standing publisher Farrar, Straus and Giroux, in an expensive, large, hardcover edition profusely illustrated with drawings and watercolors by Moskowitz. Unlike the photographs that provide verisimilitude in *A Day of Pleasure,* Moskowitz's drawings seem deliberately designed to fictionalize. Nevertheless, this volume of recollections started making available to the English reader that painful wrestling with faith and doubt that Singer's Yiddish readers had been encountering in the pages of *Forverts* in several lengthy, serialized memoirs that ran, under different series titles, between November 1974 and December 1978. Joseph C. Landis, in his 1986 study, notes that these memoirs are the voice of "I. B. Singer, the writer of seventy, recalling once again his quarrel with God in yet another autobiographical reprise, retracing the origins of his doubt and trying once again to justify his stance."

Singer reworked the same autobiographical materials for his next novel, *Shosha,* the English version of which appeared in 1978, the year he was awarded the Nobel Prize in literature. *Shosha* met with an openly hostile reception from Leon Wieseltier, who dismissed it as "a stunted novel about stunted lives" and disparaged Singer's use of the supernatural as a pandering to "that facile infatuation with the demonic that currently prevails in American culture" (*New York Review of Books,* 7 December 1978).

Set in the years immediately preceding Hitler's invasion of Poland, *Shosha* suggests that the sterile thoughts and impotent doings that preoccupy the characters of prewar Warsaw is the spiritual dead end into which worldly secularization has led. The fatalism with which these Jews await extirpation at Nazi hands is presented as a collective death-wish as much as a passive acceptance of political events outside their personal control. The narrative technique of *Shosha* calls attention to itself by employing several devices that echo the effect of a *yizker-bukh,* a Holocaust memorial volume. These were books published by survivors of Hitler's genocide and intended to memorialize and mourn the various towns and villages of Eastern Europe in which the authors had grown up; they are characterized by the kind of minute descriptive detail in which the narrative voice in *Shosha* delineates the topography of Jewish Warsaw:

> After breakfast I went to Shosha's [on Krochmalna Street] and stayed there for lunch. Then I left for my room on Leszno Street. Although it would have been quicker to go down Iron Street, I walked on Gnoyna, Zimna, and Orla. On Iron Street you were vulnerable to a blow from a Polish Fascist. I had laid out my own ghetto.

The last sentence of this passage is calculated to shock the reader with post facto recognition, because this route, like all the others detailed in the novel, can be traced on any map of the Nazi-created Warsaw Ghetto. By the time *Neshome-ekspeditsyes* (Soul-Expeditions), the serialized Yiddish version of *Shosha*, appeared in *Forverts* in 1974, Singer had been living in the United States for forty years, more than a decade longer than he ever lived in Warsaw; yet, his topographical itemization is painfully accurate. Like Singer, the narrator of *Shosha* was able to escape this horrifying cul-de-sac, but his luck, by comparison with the millions who were unable to flee, obviously remained deeply rooted in his psyche. Hence, Aaron Greidinger, Singer's fictional alter ego—making the first of many appearances as the narrator of Singer's later novels—attempts to memorize every one of Warsaw's sights and sounds in the hope that by recording them in writing he will miraculously be able to bring the destroyed world of Jewish Warsaw back to life.

Undeterred by criticism, in 1978 Singer also published *A Young Man in Search of Love,* a book he admitted in his "Author's Note" was "a continuation of *A Little Boy in Search of God.* . . . Together, these two volumes constitute a kind of spiritual autobiography which I hope to continue in the years to come." Although this book was also illustrated, this time with drawings and paintings by Raphael Soyer, Singer's open acknowledgment of his self-focus drove critics into tracking the autobiographical elements that were becoming more marked in all his new work in English. Meanwhile, Singer remained tireless in expressing his scorn for literary critics. On 11 December 1978, under the title "Why I Write for Children," *The New York Times* published as an essay remarks that had formed part of Singer's address at the banquet in Stockholm following the Nobel Prize award ceremony the night before. With tongue firmly in cheek, Singer gave a list of reasons for writing for children, each of which struck at literary concerns of the academic establishment: "Children read books, not reviews. . . . They don't read to free themselves of guilt. . . . They have no use for psychol-

ogy. . . . They detest sociology. . . . They don't expect their beloved writer to redeem humanity."

In 1979, following the publication of his Nobel Lecture in a small book including both its Yiddish and its English texts, came his eighth collection of short stories, *Old Love*. Reviewing this collection for *The New York Times* (28 October 1979), Robert Alter remarked on the contemporary value of tales of innocence "in the middle of our terrible century" and summarized the critical consensus about Singer's work at the end of the decade, concluding that Singer was "a great writer with a decidedly uneven production, who does not work equally well in all the fictional genres he has tried." Richard Burgin, writing for the *Chicago Review* (Spring 1980), examined Singer's literary quarrel with modernism, pointing out that "Singer is a writer, in an age of cultivated ambiguity, who wants us to perceive the epiphanies, doubts, and ambivalence of his characters." Burgin confessed himself "somewhat baffled by those critics who relentlessly stress Singer's devotion to traditional literary and 'moral' values while ignoring the meanings that are apparent behind the surface simplicity."

Old Love is marked less by a depiction of love as a redemptive emotion than by what Burgin identified as "the darker side of sexuality." The story "Two" explores an explicitly homosexual relationship; "Not for the Sabbath" looks at sadomasochism through the prurient eyes of Aunt Yentl; and "The Bus" combines both homosexuality and sadomasochism with a hint of incest. All three stories expose violent emotions in a way strikingly at variance with Singer's assertion in his "Author's Note" that "in love, as in other matters, the young are just beginners and . . . the art of loving matures with age and experience." Several of the tales in this volume suggest that not only curiosity about different kinds of sexuality but also active participation in them is, for Singer, part of "the love of the old and the middle-aged."

Singer opened the 1980s with the publication in English of two more stories for children: *Reaches of Heaven: A Story of the Baal Shem Tov*, once again illustrated by Moskowitz, and *The Power of Light: Eight Stories for Hanukkah*. The success of these children's books demonstrated Singer's ability to appeal to a broad spectrum of readers and validated his much-repeated insistence that "the oldest purpose of art has been to entertain. A good writer entertains a good reader."

He followed these books in 1981 with his third volume of memoirs, *Lost in America,* illustrated by Soyer. In his "Author's Note" to this volume, Singer reiterated his autobiographical purpose, though he still insisted that, since he had been obliged for personal reasons to disguise the identities of many of the people he described, he was writing "no more than fiction set

*Singer and his wife, Alma (Archives of the YIVO
Institute for Jewish Research)*

reside seems a long way either from modern America or from modern Israel."

The publication in 1982 of another children's story, *The Golem,* illustrated by Uri Shulevitz, was followed in 1983 by the publication in English translation of what became Singer's most controversial novel, *The Penitent.* Where Thomas Sutcliffe in *TLS: The Times Literary Supplement* (23 March 1984) declared it "an honest and compassionate book," Harold Bloom roundly condemned it in *The New York Times Book Review* (25 September 1983) as "a very unpleasant work, without any redeeming esthetic merit or human quality." Most unusually for Singer, he had published *Der bal-tshuve,* the Yiddish text of this novel, in Israel nine years earlier, and had even gone so far as to claim, in a public lecture in Jerusalem in May 1973, that it was "the book of his which he likes best." *The Penitent* is arguably not a novel; it belongs instead to that group of Singer's monologues that present a varied gallery of contemporary Jews who tell their idiosyncratic personal stories to a visiting Yiddish writer who bears a calculated resemblance to Singer.

The chief narrative voice in *The Penitent* belongs to Joseph Shapiro, a rich profligate who is sickened by the materialism, promiscuity, and violence of the modern world and returns to Israel to embrace a rigidly observant Jewish life. He immures himself in Me'ah She'arim, the ultra-Orthodox quarter of Jerusalem, in an attempt to cut himself off from all contaminating contact with contemporary evils that have even infected the Holy Land in its reincarnation as the secular State of Israel. What particularly disturbed many readers was the fact that Shapiro expresses his stridently antimodern opinions in words identical to those Singer had used in various published interviews. However, since the extended "Author's Note" at the end of the book is made to form an integral part of the narrative, it sets up a dialectic in which the author appears to be arguing with another version of himself about his deepest concerns. The ending of the novel disturbingly re-creates the same ambivalence as the Magician of Lublin's determination to immure himself in a cell: can the traditional values of Jewish Orthodoxy only be regained in an isolation ward?

By 1982 Singer was prepared to make a selection of what he regarded as his best stories for a volume titled *The Collected Stories.* It includes forty-seven of the more than one hundred tales he had published thus far and gives the reader approaching Singer's work for the first time a comprehensive view of his dominating thematic concerns and artistic techniques. Among others previously published, the volume included "Gimpel the Fool," "The Little Shoemakers," "The Last Demon," and "The Letter Writer," as well as hitherto uncollected

against a background of truth." The line between fiction and autobiography was now so blurred in what Singer chose to publish in English that it was virtually impossible to separate the two. In 1984, his eightieth year, Singer ensured that his three separate volumes of explicit autobiography were published in one book, under the title *Love and Exile.* Writing in the *London Review of Books* a few years later (24 October 1991), John Bayley was among many critics who fully appreciated the extent to which, in his autobiographical work as much as in fiction, Singer had succeeded in his self-imposed task of evoking for perpetuity the lost Jewish world of the Poland he had known in his youth: "In one sense, certainly, the language and the life he wrote of may still be alive, in New York and other places: but the kind of Jewishness—incarnate in speech and spirit, in herring and onion roll—where Singer's characters

pieces, including "Neighbor" and "Moon and Madness." In his introductory "Author's Note" Singer restated his favorite dicta about the danger of "experimental" writing and his firm belief in the need for the writer to be primarily a storyteller. He also gave a broad definition of what he understood by the concept "literature": "Genuine literature informs while it entertains. It manages to be both clear and profound. It has the magical power of merging causality with purpose, doubt with faith, the passions of the flesh with the yearnings of the soul. . . . While it tolerates commentary by others, it should never try to explain itself." Most critics concurred that this volume includes everything that is most representative of those literary gifts that had won Singer the Nobel Prize. Further honors followed: in 1984 he became the sixteenth member of the Jewish-American Hall of Fame, and in 1986 he was the recipient of the Handel Medallion, New York City's highest award.

The Image and Other Stories, which appeared in 1985, was equally well received. A writer for *The New York Times Book Review* (30 June 1985) asserted that this collection "splendidly confirms [Singer's] achievement," and a *TLS* critic valued Singer's frequently deployed narrative technique of setting up a listener-narrator of other people's stories as a useful distancing device, "particularly in the more disturbing or violent stories" (4 April 1986). In the "Author's Note" that had now become one of his trademarks, Singer made two contradictory assertions. He insisted that a writer "should never abandon his mother tongue and its treasure of idioms," but he also admitted that "The English translation is especially important to me because translations into other languages are based on the English text. In a way, this is right because, in the process of translation, I make many corrections." The vexed relationship between the Yiddish originals and the English translations of Singer's work later became an area of considerable literary debate.

Singer's engagement, direct or indirect, with stage and motion-picture adaptations of his work was most evident in this period. The movie rights to *The Magician of Lublin,* which Singer had sold in 1965, were realized with the release of the movie version, directed by Menahem Golan and written by Golan and Irving S. White, in 1979. This cinematic treatment was widely condemned. The *Village Voice* (19 November 1979) supplied what became the critical consensus: "Squandering some convincing location work, Golan reduces Singer to a Harold Robbins entertainment of florid compositions and bombastic copulations." Four years later, Barbra Streisand's screen adaptation of *Yentl,* written by Streisand and Jack Rosenthal, opened on 18 November 1983. This time, although the movie was widely praised in the media, its

harshest critic was Singer. On 29 January 1984, *The New York Times* published "I. B. Singer Talks to I. B. Singer About the Movie 'Yentl'," in which Singer blisteringly attacked Streisand's treatment of every aspect of his now-famous story. The controversy did no harm to the box-office takings, but it did highlight the extent to which the essence of Singer's work resisted the performing arts. Also appearing in 1984 was a more successful adaptation by Ernest Kinoy of Singer's short story "The Cafeteria," directed by Amram Nowak. This television movie was enthusiastically received and widely praised for its fidelity to the original.

In 1988 Singer published the English version of *The King of Fields,* a novel unlike any he had written before, and one that disappointed most reviewers; a widely shared opinion expressed in the *Kirkus Review* (15 August 1988) was that it was "a bad-imitation *Clan of the Cave Bear* [Jean Auel's 1980 novel]." The Yiddish text, *Der kenig fun di felder,* had been serialized in *Forverts* between 14 February and 26 December 1980. Thematically, this novel was a bizarre departure for Singer. Drawn from old Polish folklore and myth, set in the pagan world of pre-Christian Poland, and focusing on primitives groping toward some concept of ethics, this pessimistic tale questions whether murderous human nature can ever be tamed. The ethical tenets of Judaism exercise no permanent humanizing influence, for Ben Dosa, the sole Jewish character in the novel, makes only a fleeting impression on the feral people he encounters. The Lesniks, the tribe to which the protagonist Cybula belongs, suffer many hardships: they are enslaved by people calling themselves Poles, and, though briefly comforted by Ben Dosa's teachings, they are thrown into violent confusion by the inflammatory missionary sermons preached by his theological rival, a young Christian bishop. The conflict bred by subjugation and rival doctrine leaves the undeveloped people who suffer its consequences bitterly disillusioned, and the conclusion of the narrative seems once again to affirm the nihilistic conviction that death is a welcome release.

In 1988, to only lukewarm interest, Singer also published *The Death of Methuselah and Other Stories,* the tenth and last collection of his short fiction. Familiarity with his themes over three decades had sharpened critical awareness of the author's quirks, and Jay Cantor, in the *Los Angeles Times Book Review* (1 May 1988), expressed further concern at Singer's increasingly evident misogyny: "Disorder is too often, and too sourly, identified with the failings of his women characters . . . this obsession seems crabbed." Alternative sexuality is once again the theme of several stories in this collection; "Disguised," for example, indicates again Singer's interest in male homosexuality. In his "Author's Note" Singer cites traditional Jewish holy sources to justify his

Singer with his son, Israel Zamir, before the ceremony at which Singer was awarded the Nobel Prize in literature, December 1978 (from Israel Zamir, Journey to My Father, Isaac Bashevis Singer, *1995)*

fascination with human sexuality: "According to the Talmud and the Midrash, the corruption [of human beings] was all sexual. Even the animals later became sexually perverted at the time of the flood, and perhaps later in Sodom and Gomorrah." This collection is interesting also because it includes a much-watered-down English version of "The Jew from Babylon," a story Singer had first published in Yiddish as "Der yid fun bovl" more than fifty years earlier. How far this story had been reworked and, in the opinion of some critics, eviscerated for an English readership, provoked serious scholarly exploration, notably by Wolitz, of the ways in which Singer fundamentally altered the artistic principles and practice he gave his Yiddish readers as Yitskhok Bashevis.

In 1989 the American Academy of Arts and Letters recognized Singer's lifetime achievement by awarding him its highest honor, a Gold Medal, and a year later he was elected a member of the academy, the first American author who did not write exclusively in English to be so honored. Director Paul Mazursky's 1989 movie adaptation of *Enemies, A Love Story,* with screenplay by Mazursky and Roger L. Simon, opened to widely favorable reviews and became the first of Singer's works adapted for the big screen to please the critics: the movie received two Academy Award nomi-

nations, for best actress and best screenplay. By this time, however, Singer was seriously ill with Alzheimer's disease, and it is unlikely that he played any active role in the translation and publication of *Scum,* the last of his novels published in his lifetime, which appeared in 1991. The Yiddish version of this novel, titled *Shoym* (Foam), had been serialized in *Forverts* between 2 June and 16 September 1967 but not published in book form.

Scum focuses on the world-weariness of a rich, assimilated Jewish roué who returns to Poland in search of some connection to a lost past. Muted reviews greeted the publication of this novel. A reviewer for the *Los Angeles Times* (14 April 1991) found it "not quite as surprising or sharp-edged as some of Singer's more recent books," while Bayley, in the *London Review of Books* (24 October 1991), thought he identified in the novel Singer's "powerlessness to be an original artist and a man outside his race."

From the late 1980s, Singer had been showing increasing signs of mental failure. He died on 24 July 1991, but instead of being buried in Israel, in ground set aside for Jewish artists, he was buried in the Beth-El (Jewish) section of the Cedar Park Cemetery, Emerson, New Jersey. Clive Sinclair, in *TLS* (4 October 1991), reminded readers of how closely Singer had been involved in preparing the English versions of his novels. Noting that in *Scum* "there are uncharacteristically crude devices," Sinclair went on: "There is much of Singer's work that remains untranslated. Presumably, that will change now that he is dead. It is important to know when these 'new' novels were conceived, and whether their author considered that publication in book form would enhance his reputation."

Sinclair's presumption was well founded. Translations of two of Singer's earlier novels in Yiddish appeared in rapid succession after his death: *The Certificate* in 1992 and *Meshugah* in 1994. *The Certificate* (serialized as *Der sertifikat* in *Forverts* between 13 January and 27 May 1967) reworks the all-too-familiar materials of Singer's autobiography, while *Meshugah* (serialized as *Farloyrene neshomes* [Lost Souls] in *Forverts* between 9 April 1981 and 11 February 1982) records another episode in the post-Holocaust life of Singer's long-established literary double, Aaron Greidinger. Their reception was respectful rather than enthusiastic, calling attention to Singer's "deceptively spare prose" and his gift for "transforming reality into art with seemingly effortless sleight of hand" (*New York Times Book Review*, 24 November 1992). On the other hand, *Shadows on the Hudson* appeared four years later in 1998 to extraordinary acclaim. One critic for *The New York Times Book Review* (31 December 1997) hailed it as "a piercing work of fiction . . . with a strong claim to being Singer's masterpiece." The Yiddish version of this novel, *Shotns baym Hodson*, had been serialized in *Forverts* between January 1957 and January 1958.

Shadows on the Hudson bleakly examines, through a punctilious reconstruction of the period between December 1947 and mid November 1948, the lives of some Jewish refugees from Hitler fortunate enough to gain new life in America. Their adoptive country, they discover, demands of those who want its freedoms total subordination of their own values to the hegemony of American economic, social, and cultural norms. In consequence, these survivors are emotionally and spiritually dislocated, a condition symbolized by their self-perception as stunted outsiders. Singer's gift for creating dialogue ensures that the language available or denied to the characters in the novel signifies the identities they possess or lack. Those who command English are fully prepared to lose a definable Jewish identity in pursuit of instant assimilation; those few who cling to Yiddish demonstrate an unshakable sense of Jewish selfhood. Moreover, throughout the novel, the indiscriminate way in which cancer cuts down human life formulates in physical terms the central metaphysical question of the novel: where was God during the Holocaust?

By the turn of the millennium, some critical consensus about Singer's work has emerged. Widely accepted as self-evident is Alfred Kazin's 1962 contention that "Singer's work *does* stem from the Jewish village, the Jewish seminary, the compact (not closed) Jewish society of Eastern Europe. . . . For Singer it is not only his materials that are 'Jewish'; the world is so. Yet within this world he has found emancipation and universality—through his faith in imagination." Earlier critical disputes about whether Singer was a modernist or an existentialist have largely been laid to rest. Singer is clearly not modernist in his techniques, and his putative "existentialism" is now viewed as deeply personal misery about the human condition. In a 1992 article for *Judaism* Dan Miron succinctly summed up Singer's worldview: "He approached the act of literary creation with a base-experience of underlying awareness that falls under the sign of fatalism and nihilism."

The repeated thematic concerns of Singer's extensive output make clear that three things above all tormented him—his abandonment of his parents' strict religious observance, his own sexual promiscuity, and his escape from the Holocaust that destroyed the Yiddish language and the Eastern European Jewish culture. Outspokenly frank about many other aspects of his thought in scores of public interviews, Singer consistently refused to discuss the Holocaust in any but the most general terms. Yet, at the height of his fame, in the nine years between 1972 and 1981, he presented his readers with English versions of five books that all view the destruction of Eastern European Jewry through the eyes of a chief character who, like Singer, is a Yiddish writer. Since Singer escaped the Holocaust and wrote in Yiddish all his life, superficially it might seem that his work preserved both the Yiddish language and its culture. But as the number of Yiddish readers and their commitment to Yiddish culture attenuated, Singer increasingly found himself in the desolate position of writing not only of, but also for, the dead. He reversed this situation by establishing his international fame through English translations of his work, a highly alienating division of experience.

Of his enormous output in Yiddish, Singer permitted only nine books to be published in his lifetime; the rest of it is effectively buried in sixty years of *Forverts* archives. His English works, however, include more than forty volumes. This disparity is further compounded by the fact that Singer himself carefully selected specific works, from large numbers of others, that he wanted translated into English, and then collaborated with his translators and editors in preparing these English versions. Close examination of these two sets of texts—when these can be located—reveals that Singer consciously addressed two different readerships, with widely differing sets of expectations and concomitantly different attitudes of receptivity.

Singer repeatedly claimed that the essence of his work exists independently in both languages in which he published: "translation, although it does damage, cannot kill an author. If he's really good, he will come through even in translation. I have seen it my own case." Nevertheless, the existence of the Yiddish texts of some of his major work, in readily available book form, has inevitably invited critical comparison of the two versions. While the conclusions drawn from this study remain provisional, they continue to raise challenges.

A great deal of Singer's work in Yiddish remains untranslated. Most of this work was published in *Forverts,* but a fair amount of entirely unpublished material also exists in Singer's Yiddish manuscripts among his archival papers housed in the Harry Ransom Humanities Research Center at the University of Texas at Austin. The bibliographies compiled by David Neal Miller and Roberta Saltzman provide information about the texts of all Singer's work in both the languages in which he was published. Undoubtedly, more of Singer's hitherto unknown work will be made available in English. If and when it is, the question of what texts constitute the true canon of his work will become even more vexed than it is at present.

Whatever his failings, Isaac Bashevis Singer remains among the most influential and disturbing Jewish writers of the twentieth century. His enormous popularity enabled him to bring to vivid life, and to international attention, the destroyed world of the shtetl. His novels and stories made formerly indifferent, even hostile, non-Jewish readers aware of the spiritual depths of the Jewish faith and of the irreplaceable loss of the Jews of Eastern Europe. For Jewish readers, his signal importance lies in his confrontation with the need to seek a meaningful identity in a secular world far removed from traditional Orthodox observance. For the literary world at large, not least among Singer's achievements has been his influence in calling to general attention the valuable body of modern Yiddish literature from which he himself drew so deeply and to which he contributed so significantly.

Interviews:

Paul Rosenblatt and Gene Koppel, *A Certain Bridge: Isaac Bashevis Singer on Literature and Life* (Tucson: University of Arizona Press, 1979);

Joseph Sherman, "Miami Meeting: An Interview with Isaac Bashevis Singer," *Theoria,* 62 (May 1984): 1–11;

Richard Burgin, *Conversations with Isaac Bashevis Singer* (New York: Noonday Press, 1986);

Grace Farrell, ed., *Isaac Bashevis Singer: Conversations* (Jackson and London: University Press of Mississippi, 1992).

Bibliographies:

Jackson R. Bryer and Paul E. Rockwell, "Isaac Bashevis Singer in English: A Bibliography," in *Critical Views of Isaac Bashevis Singer,* edited by Irving Malin (New York: New York University Press, 1968), pp. 220–265;

David Neal Miller, *A Bibliography of Isaac Bashevis Singer, January 1950–June 1952* (New York: Max Weinreich Centre for Advanced Jewish Studies, YIVO Institute for Jewish Research, 1979);

Miller, *A Bibliography of Isaac Bashevis Singer 1924–1949* (New York: Peter Lang, 1984);

Roberta Saltzman, *Isaac Bashevis Singer: A Bibliography of His Works in Yiddish and English, 1960–1991* (Lanham, Md.: Scarecrow Press, 2002).

Biographies:

Paul Kresh, *Isaac Bashevis Singer: The Magician of West 86th Street* (New York: Dial, 1979);

Kresh, *Isaac Bashevis Singer: The Story of a Storyteller* (New York: Dutton, 1984);

Lester Goran, *The Bright Streets of Surfside: The Memoir of a Friendship with Isaac Bashevis Singer* (Kent, Ohio: Kent State University Press, 1994);

Israel Zamir, *Journey to My Father, Isaac Bashevis Singer,* translated by Barbara Harshav (New York: Arcade, 1995);

Janet Hadda, *Isaac Bashevis Singer: A Life* (New York: Oxford University Press, 1997);

Dvorah Telushkin, *Master of Dreams: A Memoir of Isaac Bashevis Singer* (New York: Morrow, 1997);

Agata Tuszynska, *Lost Landscapes: In Search of Isaac Bashevis Singer and the Jews of Poland,* translated by Madeline G. Levine (New York: Morrow, 1998).

References:

Edward Alexander, *Isaac Bashevis Singer* (Boston: Twayne, 1980);

Alexander, *A Study of the Short Fiction* (Boston: Twayne, 1990);

Marcia Allentuck, ed., *The Achievement of Isaac Bashevis Singer* (Carbondale: Southern Illinois University Press, 1969);

Alida Allison, *Isaac Bashevis Singer: Children's Stories and Childhood Memoirs* (Boston: Twayne, 1996);

Israel Ch. Biletsky, *God, Jew, and Satan in the Work of Isaac Bashevis Singer* (Lanham, Md.: University Press of America, 1995);

Irving H. Buchen, *Isaac Bashevis Singer and the Eternal Past* (New York: New York University Press / London: University of London Press, 1968);

Hugh Denman, ed., *Isaac Bashevis Singer: His Work and His World* (Boston: E. J. Brill, 2002);

Grace Farrell [as Grace Farrell Lee], *From Exile to Redemption: The Fiction of Isaac Bashevis Singer* (Carbondale: Southern Illinois University Press, 1987);

Farrell, ed., *Critical Essays on Isaac Bashevis Singer* (New York: G. K. Hall, 1996);

Lawrence Friedman, *Understanding Isaac Bashevis Singer* (Columbia: University of South Carolina Press, 1988);

Frances Vargas Gibbons, *Transgression and Self-Punishment in Isaac Bashevis Singer's Search* (New York: Peter Lang, 1995);

Alfred Kazin, *Contemporaries* (Boston: Little, Brown, 1962);

Joseph C. Landis, *Aspects of Isaac Bashevis Singer* (New York: Queens College Press, 1986);

Irving Malin, *Isaac Bashevis Singer* (New York: Ungar, 1972);

David Neal Miller, *Fear of Fiction: Narrative Strategies in the Works of Isaac Bashevis Singer* (Albany: State University of New York Press, 1985);

Miller, ed., *Recovering the Canon: Essays on Isaac Bashevis Singer* (Leiden: E. J. Brill, 1986);

Dan Miron, "Passivity and Narration: The Spell of Isaac Bashevis Singer," *Judaism,* 41 (Winter 1992);

Ronald Sanders, *The Americanization of Isaac Bashevis Singer* (Syracuse, N.Y.: Syracuse University Press, 1989);

Ben Siegel, *Isaac Bashevis Singer* (Minneapolis: University of Minnesota Press, 1969);

Clive Sinclair, *The Brothers Singer* (London & New York: Allison & Busby, 1983);

Ruth R. Wisse, *The Modern Jewish Canon* (New York: Free Press, 2000);

Seth L. Wolitz, "'Der Yid fun Bovl': Variants and Meanings," *Yiddish,* 11 (1998): 30–47;

Wolitz, "*Satan in Goray* as Parable," *Prooftexts,* 9 (1989): 13–25;

Wolitz, ed., *The Hidden Isaac Bashevis Singer* (Austin: University of Texas Press, 2001).

Papers:

The primary archive of Isaac Bashevis Singer's papers is at the Harry Ransom Humanities Research Center, University of Texas at Austin.

Peter Taylor

(8 January 1917 – 2 November 1994)

Albert J. Griffith
Our Lady of the Lake University of San Antonio

See also the Taylor entries in *DLB 218: American Short-Story Writers Since World War II, Second Series; DLB Yearbook: 1981;* and *DLB Yearbook: 1994.*

BOOKS: *A Long Fourth and Other Stories* (New York: Harcourt, Brace, 1948; London: Routledge & Kegan Paul, 1949);

A Woman of Means (New York: Harcourt, Brace, 1950; London: Routledge & Kegan Paul, 1950);

The Widows of Thornton (New York: Harcourt, Brace, 1954);

Tennessee Day in St. Louis: A Comedy (New York: Random House, 1957);

Happy Families Are All Alike: A Collection of Stories (New York: McDowell, Obolensky, 1959; London: Macmillan, 1960);

Miss Leonora When Last Seen and Fifteen Other Stories (New York: Obolensky, 1963);

The Collected Stories of Peter Taylor (New York: Farrar, Straus & Giroux, 1969);

Literature, Sewanee, and the World, Founder's Day Address, University of the South (Sewanee, Tenn.: University of the South, 1972);

Presences: Seven Dramatic Pieces (Boston: Houghton Mifflin, 1973);

In the Miro District and Other Stories (New York: Knopf, 1977; London: Chatto & Windus, 1977);

The Early Guest (a sort of story, a sort of play, a sort of dream) (Winston-Salem, N.C.: Palaemon, 1982);

The Old Forest and Other Stories (New York: Dial/Doubleday, 1985); republished as *The Old Forest* (London: Chatto & Windus/Hogarth Press, 1985);

A Stand in the Mountains (New York: Frederic C. Beil, 1986);

A Summons to Memphis (New York: Knopf, 1986; London: Chatto & Windus, 1987);

The Oracle at Stoneleigh Court: Stories (New York: Knopf, 1993; London: Chatto & Windus, 1993);

In the Tennessee Country (New York: Knopf, 1994; London: Chatto & Windus, 1994).

Peter Taylor (photograph by Bud Lee; from the dust jacket for In the Tennessee Country, *1994)*

OTHER: *Randall Jarrell, 1914–1965,* edited by Taylor, Robert Lowell, and Robert Penn Warren (New York: Farrar, Straus & Giroux, 1967);

"Acceptance by Peter Taylor [of Gold Medal for Short Story]," *Proceedings,* American Academy and Institute of Arts and Letters, second set, no. 29 (1979): 31–32;

"Reminiscences," in *The Fugitives, the Agrarians and Other Twentieth-Century Southern Writers* (Charlottesville: Alderman Library, University of Virginia, 1985), pp. 17–21;

"Tennessee Caravan," in *Tennessee: A Homecoming,* edited by John Netherton (Nashville: Third National, 1985), pp. 59–66.

During the last fifteen years of his life—capping a fifty-seven-year publishing career—Peter Taylor was awarded the Gold Medal for the short story from the American Institute of Arts and Letters (1978), a National Endowment for the Arts senior fellowship (1984), a PEN/Faulkner Award for *The Old Forest and Other Stories* (1985), a PEN/Malamud Award (1992), and an American Book Award nomination (1986), a Ritz-Hemingway Prize (1986), and a Pulitzer Prize (1987) for *A Summons to Memphis* (1986). His fiction frequently earned favorable comparisons with the work of Anthony Trollope, Henry James, and Anton Pavlovich Chekhov. Yet, when he died at age seventy-seven on 2 November 1994, the designation he had given himself years before—"the best-known unknown writer in America"—was probably still as true as ever. Like many other writers of the Southern Renaissance, Taylor often found that his regional subject matter was misunderstood as local-color nostalgia or a cultural anachronism.

Novelists are usually better known than poets or short-story writers, and Taylor was primarily a writer of short fiction. (He also wrote poetry and plays.) There is evidence that he began writing at least eight novels, but only three of these works—*A Woman of Means* (1950), *A Summons to Memphis,* and *In the Tennessee Country* (1994)—were published and marketed as novels, and the first was only thirty-five thousand words. Though widely acclaimed by reviewers, none was a best-seller or adapted for the screen. Because his many middle-length works, which are usually labeled "stories," have the thematic complexity and sociocultural depth of full-length novels, Taylor's legacy as a novelist rests on more than just *A Woman of Means, A Summons to Memphis,* and *In the Tennessee Country.*

Descended from two prominent Tennessee families with the same last name, Taylor was born on 8 January 1917, the fourth child and second son of Matthew Hillsman Taylor and Katherine Baird (Taylor) Taylor. As biographer Hubert H. McAlexander points out, the future writer was named for his father but nicknamed "Pete," and he later adopted the name Peter Hillsman Taylor. The Taylor family moved from their rural hometown of Trenton, Tennessee, to Nashville in 1924, to St. Louis in 1926, and to Memphis in 1932, as Hillsman Taylor's legal practice and business interests required. Trenton maintained a forceful presence in the family, however, through reminders such as visiting kinsfolk and the black servants who moved with the Taylors, who repeatedly traveled back to Trenton for holidays. The family was trying to maintain old tradi-

tions, values, and roles in a new age and in the new environment of rapidly changing urban centers—a recurring theme in many of Taylor's works. Much of his Southern agrarian heritage was transmitted to him through stories about the family, especially those told by his mother. A great deal of the family folklore involved his two colorful grandfathers—both lawyers and politicians and both named Robert Taylor. The paternal grandfather, Robert Zachary Taylor, and his brother, Will Taylor, were also Confederate veterans and served as models for characters in several stories, including "In the Miro District." For political characters and contexts in his fiction, Peter Taylor also drew on his mother's family, including the career of his maternal grandfather, Robert Love Taylor, who in the Tennessee gubernatorial election of 1886 ran successfully as a Democrat against his Republican brother, Alf Taylor, and their prohibition-candidate father, Nathaniel Green Taylor, a former congressman and commissioner of Indian Affairs.

After graduating from Central High School in Memphis in 1935, Peter Taylor was disappointed by his father's refusal to allow him to study writing at Columbia University, to which he had earned a scholarship, and rebelled by putting college on hold. He worked as a reporter for the *Memphis Commercial Appeal* in fall 1935, but the following spring he took two courses at Southwestern University at Memphis. One of these classes was taught by the poet and critic Allen Tate, who persuaded Taylor to try Vanderbilt University in Nashville (the school Taylor's father had originally chosen for him), where he could study with Tate's mentor, John Crowe Ransom. Both Tate and Ransom were founders of and contributors to the influential Nashville modernist literary magazine *Fugitive* (1922–1925), prominent practitioners of the formalist literary theories of the emergent New Criticism, and proponents for the anti-industrial, anti–New South philosophy of the Southern Agrarian Movement. Many of Taylor's lifetime friends had Fugitive/Agrarian/New Critical associations.

Taylor enrolled at Vanderbilt in fall 1936. The following year Ransom moved to Kenyon College in Ohio, and Taylor followed in autumn 1938, living in Douglass House, the residence for all Ransom's literary students. By the time he graduated in 1940, Taylor had published a dozen and a half pieces of fiction and poetry in a student publication, two short stories in the Oxford, Mississippi, little magazine *River,* and a poem in Ransom's prestigious *Kenyon Review.* Taylor also began "The Wanderer," his first experiment with the novel form. He abandoned the novel, and the only part he ever published was a chapter that appeared in the Kenyon student publication *Hika* (March 1940). During his undergraduate years he also formed lasting friendships with poets Randall Jarrell, whom he

*Peter Taylor and Eleanor Ross on their wedding day,
4 June 1943, with Allen Tate, who gave the bride
away (Collection of Eleanor Ross Taylor)*

knew at Vanderbilt and Kenyon, and Robert Lowell, his Kenyon roommate.

After graduating from Kenyon in 1940, Taylor and Lowell both began graduate work in English at Louisiana State University under two more writers associated with the Fugitives and New Critics, Robert Penn Warren and Cleanth Brooks. At Thanksgiving, Taylor dropped his course work to concentrate on reading and writing. During his college years Taylor had not only gained the enduring patronage of Tate, Ransom, Warren, and Brooks and formed bonds with Jarrell and Lowell, but also through them he had met other notable writers, such as Caroline Gordon (then married to Tate), Katherine Anne Porter, Andrew Lytle, and Jean Stafford (then married to Lowell).

In May 1941 Taylor was drafted into the United States Army, and the following month he reported to Fort Oglethorpe, Georgia. In spring 1943, while on leave, Taylor visited the Tates, who introduced him to poet Eleanor Lily Ross of Norwood, North Carolina, whom Taylor married just six weeks later, on 4 June 1943. The Taylors subsequently had two children, Katherine Baird Taylor

(born 30 September 1948) and Peter Ross Taylor (born 7 February 1955), both of whom became writers.

In 1944 Taylor's unit was sent to Tidworth Camp in England, where he served for the duration of the war. He was honorably discharged at the rank of sergeant in December 1945. He found his first postwar job as a reader for New York publisher Henry Holt, but by the fall of 1946 he had entered academe and begun what would be his lifelong "day job" as a creative-writing teacher. He spent much of his career from 1946 until 1967 at the University of North Carolina at Greensboro, with stints at Indiana University (1948–1949), the University of Chicago (1952), Kenyon College (1952–1957), Ohio State University (1957–1963), and Harvard University (1964). From 1967 until his retirement in 1983 he was a chaired professor at the University of Virginia, returning to Harvard as a visiting professor in 1973. He later taught briefly at Memphis State University (1983) and the University of Georgia (1985).

In spring 1947 Taylor met Lowell's editor, Robert Giroux of Harcourt, Brace, who offered Taylor a contract for two books, the first of which was *A Long Fourth and Other Stories* (1948). As Giroux recalled years later, "His prose was direct and forthright, and it got to the heart of family life in the South, the skeletons in the closet—what Southerners call 'connections'" (*The New York Times Magazine,* 1 January 1995). In his introduction Warren defined the territory Taylor was staking out for his novels as well as his short stories as "the contemporary, urban, middle-class world of the upper South," and he went on to define Taylor's themes as "Lost simplicities and loyalties, the role of woman, the place of the Negro. . . . a world vastly uncertain of itself and the ground of its values, caught in a tangle of modern commercialism and traditions and conventions gone to seed, confused among pieties and pretensions." Reviewers in general were unusually positive, agreeing with Warren's assessment of the Taylor style as "irony blended of comedy and sympathetic understanding."

Of the seven stories in *A Long Fourth and Other Stories,* two long tales, "The Scoutmaster" and the title story, bear the hallmarks of Taylor's later novellas and novels. Each of the stories includes a family in which conflict develops over an apparent breakdown in values, a sociocultural context that sets a traditional Southern way of life against the encroachments of crass modernism, and a narrative consciousness (first-person in "The Scoutmaster" and third-person in "A Long Fourth") who mentally wanders back and forth over the events, seeking resolution in some kind of epiphany. As Kenneth Clay Cathey observed in *The Western Review* (Autumn 1953), the roughly 14,600-word length of the title story permitted Taylor "more opportunity to create the exact atmosphere of contemporary middle-class family relations in all their subtlety: doubly important when we realize that the family atmosphere is the real antagonistic force in all Taylor's work."

Before publication of *A Long Fourth and Other Stories*, Taylor had completed something he thought of as a novelette, which he later said could have been "much longer" except for his habit of throwing away about half of everything he has written. "The publisher sent me a great sheaf of letters explaining why it wasn't a good novel," he told Stephen Goodwin in 1973, "and I answered by threatening to withdraw it, and the publisher wrote back saying he had decided to print it. Perhaps he still didn't like it but thought that I had other novels up my sleeve." Thus, *A Woman of Means* was published as a novel by Harcourt, Brace, in May 1950 and in England by Routledge & Kegan Paul in October 1950.

The first-person narrator of *A Woman of Means* is Quintus Cincinnatus Lovell Dudley, an adult looking back on his early teenage years in the 1920s, after his widowed father, Gerald Dudley, a traveling hardware salesman, was married to the wealthy Anna Lauterbach, daughter of a St. Louis millionaire and former wife of a brewery heir. The new marriage sets up a contrast between the traditional Southern lifestyle Quint has experienced during summer visits to Belgrove, his maternal grandmother's "run-down farm" with its Indian graveyard and trenches from the Civil War Battle of Nashville, and the modern materialism of life at his stepmother's lavish Italianate mansion in St. Louis, where Quint is introduced to the luxuries of servants, a private school, and visits to summer resorts in Michigan. His two pretty stepsisters, with their slangy speech and teenage silliness, fill him with delight, and his beautiful and charming stepmother showers him with love and attention. In fact, Quint sometimes suspects that his father married her to give Quint a new mother. Just when Quint finally feels at age thirteen that he has come into the "practical possession of a mother," the marriage seems to falter, and the doting stepmother grows increasingly neurotic, ultimately obsessing over a hysterical pregnancy.

Throughout the nonlinear narrative, Quint reflects on themes such as the country versus the city, stability versus transience, love versus money, Southern tradition versus contemporary mores, and—perhaps most important—real family versus the illusion of family. Quint's stepmother's deterioration banishes his "illusion of a family" on the day in 1927 when Charles Lindbergh's historic solo transatlantic flight is announced, and Quint, while reading about it, realizes he is "not unhappy" about his future but has a "clear image" of himself "as an independent stranger pushing through vast throngs of people."

Most reviewers liked the novel, even when they expressed some reservations. The reviewer for *Time* (15

May 1950), for example, pronounced it a "good, if not a major novel." One of the most perceptive critiques came in 1953, when Cathey said it seems "to be two short stories poorly woven together"; it contains too much exposition of the boy's early life, "which really adds nothing to the understanding of the eventual psychological change"; and it does not adequately depict the "moral *evolution*" demanded by the novel form. Taylor's own assessment, expressed in a 1977 interview with Ruth Dean, was that *A Woman of Means* was "not as good as my stories."

Taylor did not publish another novel for thirty-six years. During the 1960s he spend five years on a novel titled "The Pilgrim Sons." According to McAlexander, Taylor—having accepted a publisher's advance and working under a deadline—had a "terrible time" trying to create the novel from several long stories. In the summer of 1967, to show his good faith, he mailed approximately a hundred pages of the novel to Giroux, who had become a partner in the firm of Farrar, Straus and Giroux. That fall, a brief excerpt appeared in *The Washington Post* Sunday magazine, but two chapters Taylor submitted as stories to *The New Yorker* were rejected because, the editor said, their "construction and pace" were "entirely novelistic." One of these chapters was eventually published in *The Sewanee Review* (Spring 1969) as "Daphne's Lover," and Taylor used some other parts of the novel in some one-act dramas he was then writing. By early 1972 he had decided not to complete the novel. He tore up the novel manuscript and went back to writing short stories. *The Early Guest (a sort of story, a sort of play, a sort of dream)* (1982), first published in the Winter 1973 issue of *Shenandoah,* is a synopsis in dramatic form of the abandoned novel.

In the three and a half decades between *A Woman of Means* and his second published novel, *A Summons to Memphis* (1986), Taylor produced six short-story collections that earned him a reputation as one of the foremost masters of the American short story. He also published eleven plays in books during the same period. His stories appeared in prestigious magazines such as *The New Yorker* and *Harper's Bazaar,* bringing him scholarly and critical recognition as well as many awards and honors, including a National Institute of Arts and Letters Award (1952), a Fulbright grant to do research in Paris (1955), the Ohioana Book Award in 1960, a Ford Foundation grant to work at the Royal Court Theatre in London (1960), a Rockefeller Foundation sabbatical grant for the 1966–1967 academic year, induction into the National Institute of Arts and Letters (1969), and an honorary Litt.D. degree from the University of the South (1972). Financial rewards from his books were not as forthcoming. As a result, Taylor had wedged time for writing between the obligations of his various academic appointments.

Because it is a sequence of related stories, *The Widows of Thornton* (1954) might well have been marketed as a novel like Sherwood Anderson's *Winesburg, Ohio* (1919) and Eudora Welty's *The Golden Apples* (1949). As Taylor told the *Kenyon Alumni Bulletin* (Winter 1954), his original idea for *The Widows of Thornton* was to write stories about four or five white and black families from a country town who were now "living a modern urban life while continuing to be aware of their old identities and relationships"–showing "how old patterns, for good or bad, continued to dominate many aspects of these people's lives." Thornton, "the old dying town on the bluffs above the Tennessee River," is one of Taylor's fictional stand-ins for Trenton, Tennessee. Only two of the nine stories are set in Thornton, but the town is an inescapable influence on the lives of characters whose stories take place in transit or in Nashville, St. Louis, Chicago, or Detroit. Like the Thornton-bred Carvers of *A Summons to Memphis* and the Tuckers of *In the Tennessee Country,* the Tolliver family–which figures in three stories in *The Widows of Thornton* and later became the subject of the play *Tennessee Day in St. Louis* (1957)–has many characteristics of Taylor's family. As a whole, this Thornton saga depicts the relentless demands of traditional roles based on class, gender, and race, even when characters distance themselves from the point of origin of these roles. The longest story in the book, the seventy-five-page "A Dark Walk," is a novella in structure. It depicts the Thornton family as it lugs servants and four van loads of furniture as they follow the husband's career from city to city. Suggesting that men of that generation were able to escape to freedom only by encumbering their wives with all that was "old and useless and inherited"–making them "somehow, widows" right from the start–this story develops explicitly a thematic interest that permeates not only *The Widows of Thornton* but also Taylor's later novels and novellas.

Taylor's 1959 collection, *Happy Families Are All Alike,* marked his shift to the first-person narrative technique that became the hallmark of most of his fiction for the rest of his career. The first-person narrators in *Happy Families Are All Alike* leisurely crisscross past and present, probing one thing and ignoring another while revealing themselves to be alternately perceptive and obtuse. This digressive-progressive memoir form became a signature technique in Taylor's fiction, forcing the reader to try to penetrate a veil of subjectivity hanging over the content. The first-person narrators of Taylor's later works tend to be close to the age of the author when he created them. Their age gives them a maturity that some earlier narrators lack–but it perhaps also explains their garrulousness, as well as the suspicion of unreliability that hovers over some of them.

After *Happy Families Are All Alike,* all Taylor's volumes of short fiction except *In the Miro District and Other Stories* (1977) combined some previously uncollected stories with works from earlier collections. Of the six new stories in *Miss Leonora When Last Seen and Fifteen Other Stories* (1963), the ones with the most implication for his novel writing were the title story (about an aged and idiosyncratic schoolteacher who disappears from her hometown and seems to be "orbiting her native state of Tennessee") and "At the Drugstore" (about a thirty-five-year-old man returning to his parents' home and confronting the cycles of change). Both deal with the "mystery" in the commonplace and the difficulty of pinning down the meanings of experience. Both stories also resonate with symbolic associations of the sort Taylor also achieved in *A Summons to Memphis* and *In the Tennessee Country.* Two of the five new stories in *The Collected Stories of Peter Taylor* (1969), "Dean of Men" and "First Heat," introduce the theme of betrayal that is so important in *A Summons to Memphis* and other later writings.

Suffering from heart trouble, diabetes, and arthritis, Taylor had a heart attack in 1974, but it was only a temporary setback. "Since I've gotten sick," he told interviewer Malcolm Jones in 1980, "all I've wanted to do with my energy is write." This recommitment to writing paid off.

In the Miro District and Other Stories comprises eight stories, four of which are printed as verse. Taylor called these "broken-line prose" narratives "stoems" and was publishing other stoems in periodicals. In fact, all the fiction he wrote in the 1970s and 1980s (no matter how the texts eventually appeared on the page) started out in this broken-line format. As he told *Paris Review* interviewer Barbara Thompson in 1987, his stoems were attempts "to get interest in every line, every sentence. . . . You have the two kinds of syntax, the line-endings and the run-on line, and the regular syntax of the language. You can be saying a lot more in a short space." Though Taylor used this metrical technique in novel writing, he often admitted that he was usually unable to sustain the technique over a really long work.

Not everyone considered Taylor's experiment a success. Keith Cushman, in a review for *Studies in Short Fiction* (Fall 1977), called it "formal eccentricity" and complained, "The stories look too much like poetry to be taken as prose, but read too much like prose to be taken as poetry." Other readers, however, praised the longer prose stories of *In the Miro District and Other Stories* and the two previously uncollected stories in *The Old Forest and Other Stories,* all of which started out as stoems. As he told Robert Daniel in 1983, the year he was inducted into the American Academy of Arts and Letters, Taylor was trying "to make the language count, to make every word, every sentence, count more." "In a certain way a short story is somewhere between a novel and a poem," he told Daniel; "Chekhov's stories are really poems. The best stories can be talked about as poems in the same way. You see the structure, you see it all at once, as you can't in the novel." The virtue of compression, which he learned at Kenyon from Ransom, had always been important to Taylor, who tried to make his stories "tightly written." Paradoxically, however, as he told Thompson in 1987, his stories got "longer and longer," even while he was trying to make them "shorter and shorter." In fact, the fiction of the later part of Taylor's career demonstrates the slipperiness of the boundary between short story and novel. Reviewing *The Old Forest and Other Stories* for *The New York Times Book Review* (17 February 1985), Robert Towers said the stories have a "novelistic density of observation, analysis and reflection" that makes them "miniature novels," which "defy the conventions of brevity and concentration that we usually associate with the genre. What results is often a thickly populated microcosm of an entire society, with its assumptions, virtues, loyalties and snobberies revealed. The retrospective approach lends itself to such an effect." In fact, the mental wanderings of the first-person narrators in some of the stories in *In the Miro District and Other Stories* and *The Old Forest and Other Stories* leave readers unsure of what is objective fact and what is subjective perception. Usually there are several possible, sometimes contradictory, interpretations of the events. The most compelling examples of such stories in these collections deal with the "unchangeable codes of decent conduct" of Southern families and their relationship to the primacy of marriage and the family, the constraints of noblesse oblige, and the freedom of individuals.

"The Captain's Son" and the title story from *In the Miro District and Other Stories* explore generational responses to Southern codes of conduct, foreshadowing in form and content the novels *A Summons to Memphis* and *In the Tennessee Country*. Both stories depend for their effect on the narrator's subjectivity. Exemplifying Taylor's skillful manipulation of the first-person perspective, the ambitious "In the Miro District" has a mature narrator (in "late middle age") who reflects on events of his childhood and youth as part of a "busy, genteel, contented" family during the 1920s. Thinking specifically on the "thrusting" together of himself and his grandfather in different periods of their lives, he acknowledges "complications of feeling" from "an abrupt and unhappy" breach in the grandfather-grandson relationship that occurred when he was eighteen. He describes the problematic early forced companionship of "an old graybeard and a towheaded little boy" and the later life-changing confrontations between a censorious elder and a rebellious young adult. Yet, he and his

Randall Jarrell and Taylor in front of the duplex they owned in Greensboro, North Carolina (Collection of Eleanor Ross Taylor)

grandfather are united, despite themselves, in rejecting the control of the grandfather's daughter and son-in-law, the boy's parents. As the narrator constantly digresses, analyzes, contextualizes, interprets, speculates, and forecasts, the reader realizes there is no solid, objective evidence with which to build an independent interpretation. As Stephen Goodwin noted in *The New Republic* (7 May 1977), this narrator "experiences no epiphany, no sudden insight or intuition," and his "urgent meditation yields nothing but a story, *is* nothing but a story." "For Taylor," Goodwin continued, "the story is itself a way of knowing, of shaping knowledge; though it cannot restore the past, though it cannot unmake the divisions which existed then, it nevertheless reconciles us to that vanished world and to the present because it is as much as we can know." Writing for *The New York Times Book Review* (3 April 1977), Anatole Broyard was unimpressed with the story, attributing the traits of the narration not to the character/narrator but to the author himself. "Taylor's story," he said, "moves like a heavily-loaded wagon. He would as soon sit on his hat as compress his effects. . . .

The author is in no hurry to develop his theme, and there is in his manner a complacent, and sometimes irritating, assumption that you are more than willing to hear him out."

A willingness to "hear out" the narration is also required for the two new stories in *The Old Forest and Other Stories*–the title story and "The Gift of the Prodigal"–both digressive-progressive first-person recollections. Indeed, in "The Gift of the Prodigal" the aging widowed narrator tells not just his own story but a variety of stories he has heard over the years from his youngest child, the three-times-wed twenty-nine-year-old Ricky, who constantly unburdens himself by telling his father about the "outrageous and sometimes sordid affairs" of his disordered life. *In the Tennessee Country* includes a fuller development of this theme of a father implicitly comparing his conservative life choices with the more daring choices of his son. Moreover, this general lament for "the road not taken" permeates nearly all the works of the last part of Taylor's career. "He thought interesting people were not necessarily those who live wild lives, but those who 'could have,'" Taylor's former student Alan Williamson observed in the special Taylor issue of *The Southern Quarterly* (2000); "This interest in what is just outside the circle of the permissible is, I believe, the true subject of Peter's fiction."

What one "could have" done, how one can navigate the "circle of the permissible" without ever quite breaking out, is at the heart of the fifty-nine-page novella "The Old Forest," which first appeared in *The New Yorker* (14 May 1979). A story of youth, again told from the perspective of a mature male narrator, "The Old Forest," like many of Taylor's best works of fiction, creates a credibly authentic setting from history, personal memory, and myth and pulls unexpected, but convincing, insights from the ruminations on the manners of a given time and place. "The Old Forest" also has formidable strengths even where some of Taylor's other distinguished stories are at their weakest. It has, for instance, a dramatically rendered central incident that resonates with significance for both narrator and reader; it has three vividly individuated main characters, all of whom are ultimately seen to have values that matter; and it has an engrossing resolution that simultaneously surprises and satisfies the reader.

"I was already formally engaged, as we used to say, to the girl I was going to marry," declares narrator Nat Ramsey in the opening lines of the story. "But still I sometimes went out on the town with girls of a different sort. And during the very week before the date set for the wedding, in December, I was in an automobile accident at a time when one of those girls was with me. It was a calamitous thing to have happen–not the accident itself, which caused no serious injury to anyone, but the

accident plus the presence of that girl." The three main characters are already there in that first paragraph. Nat is the "well-brought up young man" who categorizes women by the "sort" of roles they are destined to play in service to the patriarchal society of the late 1930s. He is engaged to Caroline Braxley, the epitome of the "innocent, untutored types" whom men of Nat's class "generally took to dances at the Memphis Country Club" and "eventually looked forward to marrying." Lee Ann Deehart, the girl who is in the accident with him, is "not in the Memphis debutante set" and, consequently, despite her brightness, intellectual interests, independence, and spunk, is not the "sort" of girl a gentleman marries.

After the accident Lee Ann flees into the Overton Park woods, which become the most powerful image of the story. They are the "last bit" of an "old forest" into which "pioneer women, driven mad by their loneliness and isolation" ran off and were never seen again. Soon it becomes clear to Nat that Lee Ann must be found or his entire future might be jeopardized. Ultimately, it is Caroline, not Nat, who tracks Lee Ann to her hideaway and persuades her to tell the newspapers that she is "safe and well."

In Taylor's early fiction socially prominent heroines are generally contrasted with black servant women or with women of their own class who are perhaps of a different generation or a different marital status. In his late work Taylor began regularly to deal with distinctions between women of the "right sort" and women of the demimondaine. "That's the world that I knew growing up, the world of the so-called upper class people," Taylor told W. Hampton Sides in 1987. "I know everything that was wrong and wretched about them. But, on the other hand, they fascinate me. They represent an attitude toward the past that is terribly important to society. . . . In 'The Old Forest' I deliberately made the heroine a society girl, a debutante, even though all of us might find another character much more admirable. . . . But I said to myself, it would be more interesting to see if I can make this society girl appealing as a human being and see what her life is. I wanted to see human beings set in historical situations from which they can't escape."

In making a life for herself, the attractive Lee Ann is "what the whole world is going to be like someday," and to Nat she represents his "last moment to reach out and understand something of the world" that exists outside his own "narrow circumstances" and "narrow nature." To Caroline, Lee Ann and the other girls of her set represent the kind of freedom that men have always had but that no woman of Caroline's family or social class has ever known. Caroline at first nearly accedes to her family's expectation that, in view of possible scandal, she will end her engagement or at least postpone the wedding for a year. Then, however, she realizes, "The only power I had to save myself was to save you, and to save you by rescuing Lee Ann Deehart. . . . it was a question of how very much I had to lose and how little power I had to save myself. Because *I* had not set *my*self free the way those other girls have." Nat eventually understands that girls like Caroline "took themselves seriously . . . and took seriously the forms of the life they lived" as heirs to "the old, country manners." Once having achieved an appreciation for the limited opportunities to be found in one's inherited roles, Nat and Caroline marry; Nat fights in World War II; both cope with a series of family tragedies; and Caroline supports Nat's midlife change of career from business to academe.

A great deal of "The Old Forest" is devoted to the creation of the cultural context in which the events take place. As Madison Smartt Bell commented in *Harper's* (April 1986), Taylor had to "explain each nuance of Memphis society in excruciating detail, for its values are so alien to those of modern life that the story would otherwise be incomprehensible to modern readers." Yet, despite this culture gap, Bell noted, "the story manages to achieve a general meaning. It serves as a parable of the fecklessness of youth on the one hand, and on the other of the ultimate power of the weak and oppressed to assume control of their lives."

An independent motion-picture adaptation of "The Old Forest" by Steven John Ross reached small but appreciative audiences in 1984. This movie featured Taylor's voice-over narration and Memphis locations that (to the surprise of the movie makers) included a house Taylor had lived in as a child and a warehouse he had in mind when he wrote a scene of the story.

In many interviews Taylor expressed both his preference for writing and reading short fiction rather than novels and his resentment of the assumption that writing short stories was just preparation for novels. Talking about *In the Miro District and Other Stories* to Dean in 1977, he commented, "If I had wanted to make a killing on this last book, I could have stretched out any of these stories to 200 pages and made it into a novel." In 1983 he told Daniel, "I'm not a novelist. These pieces I'm writing now are long short stories." In the same interview, he admitted, "I'm working on what I call a book-length story. I won't say the other word." The work to which he referred became *A Summons to Memphis*—announced by Alfred A. Knopf in 1986 as the long-awaited new novel by "one of America's finest writers" and "a crowning achievement in a distinguished career." To Taylor, however, the new book was just "a story that got out of hand" (as he put it to J. William Broadway in 1985).

Dust jacket for Taylor's 1986 novel, which he described as "a story that got out of hand" (Richland County Public Library)

A Summons to Memphis was indeed Taylor's longest piece of fiction to date. As in the longer stories from *In the Miro District and Other Stories* and *The Old Forest and Other Stories,* the plot of this new novel hovers around a key incident while meandering backward and forward in time; the small group of main characters are mostly members or close associates of one family; the sociocultural aspects of setting are stressed, once again with a detailed contrast between Nashville and Memphis; and many themes introduced in previous works are brought forth for new elaboration. Foremost among the similarities, however, is the use of a mature narrator who filters all the action through his culturally conditioned sensibilities. As Taylor told Hubert H. McAlexander in 1987, "What is important is his point of view and the way he goes back and forth over the years trying to understand."

This narrator, Phillip Carver, is summoned by his two old-maid sisters to come from New York to Memphis to prevent his eighty-one-year-old father's marriage to "a respectable but undistinguished and schoolteacherish woman." Trying to piece together the chaotic information and self-serving interpretations his sisters have provided over the telephone, Philip must decide on his own stance toward the marriage. To do so he must also reexamine his feelings about his family history and often tyrannical father and take stock of his own somewhat reclusive life as a Manhattan book dealer, his current estrangement from the younger woman with whom he has lived for several years, and his noticeable degree of alienation not only from his family but also from people in general.

The aging would-be bridegroom, George Carver, emerges from Phillip's recollections as a formidable character—strong, successful, personable, attractive, witty, resilient in adversity, and full of integrity, but also pathetic. At one point, Phillip observes that "it seems almost a great beauty of my father's character that from his earliest years the boy George Carver yearned for an individuality and for personal attainments that could be in no way related to the accident of his birth, longed to succeed in some realm that he had not yet heard of and could not have heard of, yearned for some mysterious achievements" that would be "an otherness" to everything he had been taught was his or might be his. For Phillip, "such aspirations and achievements" had long represented his father's "willfulness, his selfishness, and even a certain ruthlessness." Only George Carver's "very oppositeness" to Phillip could make him an "heroic figure" to be admired without reservation. The question, though, is whether Phillip and his sisters can possibly forgive him for the "ruined lives" they blame on him.

Holly Kaplan, Phillip's lover, asserts that "our old people" must be "forgiven all their injustices and unconscious cruelties in their roles as parents," since whatever selfishness there was on their parts "had actually been required of them if they were to remain whole human beings and not become merely guardian robots of the young." Yet, Phillip and his sisters cannot easily accept, let alone welcome, their father's "selfishness." They blame their father for directly and indirectly preventing all of his children from marrying. When Philip finally arrives at the Memphis airport, having accepted the summons to thwart the octogenarian's romance, his father asks him to stand up for him at his wedding, planned for that same day. Yet, "events had conspired" to convince the intended bride that their marriage could never be happy, as "he had his children to think of," and when the two men arrive at the church, they discover that she has left on a three-month trip.

There are further events in the novel, but the real story of *A Summons to Memphis* lies in the consciousness of Phillip Carver, in his lengthy ruminations and his new and occasionally contradictory insights. Like *A Woman of Means,* this novel is not structured by a linear plot; rather, it is built on its narrator's process of presenting, interpreting, reviewing, and reinterpreting the data of his life and experience. If all this rumination never results in a clear epiphany for Phillip or the reader, that lack may not be a flaw in Taylor's execution of his design. "But after all," he told McAlexander, "how successful are we ever in understanding what has happened to us? That's what I want to suggest in the novel."

While the critical reception of *A Summons to Memphis* was generally positive, some reviewers were annoyed by the tautology of the narrator. In going back over incidents or observations to add new information or interpretive nuances, Phillip Carver often repeats dates, bits of geographical description, and other incidental facts, reintroducing them with statements such as "I have stated already . . . ," "As I have already explained . . . ," or "As I have indicated earlier. . . ." Walter Sullivan, reviewing the novel for *The Sewanee Review* (1987), called such repetition a "self-indulgence" that was sometimes "tedious." In *The New York Review of Books* (25 September 1986), Robert Towers said this way of "circling a subject repeatedly before revealing its fictional core" was effective in Taylor's stories but "leads in the novel to prolixity and repetition." John Updike, who usually expressed admiration for Taylor's fiction, complained in *The New Yorker* (3 November 1986) about the "fastidious" diction, the "portly" sentences, the "prissy, circuitous" language, and the "narrative churning" that brings up "only what is already floating on the surface." Updike appreciated, however, that Taylor's "echo of old usages and once-honored forms" often delivers what might otherwise be inexpressible.

The Pulitzer Prize and other honors that accrued to *A Summons to Memphis* led to renewed critical recognition for all Taylor's fiction. In 1991 scholars, critics, and friends of Taylor gathered for two conferences devoted solely to his work: a Peter Taylor Symposium in Baltimore on 26–27 April and a Peter Taylor Homecoming at the University of North Carolina at Greensboro on 8–9 November. Meanwhile, despite deteriorating health and partial paralysis from a stroke, Taylor kept on writing, and his final collection, *The Oracle at Stoneleigh Court: Stories,* was published in February 1993. Unified by suggestions of the occult or other kinds of mystery, the fourteen works in this volume include the title novella and two other recent long first-person narratives. Despite their more-or-less unreliable old-man narrators, these stories represent a change in direction. As Taylor told Christopher P. Mettress in an interview published in *The Craft of Peter Taylor* (1995), he had reached a time of life when he not only saw things differently but also was keenly aware that he did so. "My knowledge of mystery, if you will," he said, is "what I was trying to explore."

Jonathan Yardley of *The Washington Post* (21 February 1993) said "The Oracle at Stoneleigh Court" "surely must rank among Taylor's finest work." Taylor had originally planned the novella for separate publication, but his editor at Knopf, Judith Jones, convinced him that the work was not long enough to stand by itself and should instead be published as the title story of a new collection. The "oracle" of this work, Aunt Augusta ("Gussie") St. John Jones, appears again in Taylor's next book, *In the Tennessee Country*. Another version of this character appeared as Aunt Lottie Hathcock, in Taylor's 1950 story "Their Losses." According to Robert G. Couser, Aunt Lottie was based on one of Taylor's "most colorful relatives," Aunt Katty Williamson, who, like Lottie and Gussie, was a longtime District of Columbia resident, the widow of a politician, and a regular summer visitor to her hometown. Both the real-life aunt and the two fictional aunts were interested in spiritualism, conducted séances, and converted to Roman Catholicism. In the first part of "The Oracle at Stoneleigh Court," set in 1943, Aunt Gussie is seventy-five years old and is visited by her great-nephew, a sergeant on temporary duty in the capital. This nephew, the narrator of the story, is drawn to Gussie's occult practices, and Gussie is so taken with his "fantastically good-looking" girlfriend, Lila, that she grooms her as a "veritable reincarnation" with similar "forces" and "powers." He finally acknowledges that he has succumbed to his aunt's "spells" and recognizes his own psychic powers. Yet, like Phillip Carver in *A Summons to Memphis* (who also appears in this story as a wartime acquaintance of the narrator), this nonheroic hero will not fully engage himself with any threat to his serenity. Despite the attractions of the seductive Lila, he eventually decides to marry a safe hometown girl who lacks even "the normal quantity of secrets in her own life" and to embrace a life of "uneventful seclusion."

Near the end of "The Oracle at Stoneleigh Court," just after he has claimed an extrasensory perception, the narrator abruptly announces that from this point on he "will not be held responsible for explanation or interpretation of events that follow with seeming mystery one upon another." Speaking to Mettress, Taylor acknowledged that the narrator may not want to make too much sense of his past or have too much self-understanding. If some understanding is achieved, he said, it may be of mystery, not certainty: "I wanted there to be at the end of the story a sort of captivation—

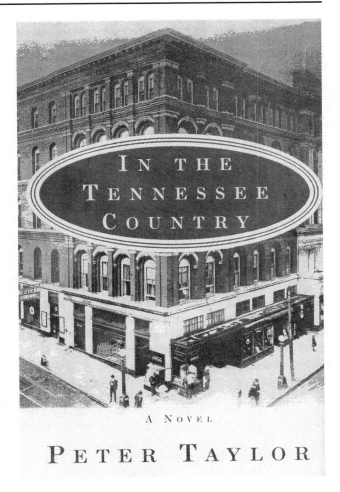

Dust jacket for Taylor's 1994 novel, inspired by family stories about the 1912 funeral train that brought the body of Taylor's maternal grandfather, Senator Robert Love Taylor, from Washington, D.C., to Tennessee for burial (Richland County Public Library)

not so much an understanding of events, but a fascination about what has occurred."

"The Witch of Owl Mountain Springs: An Account of Her Remarkable Powers," the second-longest story in the collection, is narrated by the least trustworthy of all Taylor's unreliable narrators, a gnome-like elderly bachelor and self-proclaimed amnesiac. Taylor also acknowledged multiple possibilities for interpretation in this story, telling Mettress, "Again, I've tried to look at how much of the world is concealed from us, and how much we conceal from ourselves."

"Cousin Aubrey," the third new long story in *The Oracle at Stoneleigh Court*, is related to *In the Tennessee Country*, which was published in August 1994, less than three months before Taylor's death. Both story and novel derive from a work in progress that Taylor discussed frequently in interviews during the 1980s. The inspiration for the key incident was the burial journey of 1912 in which the body of United States senator Robert Love Taylor, former governor of Tennessee and Peter Taylor's maternal grandfather, was brought by train from Washington, D.C., back to Tennessee. Taylor planned to have the narrative constructed by the senator's grandson, who would piece together family stories, going forward to the 1970s and "back 100 years before that" to trace causes and effects of this crucial episode in a family's history. Originally, the narrator was "not on the train" but had heard about it "all his life"; later, the date was changed first to 1915 and then 1916, and the narrator, then four years old, was on board.

The two versions begin with the same sentence spoken by the same narrator: "In the Tennessee country of my forebears it was not uncommon for a man of good character suddenly to disappear." Almost immediately thereafter the narratives diverge. The short story plunges into the mystery of one of those disappearing men, an "outside cousin," the illegitimate Aubrey Tucker Bradshaw, whom Taylor described as someone "awkward" and "made fun of in the family," who thus "suffered from the family." The novel begins to elaborate on the historical and geographical context not only for Aubrey's story but that of the senator's whole family and perhaps all the old gentry of Tennessee. Nevertheless, within their first few pages both versions make clear that the narrator, whose life of security has been such a contrast to Aubrey's, has become obsessed with the antihero Aubrey's disappearance. The short story efficiently and effectively explores the intrinsic interest of Aubrey's story and the significance the narrator attaches to it. The novel puts that kernel story in a grand design in which the traditions and culture of Tennessee, the saga of the senator's three daughters and their husbands, and the antithetical life choices of the academic narrator, Nathan Tucker Longfort, and his artist son Brax Longfort are extensively detailed.

Despite Nathan's constant qualifying of everything he depicts, the funeral train sequence is as memorable as anything Taylor ever wrote, evoking with humor, pathos, and irony a world already as remote as some civilization known only through an archeological dig. Effete gentility (represented by the widow, Aunt Gussie, and the senator's three married daughters) and masculine bravado (represented by the three heavy-drinking sons-in-law taking turns sitting with the corpse in the baggage car) coexist in the funeral train. Not aligned with either element is the sensitive, serious Aubrey, whom the family perceives as a "ridiculous, unmanly sort of creature" and whom the four-year-old Nathan Longfort perceives as glancing at him with

"malevolence" and a "mixture of ire and resentment." Perhaps this inexplicable hostility set Nathan off on his decades-long obsession with tracking Aubrey down and unveiling his mystery. Aubrey, who disappears after the senator's burial, continues to hover like a shadowy apparition on the periphery, showing up wraith-like at family funerals.

Most of this material was in the short story, and virtually all of it is represented in part 1 of the novel. In part 2 of the novel Nathan meanders back and forth over his childhood (dominated by his mother and two aunts, all of whom experienced early widowhoods) and recounts his youthful attempts to realize his mother's dream for him to become a painter. In part 3 Nathan tells how he abandoned art for art history and academe, while his own son, Brax, flees the family to become an artist of some serious achievement. In this section Nathan also tells how Brax was instrumental in bringing about his father's eventual reencounter with the elusive "outside cousin," now a feeble and impecunious but still proud and individualistic old man. These second and third sections, then, reveal Aubrey and Brax as alter egos of Nathan, each representing in some way the life of freedom, daring, and passion that Nathan was too full of "conformity," "dependability," "predictability," and "compromise" to attempt. Nathan learns respect for Aubrey and Brax and all the other vanished men who have plunged into "the terra incognito from which no man willingly returns." "Belatedly but firmly," Nathan says, "I resolved . . . that no one should ever search out anyone else in any way at all who has set out on that journey. It is one of the inalienable rights that people have—those that have the need or the strength for it. The rest of us have the ordinary tedium of life to deal with—to contend with. That is all."

For a work laboriously dictated by an aging author too ill to write, *In the Tennessee Country* seemed to most critics to be a worthy capstone to a distinguished career. For example, Mary Flanagan wrote in *The New York Times Book Review* (28 August 1994): "Mr. Taylor holds to the narrative contract, from the first page, full of narrative promise, to the lurking surprise, reliably delivered—though in his own good time. His writing appears to be produced without any struggle and is so graceful and lucid one has the impression that it just happened, dropping from the heavens onto the page." Her reservations, however, were also echoed by other reviewers: "My only quarrel with such mellowness, such flawless elegance, is that it is too beautiful and therefore, in places, a little dull. The debris of literary battle has been quietly and efficiently removed, leaving a tale that is often more interesting to think about than to read." *In the Tennessee Country* is Peter Taylor's appropriate last elegy for "the old ways and the old teachings" and his final demonstration of his writer's faith that as he put it in *Literature, Sewanee, and the World* (1972), "nearly everything about art is a mystery and must ever be so."

Interviews:

Malcolm Jones, "Mr. Taylor When Last Seen . . . ," *Greensboro Daily News/Record,* 27 July 1980, p. C5;

J. H. E. Paine, "Interview with Peter Taylor," *Journal of the Short Story in English,* no. 9 (Autumn 1987): 14–35;

Hubert H. McAlexander, ed., *Conversations with Peter Taylor* (Jackson: University Press of Mississippi, 1987).

Bibliographies:

Victor A. Kramer and others, "Peter Taylor," in *Andrew Lytle, Walker Percy, and Peter Taylor: A Reference Guide* (Boston: G. K. Hall, 1983), pp. 187–243;

Stuart Wright, *Peter Taylor: A Descriptive Bibliography, 1934–87* (Charlottesville: Published for the Bibliographic Society of the University of Virginia by the University Press of Virginia, 1988).

Biography:

Hubert H. McAlexander, *Peter Taylor: A Writer's Life* (Baton Rouge: Louisiana State University Press, 2001).

References:

Kenneth Clay Cathey, "Peter Taylor: An Evaluation," *Western Review,* 18 (Autumn 1953): 9–19;

Robert G. Couser, "Peter Taylor and Trenton," in *River Region Monographs: Reports on People and Popular Cul-* *ture,* edited by Neil Graves (Martin: University of Tennessee at Martin, 1975), pp. 17–24;

Critique, special Taylor issue, 9, no. 3 (1967);

Robert Giroux, "Peter's Friends," *New York Times Magazine,* 1 January 1995, p. 23;

Catherine Clark Graham, *Southern Accents: The Fiction of Peter Taylor* (New York: Peter Lang, 1994);

Greensboro Review, special Taylor issue, no. 52 (Summer 1992);

Albert J. Griffith, *Peter Taylor,* revised edition (Boston: Twayne, 1990);

Journal of the Short Story in English, special Taylor issue, no. 9 (Autumn 1987);

Hubert H. McAlexander, ed., *Critical Essays on Peter Taylor* (Boston: G. K. Hall, 1993);

David M. Robinson, *World of Relations: The Achievement of Peter Taylor* (Lexington: University Press of Kentucky, 1998);

James Curry Robison, *Peter Taylor: A Study of the Short Fiction* (Boston: Twayne, 1988);

Sewanee Review, special Taylor issue, 70 (1962);

Shenandoah, special Taylor issue, 78, no. 2 (1977);

Southern Quarterly, special Taylor issue, 38, no. 2 (2000);

C. Ralph Stephens and Lynda B. Salamon, eds., *The Craft of Peter Taylor* (Tuscaloosa: University of Alabama Press, 1995).

Papers:

The main repositories of Peter Taylor's papers are at Memphis State University, the University of Michigan, the University of North Carolina at Greensboro, and the University of Texas at Austin.

Books for Further Reading

Aldridge, John W. *Classics and Contemporaries.* Columbia: University of Missouri Press, 1992.

Aldridge. *The Devil in the Fire: Retrospective Essays on American Literature and Culture, 1951–1971.* New York: Harper's Magazine Press, 1972.

Aldridge. *In Search of Heresy: American Literature in an Age of Conformity.* New York: McGraw-Hill, 1956.

Aldridge. *Talents and Technicians: Literary Chic and the New Assembly-Line Fiction.* New York: Scribners, 1992.

Aldridge. *Time to Murder and Create: The Contemporary Novel in Crisis.* New York: McKay, 1966.

Allen, Mary. *The Necessary Blankness: Women in Major American Fiction of the Sixties.* Urbana: University of Illinois Press, 1976.

Alter, Robert. *After the Tradition: Essays on Modern Jewish Writing.* New York: Dutton, 1969.

Auchincloss, Louis. *Pioneers & Caretakers: A Study of 9 American Women Novelists.* Minneapolis: University of Minnesota Press, 1965.

Bachelard, Gaston. *The Poetics of Space,* translated by Maria Jolas. New York: Orion, 1964.

Baker, Houston A. *Blues, Ideology, and Afro-American Literature: A Vernacular Theory.* Chicago: University of Chicago Press, 1984.

Baker, ed. *Three American Literatures: Essays in Chicano, Native American, and Asian-American Literature for Teachers of American Literature.* New York: Modern Language Association of America, 1982.

Balakian, Nona, and Charles Simmons, eds. *The Creative Present: Notes on Contemporary American Fiction.* Garden City, N.Y.: Doubleday, 1963.

Baumbach, Jonathan. *The Landscape of Nightmare: Studies in the Contemporary American Novel.* New York: New York University Press, 1965.

Bell, Bernard W. *The Afro-American Novel and Its Tradition.* Amherst: University of Massachusetts Press, 1987.

Bellamy, Joe David. *The New Fiction: Interviews with Innovative American Writers.* Urbana: University of Illinois Press, 1974.

Bercovitch, Sacvan, ed. *Reconstructing American Literary History.* Cambridge, Mass.: Harvard University Press, 1986.

Berman, Ronald. *America in the Sixties: An Intellectual History.* New York: Free Press, 1968.

Bigsby, C. W. E., ed. *The Black American Writer.* De Land, Fla.: Everett/Edwards, 1969.

Blotner, Joseph. *The Modern American Political Novel, 1900–1960.* Austin: University of Texas Press, 1966.

Boelhower, William. *Through a Glass Darkly: Ethnic Semiosis in American Literature*. New York: Oxford University Press, 1987.

Bone, Robert A. *The Negro Novel in America,* revised edition. New Haven: Yale University Press, 1965.

Bradbury, John M. *Renaissance in the South: A Critical History of the Literature, 1920–1960*. Chapel Hill: University of North Carolina Press, 1963.

Bradbury, Malcolm. *The Modern American Novel,* revised edition. Oxford & New York: Oxford University Press, 1992.

Bredahl, A. Carl, Jr. *New Ground: Western American Narrative and the Literary Canon*. Chapel Hill: University of North Carolina Press, 1989.

Bremer, Sidney H. *Urban Intersections: Meetings of Life and Literature in United States Cities*. Urbana & Chicago: University of Illinois Press, 1992.

Bryant, Jerry H. *The Open Decision: The Contemporary American Novel and Its Intellectual Background*. New York: Free Press, 1970.

Byerman, Keith E. *Fingering the Jagged Grain: Tradition and Form in Recent Black Fiction*. Athens: University of Georgia Press, 1985.

Campbell, Jane. *Mythic Black Fiction: The Transformation of History*. Knoxville: University of Tennessee Press, 1986.

Carr, John, ed. *Kite-Flying and Other Irrational Acts: Conversations with Twelve Southern Writers*. Baton Rouge: Louisiana State University Press, 1972.

Chametzky, Jules. *Our Decentralized Literature: Cultural Mediations in Selected Jewish and Southern Writers*. Amherst: University of Massachusetts Press, 1986.

Christian, Barbara. *Black Women Novelists: The Development of a Tradition, 1892–1976*. Westport, Conn.: Greenwood Press, 1980.

Civello, Paul. *American Literary Naturalism and Its Twentieth-Century Transformations: Frank Norris, Ernest Hemingway, Don DeLillo*. Athens: University of Georgia Press, 1994.

Conversations with Writers, 2 volumes. Detroit: Bruccoli Clark/Gale Research, 1977, 1978.

Cook, Bruce. *The Beat Generation*. New York: Scribners, 1971.

Cook, M. G., ed. *Modern Black Novelists: A Collection of Critical Essays*. Englewood Cliffs, N.J.: Prentice-Hall, 1971.

Core, George, ed. *Southern Fiction Today: Renascence and Beyond*. Athens: University of Georgia Press, 1969.

Cowan, Louise. *The Fugitive Group: A Literary History*. Baton Rouge: Louisiana State University Press, 1959.

Cowley, Malcolm. *The Literary Situation*. New York: Viking, 1954.

Cunliffe, Marcus, ed. *American Literature Since 1900,* revised edition. London: Penguin, 1993.

Darby, William. *Necessary American Fictions: Popular Literature of the 1950s*. Bowling Green, Ohio: Bowling Green University Popular Press, 1987.

Dekker, George. *The American Historical Romance*. Cambridge: Cambridge University Press, 1987.

Drake, Robert, ed. *The Writer and His Tradition*. Knoxville: University of Tennessee, 1969.

Eco, Umberto. *Travels in Hyperreality: Essays,* translated by William Weaver. San Diego: Harcourt Brace Jovanovich, 1983.

Eisinger, Chester E. *Fiction of the Forties*. Chicago: University of Chicago Press, 1963.

Elliott, Emory, ed. *The Columbia History of the American Novel*. New York: Columbia University Press, 1991.

Elliott, ed. *The Columbia Literary History of the United States*. New York: Columbia University Press, 1988.

Etulain, Richard W., and Michael T. Marsden, eds. *The Popular Western: Essays toward a Definition*. Bowling Green, Ohio: Bowling Green State University Popular Press, 1974.

Federman, Raymond, ed. *Surfiction: Fiction Now and Tomorrow*. Chicago: Swallow Press, 1975.

Feldman, Gene, and Max Gartenberg, eds. *The Beat Generation and the Angry Young Men*. New York: Citadel, 1958.

Folsom, James K. *The American Western Novel*. New Haven: College and University Press, 1966.

Fox, Robert Elliot. *Conscientious Sorcerers: The Black Postmodernist Fiction of LeRoi Jones/Amiri Baraka, Ishmael Reed, and Samuel R. Delany*. New York: Greenwood Press, 1987.

French, Warren, ed. *The Fifties: Fiction, Poetry, Drama*. De Land, Fla.: Everett/Edwards, 1970.

Friedman, Melvin J., and John B. Vickery, eds. *The Shaken Realist: Essays in Modern Literature in Honor of Frederick J. Hoffman*. Baton Rouge: Louisiana State University Press, 1970.

Fuller, Edmund. *Man in Modern Fiction: Some Minority Opinions on Contemporary American Writing*. New York: Random House, 1958.

Gado, Frank, ed. *First Person: Conversations on Writers and Writing*. Schenectady, N.Y.: Union College Press, 1973.

Galloway, David D. *The Absurd Hero in American Fiction: Updike, Styron, Bellow, Salinger,* second revised edition. Austin: University of Texas Press, 1981.

Gass, William H. *Fiction and the Figures of Life*. New York: Knopf, 1970.

Gass. *On Being Blue: A Philosophical Inquiry*. Boston: Godine, 1976.

Gates, Henry Louis, Jr. *The Signifying Monkey: A Theory of Afro-American Literary Criticism*. New York: Oxford University Press, 1988.

Gayle, Addison, Jr. *The Way of the New World: The Black Novel in America*. Garden City, N.Y.: Anchor/Doubleday, 1975.

Gayle, ed. *Black Expression: Essays by and about Black Americans in the Creative Arts*. New York: Weybright & Talley, 1969.

Geismar, Maxwell. *American Moderns: From Rebellion to Conformity*. New York: Hill & Wang, 1958.

Gerstenberger, Donna, and George Hendrick. *The American Novel, 1789–1959: A Checklist of Twentieth Century Criticism*. Chicago: Swallow Press, 1970.

Giles, James R. *The Naturalistic Inner-City Novel in America: Encounters With the Fat Man*. Columbia: University of South Carolina Press, 1995.

Giles. *Violence in the Contemporary American Novel: An End to Innocence.* Columbia: University of South Carolina Press, 2000.

Gilman, Richard. *The Confusion of Realms.* New York: Random House, 1969.

Glicksberg, Charles I. *The Sexual Revolution in Modern American Literature.* The Hague: Nijhoff, 1971.

Gold, Herbert, ed. *First Person Singular: Essays for the Sixties.* New York: Dial, 1963.

González Echevarría, Roberto. *The Voice of the Masters: Writing and Authority in Modern Latin American Literature.* Austin: University of Texas Press, 1985.

Gossett, Louise Y. *Violence in Recent Southern Fiction.* Durham, N.C.: Duke University Press, 1965.

Green, Martin. *Re-appraisals: Some Commonsense Readings in American Literature.* London: Hugh Evelyn, 1963.

Greiner, Donald J. *Women Enter the Wilderness: Male Bonding and the American Novel of the 1980s.* Columbia: University of South Carolina Press, 1991.

Greiner. *Women Without Men: Female Bonding and the American Novel of the 1980s.* Columbia: University of South Carolina Press, 1993.

Griffin, Farah Jasmine. *"Who Set You Flowin'?": The African American Migration Narrative.* New York & Oxford: Oxford University Press, 1995.

Gruen, John. *The Party's Over Now: Reminiscences of the Fifties.* New York: Viking, 1972.

Guttmann, Allen. *The Jewish Writer in America: Assimilation and the Crisis of Identity.* New York: Oxford University Press, 1971.

Hamilton, Cynthia S. *Western and Hard-Boiled Detective Fiction in America: From High Noon to Midnight.* Iowa City: University of Iowa Press, 1987.

Handy, William J. *Modern Fiction: A Formalist Approach.* Carbondale: Southern Illinois University Press, 1971.

Harap, Louis. *In the Mainstream: The Jewish Presence in Twentieth-Century American Literature, 1950s–1980s.* New York: Greenwood Press, 1987.

Hardwick, Elizabeth. *A View of My Own: Essays in Literature and Society.* New York: Farrar, Straus & Cudahy, 1962.

Harper, Howard M., Jr. *Desperate Faith: A Study of Bellow, Salinger, Mailer, Baldwin, and Updike.* Chapel Hill: University of North Carolina Press, 1967.

Harris, Charles B. *Contemporary American Novelists of the Absurd.* New Haven: College and University Press, 1971.

Haslam, Gerald W., ed. *Western Writing.* Albuquerque: University of New Mexico Press, 1974.

Hassan, Ihab. *Contemporary American Literature, 1945–1972: An Introduction.* New York: Ungar, 1973.

Hassan. *The Postmodern Turn: Essays in Postmodernist Theory and Culture.* Columbus: Ohio State University Press, 1987.

Hassan. *Radical Innocence: Studies in the Contemporary American Novel.* Princeton: Princeton University Press, 1961.

Hassan. *The Right Promethean Fire: Imagination, Science, and Cultural Change.* Urbana: University of Illinois Press, 1979.

Hauck, Richard Boyd. *A Cheerful Nihilism: Confidence and "The Absurd" in American Humorous Fiction.* Bloomington: Indiana University Press, 1971.

Hicks, Granville, ed. *The Living Novel: A Symposium.* New York: Macmillan, 1957.

Hicks, Jack. *In the Singer's Temple: Prose Fictions of Barthelme, Gaines, Brautigan, Piercy, Kesey, and Kosinski.* Chapel Hill: University of North Carolina Press, 1981.

Hilfer, Tony. *American Fiction Since 1940.* London & New York: Longman, 1992.

Hill, Herbert, ed. *Anger and Beyond: The Negro Writer in the United States.* New York: Harper & Row, 1966.

Hobson, Fred. *Tell about the South: The Southern Rage to Explain.* Baton Rouge: Louisiana State University Press, 1983.

Hoffman, Daniel, ed. *Harvard Guide to Contemporary American Writing.* Cambridge, Mass.: Belknap Press of Harvard University Press, 1979.

Hoffman, Frederick J. *The Art of Southern Fiction: A Study of Some Modern Novelists.* Carbondale: Southern Illinois University Press, 1967.

Hume, Kathryn. *American Dream, American Nightmare: Fiction Since 1960.* Urbana: University of Illinois Press, 2000.

Hurm, Gerd. *Fragmented Urban Images: The American City in Modern Fiction from Stephen Crane to Thomas Pynchon.* Frankfurt am Main & New York: Peter Lang, 1991.

Jackson, Blyden. *The History of Afro-American Literature,* 1 volume to date. Baton Rouge: Louisiana State University Press, 1989–   .

Johnson, Charles R. *Being and Race: Black Writing Since 1970.* Bloomington: Indiana University Press, 1988.

Jones, Peter G. *War and the Novelist: Appraising the American War Novel.* Columbia: University of Missouri Press, 1976.

Karl, Frederick Robert. *American Fictions, 1940–1980: A Comprehensive History and Critical Evaluation.* New York: Harper & Row, 1983.

Kazin, Alfred. *Bright Book of Life: American Novelists and Storytellers from Hemingway to Mailer.* Boston & Toronto: Atlantic/ Little, Brown, 1973.

Kazin. *Contemporaries: Essays.* Boston: Little, Brown, 1962.

Kennard, Jean E. *Number and Nightmare: Forms of Fantasy in Contemporary Fiction.* Hamden, Conn.: Archon, 1975.

Kim, Elaine H. *Asian American Literature: An Introduction to the Writings and Their Social Contexts.* Philadelphia: Temple University Press, 1982.

Klein, Marcus. *After Alienation: American Novels in Mid-century.* Cleveland & New York: World, 1964.

Klein, ed. *The American Novel Since World War II.* Greenwich, Conn.: Fawcett, 1969.

Klinkowitz, Jerome. *The Life of Fiction.* Urbana: University of Illinois Press, 1977.

Klinkowitz. *Literary Disruptions: The Making of a Post-contemporary American Fiction.* Urbana: University of Illinois Press, 1975.

Klinkowitz. *The New American Novel of Manners: The Fiction of Richard Yates, Dan Wakefield, Thomas McGuane*. Athens: University of Georgia Press, 1986.

Klotman, Phyllis Rauch. *Another Man Gone: The Black Runner in Contemporary Afro-American Literature*. Port Washington, N.Y.: Kennikat Press, 1977.

Kort, Wesley A. *Shriven Selves: Religious Problems in Recent American Fiction*. Philadelphia: Fortress, 1972.

Kostelanetz, Richard. *The End of Intelligent Writing: Literary Politics in America*. New York: Sheed & Ward, 1974.

Kostelanetz. *Master Minds: Portraits of Contemporary American Artists and Intellectuals*. New York: Macmillan, 1969.

Kostelanetz, ed. *The New American Arts*. New York: Horizon, 1965.

Kostelanetz, ed. *On Contemporary Literature: An Anthology of Critical Essays on the Major Movements and Writers of Contemporary Literature*. New York: Avon, 1964.

Kostelanetz, ed. *The Young American Writers: Fiction, Poetry, Drama, and Criticism*. New York: Funk & Wagnalls, 1967.

Kremer, S. Lillian. *Witness Through the Imagination: Jewish American Holocaust Literature*. Detroit: Wayne State University Press, 1989.

Krim, Seymour. *Shake It for the World, Smartass*. New York: Dial, 1970.

Lebowitz, Naomi. *Humanism and the Absurd in the Modern Novel*. Evanston, Ill.: Northwestern University Press, 1971.

Lehan, Richard. *The City in Literature: An Intellectual and Cultural History*. Berkeley: University of California Press, 1998.

Lehan. *A Dangerous Crossing: French Literary Existentialism and the Modern American Novel*. Carbondale: Southern Illinois University Press, 1973.

Ling, Amy. *Between Worlds: Women Writers of Chinese Ancestry*. New York: Pergamon Press, 1990.

Lipton, Lawrence. *The Holy Barbarians*. New York: Messner, 1959.

Litz, A. Walton, ed. *Modern American Fiction: Essays in Criticism*. New York: Oxford University Press, 1963.

Lord, William J., Jr. *How Authors Make a Living: An Analysis of Free Lance Writers' Incomes, 1953–1957*. New York: Scarecrow Press, 1962.

Ludwig, Jack. *Recent American Novelists*. Minneapolis: University of Minnesota Press, 1962.

Lupack, Barbara Tepa. *Insanity as Redemption in Contemporary American Fiction: Inmates Running the Asylum*. Gainesville: University Press of Florida, 1995.

Lutwack, Leonard. *Heroic Fiction: The Epic Tradition and American Novels of the Twentieth Century*. Carbondale: Southern Illinois University Press, 1971.

Madden, Charles F., ed. *Talks with Authors*. Carbondale: Southern Illinois University Press, 1968.

Madden, David, ed. *American Dreams, American Nightmares*. Carbondale: Southern Illinois University Press, 1970.

Madden, ed. *Rediscoveries: Informal Essays in Which Well-Known Novelists Rediscover Neglected Works of Fiction by One of Their Favorite Authors*. New York: Crown, 1971.

Malin, Irving. *New American Gothic*. Carbondale: Southern Illinois University Press, 1962.

Margolies, Edward. *Native Sons: A Critical Study of Twentieth-Century Negro American Authors*. Philadelphia & New York: Lippincott, 1968.

May, John R. *Toward a New Earth: Apocalypse in the American Novel*. Notre Dame, Ind.: University of Notre Dame Press, 1972.

McHale, Brian. *Postmodernist Fiction*. New York & London: Methuen, 1987.

McNamara, Kevin R. *Urban Verbs: Arts and Discourses of American Cities*. Stanford: Stanford University Press, 1996.

Michaels, Walter Benn. *Our America: Nativism, Modernism, and Pluralism*. Durham, N.C.: Duke University Press, 1995.

Milton, John R. *The Novel of the American West*. Lincoln: University of Nebraska Press, 1980.

Moore, Harry T., ed. *Contemporary American Novelists*. Carbondale: Southern Illinois University Press, 1964.

Myers, Carol Fairbanks. *Women in Literature: Criticism of the Seventies*. Metuchen, N.J.: Scarecrow Press, 1976.

Newman, Charles. *The Post-modern Aura: The Act of Fiction in an Age of Inflation*. Evanston, Ill.: Northwestern University Press, 1985.

Newquist, Roy. *Counterpoint*. Chicago: Rand McNally, 1964.

Nin, Anaïs. *The Novel of the Future*. New York: Macmillan, 1968.

O'Brien, John, ed. *Interviews with Black Writers*. New York: Liveright, 1973.

Olderman, Raymond M. *Beyond the Waste Land: A Study of the American Novel in the Nineteen-Sixties*. New Haven: Yale University Press, 1972.

Olster, Stacey Michele. *Reminiscence and Re-creation in Contemporary American Fiction*. Cambridge: Cambridge University Press, 1989.

Panichas, George A., ed. *The Politics of Twentieth-Century Novelists*. New York: Hawthorn Books, 1971.

Parkinson, Thomas, ed. *A Casebook on The Beat*. New York: Crowell, 1961.

Pearce, Richard. *Stages of the Clown: Perspectives on Modern Fiction from Dostoyevsky to Beckett*. Carbondale: Southern Illinois University Press, 1970.

Peden, William. *The American Short Story: Front Line in the National Defense of Literature*. Boston: Houghton Mifflin, 1964. Revised and enlarged as *The American Short Story: Continuity and Change, 1940–1975*. Boston: Houghton Mifflin, 1975.

Pinsker, Sanford. *The Schlemiel as Metaphor: Studies in the Yiddish and American Jewish Novel*. Carbondale: Southern Illinois University Press, 1971.

Podhoretz, Norman. *Doings and Undoings: The Fifties and After in American Writing*. New York: Farrar, Straus, 1964.

Rocard, Marcienne. *The Children of the Sun: Mexican-Americans in the Literature of the United States,* translated by Edward G. Brown Jr. Tucson: University of Arizona Press, 1989.

Rodgers, Lawrence R. *Canaan Bound: The African-American Great Migration Novel.* Urbana & Chicago: University of Illinois Press, 1997.

Rosenblatt, Roger. *Black Fiction.* Cambridge, Mass.: Harvard University Press, 1974.

Rotella, Carlo. *October Cities: The Redevelopment of Urban Literature.* Berkeley: University of California Press, 1998.

Rubin, Louis D., Jr. *The Faraway Country: Writers in the Modern South.* Seattle: University of Washington Press, 1963.

Rubin, ed. *The American South: Portrait of a Culture.* Baton Rouge: Louisiana State University Press, 1979.

Rubin and Robert D. Jacobs, eds. *South: Modern Southern Literature in Its Cultural Setting.* Garden City, N.Y.: Doubleday, 1961.

Rubin and others, eds. *The History of Southern Literature.* Baton Rouge: Louisiana State University Press, 1985.

Ruland, Richard, and Malcolm Bradbury. *From Puritanism to Postmodernism: A History of American Literature.* New York: Viking, 1991.

Ruoff, A. La Vonne Brown, and Jerry W. Ward Jr., eds. *Redefining American Literary History.* New York: Modern Language Association of America, 1990.

Saldivar, Jose David. *Border Matters: Remapping American Cultural Studies.* Berkeley: University of California Press, 1997.

Scholes, Robert. *The Fabulators.* New York: Oxford University Press, 1967.

Scholes and Robert Kellogg. *The Nature of Narrative.* London & New York: Oxford University Press, 1966.

Schraufnagel, Noel. *From Apology to Protest: The Black American Novel.* De Land, Fla.: Everett/Edwards, 1973.

Schulz, Max F. *Black Humor Fiction of the Sixties: A Pluralistic Definition of Man and His World.* Athens: Ohio University Press, 1973.

Schulz. *Radical Sophistication: Studies in Contemporary Jewish-American Novelists.* Athens: Ohio University Press, 1969.

Scott, Nathan A., Jr. *Three American Moralists: Mailer, Bellow, Trilling.* Notre Dame, Ind.: University of Notre Dame Press, 1973.

Sherzer, Joel, and Anthony Woodbury, eds. *Native American Discourse: Poetics and Rhetoric.* New York: Cambridge University Press, 1987.

Simonson, Harold P. *Beyond the Frontier: Writers, Western Regionalism and a Sense of Place.* Fort Worth: Texas Christian University Press, 1989.

Smith, Valerie. *Self-Discovery and Authority in Afro-American Narrative.* Cambridge, Mass.: Harvard University Press, 1987.

Sollors, Werner. *Beyond Ethnicity: Consent and Descent in American Culture.* New York: Oxford University Press, 1986.

Spiller, Robert, ed. *A Time of Harvest: American Literature, 1910–1960.* New York: Hill & Wang, 1962.

Stark, John. *The Literature of Exhaustion: Borges, Nabokov, and Barth.* Durham, N.C.: Duke University Press, 1974.

Stepto, Robert. *From Behind the Veil: A Study of Afro-American Narrative.* Urbana: University of Illinois Press, 1979.

Stuckey, William J. *The Pulitzer Prize Novels: A Critical Backward Look*. Norman: University of Oklahoma Press, 1966.

Sutherland, William O. S., ed. *Six Contemporary Novels: Six Introductory Essays in Modern Fiction*. Austin: University of Texas Department of English, 1962.

Tanner, Tony. *City of Words: American Fiction, 1950–1970*. New York: Harper & Row, 1971.

Tanner. *The Reign of Wonder: Naivety and Reality in American Literature*. Cambridge: Cambridge University Press, 1965.

Tate, Claudia. *Black Women Writers at Work*. New York: Continuum, 1983.

Taylor, J. Golden, and Thomas J. Lyon, eds. *A Literary History of the American West*. Fort Worth: Texas Christian University Press, 1987.

Tilton, John W. *Cosmic Satire in the Contemporary Novel*. Lewisburg, Pa.: Bucknell University Press, 1977.

Turner, Darwin T. *Afro-American Writers*. New York: Appleton-Century-Crofts, 1970.

Tuttleton, James W. *The Novel of Manners in America*. Chapel Hill: University of North Carolina Press, 1972.

Tytell, John. *Naked Angels: The Lives and Literature of the Beat Generation*. New York: McGraw-Hill, 1976.

Waldmeir, Joseph J., ed. *Recent American Fiction: Some Critical Views*. Boston: Houghton Mifflin, 1963.

Watkins, Floyd C. *The Death of Art: Black and White in the Recent Southern Novel*. Athens: University of Georgia Press, 1970.

Watson, Carole McAlphine. *Prologue: The Novels of Black American Women, 1891–1965*. New York: Greenwood Press, 1985.

Weber, Ronald, ed. *America in Change: Reflections on the 60's and 70's*. Notre Dame, Ind.: University of Notre Dame Press, 1972.

West, James L. W., III. *American Authors and the Literary Marketplace Since 1900*. Philadelphia: University of Pennsylvania Press, 1988.

Westbrook, Max, ed. *The Modern American Novel: Essays in Criticism*. New York: Random House, 1966.

Whitlow, Roger. *Black American Literature: A Critical History*. Chicago: Nelson Hall, 1973.

Wiget, Andrew. *Native American Literature*. Boston: Twayne, 1985.

Wiget, ed. *Critical Essays on Native American Literature*. Boston: G. K. Hall, 1985.

Wilde, Alan. *Middle Grounds: Studies in Contemporary American Fiction*. Philadelphia: University of Pennsylvania Press, 1987.

Williams, John A., and Charles F. Harris, eds. *Amistad I: Writings of Black History and Culture*. New York: Knopf, 1970.

Williams and Harris, eds. *Amistad II*. New York: Knopf, 1971.

Writers at Work: The Paris Review *Interviews,* series 1–9. New York: Viking, 1958–1992.

Contributors

Barbara Bennett . . . . *Wake Forest University*

Kathryn A. Brewer . . . . *Stillman College*

Roberto Cantú . . . . *California State University, Los Angeles*

Miriam Marty Clark . . . . *Auburn University*

Ted Clontz . . . . *Northern Illinois University*

Todd F. Davis . . . . *Goshen College*

David C. Dougherty . . . . *Loyola College in Maryland*

Sara Elliott . . . . *Aurora University*

David Galef . . . . *University of Mississippi*

Samuel Gaustad . . . . *Phillips Community College of the University of Arkansas*

Wanda H. Giles . . . . *Northern Illinois University*

John M. Grammer . . . . *University of the South*

Albert J. Griffith . . . . *Our Lady of the Lake University of San Antonio*

Denis M. Hennessy . . . . *State University of New York, College at Oneonta*

Philip M. Isaacs . . . . *New York, New York*

Jacqueline C. Jones . . . . *Washington College*

Mary Ellen Jones . . . . *Wittenberg University*

Christopher J. Knight . . . . *University of Montana*

Barbara Lounsberry . . . . *University of Northern Iowa*

Bonnie Lyons . . . . *University of Texas at San Antonio*

Patrick Meanor . . . . *State University of New York at Oneonta*

Charles Nicol . . . . *Indiana State University*

Sarah A. Quirk . . . . *Waubonsee Community College*

David Sanders . . . . *Carlsbad, California*

Joseph Sherman . . . . *Oxford Centre for Hebrew and Jewish Studies*

Michael Steinman . . . . *Nassau Community College, State University of New York*

John Whalen-Bridge . . . . *National University of Singapore*

Kenneth Womack . . . . *Pennsylvania State University, Altoona*

Cumulative Index

Dictionary of Literary Biography, Volumes 1-278
Dictionary of Literary Biography Yearbook, 1980-2001
Dictionary of Literary Biography Documentary Series, Volumes 1-19
Concise Dictionary of American Literary Biography, Volumes 1-7
Concise Dictionary of British Literary Biography, Volumes 1-8
Concise Dictionary of World Literary Biography, Volumes 1-4

Cumulative Index

DLB before number: *Dictionary of Literary Biography,* Volumes 1-278
Y before number: *Dictionary of Literary Biography Yearbook,* 1980-2001
DS before number: *Dictionary of Literary Biography Documentary Series,* Volumes 1-19
CDALB before number: *Concise Dictionary of American Literary Biography,* Volumes 1-7
CDBLB before number: *Concise Dictionary of British Literary Biography,* Volumes 1-8
CDWLB before number: *Concise Dictionary of World Literary Biography,* Volumes 1-4

Cumulative Index

Cumulative Index

Villiers de l'Isle-Adam, Jean-Marie Mathias
Philippe-Auguste, Comte de
1838-1889 .... DLB-123, 192

Villon, François 1431-circa 1463?...... DLB-208

Vine Press....................... DLB-112

Viorst, Judith ?- DLB-52

Vipont, Elfrida (Elfrida Vipont Foulds,
Charles Vipont) 1902-1992 .... DLB-160

Viramontes, Helena María 1954- DLB-122

Virgil 70 B.C.-19 B.C...... DLB-211; CDWLB-1

Virtual Books and Enemies of Books Y-00

Vischer, Friedrich Theodor 1807-1887 ... DLB-133

Vitruvius circa 85 B.C.-circa 15 B.C. ... DLB-211

Vitry, Philippe de 1291-1361 .... DLB-208

Vittorini, Elio 1908-1966 .... DLB-264

Vivanco, Luis Felipe 1907-1975........ DLB-108

Vivian, E. Charles 1882-1947.......... DLB-255

Viviani, Cesare 1947- DLB-128

Vivien, Renée 1877-1909 .... DLB-217

Vizenor, Gerald 1934- DLB-175, 227

Vizetelly and Company DLB-106

Voaden, Herman 1903- DLB-88

Voß, Johann Heinrich 1751-1826....... DLB-90

Vogau, Boris Andreevich (see Pil'niak,
Boris Andreevich)

Voigt, Ellen Bryant 1943- DLB-120

Vojnović, Ivo 1857-1929.....DLB-147; CDWLB-4

Volkoff, Vladimir 1932- DLB-83

Volland, P. F., Company DLB-46

Vollbehr, Otto H. F.
1872?-1945 or 1946 .... DLB-187

Vologdin (see Zasodimsky,
Pavel Vladimirovich)

Volponi, Paolo 1924- DLB-177

Vonarburg, Élisabeth 1947- DLB-251

von der Grün, Max 1926- DLB-75

Vonnegut, Kurt 1922-
.... DLB-2, 8, 152; Y-80; DS-3; CDALB-6

Voranc, Prežihov 1893-1950 .... DLB-147

Voronsky, Aleksandr Konstantinovich
1884-1937..................... DLB-272

Vovchok, Marko 1833-1907.......... DLB-238

Voynich, E. L. 1864-1960........... DLB-197

Vroman, Mary Elizabeth
circa 1924-1967 .... DLB-33

W

Wace, Robert ("Maistre")
circa 1100-circa 1175 .... DLB-146

Wackenroder, Wilhelm Heinrich
1773-1798 .... DLB-90

Wackernagel, Wilhelm 1806-1869 ..... DLB-133

Waddell, Helen 1889-1965........... DLB-240

Waddington, Miriam 1917- DLB-68

Wade, Henry 1887-1969.............. DLB-77

Wagenknecht, Edward 1900- DLB-103

Wägner, Elin 1882-1949............. DLB-259

Wagner, Heinrich Leopold 1747-1779..... DLB-94

Wagner, Henry R. 1862-1957 .... DLB-140

Wagner, Richard 1813-1883 .... DLB-129

Wagoner, David 1926- DLB-5, 256

Wah, Fred 1939- DLB-60

Waiblinger, Wilhelm 1804-1830 ...... DLB-90

Wain, John
1925-1994 ...DLB-15, 27, 139, 155; CDBLB-8

Wainwright, Jeffrey 1944- DLB-40

Waite, Peirce and Company......... DLB-49

Wakeman, Stephen H. 1859-1924 ...... DLB-187

Wakoski, Diane 1937- DLB-5

Walahfrid Strabo circa 808-849 .... DLB-148

Walck, Henry Z. DLB-46

Walcott, Derek
1930- DLB-117; Y-81, Y-92; CDWLB-3

Waldegrave, Robert [publishing house] ...DLB-170

Waldman, Anne 1945- DLB-16

Waldrop, Rosmarie 1935- DLB-169

Walker, Alice 1900-1982 .... DLB-201

Walker, Alice
1944- DLB-6, 33, 143; CDALB-6

Walker, Annie Louisa (Mrs. Harry Coghill)
circa 1836-1907 .... DLB-240

Walker, George F. 1947- DLB-60

Walker, John Brisben 1847-1931 .... DLB-79

Walker, Joseph A. 1935- DLB-38

Walker, Margaret 1915- DLB-76, 152

Walker, Ted 1934- DLB-40

Walker and Company DLB-49

Walker, Evans and Cogswell Company... DLB-49

Wall, John F. (see Sarban)

Wallace, Alfred Russel 1823-1913 ...... DLB-190

Wallace, Dewitt 1889-1981 and
Lila Acheson Wallace 1889-1984.... DLB-137

Wallace, Edgar 1875-1932 .... DLB-70

Wallace, Lew 1827-1905............. DLB-202

Wallace, Lila Acheson
(see Wallace, Dewitt, and Lila Acheson Wallace)

Wallace, Naomi 1960- DLB-249

Wallant, Edward Lewis
1926-1962 .... DLB-2, 28, 143

Waller, Edmund 1606-1687 .... DLB-126

Walpole, Horace 1717-1797.....DLB-39, 104, 213

Preface to the First Edition of
The Castle of Otranto (1764).......... DLB-39

Preface to the Second Edition of
The Castle of Otranto (1765)........... DLB-39

Walpole, Hugh 1884-1941 .... DLB-34

Walrond, Eric 1898-1966............. DLB-51

Walser, Martin 1927- DLB-75, 124

Walser, Robert 1878-1956 .... DLB-66

Walsh, Ernest 1895-1926........... DLB-4, 45

Walsh, Robert 1784-1859............. DLB-59

Walters, Henry 1848-1931........... DLB-140

Waltharius circa 825................. DLB-148

Walther von der Vogelweide
circa 1170-circa 1230 .... DLB-138

Walton, Izaak
1593-1683 .... DLB-151, 213; CDBLB-1

Wambaugh, Joseph 1937- DLB-6; Y-83

Wand, Alfred Rudolph 1828-1891..... DLB-188

Waniek, Marilyn Nelson 1946- DLB-120

Wanley, Humphrey 1672-1726 .... DLB-213

Warburton, William 1698-1779 .... DLB-104

Ward, Aileen 1919- DLB-111

Ward, Artemus (see Browne, Charles Farrar)

Ward, Arthur Henry Sarsfield (see Rohmer, Sax)

Ward, Douglas Turner 1930- DLB-7, 38

Ward, Mrs. Humphry 1851-1920 ... DLB-18

Ward, James 1843-1925 .... DLB-262

Ward, Lynd 1905-1985 .... DLB-22

Ward, Lock and Company DLB-106

Ward, Nathaniel circa 1578-1652 ... DLB-24

Ward, Theodore 1902-1983........... DLB-76

Wardle, Ralph 1909-1988 .... DLB-103

Ware, Henry, Jr. 1794-1843 .... DLB-235

Ware, William 1797-1852........... DLB-1, 235

Warfield, Catherine Ann 1816-1877 ....DLB-248

Waring, Anna Letitia 1823-1910 ....DLB-240

Warne, Frederick, and Company [U.K.].. DLB-106

Warne, Frederick, and Company [U.S.] ... DLB-49

Warner, Anne 1869-1913 .... DLB-202

Warner, Charles Dudley 1829-1900 ..... DLB-64

Warner, Marina 1946- DLB-194

Warner, Rex 1905- DLB-15

Warner, Susan 1819-1885 ... DLB-3, 42, 239, 250

Warner, Sylvia Townsend
1893-1978.................. DLB-34, 139

Warner, William 1558-1609...........DLB-172

Warner Books DLB-46

Warr, Bertram 1917-1943............. DLB-88

Warren, John Byrne Leicester (see De Tabley, Lord)

Warren, Lella 1899-1982 .... Y-83

Warren, Mercy Otis 1728-1814 ..... DLB-31, 200

Warren, Robert Penn 1905-1989
.....DLB-2, 48, 152; Y-80, Y-89; CDALB-6

Warren, Samuel 1807-1877........... DLB-190

Die Wartburgkrieg circa 1230-circa 1280... DLB-138

Warton, Joseph 1722-1800 ....DLB-104, 109

Warton, Thomas 1728-1790.......DLB-104, 109

Warung, Price (William Astley)
1855-1911 .... DLB-230

Washington, George 1732-1799 .... DLB-31

Washington, Ned 1901-1976 .... DLB-265

Wassermann, Jakob 1873-1934 .... DLB-66

Wasserstein, Wendy 1950- DLB-228

Wasson, David Atwood 1823-1887 ... DLB-1, 223

Watanna, Onoto (see Eaton, Winnifred)

Waterhouse, Keith 1929- DLB-13, 15

Waterman, Andrew 1940- DLB-40

Waters, Frank 1902-1995.........DLB-212; Y-86

Waters, Michael 1949- DLB-120

Whitaker, Daniel K. 1801-1881 . . . . DLB-73

Whitcher, Frances Miriam
1812-1852 . . . . DLB-11, 202

White, Andrew 1579-1656 . . . . DLB-24

White, Andrew Dickson 1832-1918 . . . . . . DLB-47

White, E. B. 1899-1985 . . . DLB-11, 22; CDALB-7

White, Edgar B. 1947- DLB-38

White, Edmund 1940- DLB-227

White, Ethel Lina 1887-1944 . . . . DLB-77

White, Hayden V. 1928- DLB-246

White, Henry Kirke 1785-1806 . . . . DLB-96

White, Horace 1834-1916 . . . . DLB-23

White, James 1928-1999 . . . . DLB-261

White, Patrick 1912-1990 . . . . DLB-260

White, Phyllis Dorothy James (see James, P. D.)

White, Richard Grant 1821-1885 . . . . DLB-64

White, T. H. 1906-1964 . . . . DLB-160, 255

White, Walter 1893-1955 . . . . DLB-51

White, William, and Company DLB-49

White, William Allen 1868-1944 . . . . . DLB-9, 25

White, William Anthony Parker
(see Boucher, Anthony)

White, William Hale (see Rutherford, Mark)

Whitechurch, Victor L. 1868-1933 . . . . DLB-70

Whitehead, Alfred North 1861-1947 . . . . DLB-100

Whitehead, James 1936- Y-81

Whitehead, William 1715-1785 . . . . . . DLB-84, 109

Whitfield, James Monroe 1822-1871 . . . . . DLB-50

Whitfield, Raoul 1898-1945 . . . . DLB-226

Whitgift, John circa 1533-1604 . . . . DLB-132

Whiting, John 1917-1963 . . . . DLB-13

Whiting, Samuel 1597-1679 . . . . DLB-24

Whitlock, Brand 1869-1934 . . . . DLB-12

Whitman, Albert, and Company DLB-46

Whitman, Albery Allson 1851-1901 . . . . . . DLB-50

Whitman, Alden 1913-1990 . . . . Y-91

Whitman, Sarah Helen (Power)
1803-1878 . . . . DLB-1, 243

Whitman, Walt
1819-1892 . . . . DLB-3, 64, 224, 250; CDALB-2

Whitman Publishing Company DLB-46

Whitney, Geoffrey 1548 or 1552?-1601 . . DLB-136

Whitney, Isabella flourished 1566-1573 . . DLB-136

Whitney, John Hay 1904-1982 . . . . DLB-127

Whittemore, Reed 1919-1995 . . . . DLB-5

Whittier, John Greenleaf
1807-1892 . . . . DLB-1, 243; CDALB-2

Whittlesey House DLB-46

Who Runs American Literature? Y-94

Whose *Ulysses?* The Function of Editing. Y-97

Wickham, Anna (Edith Alice Mary Harper)
1884-1947 . . . . DLB-240

Wicomb, Zoë 1948- DLB-225

Wideman, John Edgar 1941- DLB-33, 143

Widener, Harry Elkins 1885-1912 . . . . . DLB-140

Wiebe, Rudy 1934- DLB-60

Wiechert, Ernst 1887-1950 . . . . DLB-56

Wied, Martina 1882-1957 . . . . DLB-85

Wiehe, Evelyn May Clowes (see Mordaunt, Elinor)

Wieland, Christoph Martin 1733-1813 . . . . DLB-97

Wienbarg, Ludolf 1802-1872 . . . . DLB-133

Wieners, John 1934- DLB-16

Wier, Ester 1910- DLB-52

Wiesel, Elie
1928- DLB-83; Y-86, 87; CDALB-7

Wiggin, Kate Douglas 1856-1923 . . . . DLB-42

Wigglesworth, Michael 1631-1705 . . . . . . DLB-24

Wilberforce, William 1759-1833 . . . . DLB-158

Wilbrandt, Adolf 1837-1911 . . . . DLB-129

Wilbur, Richard
1921- DLB-5, 169; CDALB-7

Wild, Peter 1940- DLB-5

Wilde, Lady Jane Francesca Elgee
1821?-1896 . . . . DLB-199

Wilde, Oscar 1854-1900
. . . . DLB-10, 19, 34, 57, 141, 156, 190;
CDBLB-5

"The Critic as Artist" (1891) DLB-57

Oscar Wilde Conference at Hofstra
University Y-00

From "The Decay of Lying" (1889) DLB-18

"The English Renaissance of
Art" (1908) DLB-35

"L'Envoi" (1882) DLB-35

Wilde, Richard Henry 1789-1847 . . . . . DLB-3, 59

Wilde, W. A., Company DLB-49

Wilder, Billy 1906- DLB-26

Wilder, Laura Ingalls 1867-1957 . . . . DLB-22, 256

Wilder, Thornton
1897-1975 . . . . DLB-4, 7, 9, 228; CDALB-7

Thornton Wilder Centenary at Yale Y-97

Wildgans, Anton 1881-1932 . . . . DLB-118

Wiley, Bell Irvin 1906-1980 . . . . DLB-17

Wiley, John, and Sons DLB-49

Wilhelm, Kate 1928- DLB-8

Wilkes, Charles 1798-1877 . . . . DLB-183

Wilkes, George 1817-1885 . . . . DLB-79

Wilkins, John 1614-1672 . . . . DLB-236

Wilkinson, Anne 1910-1961 . . . . DLB-88

Wilkinson, Eliza Yonge
1757-circa 1813 . . . . DLB-200

Wilkinson, Sylvia 1940- Y-86

Wilkinson, William Cleaver 1833-1920 . . . DLB-71

Willard, Barbara 1909-1994 . . . . DLB-161

Willard, Emma 1787-1870 . . . . DLB-239

Willard, Frances E. 1839-1898 . . . . DLB-221

Willard, L. [publishing house] DLB-49

Willard, Nancy 1936- DLB-5, 52

Willard, Samuel 1640-1707 . . . . DLB-24

Willeford, Charles 1919-1988 . . . . DLB-226

William of Auvergne 1190-1249 . . . . DLB-115

William of Conches
circa 1090-circa 1154 . . . . DLB-115

William of Ockham circa 1285-1347 . . . . DLB-115

William of Sherwood
1200/1205-1266/1271 . . . . DLB-115

The William Chavrat American Fiction Collection
at the Ohio State University Libraries Y-92

Williams, A., and Company DLB-49

Williams, Ben Ames 1889-1953 . . . . DLB-102

Williams, C. K. 1936- DLB-5

Williams, Chancellor 1905- DLB-76

Williams, Charles 1886-1945 . . . DLB-100, 153, 255

Williams, Denis 1923-1998 . . . . DLB-117

Williams, Emlyn 1905-1987 . . . . DLB-10, 77

Williams, Garth 1912-1996 . . . . DLB-22

Williams, George Washington
1849-1891 . . . . DLB-47

Williams, Heathcote 1941- DLB-13

Williams, Helen Maria 1761-1827 . . . . . DLB-158

Williams, Hugo 1942- DLB-40

Williams, Isaac 1802-1865 . . . . DLB-32

Williams, Joan 1928- DLB-6

Williams, Joe 1889-1972 . . . . DLB-241

Williams, John A. 1925- DLB-2, 33

Williams, John E. 1922-1994 . . . . DLB-6

Williams, Jonathan 1929- DLB-5

Williams, Miller 1930- DLB-105

Williams, Nigel 1948- DLB-231

Williams, Raymond 1921- . . . DLB-14, 231, 242

Williams, Roger circa 1603-1683 . . . . DLB-24

Williams, Rowland 1817-1870 . . . . DLB-184

Williams, Samm-Art 1946- DLB-38

Williams, Sherley Anne 1944-1999 . . . . . . DLB-41

Williams, T. Harry 1909-1979 . . . . DLB-17

Williams, Tennessee
1911-1983 . . . . DLB-7; Y-83; DS-4; CDALB-1

Williams, Terry Tempest 1955- . . . DLB-206, 275

Williams, Ursula Moray 1911- DLB-160

Williams, Valentine 1883-1946 . . . . DLB-77

Williams, William Appleman 1921- DLB-17

Williams, William Carlos
1883-1963 . . . . . DLB-4, 16, 54, 86; CDALB-4

Williams, Wirt 1921- DLB-6

Williams Brothers DLB-49

Williamson, Henry 1895-1977 . . . . DLB-191

Williamson, Jack 1908- DLB-8

Willingham, Calder Baynard, Jr.
1922-1995 . . . . DLB-2, 44

Williram of Ebersberg circa 1020-1085 . . DLB-148

Willis, Nathaniel Parker 1806-1867
. . . . DLB-3, 59, 73, 74, 183, 250; DS-13

Willkomm, Ernst 1810-1886 . . . . DLB-133

Willumsen, Dorrit 1940- DLB-214

Wills, Garry 1934- DLB-246

Willson, Meredith 1902-1984 . . . . DLB-265

Wilmer, Clive 1945- DLB-40

Wilson, A. N. 1950- DLB-14, 155, 194

Wilson, Angus 1913-1991 . . . . . DLB-15, 139, 155

Wright, Harold Bell 1872-1944 . . . . DLB-9

Wright, James
1927-1980 . . . . DLB-5, 169; CDALB-7

Wright, Jay 1935- DLB-41

Wright, Judith 1915-2000 . . . . DLB-260

Wright, Louis B. 1899-1984 . . . . DLB-17

Wright, Richard
1908-1960 . . . . DLB-76, 102; DS-2; CDALB-5

Wright, Richard B. 1937- DLB-53

Wright, S. Fowler 1874-1965 . . . . DLB-255

Wright, Sarah Elizabeth 1928- DLB-33

Wright, Willard Huntington
("S. S. Van Dine") 1888-1939 . . . . DS-16

Wrigley, Robert 1951- DLB-256

A Writer Talking: A Collage Y-00

Writers and Politics: 1871-1918,
by Ronald Gray DLB-66

Writers and their Copyright Holders:
the WATCH Project Y-94

Writers' Forum Y-85

Writing for the Theatre,
by Harold Pinter DLB-13

Wroth, Lawrence C. 1884-1970 . . . . DLB-187

Wroth, Lady Mary 1587-1653 . . . . DLB-121

Wurlitzer, Rudolph 1937- DLB-173

Wyatt, Sir Thomas circa 1503-1542 . . . . . DLB-132

Wycherley, William
1641-1715 . . . . DLB-80; CDBLB-2

Wyclif, John
circa 1335-31 December 1384 . . . . . . DLB-146

Wyeth, N. C. 1882-1945 . . . . DLB-188; DS-16

Wylie, Elinor 1885-1928 . . . . DLB-9, 45

Wylie, Philip 1902-1971 . . . . DLB-9

Wyllie, John Cook 1908-1968 . . . . DLB-140

Wyman, Lillie Buffum Chace
1847-1929 . . . . DLB-202

Wymark, Olwen 1934- DLB-233

Wyndham, John 1903-1969 . . . . DLB-255

Wynne-Tyson, Esmé 1898-1972 . . . . DLB-191

X

Xenophon circa 430 B.C.-circa 356 B.C. . . .DLB-176

Y

Yasuoka Shōtarō 1920- DLB-182

Yates, Dornford 1885-1960 . . . . .DLB-77, 153

Yates, J. Michael 1938- DLB-60

Yates, Richard
1926-1992 . . . . .DLB-2, 234; Y-81, Y-92

Yau, John 1950- DLB-234

Yavorov, Peyo 1878-1914 . . . . DLB-147

The Year in Book Publishing Y-86

The Year in Book Reviewing and the Literary
Situation Y-98

The Year in British Drama Y-99, Y-00, Y-01

The Year in British Fiction Y-99, Y-00, Y-01

The Year in Children's
Books Y-92–Y-96, Y-98, Y-99, Y-00, Y-01

The Year in Children's Literature Y-97

The Year in Drama Y-82-Y-85, Y-87–Y-96

The Year in Fiction. . . Y-84–Y-86, Y-89, Y-94–Y-99

The Year in Fiction: A Biased View Y-83

The Year in Literary
Biography Y-83–Y-98, Y-00, Y-01

The Year in Literary Theory Y-92–Y-93

The Year in London Theatre Y-92

The Year in the Novel Y-87, Y-88, Y-90–Y-93

The Year in Poetry . .Y-83–Y-92, Y-94, Y-95, Y-96,
. . . . .Y-97, Y-98, Y-99, Y-00, Y-01

The Year in Science Fiction
and Fantasy Y-00, Y-01

The Year in Short Stories Y-87

The Year in the Short Story Y-88, Y-90–Y-93

The Year in Texas Literature Y-98

The Year in U.S. Drama Y-00

The Year in U.S. Fiction Y-00, Y-01

The Year's Work in American Poetry Y-82

The Year's Work in Fiction: A Survey Y-82

Yearsley, Ann 1753-1806 . . . . DLB-109

Yeats, William Butler
1865-1939 . . . DLB-10, 19, 98, 156; CDBLB-5

Yellen, Jack 1892-1991 . . . . DLB-265

Yep, Laurence 1948- DLB-52

Yerby, Frank 1916-1991 . . . . DLB-76

Yezierska, Anzia
1880-1970 . . . . DLB-28, 221

Yolen, Jane 1939- DLB-52

Yonge, Charlotte Mary
1823-1901 . . . . DLB-18, 163

The York Cycle circa 1376-circa 1569 . . . DLB-146

A Yorkshire Tragedy DLB-58

Yoseloff, Thomas [publishing house] DLB-46

Young, A. S. "Doc" 1919-1996 . . . . DLB-241

Young, Al 1939- DLB-33

Young, Arthur 1741-1820 . . . . DLB-158

Young, Dick 1917 or 1918 - 1987 . . . . . . .DLB-171

Young, Edward 1683-1765 . . . . DLB-95

Young, Frank A. "Fay" 1884-1957 . . . . . . DLB-241

Young, Francis Brett 1884-1954 . . . . DLB-191

Young, Gavin 1928- DLB-204

Young, Stark 1881-1963 . . . . . . DLB-9, 102; DS-16

Young, Waldeman 1880-1938 . . . . DLB-26

Young, William [publishing house] DLB-49

Young Bear, Ray A. 1950- DLB-175

Yourcenar, Marguerite
1903-1987 . . . . .DLB-72; Y-88

"You've Never Had It So Good," Gusted by
"Winds of Change": British Fiction in the
1950s, 1960s, and After DLB-14

Yovkov, Yordan 1880-1937 . .DLB-147; CDWLB-4

Z

Zachariä, Friedrich Wilhelm 1726-1777 . . . DLB-97

Zagajewski, Adam 1945- DLB-232

Zagoskin, Mikhail Nikolaevich
1789-1852 . . . . DLB-198

Zajc, Dane 1929- DLB-181

Zālīte, Māra 1952- DLB-232

Zamiatin, Evgenii Ivanovich 1884-1937 . . .DLB-272

Zamora, Bernice 1938- DLB-82

Zand, Herbert 1923-1970 . . . . DLB-85

Zangwill, Israel 1864-1926 . . . . . .DLB-10, 135, 197

Zanzotto, Andrea 1921- DLB-128

Zapata Olivella, Manuel 1920- DLB-113

Zasodimsky, Pavel Vladimirovich
1843-1912 . . . . DLB-238

Zebra Books DLB-46

Zebrowski, George 1945- DLB-8

Zech, Paul 1881-1946 . . . . DLB-56

Zeidner, Lisa 1955- DLB-120

Zeidonis, Imants 1933- DLB-232

Zeimi (Kanze Motokiyo) 1363-1443 . . . . . DLB-203

Zelazny, Roger 1937-1995 . . . . DLB-8

Zenger, John Peter 1697-1746 . . . . DLB-24, 43

Zepheria DLB-172

Zesen, Philipp von 1619-1689 . . . . DLB-164

Zhadovskaia, Iuliia Valerianovna
1824-1883 .DLB-277

Zhukova, Mar'ia Semenovna 1805-1855 . .DLB-277

Zhukovsky, Vasilii Andreevich
1783-1852 . . . . DLB-205

Zieber, G. B., and Company DLB-49

Ziedonis, Imants 1933- CDWLB-4

Zieroth, Dale 1946- DLB-60

Zigler und Kliphausen, Heinrich
Anshelm von 1663-1697 . . . . DLB-168

Zil'ber, Veniamin Aleksandrovich
(see Kaverin, Veniamin Aleksandrovich)

Zimmer, Paul 1934- DLB-5

Zinberg, Len (see Lacy, Ed)

Zindel, Paul 1936- DLB-7, 52; CDALB-7

Zingref, Julius Wilhelm 1591-1635 . . . . . DLB-164

Zinnes, Harriet 1919- DLB-193

Zinzendorf, Nikolaus Ludwig von
1700-1760 . . . . DLB-168

Zitkala-Ša 1876-1938 . . . . .DLB-175

Zīverts, Mārtiņš 1903-1990 . . . . DLB-220

Zlatovratsky, Nikolai Nikolaevich
1845-1911 . . . . DLB-238

Zola, Emile 1840-1902 . . . . DLB-123

Zolla, Elémire 1926- DLB-196

Zolotow, Charlotte 1915- DLB-52

Zoshchenko, Mikhail Mikhailovich
1895-1958 .DLB-272

Zschokke, Heinrich 1771-1848 . . . . DLB-94

Zubly, John Joachim 1724-1781 . . . . DLB-31

Zu-Bolton, Ahmos, II 1936- DLB-41

Zuckmayer, Carl 1896-1977 . . . . DLB-56, 124

Zukofsky, Louis 1904-1978 . . . . DLB-5, 165

Zupan, Vitomil 1914-1987 . . . . DLB-181

Župančič, Oton 1878-1949 . . .DLB-147; CDWLB-4

zur Mühlen, Hermynia 1883-1951 . . . . . . DLB-56

Zweig, Arnold 1887-1968 . . . . DLB-66

Zweig, Stefan 1881-1942 . . . . DLB-81, 118

Zwinger, Ann 1925- DLB-275